C. NICOLET

THE WORLD
OF THE CITIZEN
IN REPUBLICAN ROME

Translated by P. S. FALLA

UNIVERSITY OF CALIFORNIA PRESS
Berkeley and Los Angeles

Translation from French
© P. S. Falla 1980

First published 1980 by
University of California Press

French edition
© Editions Gallimard 1976

ISBN 0-520-03545-3
Library of Congress Catalog Number 77-80474

Printed in Great Britain

CONTENTS

PREFACE TO THE SECOND
FRENCH EDITION

S INCE THIS BOOK was written and first published over four years ago, a number of new works have led me to modify slightly, or formulate more precisely, some of my conclusions on detailed points.

Our knowledge of relations between Rome and the Italians has been much improved by G. Ilari, *Gli Italici nelle strutture militari romane*, Milan, 1974, and M. Humbert, *Municipium e civitas sine suffragio*, Rome, 1978. W. Seston has elaborated and slightly modified his hypothesis concerning the passage quoted from Appian in a valuable article, 'La lex Julia de 90 av. J. C. et l'intégration des Italiens dans la citoyenneté romaine', in *Comptes-Rendus de l'Académie des Inscriptions*, 1978, pp. 529-42. P. Marchetti has developed his ideas on the introduction of the uncial *as* in 210 and the amount of soldiers' pay in several important works the conclusions of which are, however, still disputed, including *Histoire économique et monétaire de la deuxième guerre punique*, *Mémoires de l'Académie Royale de Belgique*, Brussels, 1978, and 'Paie des troupes et dévaluations monétaires au cours de la deuxième guerre punique' in *Les dévaluations à Rome, Colloque CNRS*, Rome, 1978, pp. 195-216; in the same volume, note should be taken of E. Gabba, 'Aspetti economici e monetari del soldo militare', pp. 217-25, and R. Thomsen, 'From liberal *aes grave* to uncial *aes* reduction', pp. 9-30. As regards pay the most recent study is by A. Giovannini in *Mus. Helv.* 1978, pp. 258-63, who arrives by quite different methods at the same figure as Marchetti, *viz.* 1 sesterce a day for foot-soldiers in the second century BC.

I have tried to give an overall estimate of the size and distribution of the Roman budget in 'Armée et fiscalité: pour un bilan de la conquête romaine' in *Armées et fiscalités dans le monde antique, Colloque CNRS*, Paris, 1977, pp. 435-54. I have reverted to the question of grain distributions in 'Le temple des Nymphes et les distributions frumentaires... d'après des découvertes récentes', *Comptes-Rendus de l'Académie des Inscriptions*, 1976, pp. 29-51, and 'Tessères frumentaires et tessères de vote', in *L'Italie préromaine et la Rome républicaine, Mélanges J. Heurgon*, Rome, 1976, pp. 695-716.

I have continued the overall study of the problems of civic life dealt with in this book, and have enlarged it to cover questions relating to demography, economics, society, institutions and foreign conquest, in two books which are to some extent designed to supplement the present one: C. Nicolet, *Rome et la conquête du monde méditerranéen*, Tome 1: *Les structures de l'Italie romaine*, Paris, 1977, and C. Nicolet and others, Tome 2: *Genèse d'un empire*, 1978.

In the light of various criticisms, some laudatory and others less so, I think it desirable to explain my intentions more clearly in some respects. In the first place, the precise chronological range of my enquiry is from the third to the first century BC. In the nature of things our documentation is fuller and more reliable towards the end of the period, at a time which, for various reasons, was also that of the collapse of the theoretical equilibrium of the 'mixed constitution', founded on 'geometrical equality', whose workings I have tried to describe. From 167 BC at latest, when the *tributum* was suspended, and in fact probably from the end of the Second Punic War, whole sections of this 'constitution' ceased to function one after the other. In particular the system of assemblies — which was reformed several times, at dates so uncertain that I have deliberately refrained from entering into the controversy concerning them in the present work — became manifestly inadequate after the end of the second century and above all after 89 BC. I will go further and say that, almost certainly, the structured balance of rights and duties which seemed to me to explain the principles of Roman civic life never existed in practice: it was a kind of blueprint, a theoretical model and an ideal towards which Roman institutions tended in their heyday but which they never reached. I believe I have stated this and shown it to be the case in each chapter of my book, but perhaps I have laid too much stress on the ideal reconstruction and too little on the signs of maladjustment and decline which are well known to historians.

It is because I set out to understand an ideal which was very much alive in the communal mind, even if it was never fully realized, that I deliberately made use of existing texts without enquiring, as one should do in other circumstances, whether they were always contemporaneous with what they describe or historically reliable. For my purpose the important thing was that they bore witness to a certain idea of civic relationships. Whether this idea was formally worked out in the first or the second century BC was relatively unimportant. My general approach to Roman historiography is a strongly critical one, and I am very ready to emphasize that our knowledge is scarcely reliable except for the first century BC and, at a pinch, the second. But an annalistic tradition may be significant even if it is apocryphal. Naturally in that case the most one can do is to discern general principles (e.g. the fact that the Roman franchise was unequal and based on property assessment) and not the precise details of chronological variations. None the less I have indicated the latter as far as possible, for instance in connection with the progressive introduction of the secret ballot. On this point G. V. Sumner, in his severe review in the *American Journal of Philology* (1978, p. 525), is wrong to criticize me for using the anecdote in Livy 25.3.19—4.4 about the *publicani* in 212 BC upsetting the urn so that the people could not vote; he maintains that the story is clearly anachronistic, since 'the urns were useful only for a written ballot, not introduced for *judicia* till 137'. Livy, however, makes it clear that the urn was used to draw lots to decide in which tribe the Latins should vote, and this has been strikingly confirmed by the *Lex Malacitana*. Long before the secret ballot, urns for drawing lots were used in every Roman assembly.

The present edition differs little from the first, but numerous references, dates and figures have been corrected. I am glad to acknowledge the help of my English translator, Mr P. S. Falla, in this ungrateful task.

ACKNOWLEDGMENTS

Loeb Classics, *passim*.

James H. Oliver, The Ruling Power: a study of the...Roman Oration of Aelius Aristides. *Transactions of the American Philosophical Society,* N.S., Vol. 43, Part 4, 1953. (American Philosophical Society, Independence Square, Philadelphia 6, 1959).

The Holy Bible, Revised Standard Version, Thos. Nelson & Sons, London.

Res Gestae Divi Augusti, ed. and tr. by P. A. Brunt and J. M. Moore, Oxford University Press, 1967.

Macrobius, *The Saturnalia,* tr. Percival Vaughan Davis, Columbia University Press, 1969.

Tables I and II: P. A. Brunt, *Italian Manpower 225 BC – AD 14.*

Table III: ibid.

Table IV: L. Ross Taylor, *Roman Voting Assemblies,* Ann Arbor, University of Michigan Press, 1966. This is also apparently the source of Plans I and II. Plan III is ascribed to G. Gatti and Plan IV to F. Coarelli.

E. G. Hardy, *Three Spanish Charters,* Oxford, 1912 *(Lex Malacitana)*

E. G. Hardy, *Six Roman Laws,* Oxford, 1911 *(Tabula Heracleensis = Lex Julia Municipalis)*

Gaius, *Institutes,* ed. and tr. F. de Zulueta, Oxford, 1946.

INTRODUCTION

THIS BOOK owes its origin to a feeling of surprise and remorse. The historian of Rome, especially republican Rome, is above all the historian of an oligarchy. His angle of vision is inevitably such that he is liable to treat the great Republic, that mighty engine of political absorption, in terms of a thin stratum of magistrates, generals, senators, officers and tax-farmers. If only to do justice to our sources we must, of course, study the ways in which these dignitaries were recruited, define their powers, examine their behaviour and, if possible, explain its effects. In their native simplicity or in Shakespearian enlargement, it is they who are privileged and brought into the limelight by the religious, military or political chronicles which are the essential legacy of ancient historiography. We may add, for good measure, a few 'clerks' (lawyers, orators, poets, scholars) who were also revered in a civilization based on the written word; the field is still a narrow one, and despite appearances the cast of characters is still absurdly small.

For the past 20 years I have perforce, like most other historians, concentrated on analysing the overt or hidden mechanism of the drama enacted by the favoured few.[1] Such labour is not mis-spent: it is not only legitimate but essential to study the structure, evolution and more or less regular functioning of the Roman oligarchy, and this study is still a long way from completion. The oligarchs, after all, as Ronald Syme puts it, are those who 'make history;'[2] and patient collective effort will still be needed for a long time if we are to appraise properly the role of individuals, families and institutions and the chronological thread of events.

But our concern with the leading actors should not allow us to forget the 'extras' without whom the City could never have 'taken upon itself the fate of the human race'. Rome always presented itself to the outside world in the threefold, indissoluble guise of the 'magistrates, Senate and Roman people'.[3] The oligarchy revered, or professed to revere, the body of citizens whose agent and representative it claimed to be. The generals commanded citizen armies, not passive mercenaries. The magistrates held office in theory by the 'goodwill of the people' *(populi beneficium)*, even if in practice they owed their position to family origin, factional *combinazioni* or the favour of men at the top; and the tax-farmers paid the revenues of what was sometimes an exorbitant fiscal system into the 'treasury of the Roman people'. Sincere or hypocritical deference to the collective interest of the *cives* figured as leitmotiv or alibi even at the height of the civil wars. Whether or not the mass of citizens suffered restraint or oppression in domestic matters (and this is precisely what we shall be investigating), in external affairs they were systematically exalted and defended by the class that governed them. An ordinary citizen was protected *vis-à-vis* foreigners by Roman laws and arms and enjoyed the respect belonging to a sovereign prince. This is expressed with splendid frankness in a law of 100 BC instituting a special military command for the suppression of piracy:[4]

> Let the Consul send letters to all peoples who are friends and allies of the Roman people, ordering them to ensure that Roman citizens, Latins and their Italian allies may ply their business without danger in all the cities and islands of the East and may also sail the seas in perfect safety.

There is no doubt that, as a result of this protection, the greatness of Rome rested on the loyalty, seldom withheld, of the civic base which supplied the governing oligarchy not only with an alibi but with soldiers, taxpayers and a crowd of emigrants, merchants or colonists — a master race indeed — who were destined to Romanize the world.[5]

Paradoxical as it may seem, I believe it is the Roman people itself which should arouse in the historian a feeling of surprise and remorse. The reason for surprise is that no one, as far as I know, has yet given a satisfactory answer to the simple question: what was the actual day-to-day substance of Roman citizenship, its existential content, so to speak?[6] What did it mean in practice to be a citizen — and, incidentally, why was citizenship so coveted, as it would seem, by those who did not possess it? As for remorse, ought not historians to feel ashamed of having confined their attention to a few naive stereotypes? On the one hand, scenes of grandeur: Gavius of Compsa, for instance, crucified by Verres on the shore of the Straits of Messina, in full view of Italy, and crying out passionately that he, a Roman citizen, could not have been thus tortured on Italian soil. Or the infantryman, 'Marius's mule', marching through Africa or Gaul with a pack weighing 80 pounds, digging the Fos canal between two battles and building an impregnable camp at the end of each day. Or again the Roman people on the morrow of the Cannae disaster, assembling with the whole Senate to welcome the defeated Consul and thank him for 'not having despaired of the Republic'. Then the seamier side: the citizen lost to a sense of manhood, begging a daily dole from his rich patron, selling his vote to the highest bidder, informing against his wealthy neighbour at the time of the proscriptions, and drawing his free monthly ration of corn. All these hackneyed images from our schooldays belong to a tradition which condescendingly ignores the everyday life of citizens as a class. Yet how can we understand the collective destiny of a city such as Rome, in a state of continuous geographic and demographic expansion—how can we describe and explain the rules of its political life (the *politische Grammatik* recently outlined by Christian Meier[7]) or the essential problems of socio-political cohesion, the channels and procedures of government, if we have such an imperfect idea of the lives of the rank and file of citizens. either individually or collectively? The remorse that I felt at having neglected the man in the street was not a matter of sentiment or *a priori* doctrine, but a recognition of the need to continue my studies of the political class and, as it were, to paint in the second half of the diptych.

The 'political class' and the civic mass

Having formed the project, the next step was to define more closely the precise subject and the appropriate method of research. To begin with I postulated a difference between what I called provisionally, for want of a better name, the Roman 'political class' on the one hand and the civic mass on the other, my intention being to describe the latter's condition and evaluate the part played by it in various spheres. At first sight both these categories may seem arbitrary: was there really a 'political class' in Rome, and, if so, how was it distinguished from the masses? The question is all the more legitimate since, in Roman Italy as in any ancient *civitas*, the citizens were only a minority of the total population; alongside them were half-citizens and resident aliens, as well as 'allies' and 'subjects' who, although free men, did not share in all the political and civic activities proper to Romans. In addition there was of course the mass of the non-free, who may have outnumbered the citizens by two to one.[8] From this point of view the civic body, being a fairly small proportion of the total population, may itself appear in its diversity to constitute a political class *par excellence,* enjoying various privileges. From a different angle one may question the propriety of talking about a political class in an antique city-state of the Greek type, where all kinds of offices were filled by drawing lots and each man 'obeyed and commanded, turn and turn about.' None the less I believe there is a twofold justification for speaking of a political class in Rome, which may equally well be called an oligarchy.

I have recently come to the conclusion[9] that from the very first days of the Republic the exercise of military and civil functions by officers of higher rank, tribunes, prefects and magistrates, and also less senior officials such as the *tresviri monetales* and *capitales,* was legally subject to a property qualification. The same consequently applied to membership of the Senate, since as a rule the censors and *ad hoc* magistrates drew up the list of new senators from among those who had already been magistrates. If, in exceptional circumstances, a new batch of senators was created, including some who had not previously held public office, they were required at least to be *equites.* The property qualification for appointment to the magistracy was, naturally enough, set at the higher level, the same as that required for service in the cavalry. I shall not repeat here all the arguments which have led me recently to put forward this view, which is a new one. It may suffice to make clear that the minimum qualification for *equites* was originally defined by a variable figure of which we know only that it much exceeded that which applied to the *prima classis* of heavily armed infantrymen. Around the beginning of the second century BC it was definitely fixed, in a new money of account, at 400,000 sesterces, i.e. ten times the figure for the *prima classis*. The qualification for senators and *equites* was thus the same until the time of Augustus, who, at a date between 18 and 13 BC, raised the requirement for senators and magistrates to one million sesterces, while at the same time enacting measures the effect of which was to make public office and senatorial rank virtually hereditary.[10]

The Roman oligarchy was thus not merely a *de facto* one, emerging from the mass of the people by a natural sociological process, but a *de jure,* timocratic oligarchy based on a property qualification. We should not be surprised by this: it applies more or less to all ancient cities, the most open and democratic of which were none the less based on timocratic principles. The ancients always believed that certain offices, especially those that involved the handling of public funds, should only be held by men who could offer security: almost everywhere, those desirous of occupying financial posts were required to deposit caution-money with the treasury. It was a convenient simplification to accept as candidates only members of the groups with the highest property rating. Students of the Roman constitution such as Polybius or Cicero never regarded the city as a democracy but, at the most, a 'moderate oligarchy'. As will be abundantly shown, the entire civic mass was divided into a rigid hierarchy based on property and affecting the most elementary civic activities such as voting or participating in assemblies; itwould have been paradoxical if more important activities such as the magistracy had been an exception to the rule. Thus the Roman constitution itself drew a clear line between those who were entitled to take a direct part in public affairs and those who were not.

This does not mean that the rules were not occasionally broken. Exceptions might, for instance, be made on account of military merit, and in time of civil war or revolutionary upheaval *novi homines* of the humblest extraction might arise from the mass of the people. As a rule, however, a man had to make his fortune before he could join the political class, and the citizenry was at all times deeply divided on a wealth basis.

It should, however, be made clear at once that the Roman hierarchy was never based on wealth alone. Several other considerations came into play, especially those of birth: generally speaking, freedmen, their sons and even their grandsons remained subject to various civic and political disqualifications. Individuals might, by way of exception, be exempted from these, theoretically on ground of merit but in fact often thanks to an influential patron. We see here for the first time, but not the last, an illustration of the interplay between civic or political capacity and the social hierarchy, diverse and mobile by definition and traversed by the ties of patronage.[11] In a society of this type it may often, indeed, be more advantageous to be a freedman or favoured slave of a powerful patron or master than to be an ordinary citizen without money or influence. Thus, outside the political class formally defined by property qualifications (and, of course, by the actual performance of public duties), a wider circle takes shape consisting of various groups which all share in certain forms of power. In the first place, certain functions were more markedly political in ancient cities than they are nowadays. In Rome, from around 200 BC two categories come clearly into view, the judicial and the fiscal. Ordinary Roman citizens, unlike e.g. Athenians, were always excluded from the judiciary. After 123 BC judicial office became, by an irregular but irresistible process, a privilege and sometimes a monopoly of the *equites* duly qualified by wealth, on condition that they abstained from political activity in the strict sense —a kind of implied anticipation of the 'separation of powers'.[12] By a striking dichotomy, even civil suits between Romans were to be judged by men who were not only the richest in the community but were organized in an *ordo,* a regular constitutional body whose membership and activities were closely supervised by the state.

The complex of fiscal functions is even more curious from the modern point of view. Like all ancient cities and states, Rome for a long time had no adequate administration and sought the best practical ways of procuring the collection of taxes and other necessary supplies. The lazy but convenient process of tax-farming, which was systematically adopted, assured the government of a steady revenue, the amount of which was known in advance; it did so, however, to the detriment of the public purse and above all of taxpayers.[13] A fiscal system based on this method of tax-collecting has curious effects on civic behaviour. In Rome the method had a special feature of its own in that the principal tax-farmers, who formed permanent 'companies' in each province, had to be members of the equestrian order. From the point of view of the census they thus belonged to the same class as senators. Sociologically the two groups were very close, but they were separated by profound differences of function and divided from each other by financial, administrative and political issues. In this way the equestrian order, which provided judges and tax-farmers, appears as a kind of second nobility, a privileged order with strong internal ties which remained in close political and social contact with the senatorial class and regularly supplied it with recruits. The *equites* also constituted a political or rather a governing class, which might grudgingly accept the entry of a few plebeians from below.

To stop at this point would give an incomplete picture of the Roman governing class. It has been stated time and again that the Republic had no civil service in the proper sense:[14] routine or secondary business for which a magistrate was responsible would be handled by his own slaves or freedmen. No doubt this was true at the outset. But in the later republican period the state began to create what might be called a reserve of junior functionaries in the form of lists of qualified people (still referred to as *ordines*) forming a kind of embryo civil service. These officials — scribes, apparitors and others — conducted business in direct contact with the public; they enjoyed a considerable share of power, and above all they saw to its practical application. Inexperienced magistrates, of whom there were many, relied on their professional skill, and their permanence contrasted with the annual replacement of their superiors. Thus in many cases the citizen came to regard them as the embodiment of the state.[15]

Finally, the magistrates and senators who comprised the Roman political class in the narrow sense were — as is natural in a patriarchal, slave-owning society based on patronage — aided and sometimes manipulated by their immediate entourage of relatives, friends, clients, freedmen and slaves, who managed their day-to-day business and particularly their finances, looked after technical aspects such as the drafting of speeches, letters and political documents, and very often inspired their actual decisions. Such were the narrow and hazardous channels through which plebeians, if they so desired, might work their way into the political class.

Recruitment and behaviour

It is not the object of this book to study the political class, a task which has been admirably performed by modern scholars. A full and detailed study of subsidiary connections has still to be made, but apart from this it can be said that we have a pretty good knowledge of the Roman oligarchy and particularly of the way in which it was recruited: magistrates, senators, *equites*, judges and tax-farmers have been identified, listed and studied in terms of their origins and mutual relations. This preliminary work, based in large part on the prosopographic method, is by now almost completed[16] and provides a sufficiently accurate spectrum of the governing classes of the Republic. The picture will certainly be retouched and added to, but it is already quite clear enough for our purposes.

But, while we know well enough how the ruling class was recruited, we do not know as much as we might concerning its modes of action. It is true that, in the course of the last century or more, scholars have more or less reconstructed the institutional framework of political life at the highest levels: the way in which public office was achieved and exercised, the role and powers of the Senate, provincial commands, the apparatus of justice — all these have been more and more thoroughly studied as regards both principle and practice. But the prosopographic method, on which so many hopes were built since it was pioneered by M. Gelzer and F. Münzer, has perhaps not yielded such reliable results as is generally supposed. The attempt to explain almost everything in the political life of ancient Rome by the effects of kinship, marriages and factions —which were certainly important elements, but not exclusively so —is inevitably frustrated from time to time and leads in any case to a purely empirical and cynical view of events which takes too little account of the personal convictions, laws and morality of those concerned, not to mention their need for political support and the pressure, weak though it may have been, of public opinion. Accordingly other methods or points of view, inspired for the most part by political science, have begun to challenge the monopoly of the prosopographic approach in the purely political sphere.[17] Instead of assuming *a pri. ri* that everything is accounted for by the interplay of clans and families it would be worth while, for example, to study the actual operation of the decision-making process in particular cases: this would enable us to distinguish the various degrees of responsibility, the stages and levels at which action was taken at different times and in different circumstances, the devices by which it was obstructed and so on. This kind of approach will certainly improve our knowledge of the internal workings of the Roman political class.

Political and civic life

The present work, however, has a different purpose. Since the distinction between the political class and the mass of citizens has been seen to be a relevant factor, I am concerned only to study the latter, while of course not ignoring the ever-present problem of relations between the two sections of society in the form of recruitment, mutual communication etc. However, the scope of the enquiry must be carefully defined. It is not sufficient to confine ourselves to what is called politics, i.e. essentially the taking of decisions, the exercise of power and the ways, if any, in which it is supervised. Roman institutions, as I have just said, were such that the mass of citizens took very little part in this kind of activity. Virtually excluded from military command, the magistracy and the permanent deliberating body (the Senate), ordinary citizens were no more than electors with the role of voting for one magistrate or another or for the adoption of laws; and the voting system was weighted and subdivided to such an extent that only the richest and most eminent of the citizenry had any real influence. Moreover the rules provided only for a 'yes' or 'no' vote —according to the view generally accepted by specialists in Roman public law —and thus apparently precluded discussion and debate, if not freedom of information. At all events, if we only consider the mass of citizens in their purely political role, we are likely to find out very little about them: as to this, for the present we need merely recall the patronizing and disenchanted language of Cicero:

Do not then, Cato, take from the lower class this fruit of their attention [i.e. the privilege of following us about in crowds when we seek public office]. Allow the men who hope for everything from us to have something to give us in return. If poor men have nothing but their vote, then, even if they use it, their support is valueless. Finally, as they are always saying, they cannot plead for us, stand surety for us, or invite us to their homes. *(Pro Murena* 71)

But politics was not the only field in which Roman citizenship had specific consequences. The citizen was a voter, but before that he was a soldier and, incidentally, a taxpayer. The great majority of the political debates that took place within the political class and in which he was finally called on to exercise his vote were on military or financial questions. As in all ancient cities, the citizen's well-being or otherwise was determined by services and benefits affecting his 'person and property', to use the customary formula. Civic life, thus defined as the totality of rights and duties shared in actual practice by all citizens, goes a good way beyond what is strictly called 'politics', since it is quite possible to imagine such rights and duties as deriving from decisions in which the public had little or no part. The first task was therefore to identify these rights and duties, define their interrelations and present them as a coherent system which would, if possible, cover the whole field of citizenship.

From rules to reality

It would be naive and pretentious to suggest that the objective thus defined is a new one. Ever since Rubino, and more particularly from von Jhering and above all Mommsen to De Martino,[18] historians of Roman private and public law have been improving our knowledge of the juridical content of Roman citizenship. Imposing works of scholarship, each from its own viewpoint, have painted a precise and systematic picture which can no doubt be corrected here and there but which remains a permanent addition to our knowledge. My first duty is to acknowledge the debt we all owe to these unchallengeable studies, and at the same time to express a reservation. Mommsen, very rightly, attempted to codify the 'public law' of republican Rome; De Martino traced its constitutional development on a chronological basis and in terms of political, economic and social context, while von Jhering endeavoured to distil from its institutions a 'spirit' of Roman private law. But all these writers are lawyers by background, and all of them, consciously or otherwise, tend to emphasize the rule rather than its application, the norm as opposed to what actually happened, the legislator's intention rather than the resultant fact. Roman law, especially that of the republican period, has come down to us via the age-long stratification of codes and commentaries which date from imperial or Byzantine times and reflect a constant endeavour to impose logical consistency on the relations of men and things, to embody all statutes and reconcile all conflicts in a unitary system and a universal language providing a solution to every 'problem'. This fascinating phenomenon is perhaps unique in history, and may well contain in embryo the whole evolution of law in modern times; but it does not take account of humble day-to-day reality, especially that of republican Rome. Before the lives of Roman citizens were defined and conditioned by standards which lawyers in the imperial chancery or in schools of jurisprudence laboured to fashion into a coherent system, they had been regulated for ages past by a whole series of customary practices, very different in origin and scope, often contradictory or resting on highly archaic principles of consistency and logic which are in great part hidden from us. This was still the case at the end of the republican era. Moreover, the attempt to impose logic and consistency never extended beyond what could be called Roman private law —*jus civile,* the law as it applied to citizens —corresponding more or less to our civil and criminal law. Public law, i.e. the regulation of public authority and the relations between it and the citizens, was not, strictly speaking, regarded as a matter for jurists, and in fact they took little interest in it: they regarded it as an ephemeral subject and were content to leave it to the hazards of improvisation. It is hardly surprising, therefore, if the pictures painted by modern scholars such as Mommsen, and the systems they have attempted to create, fail to give a true account of reality. Legal language is not the most appropriate medium in which to describe what is essentially contingent, variable and transitory.

In the search to discover what really used to happen, I encountered my first surprise. This was that certain practices had no juridical basis, i.e. they did not originate in any law. Examples were the duties deriving from the obligation to perform military service, or again fiscal duties, although both of these very specifically defined the citizen's condition. Even when rules of public law can be identified, one is constantly having to enquire into their real scope, how far they were applicable in practice and how far they admitted of exceptions. The object is to discover as exactly as possible what particular rights and obligations meant in daily life to those who enjoyed or were subject to them. Even if the regulations governing compulsory military service are clearly laid down, the system remains an abstraction until one tries to find out who exactly was affected by it, for how long and how regularly, at what time of year and in what geographical area. One must try to establish its demographic and financial consequences for individuals and the community, and to get some idea of the command structure and the 'works and days' of the Roman legionary at a given time and place, from the day when he was called up to that of his discharge, if ever. The same kind of enquiry is necessary if we are to understand the effect in real terms of fiscal burdens and of participation in public assemblies. This is the object I set myself in preference to examining the juridical framework, which is better known and in which I was less interested.

Thus the study is one of practical reality, and also one of extreme diversity.

It would have been a cardinal error to assume at the outset that the status of a Roman citizen was uniform and unchanging, regardless of ethnic, physical or social differences. From the point of view of legal history this may have been the case, though it is not proved; but it would have been an absurd starting-point for an enquiry into actual patterns of behaviour. Except as a cardboard abstraction, there was no such thing as 'the' Roman citizen; there were only actual citizens who at the same time were landowners, tillers of the soil, Romans of Rome or mountaineers from the Apennines, men of consular ancestry or ex-slaves who had only just gained their freedom. Roman citizenship may have worked, or been intended to work, as a melting-pot, but clearly it cannot have meant the same thing to all its possessors whatever their immediate background. There is less temptation to go wrong on this point since, as we shall see, citizenship did not even purport to entail the same rights and duties upon everyone.[19] In terms of Roman public law, it was evident from the outset that our study would have to take account of inequalities; what I had therefore to investigate was whether these inequalities were, in real life, intensified or mitigated.

A re-reading of texts

While it thus became reasonably clear what the questions were, it remained to be seen whether the available information provided answers to them; or, in other words, what was the most suitable method of going about the enquiry. Long acquaintance with Mommsen, the alpha and omega of our studies, suggested a reply which I had in fact suspected for some time: while the works that have come down to us naturally emphasize the doings of the political class, they are not altogether silent as regards the living conditions of the rank and file. Mommsen was well aware of this: as a counterpoint to his somewhat dogmatic chapters on the norms of public law, he appended exhaustive footnotes drawing attention to anomalies and the details of everyday life. The first thing to do was to follow this up by making as complete a collection as possible of the scattered notes, hints and glimpses of day-to-day reality embedded in the mass of historical, literary, epigraphic and juridical texts that we possess. This involved re-reading, from a special and rather unusual point of view, a large number of very familiar texts and some that were less so. Naturally I was much aided by various special studies on particular aspects: to mention only one or two, the works of E. Gabba, P. A. Brunt and J. Harmand on the Roman army,[20] or what may be called the American school, from Botsford to Lily Ross Taylor,[21] on the organization and development of voting assemblies. Fiscal matters, on the other hand, have been treated by fewer scholars, and in this field I had to start more or less from the beginning. In the end, having studied the documentation left to us by the ancient world either with the help of previous scholars or on my own account, I found it more enlightening than might have been expected. The sort of evidence for which I was looking was fairly frequent in the historians, starting with Polybius and Livy, and became more plentiful as one turned to areas such as the drama and satiric poetry, which are naturally closer to everyday life. To these might be added grammars and lexica, and certain works on particular subjects which their authors were at pains to treat in a descriptive and journalistic style; here I have in mind especially Varro's admirable *Res Rusticae*. Similarly speeches, judicial and political literature which presents the activity of individuals and groups in actual situations, and, of course, Cicero's unique correspondence: a 'slice of life' which, while incomplete and in many ways cryptic, is absolutely unreplaceable. It is only proper to indicate at the outset what kind of evidence I have used, and it would be worth while to make a scientific analysis, as I hope to do elsewhere, of the amount of reliance that can be placed on it. Meanwhile the reader may be assured that I have borne this question constantly in mind. My first procedure, then, was simply to re-read in a fresh light and from a different angle the sources commonly used by historians of the Roman republic. This has been a pleasant experience, and I hope a useful one. I can even say, and shall in due course endeavour to show, that the mere collating of isolated facts and scattered allusions has made it possible to correct many errors of traditional interpretation and, in some cases, to make well-known texts more intelligible. These modest achievements are, in my view, the most valuable result of the work I have undertaken.

Naturally the texts by themselves are not enough. One of my constant preoccupations has been to supply the geographical and temporal setting of the various roles and activities of the Roman citizens who are the subject of this book. Following the lead of Z. Yavetz or Lily Ross Taylor,[22] but extending my enquiry to military and fiscal questions, I have tried to trace step by step the activities and movements which gave a pattern to civic life. A striking feature is the importance of the monumental setting which the Roman city, like those of Greece and the Hellenistic world, came to create as a framework to its collective activity. Topographical problems arise at every step in an investigation of this kind. It is not only a question of 'placing' the cardinal features and key points of civic life, of estimating space and distance, but also of recognizing the constant interrelation and mutual influence between this topographical and monumental setting, in its permanence or its modifications, and the actions and events which took place there. Sometimes the material setting determined the form and eventually the significance of this or that ceremony; sometimes, on the contrary, changing institutions involved an alteration in the décor. This perpetual interplay of form and content, manner and substance, is vividly illustrated, for instance, by the study of electoral procedures and the technical arrangements connected with them.

In this very field, in the last few years our knowledge has increased by leaps and bounds. The topography of republican Rome has been more and more clearly revealed by the work of Roman and foreign archaeologists and especially the publication in a virtually definitive form of the famous fragments of the 'marble plan' of the Severian period, which has been known for a long time but only recently became available for use.[23] By a happy chance the area which has benefited most from this advance in our knowledge is the Campus Martius, where most of the ceremonies of civic life were concentrated: the census, military recruitment and exercises, most of the electoral and legislative assemblies, and the storage and distribution of public stocks of grain, all took place in specified areas within this part of Rome. Of course there are still gaps in our information, but the essential topographical facts are known. Thus I was able to pursue my enquiry in this direction too, and was able from time to time to confirm a point of detail arrived at by professional archaeologists or topographers. Most often, however, topography is the science which enables us to answer questions about procedure. My particular thanks are due to F. Coarelli, who possesses a thorough knowledge of the topography of republican Rome and was good enough to discuss these matters with me at length during my visit to Rome in March 1975.

The identification of problems

Having thus defined in broad lines the subject and method of our enquiry, it was necessary to decide in what style to treat it. As I went along, I had to re-examine preconceived ideas or working hypotheses such as cannot be dispensed with in a project of this kind. The history I was trying to write was certainly not political history in the usual sense,[24] since, as we have seen, ordinary Roman citizens had little access to the hierarchical and social spheres in which politics in the narrow sense were conducted: i.e. political debate, executive decisions and the struggle for power. Nor was my subject the history of law or institutions (though it presupposed both of these), since one of the points I wished to explore was precisely the distance and the relationship between law and fact, regulations and practice. Political anthropology and political science were perhaps more helpful, but had to be used with care. These two disciplines in all their multiple variations are always more or less concerned, respectively, with relations between power and society and with the workings of the state.[25] Naturally I had to be constantly aware of these topics, but they were not my direct concern. I had not, for instance, set out to investigate the way in which the particular form of political organization called a city evolves from some earlier form; my purpose was to discover what it meant for citizens to belong to a city that was already established and well developed. I was not concerned to follow the British school in considering the various 'functions' that politics or civic life might perform in the social field as a whole, although this is a fascinating subject and is still seldom investigated in the case of Rome. Nor, on the other hand, was I concerned with exploring the structure of the Roman state, because civic life as I had defined it went well beyond the sketchy framework of state organization. In short, while political anthropology and political science — in both of which I can only boast such knowledge as I have taught myself — have provided very useful comparisons and metaphors and some ingenious topics of discussion, it would have served no purpose to apply their methods systematically to the task in hand.

Unless, no doubt, one were to go back to the origins of these sciences. If Rome is a city on the Greek or Mediterranean model, then perhaps we should study very closely the true 'founding father' of the disciplines in question, that is to say Aristotle,[26] and deliberately place oneself inside the mental universe that he presupposes in order to explore the characteristics of the Roman city. There was no question of reverting to the difficult but instructive task of expounding the *Politics,* which so many have done before me. But previous studies[27] had convinced me that the interpretation of the origin and structure of the Roman city offered by Hellenized Romans in the last days of the Republic, or Greeks interested in Rome — from Polybius to Dionysius of Halicarnassus — conformed, rightly or wrongly, to the Aristotelian typology of cities. Why, after all, should I not trust those who knew more of the matter than I? The definition of the city as a *societas (koinonia),* a society based on an implicit contract (*Politics,* 1276 b), corresponding to the basic definition of a citizen as one who 'has the right to participate in judicial functions and in office' (1257 a 22), was implicitly accepted by Romans of the second century BC as something that went without saying, and was explicitly stated by Cicero in the following century.

Aristotle's analysis of the aspects or parts (*merè,* 1328 b) of collective life that are necessary to the survival of the city is still wholly applicable: it comprises, in ascending order of importance, economic functions (food supply and techniques), arms, the monetary system, religious ceremonies and finally, embracing all the rest, reasoned deliberation and decision (*krisis)* on matters of common concern and internal conflicts. This analysis, if one reflects on it, provides a guiding thread which makes it possible to discern the pattern of city life in concrete terms. That is to say, it offers a complete view of civic man and an adequate political anthropology. Of course, by thus attempting to summarize I am over-simplifying. In reality the theory has to be deduced from an extremely careful reading of the Aristotelian corpus, bearing in mind that Aristotle endeavoured, by a tremendous effort of synthesis, to take account of the extreme diversity of the political and constitutional forms of hundreds of Greek cities at different stages of development, which he had made it his business to collate and study. His anthropology is on the scale and in the image of the Greek world — which explains why, among other things, it is an anthropology of change and transition, seeking a 'model' which will account for the incessant adjustments that are seen to occur. The writers whom we must take as a basis — Polybius, Cicero, Dionysius — set out to measure Roman reality by Aristotle's yardstick, and their task appears simpler inasmuch as they had to do with a single city whose historical evolution is better known to us, or so we believe, than that of any Greek *polis*. A city of great size (and here already is an essential difference), but with a comparatively stable and conservative constitution, extended the mantle of the law of the Quirites over the regional diversity of all Italy. It was a city, moreover, that Polybius, followed on broad lines by Cicero and Dionysius, classed as a 'moderate oligarchy', something very close to the ideal 'mixed constitution' which Aristotle, after much argument for and against, designated as the least harmful of political regimes.

Under this constitution relations between the citizens, the magistrates and the Senate were determined empirically, as described in the celebrated analysis in Book VI of Polybius, and both Dionysius and Cicero stated and examined with care the rules governing the participation of all citizens in essential common activities, i.e. their membership of the special type of society called a city. Having studied the matter on as broad a basis as possible we were surprised and pleased to find that the logical links we sought to establish, the coherence which we believed it possible to trace, in short what appeared to us to be the fundamental and central structure, was already clearly formulated by ancient authors who, aided by the powerful instrument of Greek philosophic thought, made it their business to sift what was essential from mere anecdote. Dionysius and Cicero, like Livy after them and perhaps Polybius before them, arrived at the firm conclusion that in the last resort the whole Roman *urbs* was based on the single institution of the *census*, fundamental throughout the diversity of its consequences. To be a citizen is, as Aristotle said, to belong to a community based on an implicit contract, involving the participation of all in its duties as well as its benefits. The only problem is to determine on what principle this participation shall be based. Aristotle saw clearly that revolutions and the prosperity and downfall of cities largely depended on the strength or weakness of the *consensus* among their citizens. All the authors we are considering believed that the *consensus* among Roman citizens, at least till around 100 BC, was remarkably strong, proof against internal tension and the most redoubtable foreign enemies; and they attributed this to the excellence of the system which regulated participation in different civic activities and distributed throughout the social body the advantages and disadvantages of communal life. For once in a way, specific texts (which must naturally be assigned to their proper place in a history of culture and ideas — but this I have done elsewhere) go almost as far as one could wish to confirm the concrete, empirical evidence that I have tried to collect and arrange in the present work. It would surely be over-fastidious to decline to use this convenient instrument, which provides a logical framework and will at least save us from anachronisms. Let us give Aristotle, Dionysius and Cicero their due. They are certainly not the only thinkers from whom I have borrowed terms, concepts or 'topics', but I would nevertheless acknowledge a debt to them in particular. We shall see in due course that one can naturally put forward a different 'reading' of the Roman political system whose basis I have tried to explore; for variety's sake one may even, with a grain of salt, borrow some fashionable references to 'structure' or 'system' from Claude Lévi-Strauss or David Easton. But there is really no better way of understanding Rome than by studying Polybius, Dionysius or Cicero.

The foregoing will, I hope, explain clearly enough the purpose of this book. I have studied civic life in what appear to me to be its three main dimensions: military, fiscal and financial, and finally deliberative or electoral. In all three I have tried to bring out the profound influence of the census system and the property qualification, its principles and consequences. But it seemed to me that while the rules of participation in these three fields constituted a coherent language in the third and even the second century BC, this harmony was beginning, for various reasons that will be set out, to disintegrate towards the end of the latter century. Clearly the institution of the census ceased to meet all the needs of communication within the social and political body, as the three pillars of the republican state — the citizens' army, fiscal emulation and electoral discipline — disappeared, logically enough, one after the other. New forms of communication, channels of command and ways of securing the *consensus* came into being and, it seems to me, tended to constitute a new code, a new set of languages alongside the old code of civic behaviour. I have tried to analyse this code, but more briefly than the old one, if only because the subject is new and will require much more investigation. It seemed essential to give some outline of it, however, since otherwise a dangerously false impression would be given of the life of a Roman citizen in the last century of the Republic.

It may cause misgiving that nothing is said on the important subject of religion. No one who has read Fustel de Coulanges can ignore the religious dimension of civic affairs. But this vast subject, privileged as it is by our sources and by contemporary scholarship, is foreign to my tastes and abilities, and it is best to admit the fact openly. On the other hand, the subject-matter of this book as I have defined it extends logically to a further study, that of unofficial and non-civic groups of citizens: 'sodalities', *collegia* of all kinds, and what may perhaps legitimately be called political parties. I am well aware that these structures, whether old or new, were no less important in determining civic behaviour than was membership of a tribe or an assembly, but for lack of space I am obliged to defer a full treatment of them to a later date.

Paris, March 1975

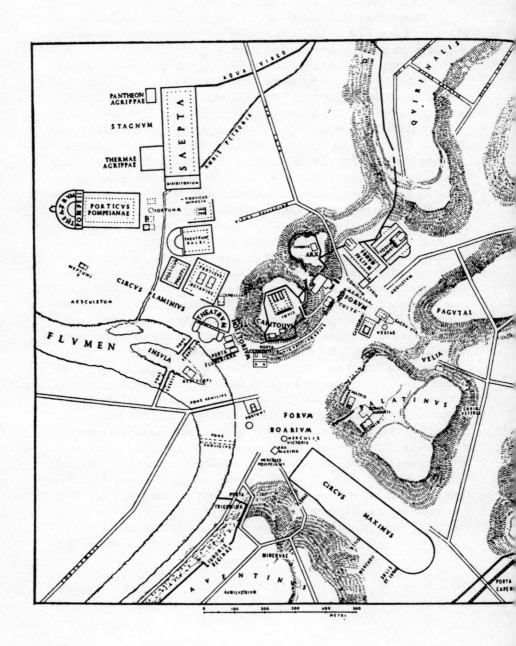

I The centre of Rome in the Augustan period.

CHAPTER I

CIVITAS
The citizen and his city

I N THE YEAR 212 the emperor Caracalla issued a 'constitution' or edict granting Roman citizenship to all free *peregrini* in the Empire. This measure was subject to restrictions, aimed no doubt at certain particularly inferior classes, and to a clause safeguarding the 'rights' of indigenous communities, i.e. local customs and especially fiscal rights. The exact scope and intentions of the *constitutio Antoniniana* (formerly known as the edict of Caracalla) are still a matter of dispute, but at all events it signifies the triumph of a particularly striking tendency in Roman civic organization which may be called 'oecumenism'. Roman citizens might have jealously preserved their own status, leaving other peoples in a state of subjection; instead they granted equal rights, more or less promptly and spontaneously, to larger and larger groups of aliens, first in Italy and later in the provinces. The broad lines of this process are unmistakable, and it is remarkable for its continuity. A recently discovered document has clearly shown that Caracalla's edict, spectacular as it was in his day, was the result of an evolution lasting over nearly two centuries. The process began on a considerable scale as far back as the reign of Augustus. The census of the year 14 (Augustus, *Res Gestae* 8. 4) registers a total civic population of 4,937,000 men, women and children; some authorities, like P. A. Brunt, think this figure too low by some 20-25%, so that the total number of citizens would be between 5,924,000 and 6,171,000. Taking six million as an approximate figure, this may represent (though here we are on much less certain ground) something between a fifth and a tenth of the total population of the Empire.

There is little evidence of resistance on the part of non-Romans to this progressive integration into the civic body of the master nation. On the contrary, the grant of citizenship was always represented or felt to be a privilege and a benefit. There is no clearer testimony to this than the pompous but impressive *Roman Oration* by a second-century rhetorician, Aelius Aristides,[1] a friend and pupil of Herodes Atticus, who spoke as follows in Rome itself, probably in about AD 143:

But there is that which very decidedly deserves as much attention and admiration now as all the rest together. I mean your magnificent citizenship with its grand conception, because there is nothing like it in the records of all mankind. Dividing into two groups all those in your empire—and with this word I have indicated the entire civilized world—you have everywhere appointed to your citizenship, or even to kinship with you, the better part of the world's talent, courage, and leadership, while the rest you recognized as a league under your hegemony.

Neither sea nor intervening continent are bars to citizenship, nor are Asia and Europe divided in their treatment here. In your empire all paths are open to all. No one worthy of rule or trust remains an alien, but a civil community of the world has been established as a free Republic under one, the best, ruler and teacher of order; and all come together as into a common civic centre, in order to receive each man his due.

What another city is to its own boundaries and territory, this city is to the boundaries and territory of the entire civilized world. (*Roman Oration* 59-61).

Making all due allowance for official rhetoric, this is not the embittered language of a vanquished people; its author is a Greek who feels himself truly Roman. While noting what he says about the social limits within which citizenship was still confined at this date, we can clearly recognize that his praise was well deserved from the ethnic, geographical and religious points of view: for in 198 Septimius Severus—a recently Romanized Semite, a man of Punic race from Leptis Magna who spoke Latin with a strong accent—became in his turn the heir of the Caesars. No power in history had ever assimilated its subject peoples to this degree.

The question that arises, however, is why there was this kind of universal attraction. What was the secret of this 'freedom of the city', and what did Roman citizenship signify in the framework of an empire?

St Paul[2] would have had an answer to this question, for the fact of his Roman citizenship stands out with especial prominence in his turbulent relations with the judicial authorities of the Roman Orient. His difficulties began at Philippi, a Macedonian city with an established Latin colony; here Paul and his companions were arrested and taken before the local magistrates, beaten with rods and put in prison. When the praetors, discovering their error, tried to set them free unobtrusively, Paul replied: 'They have beaten us publicly, uncondemned, men who are Roman citizens, and have thrown us into prison; and do they now cast us out secretly? No! let them come themselves and take us out.' (*Acts* 16:37). A similar incident occurred at Jerusalem, where Paul was rescued from the crowd by the tribune in command of a praetorian cohort, who arrested him and had him bound. The tribune had his first surprise when Paul said to him in Greek: 'May I say something to you?'—'Do you know Greek?' the tribune replied. 'Are you not the Egyptian, then, who recently stirred up a revolt and led the four thousand men of the Assassins out into the wilderness?' Paul—who, as we shall see, was skilled at building up his effects—replied: 'I am a Jew, from Tarsus in Cilicia, a citizen of no mean city.' (*Acts* 21: 37-39). The tribune nevertheless had him taken to the barracks and ordered him to be examined by scourging, 'to find out why they shouted thus against him'.

When they had tied him up with the thongs, Paul said to the centurion who was standing by, 'Is it lawful for you to scourge a man who is a Roman citizen, and uncondemned?' When the centurion heard that, he went to the tribune and said to him, 'What are you about to do? For this man is a Roman citizen.' So the tribune came and said to him, 'Tell me, are you a Roman citizen?' And he said, 'Yes.' The tribune answered, 'I bought this citizenship for a large sum.' Paul said, 'But I was born a citizen.' So those who were about to examine him withdrew from him instantly; and the tribune also was afraid, for he realized that Paul was a Roman citizen and that he had bound him. (*Acts* 22:25-9).

The third episode shows even more clearly what citizenship entailed. Paul, after his arrest at Jerusalem, was taken to Caesarea for his case to be investigated by Felix, the procurator of Judaea. Felix treated Paul benignly and kept him under a mild form of custody for two years. But when he was again accused by the Jews of Jerusalem before Felix's successor, Porcius Festus, who seemed inclined to have him tried at Jerusalem, Paul finally played his trump card:

'I am standing before Caesar's tribunal, where I ought to be tried; to the Jews I have done no wrong, as you know very well. If then I am a wrongdoer, and have committed anything for which I deserve to die, I do not seek to escape death; but if there is nothing in their charges against me, no one can give me up to them. I appeal to Caesar.' Then Festus, when he had conferred with his council, answered, 'You have appealed to Caesar; to Caesar you shall go.' (*Acts* 25:10-12).

This famous story is one of the few documents we have which illustrate the procedure of *provocatio ad Caesarem* and show exactly what was the advantage of being a Roman citizen. In the first place, it conferred a civil status that protected the individual *vis à vis* magistrates or high imperial functionaries, in the direct line of republican tradition. Roman citizenship meant above all, and almost exclusively, the enjoyment of what might be called a right of habeas corpus in the shape of an appeal to the Roman people in the person of the emperor. In its full form this privilege meant, as it did for St Paul, that local court proceedings were stopped and the accused was taken to Rome under military escort (but on a journey of such length he was not badly treated). This was the rule at least until the second century AD. For instance, when Pliny the Younger had to investigate and prosecute the Christians of Bithynia following complaints by the local priesthood, he reserved the case of those who were Roman citizens for trial in Rome.

This, then, was the principal aspect of Roman citizenship under the Empire: a civil and juridical safeguard. But there was another dimension too: citizenship was the key to advancement, the essential condition of entry into the small circle of those who governed, or rather administered the state. For this largely autonomous community was defended by an army and governed by an administration that were exclusively Roman, i.e. composed of citizens. One had to be a citizen in order to serve in the legions, even as a private soldier (but not in the auxiliary forces, which represented at least half the strength); to become an officer or NCO (even in the auxiliaries); to become a civil servant, especially, of course, a senior one of 'equestrian' rank; and, above all, to have any hope of becoming a magistrate or senator or rising to a high military or civilian post. Even so, the imperial regime, which was aristocratic on principle, put all sorts of obstacles in the way of social and political advancement. By no means all citizens were allowed to seek high office; if it was not purely hereditary, at any rate the authorities were very careful as to who was admitted to the inner circle. As for the ambitious provincial élite of whom Aelius Aristides speaks, Roman citizenship was their only means of access to the corridors of power, and as a rule it took them several generations to get there.

No doubt there were sometimes interested motives behind the progressive conferment of this privileged status on outsiders. Given the physical conditions of those days and the distances involved, the presence of Rome which seems so overwhelming to us must sometimes have been exerted in a lax fashion in outlying areas. Provincials enjoyed a large measure of autonomy, and often escaped control by the centre. Giving them the status of citizens was an elegant way of bringing them closer to the seat of power. From time to time, also, it was felt necessary to recruit men of ability; and finally, very often fiscal motives were at work. While, as we shall see, citizens were generally privileged in matters of taxation, from AD 6 onwards they alone were subjected to an estate duty the proceeds of which were devoted chiefly to military expenditure. Naturally, Caracalla's enemies put it about that this was the real reason for his 'generosity' in 212.

From our point of view, a more serious fact is that during the whole period of the Empire the nature of citizenship was undergoing change. It continued to confer a personal status which was useful especially from the procedural point of view, and it still provided access to the extremely narrow channel through which a tiny minority could aspire to administrative office; but in the heyday of the Empire it lost what had been its essential feature under the Republic, by ceasing to be a guarantee of participation in political life. In former days the humblest of citizens was a member of a collective sovereignty.

He helped to deliberate and to elect the magistrates, and by his vote was master of his own destiny and of the *res publica*. Under the Empire this power subsisted in name only. Augustus professed to restore a *respublica* which was to be, literally and for all time, the 'people's cause', but behind this fiction there gradually developed a quite different reality. This was not exactly a tyranny or even an Oriental-type monarchy (that was to come later), but a strictly oligarchic regime which soon put an end to power-sharing and political debate, though not to equity or civil liberties. It was a regime of secrecy in which decisions, wise though they might be, were taken by the emperor in his own council and prepared by administrators who, however able, were answerable to no one. The only outlet for public opinion consisted either in the closely supervised debates of a Senate virtually recruited by the emperor, or in urban riots and military pronunciamentos. There were still citizens, but civic life was extinct.

Under the Republic this was all quite different. True, citizenship was not restricted to a close community after the fashion of the Greek *polis*. The process that led to universal citizenship in imperial times began early, and the expansion of Rome made it a power on an imperial scale by the end of the fourth century BC. From its very beginning the City had absorbed alien elements and been free in granting citizenship to foreigners. But in spite of Rome's territorial expansion, and also the existence of what were in effect degrees of citizenship, the latter was not merely a guarantee of juridical status, though this was its fundamental purpose; it also conferred on its holders a political character, that of moral and physical participation in a coherent system of rights and duties, the *munera* of a citizen. Albeit in different degrees, this status belonged to every Roman citizen. Under the Empire, when citizenship betokened no more than juridical or strictly judiciary privileges, it still conferred great prestige; how much more must it have signified when it also connoted a civic function. Sure enough, it was in republican times that outsiders demanded the status of citizens most insistently; this created a political problem of the first magnitude, which was not solved until the Italian insurrection of 90-89 BC led to one of the most bitter and murderous wars in Roman history. To ascertain the underlying value, the limits and significance of this participation of citizens in their common affairs is the main object of the present study.

Roman citizenship[3]

Archaic types of community, some deriving from the most ancient structures of Indo-European peoples, certainly existed in Rome before the birth of the *Urbs* — the urban centre, seat and foundation of collective life.[4] They are only known to us indirectly, by the fugitive and enigmatic traces that they have left in the vocabulary, topography, and religious or military institutions of later times. It was certainly an anachronism and an over-simplification when the

Romans postulated the existence of a Roman 'people' and *civitas* at the very outset, at the foundation of the Roman polity. But this is of no great importance to us: the fact that the Romans traced back their corporate existence to semi-legendary times is a proof that they felt strongly the basic importance and indivisibility of these ideas. As far back as their historical memory went, the Romans believed that they had from the first been *cives,* citizens. Or rather—and this itself is significant—the word appears for the first time in the context of 'synoecism' with the Sabines (their fathers-in-law!) under the reign of Romulus, at the moment when Romans and Sabines, united in 'a single city', chose to designate themselves by the mysterious term 'Quirites':

[The Sabine women besought] their fathers on this side, on that their husbands, that fathers-in-law and sons-in-law should not stain themselves with impious bloodshed, nor pollute with parricide the suppliants' children, grandsons to one party and sons to the other. 'If you regret,' they continued, 'the relationship that unites you, if you regret the marriage-tie, turn your anger against us.'...It was a touching plea, not only to the rank and file, but to their leaders as well. A stillness fell on them, and a sudden hush. Then the leaders came forward to make a truce, and not only did they agree on peace, but they made one people out of the two. They shared the sovereignty, but all authority was transferred to Rome. In this way the population was doubled, and that some concession might after all be granted the Sabines, the citizens were named Quirites, from the town of Cures. (Livy 1.13.4)

This legendary tale contains a core of truth which is confirmed by etymology. It is striking that the birth of the *civitas* should be accompanied by invocations of kinship. The corresponding Greek words *(politeai, polites)* are derived from *polis* (formerly *ptolis*), the original meaning of which is 'citadel': to the Greeks, the citizen is essentially an inhabitant of the city. The Latin *civis,* on the other hand, is related to Indo-European roots connoting the idea of the family, an outsider admitted into the family, a guest or a friend. *Civis* is an associative term: its proper meaning is not 'citizen', but 'fellow-citizen'.[5] As soon as the city is constituted by the association of two peoples differing in race but soon intermarrying (no doubt the reflection of old rules of exogamy as between two halves of the people), it organizes itself into groups, the *curiae,* which symbolically bear a Sabine name. Etymologically these *curiae* are *co-viria,* 'men who assemble' for peace or war, just as the Romans are Quirites, i.e. no doubt *co-viri.* The same word with the same meaning is found among other Italic peoples, particularly the Volscians of Velitrae.[6] These, the most ancient divisions of the city, thus denote on the one hand a religious and political community— since, in historical times, the *curiae* are the seat of religious observances and civic and military decisions—and, at the same time, ties of blood and marriage. It is doubtless not pressing etymology too far to say that Roman citizenship, whatever aspect it wore in later times, never lost its double character of a sacral and political community based on a community of rights (*jus civile*, citizens' rights) which, among other things, strictly regulated family ties. One example, to which we shall revert, is that as soon as a Roman freedman was legally released from bondage he became a fully-fledged citizen as far as civil status was concerned, but he could only do so by joining a family, a *gens* — that of his former master, now his patron, whose name he took and whose family cult he adopted from then on. Conversely, an individual could only become or cease to be a member of a particular family within the framework of the community and with its approval: adoption was a public act affecting the whole body of citizens.[7]

Rome and Italy: municipia *and* coloniae

Citizenship, as we have said, was a unitary status: all citizens, at least after the law of the Twelve Tables (middle of the fifth century), enjoyed equal political rights. But if we consider all the inhabitants of Italy who progressively came into contact with Rome and, willy-nilly, were subjected to its power *(imperium)*, we find great and long-standing differences in their relations with the Roman polity. At the end of the period we are concerned with, however, i.e. after the Social War (war against the allies) of 91-89 BC, these differences disappear; from then on, with a few negligible exceptions, all Italians become or can become Roman citizens. This was a progressive integration, lasting over more than two generations, but was on a very large scale, doubling or trebling the number of citizens during that period. In other words, from the point of view of the integration of citizens in their own city, which is what chiefly interests us here, the Social War was an important dividing-line, after which Roman political, judicial and military life could no longer be the same. Before trying to define the scope of citizenship, therefore, we must say a few words about the evolution which, in a little over two centuries, turned the whole of Italy — which, on the scale of the ancient world, may be compared to a continent in modern times — into a single city-state, maintaining with Rome, proportionately speaking, the same admirable, paradoxical relations as Rome did two centuries later with the whole *oecumenè*, according to Aelius Aristides' description.

Rome, which thus showed itself more hospitable to aliens than any other city of the ancient world, had not always pursued an assimilationist policy. In the early days it was certainly no less exclusive, shut off and mistrustful than other cities, even towards its closest neighbours, who were often the most cordially hated. Enemy territory began at the frontier; and, just as at Gubbio in the second century the ancient rites of lustration invoked divine curses on the neighbouring Etruscans, we know that in the very earliest times a strictly guarded barrier, the *fossa Quiritium*, divided the Forum itself into the territory and domain of Roman citizens and that of the Latins. Although Rome was one of the Latin cities and belonged to their League until the fourth century, despite the ties of race and language she unalterably refused to enter into any community with them. As is well known, a pious legend disguised the relationship of hostility and, no doubt, of dependence which long prevailed between Rome and the Latin league: Rome, having in 496 defeated at Lake Regillus the Latin allies of the Tarquins who had just been expelled from the City, imposed on them a treaty, the *foedus Cassianum,* which provided for a moderate form of Roman supremacy. Very likely the true story was quite different, but the point is that Rome preserved the memory of a fundamental antagonism to Latium. Even in AD 204 the hymn sung at the secular games which were supposed to ensure the well-being of the state included the ancient formula: 'Grant that the Latins submit to us.'[8] A story illustrates the persistence of Rome's congenital mistrust of the Latins in 338 BC, on the eve of the 'Latin war' in which the Romans and their Samnite allies fought the Latins and Campanians. Before what is called their 'rebellion' (but in all probability they were in no way 'subject' to Rome at this time), the Latins sent envoys to Rome demanding that, since they shared the Romans' military and financial burdens, they should also enjoy an equal share of political responsibility:

'But, since you cannot make up your minds to bring your impotent sovereignty to a close, we — though able by force of arms to give Latium her freedom — will nevertheless concede so much to kinship as to offer terms of peace fair and equal to both sides, since the immortal gods have willed that we should be of equal strength. One consul should be chosen from Rome, the other from Latium, the senate should be drawn in equal proportions from both nations, there should be one people and one state; and that we may have the same seat of empire and the same name for all, by all means let this rather be our city, since one side must make concessions,—and may good come of it to both peoples!—and let us all be known as Romans.'

Titus Manlius, the Roman consul, reacted violently to this:

Hear, Jupiter, these wicked words! Hear ye, Law and Right! Shalt thou behold, O Jupiter, alien consuls and an alien senate in thy consecrated temple, thyself overpowered and taken captive? Are these the covenants, Latins, that Tullus, the Roman king, made with your Alban forefathers, that Lucius Tarquinius afterwards made with you? Remember you not the battle at Lake Regillus? Have you so forgot your old disasters and our goodness to you? (Livy 8.5.4-9).

Whether from pride in their military prowess or from some remnant of religious particularism, the Romans in early times reacted similarly to almost every suggestion that citizenship should be conferred on aliens who were often ex-enemies into the bargain. In 216 they replied characteristically to the Capuans who, taking advantage of the disaster at Cannae (while at the same time preparing to rebel against Rome and ally themselves with Hannibal), proposed to the Romans that the consulate should be shared between the two states:

> Legates were sent to Rome by the Campanians with the demand that, if they wished them to aid the Roman state, one of the consuls should be a Campanian. Resentment was aroused, and the legates were ordered to be removed from the Senate House. (Livy 23.6.6-7)

As we shall see later, the same resistance was manifested in 90 BC when under the pressure of a terrible war, the Senate resolved to grant citizenship to all Italians; and in AD 40, when the emperor Claudius proposed to the Senate that certain Gauls should be admitted to its membership and receive the *jus honorum* (the right to be a candidate for public office). Yet these reactions, natural and comprehensible as they were, never prevented Rome in the last analysis from obeying the tradition, so marked from its earliest times, which led it to grant citizenship to aliens and even to recent enemies, far more freely and extensively than any other nation. The impressive example of the debate in the Senate on Claudius's proposal, reported at length by Tacitus and confirmed by the Lyons inscription, shows the arguments used on either side:

> Italy, it was asserted, was not yet so moribund that she was unable to supply a deliberative body to her own capital... Was it too little that Venetians and Insubrians had taken the curia by storm, unless they brought in an army of aliens to give it the look of a taken town? What honours would be left to the relics of their nobility or the poor senator who came from Latium? All would be submerged by those opulent persons whose [Gaulish] grand-fathers and great-grandfathers, in command of hostile tribes, had smitten our armies by steel and the strong hand, and had besieged the deified Julius at Alesia...

Finally, however, the liberal principle defended by Claudius won the day:

> What else proved fatal to Lacedaemon and Athens, in spite of their power in arms, but their policy of holding the conquered aloof as alien-born? But the sagacity of our own founder Romulus was such that several times he fought and naturalized a people in the course of the same day! Strangers have been kings over us: the conferment of magistracies on the sons of freedmen is not the novelty which it is commonly and mistakenly thought to be, but a frequent practice of the old commonwealth. (Tac. *Annals* 11. 23-24)[9]

In the period we are concerned with, the Narbonian Gauls do not yet enter the picture. But the assimilation of the Italians, which was completed between 90 and 60 BC and complemented by the naturalization of the Transpadanians in 49, had its beginnings at least as early as the fourth century and eventually proved irresistible despite periodic holdups and bursts of reaction. The ways in which it was accomplished, however, differed from one period to another. The juridical processes used to enable individuals or groups to join the Roman community were multiform, as were the situations to which they were applied: for the ancients were particularly sensitive to particularism, to ethnic or religious differences and incompatibilities.[10] Relations could not be the same with Latins, men of similar race, language and religion, as they were with Etruscans, whose civilization, while admired, was foreign (though Rome had been an Etruscan city for a whole century), or with semi-barbarous Samnites who knew nothing of urban association, or again with Greeks. Moreover, in this domain, which was fundamentally one of international law, Rome always took close account of the attitude of the people in question towards Roman rule or the Roman alliance, and meted out rewards and punishments accordingly.

Some of these peoples were granted citizenship in the early days by way of reward, or benefit as it was termed. Thus the Etruscan city of Caere, which aided Rome against the Gaulish onslaught of 390, is said traditionally to have been granted citizenship without voting rights: *civitas sine suffragio*.[11] But later cases, for instance that of Anagnia (Anagni) in 306, show that by the end of the fourth century this type of limited citizenship, which we shall try to define presently, had come to be regarded as a punishment or at least a means of keeping a distrusted population under strict control:

> To the three Hernic peoples of Aletrium, Verulae, and Ferentinum their own laws were restored, because they preferred them to Roman citizenship, and they were given the right to intermarry with each other — a privilege which for some time they were the only Hernici to enjoy. The people of Anagnia and such others as had borne arms against the Romans were admitted to citizenship without the right of voting. They were prohibited from holding councils and from intermarrying, and were allowed no magistrates save those who had charge of religious rites. (Livy 9.43.23)

Similar treatment was extended to Privernum in 309 BC; the tradition which records this expatiates on the pride and dignity of these opponents of Rome, but it may well be that the real motive was to keep them under surveillance by forced integration under the appearance of equality:

> One of the deputation from Privernum,...on being asked by a certain advocate of harsher measures what punishment he thought the Privernates merited, replied, 'That punishment which is merited by those who deem

themselves worthy to be free.' The consul [replied] 'What if we remit your punishment? What sort of peace may we hope to have with you?' 'If you grant us a good one,' was the answer, 'you may look to find it faithfully and permanently kept; if a bad one, you must not expect that it will long endure.' [On this the consul commented] that only those who took no thought for anything save liberty were worthy of becoming Romans. Accordingly they gained their cause in the senate, and on the authorization of the Fathers a measure was brought before the people conferring citizenship [*sine suffragio*] on the Privernates. (Livy 8.21.2-10)

In any case, whatever its original value, *civitas sine suffragio* came to be felt as a dependent relationship. Hence the special census lists in which these communities were registered *en bloc* (like Caere, the first of them) finally came also to include full citizens who had been deprived of rights for disciplinary reasons. Without the right of voting and, as a corollary, that of seeking public office, citizenship entailed little more than military and financial obligations, plus the fact that the citizen's civil status remained assured and that he enjoyed the same juridical and judiciary protection as other citizens. The status of a *civis sine suffragio* seems to correspond closely, at least at a certain stage, to that of a *municeps* as defined by Roman jurists and antiquarians,[12] though the precise meaning of this latter term is not clear; the *municeps* was unquestionably a Roman citizen, but belonged to a non-Roman city or community which was an integral part of the city. The antiquarians and jurists give two definitions; the better is undoubtedly that of Festus, whose sources date from the end of the Republic. He states that the *municipes* were a class of persons who, although not Roman by origin, when they came to Rome shared the obligations of Romans in all respects, except as regards voting and eligibility for the magistracy (155 L). Festus also says that men of this category 'served in the legions but could not occupy posts of honour' (117).

The other definition, by Aulus Gellius, is much later and no doubt refers to a Roman development subsequent to 89 BC, perhaps interpreted in the light of an ancient practice of Greek international law that was in force throughout the Eastern part of the Empire: the *isopoliteia,* or potential right of citizenship, which some cities granted to foreigners individually or as part of a treaty settlement.

Municipes are Roman citizens from free towns, using their own laws and enjoying their own rights, merely sharing with the Roman people an honorary *munus,* or 'privilege' (from the enjoyment of which privilege they appear to derive their name), and bound by no other compulsion and no other law of the Roman people, except such as their own citizens have officially ratified. We learn besides that the people of Caere were the first *municipes* without the right of suffrage, and that it was allowed them to assume the honour of

Roman citizenship, but yet to be free from service and burdens, in return for receiving and guarding sacred objects during the war with the Gauls. (Aulus Gellius 16.13.6)

Whatever the exact juridical nature of the status of *municeps,* it was certainly used by Rome to bind closely to herself a large number of Italian peoples. In 338, at the close of the last Latin war, she dissolved the Latin League and offered or imposed the rank of *civitas sine suffragio* on many old Latin cities. At the end of the fourth century and the beginning of the third the same status was conferred willy-nilly, as we have seen, on many cities of the Hernici, Aequi and Volsci, and later on the Sabines and Umbrians. Above all, whatever disagreement there may be on details, this was the condition imposed on the most important region of Italy, whose entry into the Roman orbit was decisive from the point of view of future conquests: Campania with its rich and populous chief city of Capua, which had for a long time rivalled Rome and made a last brief effort to challenge her authority during the second Punic war. The Campanians became citizens in the sense that they served in the Roman army and that some of them (perhaps those who chose to settle in Rome) could attain full citizenship and even become magistrates and senators. On the other hand, the mass of simple *cives* who remained in their homes certainly became citizens *sine suffragio.* They were allowed to keep their own laws and magistrates: Capua in 216 still had its Senate and eponymous magistrates, the *meddices,* but their authority was confined to local affairs. After the battle of Cannae in that year it was precisely its external freedom of action, its independence in the diplomatic sense, that Capua sought to recover.[13]

Another method used by Rome at a very early date to strengthen its hold on certain parts of Italy was by colonization *(deductio,* as it was called), somewhat in the Greek manner, whereby groups of families, usually of demobilized ex-soldiers, were settled in strategic spots on confiscated territory.[14] This was not a spontaneous process but an official one, decided on at Rome and by Rome for its own needs and consecrated by formal rites. Despite the name *coloni* (tillers of the soil), the purpose of these settlements was essentially military. The first colonies, composed of citizens, were established along the sea-coast—hence their name *coloniae maritimae*—first of Latium and Campania and, in the second century, of southern Italy and the Adriatic. Each colony consisted of no more than 200 or 300 families, no doubt because they were regarded, as we shall see, as an integral part of the civic body, fragments of Rome outside Roman territory, and it was hard to apply this paradoxical concept to groups of any size. However, these principles were departed from in a second phase which began shortly before the second Punic war. Colonies were established in inland areas, especially those newly conquered from the Gauls in the Po valley, and the numbers of colonists were much greater. Finally a third phase began in the time of Caius Gracchus, towards the end of the second century: colonies were now regarded essentially as a way of providing land for dispossessed citizens, or of bringing land into cultivation. Throughout these different phases, colonization remained a highly effective means of Romanization and integration. As Aulus Gellius put it:

[The colonies are different from the *municipia:*] for they do not come into citizenship from without, nor grow from roots of their own, but they are, as it were, transplanted from the State and have all the laws and institutions of the Roman people, not those of their own choice. (Aulus Gellius 16.13.8)

Colonies in the strict sense were, so to speak, a detached part of the Roman army encamped on foreign soil. The military and political link with the mother city appeared in the archaic solemnity of the foundation rites, the procedure for recruiting colonists, their ceremonial march and spectacular entry into occupation of the new home. Tacitus regretted the abandonment of these customs:

Veterans were drafted into Tarentum and Antium, but failed to arrest the depopulation of the districts, the majority slipping away into the provinces where they had completed their years of service; while, as they lacked the habit of marrying and rearing families, the homes they left behind them were childless and without heirs. For the days had passed when entire legions — with tribunes, centurions, and privates in their proper centuries — were so transplanted as to create, by their unanimity and their comradeship, a little commonwealth. The settlers now were strangers among strangers; men from totally distinct maniples; leaderless; mutually indifferent; suddenly, as if they were anything in the world except soldiers, massed in one place to compose an aggregate rather than a colony. (*Annals* 14.27)

The 'ancient' custom, to be exact, dated rather from the last hundred years of the Republic, especially the *deductiones* of Sulla, Caesar and the triumvirs (Appian, *B. Civ.* 2.120, 133: 3.81). In any case, the Roman colony was a community in its own right, with institutions of its own, generally modelled on those of Rome. Only one colonial charter has survived, that of the Julian colony of Urso (Osuna) in Spain, and its conformity with Roman public law can be verified.[15] But, as far as civil law went, the colonists were naturally on the same footing as Roman citizens and were bound by Roman legislation. The only, small exception related to the military *munus* of the maritime colonies: as it was their special task to guard a portion of the coast, both by sea and by land, they were exempt from other duties (but this was no more than a division of responsibilities). In emergencies, moreover, additional tasks were imposed on these colonies: e.g. in 207, or in 191 during the war with Antiochus (Livy 27.38.3).

What is remarkable from the point of view of the extension of civic rights is that, when colonies were established, non-Romans were permitted to join them and thus became Roman citizens. This happened at Antium, a Latin city, when a maritime colony was created alongside the town in 338 (Livy 8.14).

The nomen latinum

To a greater extent than by direct integration, conferring citizenship *optimo jure* or *sine suffragio,* or by the foundation of colonies, Rome consolidated its hold on Italy by an original process employed on a very large scale, that of 'Latin' colonies.[16] These were new communities based on the same principle as Roman colonies, but much larger and more numerous, which were granted a juridical status similar to that accorded to the former cities of the Latin League after it was defeated and dissolved by Rome in 338. As a result of this the *nomen latinum* ceased to designate an ethnic group with geographical boundaries and came to denote a particular status with a *jus* granted irrespective of ethnic or territorial factors. As we shall see, 'Latins' thus defined were halfway between citizens and 'allies' or subjects; there was a kind of waiting-room occupied pending the acquisition of full citizenship by a great many inhabitants of Italy until 89 BC and, under the Empire, by most of the provincial cities. The Latins, old or new, were certainly not citizens: this is shown by their official designation, 'allies of the Latin name', and by the details of their civil status: they were not registered as members of a Roman tribe but, as we shall see, were listed separately, like the other allies. Some of them—the old Latin cities—were linked to Rome by an ancient treaty *(foedus),* so that in a sense the Latins can be called *foederati:* their relations with Rome were thus governed by specified rights and obligations. But the new Latin colonies were on a different footing. From 338 to the end of the second century Rome founded numerous colonies throughout Italy (Livy says there were 30 at the time of the second Punic war), enjoying a much more flexible regime than that to which colonies were subjected. For the Latins were not affected by the paradox which for a long time characterized the status of Roman colonies, whose members, although full citizens, lived outside the only place in which their political and even civil rights could be fully exercised. The Latins, not being Romans, lived under their own laws and possessed their own juridical system, public and private. Procedures governing their relations with Roman citizens were laid down at least as early as 241 BC, when the Romans created the office of praetor 'to pronounce on matters of law as between citizens and *peregrini*'; the Latins enjoyed certain guarantees such as privileged civil rights of trading *(commercium)* and matrimony *(conubium),* but could not share fully in the *munera* (rights and obligations) of Roman citizens. They contributed to the majesty of Rome, but in a manner prescribed once and for all by the *foedus* or *lex* under which their communities were founded. They served in the auxiliary forces, but their collective obligations were generally fixed in advance, both in fiscal and in military matters. This was advantageous to Rome, which could thus evaluate the resources at its disposal, and also to the colonies, who knew where they stood and could doubtless share out the obligations among individual citizens as they thought fit. The *jus latinum* thus appears as a very flexible form of autonomy under which Rome was assured of the colonies' loyalty by the mutual observance of a charter. It is notable, moreover, that from the very first occasion when such a colony was founded, that of Cales in 338, Roman citizens were allowed to register as members of a Latin colony, as were all other inhabitants of Italy. Cicero bears witness to this well after the Social War: 'Those who, being Roman citizens, migrated to Latin colonies, could not become Latins unless they deliberately chose to do so, and sent in their names for enrolment.' (*De Domo* 78; cf. *Pro Caecina*). Later still, the jurist Gaius compared the condition of freedmen who had become 'Junian Latins' to that of the 'free Roman citizens who became colonial Latins, having left the City to take part in the foundation of a Latin colony'.

Naturally the Romans who were thus prepared to relinquish their citizenship were chiefly proletarians attracted by the prospect of an apportionment of fertile land in the new colony. For the Latin colonial foundations were much more extensive as well as more populous than Roman colonies, and each member received a sizable allotment, especially in the Po valley. This no doubt explains, as E. T. Salmon and P. Brunt have pointed out,[17] why the Roman authorities accepted and no doubt expressly permitted the depletion of the body of citizens that the system entailed: the individuals concerned were not rich enough for their loss to be of any consequence, and, on the other hand, the amount of land granted to them in their new abode (up to 50 *jugera* for the infantrymen at Aquileia in 181: Livy 40.34.2) made them liable for military service.

In any case, the system of Latin colonies was an immense success for nearly two centuries. In the first place they were all centres of Romanization, since a large proportion of their inhabitants were no doubt Romans; at the same time they were a melting-pot in so far as they consisted of former *socii* of diverse origin linked by a new juridical status. According to Livy there were as many as 30 Latin colonies at the time of the second Punic War, and collectively they formed the backbone of Roman domination in Italy. Their loyalty to Rome was complete—whereas the allies sometimes deserted to throw in their lot with Hannibal, and some *cives sine suffragio,* like the Campanians of Capua, actually rebelled against Rome—and this was recognized by the Carthaginians as one of the underlying causes of their own failure. Hannibal's adversary Hanno perceived this, to judge from the words Livy puts into his mouth on the morrow of Cannae:

'I should like either Himilco or Mago to answer, in the first place, whether any state among the Latins has revolted to us, although the battle of Cannae meant the utter destruction of the Roman power, and it is known that all Italy is in revolt; in the second place, whether any man out of the 35 tribes has deserted to Hannibal.' (Livy 23.12.15)

No doubt, as the war continued, some Latin colonies found the financial and military burden more and more onerous. In 209, when the reinforcements sent to Sicily were nearly all Latins or allies, 12 out of the 30 colonies protested to the Senate and demanded that their obligations be reduced. It is worth quoting Livy's account in full, as it shows the exact nature of the colonies' burdens and their relationship with Rome:

Complaints began to be heard among Latins and allies in their gatherings: that for over nine years they had been exhausted by levies of troops and their pay; that almost every year they fought in a disastrous defeat. Some, they said, were slain in battle, others carried off by disease. The townsman who was enlisted by the Roman was lost to them more completely than a man taken captive by the Carthaginian. For with no demand for a ransom the enemy sent him back to his native town; the Romans, however, transported him out of Italy, really into exile rather than into military service. For the eighth year now the soldiers from Cannae were growing old there, certain to die before the enemy, who at the very moment was in the flower of his strength, departed out of Italy. If the old soldiers should not return to their native places, and fresh soldiers continued to be levied, soon no one would be left. Accordingly what the situation itself would soon refuse, before they should reach the extreme of desolation and poverty, must be refused the Roman people. If the Romans should see the allies unanimous to this effect, surely they would think of making peace with the Carthaginians. Otherwise never, so long as Hannibal lived, would Italy be rid of war. Such were the matters debated in their meetings.

There were at that time 30 colonies of the Roman state. Of these, while delegations from them all were at Rome, 12 informed the consuls that they had no means of furnishing soldiers and money. These were Ardea, Nepete, Sutrium, Alba, Carsioli, Sora, Suessa, Circeii, Setia, Cales, Narnia, Interamna. The consuls, deeply impressed by what was unheard of, wishing to deter them from so abominable a move, and thinking they would accomplish more by upbraiding and rebuking them than by soft words, told them that they had dared to say to the consuls what the consuls could not bring themselves to utter in the Senate. For it was not a refusal of burdens and of military service, but an open revolt against the Roman people. Accordingly they should return to their colonies promptly, and, since they had spoken of so great a crime, but had not yet ventured to commit it, they should deliberate with their people as though nothing had been settled. Let them remind them that they were not Capuans nor Tarentines, but Romans, sprung from Rome and sent thence into colonies and on land captured in war, to increase their race. All that children owed to their parents they owed to the Romans, if there was any filial affection, any memory of their former city. Let them therefore deliberate again; for their present reckless proposal tended to betray the Roman empire, to give over the victory to Hannibal. The consuls by turns kept on for a long time in this strain; but the deputies, still unmoved, said that they had nothing to report back home, nor did their senates have anything new to decide upon, in towns where there were neither soldiers to be enlisted nor money to be furnished for pay. The consuls, finding them unyielding, brought the matter before the Senate; and there such terror was inspired in the minds of the members that a great many of them said the empire was at an end; that the same thing would be done by the other colonies, the same by the allies; that they all had conspired to betray the city of Rome to Hannibal.

The consuls exhorted and comforted the Senate, and said that the rest of the colonies would be loyal and dutiful as formerly; that even the colonies which had abandoned their duty would have respect for the empire, if legates were sent about among them to upbraid, not to entreat. Permission having been given the consuls by the Senate to act and do as they thought to be in the interest of the state, after first sounding the temper of the other colonies, they summoned their legates, and asked them whether they had any soldiers in readiness according to the compact. On behalf of the 18 colonies Marcus Sextilius, of Fregellae, replied that they had soldiers in readiness according to the compact, and would give more if more were needed, and would exert themselves to do whatever else the Roman people might command and desire. To that end, he said, they did not lack means and had even a surplus of spirit. The consuls began by saying that to do the men justice it did not seem enough that they should receive praise from the lips of the consuls only, without having the entire Senate first return thanks to them in the Senate House; and then they bade them follow into the Senate. After addressing them in a decree as complimentary as possible, the Senate instructed the consuls to bring them before the people also, and along with the many other conspicuous services they had rendered to the senators themselves and their ancestors, to recount their recent service also to the state. Even now, after so many generations, they shall not be passed over in silence or defrauded of their praise. It was the men of Signia and Norba and Saticula and Fregellae, and of Luceria and Venusia, and of Brundisium and Hadria and Firmum and Ariminum, and on the other sea, the men of Pontiae and Paestum and Cosa, and in the interior, the men of Beneventum and Aesernia and Spoletium, and of Placentia and Cremona. With the aid of these colonies at that time the empire of the Roman people stood fast, and thanks were rendered to them in the Senate and before the people. Of the other 12 colonies, which refused to obey orders, the senators forbade any mention to be made; their legates should neither be dismissed nor detained nor spoken to by the consuls. That silent rebuke seemed most in keeping with the majesty of the Roman people. (Livy 27.9-10)

Livy's account shows that the colonies' obligations were prescribed by a *formula* which specified the number of troops and amount of money to be contributed. It also shows that, at least at the time of year when the Senate and magistrates debated the amount of the *supplementum* and the tribute (i.e. the needs of the current campaign in respect of men and money), the colonies sent delegations to Rome to take part in the discussion. Such delegations, curiously enough, are the only form of 'representational' regime that existed in ancient times; they show Rome to have been a state of a federal type, at least in its relations with its colonies and allies. We meet with them on other occasions: e.g. in 338, on the outbreak of the Latin war, the *decem principes* of the Latins formed an embassy to Rome, and in 193, over the levies for the Ligurian war:

Minucius, the consul...sent notice to the allies of the Latin confederacy, that is, to their magistrates and ambassadors, who were under the obligation to furnish soldiers, that they should meet him on the Capitoline. For these he made up a list amounting to 15,000 infantry and 500 cavalry, in accordance with the quota of young men in each state. (Livy 34.56.5-6)

Similar delegations, as we shall see, were sent at other times to remonstrate over particular issues.

Livy also throws light on the condition of the Latins by describing the measures taken five years later against the ten rebellious colonies of 209:

While they were discussing the men needed to recruit the legion in the provinces, certain senators suggested that, since now by favour of the gods fear had at last been removed, it was time for them no longer to tolerate what had been endured as best they could in critical circumstances. As the Senate was alert and in suspense, they added that the 12 Latin colonies which had refused to furnish soldiers in the consulship of Quintus Fabius and Quintus Fulvius had been exempt from service now for about five years, as though it were an honour and a favour bestowed upon them, whereas in the meantime good and obedient allies, in return for their loyalty and submission to the Roman people, had been exhausted by successive levies every year. These words revived the memory of an affair almost obliterated and correspondingly inflamed the anger of the senators. Accordingly, allowing the consuls to bring up no other question first, they decreed that the consuls should summon to Rome the magistrates and ten leading citizens in each case from Nepete, Sutrium, Ardea, Cales, Alba, Carsioli, Sora, Suessa, Setia,

Circeii, Narnia, Interamna, these being the colonies concerned; that they should order them to furnish double the maximum number of infantry that each of those colonies had ever furnished to the Roman people since the enemy was in Italy, and also 120 horsemen in each case. If any colony should be unable to make up that number of horsemen, it should be permitted to give three foot-soldiers for one horseman. Men having the largest means should be chosen for infantry and cavalry and sent to any place outside Italy where supplements were needed. If any delegation should refuse, it was decided that the magistrates and envoys of that colony should be detained, and that if they asked for a hearing in the senate, it should be refused until they had done what was required of them. It was further ordered that a tax of one *as* for each thousand be laid upon those colonies and exacted every year, and that a census be taken in those colonies on the basis of a census-list furnished by the Roman censors. They resolved also that it be the same which was administered to the Roman people, and that it be sworn to by the censors of the colonies and brought to Rome before they laid down their office.

In accordance with this decree of the Senate the consuls summoned the magistrates and leading citizens of those colonies to Rome and required of them soldiers and the tax. Thereupon they outdid each other in refusing and loudly protesting. They said that such a number of soldiers could not be made up; that even if the normal number were required according to the original compact, they could hardly reach it. They begged and implored that they be permitted to go before the Senate and make their plea. No such offence, they said, had been committed that they deserved to perish. But even if perish they must, neither their crime nor the anger of the Roman people could enable them to furnish more soldiers than they had. The consuls, disinclined to yield, ordered the envoys to remain at Rome, the magistrates to go to their homes in order to conduct levies, adding that unless the number of soldiers demanded of them was first brought to Rome, no one would give them a hearing in the Senate. Thus, after their hopes of appearing before the Senate and of making their plea had been shattered, a levy was carried out in those 12 colonies without difficulty, since owing to long exemption the number of younger men had increased. (Livy 29.15-16)

This shows how the sanction consisted in multiplying the figures prescribed by the treaty or charter, a procedure also applied to Roman citizens. As we shall see when we come to discuss fiscal questions, the imposition of a fixed annual *stipendium* was also a sanction, as the Roman tribute was not levied in this way. Finally, the imposition of Roman assessment standards on the colonies shows that they had previously enjoyed some privileges in this respect, similar perhaps to those of the Hernician city of Aletrium, which, before the Social War, was able to exempt from public service the son of a local magistrate and benefactor.[18] As we have seen, the richer citizens of these colonies were to be subjected to a larger fine, and it is therefore understandable that the Romans wanted to keep a close eye on the workings of the local census.

But these military and financial protests must not be mistaken for acts of rebellion; as we shall see, they were echoed during the same period by Roman citizens themselves.

During all this time, as late as the beginning of the second century, the *nomen latinum* was enough of an advantage for most Latin cities to wish to retain it. When Rome desired to reward the heroism of the Praenestine cohort which had withstood the siege of Casilinum,

> the Roman Senate voted to the Praenestine soldiers double pay and exemption from service for five years. Though rewarded for their courage with the gift of Roman citizenship, they made no change. (Livy 23.20.2)

We may note, however, that towards the beginning of the second century a contrast can be perceived between the Latins who remained in their own cities for the sake of the privileges they enjoyed there, and the increasing number who took advantage of the *jus migrationis* to settle in Rome. A Latin living in Rome, though in principle a non-citizen, could to some extent be admitted into the civic community; although not enrolled in any tribe, he voted on each occasion, as Livy tells us, with a tribe selected by lot. This procedure applied in reverse to Roman citizens temporarily resident in Latin colonies, as appears from a provision in the municipal charter of Malaca (Málaga), dating, it is true, from imperial times: 'Every person holding the *comitia* in the said *municipium* for the election of duumvirs or aediles or quaestors shall out of the curiae appoint one by lot, in which resident aliens, being Roman or Latin citizens, shall register their votes, and for such persons the registration of votes shall be in that curia'.[19]

There was a strong temptation, therefore, for those who had settled permanently in Rome to consider themselves citizens and enrol on the census lists. The Romans themselves did not object, for the censors accepted these declarations. But the Latin cities concerned objected to the loss of their citizens, as their financial assessment remained the same while the number of taxpayers decreased. On two occasions, in 186 and 177, the Senate was obliged to give satisfaction to such complaints:

> Ambassadors from the allies of the Latin confederacy, who had assembled from all Latium in great numbers from every side, were granted an audience by the Senate. When they complained that a great number of their citizens had migrated to Rome and had been assessed there, Quintus Terentius Culleo the praetor was instructed to search them out, and, on receiving from the

allies proof that any person or the father of such person had been assessed among the allies in the censorship of Gaius Claudius and Marcus Livius or after that censorship, to compel such persons to return to the places where they had been registered. As a consequence of this investigation 12,000 of the Latins returned home. (Livy 39.3.4)

In 177 the practice was extended: a law, the text of which has not come down to us, provided that Latin allies could become Roman citizens by simple registration provided they left children in their own cities. The Latins evaded this by selling their children to Roman citizens who immediately freed them, so that they too became citizens. Latins who had no children doubtless made a fictitious sale of their own persons. To satisfy the Latin cities, the Senate ordered the consul C. Claudius to enact a law obliging persons who had been registered as Latins under the censorship of M. Claudius and T. Quinctius to return to their own cities (Livy 41.9.9). A *senatus consultum* provided additionally that manumission before a magistrate would in future not be valid unless accompanied by an oath that its purpose was not to effect a change of citizenship.

During the whole period, the status of a Latin from the point of view of civil law was so advantageous that many preferred it to Roman citizenship. In 192, for example, it was seen that many were enabled by it to evade the Roman law on usury: this might suit the convenience of both borrowers and lenders, but above all it permitted the latter to charge extortionate rates of interest:

> A way of evasion was opened because accounts were transferred to allies [and Latins], who were not under the operation of these laws. When a method of curbing this practice was sought, it was determined that [after a fixed day] whatever allies should have lent money to Roman citizens should make a public statement to that effect, and that proceedings regarding money so loaned after that date should be governed by the laws of whichever state the debtor should elect. Then... Marcus Sempronius, tribune of the people, with the authorization of the Senate proposed to the assembly, and the assembly voted, that the allies of the Latin confederacy should have the same law regarding the loan of money that applied to Roman citizens. (Livy 35.7)

Another well-known instance is that when the Romans adopted the *Lex Furia* on bequests (at an unknown date) and, in 169, the *Lex Voconia* on the capacity of women to inherit property, the Latin cities were free under their treaties to reject this legislation (Cicero, *Pro Balbo* 21).

The Italian question in the first century BC

The situation began to alter, however, towards the end of the second century, and this is one of the major themes of Italian history in Roman times. What was previously thought of as a privilege accorded generously in return for military and financial aid that involved no great sacrifice, came to be regarded as a state of inferiority to which the greater part of the Italian population was relegated by Rome. The Italians' discontent is very evident during the tribunate of Tiberius Gracchus, but must have made itself felt at an earlier date. No doubt there were several reasons for its coming to a head, but the basic cause lay in the transformation, to be described in more detail later, of the status of full citizenship, as successful conquests made it possible to alleviate the traditional obligations of the Roman citizen. In 167 he was exempted from direct taxation — the *tributum* — while military levies, which were less and less popular, were considerably reduced. As the citizens were refractory, the burden tended to be shifted on to the lower classes, who were, to some extent at least, volunteers attracted by the lure of booty. More important still, from the time of T. Gracchus onwards public policy was increasingly based on the new idea that a citizen had a right to be economically assisted by the state: large-scale grants of land took place, soon followed by distributions of grain and other benefits. In short, Roman citizenship came to be first and foremost a matter of privilege. Meanwhile the position of the Latins and allies continued to be governed by old charters, the terms of which were endurable as long as the Romans performed their share of obligations, but were less and less so in the new political situation. A gulf opened between the Italians and the Romans. We now know for certain that only citizens benefited from the redistribution of land under the *Lex Sempronia* of 133, but it seems very likely that the surplus land was confiscated from all those to whom the *ager publicus* was leased, whether citizens, Latins or allies: this was shown by the growth of the protest movement led by Scipio Aemilianus in 129. Again, it is almost certain that practically the whole brunt of the external wars of the pre-Gracchan period was borne by the Latins and allies: cf. for instance the *dilectus* (levy) of Scipio on his departure for Numantia in 134.[20] From that time onwards the burden of campaigning fell on the allies and especially the Latins. No doubt they always shared in the booty, but exclusion from full citizenship deprived them of the new advantages that were beginning to accrue from the adoption of Hellenistic ways and customs.

At the same time, non-citizens were being less and less well treated by Roman magistrates. Methods of command had always been brutal, and there was not much change in these: during the second Punic War, Roman officers were particularly severe to rebel cities, as is shown by Fulvius Flaccus' punishment of Capua in 212. But this kind of severity was meted out to citizens as well, and had long been taken for granted. Around the beginning of the second century, however, the guarantees affecting individual citizens were greatly strengthened; rights of appeal and the juridical protection of the individual were specified in a series of laws which soon came to be regarded as the essential core of Roman *libertas* and the keystone of the constitution. The

Latins and allies were outside the scope of these laws, as they were not formally part of the body politic. This being so, Roman magistrates and pro-magistrates were inevitably tempted to abuse their powers, and according to orators and historians such abuses were a fundamental cause of Italian discontent. An unhappy precedent was set in 173 by the consul L. Postumius, who, in revenge for disrespect allegedly shown him by the Praenestines—a loyal community if ever there was one—sent a message to the city

> to the effect that the magistrate should come out to meet him, that they should engage at public expense quarters for his entertainment, and that when he should leave there transport animals should be in readiness.... The anger of the consul, even if it was while he was in office, and its silent acceptance by the Praenestines, whether too modest or too fearful, established, as by an approved precedent, the right of magistrates to make demands of this sort, which grew more burdensome day by day. (Livy 42.1.7-12)

In 125-123, when Italy was already up in arms, political orators were in no doubt that behaviour of this sort was the basic cause of the revolt. C. Gracchus told a similar story in 123 in a well-known speech supporting a proposal to confer Roman citizenship on Latins and the legal status of Latins on the allies:

> 'The consul lately came to Teanum Sidicinum. His wife said that she wished to bathe in the men's baths. Marcus Marius, the quaestor of Sidicinum, was instructed to send away the bathers from the baths. The wife told her husband that the baths were not given up to her soon enough and that they were not sufficiently clean. Therefore a stake was planted in the forum and Marcus Marius, the most illustrious man of his city, was led to it. His clothing was stripped off and he was whipped with rods. The people of Cales, when they heard of this, passed a decree that no one should think of using the public baths when a Roman magistrate was in town. At Ferentinum, for the same reason, our praetor ordered the quaestors to be arrested; one threw himself from the wall, the other was caught and beaten with rods.' (Aulus Gellius 10.3)

More than half a century earlier, in about 190, Cato had denounced such behaviour and upbraided Q. Thermus for having inflicted a scourging on the *decemviri* of an allied city whom he accused of neglecting his travel arrangements.[21]

The Italian question, as a result, presented itself time and again in political and even military terms. In 125 Fregellae revolted—a move so desperate, to all appearances, that the Romans wondered if the townsfolk were not reckoning on some powerful aid in Rome itself; suspicion apparently fell on the consul M. Fulvius Flaccus, who in that year had proposed (Valerius Maximus 9.5.1) that the Italians should be given Roman citizenship and that any who refused it should at least enjoy the right of *provocatio*. Gaius Gracchus, a friend and protégé of M. Fulvius, revived this proposal in 122, particularly as far as the Latins were concerned. It was defeated by the opposition of the consul C. Fannius, who appealed to the most selfish instincts of the urban plebs: 'If you give the city to the Latins, do you think you will have as much room as you have now at public meetings like this one, or at the games, or for your festivities? Don't you see that they will crowd you out?'[22] The Senate thereupon decided—as it had, for very different reasons, in 177—to expel the Latins and allies from Rome. Another 20 years' quiet was secured by allowing the Italians to take part in colonizing Africa and Cisalpine Gaul; while in 122 the Senate and the tribune Livius Drusus took steps to protect the Latins against the excesses of military discipline. But a fresh storm brewed up towards the year 95, when the two consuls passed a law obliging Latins and allies who attempted to pass themselves off as citizens to revert to their proper status. This, according to Asconius, was the primary cause of the ensuing war.[23] The Italians' last hopes of a peaceful solution were reposed in Livius Drusus, son of the tribune of 122, who proposed one or more laws for their enfranchisement. When civil war became imminent they apparently bound themselves to Drusus by a solemn, archaic oath, the text of which, somewhat distorted, can be read in Diodorus:

'I swear by Jupiter Capitolinus, by Vesta of Roma, by Mars her ancestral god, by Sol the founder of the race, and by Terra the benefactress of animals and plants, likewise by the demigods who founded Rome and by the heroes who have contributed to increase her empire, that I will count the friend and foe of Drusus my friend and foe, and that I will spare neither property nor the lives of my children or parents except as it shall be to the advantage of Drusus and of those who have taken this oath. If I become a citizen by the law of Drusus, I shall consider Rome my country and Drusus my greatest benefactor.' (Diodorus 37.11)

A document of this kind is suspect, however: it may be a piece of anti-Italian propaganda by Drusus' enemies, who truckled to the selfishness of the urban plebs and held out as long as they could against the extension of the franchise. There was a witch-hunt, as usually happens on such òccasions, with the demagogues scenting treachery everywhere. An emergency law was passed, the *Lex Varia de majestate,* against 'those who had incited the allies to arms'. The following passage from *Rhetorica ad Herennium* (by Cornificius?), with its clear references to complicity within the city, may be part of a speech advocating this law or prosecuting somebody under its terms:

'Men of the jury, you see against whom we are waging war—against allies who have been wont to fight in our defence, and together with us to preserve our empire by their valour and zeal.... Their nearness to us and their alliance with us in all affairs enabled them to learn and appraise the power of the Roman people in every sphere. When they had resolved to fight against us, on what did they rely in presuming to undertake the war, since they understood that much the greater part of our allies remained faithful to duty, and since they had at hand no great supply of soldiers, no competent commanders, and no public money?...Someone will ask: "What of the Fregellans? Did they not make the attempt on their own initiative?" Yes, but these allies would be less ready to make the attempt precisely because they saw how the Fregellans fared....Have they, then, in taking up arms, been impelled by no motive? Have they relied on no hope? Who will believe that any one has been so mad as to dare, with no forces to depend on, to challenge the sovereignty of the Roman people? They must, therefore, have had some motive, and what else can this be but what I say?' (*Rhet. ad Her.* 4.9.13)

The Social War was bitter and long drawn out, and engulfed most of central Italy. In many ways it resembled a civil war. Not all Romans were intransigent: Marius and his friends, in particular, were anxious for reconciliation, as is shown by his celebrated meeting, between the battle-lines, with the Marsic commander Pompaedius Silo.

Marius led his army into Samnite territory and encamped over against the enemy. Pompaedius, who had assumed full command of the Marsic forces, also advanced with his troops. As the armies came close to one another their grim belligerency gave way to peaceful feelings. For as they reached the point where features could be distinguished, the soldiers on both sides detected many personal friends, refreshed their memory of not a few former comrades in arms, and identified numerous relatives and kinsmen, that is to say, men whom the law governing intermarriage had united in this kind of friendly tie. Since their common bonds compelled them to give voice to friendly greetings, they called one another by name and exchanged exhortations to abstain from murdering men bound to them by close ties. Laying aside their weapons, which had been placed in hostile poses of defence, they held out their hands in sign of friendly greeting. Seeing this, Marius himself advanced from the battle line, and when Pompaedius had done the like they conversed with one another like kinsmen. When the commanders had discussed at length the question of peace and the longed-for citizenship, in both armies a tide of joyous optimism surged up and the whole encounter lost its warlike air and took on a festive appearance. And inasmuch as the soldiers too had in private conversations been urging peace, they were all glad to be relieved of the necessity of mutual slaughter. (Diodorus 37.15)[24]

The war in fact ended with the satisfaction of the Italian demands, which were supported by a majority of the Senate. Three or four laws dating from 90, 89 and perhaps 88 provided various ways in which Italians of different categories could gradually achieve full citizenship. Any free inhabitant of Italy and any free community could henceforth, if they wished, be integrated in the *civitas Romana* in the way that had long been open to the *municipia*. Their citizenship would be given specific form by census registration and, above all, enrolment in a tribe. This seems to have been the profound desire of the great majority of Italians, who had only opted for complete independence (with a rival state, a federal capital and institutions of its own) because for a time they despaired of making the Romans see reason. The war was over fairly quickly, however, although in some areas armed resistance, encouraged by the Roman civil wars, persisted as late as the year 82. Hatred and hardships were soon forgotten, so strong was the desire for Roman citizenship among the allies, both the upper class and the masses. To the former, as we shall see, it meant an opportunity of entering politics and taking part in government; while to ordinary individuals it signified juridical protection of every kind, in Rome or in the provinces, and the fiscal and economic privileges they had long coveted.

There were, however, some problems to be solved, first and foremost the harmonization of laws. A very few cities such as Neapolis (Naples) and Heraclea in Lucania, which already enjoyed an advantageous treaty with Rome, at first wondered if they would not do better to abide by the arrangement which left them their old institutions and considerable autonomy in the sphere of private law (Cicero, *Pro Balbo* 21). Then there were practical problems of the administrative and constitutional organization of the old Latin colonies or allied cities, now assimilated to Roman *municipia* of long standing: it was a long time before balanced arrangements could be worked out. Finally, all the new citizens had to be gradually integrated in the elaborate machinery of the census, outside which there could be no real exercise of civil rights. As full citizens they were prospective army recruits, taxpayers and electors, and particularly in this last field the influx of new citizens threatened to cause disequilibrium. Most of them belonged to cities which had hitherto had their own system of social classification and access to political rights. As we shall see, one of Rome's first measures was to standardize the method of registration on the Roman pattern but to have it carried out locally (at any rate in a new *municipium* such as Heraclea, but no doubt more or less everywhere), the results being then reported to Rome. None the less, the years after the Social War were a time of civil disturbance aggravated by the fact that the archives had been destroyed by fire, and it was not until the great census of 70-69 that practically all the new citizens were finally registered. As G. Tibiletti and T. P. Wiseman have shown, the intervening delay and even obstruction was probably due to certain political leaders and to the reluctance of former citizens to have their votes in the *comitia* swamped by new electors. So lively were their fears that an attempt was made between 90 and 87 to draft the legal provisions implementing the right of citizenship in such a way that the number of tribes to which the new citizens might belong was limited to eight or even three; we shall return to this in a later chapter. Again, a considerable section of Roman opinion — essentially the urban plebs and some of the prouder nobles — for a long time made no secret of its contempt for the Italians. In aristocratic circles this contempt extended even to such a man as Cicero, whose native city, Arpinum, had enjoyed *civitas sine suffragio* since 306 and full citizenship since 188! Cicero's grandfathers were *equites,* he was by marriage a cousin of Marius, who had been consul six times, yet a Clodius or a Torquatus spoke of him scornfully as a 'foreign king' or a 'newcomer to Rome'. Such manifestations of snobbery, however, weighed little against compared to the mounting influence of the new citizens. Men from all over Italy were prominent in the *comitia*, the army and the magistracies, not to speak of the business world and Roman settlements in the provinces, and their influence was deliberately relied on by successive statesmen: Pompey, Caesar, Cicero himself, Lucius Antonius in 43 and finally Octavian Augustus. As Cicero proudly said to Antony (Philippics 3.15), 'How few of us [senators] do not come from the *municipia!*'; he had said the same in 63 to Manlius Torquatus, the adversary of his client Sulla (*Pro Sulla* 24). The best example of this spectacular assimilation of the Italians, including those who had taken up arms against Rome, is the fabulous career of Ventidius Bassus, the first Roman to triumph over the Parthians:

He was born in Picenum in a humble station, and with his mother taken prisoner by Pompeius Strabo, father of Pompey the Great, in the Social War, in the course of which Strabo subdued the Aesculani. Afterwards, when Pompeius Strabo triumphed, the boy also was carried in his mother's arms amid the rest of the captives before the general's chariot. Later, when he had grown up, he worked hard to gain a livelihood, resorting to the humble calling of a buyer of mules and carriages, which he had contracted with the State to furnish to the magistrates who had been allotted provinces. In that occupation he made the acquaintance of Gaius Caesar and went with him to the Gallic provinces. Then, because he had shown commendable energy in that province, and later during the civil war had executed numerous commissions with promptness and vigour, he not only gained Caesar's friendship, but because of it rose even to the highest rank. Afterwards he was also made tribune of the commons, and then praetor. [After the civil war] he not only recovered his former rank, but gained first the pontificate and then the consulship. At this the Roman people, who remembered that Ventidius Bassus had made a living by taking care of mules, were so indignant that these verses were posted everywhere about the streets of the city:
A portent strange has taken place of late;
For he who curried mules is consul now.
Suetonius Tranquillus writes that this same Bassus was put in charge of

the eastern provinces by Mark Antony, and that when the Parthians invaded Syria he routed them in three battles; that he was the first of all to celebrate a triumph over the Parthians, and when he died was honoured with a public funeral. (Aulus Gellius 15.4)

Thanks to the extension of the movement towards granting Roman citizenship, which was only impeded for a short time, the Italians were able, without injury to their local patriotism and particularism, to become members of a new *patria* with an exclusive claim to world domination. They could still be at heart men of Arpinum, Capuans or Gauls from Mantua, while at the same time enjoying a Roman citizenship which did not impose any artificial uniformity: Neapolis continued to speak Greek for two centuries, while Arpinum kept its original *collegium* of three aediles. Over and above their own *patria* they now belonged as of right to a legal community in which political rights could be freely exercised until the last days of the Republic, before power was appropriated by a single man. Cicero, himself a man from Arpinum with its old local associations, described the situation in precise and moving terms in an imaginary dialogue with his friend, Atticus:

Atticus: But what did you really mean by the statements you made a while ago, that this place, by which I understand you to refer to Arpinum, is your own fatherland? Have you then two fatherlands? Or is our common fatherland the only one? Perhaps you think that the wise Cato's fatherland was not Rome but Tusculum?
Marcus: Certainly I think that he and all natives of Italian towns have two fatherlands, one by nature and the other by citizenship. Cato, for example, though born in Tusculum, received citizenship in Rome, and so, as he was a Tusculan by birth and a Roman by citizenship, had one fatherland which was the place of his birth, and another by law. Just as the people of your beloved Attica, before Theseus commmanded them all to leave the country and move into the city (the *astu,* as it is called), were at the same time citizens of their own towns and of Attica, so we consider both the place where we were born our fatherland, and also the city into which we have been adopted. But that fatherland must stand first in our affection in which the name of republic signifies the common citizenship of all of us. For her it is our duty to die, to her to give ourselves entirely, to place on her altar and, as it were, dedicate to her service all that we possess. But the fatherland which was our parent is not much less dear to us than the one which adopted us. Thus I shall never deny that my fatherland is here, though my other fatherland is greater and includes this one within it; [and in the same way every native of an Italian town, in my opinion,] has [two] citizenships but thinks of them as one citizenship. (*De Legibus* 2.25)[25]

The two patriae

This idea that the Roman *patria* is greater than local homelands and contains them all is no doubt a reflection, in terms of political philosophy, of the idea of the *majestas populi Romani* which had been a feature of international law for nearly two centuries. From the end of the third century onwards this doctrine figured in the treaties concluded by Rome, for instance with the Aetolians; it might well appear overweening, implying as it did that the two parties were essentially unequal and that the wishes of one of them must prevail over the other. The Aetolian envoys received a sharp lesson in 191 when they sent envoys to 'surrender to the good faith' of the Romans in the person of Manius Acilius Glabrio:

> When they came before the consul, Phaeneas, the leader of the embassy, spoke at length and with manifold devices with which to soften the heart of the conqueror, and concluded by saying that the Aetolians entrusted themselves and all their possessions to the good faith of the Roman people. When the consul heard this he replied, 'Consider again and again, Aetolians, whether you are submitting on these conditions.' Then Phaeneas displayed the decree in which this was explicitly stated in writing. 'Since, then,' the consul said, 'you are submitting on these terms, I demand that Dicaearchus your fellow-citizen and Menestas of Epirus'—he had entered Naupactus with a garrison and compelled it to revolt—'and Amynander with the chiefs of the Athamanes, by whose advice you revolted from us, be delivered to me without delay.' Phaeneas interrupted while the Roman was still speaking: 'We have not delivered ourselves into slavery but have entrusted ourselves to your good faith, and I feel sure that you err from ignorance in giving us orders which are inconsistent with the customs of the Greeks.' To this the consul replied: 'By Hercules, I care little what the Aetolians regard as properly consistent with the customs of the Greeks, since I, in the Roman way, am delivering an order to men who a moment ago surrendered by their own decree and had previously been conquered by armed force; therefore, unless my order is immediately executed I shall at once order you to be put in chains.' He directed the chains to be brought and the lictors to stand by. Then the haughty spirit of Phaeneas was broken and that of the other Aetolians, and they finally perceived in what condition they were. (Livy 36.28.1-7)

The treaty which the Aetolians finally obtained was less harsh, but it still contained the 'supremacy' clause attested by both Polybius (21.32.2) and Livy (38.11):

The people of the Aetolians shall uphold the sovereignty and dignity of the Roman people without fraud; they shall permit no army which is being led against the allies and friends of the Romans to cross their borders and shall aid such an army in no way; they shall regard as enemies the same persons whom the Romans so regard, shall take up arms against them and make war upon them in company with the Romans; [etc.].

A similar clause figured in nearly all Roman treaties, even those with friends of long standing such as Gades in Spain (205):

This clause also was added, which is not found in all treaties, 'Let them uphold the greatness of the Roman People in a friendly way.' (Cicero, *Pro Balbo* 35)

This might have signified domination pure and simple, but in the long run it did not, because *majestas* was defined by Rome in a precise fashion which effectively confined it to diplomatic and external relations, while avoiding any interference in matters of private law, customs or institutions. Cicero made this very clear when he recalled that in this more or less 'reserved' sphere the right to accept or refuse any part of Roman law was conceded by Rome both to her allies and to the new citizens integrated in 90-89. This 'guarantee' or 'endorsement' (*fundifactio*) recognized the sphere of individual relations, the family, customs and religion as an essential though subordinate aspect of public life: these constituted the 'natural *patria*' of which Cicero speaks. Embracing them, but at a higher level, was the national or imperial *patria* embodied in Rome and the right of a Roman citizen:

When the Roman People have made any law, and if this law is of such a kind that it seems likely to give certain states, whether bound to us by treaty or free, an option to decide themselves, not with reference to our but to their own concerns, what legal principle they desire to adopt, in that case we clearly ought to ask whether these states have, or have not, 'given consent' (*utrum fundi facti sint an non*). But when it is a question of our own State, of our Empire, of our wars, of our victory or of our welfare, our forefathers did not desire that states should 'give consent. (Cicero, *Pro Balbo* 22)[26]

Since Rome was the common *patria* of Italy and, ultimately, of the whole human race, it can be seen that this conception was neither brutal nor imperialistic, though it might at first appear so; for the 'higher interests' of the Roman people were soon to become no more than joint manifestations of its *majestas*, that is to say of the *raison d'État* to which every nation or city lays claim as a guarantee of its own survival. By making it easily reconcilable with the autonomy of laws and customs, Rome created an original conception of citizenship: not dual citizenship (since *civitas Romana* excludes any other, independent *civitas*) but, so to speak, a citizenship at two levels. Roman citizenship bore within itself the notion of cosmopolis that was almost realized by the Empire, rival of the *Civitas Dei*, and the oecumenism which it bequeathed directly to the Catholic tradition.

TABLE I

Roman census figures, 508 BC — AD 14

508	130,000	Dionys. 5. 20
503	120,000	Hieronym. *Ol.* 69. 1
498	157,700	Dionys. 5. 75
493	110,000	Dionys. 6. 96
474	103,000	Dionys. 9. 36
465	104,714	Livy 3. 3 ('excluding widows and orphans')
459	117,319	Livy 3. 24; Eutrop. 1. 16
393/2	152,573	Pliny *NH* 33
340/39	165,000	Euseb. *Ol.* 110. 1
323	150,000	Oros. 5. 22. 2; Eutrop. 5. 9 (the MSS of Livy 5. 19 give 250,000)
294/3	262,321	Livy 10. 47
289/8(?)	272,000	*Per.* Livy 11
280/79	287,222	Ibid. 13
276/5	271,224	Ibid. 14
265/4	292,234	Eutrop. 2. 18 (*Per.* Livy 16 gives 382,233)
252/1	297,797	*Per.* Livy 18
247/6	241, 712	Ibid. 19
241/0	260,000	Hieronym. *Ol.* 134. 1
234/3	270,713	*Per.* Livy 20
209/8	137,108 (or 237,108)	Livy 27. 36 and *Per.*
204/3	214,000	Livy 29. 37 and *Per.*
194/3	143,704 (or 243,704)	Livy 35. 9
189/8	258,318	Livy 38. 36
179/8	258,794	*Per.* Livy 41
174/3	269,015	Livy 42. 10 (*Per.* 42: 267,231)
169/8	312,805	*Per.* Livy 45
164/3	337,022	Ibid. 46 (Plut. Paul. 38)
159/8	328,316	Ibid. 47
154/3	324,000	Ibid. 48
147/6	322,000	Euseb. Armen. *Ol.* 158. 3
142/1	322,442	*Per.* Livy 54
136/5	317,933	Ibid. 56
131/0	318,823	Ibid. 59
125/4	394,736 (294,336?)	Ibid. 60
115/4	394,336 (?)	*Per.* Livy 63
86/5	463,000 (or 963,000?)	Hieronym. *Ol.* 173.4
70/69	910,000	Phlegon of Tralles, F. 12. 6; *Per.* Livy 98
28	4,063,000	*Res Gestae* 8. 2
8	4,233,000	Ibid. 8. 3
14AD	4,937,000	Ibid. 8. 4

These figures represent, in principle, the total number of adult male citizens. But their detailed interpretation is extremely complicated, and I shall not go into it here. (Source: P. A. Brunt, *Italian Manpower...*, pp. 13-14)

CHAPTER II

CENSUS
The integrated citizen

T HE FIRST and most important sign of the citizen's integration in a restrictive community was his enrolment in the *census*.[1] This word designates several things: firstly, a 'census' in the modern sense, the numbering of all citizens who together constitute the civic community. Secondly, within this enumeration it denotes the division of citizens into a number of categories: these varied a great deal at different periods, but were always egalitarian from one point of view and hierarchical from another. They were egalitarian because their effect was to define a personal status (the *civitas romana*) which was juridically complete and which, from the time of the codification of the Twelve Tables in 450 BC, implied the equality of rights (*finis aequi juris,* in Tacitus's phrase), i.e. of the juridical capacity of every citizen. But the system was also hierarchical in that outside the relatively narrow sphere of private law there extended, as in concentric circles, the various forms of participation in public affairs such as religion, finance, the army and politics in the stricter sense, i.e. participation in debates and decisions, magisterial office etc. Clearly all citizens, even if they were held to be perfectly equal before the law, could not reasonably be treated on the same footing in respect of all these activities. Nature herself forbade it: young and old people, the well and the sick could not perform the same tasks or be subject to the same obligations. In all these spheres, the Romans were not offended by inequalities due to wealth or natural circumstances; nor were most ancient communities, apart from a few short-lived experiments in total democracy. In this way, Roman citizenship combined legal equality with social and political inequality; and the complex of operations known as the *census* was designed to achieve this double result as rationally as possible. The contrast is very clearly defined by the elder Cato in a passage from an otherwise unknown speech recorded by Festus (408, 33 L): 'As regards law, liberty and the commonwealth, it is proper that we should all enjoy them equally and in common; but as for glory and honours, it is for each man to obtain them as best he can.'

On the one hand, an enumeration; on the other, a record of names, property and other qualifications enabling citizens to be classified according to a logical system (*ratio*) so that a proper share of public rights and duties could be assigned to them—such was the *census,* which the Romans regarded as one of the fundamental institutions of their state:

' [King Servius Tullius] intended that posterity should celebrate himself as the originator of all distinctions among the citizens, and of the orders which clearly differentiate the various grades of rank and fortune. For he instituted the census, a most useful thing for a government destined to such wide dominion, since it would enable the burdens of war and peace to be borne not indiscriminately, as before, but in proportion to men's wealth. He distributed the people into classes and centuries according to the following scale, which was based upon the census and was suitable either for peace or war. (Livy 1.42.4-5)

Not that Rome was the only ancient community to have such an institution; practically all the Greek and Italic cities numbered their citizens and assessed their wealth in the same way. Utopian 'constitutions' drawn up in the fourth century by Plato and other philosophers show how fundamental a part was played by the notion of property qualifications in the assignment of responsibilities and the election of magistrates. When Aristotle in his *Politics* (*c.* 340 BC) analysed most of the constitutions that existed in his day in order to formulate a treatise on political science, he concluded that the best and most balanced constitutions were those 'founded on property'. But, while we know that many archaic Greek constitutions (like Solon's at Athens) and even classical ones were based on this criterion, in none of them was its role so clear as in ancient Rome.[2]

The Greek word *timema* comes from the same root as *timan,* to value or estimate, as does *timè,* signifying 'honour' or 'public office'. The Latin *census,* on the other hand, is connected with *censere,*[3] which in classical times meant 'estimate', 'express an opinion' or 'appreciate'. The problem of ascertaining which of these is the basic sense has been elucidated by comparison with Sanskrit, where the root *śams* (from which may be inferred an Indo-European **kens*) means to evoke in speech, or almost to call a thing into existence by naming it. The eminent philologist G. Dumézil speaks of 'siting a man, an act or an opinion etc. in his or its correct place in the hierarchy, with all the practical consequences that this entails, and doing so by a just public assessment, by a solemn act of praise or blame' (*Servius et la fortune,* 1942, p. 188). This accurate definition, supported by numerous texts, has the merit of emphasizing at the outset a permanent characteristic of the Roman city, viz. that an individual's status does not depend solely on objective criteria, even as defined in a law or regulation, but largely on the assent of the community expressed by its competent magistrates in a solemn declaration expressed in words of praise or blame and summed up in a designation (*nomen*). In order for the status to exist it must be formulated and express a consensus of opinion. No doubt the status exists before the title, but, conversely, the bestowal of a title (the minimum one of *civis* for those to whom it is due, and the whole range of honorific titles above it) largely creates the status; it invests the individual concerned with a whole range of very precise duties and privileges which, in effect, endow him with a second nature. Hence the ritual and formalistic character of the series of solemn obligations by which the city—in abstract theory an aggregate of equal and independent legal agents—becomes an organic and rational structure, every member of which receives a designation assigning him his proper place in a system of reciprocal relationships.

As we have said, the census served much more than a purely demographic purpose. Certainly it was intended to enumerate the free population as accurately as possible, but in the ancient world, as in our own day, totals meant little until they were broken down by categories. As we saw in Chapter One, citizenship was the privilege of a minority at all periods of the Roman state. Only during the decades which followed the Social War (91-89 BC) was it extended by degrees, with some exceptions, to peninsular and Cispadane Italy. Before this process was complete, however, the population had included, besides slaves and foreigners, an intermediate category of 'subjects' comprising Latins (*nomen latinum*) and allies (*socii*). As we have also seen, until about the year 200 there was a 'reduced' form of citizenship known as *civitas sine suffragio*. The census took account of all these categories, and the figures that have come down to us—particularly those dating from the military situation in 225, during the war with the Gauls (Table II)—partly reflect these geographical and juridical distinctions.

TABLE II

The free population of Italy in 225 BC

	Juniors	Adult males (corrected)	All free persons	Territory in sq. km.	Numbers per sq. km.
Romans	205,000	300,000	923,000	25,615	36
Latins	85,000	134,000	431,000	10,630	40
Italians	276,000	441,600	1,398,000		
Total	566,000	875,600	2,752,000	107,810	25.5

(Source: P. A. Brunt, *Italian Manpower...*, p. 54)

But there were also differences of status among the ranks of full citizens (*cives optimo jure*), and it was even more important to register these distinctions than to number the population. The total number of *capita civium* represented the potentiality of the state, while their division into separate lists reflected their different functions within the state. The census was designed to furnish both types of information. It had, moreover, a military, a financial and a political aspect, which Roman tradition presents as being complementary and contemporaneous with each other. There has been much debate, some of it quite recent,[4] as to which of these aspects may have come first, but in fact they can only be isolated by placing the matter in false perspective. Naturally a citizen's wealth was taken into account when it was a question of assigning him a place on the battlefield or in the assembly, or deciding his fitness for this or that office. But wealth was not the only consideration: it might be reinforced, or the lack of it corrected, by physical, moral and social factors. Livy expresses this well in the above-quoted phrase, 'the various grades of rank and fortune'. Heredity, for instance, while it did not constitute a legal title to a particular magistracy, was at least a recommendation to it.[5] Moral character played a part in admission to the privileged orders of the *equites* and senators, from which one might be expelled by the censor's opprobrious *nota*. That wealth was not the only criterion is shown most clearly by the fact that until the end of the Republic the father was responsible for registering his children and hence for their being enrolled in particular lists, e.g. that of the *equites*. Here it was the father's wealth that counted, yet the son who enjoyed the benefit. The census went much further than merely ascertaining a citizen's wealth and classifying him accordingly; it also determined his military and fiscal obligations and political privileges, but it cannot be said that any of these decisions were historically prior to others. Ancient historians show this clearly by their accounts of the origin of the census; we may instance three authors dating from the end of the first century BC: Livy, Cicero and Dionysius of Halicarnassus. According to old tradition the census was introduced by Servius Tullius, a king of the 'Etruscan dynasty', in the sixth century BC; we should take due account of this, but it is doubtful whether the form in which the institution is described really dates from such early times. The monetary scales, for instance, are those of the end of the third century or the beginning of the second. The military equipment, on the other hand, would seem to be appropriate to a hoplite in the fifth or fourth century BC, and there is nothing implausible about ascribing the system to an Etruscan king; as Festus tells us (358 L): 'The Etruscan ritual books prescribed rites for founding cities, consecrating altars and sanctuaries, protecting the legal and religious status of walls and gates; the distribution of tribes, curiae and centuries, the formation and disposition of armies'. In other words, the Etruscan ritual comprised all the essential features of the Roman census. It is thus very probable that the latter, in all three of its aspects, went back to the remotest antiquity, but that the practical forms of classification—i.e. types of military equipment, the assigning of roles in accordance with combat tactics, the criteria used to determine differences of wealth and status, and the system of political organization itself—varied from one age to another. It is not our task here to reconstruct these variations, which can only be done with great caution; but we shall see in detail how the military, fiscal and political integration of the citizen took place during the period with which we are concerned. The traditional Roman account of the original census is a different matter; we shall, however, begin by taking some notice of it, as in its schematized way it gives a good insight into the logic of the system.

Livy's description of the Servian organization by 'centuries' is given below. That of Dionysius is very similar: he converts the sums of money into Greek equivalents at the rate of 1 drachma = 1 *denarius* = 10 *asses*, and differs slightly in the place he assigns to the centuries of craftsmen and military musicians.

Out of those who had a rating of 100,000 *asses* or more Servius made 80 centuries, 40 each of seniors and of juniors; these were all known as the first class; the seniors were to be ready to guard the city, the juniors to wage war abroad. The armour which these men were required to provide consisted of helmet, round shield, greaves, and breast-plate, all of bronze, for the protection of their bodies; their offensive weapons were a spear and a sword. There were added to this class two centuries of mechanics, who were to serve without arms; to them was entrusted the duty of fashioning siege-engines in war. The second class was drawn up out of those whose rating was between 100,000 and 75,000; of these, seniors and juniors, 20 centuries were enrolled. The arms prescribed for them were an oblong shield in place of the round one, and everything else, save for the breast-plate, as in the class above. He fixed the rating of the third class at 50,000; a like number of centuries was formed in this class as in the second, and with the same distinction of ages; neither was any change made in their arms, except that the greaves were omitted. In the fourth class the rating was 25,000; the number of centuries was formed, but their equipment was changed, nothing being given them but a spear and a javelin. The fifth class was made larger, and 30 centuries formed. These men carried slings, with stones for missiles. Rated with them were the horn-blowers and trumpeters, divided into two centuries. The rating of this class was 11,000. Those who were assessed at less than this amount, being all the rest of the population, were made into a single century, exempt from military service. When the equipment and distribution of the infantry had been thus provided for, Servius enrolled 12 centuries of knights out of the leading men of the state. He likewise formed six other centuries — three had been instituted by Romulus — employing the same names which had been hallowed to their use by augury. For the purchase of horses they were allowed 10,000 *asses* each from the state treasury, and for the maintenance of these horses unmarried women were designated, who had to pay 2,000 *asses* each, every year. All these burdens were shifted from the shoulders of the poor to those of the rich. The latter were then granted special privileges:

for manhood suffrage, implying equality of power and of rights, was no longer given promiscuously to all, as had been the practice handed down by Romulus and observed by all the other kings; but gradations were introduced, so that ostensibly no one should be excluded from the suffrage, and yet the power should rest with the leading citizens. For the knights were called upon to vote first; then the 80 centuries of the first class: if there were any disagreement there, which rarely happened, it was provided that the centuries of the second class should be called; and they almost never descended so far as to reach the lowest citizens. (Livy 1.43)

Livy thus describes the division of the citizens, on a basis of age and wealth, into five classes and 193 centuries; both these are spoken of as regular military units, since their equipment is specified. From this he proceeds directly to the electoral aspect, showing the same classes and centuries voting in hierarchical order. The detailed description of the centuries' equipment, plus the striking fact that the basic unit of the legion was also called a century, even if it only consisted of 60 men, led scholars for a long time to seek an exact correspondence between the Servian system of 193 centuries and the Roman army in the field, which first consisted of one legion, later of two and afterwards of four. Unfortunately it is very difficult to make the two schemes coincide, and the attempt to do so may well be based on a false premise. A neglected passage in Dionysius is the only one in classical literature to present a detailed account of the Servian system calculated to resolve the difficulties that have been met with. True, Dionysius is a late author, he is verbose and apt to embellish or gloss the raw material of tradition; but as we shall see in the chapter on military affairs, the logical system he presents has the great merit of agreeing precisely with what we know of the procedure of the levy (*dilectus*). After describing the centurial system in very similar terms to those of Livy and Cicero he continues:

In pursuance of this arrangement Servius levied troops according to the division of the centuries, and imposed taxes in proportion to the valuation of their possessions. For instance, whenever he had occasion to raise 10,000 men, or, if it should so happen, 20,000, he would divide that number among the 193 centuries and then order each century to furnish the number of men that fell to its share. As to the expenditures that would be needed for the provisioning of the soldiers while on duty and for the various warlike supplies, he would first calculate how much money would be sufficient, and having in like manner divided that sum among the 193 centuries, he would order every man to pay his share towards it in proportion to this rating. Thus it happened that those who had the largest possessions, being fewer in number but distributed into more centuries, were obliged to serve oftener and without any intermission, and to pay greater taxes than the rest; that those who had small and moderate possessions, being more numerous but distributed into fewer centuries, served seldom and in rotation and paid small taxes, and that those whose possessions were not sufficient to maintain them were exempt from all burdens. (Dionys. 4.19)

This text is not free from ambiguity: in particular, it does not say whether the levy was shared equally among the centuries, i.e. whether each of them had to provide the same number of soldiers or contribute the same sum of money. We may be inclined to think so; but in any case it is quite clear that according to this text the system of centuries does not represent the army under arms but a cadre on the basis of which soldiers are recruited and the tax levied. In particular, the number of citizens in a century might evidently vary to any extent: this is expressly stated by Cicero, Dionysius and Livy as regards the last century, that of the *capite censi*, which was larger than all those of the first class put together (*De Republica* 2. 40). As Roman military history shows in detail, the army establishment was never fixed or permanent, just as the annual yield of taxation was never fixed once and for all. As was natural, and as Dionysius rightly says, these varied considerably from year to year in accordance with changing needs.[6] We can thus see the logic and flexibility of the system. The principle was, it appears to me, that each of the units represented (on the model of the fiscal units of fourth-century Athens) a more or less equal taxable capacity, which would thus have been roughly one two-hundredth part of the total taxable capacity of the Roman state. Using the figures provided by Cicero this would mean that the total wealth of citizens of the last century, possessing between 1,500 and 11,000 *asses* each, was approximately equal to the total for one of the first centuries (or, no doubt, for two of them, one of *juniores* and one of *seniores*), which is quite plausible. In any case it is clear that the first classes of centuries had fewer members than the last, and, as they had to furnish a proportionately larger contingent, each man had to serve more often and for a longer time. In short, the century was only a reservoir of military strength: it did not consist of men under arms but of men who might be called up, and it provided a source of men and money which could be drawn upon to a given extent as and when need arose. In the chapters on taxation and the army we shall see that even when the services required had become much more varied than in Dionysius's day (different types of arms, obligation to provide equipment as well as military service), the census categories were still the essential basis on which a citizen's rights and duties were assessed. Contrary to what is sometimes maintained, the obligation of enrolment did not come to an end in 168, when the *tributum* ceased to be levied (until 43 BC at least), nor in 107, when Marius raised a force for the war against Jugurtha without taking account of census categories. These decisions, taken in the light of circumstances which might or might not recur, were not intended to prejudice the future or to set up any new principle; the citizens were not relieved of the *tributum* for all time, nor the rich permanently exempted from military service. The lists were accordingly kept in being; and, as we shall see, the census was doubly necessary for enrolment in what may be called electoral lists, those of the tribes and those of the centuries. It has been too readily asserted that participation in the *comitia centuriata* was severely restricted; in actual fact voting rights were important up to the end of the Republic, and a citizen's place in the *comitia* depended on the census. The latter also, as we shall see, was the basis of qualification for admission to the higher orders of the state—the equestrian order first of all—and the magistracy. It is true that the full census could not always be carried out, and there were interruptions from Sulla's time onwards; but this was always largely due to political troubles, and was felt as something that ought to be remedied as soon as possible. Some may have wished to see the censors' coercive powers abolished or reduced: in 58 the demagogue Clodius obtained the passage of a law *de notione censoris* which considerably limited the censors' arbitrary powers in regard to classification and the sanctions connected therewith, by making them subject to a preliminary formal sentence. This law was no doubt concerned first and foremost with senators; Clodius wanted to reassure those who might feel threatened with expulsion, and was anxious above all for his own position. But Dio Cassius expressly says that the limitation applied to the censors' power over all orders in the state: 'He forbade the censors to remove anybody from any order or to censure anyone [this certainly means to deprive him of the vote] unless he were first tried and convicted before them both.' (38.13.2). Although opposed by conservative elements, this law remained in force for six years. Cicero proposed its abrogation several times, in his speech to the Senate *De Provinciis Consularibus* in 56 and in his treatise *De Legibus,* written in about 54-52. It was repealed in 52 by the *Lex Caecilia* proposed by the consul Q. Caecilius Metellus Pius, certainly with Pompey's agreement, on the ground that it had prevented the expulsion of undesirables from the two higher orders. As Dio observes,

> It looked as though the consul had done this out of favour to the censors, since he had restored the authority which they formerly had; but it turned out to be the opposite. For in view of the fact that there were many unworthy men both in the equestrian and in the senatorial order, so long as they had not been allowed to expel anyone who had been either accused or convicted, no fault was found with them on account of those whose names were not expunged. (40.57.1-2)

In 50 BC the censors, especially Appius Claudius, took fairly rigorous measures, and the resentment these aroused was certainly one reason for the civil war which broke out at the end of that year.

Ideological basis of the census

The elaborate apparatus of the census was regarded as one of the main foundations of civic life. As its military and religious aspects show, it undoubtedly went back to a very remote past and was perhaps rooted in the socio-political organization of the Indo-European community; it gave the city its essential structure and corresponded to an ideology which had become more elaborate and specific with the passage of time. The philosophers who were interested in civics and political thought, Plato and Aristotle in particular, treated it as of key importance, agreeing as it did with an explicit theory of participation in public life. Both Plato and Aristotle thought that the best constitutions were those based on the census (*apo tou timematos*), i.e. in which rights and duties were related to the classification of citizens according to their wealth and acknowledged valour and practically nothing else. Such timocratic constitutions, of which Rome was a perfect example, were compatible with that 'moderate democracy' which was regarded as a desirable model. Athens herself, one of the most democratic of Greek cities in the fifth and fourth centuries, maintained the system of classes based on property and saw no reason why certain functions should not be confined to the richest citizens; while oligarchic and aristocratic constitutions paid even more attention to these hierarchical classifications. Rome never purported to be a democracy, even though, from the end of the second century, some political leaders—including C. Gracchus, if we may believe Diodorus Siculus—tried to modify some aspects of its constitution in a more democratic sense. None of them, however, tried to do away with the census as such; and in fact it represented a skilful balance of democratic and aristocratic elements. The strictly hierarchical system would have been shocking and no doubt unendurable if it had been completely one-sided, with nothing but privilege on the one hand and subjection on the other. A society of this type, known to us from medieval and modern times, would have been contrary to the essential nature of Rome, which could only survive on the basis of broad consensus. The census regime, on the other hand, was thought to represent a more perfect and beneficial equality than the simple 'arithmetical' type to be found in some extreme democracies. By way of distinction, the census type of equality was called by philosophers 'geometrical' or 'proportional', meaning that each individual's rights and duties conformed, so to speak, to a constant ratio. The rich enjoyed more 'honours', i.e. they had a virtual monopoly of high office and even of decision-taking in public assemblies, but equally they had more duties, being more often called on to serve the state either financially or in person. This, according to Dionysius, was what Servius Tullius intended:

> Tullius made none of these regulations without reason, but from the conviction that all men look upon their possessions as the prizes at stake in war and that it is for the sake of retaining these that they all endure its

hardships; he thought it right, therefore, that those who had greater prizes at stake should suffer greater hardships, both with their persons and with their possessions, that those who had less at stake should be less burdened in respect to both, and that those who had no loss to fear should endure no hardships, but be exempt from taxes by reason of their poverty and from military service because they paid no tax. (4.19.3)

The poor were exempted from the principal obligations of public service, and it was only right that in compensation they were virtually excluded from political influence by the finely calculated voting system of the *comitia centuriata;* this did not deprive them of the suffrage (which would have been tyrannical, *superbum,* as Cicero points out) but did exclude them from decision-taking. The exclusion, however, was glossed over; for, Dionysius goes on to say:

They all thought that they had an equal share in the government because every man was asked his opinion, each in his own century; but they were deceived in this, [for the system gave a definite advantage to the rich]... The rich, though paying out large sums and exposed without intermission to the dangers of war, were less inclined to feel aggrieved now that they had obtained control of the most important matters and had taken the whole power out of the hands of those who were not performing the same services. The poor, who had but the slightest share in the government, finding themselves exempt both from taxes and from military service, prudently and quietly submitted to this diminution of their power; and the commonwealth itself had the advantage of seeing the same persons who were to deliberate concerning its interests allotted the greatest share of the dangers and ready to do whatever required to be done. (4.21.1)

Thus the proportional equality brought about by the census was regarded as a factor of social cohesion, helping to bring about the consensus. This was exactly what Plato maintained in the *Laws,* when devising the best possible constitution for his imaginary colony of Magnetes. Ideally, he said, all men would be equally wealthy:

Since this, however, is impossible, and one man will arrive with more money and another with less, it is necessary for many reasons, and for the sake of equalising chances in public life, that there should be unequal valuations, in order that offices and contributions may be assigned in accordance with the assessed valuation in each case—being framed not in proportion only to the moral excellence of a man's ancestors or of himself, nor to his bodily strength and comeliness, but in proportion also to his wealth or poverty—so that by a rule of symmetrical inequality they may receive offices and honours as equally as possible, and may have no quarrelling.

For these reasons we must make four classes, graded by size of property. (744 b)

Aristotle, though his approach in the *Politics* is quite different, reached more or less the same conclusion:

It is for this reason that it is advantageous for the form of democracy spoken of before, and is a customary institution in it, for all the citizens to elect the magistrates and call them to account, and to try lawsuits, but for the holders of the greatest magistracies to be elected and to have property qualifications, the higher offices being elected from the higher property grades... And a state governed in this way is bound to be governed well, for the offices will always be administered by the best men with the consent of the people and without their being jealous of the upper classes. (VI.2.1318 b, 26)

This kind of argument, representing an advanced stage of political thought, was naturally used by the Romans in the first century BC, particularly Cicero, who, as we shall see in the context of elections, never lost an opportunity of emphasizing the advantages of the centurial system. His opinion is summed up in a phrase in *De Republica* I. 43: 'Equality itself is inequitable, since it allows no distinctions in rank.' Such philosophical arguments had been known to the Romans long before this. The idea of proportional and even of progressively increasing burdens was applied, for example, in 214, when an extraordinary contribution in kind was demanded, after the manner of a Greek 'liturgy', for the fitting-out of the fleet. Not only did the richer citizens have to provide and maintain seamen in a number proportionate to their census rating, but within a single census category, that of the *equites* and senators, the latter, by reason of their office, were assessed at a higher rate than the former. In 210, instead of repeating this procedure, the Senate adopted the proposal of the consul M. Valerius Laevinus for voluntary contributions in the form of a loan. The consul justified this in terms which strikingly bring out the responsibility of the most prominent citizens and the need for them to make sacrifices in order to secure the consent of the population as a whole:

As magistrates are superior to the senate in dignity, and as the senate is superior to the people, so ought they to be leaders in shouldering all that is hard and drastic. If there is a duty which you wish to lay upon an inferior, and you first set up the same obligation as against yourself and your family, you more readily find everyone submitting. And the outlay is not burdensome when they see every prominent man taking upon himself more than his share in it. (Livy 26.36.2)

As we shall see, the Servian constitution was still largely in force in Rome in the last century of the Republic, at least as regards the electoral system and also, potentially at all events, in its fiscal and military provisions. Its principles were at times disputed by C. Gracchus and other politicians after him; but despite some modifications, not all of which were lasting, the system remained virtually unchanged. Even under the Empire politics continued to be based on property qualifications, and Augustus himself accentuated this aspect.

How the census was carried out

Much has been said about the earliest origins of the census as an incantatory operation intended, by a just distribution of praise and blame, to ensure that everyone was rated at his true value and assigned his rightful place within the city. The military and economic aspects of this value were closely allied from the outset. Perhaps, as G. Dumézil suggests, we should imagine some kind of after-battle ceremony in ancient times, linked with the sharing of the spoils and culminating in a kind of solemn and public 'new deal'.[7] Such would be the interpretation of the episode related by Livy after the heroic resistance of Manlius Capitolinus during the siege of Rome by the Gauls in 390/386:

> At dawn the trumpet summoned the soldiers to assemble before the tribunes. Good conduct and bad had both to be requited. First Manlius was praised for his courage and presented with gifts, not only by the tribunes of the soldiers, but by agreement amongst the troops, who brought each half a pound of spelt and a gill of wine to his house, which stood in the Citadel. ...Then the watchmen of the cliff which the enemy had scaled without being discovered were called up. Quintus Salpicius, the tribune, announced his intention to punish them all in the military fashion; but deterred by the cries of the soldiers, who united in throwing the blame upon a single sentinel, he spared the others. This man was guilty beyond a doubt, and was flung from the Tarpeian rock with the approval of all. (Livy 5.47.7-10)

Here it is noteworthy that the guilty man is not punished under military regulations but is 'magically' expelled from the city; and we shall see in due course that the censors had no power to punish a citizen except the negative one of excluding him from a social category.

In historical times the main characteristic of the census is that it was, in principle, mandatory. All citizens were summoned, and were obliged to take part. This formal obligation is attested by specific rules, such as the ancient formula quoted by Varro:

> Now first I shall put down some extracts from the Censors' Records:

'When by night the censor has gone into the sacred precinct to take the auspices, and a message has come from the sky, he shall thus command the herald to call the men: "May this be good, fortunate, happy and salutary to the Roman people—the Quirites—and to me and my colleague, to our honesty and our office: Call hither to me all the citizen soldiers under arms [*armatos:* capable of bearing arms?] and private citizens as spokesmen of all the tribes, in case anyone wishes a reckoning to be given for himself or for another."' (*De Lingua Latina* 6.86)

The summons is thus addressed to all Quirites, i.e. all citizens. The text presents several problems that we shall not go into here—the non-mention of *equites*, the meaning of *armatos* etc.—but in any case it is clear that all are required to present themselves. This regulation went back to Servius Tullius:

Upon the completion of the census, which had been expedited by fear of a law that threatened with death and imprisonment those who failed to register, Servius issued a proclamation calling on all Roman citizens, both horse and foot, to assemble at daybreak, each in his own century, in the Campus Martius. (Livy 1.44.1)

After he had made these regulations [for the citizens to be numbered by means of coins or counters], he ordered all the Romans to register their names and give in a monetary valuation of their property, at the same time taking the oath required by law that they had submitted a true valuation in good faith; they were also to set down the names of their fathers, with their own age and the names of their wives and children, and every man was to declare in what tribe of the city or in what district of the country he lived. If any failed to give in their valuation, the penalty he established was that their property should be forfeited and they themselves whipped and sold for slaves. This law continued in force among the Romans for a long time. (Dionys. 4.15.6)

The sanctions are confirmed by Cicero, who says: 'By selling a man who has evaded the census, the state decrees that, whereas those who have been slaves in the normal way gain their freedom by being included in the census, one who has refused to be included in it although free has of his own accord repudiated his freedom.' (*Pro Caecina* 99)

Dionysius' account is confirmed by the *Tabula Heracleensis*, an inscription which probably dates from the decade 80-70 and lays down rules for the conduct of the census of citizens of *municipia* and colonies during the period after the Social War. As the procedure is expressly modelled on that of Rome itself, we may record it here:

In all *municipia, colonia,* or *praefecturae* of Roman citizens, such as are or shall be within Italy, those persons who shall hold the highest magistracy or competence within such communities shall, at the time when the censor or any other magistrate at Rome shall take a census of the people, and within the 60 days next following upon their knowledge of such census being taken at Rome, proceed to take a census of all those persons belonging to their respective *municipia, coloniae,* or *praefecturae* who shall be Roman citizens; from all such persons, duly sworn, they shall receive their gentile names, their *praenomina,* their fathers or patrons, their tribes, their *cognomina,* their age, and a statement of their property, in accordance with the schedule set forth by the magistrate about to take the census of the people at Rome; all such particulars they shall cause to be entered in the public records of their respective communities, and shall despatch the said papers to the officials then taking the census at Rome by the hands of delegates, selected for that purpose by a majority of the *decuriones* or *conscripti* present at a meeting convened for such selection; they shall further see that, within 60 days of the date on which the aforesaid magistrates shall have completed the census of the people at Rome, the said delegates shall reach the said magistrates, and deliver the papers of their respective *municipia, coloniae,* or *praefecturae.* Thereupon, the said censor, or whatever magistrate shall take the census of the people at Rome, shall, within the five days next following upon the arrival of the said delegates from their respective communities, receive in all good faith the said census papers delivered by the said delegates; he shall further see that the particulars contained in the said papers shall be entered in the public records, and that such public records shall be preserved in the same place with the other records in which the census of the people is registered and inscribed. (*CIL,* I² 593, 1.142)

Clearly a whole bureaucratic apparatus must have been required in order to carry out these operations under the censors' supervision. In the first place, where were they held? The census of citizens, excluding *equites* and the compilation of the Senate list, took place on the Campus Martius, a large area outside the *pomerium,* because the object of the census was to draw up the order of battle, and citizens under arms were not allowed to assemble inside the *pomerium.* From 435 BC this area was covered by a hugh complex of buildings and gardens, the Villa Publica. We now know exactly where it was located:[8] viz. east of the portico which in Republican times surrounded the Area Sacra of the Largo Argentina, and south of the voting enclosure known as the *saepta* — the southern wall of which, the *diribitorium,* was excavated in the nineteenth century under the Corso Vittorio Emmanuele, west of the Gesù. The Campus Martius must have extended as far south as the Circus Flaminius, which, we now know, ran parallel with the Tiber bank, and its boundary cannot have been far from the temple of Bellona, which is very probably to be identified with the temple next to that of Apollo,[9] near the Portico of Octavia and the Theatre of Marcellus. In any case, during the famous session of the Senate in the temple of Bellona in 82, shortly after Sulla's entry into Rome, those inside it could hear the screams of 8,000 prisoners whom Sulla cold-bloodedly caused to be executed after confining them in the Villa Publica.[10] The latter cannot have measured less than about 400 by 300 metres. As the word Villa suggests, a great part of this consisted of gardens, whose shade was much appreciated in the first century (Varro, *RR* 3.1.2). There were also buildings, however; first and foremost those of the Villa itself, which must have been able to contain a large number of people, e.g. victorious generals and their attendants awaiting the triumphal procession (and hence debarred from coming within the *pomerium*) and certain foreign ambassadors. Coins show it as a two-storied building with an arcaded portico on the ground floor and a gallery above (Crawford, No. 429). Some of the census formalities were certainly carried out inside this building, but we do not know which.

The censors, however, moved about during their long term of office, and the operations over which they presided were held in different places. The conclusion of the census, the *lustrum,* with the sacrifice of a pig, a sheep and a bull, followed by a ceremony of purification, took place in the presence of the 'army', therefore certainly on the Campus Martius (Livy 1. 44) and at the altar of Mars (Festus 189 L; Livy 40.45.8); but the *lectio* of the Senate, for instance, after the scrutiny of the list, must have terminated in a kind of solemn 'reading' in one of the buildings in which the Senate usually assembled. Operations affecting the equestrian order, which were also preceded by a scrutiny of the record, took place inside the *pomerium,* much nearer the Forum. The *probatio* or review of the *equites,* which until 70 at least (with some interruptions) included a parade before the censors, took place in the Forum itself (Plut., *Pompey* 22). For these operations connected with the Senate and the *equites* the censors most probably had a kind of permanent office in a building called the Atrium Libertatis. When, in 169, the *tribunus plebis* P. Rutilius threatened to bring the censors C. Claudius Pulcher and Ti. Sempronius Gracchus to trial because of the way they had treated the *equites,* the censors

mounted to the Hall of Liberty and, having there sealed the public accounts and closed the account-room and sent away the public slaves, declared that they would transact no public business until the judgment of the people had been passed upon them. (Livy 43.16.13)

In 168 it was in the Atrium Libertatis that lots were drawn to select the tribe to which the censors proposed to assign the freedmen (Livy 45.15.5). It too was quite a large building, with room e.g. for the hostages from Tarentum and Thurium in 212 (Livy 25.7.12); but in the first century BC it is only mentioned as the place in which Milo's slaves were detained and tortured (Cicero, *Pro Milone* 59).

It stood to the north of the Forum Romanum, probably near the site of the future Forum Augustum, between it and the Forum Caesaris.[11] In the second century it was used to house other documents of interest to the censors, e.g. a map of the *ager publicus* in Campania (Granius Licinianus 10 F). But the censors were of course also concerned with the *aerarium,* especially in all matters relating to their financial duties. The *aerarium,* situated beneath the temple of Saturn, was also a public record office, at least until the *Tabularium* was built in the second century; it was itself rebuilt in 78 BC. Thus in 202 the censors, after performing their duties, proceeded to the *aerarium* to pronounce the ritual oath and present to the *quaestors* the list of those (the *aerarii*) whom they had expelled from their centuries while leaving them subject to tax (Livy 29.37). It is probable that in the first century the censors' records were kept in various places, since, as we saw, the *Tabula Heracleensis* merely states that the census records of the *municipia* shall be stored in Rome 'in the same place' as those of the Roman census.

The only place in which we have actual evidence that census records were stored in the first century BC is the temple of the Nymphs. The building, situated apparently *in Campo,* has recently been identified[12] with the unknown temple in the Via delle Botteghe Oscure which is exactly reproduced in the marble plan of Rome in the centre of the *Porticus Minucia frumentaria*; this portico was built on the site of the Villa Publica in the early days of the Empire. The temple, many times rebuilt, bears traces of having been destroyed and restored in the middle of the first century BC. Now Cicero tells us several times that one of Clodius's crimes was to set fire to the temple of the Nymphs, in order 'to erase the records of the censor's registration that were printed in the national rolls' (*Pro Milone* 73). As we shall see later, the documents were in fact not census records but lists of beneficiaries of the grain distribution. But in any case the temple was used to keep records in, and was no doubt situated within the Villa Publica.

The next question is that of staff. The censors had at their disposal scribes, heralds (*praecones*), *nomenclatores* whose duty was to know the names of citizens, and summoners (*viatores*). They had no lictors, since in principle they did not possess the *imperium.* All these officials were recruited from the ranks of public slaves or freedmen or the order of scribes, which consisted, as we shall see, of men who purchased their 'commission' (*decuriam emere*) and played an important part in the machinery of government. Among employees who served the censors in particular, two categories are noteworthy: the receivers of sworn returns (*juratores*) and investigators (*inquisitores*). The existence of the former is explained by the special importance attached to oath-taking in the declaration which all citizens were required to make. At the census of 184, for instance, they had the duty of drawing up a list of objects of special value which the censors wished to assess separately (Livy 39.44.2); they dealt directly with the citizens, such as the character in Plautus (*Trinummus* 872) who says: 'When my taxes were due, I made the receiver a true declaration' (*Census cum sum, juratori recte rationem dedi*). The *inquisitores*, on the other hand, are not attested until the age of Augustus and Claudius. They were evidently supposed to conduct investigations on their own initiative, without contacting the public; under the Empire they became increasingly officious and aroused discontent. For instance:

As censor, too, Augustus showed a remarkable tolerance which won him high praise. A Roman knight was being reprimanded by him on the ground that he had squandered his property, but was able to show publicly that he had in fact increased it. The next charge brought against him was failure to comply with the marriage laws. To this he replied that he had a wife and three children and then added: 'I suggest, Sire, that in future, when you have occasion to inquire into the affairs of respectable persons, the inquiry be entrusted to respectable persons.' (Macrobius, *Saturnalia* 2.4)

Duty to attend the census

Throughout the Republican period, and until the enactment by Augustus of the Leges Aelia Sentia (AD 4) and Papia Poppaea (AD 9), the census was the only regular means by which a Roman could establish his identity and be recognized as a citizen. The two measures referred to introduced a fundamental change by obliging citizens, in the interval between censuses, to declare to magistrates or governors (according to whether they lived in Rome or the provinces) the names of their children who were free-born citizens, including bastards by slave women.[13] A register was kept of these declarations, and thus it became possible for the census procedure to be replaced in future by a simple collation of records. As in modern times, duplicates of the register entry were issued to those who required them, and half a dozen of these have fortunately survived in Egyptian papyri. One of the fullest reads:

Done at Alexandria in Egypt in the consulate of P. Marius and L. Alfinius Gallus [AD 62], on the 10th day before the calends of August, in the eighth year of the reign of the Emperor Nero Claudius Caesar Augustus Germanicus, on the 29th day of the month of Ephip.
Certified copy of an entry in the register at the Grand Palace of declarations of those having children:
L. Julius Vestinus, prefect of Egypt, has registered the names of those who have declared their children under the Lex Papia Poppaea and the Lex Aelia Sentia. In the consulate of P. Marius and L. Afinius Gallus, AD XV Kal. Aug.
L. Valerius Crispus, son of Lucius, of the Pollian tribe, whose census rating is 375,000 sesterces, declares the birth of a son named L. Valerius Crispus, son of Lucius, of the Pollian tribe, by Domitia Paulla daughter of

Lucius. AD III Kal. Iul. [here follow abbreviations which may mean 'Roman citizen; see daily register' or 'certified copy of entry in daily register'].

Under the Republic, however, this procedure did not exist and such declarations could only be made at the regular census, held in principle every five years. Citizens were obliged to attend the ceremony in Rome, except after the Social War, when the inhabitants of *municipia* and Italian colonies were permitted to register with local censors, copies of the records being sent to Rome (cf. above). Importance was clearly attached to the summoning procedure and to personal attendance, and infringement could be visited with the legal penalties referred to above; at the time we are concerned with, these were apparently very rare, as no example is known to us. The state could, however, allow citizens to register by proxy: as we saw, the official formula contains the words 'in case anyone wishes a reckoning to be given for himself or for another'. There is further evidence of this in a letter of Cicero's relating to the census of 61-60 BC: on 20 January he wrote to Atticus in Greece:

> I will see to it that notice is given and posted up everywhere, that you may not be entered on the census list as absent. But to get put on the roll just before the census is too thoroughly tradesman-like. So let me see you as soon as possible. (*Ad Att.* 1.18.8)

By 'everywhere' Cicero probably means Atticus's various estates in Italy. It has been asked why Atticus should not have used a proxy, but was not Cicero offering to act in precisely this capacity? Naturally one could always be registered *in absentia* on the ground of *force majeure*, and it was still more legitimate to use a proxy as suggested in the formula quoted by Varro. What Cicero means is that to do so might be to Atticus's disadvantage and would be an unworthy procedure, typical of the second-rate people of whom there were so many about and whom he stigmatizes as 'tradesmen'. The reason why it might be disadvantageous will appear from the census formalities themselves: the main point is that while the censors might accept a declaration made *in absentia*, it did not automatically guarantee the citizen his due place in the civic hierarchy. The censors might at any time rule otherwise, and a citizen who valued his position owed it to himself to appear in person if he possibly could. In some cases, as we know, people were reluctant to take the trouble, but in others they made great efforts to be present: crowds flocked to Rome to be registered in 70 BC, when admittedly a long interval had elapsed since the previous census. In his first speech against Verres, Cicero exclaims: 'I will not permit the settlement of this case to be delayed until after the departure from Rome of these multitudes that have simultaneously assembled from all parts of Italy to attend the elections, the games and the census.' (I *Verr.* 1.54) Elsewhere he says that the people, who used to dislike hearing the censors so much as mentioned, were insisting that the office should be restored (*In Caecilium* 8). The reason will be clear from the previous chapter: nearly 400,000 new citizens who became legally entitled to registration in 86 and the ensuing decade were finally enrolled at the census of 70. At last the Italian masses were part of the Roman city. It was certainly not by chance that a politician such as Pompey, with a sensitive nose for public opinion, took advantage of their enthusiasm and of the crowds present in Rome: when already consul-designate he subjected himself to the traditional formalities and, with calculated simplicity, underwent enrolment with the whole of Italy looking on.

Another reason which might induce citizens, especially the senators and *equites*, to be punctilious over registration was that, strictly speaking, enrolment in these privileged classes was confined to those officially domiciled in Rome. Certainly an *eques* might habitually live in the provinces and own estates there; but if he took up his abode there for good and all and did not come to Rome for the census at least, he could not be effectively registered as a member of the privileged voting class. This meant, at least after 123 BC, that he forfeited the important right to be inscribed by the *praetor urbanus* in the *album* of judges in the criminal courts (which were in fact political), and thus lost all political influence. This is clearly shown by a clause, preserved epigraphically, of the law of 123 (no doubt a Gracchian measure) on the judiciary, which confined the office of judgeship to citizens with an equestrian rating (or belonging to the equestrian centuries): it expressly excluded magistrates, senators and their close relations, any who could not be senators by reason of an indictment or conviction, and finally 'any who are not domiciled in the City of Rome or within a mile therefrom,... or who shall be overseas.'[14] Thus all Romans who had settled in the provinces were excluded, however rich they might be, unless they came to Rome for registration. When many citizens were absent for reasons beyond their control, for instance during a military campaign, the censors might send officials to collect declarations on the spot, as happened in 204 (Livy 29.37.5),[15] perhaps in order to have a more exact idea of the number of citizens. There might also be another motive: as Velleius tells us (2.7), the Romans were so anxious lest a colony should assert its independence and become a rival to the mother city (as Carthage did of Tyre) that, until 89 at least, they summoned all Roman citizens from the provinces back to Italy that they might be enrolled upon the census lists.

The declaration

As the *Tabula Heracleensis* shows, this had to be made by the *paterfamilias*, who stated his name and gave an account of his property. Probably he also had to register his wife; a formula for this purpose occurs in a story by Aulus Gellius:

The censor was administering the usual oath regarding wives, which was worded as follows: 'Have you, to the best of your knowledge and belief, a wife?' The man who was to take the oath was a jester, a sarcastic dog, and too much given to buffoonery. Thinking that he had a chance to crack a joke, he replied: 'I indeed have a wife, but not, by Heaven! such a one as I could desire.' Then the censor reduced him to a commoner for his untimely quip, adding that the reason for his action was a scurrilous joke made in his presence. (4.20)

It is not surprising to learn from Cicero (*De Or.* 2.260) that the severe censor on that occasion was Cato, and that the incident was recalled by Scipio Aemilianus when he held the same office in 142; he had good reason to remember it, as the humorist was a member of his own family.

As regards children *in patria potestate,* the position is less clear. It was of importance, however, since young men of 17 and upwards formed the core of the army levies. At times they were required to attend the census, for instance in 169 at the time of the levy for the Macedonian war: to aid the magistrates responsible for the levy, the censors announced that they would add to the declaration formula (*lex censui censendo*) an additional oath to be sworn by all those aged under 45:

'Have you, in accordance with the proclamation of Gaius Claudius and Tiberius Sempronius the censors, come forward for the levy, and as often as there shall be a levy, as long as these censors shall hold office, if you have not entered the army, will you come forward for the levy? (Livy 43.14.5)

The censors in that year also required the names of all soldiers mobilized for the Macedonian war who had returned to Italy with or without regular leave, and ordered them to report before they returned to the province:

The names of those who were subject to the authority of father or grandfather should be reported to the censors. Through this proclamation of the censors, and through their letters sent about throughout the markets and hamlets, so large a crowd of men of military age assembled at Rome that the unusual throng was burdensome to the city. (Livy 43.14.8)

Evidently 'minors' *in patria potestate* were not required to appear in person. In ancient times a father who registered his son was called *duicensus,* 'registered twice over' (Festus 58 L). A clear distinction must therefore be made between the total number of *censi,* i.e. citizens present at the census, and the lists drawn up by the censors on the basis of their declarations: e.g. those of the *juniores,* the figures for whom were obtained indirectly. The only women and children who appeared on lists of their own were widows and orphans, since they were not subject to anyone's *potestas* or at least not that of the natural head of the family. In some years, as the table shows, the register indicates that they are not included in the figures (e.g. in 131: *Per.* Livy 59). They had to be registered, however, as they might own property and thus be liable for tax. Traditionally certain charges (liturgies) were imposed on them, such as paying for the maintenance of the cavalry. On one occasion at least (in 214, during the crisis of the second Punic War) the treasury floated a kind of forced loan on widows' and orphans' property.

Dionysius also says that the *paterfamilias* declared his slaves. This is very likely, but we have no direct information as to the number of slaves in Rome at any time, except for one figure, also from Dionysius, unfortunately for a half-legendary period (Dionys. 9.25.2; cf. Chap. One). One of the commonest ways of freeing a slave was to make a declaration before the censor, which took effect immediately.

The most important feature of the census, however, was the declaration of property. Its purpose was not only fiscal, as we have seen, since until 106 at least it determined very precisely the nature of the citizen's military obligations. It was also essential to the political life of the city, as it determined the citizen's place in the *comitia* and indeed his eligibility for most political functions. It is hard to say exactly what kinds of property originally had to be declared. Since the last century at least, ethnologists and jurists have supposed that there was a period in the earliest days of the City when individual property consisted essentially of cattle (hence the derivation of *pecunia* from *pecus*), the land at that time being still collectively owned by the City or the *gens*. It is scarcely possible to say when landed property became subject to the law of ownership that we are acquainted with (*dominium ex jure Quiritium*) and hence a matter for the census, but this must have been at an early date, as according to Cicero the *locupletes* (men 'rich in lands') were assimilated to the *assidui* (those who paid taxes and were liable for military service) as far back as Servius Tullius's reign in the sixth century. Mommsen, followed by others, believed that originally only landowners were liable for military service and regularly enrolled among the tribes, and that other property-owners (of real estate) were registered on separate lists as taxpayers (*aerarii*) only. Thus, on this view, the census originally took account only of a particular kind of property, the *bona censui censendo*; and this would accord with the distinction in old Roman law between *res mancipi* and *res nec mancipi,* i.e. things which were transferable only by formal mancipation and those which could be transferred by mere delivery. To the former category belonged estates in Italy, the praedial servitudes relating to them, and all property directly connected with the cultivation of land, including cattle and slaves, but not smaller livestock, furniture and money.[16] Naturally this distinction survived only as an archaeological curiosity, and no doubt from the fourth century onwards the whole of one's personal property had to be declared and assessed. The censor retained the power, for punitive purposes perhaps, to assess land at a higher value and to discount certain other types of property. Clearly the tendency was to take increasingly full account of the whole of the individual's patrimony. Some documents enable us to identify particular items, e.g. uncoined metal (Festus (322 L) tells us that the censor classified this as *rudis*) and luxury articles, slaves or vehicles above a certain value: as we shall see, the censor could impose his own assessment of the latter. The list also included ready cash, as the example of Decianus will show, and of course house property in the city and countryside. Its value was probably assessed by surface area, as several documents speak of the 'number of tiles' involved: thus in 43 senators were taxed at the rate of ten *asses* (four obols) per tile:

> Since there was need of much money for the war, they all contributed the twenty-fifth part of the wealth they possessed and the senators also four obols for each roof-tile of all the houses in the city that they either owned themselves or occupied as tenants. (Dio. 46.31.3)

Cicero estimated the yield of this tax at 60 million sesterces. At Tarento, in the decade 80-70 or thereabouts, magistrates and *decuriones* were required to own a house of not less than 1,500 tiles in the city itself. As we shall see in another chapter, at the time of the civil wars it became necessary to assess the rental value of urban and rural property or at any rate the income derived from it, although taxation always fell on capital and not on income. The number of one's slaves also had to be declared—this is covered by the formula 'money and *familia*', quoted by Cicero—and, again during the civil wars, slave-owners were taxed as such (Dio 47.17.4). Finally, the declaration might contain a debit item: debts had to be declared, and were deducted from the total. One might suppose that, on the same principle, creditors would be required to declare debts owed to them; but there is no direct evidence of this, as there is in the case of debts:

> [The tribunes protested at the cancellation of the election of censors for religious reasons, which they said was] an intolerable mockery of the plebs. The senate, they said, was seeking to avoid the evidence of witnesses and public records regarding the property of every man, because they did not want it to be seen how great was the volume of debt, which would show that half of the state had been ruined by the other half. (Livy 6.27.6)

Much later, in 52 BC, we learn that Milo, in making his declaration (*professio*), deliberately undervalued his debts and was attacked for doing so:

> For he had declared, according to ancient usage, that his debts amounted to six million sesterces. Clodius maintained vehemently that one who was in

reality crippled by debt and regarded the Republic as his prey ought not to be allowed to stand [for the consulate]. Cicero took up Milo's defence against this accusation. (*Scholia Bobbiensia,* 341 Or. = 169 St.)

We see here the mechanism and the underlying reason for the declarations at a time when their military and fiscal *raison d'être* had largely disappeared. The upper ranks of society were obliged to furnish evidence that they possessed a certain minimum degree of wealth; a great part of this would naturally consist of property of especially valuable kinds that were required to be declared (*bona censui censendo*), since only such property afforded a sufficient guarantee of the value of the individual's patrimony. This explains why some men were anxious to have particular kinds of property registered, albeit at their own financial risk. For, just as a census declaration did not prove that the man in question was a citizen, but only that he considered himself to be one and wanted his status recognized, so the declaration of a property was not itself a proof of the legal value of that property; at most it signified that the declarer was prepared to accept the fiscal and political consequences of the wealth he claimed to possess.

This is well shown by the case of Appuleius Decianus in 59 BC. Decianus was the son of a *tribunus plebis* who was killed in the civil wars around the year 90; he lived in Asia, where he owned much land and had considerable business interests. His father had been a senator, and he himself was an *eques*. Involved in a lawsuit against the proconsul Flaccus, he was sharply attacked by the latter's defender Cicero, who accused him of having acquired estates at Apollonis by corrupt means:

But you say you made returns of these estates in the census [no doubt that of 61 BC]. I omit the fact that they belonged to others, that they had been taken by violence, that they were declared by the people of Apollonis not to belong to you, that the Pergamenes refused to register them, even that they were reinstated by our magistrates, that you held them without right either of ownership or of possession. I ask these questions: are those estates capable of being returned in the census, do they admit of a legal right, are they in your formal possession or not, can they be entered as surety at the treasury or with the censor [in connection with a public contract]? Finally, in what tribe did you register those estates? You rendered yourself liable, had some crisis occurred, to have those same estates assessed for tribute at both Apollonis and Rome. But let that pass; you were full of your own importance, you wanted to be assessed for a large area of land, and land at that which cannot be divided among the Roman commons. You also declared 130,000 sesterces in cash. ...You declared Amyntas' slaves but you did not cause him any loss by doing so, for he still owns those slaves. Admittedly, he was afraid at first when he had heard that you had declared his slaves and took legal advice.

The unanimous opinion was that if Decianus was able to make other people's slaves his own by declaring them, he would have the largest household of any of us. (*Pro Flacco* 79-80)

This throws a clear light on the working of the census. The estates in question, being in Asia, did not strictly have to be declared. In declaring them, or at least reckoning them as part of a total, Decianus had a double purpose: he wished, if possible, to have the property recognized as his, and also to swell the amount of his declared capital, either out of vanity (*gloriosus es*) and in order to preserve his status as an *eques*, or because of some secret ambition. For the sake of this he accepted the negligible risk of having to pay tax on the estates.

Sometimes a citizen, for converse reasons, would conceal his wealth. Some time before 75 — no doubt at the census of 86 — the senator P. Annius Asellus did so because he wanted to appoint his daughter his heir, which the *Lex Voconia* of 169 forbade in the case of inheritances of the first class. Some have fastened on the statement that Annius 'did not register' (*neque census esset*), and have drawn hazardous conclusions to the effect that registration was not compulsory. But Annius could not possible have made no declaration at all, if only because he was a senator and had to figure on the Senate list drawn up by the censors. What the statement means is only that when he died in 75 there had been no census since 86 or even perhaps 90-89, a lapse of 15 years, so that the property he wished to bequeath to his daughter escaped the provisions of the *Lex Voconia*. For Cicero himself tells us that Voconius confined its application to the future so as not to infringe the rights of existing heiresses:

You might well have followed the example of Quintus Voconius himself, then: for his law did not deprive any girl or woman of her position of heiress if she had it already; it merely enjoined that no one, registered after the year of the censors named, should make a girl or woman his heiress in future. (*II Verr.* 1.107).

The declaration, then, was the first stage of the census operation; but it was not the end of the matter, being intended as the basis of an estimate by the censors of the total value of the individual's property. This estimate, moreover, might intentionally differ from the real value, for instance in the case of luxuries which the censors wished to prevent or punish. This is what happened when Cato was censor in 184:

In accepting assessments his censorship was stern and harsh towards all ranks. Jewels and women's dresses and vehicles which were worth more than 15,000 *asses* he directed the assessors to list at ten times more than their actual value; likewise slaves less than 20 years old, who had been bought since the previous *lustrum* for 10,000 *asses* or more, he directed to be assessed at ten times more than their actual cost, and he ordered that a rate of three *asses* per thousand should be applied to all these articles. (Livy 39.44.3)

As Livy suggests and Plutarch (*Cato Major* 18.3) expressly says, this was a fine and not a tax: the censors had in fact no power to impose taxes. The property having been assessed at ten times its value, the fine amounted effectively to 3 per cent. This would be added to the ordinary tax, the *tributum*, which was calculated at a variable rate on the whole assessment; the offending items were thus taxed twice over.

It might also happen that the censors would assess the whole of a man's property at a higher figure than its real value; this, as we shall see, was always a punishment in the form of a surtax. In any case, the operations described resulted in a figure representing the total amount of the citizen's official rating. We have few examples of such individual ratings from censorial documents; we may know the extent of a certain person's wealth, e.g. at his death, but this is not necessarily the same as his *aestimatio*. We also have the figures of categories adopted by the censors, e.g. those of the classes of the centuriate system, or the figure adopted as a criterion on one occasion or another. The register entry from Alexandria, quoted above, is a clear example, as L. Valerius L. f. Pol. Crispus gives his own rating as 375,000 sesterces, which was no doubt the officially recorded figure.

The exact extent to which wealth had to be declared is a matter of dispute. Below a certain minimum the citizen was exempt from taxation and military service, and therefore presumably from the obligation to furnish an account of his possessions. But it is not certain that the two limits coincided, and they may well have varied at different times. We shall return to this question when we discuss the composition of lists.

Moral censorship

While age and wealth were the main criteria as far as the lists were concerned, it must always be borne in mind that the census was also a moral and political operation, the fountain of 'honour' in the etymological sense. The censors' primary function, in fact, was to assign to each citizen a place not only in the order of *fortuna* but also in that of merit or demerit. Hence the importance of the *regimen morum* entrusted to them, and of the citizen's duty to appear before them and submit to moral and physical examination and possible questioning. Although the censors had no *imperium* they had a discretionary power (*arbitrium*) in this respect, and their disapproval could be expressed in what was to all intents and purposes a sentence (*nota*), which might be accompanied by a fine.[17] In principle they were mainly concerned with a man's civic behaviour, but it was difficult to draw a line between this and private morals; at a very early date it was considered that the citizens on whom the state chiefly depended — the soldiers, but especially the *equites* and of course the senators — must be above reproach in their private lives as well. The City claimed the right to examine a man's most secret acts, on the ground that virtue is indivisible and that a bad man cannot be a good citizen. The higher a man's position in the hierarchy of the census, which purported to be the model of the social hierarchy, the more rigorously his morals should be judged. As Cicero says in *De Legibus* (3. 7-10), it was the censors' task to 'prohibit celibacy' and 'regulate the morals of the people', while 'the senatorial order must be free from dishonour'. By way of comment he adds the following story:

> The reply made by our friend, the eminent Lucius Lucullus, to a criticism of the luxury of his villa at Tusculum was considered a very neat one. He said that he had two neighbours, a Roman knight living above him, and a freedman below; as their villas also were most luxurious, he thought that he ought to have the same privilege as members of a lower order. But, Lucullus, do you not see that even their desire for luxury is your own fault? If you had not indulged in it, it would not have been permissible for them to do so. For who could have endured seeing these men's villas crowded with statues and paintings which were partly public property and partly sacred objects belonging to the gods? Who would not put an end to their inordinate desires, if those very men whose duty it was to put an end to them were not guilty of the same passions? For it is not so mischievous that men of high position do evil — though that is bad enough in itself — as it is that these men have so many imitators. (3.30)

It would be quite wrong to suppose that this moral supervision came to an end when, in imperial times, the senatorial and the equestrian order were reconstituted and new timocratic conditions attached to them. At no time, under the Republic or the Empire, was an assessment of property by the census automatically sufficient to assure a man of inscription in an *ordo;* and the emperors, who inherited the censors' authority, were as strict on morality as their predecessors. However, from Augustus's time onwards, the moral test was essentially for *equites* and perhaps citizens of a somewhat lower financial rating who were to have the power to try certain cases in Rome, or so Pliny tells us (*N.H.* 29.8.18):

> Panels of judges are tested according to custom by the censorial powers of the Emperors; their examination invades the privacy of our homes; to give a verdict on a petty sum a man is summoned from Cadiz and the Pillars of Hercules.

But the most striking evidence is certainly that contained in an application for the title of *eques* submitted by a Greek from Asia, which has survived by chance together with Hadrian's comment:

> The applicant said that he had sufficient wealth for the equestrian dignity but that when he applied for it two years ago he had been passed over on the ground that he had been ordered by the governor to leave the *municipium* for a year on account of a charge brought against him by his slaves. To this Hadrian replied: 'to apply for the *equus publicus* a man must be above all suspicion; as to what your slaves may do, examine them yourself as if you were the emperor.'[18] (Pseudo-Dositheus, *CGL*, 3.33.1-25)

Other citizens, who could not aspire to equestrian rank, were examined less severely or not at all. At Augustus's census of AD 4 it was decided to assess only citizens worth at least 200,000 sesterces (Dio 50.13 and 56.28.6). Even for the Republican period we are much better informed about the moral standards required of the upper orders than those expected of ordinary citizens. The 'censorial severity' which figures so prominently in Roman politics and historiography was not so much a matter of repressing the lower classes as of upholding the traditional values of the governing class, in accordance with the doctrine of 'geometrical inequality' of which we have spoken.

The censors' arbitrary power was subject to certain legal forms, for the good reason that their moral judgement involved not only civic and political consequences but also judicial ones: the *ignominia* was a mark of disgrace, in many ways equivalent to that resulting from a legal sentence. As a rule, however, the censors' disapproval was expressed by removing the person concerned from the Senate or the equestrian order or his place in a century or tribe: that is to say, it chiefly affected his political status. Judicial consequences in the strict sense — for instance exclusion from testimony or ineligibility to act as an arbiter — were only secondary; nevertheless the censor's *nota* was couched in quasi-judicial form, with citation, accusation, evidence, and defence if any, sometimes with the help of lawyers, as is shown *e contrario* by Claudius's decision during his period as censor:

> He would not allow anyone to render an account of his life save in his own words, as well as he could, without the help of an advocate. (Suetonius, *Claudius,* 16)

Even when the censors were convinced of a man's guilt they did not usually inflict penalties unless he was formally accused:

> During his term as censor Scipio Africanus was holding the census of knights, when G. Licinius Sacerdos came forward; whereupon, in a loud

voice so as to be heard by the whole assembly, Scipio said that he knew that Licinius had committed deliberate perjury; and that if anyone wished to bring an accusation against him, he would give his evidence to support it. But, as no one brought an accusation, he bade Licinius 'lead past his horse' [i.e. confirmed his rank as an *eques*]. (Cicero, *Pro Cluentio* 134)

The sources offer a fairly large number of examples from which we can draw up a list of crimes and misdemeanours such as were liable to incur a censorial *nota* or penalty. The most obvious ones were connected with the infringement of military discipline, without prejudice to sanctions that might be inflicted by the army authorities themselves. For instance, in 264 some *equites* refused to obey an order which they thought derogatory:

> Four hundred young men, a large proportion of the equestrian order, received a *nota* from the censors M. Valerius and P. Sempronius for refusing to obey an order to dig trenches. (Valerius Maximus 2.9.7)

But Frontinus tells us (4.1.22) that the consul himself requested the censors to apply this sanction. The censors might also impose penalties for acts that were not a formal breach of discipline:

> Africanus as censor removed from his tribe that centurion who failed to appear at the battle fought under Paullus, though the defaulter pleaded that he had stayed in camp on guard, and sought to know why he was degraded by the censor: 'I am no lover of the over-cautious [*nimium diligentes*], was the answer of Africanus. (Cicero, *De Oratore* 2.272)
>
> [Africanus] deprived a young knight of his horse because, at the time when war was being waged against Carthage, this young man had given an expensive dinner for which he had ordered a honey-cake to be made in the form of the city, and, calling this Carthage, he set it before the company for them to plunder. When the young man asked the reason why he had been degraded, Scipio said, 'Because you plundered Carthage before I did!' (Plutarch, *Apophthegms of Scipio (Moralia)* 11)

But it was at times of grave national crisis, such as the second Punic War, that the censors' severity reinforced the powers of the magistrates and the Senate in military matters. In 214 the censors turned their attention to those senators and *equites* who, after Cannae, had despaired of the Republic and thought of leaving Italy:

> First they summoned those who after the battle of Cannae were said to have abandoned the state. The foremost among them, Marcus Caecilius Metellus, happened at this time to be quaestor. Inasmuch as he and the rest

of those guilty of the same offence, on being ordered to plead their cases, proved unable to clear themselves, the censors gave their verdict that in conversation and formal speeches they had attacked the state, in order to form a conspiracy to desert Italy. Next after them were summoned those who had been too crafty in interpreting the discharge of an oath—those of the captives who, after setting out and then returning secretly to Hannibal's camp, thought the oath they had sworn, that they would return, had been discharged. From these men and those mentioned above, their horses, if they had such from the state, were taken away, and all were ejected from their tribes and made *aerarii*. ... And to this relentless stigma of the censors was added a severe decree of the senate that all those whom the censors had stigmatised should serve on foot and be sent to Sicily, to the remnant of the army of Cannae. For this class of soldiers the term of service was not at an end until the enemy should be driven out of Italy. (Livy 24.18.3.-10)

In 209 the censors reverted to this matter:

From all those who, as horsemen belonging to the legions from Cannae, were in Sicily—and there were many of them—their horses were taken away. To this severity the censors added also prolonged service—that the years previously served with horses furnished by the state should not be reckoned, but that they must serve 10 years, furnishing their own mounts. Furthermore they sought out a great number of men who were bound to serve in the cavalry, and reduced to the grade of *aerarii* all those who at the beginning of the war had been 17 years old and had not served. (Livy 27.11.14-15)

It was not until 169 that the censors again intervened so directly in military matters: we have already mentioned their action in ordering all citizens to take an oath and submit to the *dilectus,* and their supervision of men on leave from Macedon (Livy 43.14). But they probably took an equally strong line in 167-133, when recruitment was beset by increasing demographic, economic and political difficulties. Evidence is lacking in our sources, but Scipio's very severe censorship in 142, though perhaps exceptional, is nevertheless significant.

But moral supervision extended to many other fields as well. Especially in later times, the censors punished dereliction of duty on the part of magistrates, judges and officials: a *tribunus militum* for disbanding a cohort without authority, a magistrate for convoking the Senate unconstitutionally, a quaestor for leaving his province before the due date, judges for taking bribes, etc. Other cases related especially to political behaviour: e.g. the censors in 169, C. Claudius Pulcher and Ti. Sempronius Gracchus, demoted P. Rutilius, a tribune of the plebs, from *eques* to *aerarius* and moved him to another tribe because, during his tribunate and at the beginning of their term of office, he proposed a law rescinding the edict under which they had farmed out the taxes and public works (they had sought to eliminate the tax-farmers of the previous census); in addition he had publicly arraigned C. Claudius and almost secured his condemnation (Livy 43.16; 44.16.8). Certainly censorial sanctions, especially against senators and *equites,* tended to become more and more 'political' in the narrow sense; this applied in large measure to the wholesale expulsion of senators from the Senate in 115, 70 and 51. But things were not so in earlier times, even towards the third and second centuries BC. At that time the censors' authority extended to some areas of private life. As Dionysius says:

The Athenians gained repute because they punished as harmful to the state the indolent and idle who followed no useful pursuits, and the Lacedaemonians because they permitted their oldest men to beat with their canes such of the citizens as were disorderly in any public place whatever; but for what took place in the homes they took no thought or precaution, holding that each man's house-door marked the boundary within which he was free to live as he pleased. But the Romans, throwing open every house and extending the authority of the censors even to the bed-chamber, made that office the overseer and guardian of everything that took place in the homes; for they believed that a master should not be cruel in the punishments meted out to his slaves, nor a father unduly harsh or lenient in the training of his children, nor a husband unjust in his partnership with his lawfully-wedded wife, nor children disobedient toward their aged parents, nor should brothers strive for more than their equal share; and they thought there should be no banquets and revels lasting all night long, no wantonness and corrupting of youthful comrades, no neglect of the ancestral honours of sacrifice and funerals, nor any other things done contrary to propriety and the advantage of the state. (Dionys. 20.13.2-3)

This description (which enumerates most of the grounds for censorial *notae* for which we have evidence) follows a celebrated example of severity on the part of Fabricius Luscinus, who expelled P. Cornelius Rufinus from the Senate for possessing a silver vessel weighing 10 pounds.

The first area, and perhaps the most important, in which the state claimed authority over family life was that of population. Ancient cities, as soon as their initial struggle for existence was over, were obsessed by fears of insufficient manpower. As we have seen the organization of the census conferred a definite advantage on those who had children; with the lowest property class a distinction was made between *capite censi,* who had only themselves to declare, and those who also had children and were relatively privileged on that account. As to the richest class, it was thought their duty to provide the city with manpower. By the second century the situation had become so disquieting that Q. Caecilius Metellus Macedonicus, who was censor in 131, delivered a famous speech urging compulsory marriage:

In that speech these words were written: 'If we could get on without a wife, Romans, we would all avoid that annoyance; but since nature has ordained that we can neither live very comfortably with them nor at all without them, we must take thought for our lasting well-being rather than for the pleasure of the moment.' (Aulus Gellius 1.6.2)

This edifying appeal to duty and resignation to the will of nature was long remembered: Augustus urged people to re-read it when, in 18 BC he promulgated the *Lex Julia* 'on the marriage of the upper orders', with penalties for senators and *equites* who refused to marry and beget children (Suetonius, *Aug.* 89.2). This law was resisted for a long time. In AD 9, when Augustus was at a theatre, the *equites* present urged him to repeal it. By way of reply, he sent for the children of Germanicus and exhibited them, some in his own lap and some in their father's, intimating by his gestures and expression that they should not refuse to follow that young man's example. (Suetonius, *Aug.* 34)

We have seen that the censors could inflict penalties for perjury and excessive luxury (which was later also subjected to the judicial sanctions of the sumptuary laws). Other misdeeds within their purview were the maladministration of property and even bad farming methods:

If anyone had allowed his land to run waste and was not giving it sufficient attention, if he had neither ploughed nor weeded it, or had neglected his orchard or vineyard, such conduct did not go unpunished, but was taken up by the censors, who reduced such a man to the lowest class of citizens. So too, any Roman knight, if his horse seemed to be skinny or not well groomed, was charged with *impolitia,* a word which means the same thing as negligence. (Aulus Gellius 4.12)

[In 179] the censor Lepidus had taken a horse from Marcus Antistius of Pyrgi. Antistius's friends made an outcry and kept asking what answer he should give his father to explain why his horse had been taken away from him, a first-class farmer, and an extremely economical and moderate and thrifty person. His reply was simply: 'I don't believe it is so.' (Cicero, *De Oratore* 2.287)

This concern for the state of the economy and agriculture should be distinguished from the fact that a senator or *eques* whose patrimony was lost or impaired might be reduced to a lower rank of society. This was not so much a moral penalty as a reflection of the fact that he no longer possessed the necessary property qualification. Even in this case, however, the moral aspect was not lost sight of: as I have said, it always in some degree modified the working of the timocratic principle. The circumstances that had deprived a man of his fortune were enquired into, and if it appeared to be a matter of ill-luck and not his own fault, he might exceptionally be allowed to keep his former rank. This happened several times during the civil wars: in 45 we find Cicero writing a letter on behalf of C. Curtius, who had apparently been a senator since the previous year and whose lands were threatened with confiscation under an agrarian law, which would probably mean that he could not become a senator:

> Now Curtius has a holding in the territory of Volaterrae into which, just as though he had been shipwrecked, he had collected all that was left to him. But just at this moment Caesar has chosen him to be a member of the Senate—a rank, which, if he loses that holding of his, he cannot easily maintain. Now it is very hard upon him that, though he has been raised higher as regards rank, he should be in a lower position as regards means; and it is shockingly inconsistent that the very man who is a senator by Caesar's favour should be ejected from land that is being distributed by Caesar's order. (*Ad Fam.* 13.5.2)

Augustus himself took measure to ease the lot of many who had been impoverished by the civil wars:

> Since many knights whose property was diminished during the civil wars did not venture to view the games from the 14 rows [reserved to them by the *Lex Roscia* and the *Lex Julia*] through fear of the penalty of the law regarding theatres, he declared that none were liable to its provisions, if they themselves or their parents had ever possessed a knight's estate. (Suetonius, *Aug.* 40)

In other words, if he did not leave them their title of *eques,* at least he allowed them to retain the external marks of honour (*ornamenta*) associated with it.

That the census always took account of civic morality as well as financial standing is confirmed by the fact that certain trades and activities were officially regarded as degrading. It is not clear to what extent citizens were obliged to disclose the nature of their livelihood; but the higher orders, at any rate, were subject to very strict laws or customs concerning 'disparagement' or conduct unbefitting their class. At least from 218 onwards senators were theoretically forbidden by a *plebiscitum,* the *Lex Claudia,* to pursue any kind of activity for gain (*quaestus*);[19] this had already become a dead letter by the time of the elder Cato, who lent money on bottomry, but the moral stigma remained. The upper orders largely lived on the income from their estates, and later, in the case of some *equites,* by tax-farming or accepting contracts for public works; this was not regarded as demeaning. Commerce, craftsmanship, and working for a wage or salary were not considered derogatory but were regarded as a bar to political activity, on the part of *equites* as well as senators. However, as a famous passage in Cicero's *De Officiis* makes clear,[20] it was all a question of scale: big business might be acceptable if the resulting fortune was invested in real estate. Banking might or might not be respectable, according to the degree of usury practised. Here again public opinion was more tolerant than the law, at least in the last century of the Republic. Atticus's uncle Q. Caecilius, a notoriously grasping money-lender, was not deprived of his rank or molested on that account, whereas Augustus censured certain *equites* who borrowed money at low interest and invested it at a higher rate (Suetonius, *Aug.* 39). It would seem that citizens were in fact questioned as to their source of income, as Livy says of the census of 179 that 'the censors changed the method of voting and constituted the tribes according to districts and to the classes and situations and occupations of the members.' (40.41.9)

In any case the censors agreed with the law in regarding certain occupations as degrading, e.g. acting, gladiatorial shows and of course prostitution. The story of D. Laberius is familiar: a well-known author of mimes, who was also an *eques* and proud of his title, he was obliged by Caesar to perform on the stage; by so doing he forfeited his rank, but Caesar at once restored it. His eloquent lament has been preserved by Macrobius:

> I, whom no soliciting, no bribe, no threat, no violence, no influence, could ever have moved from my rank when I was young—how easily I am made to fall from my place now, in my old age, by a man of high position! ...For twice 30 years I have lived without reproach; I left my household gods today a Roman knight and I shall return home—a mime. In very truth, today I have lived a day too long. (*Saturnalia* 2.7)

It is quite understandable that the upper orders were subject to rules of this kind, not only because, as Cicero points out, they were expected to set an example, but because membership of an *ordo* was the precondition of engaging in certain public activities: under the Republic a candidate for office had to be an *eques*, and from C. Gracchus's time onwards only an *eques* could sit as a juryman in criminal cases. Probably the same condition applied to being a *publicanus*—one of the select band of managers of large provincial companies —although not to contracting for ordinary public works. Under the Empire only an *eques* could serve as a *tribunus militum* or prefect or, in some cases, a *procurator* of the *princeps*. The state or its ruler wanted to know whom they were dealing with: their servants must be rich, which in itself was a guarantee to some extent, but they must be honourable as well. Qualifications of this sort applied to enrolment in the first class of the census. We shall see that the censors had the power to expel a man from the class to which his wealth entitled him, and this explains why the agrarian law of 111 laid down that only men of the first class might, for example, adjudicate fiscal disputes between *publicani* and *coloni* on the *ager publicus*.

Censorial sanctions

The registration process, the declaration and assessment of wealth, the attendance of citizens at the census and the enquiry into their morals — all these culminated in the essential operation of the compilation of lists in which each citizen found his proper place. There were several overlapping lists for different purposes. To begin with, as we saw, there was the total of male adult citizens, whether possessed of the vote or not (during the period before 89 BC), including freedmen and proletarians or *capite censi*.

This total, being the most significant, is the one most often cited by our sources. However, women and orphans were also counted (as they were liable to tax), and they are sometimes included in the total, so there was presumably a separate list of them. The state, however, also required more detailed lists of specific categories. For instance, it needed to know who was liable for ordinary military service, bearing in mind that, exceptionally, even *proletarii* and *capite censi* might be called up. Those so liable were called *assidui*, literally 'settled men', i.e. those rich enough to pay taxes and therefore liable to serve in the army. But some might be physically unfit, so that the lists of *assidui* and of those capable of bearing arms were not identical. The latter were subdivided into age groups: on the one hand the *juniores*, aged from 17 to 45, and on the other the *seniores*, aged over 45. These lists must evidently have been revised annually in one way or another, as the consuls would require them for the levy. The censors and their officials seem to have carried out preparatory work, as we find that from time to time retrospective enquiries were carried out, e.g. to identify all who had reached the age of 17 by a certain date. These *tabulae juniorum* were clearly an essential document for military purposes (Livy 24.17.1; Polybius 2.23.9 and 6.19.5). But there were many other classifications as well. In the first place there was a distinction between those who were to serve in the infantry and cavalry respectively: this was the basis of the whole aristocratic structure of the Roman state.[21] The essential criterion was the upper assessment, i.e. that of the richest members of the first class; but here again the censors had to see to the personal enrolment of the young man *'qui equo merere debet'*, as is shown by the exemption granted in 186 to the young P. Aebutius, denouncer of the Bacchic *thiasoi*, so that the censor 'should not assign him a public horse [i.e. make him liable to military service] without his consent' (Livy 39.19.4). These lists, as we have seen, existed during the second Punic War. The *equites* also had to undergo a second check: after their regulation ten years' service, when they were about 27, they had to appear before the censor with the horse furnished by the state, and render an account of their campaigns and conduct. The censors might then order them to return the horse, with or without *infamia*, whereupon they would cease to be *equites* and would revert to the first class; or else they were permitted to keep the horse (by the formula *traduc equum*) and continue to be members of the privileged centuries of *equites*, whose influence in the *comitia* was considerable. This 'review' (*recognitio equitum*) was, together with the compilation of the Senate list, an essential feature of the census. It was performed in a separate ceremony in the Forum and not the Campus Martius, and was the more important in that, until the year 129 or 123, the senators, who were nearly all former *equites*, were privileged to retain their places in the equestrian centuries, among the *seniores*, so that they too must have been present at the ceremony. An instructive incident took place at the census of 204:

They began to take the census of the knights; and it happened that both of the censors had horses from the state. When they had reached the Pollia tribe, in which stood the name of Marcus Livius, and while the herald was hesitating to summon the censor himself, Nero said, 'Summon Marcus Livius!' And, whether still nursing their ancient quarrel, or priding himself on an ill-timed display of strictness because he had been condemned by a verdict of the people, he ordered Marcus Livius to sell his horse. Likewise Marcus Livius, when they had reached the Arniensis tribe and the name of his colleague, ordered Gaius Claudius to sell his horse for two reasons: one because he had given false testimony against Livius, the other that he had not honestly been reconciled with him. Equally shameful at the close of their censorship was their contest in each besmirching the other's reputation even to the detriment of his own. When Gaius Claudius had taken the oath that he had complied with the laws, upon going up into the Treasury and giving the names of those whom he was leaving as mere tax-payers, he gave the name of his colleague. Then Marcus Livius came into the Treasury, and except for the Maecia tribe, which had neither condemned him nor after his condemnation voted for him either for consul or for censor, he left the entire Roman people, 34 tribes, as mere tax-payers, alleging that they had both condemned him, an innocent man, and after his condemnation had made him consul and censor, and could not deny that they had erred either once in their verdict or twice in the elections. He said that among the 34 tribes Gaius Claudius also would be a mere tax-payer; and that if he had a precedent for twice leaving the same man a mere tax-payer, he would have left Gaius Claudius among them with express mention of his name. (Livy 29.37.8)

This review of the equestrian order is the subject of many accounts. On one such occasion C. Gracchus had to answer a charge relating to his term of office as quaestor. Suspended by Sulla, the review was ceremonially restored by Pompey at the census of 70 BC, as it gave him an opportunity to demonstrate the exceptional nature of his own career and his respect for the law:

It is customary for a Roman knight, when he has served for the time fixed by law, to lead his horse into the forum before the two men who are called censors, and after enumerating all the generals and imperators under whom he has served, and rendering an account of his service in the field, to receive his discharge. Honours and penalties are also awarded, according to the career of each.

At this time, then, the censors Gellius and Lentulus were sitting in state, and the knights were passing in review before them, when Pompey was seen coming down the descent into the forum, otherwise marked by the insignia of his office, but leading his horse with his own hand. When he was near and could be plainly seen, he ordered his lictors to make way for him, and led his horse up to the tribunal. The people were astonished and kept perfect silence, and the magistrates were awed and delighted at the sight. Then the senior censor put the question: 'Pompeius Magnus, I ask thee whether thou hast performed all the military services required by law?' Then Pompey said with a loud voice: 'I have performed them all, and all under myself as *imperator.*' On hearing this, the people gave a loud shout, and it was no longer possible to check their cries of joy, but the censors rose up and accompanied Pompey to his home, thus gratifying the citizens, who followed with applause. (Plutarch, *Pompey* 22.4-6)

The most important lists of all, however, were of course those on which the electoral organization was based. We shall return to them in detail in a later chapter. On the one hand there were the 35 tribes (from 241 onwards), which were essentially geographical divisions and might to some extent be compared with electoral districts.[22] They were not geographically self-contained, however; as we have seen, a community might be attached to a particular tribe even though its territory was not contiguous. Moreover the tribe was also to some extent a personal grouping. Men who lived in Rome but who originally came from the *municipia* continued to be registered in their tribe of origin, especially as far as the upper orders were concerned; the urban tribes, as we shall see, were regarded as inferior. On the other hand the censors had the all-important power to inflict sanctions on individuals or groups by transferring them from one tribe to another. In the case of individuals this was a perfectly normal procedure, one penalty among other possible ones, the point being that the tribes were not equal from the electoral point of view; they voted in a certain order, and those which voted last were in a less favourable position. The tribes were also unequal demographically: they varied from a few hundred citizens to tens of thousands, and the voice of an individual might either dominate the rest or be swallowed up in the crowd. A citizen could not be expelled from the tribal system altogether, since belonging to a tribe was the proof and essential feature of citizenship, but he could be compulsorily transferred from one to another. Again, the censors might assign certain groups to a particular tribe: geographical groups, such as alien communities who were admitted to the City, or social ones such as freedmen. However, at a fairly early date these matters were recognized as political and therefore subject to regulation concurrently by the censors and by the law, that is to say the people. In 89 and 88, for instance, laws were passed providing that new citizens should vote in only eight or ten tribes. In 66, 63 and 58 there were laws or proposed laws about the position of freedmen in this respect (cf. below, p. 227).

But the electoral system did not consist merely of tribes: the citizens were also divided into classes and centuries. Originally perhaps there was only one class, that of the *assidui*; but from the fourth century BC to the Empire the complete system comprised five classes based essentially on the census. Each class was divided into a certain number of centuries, grouped according to age. In addition there were 18 centuries of *equites* and four or five specialized ones of craftsmen or trumpeters. This added up to 193 units, which originally provided a basis for recruitment to the army and payment of the *tributum*, but in the second and first century were no longer of practical significance except from the electoral point of view. They did, however, retain considerable prestige: quite apart from the *comitia*, it was no small thing to belong to the equestrian centuries or the first class of the census. In this field also, it would be wrong to suppose that a man's classification was purely a function of his wealth. Just as an individual might be moved from one tribe to another, though not excluded from every tribe, he might be ranked in a lower or less privileged century than that to which his fortune entitled him. A scholiast of Cicero who is our sole source for this information tells us that:

> The censors penalized citizens in the following manner: one who was a senator was expelled from the Senate, while a knight had his 'public horse' taken away. If the man was a plebeian he was inscribed on the *tabulae Caeritum* and made an *aerarius*, which meant that he was no longer enrolled on the list of his century. He remained a citizen only in the sense that he paid his contribution to the Treasury as an individual. (Pseudo-Asconius, p. 103, Or.)

The scholiast evidently wished to explain the use of the old word *aerarius*, which is obviously connected with *aes* and signifies a taxpayer. All citizens were liable for tax, but the term *aerarii* was applied to those who were taxpayers and nothing else, and who paid tax at a higher percentage of their census rating. The working of the financial sanctions is well shown by the example of the former dictator Mamercus Aemilius Mamercinus, who was punished for trying to curtail the censor's term of office: 'The censors...removed him from his tribe, and assessing him at eight times his former tax, disfranchised him.' (Livy 4.24.7)

But, as a citizen could not be excluded from the centuries altogether unless he were also deprived of his citizenship, a special century appears to have been created, to which the prospective expellees were assigned on voting day. This century does not figure in the canonical list transmitted by the sources which describe the Servian system (except a Latin papyrus of Oxyrhynchus), but it is mentioned by the lexicographers:

The 'non-voters' century', as it is called, is said to have been instituted by King Servius Tullius: those who did not vote in their own centuries could vote in this one, so that no citizen was legally excluded from voting. But no one was registered in this century; there was no centurion [head of a century] and there was no such thing as a 'member' of it, because no one was assigned to it permanently. (Festus, p. 184 L).

Whatever the position as to their voting rights, the *aerarii* also figured on the list of citizens *sine suffragio* (which existed until about the beginning of the second century), known as *tabulae Caeritum* (cf. Chapter One, p. 27); this meant that they had become mere taxpayers.[23]

Such were the principal lists drawn up on the basis of the census. The citizens were classified in a number of different ways, and despite the margin of error and any laxness on the censors' part it was, in normal times, very difficult to evade registration. In any case, it was only the poorest or remotest citizens who wished to evade it. The upper orders — senators, *equites,* publicans, scribes, *apparitores* etc.— had least chance of doing so, since their civic status was manifest to all by virtue of a whole system of titles, visible marks and details of behaviour. For a long time the wearing of the toga distinguished all Roman citizens from others. The effect of the system was that a man was, so to speak, on duty at every moment of the day, and everything he said and did was subject to public inspection and approval. The dividing line between public and private life was never clearly drawn in Rome. It only began to acquire significance as the motive forces of the old Republic lost their efficacy, which was a slow and gradual process. The citizen was relieved of his main fiscal obligation in 167; he eventually became virtually exempt from compulsory military service — but not before the reign of Tiberius — and ceased to have a voice in political decisions. But this disengagement from public life was never officially recognized, and did not affect all classes to the same extent at any given time. Its detailed history will be studied in the remainder of this book.

The whole censorial process, concerning which I have collected a large amount of literary and juridical evidence, is vividly illustrated by a remarkable archaeological document, fortunately preserved intact: the famous relief in the Louvre, known incorrectly as the 'altar-frieze of Domitius Ahenobarbus'[24]. Recent studies have shown that this was part of a frieze decorating the very broad base of a series of religious statues (another part of the frieze, now in the Munich museum, shows Neptune with Amphitrite, nereids and tritons). The frieze was originally in a temple of the Republican period, the ruins of which can still be seen under the church of San Salvatore in the southern part of the

Campus Martius; this temple is almost certainly identical with a temple of Neptune, built probably in the last years of the third century BC or at the beginning of the second. The statues and their base are, however, much later than the temple itself. The portion of the frieze now in the Louvre unmistakably depicts the whole censorship process from beginning to end; as M. Torelli has recently shown,[25] it can be considered as illustrating a formula of the type: 'X (the dedicator of the temple) performed the census, completed (*condidit*) the lustrum and dedicated this temple to Neptune'. The frieze enables us to follow the process in great detail. The key portion in the centre shows the final sacrifice of a pig, a sheep and a bull (*suovetaurilia*) being performed at an altar by the censor and his acolytes (*camilli*). The god Mars, as would be expected, is standing at the left of the altar. To left and right of this religious scene are four figures in civilian clothes and five in uniform. As we have seen, the essential purpose of the census is a military one, the division (*discriptio*) of citizens into a certain number of military categories, horse and foot. Here we see four foot-soldiers and, on the extreme right, a cavalryman about to mount his horse. The rhythm of the scene is very marked: on the left, a citizen in civilian clothes, bearing tablets in his left hand, is approaching a man seated beside a pile of registers; he has an open register on his knees and is writing in it at the citizen's direction. The scene is both lively and specific: the citizen is in the act of making his *professio* to the receiver of returns (the *jurator*), and is holding the *codex* on which he has noted the relevant data. We next come to the *discriptio:* a census official lays his right hand on the citizen's shoulder (this time the latter is not holding a *codex*) and directs him to take his place in a particular hierarchy. Then, continuing from left to right, we see the four infantrymen in matching equipment and the horseman with his back to us; he has no shield, and his helmet seems to be of different design from that of the foot-soldiers, with a larger rear-peak. He, no doubt, symbolizes the class of *equites*. It may be wondered why there are only four classes of infantry, whereas the canonical accounts of the Servian system mention five. Either the symbolism is not so rigid and the exact number is thought unimportant, or perhaps the second citizen on the left, wearing a toga, stands for the fifth class, which was called up rather infrequently. Another possible interpretation is suggested by Polybius, who tells us that in his day the legionaries were divided by age and wealth into four categories—*velites, hastati, principes* and *triarii*—which did not exactly correspond to those of the census. He adds, unfortunately, that the four types of soldiers had different kinds of offensive and defensive weapons, and that the coat of chain-mail (*lorica*) was only worn by *hastati* of the first census class (6.23.15), whereas all the soldiers on the frieze are wearing this type of cuirass; they also have a long *scutum* of the Gaulish type and the *gladius* or Hispanic short sword. This uniformity of equipment, together with the general style of the relief, is a valuable indication of its date. It must be fairly early, since it depicts a time when the system of military service based on property rating had not entirely disappeared; and it belongs to a period during which the lustrum was celebrated, which excludes the years from 70 to 28. On the other hand, the uniformity of equipment shows it to be subsequent to the various *leges militares* of the Gracchian era (*Lex Sempronia, Lex Junia* of 109). All the evidence therefore points to a date around the beginning of the first century BC.

CHAPTER III

MILITIA
The army and the citizen

LIKE ALL ANCIENT CITIES, but perhaps to a greater extent than any other, Rome was a community of warriors. This applied to practically all citizens: it does not appear that military service was ever confined, as a privilege or a duty, to any particular group. Rome differed in this from the Indo-European societies of proto-historical times, which in various forms and degrees practised what has been called the system of 'functional tripartition' whereby military, politico-religious and economic tasks were divided among more or less distinct and usually hereditary groups.[1] Even archaic Greek society — at least as reflected in the Homeric tradition, distorting and interpretative though it is — shows traces of this division of functions: one can, at any rate, identify without too much difficulty a recognizable class of 'professional warriors' represented by the Homeric kings and their trusty companions, who are evidently no more than a small, dominant, specialized group within society as a whole. While many questions arise as to the exact interpretation of this picture, and much might be said about conditions in Mycenaean times as the Pylos tablets are beginning to reveal them to us, it seems certain that a military society of this type, aristocratic and highly specialised, was long prevalent among the various Greek cities. It stands in sharp contrast to the hoplitic system found in Sparta around the seventh century and in Athens towards the end of the sixth, which reflected a profound transformation of military technique: Mycenaean chariots and single combat on the Homeric model have given place to collective manoeuvres by a body of heavily-armed infantrymen, who submit freely to discipline because they are also citizens. Although one of these two phases evolved from the other, they represent two quite different conceptions of society. The precise causes of the evolution are no doubt impossible to trace, but a great many economic, political and military factors operated in various ways to bring about the hoplitic system in which military and civic participation are inextricably linked.[2]

Even if Rome in its earliest days practised an aristocratic system in which the business of fighting was reserved to a functional, hereditary group, there is scarcely any trace of it in the records.[3] On the contrary, the Roman tradition emphasizes themes which in the course of time became positive obsessions, pervading the citizen's subconscious as well as the official ideology. In this system the Roman, any Roman, is first and foremost a warrior, or rather a soldier — i.e. not so much a fighting man eager for individual exploits as a disciplined citizen forming part of a machine whose redoubtable efficiency is the result of its coherence. This essential military vocation presents several aspects. The first is blind devotion to one's native land, which may be said to reflect the conservative instinct: it is, in a sense, passive, although the individual's subordination to the community was carried to a much higher degree in Rome than in other cities. But Roman warfare, like Janus, was two-faced. Its most defensive and desperate moments, at any rate as they were recalled by the historians, were accompanied by an instinctive confidence in Roman destiny which was largely religious in origin and found expression in unperturbed aggressiveness. From the end of the war with Hannibal, the public mind of Rome was dominated by the conviction that it was the City's destiny to rule over the whole world — a conviction admirably expressed in Virgil's famous words, written at a time when Rome's conquests were, by and large, coming to an end: 'Remember thou, O Roman, to rule the nations with thy sway: these shall be thine arts — to impose the law of peace, to spare the humbled and to tame in war the proud.' (*Aeneid* 6. 851-3)

There is no more typical illustration of this state of mind, with its aggressive self-confidence and complete subordination of the individual to the community, than the decisions taken at the height of the Second Punic War, immediately after the catastrophe at Cannae. For a time after the battle some commanders, fearing the capture of Rome, prepared to flee from Italy, but at once they were forcibly prevented by others (Livy 22.53.5-13). At Rome itself the magistrates and Senate reacted with the constancy and determination which, 75 years later, so impressed Polybius that he devoted his whole work to investigating its causes. Due allowance should be made for the enthusiasm of annalists: the tradition which idealized the past no doubt concealed many hesitations, public and private debates, and the loss of nerve by this or that group or individual. But the essential fact is that at that crucial moment Rome refused to discuss terms of peace with Hannibal, and the whole of public opinion finally rallied behind the Senate. The indulgence shown to Terentius Varro, the general who was at least partially to blame for the defeat and who himself survived it, was a kind of pledge that Cannae would be avenged:

In that very hour there was such courage in the hearts of the citizens that when the consul was returning from that defeat for which he himself had been chiefly responsible, a crowd of all sorts and conditions went out to meet him on the way, and gave him thanks because he had not despaired of the state. (Livy 22.61.14-15)

More significant still, perhaps, was Rome's refusal on that occasion to ransom the prisoners in Carthaginian hands. Hannibal, like a good Hellenistic general, expected his victory to be followed by negotiations. Under the more or less established rules that governed international relations in the Greek world at that time, Rome should have capitulated, yielded a large part of her territory, abandoned her diplomatic and military pretensions and, no doubt, conceded to Hannibal some kind of protectorate over Italy and Sicily; on the other hand she would have preserved her own existence and autonomy, though not independence, and no doubt her economic prosperity. The first move in this direction would have been to ransom her prisoners by means of public and private funds, as was the normal procedure of Greek states. Many Romans were naturally tempted to do so—the prisoners and their relatives first and foremost. Nevertheless, and no doubt after a long debate, the Senate rejected the proposal in the presence of the prisoners' own representatives sent by Hannibal:

After the speech of Manlius, though most of the senators, too, had relatives amongst the prisoners, yet, besides the example of a state which had shown from of old the scantiest consideration for prisoners of war, they were also moved by the greatness of the sum required, not wishing either to exhaust the treasury, on which they had already made a heavy draft to purchase slaves and arm them for service, or to furnish Hannibal with money—the one thing of which he was rumoured to stand most in need. (Livy 22.61.1-3)

When a city accepts without a murmur such a hard decision on the part of its public authorities, it deserves to win victories—such at least was Polybius' opinion. At a time when the civic population of Rome was putting forward such an effort, the system of national defence in most Greek cities and also Carthage was quite different: mercenaries were used at all levels, from the general staff to the rank and file. The nucleus of Hannibal's army was Carthaginian: it was the most dependable part of his force, but was very small; the most important contingents were Greeks, Numidians, Gauls and Italians, whose technical skill was purchased at high cost. It is an important fact, and is often insufficiently noticed, that in Rome, although the army was largely composed of volunteers after 106 BC, and altogether so from Augustus' time onwards, these volunteers, who thus became professionals, were at all events Roman citizens—and, incidentally, were underpaid. Only the auxiliary troops, comprising 50 or 60 per cent of the whole force according to circumstances, were non-Romans; and in their status, the manner of their recruitment and the elaborate arrangements for integrating them into the Roman state they differed totally from the unreliable, unassimilable mercenaries of the Hellenistic world. Finally, and this is perhaps the most important point, while military service ceased to be compulsory for ordinary citizens during the first century BC, it was still a precondition of appointment to public office or, under the Empire, to senior posts in the civil service.[4] Thus throughout Roman history the upper class was subject to military obligations and permeated by the military spirit. Even when Rome had conquered the world, she never quite demobilized.

The obligation to serve in the army was not specified in any law. Long after the army had in effect been placed on a professional footing, in time of national emergency (such as the loss of Varus's three legions in the Teutoburger Wald in AD 9) no special law was necessary to re-enforce conscription. The latter was in fact regarded as part of the City's very being, an integral part of the *mos majorum* which preceded all laws.[5] As we shall see, anyone who evaded it in any way was liable to the severest penalties; but in the course of Roman history there are very few examples of individuals or groups refusing to serve in the army. To understand these cases we must bear in mind that the part played by military service changed fundamentally towards the end of the second century BC. Until then, by virtue of the rules of civic integration embodied in the census system, the burden of military duties fell especially, though not exclusively, on the rich; very poor citizens, and those of modest means, were as a rule exempt, and it was quite exceptional for non-citizens or those recently freed to be affected by it. This discrimination against the rich was justified by the principle of 'geometrical equality' and the belief that the only good soldiers were rich men to whom the safety of the state was of genuine concern. Moreover, since in practice they alone took the political decisions on which peace or war might depend, it seemed right for them to bear the consequences. But this is only a partial explanation, for participation in the defence of the state was not merely a duty or a burden. It was also a privilege, to an extent that we shall try to assess more precisely: it meant a share of booty in the event of victory, and an opportunity for the individual to gain distinction by exhibiting his courage and patriotism. Service and reward, praise and hardship were connected by the workings of a subtle and archaic code of honour, which is not fully clear to us but which we can perceive vividly in operation on certain occasions. Hence during the whole long period when, in theory, military service was a prerogative of the well-to-do, this never precluded an element of spontaneity and the enlisting of volunteers.

In the first century BC the climate changed. The key event is Marius's celebrated levy of 107 when, contrary to all expectation, he was put in command of the force which had been fighting inconclusively for five years in Africa.[6] Marius set a precedent by ignoring property qualifications and accepting as many volunteers as cared to come forward. From then on the Roman army ceased to be a militia of rich bourgeois, serving voluntarily or not as the case might be, and became increasingly an army of indigent volunteers. With hindsight the importance of this change has been pushed so far as to ascribe to it all the political and social crises, the civil wars and *coups d'état* which finally gave birth to the Empire. As we shall see, things were no doubt less dramatic than this. Marius's reform was no more than the culmination of a long-standing recruiting crisis; its consequences were undeniably profound, but they were not immediate. All the same, such an abrupt change in the sociological basis of recruitment and the terms of service inevitably produced changes of mentality and behaviour which made the Roman armies of the first century BC very different from those of earlier times, as well as transforming relations between them and the City as a whole.

The civic cadres of military life

In Roman eyes a soldier and a citizen were the same thing. Every lad of 17 was enrolled, as a *juvenis,* on the list of those subject to call-up. The obligation extended, potentially at any rate, to everyone: the effect of discrimination on property grounds was not to exempt the poorest classes completely and legally from military service, but only to make it very unlikely that they would be mobilized. True, the Servian system as described by Livy, Cicero and Dionysius included an 'unarmed' century, the last, for citizens who owned less than 11,000 *asses* (Livy) or, according to Dionysius, 12,500; the figure varied from one date to another, for Cicero and, in particular, Polybius speaks of 4,000 and 1,500 *asses.*[7] Those in this category were called *proletarii* and/or *capite censi,* men assessed on their person only. Very likely the various figures denote the successive lowering of the limit as recruiting became more and more difficult. A first reduction from 11,000 to 4,000 *asses* may have taken place towards 214 BC, in the midst of the Second Punic War, and a further one around the time of the Gracchi. When Marius swept away the property qualification altogether he was not performing a revolutionary act but setting the seal on a long-standing tendency. The increasing shortage of 'qualified' manpower was certainly a major phenomenon between the Second Punic War and Marius's time, and the property requirement was correspondingly relaxed. But in emergency the City was quite ready to call on its poorest citizens and even more suspect characters, such as freedmen or convicted criminals. The earliest known example goes back to 280, at the beginning of the war against Tarentum: 'Then for the first time the proconsul Marcius [Philippus] armed the *Proletarii.*'[8] But in fact, as we shall see, there were at least two types of levy: a regular one, in normal circumstances, in which the forms and requirements of the census were adhered to, and a *levée en masse (tumultus)* in which all the City's manpower was called up in the event of an unexpected enemy onslaught. In 296, for instance, at the end of the Samnite wars,

News came from Etruria that after the withdrawal of Volumnius' army the Etruscans had been induced to arm; Egnatius, the Samnite general, and the Umbrians were being invited to join in the revolt, and the Gauls were being tempted with great sums of money. Alarmed by these reports, the Senate ordered that a cessation of the courts should be proclaimed, and that a levy should be held of every sort of men. Not only was the oath administered to free citizens of military age, but cohorts were also formed out of older men, and freedmen were mustered into centuries. (Livy 10.21.3)

In later times it became the rule to call up freedmen, but only for the navy, which the resources of the old 'naval colonies' no longer sufficed to equip. Thus in 217:

A vast number of men had been enrolled in Rome; even freedmen who had children and were of military age had taken the oath. Of this urban levy those who were less than 35 years old were sent on board the ships; the others were left to garrison the City. (Livy 22.11.8)

In 181, to fit out a fleet against the Ligurian pirates and those of the Ionian Sea:

The consuls were directed to secure the election of a board of two for this purpose; 20 ships, launched from the yards, would be manned by Roman citizens who had been slaves, serving as marines, employing free-born citizens only as commanders. (Livy 40.18.7)

The same thing happened in 171 (42.27.3). Sometimes, however, it was necessary to go further. The disaster of Cannae forced Rome to break with her most sacred traditions and to accept slaves as volunteers:

The levy wore a strange appearance, for owing to the scarcity of free men and the need of the hour, they bought, with money from the treasury, 8,000 young and stalwart slaves and armed them, first asking each if he were willing to serve. (Livy 22.57.12)

This slave army is celebrated in the annals of the war for its valour and loyalty. Commanded by Ti. Sempronius, grandfather of the Gracchi, the force took the name of 'Sempronians' and fought with distinction at Beneventum. None the less, its existence in the midst of a civic militia of the traditional kind presented awkward problems of morale, as its general commendably realized:

It was the commander's greatest concern, and he instructed the lieutenants and tribunes to the same effect, that no reproach as to any man's previous lot should sow strife between the different classes of soldiers; that the old soldier should allow himself to be rated with the recruit, the freeman with the slave-volunteer; that they should consider all to whom the Roman people had entrusted its arms and standards as sufficiently honoured and well-born. (Livy 23.35.7)

The anomalous situation (for the men, although soldiers, were still not free) continued for two years. In 214 some of them began to complain and to demand recompense. The general, after taking the Senate's advice and extolling the men's services, promised freedom to any who killed an enemy and brought back his head, if they were victorious in the battle about to begin (24.14.5); this promise nearly led to the Romans losing the battle. After the victory Gracchus freed them all, while punishing according to regulations those who had not fought bravely enough. Their triumphant return to Beneventum was celebrated by a huge public banquet at which they wore the caps of freedmen (24.16.17). But the sequel was to show that they were still slaves at heart, for on Gracchus's death they deserted *en masse,* as if they only considered themselves bound personally to their commander and liberator and not to the Republic (25.20.4 and 22.3). They had to be sought out and re-enlisted, apparently without being penalized in any way. In 214 slaves were again called into service, this time in order to man a new fleet. Instead of giving them their freedom, however, a more flexible method was adopted, similar to the Greek system of 'liturgies': the richer citizens and senators were required, each in proportion to his wealth, to furnish from among their own slaves, of whom they remained the owners, a certain number of seamen with their pay and equipment for a given period (Livy 24.11.7-9). Finally, in 216, as the emergency continued, another expedient was adopted:

> The dictator M. Junius Pera...stooped to that last defence of a state almost despaired of, when honour yields to necessity: namely, he issued an edict that if any men who had committed a capital offence, or were in chains as judgment debtors, should become soldiers under him, he would order their release from punishment or debt. (Livy 23.14.2).

All in all, as will be seen, the recourse to non-citizens or even those recently enfranchised was quite exceptional; it also occurred in the Greek city states, but there too it was an emergency measure, for instance when Abydos was struggling for survival against Philip of Macedon (Polybius 16.31-33). In principle the city was supposed to rely on its own citizens and, as far as possible, on those whose birth and wealth marked them out for a military career.

Military training

The Roman's whole upbringing was designed to inculcate military attitudes and habits. The traditional private education (there were no public schools till the end of the Republic) included physical exercises which were in fact paramilitary,[9] and it was because country life best fitted a young man for these exercises that the Romans ascribed a special social value to farming: as the elder Cato said in the preface to his *De re rustica,* 'It is from the farming class that the bravest men and the sturdiest soldiers come.' The same Cato gave his eldest son a purely military upbringing, teaching him to throw the javelin, to fence, ride and box, to endure heat and cold and to swim across an icy, swift-flowing river (Plutarch, *Cato* 20). We may perhaps suppose that this training was administered in Rome itself, on the Campus Martius, and that the river was the Tiber; for, Vegetius tells us (1.10), 'the ancients sited the Campus Martius near the Tiber so that young men sweating after their exercises might wash and clean themselves at once.' The exercises in question were certainly no joke. Even in the last century of the Republic, when ordinary citizens were no longer liable for call-up, they continued to be socially obligatory for young men of the upper orders, sons of *equites* and senators, who had to serve in the army if they aspired to public office.[10] The time for performing the exercises was the first year or two after assuming the *toga virilis;* on the Campus Martius well-born young Romans in Cicero's day were closely watched by their fathers, for its social promiscuity offered many temptations. As Cicero recalls (*Pro Caelio* 12):

> When I was young, we usually spent a year 'keeping our arms in our gown' and, in tunics, undergoing our physical training on the Campus, and, if we began our military service at once, the same practice was followed for our training in camp and in operations.

Horace reproaches Lydia for distracting her lover Sybaris from his indispensable rendezvous with military life: 'In the name of all the gods, tell me, Lydia, why thou art bent on ruining Sybaris with love; why he hates the sunny Campus, he who once was patient of the dust and sun; why he rides no more among his soldier companions, ... and fears to touch the yellow Tiber' (*Odes* 1.8; cf. 3.12).

Such, in any case, was the proper education of a young citizen during the Second Punic War. C. Sempronius Blaesus, attacking Cn. Fulvius for the loss of an army in Apulia, holds up the example of Ti. Gracchus with his slave army and upbraids him for being defeated in spite of having 'an army of Roman citizens, men well born and brought up as free men' (Livy 26.2.11). Six centuries later, seeking to revive the past glories and virtues of Rome, Vegetius urges that as far as possible the army should be recruited from men 'of good birth and good morals'; for 'a well-born man will generally make a good soldier, since honour prevents him from fleeing and thus obliges him to conquer.' (1.10)

The dilectus[11]

The young Roman was thus prepared for the call-up by moral pressure and intensive physical training. Before describing the enlistment procedure we must recall certain principles. The Roman had to consider himself liable for service during almost the whole of his active life: from the time he was enrolled as a *junior* at 17 to the age of 60. (He became a *senior* at the age of 46.) After 60 he was 'free of all civic duties', as Varro tells us (*Nonius* 523.24), including military service. The general retirement age of 60 is attested for judges and municipal *decuriones,* and senators could, if they wished, retire at that age while keeping their title (Seneca, *De brevitate vitae* 20.4). Naturally the conscript citizen could not and did not, any more than in a modern state, spend all his life actually under arms. It must be noted that Rome had no standing army until about the end of the second century BC, so that during that period, if she were at any time at peace with all her neighbours, she might have no army in being at all. This, however, was extremely rare. We have one example from 347, when 'what did the most to lighten the burden [of distress] was the omission of the war-tax and the levy' (Livy 7.27.4).

The most usual situation, however, was that each year the City was involved in limited wars requiring relatively small forces. The machinery for providing these was the *dilectus,* the very name of which shows that it was a 'selection' and not a mass levy. There was in fact a difference between theory and practice: any Roman from 17 to 60 might be called up, but it very seldom happened that all those liable were actually mobilized.[12] Even in theory, no one was obliged to serve for the full 43 years: at the time of the Second Punic War the maximum was probably 16 or 20 campaigns. A man who had fought as many times as this might be still on the list of *juniores,* but he had discharged his obligation to the state: he was *emeritus* and need not serve again unless he chose to do so as a volunteer. If he was an *eques* and hence a cavalryman, the required number of campaigns was reduced to ten. The term 'campaigns' is used because we do not know whether or not the term of service had to be continuous. The question had little significance as long as the Romans were fighting annually in Italy: the soldier would return to his home in winter and take the field again, if necessary, in spring. But in the later period of overseas conquests and long wars in distant lands, armies could not be disbanded and reassembled once a year. Service tended to be continuous, and this brought about a change in the conditions of army life and the soldier's mentality. Thus, while the army was basically a conscript one, the Republic came to maintain a regular force as well. (The Second Punic War, which lasted 17 years, was immediately followed by wars in Greece and Asia, while several legions were tied down in Spain throughout the second century.) The annual *dilectus* was still held, but it was only a *supplementum* to make up for those discharged after completing their term of service, to replace casualties or provide reinforcement. There was no legal difference from the citizen's point of view between peace-time and wartime; or rather, the levy took place because the city was in a more or less permanent state of war. Thus there was no distinction, as in a modern state, between peace-time military service and mobilization for war. The Roman army was perpetually mobilized. It is not surprising therefore that its strength was not prescribed by law: it was variable by definition, depending on circumstances. As we shall see, exactly the same was true of the direct tax, the *tributum.* It was not for the people to make rules governing the length of service or the level of taxation; the magistrates and their council, i.e. the Senate, were responsible for taking decisions in both fields as the situation might require.

The magistrates (usually the consuls) submitted an estimate of the men and money they required to the Senate, which passed a decree accordingly. Thereupon the consuls, as commanders of the army, carried out the *dilectus* so as to provide the required forces, the cost of supplying which had likewise been approved. The citizens were not consulted on these matters as a rule: they could only obey, though in rare cases they might challenge the magistrates' decision through their tribunes, or even actually rebel.

The regular *dilectus,* then, was a selection from a given category of citizens. The consuls might summon only certain men to attend, and might recruit only some of them. On the other hand, the *dilectus* gave everyone an opportunity to assert his rights and claim any exemption to which he was entitled, e.g. on grounds of health or religion or of having already served his term. The operation was a fairly long and complicated one, and various short cuts were devised; the best-known of these, the *tumultus,* made it possible to enrol practically all the physically fit without considering exemption claims or allowing the tribunes to intervene.

The *dilectus* began with a summons in the form of an edict, warning citizens to prepare to assemble on a date usually fixed 30 days ahead (approximately a *trinundinum);* during the interval a red flag was flown from the Capitol by way of reminder (Festus 92 L). At least until the Second Punic War, the first part of the recruiting operation took place on the Capitol itself: this was an actual roll-call of those liable for service, to ascertain that they were present and physically fit and to examine any claim for exemption that they might have. All were thus called, but not all were chosen: the magistrate selected those he needed from the point of view of numbers and quality. This, at least, was the practice around the time of the Second Punic War. Polybius describes the procedure in detail, though in a somewhat schematic way:

> On the appointed day, when those liable to service arrive in Rome, and assemble on the Capitol, [the military tribunes] draw lots for the tribes, and summon them singly in the order of the lottery. From each tribe they first of all select four lads of more or less the same age and physique. When these are brought forward the officers of the first legion have first choice [etc]. (6.19.6–20.4)

Polybius here omits an essential feature of the regular *dilectus,* that of the examination of each man's status from the military point of view: his description starts from the point where the tribunes have before them only those who are definitely being called up. What were in fact the citizen's rights in this respect? In the first place, there were heavy penalties for disobeying the summons itself; the worst of these was to be sold into slavery:

> The consul Manius Curius found it necessary to order an immediate levy, and when no young men answered the summons he had lots cast for each tribe and announced the first citizen's name to be drawn from the urn. When the man failed to appear, the consul had his property sold by auction. The man, learning of this, hastened to the consul's court and appealed to the college of tribunes. Curius then declared that the Republic had no use for a citizen who could not obey orders, and gave order that not only his goods but he himself should be sold. (Valerius Maximus 6.3.4)

A similar incident occurred during the Social War. It was at this preliminary stage that the citizen had his only chance of escaping the mobilization order or refusing to comply, by appealing to the tribunes of the plebs. The annals describe many such incidents in the fifth and fourth centuries, illustrating the semi-legendary conflict between patricians and plebeians. According to them the tribunes might either stop proceedings by opposing the levy altogether, or (which came to practically the same thing) declare that they would use their legal powers to aid anyone who refused to be called up or take the oath. One recourse that was then open to the consul was to declare a *tumultus* (state of emergency), which overrode the obligation to examine appeals by the tribunes on behalf of men who objected to being enlisted. This procedure, which was perhaps the basis of M. Curius's action quoted above, is not well attested until the second century. In 193, for instance:

> Numerous soldiers who were in the city legions appealed to the tribunes of the people to look into the cases of those who had claimed exemption from military service on the ground of completed service or illness, but despatches from Tiberius Sempronius put an end to their attempt. He reported that 10,000 of the Ligures had entered the territory of Placentia and had laid it waste with fire and slaughter up to the very walls of the colony and the banks of the Po, while the nation of the Boi was also considering a rebellion. For these reasons the senate decreed that a state of civil war existed, and that the tribunes of the people should not investigate the cases of soldiers to prevent their mustering according to the proclamation. They added also that the allies of the Latin confederacy who had been in the army of Publius Cornelius and Tiberius Sempronius and had been discharged by those consuls should assemble on the day and at the place in Etruria which the consul Lucius Cornelius had announced in his proclamation. They also decreed that the consul Lucius Cornelius, on his way to the province, should enlist,

in the towns and rural districts along his route, whatever soldiers he saw fit, should arm them and lead them with him, and should have the privilege of discharging whichever of them he desired and at whatever time. (Livy 24.56.9-13)

But the consuls had other means at their disposal. In the first place, they might play on the internal divisions of the college of tribunes; the story of the tribune M. Menenius in 407, if confirmed, would be an example of this:

[The other tribunes] proclaimed in the name of the college that they would support the consul Gaius Valerius if he resorted, despite the veto of their colleague, to fines and other forms of coercion against those who refused to serve. (Livy 4.53.7)

Dionysius suggests another procedure, which may explain why, from about 100 BC, the *dilectus* was apparently transferred from the Capitol to the Campus Martius, outside the area of the tribunes' authority:

[The consuls L. Valerius and M. Fabius, in 493 BC,] having taken office, appointed a day on which all who were of military age must appear. [But] the poorest citizens refused either to comply with the decrees of the senate or to obey the authority of the consuls, and, going in great numbers to the tribunes, they demanded their assistance. [One of the tribunes, C. Maenius, promised to] hinder the levy with all his power. [But] the consuls, going outside the city, ordered their generals' chairs to be placed in the Campus Martius; and there they not only enrolled the troops, but also fined those who refused obedience to the laws, since it was not in their power to seize their persons. If the disobedient owned estates, they laid them waste and demolished their country-houses; and if they were farmers who tilled fields belonging to others, they stripped them of the yokes of oxen, the cattle, and the beasts of burden that were used for the work, and all kinds of implements with which the land was tilled and the crops gathered. (Dionys. 8.87.3-5, abridged)

During the period for which we have reliable historical evidence, i.e. after the Second Punic War, there is no instance of the tribunes preventing the *dilectus* altogether, but only of their intervening on behalf of individuals who had formally appealed to them. Such cases might lead to a sharp political conflict; in 151,

When the consuls Lucius Licinius Lucullus and Aulus Postumius Albinus were conducting the levy strictly and exempting no one as a favour, they were thrown into prison by tribunes of the people who were unable to obtain exemption for their friends. (Livy, *Per.* 48)

But Appian gives a somewhat different version:

Since many had complained that they had been treated unjustly by the consuls in the enrolment, while others had been chosen for easier service, it was decided now to choose by lot [those who were to serve in Spain]. (*Iber.* 49)[13]

In 138, again in dramatic circumstances (the consuls, moreover, had caused a deserter to be condemned, beaten with rods and sold into slavery),

Because tribunes of the commons did not succeed in obtaining the right to choose ten men apiece for exemption from the levy, they ordered the consuls taken to gaol [but, on a petition from the people, they refrained from fining them.] (Livy, *Per.* 55)

As will be seen, when matters were going properly any citizen who wished to claim exemption had to apply to the consuls, who had supreme responsibility for the levy and whose duty it was to examine particular cases (*causas cognoscere*). Legal exemption was very rare, and it is noteworthy that until Marius's time all Romans were fully equal as far as the blood-tax was concerned. The law only exempted the members of certain priesthoods or those whom it was desired to reward for outstanding services: e.g. the Praenestines who resisted Hannibal so valiantly at the siege of Casilinum (Livy 23.20.2) and were exempted for five years, or the young P. Aebutius, who denounced the Dionysiac associations in 189. Much later, in 123, a law against peculation provided that non-citizens who successfully charged a magistrate with embezzlement should be exempted from military service whether or not they accepted enfranchisement for themselves and their children.[14] In the same way the publicans who, in 215, demanded exemption for the duration of their contract to supply the armies were certainly an exceptional case, and at least one of them later gave evidence of a taste for war by raising a private army at his own expense.[15]

But other cases might arise, and the first step in considering them was to ascertain a man's military record. As we have seen, those who had fought in 16 campaigns were legally exempt; in some cases the commander-in-chief might decide, on his sole responsibility, that a lesser number sufficed. Soldiers thus released were called *emeriti* and could not be called up in future against their will. But, especially towards the beginning of the second century, the supreme commanders (e.g. Quintus Metellus: cf. Valerius Maximus 9.4.7) acquired the right to give a 'free discharge' to some who had not served for the full period. This could always be overruled by the other consul, as was shown at the levy of 169 BC:

> Since it was rumoured that many were absent on leave from the legions in Macedonia without specific reason because of the popularity-hunting of the generals, the censors proclaimed, as regards the soldiers enrolled for Macedonia in or after the consulship of Publius Aelius and Gaius Popilius, that whoever of them were in Italy should, having first appeared before the censors, return to their province within 30 days, and that the names of those who were subject to the authority of father or grandfather should be reported. They would also review, they said, the reasons for discharges, and those whose discharge before completion of their military service seemed to result from indulgence they would order to be enrolled as soldiers. In consequence of this proclamation of the censors, and their letters sent about throughout the markets and hamlets, so large a crowd of men of military age assembled at Rome that the unusual throng was burdensome to the city. (Livy 43.14)

When all claims to exemption had been investigated, with or without the aid of the *tribuni plebis,* the enrolment took place in the way described by Polybius, the military tribunes selecting men on the consul's behalf. But the recruits were not brought on to the strength at once: the consul ordered them to report at a given date to their respective enrolment centres, generally in the area where each man was to serve. In 193, for instance, the new recruits had to present themselves at Arretium (Arezzo) within ten days (Livy 34.56.3), and in 191, for the war against Antiochus, at Brundisium (Brindisi):

> The consul Manius Acilius issued an edict to the soldiers whom Lucius Quinctius had enlisted and those whom he had requisitioned from the allies of the Latin confederacy, whom he was to take with him to his province, and to the military tribunes of the first and the third legions, that they should all assemble at Brundisium on the Ides of May (Livy 36.3.13)

Anyone who disobeyed this summons or arrived after the due date was treated as a deserter (*infrequens*).

The oath

Between the ceremony in Rome and their actual enrolment in the field, the recruits took the oath (*sacramentum dicere*) which in common language became a synonym of military service.[16] It was in fact the keystone of the system from a religious, legal and civic point of view. The term *sacramentum* itself was an indication of its solemnity: it is not the ordinary word for 'oath', which was *conjuratio* or *jusjurandum*, but had religious implications, signifying that anyone who violated it was *sacer*, 'accursed'. Once a soldier had taken the oath he was linked by the strongest ties to the Republic, his commander and his comrades. In addition, the oath alone legitimized his status as a soldier (*miles*) and his right to perform acts of war. There is evidently a trace here of the rites known to the most ancient Indo-European societies by which the soldier was associated with an aspect of divinity. These rights, in a strikingly cruel form, are attested as late as the fourth century in Italy, e.g. when the Samnites wished to recruit forces with especial ceremony. Here is Livy's famous description of the oath taken by the 'linen legion':

> The enemy...had likewise invoked the assistance of the gods, initiating, as it were, their soldiers, in accordance with a certain antique form of oath. But first they held a levy throughout Samnium under this new ordinance, that whosoever of military age did not report in response to the proclamation of the generals, or departed without their orders, should forfeit his life to Jupiter. Having done this they appointed all the army to meet at Aquilonia, where some forty thousand soldiers, the strength of Samnium, came together.
>
> There, at about the middle of the camp, they had enclosed an area approximately 200 feet in diameter with wicker hurdles, and roofed it over with linen. In this place they offered sacrifice in accordance with directions read from an old linen roll. The celebrant was one Ovius Paccius, an aged man, who claimed to derive this ceremony from an ancient ritual which the Samnites had formerly employed when they had secretly planned to take Capua from the Etruscans. On the conclusion of the sacrifice, the general by his apparitor commanded to be summoned all those of the highest degree in birth and deeds of arms; and one by one they were introduced. Besides other ceremonial preparations, such as might avail to strike the mind with religious awe, there was a place all enclosed, with altars in the midst and slaughtered victims lying about, and round them a guard of centurions with drawn swords. The man was brought up to the altar, more like a victim than a partaker in the rite, and was sworn not to divulge what he should see or hear. They then made him take an oath in a certain dreadful form of words, whereby he invoked a curse upon his head, his household, and his family, if he went not into battle where his generals led the way, or if he either fled from the line himself or saw any other fleeing and did not instantly cut him down. Some at first refused to take this oath: these were beheaded before the altars, where they lay amongst the slaughtered victms, as a warning to the rest not to refuse. (Livy 10.38)[17]

The Romans, who inherited the same cultural and religious outlook as the Samnites, also regarded warfare as a 'consecrated service', as Papirius Cursor called it in 325 (Livy 8.34.11), transforming a citizen into a warrior and sealing a pact between him and the gods of his mother city, the state, his commander and his fellow-soliders, so that only death or a regular discharge could loosen the sacred bond. All those selected were henceforth united in this way, and, conversely, a man could not fight even as a volunteer without first taking the oath. War was a matter for the community, and an individual could not take part in it unless he had been formally taken into its bosom. Cato warned his son, who had been discharged and wanted to re-enlist, that he must not forget to take the oath again, without which he could not be a lawful combatant.[18] The terms of the oath, which went back to the remotest antiquity, were codified and no doubt re-phrased in 216:

> When they had finished the levy, the consuls waited a few days for the soldiers from the allies and the Latins to come in. An oath was then administered to the soldiers by their tribunes, a thing they had never done before. For until that day there had only been the general oath to assemble at the bidding of the consuls and not depart without their orders; then, after assembling, they would exchange a voluntary pledge amongst themselves — the cavalrymen in their decuries and the infantry in their centuries — that they would not abandon their ranks for flight or fear, but only to take up or seek a weapon, either to smite an enemy or to save a fellow citizen. This voluntary agreement amongst the men themselves was replaced by an oath administered formally by the tribunes. (Livy 22.38.3)

> The enrolment having been completed in this manner, those of the tribunes on whom this duty falls collect the newly-enrolled soldiers, and, picking out of the whole body a single man whom they think the most suitable, make him take the oath that he will obey his officers and execute their orders as far as is in his power. Then the others come forward and each in his turn takes his oath simply that he will do the same as the first man. (Polybius 6.21.1)

The first promise was to report for enrolment at the appointed place and time. An ancient author has fortunately preserved the exact wording:

> Unless there be any of the following excuses: a funeral in his family or purification from a dead body (provided these were not appointed for that day in order that he might not appear on that day), a dangerous disease, an omen which could not be passed by without expiatory rites, an anniversary sacrifice which could not be properly celebrated unless he himself were present on that day, or violence or the attack of enemies, or a stated and appointed day with a foreigner; if anyone should have any of these excuses, then on the day following that on which he is excused for these reasons he shall come and render service to the one who held the levy in that district, village or town. (Aulus Gellius 16.4)

The soldier had to take a second oath when he actually joined his unit, but this related to less important matters of discipline such as not committing any theft in or outside the camp. This is attested by Polybius (6.33.1), and again Aulus Gellius has preserved the text:

> In the army of the consuls Gaius Laelius, son of Gaius, and Lucius Cornelius, son of Publius, and for ten miles around it, you will not with malice aforethought commit a theft, either alone or with others, of more than the value of a silver sesterce in any one day. And except for one spear, a spear-shaft, wood, fruit, fodder, a water-skin, a purse and a torch, if you find or carry off anything there which is not your own and is worth more than one silver sesterce, you will bring it to the consul Gaius Laelius, son of Gaius, or to the consul Lucius Cornelius, son of Publius, or to whomsoever either of them shall appoint, or you will make known within the next three days whatever you have found or wrongfully carried off, or you will restore it to him whom you suppose to be its rightful owner, as you wish to do what is right. (16.4)

Discipline

From this point onwards the civilian disappears and only the *miles* remains. We shall not attempt to trace every detail of his life in camp and on the battlefield, but only to discover what responsibilities, rights and duties fell on him in this new phase of his communal life.[19] Formidable though military discipline was in the ancient world, we should not suppose that a Roman soldier ceased to think and act as a citizen. Even in the last century of the Republic, when the army was to all intents and purposes a professional one, it was not divorced from the life of the City, if only because some of its leaders involved it in civil wars, and it is not to be imagined that this did not lead to protests and recalcitrance on the part of some soldiers. But we have not yet reached that point in the story: the army continued to be a bourgeois militia at least until the Second Punic War, and the citizens who served in it could hardly forget that they had recently been civilians and, for the most part, soon would be again. In strict law the army, even in the field, was in certain circumstances regarded as a kind of extension of the City itself, and behaved accordingly; the Greek democracies normally took a similar view. In 357, for instance, a law was formally passed by citizen-soldiers encamped far from Rome at Sutrium. The tribunes of the plebs could not intervene at the time but had the procedure banned for the future, and it did not recur (Livy 7.16.8). But in some cases, albeit exceptionally, the soldiers might act as civilians once again. This occurred, for instance, in Spain in 211; the two proconsuls had been killed, and the defeated and isolated army elected its own general:

So pre-eminent was a mere Roman knight in his personal influence with the soldiers and in the respect they paid him that, after they had fortified a camp on this side of the Hiberus and decided that a commander of the army should be chosen in an election by the soldiers, relieving each other as sentries on the wall and in outpost duty until all had cast their votes, they unanimously conferred the high command upon Lucius Marcius. (Livy 25.37.5-6)

Marcius, writing to the Senate after this event, imprudently styled himself pro-praetor, which many took amiss:

It was a bad precedent, they said, for generals to be chosen by armies, and for the sanctity of elections with the required auspices to be removed instead to camps and the provinces, far from laws and magistrates, at the bidding of reckless soldiers. (Livy 26.2.3)

There is no doubt that Roman military discipline was extremely severe: the *imperium* could be exercised in ferocious ways which legend or tradition has recorded and perhaps embellished. Manlius Torquatus, consul in 340 and surnamed *imperiosus*, put to death his own son, who was a prefect or tribune, for disobeying his orders and engaging, victoriously, in single combat with an enemy.[20] At the time we are concerned with there was, properly speaking, no code of military regulations but only a set of customs to which the name *disciplina* was given and which had nothing to do with public or private law: certain crimes related only to army life and had no civilian counterpart, and some others were punishable by death in the army but not in civil life. Thus the unofficial military code was marked by greater severity, specific penalties, and procedures of its own such as collective punishment and sentences of death determined by lot (decimation). Strictly military offences were, of course, first and foremost disobedience, cowardice and desertion, but also slackness on guard and sentry duty, losing the tablet on which the password was inscribed etc. Capital crimes in military as opposed to civilian life were, for instance, theft, sexual offences and false witness. The scale of punishments was in proportion to the rest of the code, and the military tribunes could inflict fines, stoppage of pay, flogging, the bastinado and death.[21] But this rigid discipline was endurable, that is to say effective, for two reasons: one is spelt out by Polybius, while the other is implicit in the data available to us.

The first reason was that the whole object of discipline was to exalt the soldier's devotion and courage: it was a skilful blend of punishments and rewards. Sometimes the former were such as only to impugn the guilty man's honour, while rewards and chances of promotion were so calculated that the private soldier was not merely the butt of a brutal system but was imbued with a sense of responsibility. The procedure is thus described by Polybius:

A court-martial composed of all the tribunes meets to try him, and if he is found guilty he is punished by the bastinado (*fustuarium*). This is inflicted as follows: the tribune takes a cudgel and just touches the condemned man with it, after which all in the camp beat or stone him, in most cases dispatching him in the camp itself. But even those who manage to escape are not saved thereby; for they are not allowed to return to their homes, and none of the family would dare to receive such a man in his house. So that those who have once fallen into this misfortune are utterly ruined. The same punishment is inflicted on the *optio* and on the *praefectus* of the squadron, if they do not give the proper orders at the right time to the patrols and the *praefectus* of the next squadron. Thus, owing to the extreme severity and inevitableness of the penalty, the night watches of the Roman army are most scrupulously kept.

While the soldiers are subject to the tribunes, the latter are subject to the consuls. A tribune, and in the case of the allies a *praefectus,* has the right of inflicting fines, of demanding sureties, and of punishing by flogging. The bastinado is also inflicted on those who steal anything from the camp; on those who give false evidence; on young men who have abused their persons; and finally on anyone who has been punished thrice for the same fault. Those are the offences which are punished as crimes, the following being treated as unmanly acts and disgraceful in a soldier—when a man boasts falsely to the tribune of his valour in the field in order to gain distinction; when any men who have been placed in a covering force leave the station assigned to them from fear; likewise when anyone throws away from fear any of his arms in the actual battle. Therefore the men in covering forces often face certain death, refusing to leave their ranks even when vastly outnumbered, owing to dread of the punishment they would meet with; and again in the battle men who have lost a shield or sword or any other arm often throw themselves into the midst of the enemy, hoping either to recover the lost object or to escape by death from inevitable disgrace and the taunts of their relations.

If the same thing ever happens to large bodies, and if entire maniples desert their posts when exceedingly hard pressed, the officers refrain from inflicting the bastinado or the death penalty on all, but find a solution of the difficulty which is both salutary and terror-striking. The tribune assembles the legion, and brings up those guilty of leaving the ranks, reproaches them sharply, and finally chooses by lot sometimes five, sometimes eight, sometimes twenty of the offenders, so adjusting the number thus chosen that they form as near as possible the tenth part of those guilty of cowardice. Those on whom the lot falls are bastinadoed mercilessly in the manner above described; the rest receive rations of barley instead of wheat and are ordered to encamp outside the camp on an unprotected spot. As therefore the danger and dread of drawing the fatal lot affects all equally, as it is uncertain on whom it will fall; and as the public disgrace of receiving barley rations falls on all alike, this practice is that best calculated both to inspire fear and to correct the mischief.

They also have an admirable method of encouraging the young soldiers to face danger. After a battle in which some of them have distinguished themselves, the general calls an assembly of the troops, and bringing forward those whom he considers to have displayed conspicuous valour, first of all speaks in laudatory terms of the courageous deeds of each and of anything else in their previous conduct which deserves commendation, and afterwards distributes the following rewards. To the man who has wounded an enemy, a spear; to him who has slain and stripped an enemy, a cup if he be in the infantry and horse trappings if in the cavalry, although the gift here was originally only a spear. These gifts are not made to men who have wounded or stripped an enemy in a regular battle or at the storming of a city, but to those who during skirmishes or in similar circumstances, where there is no necessity for engaging in single combat, have voluntarily and deliberately thrown themselves into the danger. To the first man to mount the wall at the assault on a city, he gives a crown of gold. So also those who have shielded and saved any of the citizens or allies receive honorary gifts from the consul, and the men they saved crown their preservers, if not of their own free will, under compulsion from the tribunes who judge the case. The man thus preserved also reverences his preserver as a father all through his life, and must treat him in every way like a parent.

By such incentives they excite to emulation and rivalry in the field not only the men who are present and listen to their words, but those who remain at home also. For the recipients of such gifts, quite apart from becoming famous in the army and famous too for the time at their homes, are especially distinguished in religious processions after their return, as no one is allowed to wear decorations except those on whom these honours for bravery have been conferred by the consul; and in their houses they hang up the spoils they won in the most conspicuous places, looking upon them as tokens and evidences of their valour. (Polybius 6.37-39)[22]

The second reason for the effectiveness of Roman discipline is that the army was not a state within the state. In the first place, the soldiers were citizens possessed of political rights which they had exercised or would in future exercise in Rome. The election of officers (*tribuni militum*) and army commanders (quaestors, praetors, consuls) depended on them either directly or indirectly (e.g. through their relatives). The consuls had always to remember that they were only the magistrates of a city in which the body of citizens played an important part. As we shall see, one of the latter's most remarkable achievements in the civilian sphere was the recognition of the right of *provocatio* which in practice prevented the magistrates from condemning a citizen to the death penalty without first allowing him to appeal to the people. This right, first enacted no doubt around the year 300, was elaborated by the Leges Porciae at the beginning of the second century. It has been asserted that the right of *provocatio* was then extended to the army, so that defendants would have had to be brought to Rome and would have escaped execution. This is doubtful, however, and there are examples of decimations subsequent to the Leges Porciae. But it would seem that citizens at least were exempt from capital punishment at the sentence of a military court (*consilium*). In any case the soldier, as a past or future elector, could not have felt deprived of all rights. Matters of recruiting and discipline were the legislative concern of tribunes of the people like C. Gracchus and even, in 122, of his senatorial adversary Livius Drusus. The City and its army were not in watertight compartments.

There was another reason, perhaps even stronger. Roman discipline was not all one way: it was just as severe towards junior officers (centurions) and senior ones (tribunes, *praefecti* and even legates or deputy commanders) as towards private soldiers. Until the middle of the second century at least, the misdeeds of officers were punished no less harshly than those of their men. The most famous examples of military discipline quoted by Valerius Maximus (2.7.1-15) largely involve high officers: the outstanding case is perhaps that of Q. Fabius Rullianus, *magister equitum* to the dictator Papirius Cursor in 325, who narrowly escaped being executed for fighting a battle (which he won) in breach of orders.[23]

CHAPTER IV

ARMA ET TOGA
The army and the body politic

The demographic aspect

I S IT POSSIBLE to form an idea of the military burden sustained by the Roman population at various times during the last three centuries of the Republic?[1] Cautious though one must be in demographic studies of the ancient world, the sources suffice to indicate an order of magnitude. We must first consider some figures in order to judge the exact impact of military service on the citizens, and understand their varying reactions in different circumstances. According to the most conservative estimates the total free population of Roman Italy in 225 BC must have been of the order of 2,752,000, of whom citizens and their families may have totalled 923,000. Adult male citizens, i.e. *juniores* and *seniores* capable of bearing arms, must have numbered about 300,000, including 205,000 *juniores*. Taking the number of legions raised during the first years of the Punic War we find, allowing for losses, that from the beginning of the war to 215 Rome had mobilized about 108,000 citizens in the legions, 50,000 of whom lost their lives. Thus those mobilized were over 10 per cent of the total population and about 35 per cent of the adult males, while losses amounted to almost half of these figures. In modern times, armies and casualties on this scale are not met with until the mass mobilization and slaughter of the First World War. But we must also bear in mind the fundamental principle of the *dilectus,* the brunt of which was originally borne by the rich and middle classes as opposed to the very poor. The burden on those classed as rich was proportionately higher, and it is probable that the minimum property qualification for recruitment (in the fifth class) was lowered from 11,000 to 4,000 *asses* as early as 214, on the occasion of a general monetary and fiscal reform. This made it possible in that year to raise the number of legions under arms from 15 to 20: Rome had to mobilize her poorer citizens and even, as we have seen, 8,000 slaves to whom she promised the franchise. By this means the total strength of the legions was raised to 75,000, and two years later to 80,000. But the rest of Italy was also involved in Rome's war effort. The allies and Latin colonies must have contributed somewhat more than Rome itself; after the defections of 216 they were required to furnish about the same number of troops. The free population of the allied cities in 225 was nearly twice as great as that of Rome — perhaps

1,840,000 in all, but in their case too the military burden was very unequally distributed. The colonies, as we have seen, were obliged by their charters to contribute a fixed contingent; this no doubt bore heavily on them, witness the 'revolt' of the twelve colonies in 209. Altogether we may estimate that from 214 to the end of the war in 203 some 75,000 citizens were killed in action, bringing the total losses in 16 years of war to 120,000. Taking account of demographic factors and the natural deaths that would have occurred in any case, the 'net losses' due to the war would thus amount to 50,000 citizens, or 6 per cent of the population. This is a higher proportion than French losses in 1914-18, which were nearly two million dead out of a population of about 40 million. Recalling the traumatic effect of these losses in terms of French politics, demography and national psychology, we can easily imagine that the Second Punic War was no less momentous in its effect on Rome.

The defeat of Hannibal delivered Rome from a nightmare and from a heavy drain on its manpower, but the burden of conscription was not much relieved. For reasons we need not go into here, the Republic was involved in a series of interventions in Macedon, Greece and later Asia Minor, not to mention its permanent military presence in Spain. Only twice between 200 and 168 did the number of legions under arms fall as low as six; generally there were ten and at times 13—e.g. in 190, representing a total for that year of perhaps 71,000 or 65,000 citizens and 110,000 or 105,000 allies. It has been thought that these figures may be too high, as they assume that all the legions were at the full strength permitted by law, which is not certain. But, even making allowance for this, it seems established that in each year one-tenth or even more of the adult males of Italy were under arms—a heavy burden, both demographically and economically. We are not well informed as to the subsequent period, but here too an order of the magnitude can be predicated. Between 167 and 91 there were never less than four legions under arms; the figure rose to ten or 12 during three or four years of war in Spain (149-146), nine for the Numantian war, and 11 during the dark days of the Jugurthan and especially the Cimbrian War (104-101). Although the actual burden cannot be estimated, it was clearly no less grave than in previous times. This, moreover, was the period when conscription was most violently resisted in every way: as we have seen, in 151 and 138 it gave rise to acute political conflict between consuls and tribunes of the plebs. Citizens liable for service tried to escape the call-up either by appealing legally to the tribunes or by taking advantage of the patron-client system: thus Appian accuses the consuls in 151 of granting 'favours' to their friends and enabling them to dodge service in Spain (*Hisp.* 49). By 123 the pressure on the City's manpower had become so severe that C. Gracchus had to propose a law 'that no one under 17 should be enrolled as a soldier' and that 'clothing should be furnished to the soldiers at the public cost' (Plutarch, *C. Gracchus* 5). These obstructions to recruiting were no doubt repealed by Metellus and M. Junius Silanus at the height of the Jugurthan war (Asconius 68 C).

Ten per cent of the male population under arms, and at times of crisis up to 20 per cent — figures like these imply that there must have been some reduction in the length of service, for such a proportion of the city's manpower could not have been kept in the field for years on end. To do so would indeed have solved the problem of recruitment at a stroke, but clearly some rotation had to be observed. During the Punic War it was all hands to the pump, and some unfortunate classes were made to serve for an extraordinary length of time: at least three legions served for 12 years, another for ten and four more for nine (Toynbee II.71). The average worked out at seven years, apart from the legions in Spain and Sardinia, which it was impossible to relieve; but their case was so exceptional that in 200 they were given grants of land by way of compensation: as Livy tells us, 'Regarding land for Scipio's soldiers it was decreed that each should receive two *jugera* of land [about one and a third acres] for each year of their service in Spain or Africa (31.49.5; cf. 32.1.6).

The average also does not take account of the private soldiers, cavalrymen and officers who were punished for their conduct at Cannae: in 209, for example, the *equites* who had fought in that battle and were now in the infantry in Sicily were not only 'deprived of the public horse', i.e. expelled from the equestrian centuries, but also obliged to serve for an additional ten years, mounted at their own expense (Livy 27.11.14).

It is typical of what was still a citizen army that this punishment, including the extension of service, became a political problem. In 212 a deputation of the Cannae legions, consisting of *equites*, the most distinguished centurions and the élite of the infantry, visited the consul M. Marcellus in Sicily to appeal against the Senate's decree; they did not plead to have their term of service reduced, but to be allowed to take part in the fighting. Their argument is interesting:

> Others who survived that disaster, the men whom we had as our tribunes of the soldiers, now canvass for offices, we have heard, and hold them, and govern provinces. Can it be, conscript fathers, that you so readily pardon yourselves and your sons, but are cruel to us who are creatures of no account? (Livy 25.6.8-9)

But these were extreme cases. During the second century every effort was made to keep the average period of service down to six years: this was relatively easy for operations in Cisalpine Gaul or in the East, much less so in Spain. In 184, for example, a decree of the Senate provided for the discharge from the army in Spain of all those who had 'served their full term' (ten or 16 years?), and all who had distinguished themselves in battle (Livy 39.38.8). Levies at that time were extremely irregular: the satirical poet Lucilius speaks of 'a soldier in the land of Spain, serving for thrice six years or so' (509 W). Sometimes there might be enough volunteers to meet requirements: it depended on the reputation of the general who was to take command, or the prospects of booty. Thus the levies in 171 for the third and last Macedonian war were at first very easy:

> Licinus was enrolling the veteran soldiers and centurions; likewise many enlisted voluntarily, because they saw that those who had served in the former Macedonian campaign or against Antiochus in Asia had become rich. (Livy 42.32.6)

The same was true of the Second Punic War (Appian, *Pun.* 75). At other times the result was more disappointing. From 169 onwards, as the war in Macedon dragged on, the flow of volunteers dried up, and the consuls complained of the lack of recruits. The praetors thereupon intervened, talking of politically-minded consuls who never enrolled a soldier against his will, and offering to conduct the levy themselves (Livy 43.13). As we have seen, the consuls for that year gave them valuable help by drawing up the lists with particular care, administering the oath in very strict terms and doing everything possible to rout out shirkers and those absent without leave. Similar difficulties were met with in 154-151: not only was there a shortage of recruits, but even the higher ranks could not be brought up to strength until Scipio himself volunteered; then, as we read in Polybius:

> Those who previously shirked their duty, ashamed now of being shown up by a comparison of their conduct with his, began some of them to volunteer for the post of legate and the rest to flock in groups to enrol themselves as soldiers. (25.4.14)

As we shall see, there was no fundamental change when proletarians were admitted to the army as recruits by Marius in 107; this made it easier for the time being to recruit on a voluntary basis, but the number of men involved was hardly more than 5,000. Conscription remained in force during the first century, especially at the time of the civil wars; and the demographic burden of soldiering was not in fact reduced until Augustus established a regular standing army.

The fact that such a large proportion of the citizens were serving soldiers goes far to explain certain aspects of foreign policy. War had to be declared by a law for which the citizens voted. In wartime the people decided, by the election to the consulate, who would be in charge of operations for the coming year. This led to debates and conflicts in which the interests of future recruits might play a part. For example, at the election in 216 of C. Terentius Varro, who favoured an aggressive strategy, Fabius and the nobles were accused of dragging out the war (Livy 22.34). Sixteen years later the people displayed their reluctance even more clearly by at first refusing to renew the declaration of war on Macedon:

[The citizens] were worn out by a war of long duration and great severity, so weary were they of hardships and perils; furthermore, Quintus Baebius, the tribune of the plebs, pursuing the once-usual course of attacking the Fathers, had taunted them with sowing the seeds of war upon war, that the common people might never enjoy peace. (Livy 31.6.3-4)

The consul P. Sulpicius, with some difficulty, persuaded the citizens to change their minds by making a speech which painted the situation in dark colours and raised the spectre of a Macedonian invasion of Italy.

Economic aspects: equipment, pay and booty

The original, hoplitic type of army was composed of the rich and the fairly well off. Citizens were supposed to be able to afford their own equipment, which accordingly differed from one 'class' to another: the richest served in the front line and were the most heavily armed. Naturally we know next to nothing of any standardization of equipment, how it was stored in peace-time and what it cost in real terms.[2] The citizen-soldiers were also supposed to provide for their own subsistence while on campaign. Later this became inadequate and a pay system was introduced; we may also assume, though there is no confirmation of this, that the state provided arms and equipment, of course at the soldiers' expense. According to tradition soldiers first received pay during the siege of Veii in 406-396, the first campaign which lasted for several years and kept the soldiers away from home for several winters. But this has been doubted (the whole account of the siege of Veii is highly suspect), and it is thought that the introduction of payment probably occurred later, towards the end of the fourth century or even the beginning of the third; it presupposes the existence of money, which is very unlikely in Rome before that time.[3] In any case, as we shall see when discussing fiscal matters, the pay system was a definite step towards equalizing the burdens of war. The necessary funds were provided collectively by the *assidui* or taxpayers; these were defined by the same property criterion as those liable for military service, but were more numerous than they (since the *assidui* included the old and unfit) and, *a fortiori*, than those called up for any one campaign. The pay system, while still confining military service to those of sufficient means, made it possible to apportion the cost more fairly between those who actually served and those who were exempt. According to tradition there was opposition when it was introduced, as the *tribuni plebis* complained that 'the money could only be got together by imposing a tribute on the people' (Livy 4.60.4). But the senators set the example, the system was adopted, and the soldiers' pay, together with the *tributum* levied for the purpose, became a familiar institution.

We do not know what the original rate was, but Polybius gives figures for the time of the Punic Wars or immediately afterwards: 'The foot-soldier receives two obols a day, a centurion twice as much, and a cavalry-soldier a drachma' (6.39.12). Polybius's conversion of Roman money into Greek for his readers' benefit creates a problem of interpretation, but the text probably means that the foot-soldier's daily pay was one-third of a silver denarius. As we shall see, the amount apparently remained unchanged until Caesar doubled it. But account must also be taken of the variations in weight and accounting to which Roman currency was subject from the end of the second century to the time of the Gracchi. We now know that the denarius was introduced as such in about 213 BC, when it was worth ten bronze *asses:* this refers to the *as sextantarius,* weighing one-sixth of a Roman pound, or about 40 grammes. But the value of the *as* was reduced during the second century BC, so that finally it weighed only one ounce (the twelfth part of a pound), and it was decreed that the denarius would henceforth be equivalent to 16 *asses* except for the purpose of soldiers' pay, where the former parity of ten *asses* was maintained. Unfortunately the date and exact scope of this last measure are not very clear.[4] It would seem to have been intended to benefit soldiers, but at what rate were they paid? It may be, as a young scholar has recently argued, that the reduction of the bronze *as* to one-twelfth of a pound and the re-tariffing of the denarius at 16 *asses* instead of ten did not take place around 150 BC, as has hitherto been thought, but during the Second Punic War. Polybius's two obols a day would then represent four *asses* or a *sestertius;* the soldier's annual pay would have been between 88 and 94 denarii, and this would have been kept unchanged when the danarius was re-evaluated at 16 *asses.*

We learn from Suetonius that Caesar doubled the soldiers' pay, and from Tacitus that it amounted to ten *asses* at the death of Augustus, who made no change in it.[5] It would thus appear that the rate began at four *asses* (= 88 or 94 denarii) in about 214, that it was raised slightly to five *asses* (112.5 denarii) during the second century, perhaps in the time of the Gracchi or Marius, and then doubled by Caesar to ten *asses* (225 denarii). In any case these figures only serve as a rough guide. As we shall see, in the first century BC they were a very small sum compared with the wages of a manual worker who, though a slave, might earn up to 12 *asses* a day.[6] But it must be remembered that the soldier's *stipendium* was not intended to be a wage; in an army based on property, the citizen was supposed to serve at his own expense, to have capital and an income of his own. His pay was merely an allowance to cover subsistence and perhaps equipment. Polybius goes on to say that:

> The allowance of corn to a foot-soldier is about two-thirds of an Attic medimnus a month; a cavalry-soldier receives seven medimni of barley and two of wheat. Of the allies the infantry receive the same, the cavalry one and one-third medimnus of wheat and five of barley, these rations being a free gift to the allies; but in the case of the Romans the quaestor deducts from their pay the price fixed for their corn and clothes and any additional arms

they require. (6.39.12-15)

As we have seen, C. Gracchus in about 123 tried to alleviate the troops' distress by providing them with free clothing. Certainly in the second and first century their pay could not be considered an attraction or even a serious compensation for years of service. It is symptomatic of the gradual decline of the Roman military system during the second century that, while more and more needy citizens had to be called up for seven years or even longer, no attempt was made to improve the economic conditions of service. These grew steadily worse until Caesar's time, and their effect was very different once the army had become almost wholly professional and largely proletarian in composition.

It must also be noted, however, that the soldier's pay was far from being all he got out of military service, even before the army was professionalized. War was a *munus:* the citizen shared its dangers and the risk of loss, but also any profits there might be, in proportion to his stake. This is why a centurion was paid more than an infantryman, and a cavalryman more than a centurion. War was expected to bring profit to the Roman state as a whole and to each of its citizens individually; these profits included the exaction from the defeated enemy of an indemnity for war expenses, including the cost of paying troops. Later, when wars no longer took place on Italian soil, it became usual for armies to live off the countryside (in contrast to the terms of the oath quoted in the previous chapter), and a whole system of garrisons and billeting orders increasingly threw the financial burden of maintaining an army on the subject peoples.[7]

But the chief allurement was booty. Rome, like all ancient cities, asserted the right to plunder as part of international law, on the principle that the persons and possessions of the conquered became the victors' property. This law, however, was codified, and thus mitigated in practice. A distinction was drawn, for instance, between the enemy camp with its baggage and the goods owned by the civilian population of a conquered city or state. The first could be plundered as a matter of course, and this practice was never defined by regulations. Civilian property was on a different footing and was much more important, as it comprised in theory persons, livestock, buildings and the land itself. Many documents show that international treaties throughout the Mediterranean world laid down precise regulations for pillage in the case of alliances and joint victories. Such clauses figure in the treaties of the sixth and fifth centuries between Rome and Carthage, and also in the first treaty of 212 BC between Rome and the Aetolians, known to us from Livy (following Polybius) and a recently discovered inscription:

Of the cities between the Aetolian border and Corcyra the soil and buildings and city walls, together with their territory, were to belong to the Aetolians, all the rest of the booty to the Roman people. (Livy 26.24.11)

The epigraphic text shows that a distinction was drawn between joint military operations and those conducted severally by the two parties.[8] An important detail indicates that there was one way only for the vanquished to avoid the total loss of their property: all the treaties speak of 'cities taken by force', i.e. those which reject a summons to surrender. Only by capitulation, as a rule, could the persons and property of the weaker side be safeguarded. The Romans quite often accepted a form of surrender, known as *deditio in fidem*, whereby the vanquished or weaker party committed the whole of its population, its property and its gods to the discretion and 'good faith' of the Roman people. Usually the latter would then at once perform a *redditio* by which they restored to the conquered people their personal freedom and most of their property, except for a portion of their goods or territory which was annexed to Rome. In this way, over the centuries, the land of Italy came to belong to the Roman state. But this kind of booty was not of immediate advantage to the Roman people, especially the soldiery. What the latter usually expected from a campaign was instantly available loot in the form of prisoners, livestock, articles of use and, most important of all, precious metals, whether coined or otherwise.

In theory this plunder did not belong to the individual soldier but the community. We have seen the text of the oath against stealing, recorded by Cincius and quoted in Aulus Gellius, 16.4.2; perhaps this applied to booty also? In any case, the actual collection of booty was a collective operation conducted by the Romans in their usual methodical way, as reported by Polybius (though perhaps it was not quite as disciplined as he makes out):

The Romans after the capture of a city manage matters more or less as follows: according to the size of the town sometimes a certain number of men from each maniple, at other times certain whole maniples are told off to collect booty, but they never thus employ more than half their total force, the rest remaining in their ranks either outside or inside the city, ready for the occasion. As their armies are usually composed of two Roman legions and two legions of allies, the whole four legions being rarely massed, all those who are told off to spoil bring the booty back, each man to his own legion, and after it has been sold the tribunes distribute the profits equally among all, including not only those who were left behind in the protecting force, but the men who are guarding the tents, the sick and those absent on any special service. I have already stated at some length in my chapters on the Roman state how it is that no one appropriates any part of the loot, but that all keep the oath they make when first assembled in camp on setting out for a campaign. So that when half of the army disperse to pillage and the other half keep their ranks and afford them protection, there is never any chance of the Romans suffering disaster owing to individual covetousness.

For as all, both the spoilers and those who remain to safeguard them, have equal confidence that they will get their share of the booty, no one leaves the ranks, a thing which usually does injury to other armies. (Polybius 10.16)

What was then done with the booty? In principle, it would seem that the individual soldiers had no right to it; for we often find that a general, sometimes by way of punishment, would refuse to share out any of it and would turn over the whole lot to the treasury (Livy 4.53.10). Thus in 293, at the time of Papirius's triumph over the Samnites:

Of heavy bronze there were carried past 2,533,000 pounds. This bronze had been collected, it was said, from the sale of captives. Of silver which had been taken from the cities there were 1,830 pounds. All the bronze and silver was placed in the Treasury, none of the booty being given to the soldiers. The ill-feeling which this gave rise to in the plebs was increased by the gathering of a war-tax to pay the troops. (Livy 10.46.5)

But in the same year the other consul, Sp. Carvilius, behaved in a very different fashion with the Etruscan booty:

Of heavy bronze he lodged in the Treasury 380,000 pounds; with what remained he contracted for a temple to Fors Fortuna to be erected from the general's spoils, near the temple of that goddess dedicated by King Servius Tullius, while to the soldiers he apportioned from the rest of the booty 102 *asses* each, and as much again to the centurions and horsemen. These allowances were all the more welcome because of the parsimony of his colleague. (ib. 14-15)

In fact, as I. Shatzman has recently shown,[9] the whole matter lay within the general's discretion. He could, according to his own pleasure or rather to circumstances, either make everything over to the treasury, or keep it all for the soldiers, or divide the proceeds. The Senate approved of generals who contributed at least the greater part of it to public funds. A typical case was that of L. Aemilius Paullus, the conqueror of Perseus of Macedon, who brought home unprecedented sums including 120 million sesterces' worth of gold and silver alone (Livy 45.40.1). The amount surrendered to the treasury was such that the authorities were able thereafter to suspend the *tributum* altogether: Roman conquest was paying for itself. Paullus, on the other hand, was relatively stingy in his gifts to the soldiers of his army: on the day of his triumph the infantry received 100 denarii a head, the centurions 200 and the cavalry 300 (Livy 45.40.1). This was partly by way of rebuke to those who had complained of the hardships of campaigning and tried to prevent his being granted a triumph at all:

[Servius Galba reminded the tribunes of L. Aemilius's] harsh enforcement of military duties; more toil and more danger had been imposed, he said, than the situation demanded; on the other hand, rewards and honours had been without exception restricted; if success attended this sort of leadership, military service would be more dreadful and full of hardships in wartime, and after victory would be left without funds or honours. (Livy 45.36.3-4)

We shall see later the contrasting example of Manlius Vulso, who at his triumph in 187 used the spoils of war to reimburse part of a tax previously paid by the citizens.

However cautious some generals may have been, during the period after the Second Punic War the army received increasingly large sums on the occasion of successive major victories in the West and East, as is shown by the following Table (source: P. A. Brunt, *Italian Manpower,* p. 394).

TABLE III

DISTRIBUTIONS OF MONEY TO SOLDIERS, 201-167 BC
All figures represent *denarii*

DATE	SUMS GIVEN			SOURCE AND REMARKS
	Pedites	Centurions	*Equites*	
201	40			Livy 30.45.3. Scipio's triumph *ex Africa*.
200	12			31.20.7. Ovation from Spain.
197	7	14	21	33.23.7 ff. Triumph from Gaul.
196	8	24	24	33.37.11 f. Triumph from Gaul.
194	27	54	81	34.46.2 ff. Cato's triumph from Spain.
	25	50	75	34.52.4 ff. Flamininus' triumph from Greece and Macedon.
191	12.5	25	37.5	36.40.12 f. Triumph from Gaul.
189	25	50	75	37.59.3 ff. L. Scipio's triumph from Asia.
187	25	50	75	39.5.14 ff. Fulvius Nobilior from Greece.
	42	84	126	39.7.1 ff. Manlius from Asia.
181	30			40.34.7 f. L. Paullus from Liguria.
180	50	100	150	40.43.5. Q. Fulvius Flaccus from Spain.
179	30	60	90	40.59.2. Q. Fulvius Flaccus from Liguria.
178	25	50	75	41.7.1 ff. From both Spains.
177	15	30	45	41.13.6 f. From Liguria.
167	100	200	300	45.40.1 ff. L. Paullus from Macedon. (Plut. *Aem.* 29 says that in Epirus his soldiers got only 11 drachmae each.)
	45	90	135	45.43.4. Anicius from Illyria.

We also know that these end-of-campaign donatives were accompanied by a grant of double pay, e.g. in 187 (Livy 39.7.1) and 180 (40.43.5).

Even if the sums listed in the Table are far from equalling those received by the semi-professional armies of the first century BC, they are certainly not negligible, and we can understand better why (as mentioned above) so many volunteered for service in Macedon in 171.

In addition to donatives and regular rewards, war offered a further prospect of gain: from the end of the Second Punic War onwards, some Roman soldiers were able to make a fortune out of trading. There is a striking example from the year 196, when the Roman army spent its first winter in Greece after defeating Antiochus. Some soldiers (Livy says they were Italians, i.e. allies) were involved in the murder of the pro-Macedonian beotarch.

> [This] aroused the Thebans and all the Boeotians to a frenzy of hatred against the Romans, for they thought that Zeuxippus, a leading man in the state, would not have committed such a crime without the cognizance of the Roman commander. They had neither army nor leader for a rebellion; so, turning to what was most like war, to brigandage, they killed some soldiers in the taverns and others as they travelled about on various errands during the winter season. Some on the public highways were lured by decoys into ambushes, some were brought by trickery to deserted inns and murdered; moreover, such crimes were committed not only from hatred but also from greed of booty, because the soldiers, who were usually travelling on business, had money in their purses. (Livy 33.29.1-4)

The sale of loot after a battle brought the soldier into contact with a whole world of camp-followers, sutlers, slave-dealers and middlemen of all sorts. Roman generals tried every now and then to get rid of this floating population, with its disastrous effects on discipline. There are two well-known examples, that of Scipio when he took command at the siege of Numantia in 134, and Metellus in Numidia in 111:

> Scipio... went in advance with a small escort to the army in Spain, having heard that it was full of idleness, discord, and luxury, and well knowing that he could never overcome the enemy unless he first brought his own men under strict discipline.
>
> When he arrived he expelled all traders and harlots; also the soothsayers and diviners, whom the soldiers were continually consulting because they were demoralized by defeat. For the future he forbade the bringing in of anything not necessary, even a victim for purposes of divination. He also ordered all wagons and their superfluous contents to be sold, and all pack animals, except such as he himself permitted to remain. For cooking utensils it was only permitted to have a spit, a brass kettle, and one cup. (Appian, *Hisp.* 84-5)

Metellus encountered similar trouble in Numidia:

> When Metellus reached Africa, the proconsul Spurius Albinus handed
> over to him an army that was weak, cowardly, and incapable of facing either
> danger or hardship, readier of tongue than of hand, a plunderer of our allies
> and itself a prey to the enemy, subject to no discipline or restraint...His
> camps were not fortified, nor was watch kept in military fashion; men absented
> themselves from duty whenever they pleased. Camp-followers and soldiers
> ranged about in company day and night, and in their forays laid waste the
> country, ransacked farmhouses, and vied with one another in amassing booty
> in the form of cattle and slaves, which they bartered with traders for foreign
> wine and other luxuries. They even sold the grain which was allotted them
> by the state and bought bread from day to day. In short, whatever disgraceful
> excesses resulting from idleness and wantonness can be mentioned or imagined
> were all to be found in that army, and others besides. (Sallust, *Jugurtha* 44)

As can be seen, commercial and military activity were not sharply opposed.
Roman imperialism had a dual character, and, apart from the great defensive
wars in which the city's fate and that of all its citizens was at stake, every
warlike expedition had both a political and a financial purpose. The legitimate
and traditional object of campaigning was booty, and this offered far greater
prospects of gain than a soldier's pay. Plunder finally became an end in itself,
which might be jeopardized by victory or a too successful pacification of the
enemy. Moreover, the transactions to which it led introduced the soldier to
other activities not directly connected with war, and gave him the idea of
setting up as a dealer after the fashion of those who visited his camp. Over a
long period we shall come across typical careers of ex-servicemen turned
negotiatores: the two professions are by no means incompatible and basically
involve the same behaviour and attitudes. The soldiers on leave in Boeotia in
196 became usurers as a matter of course; conversely, as we know from an
inscription, the *negotiatores* of Delos mobilized spontaneously in 69 when the
island was raided by the pirate Athenodoros, one of them taking command of a
Milesian trireme.[10] Again, traffickers who had ventured into the rich country
of Gaul before the Roman invasion put themselves at Caesar's disposal as
spies, interpreters or even officers when he set about conquering it.[11] Pillage
and commerce were two complementary and interconnected methods of
exchange and the transfer of wealth, and it was a long time before the ancient
world established a clear distinction between them.

Tensions and methods of command

If we relied wholly on Polybius's description and analysis of the Roman military system we should have a somewhat idealized picture, as is shown by many parts of Polybius's own narrative. After the Second Punic War and the terrible days of national peril were over, and as the scene of war shifted to far-off Spain and the East, the soldier's mentality also changed; in the nature of things, the army was transformed from a civic militia into a force more like those against which it fought. Protracted operations and long periods of service far from home gave birth to a new type of soldier who could no longer be led by traditional methods. A new kind of relationship grew up between the generals and the rank and file, which had less in common with the Roman tradition than with professional armies of the Hellenistic type. Not that the Roman army, while all its campaigns were still in Italy, had always been a model of discipline and civic spirit, as Polybius would have us believe. The conquest of Italy was marked by several murky episodes which prove the contrary. There was, for instance, the strange revolt of 342 BC,[12] the historical facts of which are more than doubtful, but which is none the less significant. A Roman army, wintering at Capua after that city had allegedly surrendered, was attracted by its fabulous delights (is this a piece of anticipation?) and resolved to capture the town as its inhabitants, in 440, had themselves captured it from the Etruscans. Afterwards the army, feeling itself exposed to attack, marched on Rome itself, obliged T. Quinctius to place himself at its head, and was finally brought to a stop and pacified by T. Valerius Corvus, who had been appointed dictator in the emergency. The story ends with the people voting measures of clemency and new provisions concerning recruitment (no one to be discharged from the army without his consent), pay (that of the *equites* to be reduced) and the military tribunate (a former tribune shall not revert to the rank of centurion). This curious tale is a blend of archaic features that are very comprehensible in the context of fourth-century Italy (a mercenary army 'capturing' a city), together with social grievances (usury in Rome), and certainly reflects memories of substantial changes in military institutions (but army service is still represented as a much sought-after privilege).

A very different story is that of the mutiny,[13] in 206, of Scipio's troops encamped at the mouth of the Sucro (Livy 28.24). This was due to false news of the general's death, delay in paying the soldiers, and their desire for leave of absence or permission to go to Africa. They did not revolt openly at first, but on receiving the news of Scipio's death they elected as their leaders two common soldiers who usurped the insignia of command. Their officers were clearly disconcerted by this unfamiliar problem, and uncertain how to handle it. Having persuaded the rebel army to come to Nova Carthago (Cartagena), Scipio rebuked them in these terms:

'Mercenary troops may indeed sometimes be pardoned for revolting against their employers, but no pardon can be extended to those who are fighting for themselves and their wives and children.' (Polybius 11.28.7)

But, while addressing them as citizen-soldiers, the commander treated them as an irresponsible mob; to terrorize them and restore discipline he used a repertoire of tricks and dramatic effects more typical of a Hellenistic war-lord than a Roman *imperator*. The tribunes were first ordered to identify the ringleaders, and, after inviting them to their houses, to disarm them and place them under guard; then reliable troops who had been posted at the city gates surrounded the mutineers, whom Scipio harangued as follows:

'[Coriolanus once made war on his own country, not without cause; but] in your case what grievance, what anger spurred you on? Was delay of a few days in receiving your pay owing to the illness of your general a sufficient reason why you should declare war on your country, why you should revolt from the Roman people to the Ilergetes, why not one thing divine or human should be to you inviolable?

'Insane you surely were, soldiers, and no more critical ailment attacked my body than your minds. I shrink from recalling what men believed, what they hoped, what they desired. Let forgetfulness carry away and cancel everything if possible; if not, let silence somehow cover it all. I would not deny that my speech has seemed to you severe and cruel; how much more cruel do you believe your acts are than my words? And you think I ought patiently to bear what you have done: on your side can you not bear patiently even the telling of the whole story? But even those acts themselves will not be the subject of further reproaches. May you forget them as easily as I shall forget them! Accordingly, so far as the mass of you are concerned, if you repent of your mistake, that is to me a quite sufficient punishment. Albius of Cales and Atrius the Umbrian and the rest of those who brought about a wicked mutiny will atone with their blood for what they have done. To you the spectacle of their punishment, if your minds have returned to health, ought not only to bring no bitterness but even joy. For there are no men whom they have treated in a more hostile and unfriendly spirit than yourselves.'

Scarcely had Scipio made an end of speaking when, in accordance with previous orders, their eyes and ears were assailed by terrifying sights and sounds everywhere. The troops who had encircled the assembly crashed swords against shields. The herald's voice was heard, calling out the names of those condemned in the war-council. They were being dragged out into the centre stripped, and at the same time everything requisite for punishment was being brought out. Bound to a stake they were scourged and beheaded, while the spectators were so paralysed by fear that not only was no fierce protest against the severity of the punishment heard, but not even a groan. Then all the bodies were dragged away from the centre, and after the ground had been cleansed the soldiers, summoned by name, in the presence of the military tribunes, swore allegiance to Publius Scipio; and as each man was called his pay was counted out to him. Such was the end and outcome of the mutiny of the soldiers which began at Sucro. (Livy 28.29)

Even if Polybius and Livy embellished their account in order to improve Scipio's image, the conclusion of the story shows that after acting like a Hellenistic condottiere he recalled that his army was in fact composed of citizens: his speech is an appeal to the *mos majorum,* to their civic spirit and patriotism. The mutineers were identified, duly tried by a *consilium* and executed in the traditional manner. The main body of the troops were spared and a new oath administered in traditional form. The same kind of thing happened two years later at the capture of Locha in Africa. The town had surrendered, and Scipio gave the signal to withdraw and cease fighting, but the soldiers ignored his orders and, contrary to all regulations, began to slaughter the inhabitants and sack the town. Scipio had the booty confiscated and put to death three centurions selected by lot from among the culprits (Appian, *Pun.* 15). Here again the commander acted with distinct moderation. Another example is the mutiny encountered by P. Villius Tappulus on his arrival in Macedon in 199, when 2,000 'volunteers', former soldiers of Scipio's army who had come from Africa by way of Sicily, complained that they had been pressed into service although their time had already expired, and had been put on board by the tribunes in spite of their protests. The consul promised that if their request for a discharge was couched in moderate language he would forward it with a recommendation to the Senate (Livy 32.3.1-7).

In short, a Roman general saw his army as a body of citizens and naturally had an eye to the next elections and how his men would behave when they returned to civilian life. An excellent illustration of the interdependence between magistrates and the troops under their command is afforded by Aemilius Paullus's triumph in 167 after his victory over Perseus. A law was to be voted on the day of the triumph, confirming him in his command. But Paullus was not popular with the troops, as he had tightened up discipline and distributed less booty than he might have. When the proposed law was debated in the assembly, an officer opposed it and persuaded the ex-soldiers to do likewise. It required a long speech from the former consul M. Servilius to make them reverse their vote.[14] Discipline and civic spirit won the day, but the soldiers had proved that they were still citizens.

A new type of soldier

At the beginning of the second century the conditions of war began to alter, and with them the composition and conduct of the army. Italy was henceforth safe from invasion; the motherland was no longer in danger. Wars were fought overseas, with easy gains followed by disappointing reverses. As we saw apropos of the *dilectus,* enthusiasm might give place to hesitation and refusal according to the military outlook or the consuls' attitude. The prospect of gain tended to turn the army into a professional one, but its cadres were still those of a citizens' militia and there were no straightforward rules governing recruitment and promotion. The ambiguity of the situation is well shown by the incident of the Macedonian levies in 171. Volunteers came forward in large numbers, but Licinius ill-advisedly refused to re-engage in their former rank ex-*primipilares* (chief centurions) who had in effect become regular soldiers. The veterans protested and appealed to the tribunes; one of them, who spoke with exemplary dignity, is graphically depicted in Livy's account:

Licinius also enrolled the veteran soldiers and centurions; likewise many enlisted voluntarily, because they saw that those who had served in the former Macedonian campaign or against Antiochus in Asia had become rich. When the military tribunes who were appointing centurions were assigning men as they came, 23 veterans who had held the rank of chief centurion appealed to the tribunes of the people. Two of these magistrates, Marcus Fulvius Nobilior and Marcus Claudius Marcellus, referred the matter back to the consuls; for, they said, the investigation belonged to those to whom the levy and the war had been committed; the other tribunes said they would investigate the matter of the appeal, and if wrong was being done, they would come to the aid of their fellow-citizens.

The investigation took place at the benches of the tribunes; thither came the ex-consul, Marcus Popilius, as counsel for the centurions, the centurions themselves, and the consul. At the request of the consul that this investigation take place before an assembly, the people were summoned to an assembly. On behalf of the centurions Marcus Popilius, who had been consul two years before, addressed the people as follows: These soldierly men had ended their regular military service and had also lost their physical vigour because of age and unremitting labour; however, they had no objection to contributing their services to the state. This one request they did make, that they should not be assigned ranks lower than those they had held during their regular service. Publius Licinius the consul ordered to be read the decrees of the senate, first that in which the senate authorized the war against Perseus, then that in which it resolved that as many former centurions as possible be enrolled for this war, and no exemption from service be granted to any under 51 years of age. Then he made the request that, in a new war, at so little a distance from Italy, against a very powerful king, the people should not hinder the military tribunes who were holding the levy or prevent the consul from assigning such rank to each man as was in the best interests of the state. If there were any doubtful point in this matter, let them refer it back to the senate.

After the consul had said what he wished, Spurius Ligustinus, one of the men who had appealed to the tribunes of the people, asked of the consul and the tribunes that he be permitted to address a few words to the people. With everyone's permission he is said to have spoken as follows:

'I, Spurius Ligustinus of the tribe of Crustumina, come of Sabine stock, fellow-citizens. My father left me an acre of land and a little hut, in which I had been born and brought up, and to this day I live there. When I first came of age, my father gave me as wife his brother's daughter, who brought with her nothing but her free birth and her chastity, and with these a fertility which would be enough even for a wealthy home. We have six sons and two daughters, both of whom are now married. Four of our sons have assumed the toga of manhood, two wear the boys' stripe. I became a soldier in the consulship of Publius Sulpicius and Gaius Aurelius. In the army which was taken over to Macedonia I served two years as a private soldier against King Philip; in the third year, for my bravery, Titus Quinctius Flamininus made me centurion of the tenth maniple of the advance formation. After the defeat of Philip and the Macedonians, when we had been brought back to Italy and discharged, immediately I set out for Spain as a volunteer soldier with Marcus Porcius the consul. No one, of all the generals now living, was a keener observer and judge of bravery, as those know who have had experience of him and other leaders, too, through long service. This general judged me worthy to be assigned as centurion of the forward first century of the advance formation. For the third time I enlisted, again voluntarily, in the army which was sent against the Aetolians and King Antiochus. By Manius Acilius I was given the rank of centurion of the forward first century of the main formation. When King Antiochus had been driven out and the Aetolians beaten, we were brought back to Italy; and twice after that I was in campaigns where the legions served for a year. Then I campaigned twice in Spain, once when Quintus Fulvius Flaccus was praetor, and again when Tiberius Sempronius Gracchus held that office. I was brought home by Flaccus along with the others whom he brought with him from the province for his triumph because of their bravery; I went back to the province because Tiberius Gracchus asked me. Four times within a few years I held the rank of chief centurion; 34 times I was rewarded for bravery by my generals; I have received six civic crowns. I have done 22 years of service in the army, and I am over 50 years old. But if all my years of service had not been completed and my age did not yet give me exemption, still, since I could give you four soldiers in my place, Publius Licinius, it would be fair to discharge me. But I should like you to accept these things that I have said on my side of the case; for my part, as long as anyone who is enrolling armies considers me fit for service, I will never beg off. Of what rank the military tribunes think me worthy is for them to decide; I shall see to it that no one in the army surpasses me in bravery; and that I have always done so, both my generals and those who have served with me are witnesses. As for you, fellow-soldiers, even though you are within your rights in this appeal, since when you were young you never did anything against the authority of the magistrates and the senate, you ought now also to submit to the consuls and the senate, and to consider every place honourable in which you will be defending the state.'

When he had said this, Publius Licinius the consul praised him at some length and took him from the assembly to the senate. There also thanks were expressed to him by authorization of the senate, and the military tribunes gave him for his bravery a chief centurionship in the first legion. The other centurions gave up their appeal and obediently responded to the levy. (Livy 42.32.6-35.2)

CHAPTER V

MILES IMPROBUS
Rome and her army

The army and the proletariat

IT IS IMPORTANT to ascertain the scope of the change in the recruiting system brought about by Marius in 107 BC when he decided, as Sallust tells us, to enrol soldiers 'not according to the classes in the manner of our forefathers, but allowing anyone to volunteer (*uti cujusque libido erat*), for the most part the proletariat' (*Jugurtha* 86).[1] Sallust himself proposes two explanations of the change: either, he says, there were not enough rich men, or else the ambitious Marius wished to reward the kind of people to whom he owed his election. We should first note, with P. Brunt, that the innovation related only to a limited number of recruits: the Senate had authorized the new consul to raise reinforcements, certainly not more than 5,000 or 6,000 men, for the legions already in Africa. No doubt they expected him to run into the same difficulties and incur the same unpopularity as all the other generals. But Marius foiled their expectation in various ways. Firstly he appealed to ex-soldiers of Latin status whom he had known in the army either personally or by repute, and persuaded them to re-enlist. His second and most important device was to make political speeches appealing for volunteers, the tenor of which is summarized in a celebrated passage of Sallust (*Jugurtha* 85): 'Do you, who are of military age, join your efforts with mine and serve your country.' Marius, however, did not play on the soldiers' professional sentiments but appealed to Roman patriotism of the most austere, Catonian brand. Ignorant and unskilful generals of noble birth, he said, had brought the state to the verge of ruin; the war must be won and Rome saved. A citizen was first and foremost a soldier, delighting in the hardships of war. The new feature was that he would henceforth be democratically commanded, by men who would share those hardships as they had done in the past. In speaking thus, Marius was addressing citizens on an essentially civic note. The appeal to volunteers certainly included a promise of victory and the spoils of war, but, as we have seen, there was nothing new in that. Clearly no one, least of all Marius, foresaw in 107 that the professionalization of the army would open the door to civil wars more than 30 years later. Valerius Maximus contends that until Marius's time the *capite censi* were not allowed to serve in the army because their poverty made them untrustworthy; actually some of them were so allowed, but the reason why they were excluded in principle was so that everyone's rights and duties should be balanced. Valerius Maximus's explanation is anachronistic: it is natural enough in a man of the civil war generation, but that was a long way off in 107.

Nevertheless, an impulse for change was given in that year, and the composition of Roman armies changed progressively from then on, as did their mentality and civic attitude.

Recruitment in the first century BC

It should not be thought that after 107 all Roman armies consisted entirely of volunteers. Several times during the first century the magistrates were authorized to carry out a *dilectus* of the traditional kind, either for foreign or civil wars. The size of the forces that were necessary suffices to show that volunteer recruitment would not have been enough. In 90 and 89, for example, at the time of the insurrection of the Italian allies, Rome must have mobilized nearly 150,000 men, a force slightly larger than that of the enemy. The first step was a senatorial decree authorizing the consuls to levy 100,000 on the ground of national emergency (*tumultus*).[2] As we know, the shortage of manpower was such that even freedmen were enrolled. Similar measures are attested on several other occasions, even apart from the civil wars: in 64, in Umbria, for the troops which were to serve in Gaul under Murena's command (Cicero, *Pro Murena* 42); in 61 (*Ad Att.* 1.19.2); in 58, when Piso was preparing to depart for his proconsulate in Macedon. In all these cases the *dilectus* was evidently compulsory; Cicero, for instance, commends Murena for taking advantage of the Senate's permission to be 'liberal', i.e. presumably to grant exemptions freely. In 61, when the Gauls were threatening war, the Senate decided that 'troops would be levied and no exemptions considered'; this was evidently a regular mobilization, though unfortunately we do not know the total numbers involved. In 58 the army that was to fight in Macedon was recruited, Cicero tells us, 'by the strictest of levies and the most merciless of conscriptions' (*De provinciis consularibus* 5). But it was of course in times of unrest or civil war that mobilization once again took on a pressing character. In 52, for example, the levy carried out in Italy by several *conquisitores* under Pompey's orders was directed against Milo and his bands of supporters (*Pro Milone* 67). When civil war broke out in 49 the Senate authorized Pompey to levy 130,000 men (Appian, *B. Civ.* 2.34); he had too little time to do so, but the figure shows that it cannot have been merely a question of volunteers. Evidence from Cicero and others confirms this: as Cicero wrote to Atticus (7.13.2), 'So far the levy has found unwilling recruits, afraid of war'. Caesar was not outdone, even though he began with a larger core of seasoned professional troops. Altogether, between 49 and 31 nearly 420,000 men were called up in Italy for civil wars, not counting levies of citizens in the provinces and of course auxiliaries.

Such mobilizations of course affected all classes. Q. Horatius Flaccus, son of a rich and respectable freedman, was a tribune in the army of Brutus and Cassius after Caesar's death, though fighting was by no means to his taste. Sometimes, however, the civil wars with their political background aroused warlike passions in unlikely quarters, as worthy people breathed fire and slaughter against their neighbours (Cicero, *Ad Att.* 9.2.3). The upper classes, rich bourgeois or *equites*, were to provide the officer corps of these inflated armies, though they were not always keen on doing so. But the call-up also affected the lowest classes, and it then often reflected the archaic structures of a society in which the ties of patronage and economic dependence were very strong. There is a good example in 49, when the fleet of Domitius Ahenobarbus, fighting on Pompey's side, was entirely manned by 'farmers and herdsmen' whom Ahenobarbus had recruited, willingly or otherwise, on his own estates; these, at any rate the farmers or sharecroppers, were not slaves but free men (Caesar, *B. Civ.* 1.56.3). But perhaps the provinces furnish the best examples of how mobilization affected every social class, and of the abuses and opposition they aroused. In Italy, Caesar's swift victory at the beginning of 49 very soon brought the situation back to normal; but in 46 the greed and maladroitness of L. Cassius Longinus, governor of Spain on Caesar's behalf, provoked some of the leading local Romans to rebel and even to plot against his life. According to the author of *Bellum Alexandrinum,* his unpopularity was due to his recruiting activities: on being ordered to Africa by Caesar,

> He held a levy of Roman knights. These were conscripted from all the corporations and colonies and, as they were thoroughly scared of military service overseas, he invited them to purchase their discharge. This proved a great source of profit, but the hatred it produced was still greater. (*Bell. Alex.* 56.4)

Still, when all is said and done, the civil war period is exceptional. Clausewitz's dictum that war is the continuation of politics by other means applies more to civil war than to any other kind, and we shall study it in another chapter from the point of view of citizen participation. These mobilizations of mass armies cannot disguise the basic fact that in the first century BC the Roman army, as a result of Marius's cautious innovation in 107, became an army of volunteers and almost of professional soldiers.

This term in itself does not mean much: an army of professionals may, according to circumstances, be animated by the highest civic and military virtues or, on the contrary, given to every kind of excess. It may be a closed aristocratic caste or a receptacle for the dregs of the population. The armies of the Republic in the first century BC in fact exhibited all these features; it was not until the Empire that a career structure emerged with regulations governing recruitment and promotion, so that for a time the army was unified and stabilized. During our period conscription was used sporadically for both foreign and civil wars, but voluntary recruitment was the norm. The length of service was not fixed; the average was perhaps 8-10 years, less than is often supposed. But some troops might remain with the colours much longer than this, often in remote provinces, which of course increased the tendency for the soldiers' links with Italy to be weakened.

In these armies a special class of men should be noted, the *evocati* who stayed on or re-enlisted after their time had expired.[3] These were certainly volunteers, and received privileged treatment as far as pay and duties were concerned. They were a *corps d'élite* and often formed the nucleus of a provincial army, like Cicero's in Cilicia in 51. They owned horses, although they were not reckoned as belonging to the cavalry. Octavius at Mutina (Modena) made them into a sort of praetorian guard 10,000 strong.

Where did most of the soldiers come from? To begin with, an important point is that Senate decrees generally indicated in what area a general was entitled to raise troops. Very occasionally we hear of urban levies in this period, e.g. in 55 according to Dio Cassius (39.39.1). But the account shows that the city population had little liking for military service, and that of Rome itself had a bad reputation in the first century: it produced such hotheads as C. Titius or Titinius, a Forum agitator who raised a revolt against L. Cato, consul in 89, and escaped punishment thanks to the tribunes' intercession (Dio, fragment 100).[4]

As a rule, the levies for a particular army took place on a regional basis. This might be one of the provinces, the call-up being of course confined to Roman citizens. It Italy the Senate would often designate a region, such as Picenum, Umbria, Campania or Apulia. The best-known army, that of Gaul, was essentially drawn from the Cisalpine province granted to Caesar. Its inhabitants were Gauls rather than Italians; they had been culturally Romanized for some time past, but had become citizens at a fairly recent date. Crassus' army at Carrhae, for instance, consisted chiefly of Lucanians (Pliny, *N.H.* 2.147). Pompey, at the time of the civil war of 82, had raised a whole army among his father's clients in Picenum. Altogether the Roman armies, at least the rank and file, consisted mostly of countrymen and, in the years after the Social War, of recently naturalized Italians. Their ways were still barbarous and uncouth: at Asculum in 90, at the beginning of the insurrection, Italian peasants such as these had savagely massacred the Romans who fell into their hands and even, according to Dio (frag. 98.3), scalped the wives of those who refused to join them. The Roman armies of the first century BC were in general more ferocious than the citizen armies of the previous century for both social and geographical reasons. Their rusticity and brutality came to the fore on many occasions, especially in the civil wars. Cicero, when he wanted to flatter them, used polite terms such as 'men who, though country-bred, are yet very gallant soldiers and very excellent citizens' (*Ad fam.* 11.72.2), but in a more sincere vein he spoke of 'rough countrymen, if men they are and not rather beasts' (*Phil.* 8.9; 10.22).

The army thus recruited took on a different personality and a new style of behaviour. As a professional body it became first and foremost a fighting machine, a body of men to whom war was an end in itself and not a mere episode. In extreme cases such an army becomes a roving band, obedient to no authority and divorced from any link with civilian life. There are two picturesque examples of this. When Pompey arrived in Africa in 81 to combat Marius's supporters,

> Some soldiers, it would seem, stumbled upon a treasure and got considerable amounts of money. When the matter became public, the rest of the army all fancied that the place was full of money which the Carthaginians had hidden away in some time of calamity. Accordingly, Pompey could do nothing with his soldiers for many days because they were hunting treasures, but he went about laughing at the spectacle of so many myriads of men digging and stirring up the ground. (Plutarch, *Pompey* 11)

The second example is that of the desperadoes who became known as Fimbrians—an army sent by Marius's supporters to Asia in 86 to fight both Mithridates and Sulla. Its general, Valerius Flaccus, was killed by his men at the instigation of the legate Flavius Fimbria, who proceeded to make war on his own account. This body finally deserted and joined Sulla's force in 85; Sulla left them to garrison the province of Asia, no doubt by way of punishing the inhabitants:

> Sulla now laid a public fine upon Asia of 20,000 talents, and utterly ruined individual families by the insolent outrages of the soldiers quartered on them. For orders were given that the host should give his guest four tetradrachms every day, and furnish him, and as many friends as he might wish to invite, with a supper; and that a military tribune should receive 50 drachmas a day, and two suits of clothing, one to wear when he was at home, and another when he went out. (Plutarch, *Sulla* 25)

When hostilities resumed in 79 the Fimbrians, who formed the core of the army of Asia, gave plenty of trouble to Lucullus, their new commander, who tried to take them in hand. Plutarch paints a vivid picture:

> The Fimbrians had become unmanageable through long lack of discipline. These were the men who, in collusion with Fimbrius, had slain Flaccus, their consul and general, and had delivered Fimbrius himself over to Sulla.

They were self-willed and lawless, but good fighters, hardy, and experienced in war. (Plutarch, *Lucullus* 7.2)

As the fighting continued, and despite its success, the Fimbrians became more and more unruly. Pompey and his party followed the situation attentively from Rome, where they may have received information in letters, and decided to make a change in the high command and also disband some of these soldiers (Plutarch, *Lucullus* 33). Pompey also used P. Clodius to undermine the Fimbrians' morale by emphasizing the severity and integrity of Lucullus, who refused to divide all the spoils of war among his men (ibid. 34). Shortly before Pompey himself arrived in 66, the Fimbrians openly mutinied and refused to march:

> The rebels went so far in their outrageous treatment of their general that, at the close of the summer, they donned their armour, drew their swords, and challenged to battle an enemy who was nowhere near, but had already withdrawn. Then they shouted their war-cries, brandished their weapons in the air, and departed from the camp, calling men to witness that the time had expired during which they had agreed to remain with Lucullus.
>
> The rest of the soldiers [those who had not been serving for so long] Pompey summoned by letter (*evocatio*). (Plutarch, *Lucullus* 36.6)

Of course the Roman armies, however rustic and 'professional' they had become, were not all of this type. The Fimbrians no doubt belonged to the first levy in Italy carried out after the Social War, and had only recently become Roman citizens. A different general, such as Caesar, could turn an army which had been kept in the field nearly as long into an effective fighting force without letting it become its own master. Much of the secret lay in Caesar's style of command, which was also a matter of policy. He rode his troops with a light rein, and did not enforce strict discipline except in the face of the enemy; he laid stress on *esprit de corps* and the sense of honour (the general's as well as that of his men), and knew how to appeal to patriotism and even to civic spirit. Above all, unlike Lucullus but like his own uncle Marius, Caesar made a point of sharing the men's toil and hardship; more perhaps than his rival members of the senatorial aristocracy, he showed concern for the physical and economic conditions of the common soldiers' life. It may have been at the beginning of the Gallic War that he doubled their pay: before long, the success of the campaign allowed him to maintain the army at his own expense without help from the Senate, and therefore he could pay it what he liked. Caesar's army, of course, was as much actuated by the hope of gain as any Roman army of its time; like Pompey, he did everything he could to enrich his soldiers, e.g. by allowing frequent pillage. In any case, he was always able to keep them on his side; too much so, perhaps, since in 49 they showed no hesitation in following him when he crossed the Rubicon and became a rebel. As we shall see, his speech on that occasion, as reported by himself, paid a high compliment to their civic sense and even their political awareness; but, even if the facts are correctly stated, it is doubtful whether the speech was really addressed to that audience. Suetonius relates a more significant anecdote in the same context: when Caesar's army agreed to cross the Rubicon it was partly because the men mistakenly believed that he was offering each of them 'a knight's estate' (i.e. 400,000 sesterces).5

In any case, it is certain that during our period relations between the army and its commanders underwent a great change. Since, from 88 onwards, the supreme leaders themselves did not hesitate to use the army for political ends and thus to set an example of indiscipline, they could scarcely exact too high a standard from their troops (Plutarch, *Sulla* 12). Now and again, it is true, the old-fashioned system raised its head again: in the war against Spartacus, Crassus revived the practice of decimation to punish deserters. Lucullus in similar circumstances was content to impose the humiliating 'fatigues' that were already customary in Polybius's time: 'He bade them dig a 12-foot ditch, working in ungirt blouses, while the rest of the soldiers stood by and watched them' (Plutarch, *Lucullus* 15). The only new and interesting piece of information about discipline in this period dates from 43, when the legions returning from Macedon mutinied against Antonius at Brundisium on the ground that he was disloyal to Caesar and was not promising them sufficient rewards.

Antony rose and departed, saying, 'You shall learn to obey orders.' Then he required the military tribunes to bring before him the seditious characters (for it is customary in Roman armies to keep at all times a record of the character of each man) [*anagraptos estin aiei kath' hena andra ho tropos*]. From these he chose by lot a certain number according to military law, and he put to death not every tenth man, but a small number. (Appian, *B. Civ.* 3.43; the incident is also recorded by Cicero.)

It is known for certain that these 'record cards' existed, and that they served both a disciplinary and a political purpose. They were used when a man was court-martialled, for instance in Africa in 46, when Caesar set about reasserting his authority over army cadres:

These legions were then disembarked. Now Caesar had in mind the lack of discipline of old among the troops in Italy and the plundering exploits of certain individuals; and he had some ground for complaint, though only a trifling one, in the fact that C. Avienus, a military tribune of the Tenth legion, had commandeered a vessel from the convoy and filled it with his own household slaves and beasts of burden, without transporting a single soldier from Sicily. Accordingly, on the following day Caesar paraded the tribunes and centurions of all his legions and thus addressed them from the platform. 'I could have wished above all things that people would at some time or other have set bounds to their wanton and irresponsible behaviour, and had regard for my own leniency, moderation and forbearance. However, since they set themselves no limit or boundary, I myself will set them a precedent in accordance with military custom, so that the remainder may behave differently. You, C. Avienus, in Italy have stirred up soldiers of the Roman people against the state and have committed acts of plunder in various municipal towns; you have proved useless to me and to the state and have embarked your own household slaves and beasts of burden instead of troops, so that thanks to you the state is short of troops at a critical time. For these reasons I hereby discharge you with ignominy from my army and direct that you leave as soon as possible and be quit of Africa this day. You also, A. Fonteius, I dismiss from my army, for having proved a mutinous military tribune and a disloyal citizen. T. Salienus, M. Tiro and C. Clusinas, you have attained your ranks in my army, not by merit, but by favour; your conduct has been such as to prove you neither brave in war, nor loyal nor competent in peace, and more eager to stir up mutiny among the troops against your commander-in-chief than to preserve respect and discipline. On these counts I deem you to be unworthy to hold rank in my army, and I hereby discharge you and direct that you be quit of Africa as soon as possible.' Thereupon he handed them over to the centurions, assigned them each no more than a single slave, and had them embarked separately in a ship. (Caesar, *De Bello Africo* 54)

This punishment, which was after all a moderate one, would doubtless have made little impression on the tribunes and centurions who, 10 years later, laughed in Octavius's face when he offered them, by way of reward, the office of *decuriones* in their local *municipia* (Appian, *B. Civ.* 5.128). However, perhaps one should not exaggerate the value of this evidence. The epigraphy of the triumvirate and early Empire shows that military tribunes and centurions were not so disdainful of these civic honours as Appian suggests. Despite the large-scale recruiting of volunteers, the frequency of wars and the *dilectus* in the last century of the Republic made it very unlikely, as it had always been, that a citizen would manage to avoid conscription all his life. For one thing, a man's army record at all times had a more or less decisive effect on his civilian career; this was obviously so in the case of the senatorial and equestrian orders. Even the least military-minded, Cicero for instance, owed it to themselves to perform at least a year's service, without which they were ineligible for the magistracy. Many important political careers were founded on military valour, especially after the time of Sulla and Caesar. But the same was true at a lower social level. The *Lex Julia Municipalis*,[6] which probably dates from 75-70 BC, lays down precise conditions for appointment to local magistracies:

No person who is or shall be less than 30 years of age, shall, after the first day of January in the second year from this date, stand for or accept or hold the office of duumvir or quattuorvir or any other magistracy in a *municipium* or *colonia* or *praefectura* unless he shall have served three campaigns on horseback in a legion, or six campaigns on foot in a legion, such campaigns being served in a camp or a province during the greater part of each several year, or during two consecutive periods of six months, which in any year may be counted as equivalent to two years, or unless he shall be entitled by the laws or *plebiscita* or by virtue of a treaty to exemption from military duty, whereby he is freed from compulsory service. (89-94). The list of those ineligible to serve in a local senate or hold public office in a municipality includes those persons who for any dishonourable cause have lost or shall lose their rank in the army, or whom a general for such cause has cashiered or shall cashier. (120-1)

In short, military and civil society were at all times closely interconnected.

The army and politics: the civil wars

In the last resort, did the army ever intervene directly in Roman political life in the first century BC as a specific element distinct from the civilian mass? Paradoxical as it may seem in a period of civil wars,[7] the answer would seem to be 'No'. We must explain our meaning here: when a state undergoes four armed conflicts in half a century (from 88 to 30 BC), with up to 40 legions involved in pitched battles, sometimes for several years in succession, it is clear that the army or armies have become a decisive element in political conflict. It is our task, therefore, to interpret these civil wars from the point of view of political typology. Several points arise here, to which we shall revert when framing our conclusions.

In the first place, all these wars originated at the highest military level. Marius, Sulla, Caesar, Pompey and the triumvirs were generals and politicians sufficiently well advanced in their career to exercise high military command, which was only one of the stakes in the ruthless competition between them. The armies intervene at a moment when the traditional political game comes to a stop, as one or other protagonist finds that there is no legal way in which he can pursue his objective. But they do not intervene of their own accord; their leaders involve them in the conflict, and these leaders, as we have said, are not military men pure and simple: they are much less professionalized than the middle cadres or even the hard core of the rank and file. It is a remarkable fact that throughout the period we find no instance of an insurrectional military movement instigated from below (whether by officers or private soldiers) with the object of setting up a 'military government'. Nor is this all. With the Roman governing class there was no distinction between civil and military functions, inasmuch as the normal career presupposed a succession and alternation of the two; but in the first century BC a degree of specialization none the less became apparent. Some men, having occupied a series of high offices including civilian ones, chose to exercise military command for prolonged periods during the interval between one civilian job and the next: these were what Sallust calls *homini militares*, almost professional soldiers. They form a fairly well-defined group, among whom we may mention Afranius, Petreius, and later on Licinius Murena or Labienus.[8] It is the more noteworthy that while these men naturally played a part in the civil wars, as both sides valued their military skill, they did not really belong (except perhaps Labienus) to the class of 'political general staffs' and scarcely ever figure in the first rank of events.

A second point: as we have seen, the armies that fought in the civil wars, especially in 49 and 44, naturally comprised a substantial core of genuinely professional troops, often a whole provincial army (such as that of Gaul in 49). At the outset of any civil war there is a mobilization of fresh forces, sometimes on a considerable scale. No doubt in some cases ex-soldiers were preferred, e.g. when Octavius levied an army from among Caesar's veterans in Campania in 44. But as a rule the new armies consisted of civilians hastily enrolled and trained, who only took part in the fighting because they were given no choice. In short, the civil war, which was a prolongation of earlier political and even social conflicts, was not so much an intervention of the army in civilian life as a politicization of the armies as regards both composition and outlook. This, at all events, was so at the beginning. In time the new recruits might come to resemble professionals and finally adopt their attitude altogether. It could then happen that the soldiers and even the officers on either side felt they had more in common with each other than with civilians of any party, including their own commanders. This did not apply to the armies of Caesar and Scipio in Africa in 46, which had a strong *esprit de corps* and were partisan to the point of mutual hatred. But it was true, three years later, of the armies of Antonius and Octavian, each of which was no more than a part of Caesar's former army. At that time the troops did intervene, their action being one of the few spontaneous movements, originating at a middle or lower level, that are met with in the history of this period. But it is significant that the purpose of the movement was to put an end to fratricidal struggle and induce their leaders to make peace. This was seen at the siege of Perusia (Perugia) in 41, after Lucius had capitulated and brought his forces over to Octavian in good order, with a report informing him of their strength:

> [Octavian] ordered the veterans to draw nearer, intending, it seems, to reproach them for their ingratitude and to strike terror into them. It was known beforehand what he was about to do, and his own army, either purposely (as soldiers are often advised beforehand), or moved by sympathy

as for their own relatives, broke from the formation in which they had been placed, crowded around Lucius' men as they approached their former fellow-soldiers, embraced them, wept with them, and unceasingly implored Octavian on their behalf — the new levies sharing in the outburst of feeling, so that it was impossible to distinguish or discriminate between them. (Appian, *B. Civ.* 5.46)

A similar scene took place in 39, shortly before the treaty of Brundisium. According to Appian, the veterans recruited by Octavian had joined his army in the secret hope of reconciling him with Antonius. Negotiations began, through Cocceius, immediately after the news of Fulvia's death was received; at this point the army intervened directly, choosing 'deputies' from among its ranks to negotiate the terms of agreement.

The reason for the change was that since Caesar's death in 44 the whole army had come to represent a political force, almost a party. All the troops — what remained of the old nucleus of the army of Gaul, the men recruited in 49 or even Pompey's old supporters who had gone over to Caesar, those under arms in 44, and the freshly demobilized troops stationed in or around Rome and about to leave for the colonies allotted to them — all these shared a lively feeling of being the main beneficiaries of Caesar's regime, and believed that his murder had compromised all the advantages that they had been granted or promised. Both officers and men regarded themselves as Caesar's only true heirs *vis à vis* the other political forces in the City; they also felt, with reason, that they were generally unpopular. We have shown elsewhere that in the first weeks after Caesar's death the question of the veterans and the implementation of his plans for colonial *deductiones* was perhaps the fundamental issue in the political and propaganda struggle between the 'liberators' and constituted authority in the person of the consul Marcus Antonius. Both sides were at pains to conciliate the menacing force that the veterans represented. Brutus and Cassius hastened to proclaim that Caesar's wishes concerning them would be respected. The army, out of self-interest and gratitude to Caesar, came by degrees to regard itself as the guardian and guarantor of a kind of posthumous Caesarism and to appraise from this point of view the conduct of the political leaders. When Antonius, the consul in office, forbade the young Octavian to seek election to the tribunate, the military tribunes of the consular army sent a delegation which, according to Appian, spoke to him as follows:

'We, O Antony, and the others who served with you under Caesar, established his rule and continued to maintain it from day to day as its faithful supporters. We know how his murderers equally hate and conspire against us and how the Senate favours them. But after the people drove them out we took fresh courage, seeing that Caesar's acts were not altogether without friends, were not forgotten, were not unappreciated. For our future security we put our trust in you, the friend of Caesar, after him the most experienced of all as a commander, our present leader, and the one most fit to be such.' (*B. Civ.* 3.32)

It is of great interest that the army, rightly or wrongly, believed itself to represent the Caesarian 'party' *par excellence,* but the degree of political consciousness in the soldier's attitude should not be overrated. They were not interested in imposing a particular regime, but in preserving their material advantages and privileges. We shall see in the next chapter that in 43-40 soldiers or ex-soldiers were the chief if not the only beneficiaries of the biggest transfer of property in all Roman history. The property of the triumvirs' opponents was confiscated, taxes were multiplied, collective confiscations were made from Italian cities, individuals were murdered and despoiled; and, as Dio Cassius clearly states, the sole ultimate beneficiaries of all this were the military. In proportion to their good fortune they were detested not only by the rich but, before long, by a majority of the people of Italy. This mounting hatred and resentment made the soldiers still more attached to their leaders, as their privileges depended on keeping the latter in power. Appian makes this point again very clearly towards the end of his account of the civil wars:

They were contemptuous of their rulers in the knowledge that they needed them to confirm their power, for the five years' term of the triumvirate was passing away, and army and rulers needed the services of each other for mutual security. The chiefs depended on the soldiers for the continuance of their government, while, for the possession of what they had received, the soldiers depended on the permanence of the government of those who had given it. Believing that they could not keep a firm hold unless the givers had a strong government, they fought for them, from necessity, with good-will. (*B. Civ.* 5.13)

This was not, however, the first instance of the army intervening directly in politics. Civil war was only the extreme form of a much more pervasive presence whereby the army had, on various occasions, made its weight felt in the City's affairs without actually fighting. In some cases the soldiers were only making legal use of their rights as citizens. The first example, even before the army was proletarianized, was a campaign of letter-writing by the army of Africa in 108 in support of Marius's election to the consulate:

In this way Marius induced Gauda and the Roman knights, both those who were in the army and those who were doing business in the town, some by his personal influence, the most by the hope of peace, to write to their friends in Rome in criticism of Metellus' conduct of the war and to call for Marius as a commander. As a result many men supported Marius' canvass for the consulship in a highly flattering fashion. (Sallust, *Jugurtha* 65.4-5)

Six years later, however, the soldiers adopted different means: at the tribunicial elections of 101 for 100, L. Appuleius Saturninus stood for the second time but encountered an unexpected rival whose candidature would have made his re-election impossible. Saturninus and Glaucia, the praetor-designate, had recourse to murder 'with the support of C. Marius and his soldiers' (Livy *Per.* 69); they were certainly aided by Marius's veterans, who were in a position to intervene as they were in Rome for his triumph. In the following year these veterans, who were of rural stock, were again solicited by Saturninus to help pass his agrarian law for the distribution of land in Cisalpine Gaul; he feared the opposition of the urban plebs, either because they were in the hands of the nobles or because of their hostility to the Latins and allies whom the law would benefit. A battle with clubs ensued, in which the veterans won the day.[9]

In 88 the army for the first time intervened directly, not against another army but against the civil government. Sulla, who was then consul, was to be put in command of a new army mustered in Campania to prosecute the war against Mithridates. Marius persuaded the tribune P. Sulpicius Rufus to pass a law entrusting the command to him instead of to Sulla. The latter, however, at once placed himself at the head of the army and persuaded the troops to march on Rome, giving them to understand that Marius was setting out with forces of his own. What followed was highly significant: all the officer corps (magistrates and, no doubt, military tribunes) were horrified and abandoned Sulla, whereas the rank and file followed him enthusiastically; yet marching on Rome was an act of unprecedented gravity. To the envoys who met him on the road and asked why he was marching with armed forced against his country, Sulla replied 'To deliver Rome from her tyrants' (Appian, *B. Civ.* 1.57).

This was the first direct intervention of the regular army against a political decision by the Roman people. Six legions under Sulla's command formed a semicircle in front of the city gates. Marius's supporters had a few hastily levied troops, aided at first by citizens posted on the roof-tops. Sulla thereupon ordered his men to set fire to the houses. In the end the people refused further help to Marius's men, who had to evacuate the city. It was occupied and terrorized by Sulla's troops, which maintained order with a semblance of impartiality:

> Sulla advanced to the Via Sacra, and there, in sight of everybody, punished at once certain soldiers for looting things they had come across. He stationed guards at intervals throughout the city, he and Pompeius keeping watch by night. Each kept moving about his own command to see that no calamity was brought about either by the frightened people or by the victorious troops. (Ibid. 1.58)

Under pressure from this victorious army the Senate declared Marius and 12 others to be 'public enemies', and the *comitia* were summoned to vote certain oligarchic measures. As Appian says,

> Now the first army of her own citizens had invaded Rome as a hostile country. From this time the seditions were decided only by the arbitrament of arms. (Ibid. 1.60)

In the very next year (87) Sulla's example was imitated by the consul L. Cornelius Cinna. Expelled from Rome during a riot against his proposed law on voting by new citizens, and deprived of his office by the Senate, he made his way to the army at Capua and enlisted its support, including that of the tribunes and centurions, in a speech appealing to the men's civic sentiments and urging them to defend the cause of legality against the Senate's decision (Appian, *B. Civ.* 1.65). It is remarkable that, 40 years later, when Caesar was in a very similar situation before crossing the Rubicon, he addressed to his soldiers, about to be rebels, a political speech explaining at length why the *senatus consultum ultimum* that had just been passed against his friends in Rome was illegal and contrary to tradition.[10] Caesar's speech is, of course, reported by himself and does not figure in Suetonius's more down-to-earth account. He may have been appealing to public opinion over his soldiers' heads, but in any case he evidently did not see anything improbable in the self-painted picture of a general addressing his troops.

The events of 88 were repeated several times during the civil wars, and Rome was captured and recaptured in 82, 49 and 43 by factious armies with the same scenes of terror, revenge and the repression of opponents. Appian has a striking description of the arrival in Rome of the joint forces of Antonius, Octavian and Lepidus in 43 after the 'constituent triumvirate' had been formed in Cisalpine Gaul: Rome was the proper place in which to seek endorsement of their action, but this is how they went about it:

> The triumvirs entered the city separately on three successive days, Octavian, Antony, and Lepidus, each with his praetorian cohort and one legion. As they arrived, the city was speedily filled with arms and military standards, disposed in the most advantageous places. A public assembly was forthwith convened in the midst of these armed men, and a tribune, Publius Titius, proposed a law providing for a new magistracy for settling the present disorders, to consist of three men to hold office for five years, namely, Lepidus, Antony, and Octavian, with the same power as consuls. (*B. Civ.* 4.7)

The composite army was not used only to bring about, in irregular fashion, the *Lex Titia* which legalized the triumvirate retrospectively and authorized it to proscribe citizens by proclamation, but also and above all to execute repressive sentences:

When the lists were published, the gates and all the other exits from the city, the harbour, the marshes, the pools, and every other place that was suspected as adapted to flight or concealment, were occupied by soldiers; the centurions were charged to scour the surrounding country. (4.12)

The vivid account of the many proscriptions in Book Four of Appian's *Bella Civilia* throws unexpected light on the professional soldiers' behaviour: they seem to have been less ferocious than the delators or slaves who hunted down outlaws for the sake of reward. The rustic soldiery as a rule carried out their orders obediently and without concern for the victims, but sometimes showed mercy out of greed or respect for those of high rank. The centurions who were ordered to kill Lepidus's brother Aemilius Paullus and Antony's uncle Lucius Caesar hesitated to carry out their task. Those ordered to kill a certain Acilius were suborned by a promise of much money and actually found him a boat in which to cross to Sicily. Another outlaw, Minucius Reginus, who tried to escape through the city gate disguised as a charcoal-dealer was recognized, but not betrayed, by a soldier who had served under him in Syria: 'Go on your way rejoicing, general, for such I ought still to call you' (4.40).

Apart from the civil wars, between 88 and 40, the army affected political life on several occasions: in the first place quite legally, through the votes of soldiers stationed near Rome and awaiting their general's triumph or their own discharge. Cicero bears witness to this in his speech of 63 in defence of Murena, who owed his consulship to the votes of Lucullus's army:

> The army of Lucius Lucullus which had assembled for his triumph was at hand to help Lucius Murena in the election, and his praetorship supplied the magnificent games whose absence handicapped his campaign for that praetorship. Do you really think that this help and assistance for the consulship is unimportant? I mean the goodwill of the soldiers and their voting power which derives its strength from their very number, from their influence with their friends and, most important of all, from the great weight that they carry with the whole people of Rome in electing a consul. Generals, not interpreters of words, are chosen at consular elections. Hence, talk like this is important: 'He saved my life when I was wounded; he gave me a share of the booty; he was our leader when we took the camp and engaged the enemy; he never asked a soldier to endure more hardship than himself; he was lucky as well as brave.' (*Pro Murena* 37-8)

This appreciation is noteworthy, as it refers to the *comitia centuriata* in which the only votes of consequence were those of the centuries of the first class, and it shows that soldiers — at any rate those returning victoriously from the East with plenty of money — could be influential in that body. Sometimes an army might be disbanded or large numbers of soldiers given leave and sent to turn the scale in an election: Caesar in this way helped Crassus and Pompey to become consuls in 55 (Plutarch, *Pompey* 51.3), the soldiers he sent being led by Crassus's son (Dio, 39.31). He did the same in 54 for Memmius, who, however, failed to be elected (Cicero, *Ad Att.* 4.16.6. and 17.3).

An equally legal role of the army, but a less peaceful one, was to prevent or quell disorder at the request of the government of the day. This was a particularly delicate matter; Rome, like all ancient cities, had no police, but, as we shall see in Chapter VIII, the people and citizens were protected by legal guarantees against the use of force, at least within the city area in which the tribunes of the plebs enjoyed the right of *provocatio*. After 121 the Senate could, by an emergency decree (*senatus consultum ultimum*), proclaim a kind of martial law empowering the magistrates to suspend *provocatio* and use force in specified cases such as a threat of sedition, the occupation of public buildings etc.[11] In some instances, when troops were not available, the citizens were armed in their respective *ordines* — senators, *equites, tribuni aerarii* etc. — but after 107 the army often came into action in this way. It did so, for instance, in 63, at the end of Cicero's consulate, when clear evidence reached Rome concerning the armed conspiracies organized by Catiline throughout Italy after the failure of his third attempt at the consulship. Armed with a *senatus consultum ultimum* dated 21 October, Cicero stationed military detachments in Rome itself (Appian, *B. Civ.* 2.3). He had Catiline's accomplices arrested and confined in the praetors' houses, and when their slaves and numerous 'artisans' (ibid. 2.5) tried to set them free he placed the houses under military guard. Outside the City and in the provinces two generals (Q. Marcius Rex and Q. Metellus Creticus) were waiting with their armies to know the dates on which their triumphs were to be held; these were despatched to combat the rebel forces in Etruria and Apulia respectively (*In Catilinam* 1.1.1; Plutarch, *Cicero* 16.1). The army was used to the full, as Catiline's conspiracy led to a regular civil war: several thousand men were engaged at the battle of Faesulae (Fiesole), under the nominal command of the consul Marcus Antonius. At the same time Cicero proudly insisted, in Rome from 9 November onwards, that he had vanquished the conspirators 'in a toga', i.e. as a civilian, without having recourse to a 'state of emergency' (*tumultus*) (*In Cat.* 2.28; 3.23). This did not refer to military measures, which no one denied his having used, but to the execution without trial of six highly-placed accomplices, a measure which Cicero justified in political terms, congratulating himself on having received unanimous support with *equites* and scribes intervening unofficially in his favour.[12] The expression 'a consul in a toga' was a clear warning to Pompey's partisans, who wanted the Senate to pass a decree recalling their leader from the East so that he might play Sulla's role at the head of his army. Cicero had forestalled them by his skilful policy, and wanted to make the lesson quite clear. He had averted a civil war *à la* Sulla, but he too had had to use the regular army to maintain public order and crush the conspiracy.

The army was again called in in 52 after the long series of riots, revolts and street battles which preceded and followed the murder of Clodius by Milo. By a first *senatus consultum* Pompey as proconsul was ordered to 'take care for the safety of the state' and authorized to levy troops in Italy. A month later he was designated sole consul and immediately proposed several repressive laws. When these were openly criticized by the tribune M. Caelius, Pompey declared that if necessary he would use armed force to defend the state; he also stationed a large military guard at his own house. Then, on the second day of Milo's trial, the sixth before the Ides of April, as Asconius records (p. 40-1 C), 'the shops were shut throughout the City and Pompey placed guards in the Forum and at all the entrances to it. He himself took up a position near the *aerarium,* surrounded by picked troops'.

However, it was not until the time of the second triumvirate that a riot was put down by main force. This was in 40, when Octavian was preparing, against Antony's advice, to make war on Pompey's son Sextus. There was a famine in Rome, and the riot was occasioned by an edict introducing a new tax on slaves and an estate duty (Appian, *B. Civ.* 5.67; cf. p. 183 below).

But the army's action was not confined to cases in which it was officially called in. The civil wars in fact visited on Italy itself all the 'horrors of war' which had till then only been inflicted by foreign enemies. As we have seen, the military oath administered during the Second Punic War contained fairly severe safeguards against pillage and petty theft. The militias of the third and second centuries, consisting of fairly well-to-do citizens of decent upbringing under the command of generals closely superintended by the Senate, probably behaved well enough, at all events in Roman territory. There were of course exceptions, like the exactions of Q. Pleminius's army at Locri in 206, which finally provoked a kind of civil war between the legate's troops and those of two military tribunes who tried to restrain them. Pleminius was arrested and mutilated by order of the tribunes; then, set free by Scipio's intervention, he arrested them in his turn and had them tortured and put to death.[13] But Locri was a Greek city and, what is more, had gone over to Hannibal. In the first century BC, however, incidents of this kind were multiplied as the armies marched and fought all over Italy. First, in 90-89, the insurrection of the allies led to a savage, pitiless war on all fronts with one or two exceptions such as that commanded by Marius, where there was much sympathy for the insurgents. When towns surrendered after a siege or were taken by storm they were sacked and their inhabitants slaughtered or sold into slavery. Then came the civil wars, Lepidus's march on Rome, the Servile Wars and, soon after, Catiline's conspiracy. The exactions and sufferings due to the presence in the countryside of armies, whether regular or not, were still a vivid memory in 66. Cicero reminded an audience of the hatred aroused in the provinces by the Roman military presence:

Who does not know how great is the ruin which, owing to this avarice on the part of our generals, is caused by our armies in every place to which they go? Think of the tours which of late years our generals have made in Italy itself through the lands and the towns of Roman citizens, and then you will more easily judge what, it seems, are their practices among foreign peoples. (*Pro lege Manilia* 37-38)

In particular, the provision of winter quarters (*hiberna*) was always a grievous burden on the towns concerned. As we saw, this was one of the means used by Sulla to terrorize Asia and keep it in subjection after Mithridates' invasion. Even during the Second Punic War, when the armies were still highly patriotic, billeting was an affliction to the Latin colonies; after the defeat at the Trebia Scipio 'led his army in silence to Placentia and thence...to Cremona, so that one town might not be overburdened with furnishing winter quarters for two armies' (Livy 21.56.8). According to Cicero the *hiberna* of the army of Macedon commanded by Piso in 56 were particularly odious:

Did you not, after handing over your winter quarters to your lieutenant and your prefect, utterly destroy those wretched communities, which were not only drained of all their wealth but were also forced to submit to the degradation of your lustfulness? (*In Pisonem* 86)

A brief but significant example shows that the quartering of troops in Italy, during the civil wars, was as much feared by the inhabitants as it was by those of the provinces. During the first Spanish campaign in 49 one of the legions of Terentius Varro, a legate with Pompey's forces in Spain, abandoned its camp and withdrew to Hispalis:

One of the two legions, which was called the Native Legion, removed its colours from Varro's camp while he was standing by and looking on, and, withdrawing to Hispalis, bivouacked in the forum and porticoes without harming anyone. The Roman citizens of the district approved this action so highly that every one of them most eagerly welcomed the men with hospitable entertainment in his own house. (Caesar, *B. Civ.* 2.20)

The legion, it is true, was a locally recruited one; but the astonishment caused by its behaviour shows how exceptional this must have been.[14]

We may attempt to sum up. At all times Roman political life, like that of all cities governed on a timocratic basis, was shaped by the exigences of war. The soldier, during his time in the army, was subjected to the strict discipline and strong traditions of a first-class war machine, but he none the less remained a citizen. He elected, at least indirectly, his senior officers and generals, and the military order was an exact reflection of that which prevailed in civil life.

Recruited in accordance with the hierarchy of social rank and property rating, conditioned by an education which laid stress on warlike virtues and patriotism, he had little reason to be discontented with a command structure imbued with the City's traditional values and the system of patron-client relationships. Up to and including the first century BC, revolts and mutinies were extremely rare. Any tension that might arise between commanders and their men, particularly over the division of spoils, was more likely to find expression after the return to civilian life than in the army itself. In any case, this army of the Republic remained at all levels eminently loyal and obedient to the supreme authority of the Senate, the magistrates and the people. There was an almost perfect identity between the City and its army. At the end of the second century a gulf began to open between a high command (reserved to the *nobilitas*) which was much more refractory, corrupt and subject to rivalry, and the rank and file which gradually became professionalized after Marius's reform. But the latter's own career was an embodiment of the traditional military virtues and was largely an exemplification of the old-fashioned maxim that *virtus* would get one to the top. It was not Marius—the first *novus homo* to become a consul thanks to the soldiers' vote, and the first general to recruit among the *proletarii*—who set the example of using the army against the civil power. Sulla, a patrician who had come down in the world, a brilliant soldier and an opportunist politician, was the first to adopt this course in 88, as a means of keeping his command. For the next nine years the army would be made use of by both camps, at a time when the new recruiting system and especially the mass enfranchisement of Italians were breeding a new type of Roman soldier—a type of which the Fimbrians who murdered their general and mutinied against Lucullus are a sadly famous example. At this time there was still a clear difference between a colonial force used for service in the provinces, such as the Fimbrians or Sulla's army, and those raised for unexpected wars in Italy. Marius's veterans who, in 101, enforced the adoption of the agrarian *Lex Appuleia* were land-hungry peasants. Sulla's men, enriched in 81 at the expense of their fellow-citizens, were allotted fertile lands in Italy but did not succeed in putting down roots or maintaining themselves; by 63 most of them were destitute and ready to throw themselves into a new civil war.[15]

The soldiers, recruited henceforth from rural parts of Italy which had recently acquired citizenship, were to an increasing extent foreigners in Rome. They could be summoned there to keep order in a brutal fashion without the least hesitation. In the years 60-50 or thereabouts, the hard core of the Roman army was formed by the 11 legions from Gaul, recruited chiefly in the Cisalpine province, whom Caesar had gradually turned into a magnificent fighting force with an incomparable *esprit de corps*, full of gratitude towards the charismatic leader who had brought them victory and made them rich, and had always taken care to appear as the champion of justice and popular sovereignty. Following his example, his soldiers showed intelligent moderation towards their adversaries in the conduct of the civil war, a fact which explains the ease with which Caesar was able to enlarge the nucleus of veterans in his army. When he died in 44, although several strata could be discerned in the army it appeared for the first time sociologically and politically unified. Victory enabled Caesar to bestow or promise the richest rewards in land and money. The army was itself the nucleus of Caesar's 'party', indifferent or hostile to the turmoil of politics and the fate of the urban plebs. By virtue of its strength and size it represented the essence of power, and accordingly for the next 10 years it was within the army that the struggle for power was chiefly played out. Professional military leaders like Antonius and accidental ones like Octavian had first of all to assure themselves of the army's loyalty; they managed to remain in power in so far as they were able to keep it on their side, using Caesar's name and memory as far as each of them was able.

The best way of keeping the army on one's side was to make it rich, and the years from 44 to 40 witnessed a revolution of unexampled ferocity whereby 400,000 or 500,000 soldiers or ex-soldiers came into possession of a considerable slice of the wealth of Italy, with predictable consequences in the demographic, economic, social fields and even in the realm of geography. In the last resort the sole victor of the civil wars was the *miles impius,* more terrible than any foreign foe. This, in our view, sufficiently explains the fate which befell the Republic. The power that emerged from those years of madness could be no other than military, that of an *imperator* at the head of 40 legions. But public weariness and accumulated hatred of the military 'revolution' were such that if the leader wished to assert his authority and remain in power he must put an end to the fear of such excesses for ever. The essential features of Augustus's policy were to proclaim solemnly the 'end of civil wars' and to make this promise a reality by sending the army to confront distant barbarians at the frontiers of a huge empire; at the same time it was reduced in size, placed on a long-service footing and financed in a regular manner by a special fund based on public consent. In this way the *princeps* presented himself as the guarantor if not the avenger of the civilian population, while the army in its remote outposts was once more the bulwark of the nation. It was at the same time the mainstay of the quasi-absolute power of its leader, but it supported him by its absence rather than its presence. With the army safely away, a *respublica* could once more function in apparent freedom; such, at least, was the unanimous desire of a generation weary of war and murder. The illusion lasted three-quarters of a century, until the military revolt which brought about Nero's death and continued after it. This revealed to the world the secret of the Empire, that it was not in Rome but at army headquarters that emperors were made: *evulgato imperii arcano posse principem alibi quam Romae fieri* (Tacitus, *Hist.* 1.4.2).

CHAPTER VI

AERARIUM
The citizen and the treasury

OUR STUDY of how the Roman lived and died as a soldier has shown, among other things, that although the new recruiting system of the first century BC provided in large measure for voluntary service, especially by the proletariat, Roman society as a whole continued until imperial times to be profoundly marked by the old military structure of the City, which was fundamentally an association for defence purposes. Whatever the part played by cupidity or political ambition, it is still true to say that up to the last days of the Republic citizens were ready to shed their blood for the *patria*. Some, as we have seen, embraced a military career with enthusiasm, realising that bravery or good fortune might secure them rich rewards from foreign conquest or the hazards of civil war. In any case it was unthinkable that Rome or any other city should be left *inermis*, without defences.

In any political community, however, the citizens or subjects also have the less exhilarating obligation of paying taxes.[1] Rome had an exchequer like any other state, and it had to balance receipts and expenses in order to survive. How far were the citizens involved in this? Some would say 'not at all', as the spoils brought back by Aemilius Paullus after his victory over Perseus of Macedon in 167 made it possible to dispense with the *tributum*, which was only restored in 43 (for seven years, it would seem), under the ill-starred consulate of Hirtius and Pansa. This picture of a privileged civic body is complemented by that of the ferocious exploitation of the subject peoples, i.e. the provinces. The City having managed to export all its financial problems, there should be no occasion to enquire into them further.

This view is not entirely without foundation. As we shall see, Rome, like other cities, did tend whenever possible to shift its financial burden on to others and particularly on to its own provinces. This did not mean, however, that it felt free to increase the burden to the maximum. On the contrary, except in time of emergency such as rebellion or civil war, care was taken to keep the City's financial demands to a reasonable level. During the period we are concerned with, the imposition of financial burdens on the provinces came to be defended in theory as the counterpart of the advantages they derived from belonging to the Roman empire; Roman rule and Rome's demands were thus justified together. With various transpositions, this theory has remained the basis of all modern fiscal doctrine.

But, even during the long period when the *tributum* was unnecessary, it should not be thought that fiscal matters were outside the citizen's purview. In the first place, the suspension of the *tributum* in 167 was not the result of a formal decision, but merely of the abundance of booty which made it superfluous for more than a century.[2] The *tributum* was not abolished in law: it could have been reimposed at any time in case of need, and the citizens would have been regularly subjected to it. The ancients regarded taxation as a necessary evil; if it could be dispensed with in given circumstances, so much the better, but provision must always be made for it. Cicero makes this clear in *De Officiis*, written in 44 for the benefit and instruction of his son, who was to be consul one day:

> The administration should also put forth every effort to prevent the levying of a property tax, and to this end precautions should be taken long in advance. Such a tax was often levied in the times of our forefathers on account of the depleted state of their treasury and their incessant wars. But if any state (I say 'any', for I would rather speak in general terms that forebode evils to our own; however, I am not discussing our own state but states in general)—if any state ever has to face a crisis requiring the imposition of such a burden, every effort must be made to let all the people realize that they must bow to the inevitable, if they wish to be saved. (*De Off.* 2.74)

Thus the Romans knew that they were exempt from direct taxation only in so far as the City's revenues were plentiful and well administered.[3] Accordingly they always lent an attentive ear to arguments concerning finance and the balancing of the budget. This was not only true of ruling circles in the narrow sense, the magistrates and the Senate, who bore direct responsibility; it also applied to ordinary citizens, at least those who took part in public debate and voted on legislation, elections or lawsuits. When financial matters were under discussion—as they often were, e.g. in connection with a law or the investigation of a promagister's activities—we feel that the speaker had no difficulty in holding the audience's attention: the citizens took a direct interest in the state of the public purse, not only because they stood to benefit from it but also because it was not they but others who provided the funds. Cicero gives an example in his speech of 66 BC in favour of the *Lex Manilia* putting Pompey in charge of the war against Mithridates. He urges the citizens to conduct the war with resolution,

> Especially since your chief sources of revenue are involved! For while the revenues of our other provinces are barely sufficient to make it worth our while

to defend them, Asia is so rich and fertile as easily to surpass àll other countries in the productiveness of her soil. ... If you wish to retain what makes war possible and peace honourable, it is your duty to defend this province not only from disaster but from fear of disaster. (*Pro lege Man.* 14)

In the same way, arguing three years later against the agrarian law proposed by Servilius Rullus, Cicero expatiated on the financial aspect: by splitting up into small holdings the *ager publicus* of Campania, on which concessionaires paid rent (*vectigal*) to the treasury, this law would bankrupt the state and deprive citizens of their income:

Will you allow the one most beautiful estate belonging to the Roman people, the source of your wealth, the ornament of peace, the support in war, the basis of your revenues, the granary of the legions, your relief of the corn supply — will you allow it to perish? When all your other revenues failed you in the Italian war, have you forgotten how many armies you supported by the income from Campanian territory? (*De lege agraria* 2.80)

The threat could not be presented in clearer language.

Moreover, while a Roman citizen in Italy was exempt from direct taxation for the time being, he was not free of all financial obligation to the state. Italy, like the provinces, was subject to indirect taxes (customs, tolls, pasture rights, duties on certain legal acts such as manumission, various monopolies), of which we are fairly well informed (cf. p. 170 below). We cannot estimate the total return from these, but two statements by Cicero indicate that they constituted a heavy enough burden to arouse resistance, so that customs and tolls were for the most part abolished in 60, though they were reimposed in 46. As we shall see, these dues were collected in almost as arbitrary a manner in Italy, where everyone was a citizen, as they were in the provinces. Finally, it must be recalled that while Roman citizens were dispensed from the *tributum* — which was essentially a tax on their land holdings in the *ager romanus* until 89 BC, and anywhere in Italy after that date — they were not at all times exempted in respect of all their estates in the provinces. Many of them had emigrated to Spain, Sicily, Gaul, Africa or the East, and others who still lived in Rome or their home *municipia* owned property overseas.[4] The status of these lands no doubt varied considerably; often they paid little or no tax, but in many other cases they did, and the citizen, though exempt in Rome and the rest of Italy, was subject to fiscal law in the provinces; there are striking examples of this, all the way from Sicily to Asia. Thus he was far from being able to ignore fiscal problems, which demanded his attention at every turn. While these problems may have been less crucial and dramatic in our period than at other times in Roman history,[5] it is no accident that they figure prominently in our sources — not only in technical literature, but in contexts which show how sensitive and even nervous public opinion was in matters of this kind.

So far, then, we find an acute consciousness of fiscal problems, combined with a kind of *sacro egoismo,* as though the whole object of financial policy was to thrust the burden as far as possible on to others. Up to this point there is no suggestion of solidarity or considerations of fiscal justice. In this respect, however, Rome was no exception to the rest of the ancient world. Far from being unusually rapacious, her behaviour, like that of any other city, conformed to the logical implications of the civic system itself. No doubt, in the course of history particular circumstances might lead to all sorts of variations in the financial administration of cities; but Greek theorists at all times held certain simple ideas on the nature and purpose of the *polis* which found expression in what they considered to be the normal organization of public finance.[6] In the first place the city was first and foremost an association, a *societas,* and as such was only justified by the common interest of its members. No doubt philosophers and jurists from Plato and Aristotle to Cicero pointed out the narrowness and inadequacy of a definition so utilitarian that it would have reduced the city to the level of a gang of brigands (Aristotle, *Politics* 1280 a-b); they depicted the state as a specific and primary form of association transcending all others and devoted to a supreme moral end which might be called justice, virtue or simply the *utilitas communis,* the common interest conceived and felt as something different from the interest of each individual citizen. Blind egoism was no doubt curbed by this view of the state, which we find in Cicero and which was largely inspired by Aristotle and the Late Stoa. But when Cicero abandons pure speculative philosophy and addresses himself to citizens in the Forum, or even when he composes *De Officiis* by way of guidance to a future statesman, criteria of immediate self-interest once more come into the foreground and it becomes very hard to distinguish between the general, collective interest of the city and the particular, individual interest of citizens.

In principle, then, a city was expected to live off its own regular revenues. These were, first and foremost, those from land, including buildings etc., of which the city enjoyed the benefit in the same way as a private owner would. It could rent or farm out its territory, cultivate it directly or even, in rare cases, dispose of it altogether. Added to such revenues are the proceeds of what we should call indirect taxes of various kinds (the Greek word is *telè* as opposed to *phoros* and *eisphora,* which denote special taxes or tribute), but which the ancients no doubt thought of as a kind of extension of the city's right of eminent domain over all its territory: customs, tolls, rights of user, harbour dues and so forth. Considering these various types of revenue, the ancients drew a clear distinction between a 'despotic' fiscal system which involved direct personal taxation, and a 'civic' type which did not. This is shown by the Pseudo-Aristotle's *Oeconomica,* a financial treatise written probably towards the end of the fourth century BC,[7] when the Greeks were beginning to explore the wide field of exploitation opened up by Alexander's conquests. This gives the following account of a 'satrapic economy', in which despotic power is exercised directly in Oriental fashion:

> Taking these [revenues] in turn, the first and most important of them is revenue from agriculture, which some call tithe (*dekatè*) and some produce-tax (*ekphorion*). The second is that from special products; in one place gold, in another silver, in another copper, and so on. Third in importance is revenue from markets, and fourth that which arises from taxes on land and on sales. In the fifth place we have revenue from cattle, called tithe or first-fruits (*epikarpia*); and in the sixth, revenue from other sources, which we term poll-tax (*epikephalaion*), or tax on industry (*kheironaxion*). (*Oecon.* 2.1.4)

Thus it was a normal feature of non-Greek financial systems, alien to the *polis*, to impose both a regular poll-tax (*epikephalaion*) and a tax on landed property (*ekphorion*). The first of these was pre-eminently a mark of servitude and was at all times repugnant to the civic ideal of both Greeks and Romans; Roman tradition assigns it to the most tyrannical phase of the Etruscan monarchy, at the dawn of the City's history. The second, in so far as it was regular and permanent, was considered almost equally degrading and was in any case not a normal part of civic life. Thus the *Oeconomica* briefly and eloquently describes a 'civic' economy as follows:

> Of our third kind of administration, that of a free state, the most important revenue is that arising from the special products of the country. Next follows revenue from markets and occupations; and finally that from every-day transactions. (2.1.5)

The tributum: a tax or a loan?

These ordinary revenues were supposed, in a normal year, to suffice for the city's ordinary expenditure, which was very small. Opposed to them was the *tributum*, an extraordinary tax levied directly on the citizens. In republican times this term was sometimes applied to what the Greeks called a *phoros*, i.e. a tribute imposed on a whole city by a foreign power. Republican Rome was fortunate enough to undergo this humiliation once only in its history, when it was besieged and captured by the Gauls. Not until the dark days of the Lower Empire were such indemnities again met with. Ancient historians also use the word of personal taxes or services imposed on the Romans, according to tradition, by the Etruscan kings; but there is no certainty about this, except the fact that it was regarded with horror as a tyrannical practice. In our period the word *tributum* denoted a very specific institution, namely an extraordinary direct tax levied on citizens to meet the expenses of a war. It was so limited in its object and so closely connected with military necessity that its origin was traditionally linked with the siege of Veii in 406-398, the first occasion on which a Roman army had to serve for a longer period than the usual brief campaigns. This new development led the Senate to propose that soldiers be paid from public funds, and the idea of a *tributum* arose in the same connection:

[The Senate] decreed, without waiting for any suggestion by the plebs or their tribunes, that the soldiers should be paid from the public treasury, whereas till then every man had served at his own costs.

Nothing, it is said, was ever welcomed by the plebs with such rejoicing. Crowds gathered at the Curia and men grasped the hands of the senators as they came out, saying that they were rightly called Fathers, and declaring that they had brought it to pass that no one, so long as he retained a particle of strength, would grudge his life's blood to so generous a country. Not only were they pleased at the advantage that their property would at least not diminish while their bodies were impressed for the service of the state, but the voluntary character of the offer, which had never been mooted by plebeian tribunes nor extorted by any words of their own, multiplied their satisfaction and increased their gratitude. The tribunes of the plebs were the only persons who did not partake in the general joy and good-feeling of both orders. They said that the measure would neither be so agreeable to the Fathers nor so favourable to the whole body of the citizens as the latter believed; it was a plan which at first sight promised better than experience would prove it. For how could the money be got together, save by imposing a tribute on the people? The senators had been generous at other men's expense; and even though everyone else should agree to it, those who had already earned their discharge would not endure that others should serve on better terms than they had themselves enjoyed, and that men who had paid their own expenses should now also contribute to the expenses of others. Some of the plebs were influenced by these arguments. Finally, when the assessment had already been proclaimed, the tribunes announced that they would protect anybody who should refuse to contribute to a tax for paying the soldiers.

The Fathers, however, had made a good beginning and persevered in supporting it. They were themselves the first to contribute, and since there was as yet no silver coinage, some of them brought uncoined bronze in wagons to the treasury, and even made a display of their contributing. After the senators had paid most faithfully, according to their rating, the chief men of the plebs, friends of the nobles, began, as had been agreed, to bring in their quota. When the crowd saw that these men were applauded by the patricians and were looked upon as good citizens by those of military age, they quickly rejected the protection of the tribunes and vied with one another who should be the first to pay. And when the law was passed declaring war on the Veientes, an army consisting in great part of volunteers marched, under command of the new military tribunes, upon that city. (Livy 4.59.11-60.8)

Anachronistic though it is, Livy's account brings out the major aspects of the history of the *tributum*. The tax was decreed by the Senate and fell chiefly on the rich; it was paid by men liable for military service, for the benefit of those actually called up (thus by a majority for a minority); and it was opposed by some plebeians, incited by the tribunes. The 'voluntary' example of the richest and most important men in the City was of clear moral value. All these features gave a special character to the *tributum,* which appears as the counterpart of a 'bounty', the new institution of pay. Many questions arise as to its exact nature. Modern scholars have long debated, for instance,[8] whether it was a true tax as we understand the term, i.e. an imprescriptible claim by the state upon its citizens in token of its regality: in the words of Gaston Jèze, 'a monetary payment exacted from individuals definitively and without return, for the purpose of meeting public charges'. If this is a close enough definition of what is meant by a tax in modern times,[9] it may indeed be questioned how far the *tributum* was a true tax, for it is not clear how far it was compulsory and definitive and whether there was in fact no specific return for it. As Huschke and Marquardt first suggested, it ought perhaps to be considered rather as a kind of voluntary 'contribution' or even a loan. But does the distinction mean anything in terms of the City's constitution at the period we are concerned with? The notion of a tax as defined by Gaston Jèze was only known to the ancients in the context of provincial finances, i.e. in respect of conquered peoples who, in return for their freedom and an assurance of protection, were obliged to make a 'monetary payment' in recognition of Roman sovereignty. Later this conception was extended to the whole Empire, in so far as the distinction between the 'master race' and its subjects fell into oblivion. In our period, as in the case of Greek and Hellenistic cities, the question has no meaning; an *eisphora* or a *tributum* is by definition extraordinary and exceptional, as it is only levied in wartime. It has a precise and limited purpose, not a general one. Furthermore, as we shall see, the *tributum* might actually be reimbursed; so what becomes of its regalian character?

The *tributum,* to begin with, was not a permanent institution. Thus, in 347 BC, 'what did the most to lighten the burden was the omission of the war-tax and the levy' (7.27.4). And, as we have seen, the *tributum* was suspended in 167 not because Rome was at peace, but because the public coffers were full. Again, it had a precise, limited purpose, that of providing the means to pay and equip the army, which goes far to explain the way in which it was originally organized. By this direct, obligatory connection with a certain kind of expenditure it comes closer to what the Greeks called a 'liturgy'—an expense directly undertaken by private persons for the benefit of the state—than to a modern tax. And, most remarkable of all, this so-called tax might in some circumstances be refunded.

There are several examples of this. In 503 during the Sabine war, Dionysius records, 'the booty having been sold at public auction, all the citizens received back the amount of the contributions which they had severally paid for the equipment of the expedition' (5.47.1). This is an interesting statement, even if its historical accuracy is doubtful. Still more explicit are the words ascribed by the same author to Fabricius, that model of antique virtue, after his triumph over the Samnites in 293: 'I ... plundered many prosperous cities from which I enriched my entire army and gave back to the private citizens the special taxes which they had paid in advance for the prosecution of the war' (Dionys. 19.16.3: we shall revert to this text, which may be a valuable indication of the way in which the *tributum* was levied). But the clearest instance of all belongs to a much more reliable period. In 186, at the time of Manlius Vulso's triumph over the Galatians,

> Manlius's friends were able to curry favour with the people as well; at their instance the senate decreed that, as regards the tax (*stipendium*) which had been paid by the people into the treasury, whatever portion was in arrears should be paid out of the money which had been carried in the triumph. The city quaestors, displaying fidelity and diligence, paid 25½ per thousand *asses*. (Livy 39.7.4-5)

The text is not free from ambiguity, if only because Livy refers to *stipendium* where we would have expected *tributum*; but in his time *stipendium*, which originally meant the soldiers' pay, had come to be commonly used in the sense of 'tax': cf. its very precise use at 33.42.3. The phrase *stipendium collatum a populo in publicum* cannot really mean anything but *tributum*. As to the reimbursement at the rate of 2.55 per cent, many interpretations have been offered, but again it cannot signify anything but a return to each taxpayer of a sum proportionate to his capital. Given the precedent of 293 BC, this must be regarded as a refund of tax — which is the less surprising if one recalls that, 21 years later, another triumph made it possible not to repay past taxes but to suspend future ones indefinitely.

Assessment and collection of the tributum

Ancient lexicographers and antiquarians claim to distinguish between several kinds of *tributum*. Firstly there was a *tributum in capita* (Festus, p. 500 L), which we might call a poll-tax and which they assign to the royal period; but if it existed, which is far from certain, it was a badge of servitude and naturally disappeared under the Republic. Secondly there was an 'emergency' or 'improvised' levy (*tributum temerarium*), when every citizen was commanded to turn over the whole of his property, for instance after the capture of Rome by the Gauls and in 210 during the Second Punic War (Festus, p. 500 L). But the normal kind, and the only one that is well attested, was the *tributum ex censu*, of which Varro says: '*Tributum* ("tribute") was so called from the *tribus* ("tribes") because that money which was levied on the people was exacted *tributim* ("tribe by tribe") in proportion to each citizen's financial rating in the census' (*De lingua latina* 5.181).

Thus each citizen (*singuli*) had to pay 'in proportion to his rating'. Livy uses the phrase *pro habitu pecuniarum*, 'according to the state of his wealth', which comes to the same thing; and Dionysius of Halicarnassus, describing at length the 'constitution' of Servius Tullius, the archetype of the censor, shows that the census was in fact the basis on which the *tributum* was assessed—though this is an anachronism, since soldiers' pay and the *tributum* date back only to 406 and the censorship to 445, not to the Servian era. Thus the *tributum* was a direct contribution assessed as a proportion of declared wealth (i.e. capital). It conformed absolutely to the logic of the timocratic system which prevailed in most cities, whereby financial burdens, military duties and political rights were proportionate to wealth. The implicit or explicit ideology of 'geometrical equality' which underlies and justifies the system goes back to Plato and perhaps Pythagoras; it is well expressed in the words that Dionysius puts in the mouth of Servius, the founder of the system:

'In order to lighten for the future the burden of the war taxes you pay to the public treasury, by which the poor are oppressed and obliged to borrow, I will order all the citizens to give in a valuation of their property and everyone to pay his share of the taxes according to that valuation, as I learn is done in the greatest and best governed cities [e.g. Athens under Solon]; for I regard it as both just and advantageous to the public that those who possess much should pay much in taxes and those who have little should pay little.' (Dionys. 4.9.7)

Certain citizens were exempt from this proportional tax: those of the last 'century' (a kind of sixth class below the five property-ratings), the *proletarii* or *capite censi*, were neither taxed nor liable for military service. No one paid tax who was not financially qualified to bear arms. Those who paid it were called *assidui*, and some ancient authors derived the word from *as*:

In former times the word *assiduus* was applied to those who had to contribute to the expenses of the treasury by paying *asses*, and in this way took an 'assiduous' part in public affairs. (Isidore, *Or.* 10.17)

Others rightly connected the word with *sedere*, 'sit', and took it to mean 'one who is settled or permanently present': thus Festus, 8 L. But in ordinary language *assiduus,* which at first signified 'taxpayer', came to mean simply 'rich'. The distinction was one of law as well as of fact: in the Twelve Tables, dating from about 450, we find that only a taxpayer can stand surety (*vindex*) for a debt incurred by another taxpayer, whereas any citizen could do so in the case of a *proletarius* (Aulus Gellius 16.10.5).

In census terms, 'proportionate' did not relate simply to the actual value of a man's capital. As we saw in Chapter II, the census was a complex operation for the classification of citizens, and wealth was not the only factor that came into play. While it was for the citizen to make a detailed declaration of his property and to estimate its value, the censors might alter this estimate of their own accord. Thus, as we saw, in 184 Cato and his colleagues rated at ten times their declared value certain luxury items (jewels, vehicles, highly-priced slaves) of which they disapproved, and imposed on them a 3 per cent fine (not a tax, as is often said). This deliberate over-valuation likewise multiplied by ten the value of any *tributum* based upon it. Another significant example, though of early date: in 434 the censors, to avenge themselves on the dictator Mam. Aemilius Mamercinus, who had sought to reduce their term of office, 'removed him from his tribe, assessed him at eight times his former tax and made him an *aerarius*' (disfranchised him) (Livy 4.24.7). As we have seen, the *aerarius*—he who is a taxpayer and nothing more—was a man who had been expelled from his own century and relegated to a supernumerary one with no electoral influence. In this case, additionally, his property rating and therefore his tax liability was multiplied by eight. Thus it may almost be said that the *tributum* was not only a proportional tax but in some cases a progressive one, since at the censors' discretion it might be assessed at a higher rate on certain taxpayers or on certain kinds of property.

How was the tax calculated on the basis of the census? It is generally supposed that the *tributum* was a coefficient tax, and the normal rate is thought to have been a tenth of one per cent of a man's declared capital. But the evidence for this is very slight. The recalcitrant Latin colonies in 204 (p. 35 above) were made to pay an annual *stipendium* (i.e. *tributum*) of one *as* per thousand; but this was a punishment meted out to Latins, and is not likely to represent the rate of the *tributum* imposed on citizens. We have also seen that the rate of 3 per thousand levied on certain luxuries at the census of 184 did not apply to the *tributum*, which the censors were neither entitled to assess nor to collect, but was specifically a fine. Finally, the rate, mentioned by Livy, of the reimbursement at the triumph of Manlius Vulso in 184 is no indication of the rate of tax.

It is very unlikely that the rate of the *tributum* was laid down for all time. In the first place, a coefficient tax of this kind appears very late in fiscal history and is quite foreign to ancient systems: there is no known equivalent in the Greek or Hellenistic world.[10] Secondly, we have seen that the *tributum* was by definition a non-permanent tax. There was nothing to say that it would be automatically repeated from one year to the next, and in fact this did not happen to any considerable extent save during the Second Punic War, when it caused lively protest, as we shall see.

The logic of the procedure by which the *tributum* was imposed and collected in fact excluded the principle of a fixed rate. Once again this is shown clearly by Dionysius' account, anachronistic though it is, of the establishment of the census by Servius Tullius:

> As to the expenditure that would be needed for the provisioning of the soldiers while on duty and for the various warlike supplies, he would first calculate how much money would be sufficient, and having divided that sum among the 193 centuries, he would order every man to pay his share towards it in proportion to his rating. Thus it happened that those who had the largest possessions, being fewer in number but distributed into more centuries, were obliged to serve oftener and without any intermission, and to pay greater taxes than the rest. (Dionys. 4.19.1-4)

What we have is clearly a spreading of the burden in a way that was common in European monarchies in the Middle Ages and in more recent times. An estimate of actual needs is taken as a basis, and the taxpayers are required only to furnish this amount in accordance with accepted rules (*proportione census*). The total yield of the tax is thus variable by definition, and, assuming that the number of taxpayers and the assessment of their wealth remained fixed (as it did for at least five years, from one *lustrum* to the next), the amount required from each therefore varied also. What remained constant in principle was the proportion of the total that each was obliged to pay; but this might signify, according to needs, a varying percentage of the wealth assessed. Probably the usual rate was of the order of one, two or three per thousand, but the norm should have been less, since in 204 the rate of one per thousand was imposed as a punitive measure (but one which was to be repeated annually, perhaps in perpetuity). There must have been years in which the rate, for various reasons, was much lower, whereas in times of grave emergency it would be much increased. To take only one example, in 215:

> The Senate, on the first day on which it was in session on the Capitol, decreed that a double tax should be imposed that year and the normal tax collected at once, and that from it pay should be given in cash to all the soldiers. (Livy 23.31.1)

This can only mean that a *tributum* was imposed at the same rate as in the previous year and that it was decided to levy a second one of the same value. It may be, as some have suggested, that an extra contribution of this kind was formally regarded as a loan, and that such loans (for there were later instances too) were taken into account when citizens were 'reimbursed' in 187 thanks to Manlius Vulso. This would mean that in 215 the tax which originally resulted from the repartition of a sum fixed in advance became, for one year at least, a coefficient tax, in the sense that its rate was arbitrarily doubled. But this doubling must itself have been due to an approximate doubling of the total sum required.

It is quite probable that originally the system of load-sharing was carried even further. As we have seen, the lexicographers regard the tribe as the basic unit for tax-collecting purposes, and this is confirmed by Livy and Dionysius for the period of Servius Tullius. But the text quoted above shows that, for a time anyway, the century also became a basis, and so consequently did the class, as the five property-classes were merely a grouping of centuries. Thus the tribes and centuries both appear to have been fiscal units, and this again is logically in accordance with the city system. In Greek cities as in Rome, and no doubt for the same technical reasons, administrative tasks were for the most part devolved as far as possible on to smaller groups in which the citizens' collective responsibility was more directly engaged. The *dilectus* took place on a tribal basis; so did elections, and often the free distribution of wheat and oil, as a celebrated inscription from Samos shows.[11] This certainly simplified operations and their supervision. But in addition there is at least one example in antiquity of a fiscal system based on sub-units which served as the framework both for the assessment of wealth and for the actual tax-collection. These were the groups created at Athens from the fourth century onwards under the name of *summoriai* (co-partnerships or companies) for the payment of the *eisphora*, an irregular and extraordinary war-tax corresponding exactly to the Roman *tributum*. The *summoriai* had a remote precedent in the *naucrariai* of archaic and classical times, divisions of citizens which were severally responsible for providing ships and fighting men. Between 378 and 354 the system of *summoriai*, as far as it can be reconstructed, comprised 400 fiscal units representing — this was its original feature — more or less equal shares of the state's capital. Each *summoria* had a taxable capacity of approximately 15 talents, and whenever an *eisphora* was decreed it had to pay 25 *minae*; this worked out to a rate of 27 per mille. Each *summoria*, of course, included both rich and poor citizens, who contributed to the quota in proportion to their individual rating (*timema*). The system was a simple and flexible one and greatly simplified accounting.[12]

It is significant, in my view, that Dionysius in his description of the Servian system uses the word *summoria* to designate either tribes or classes. The term was far from being an everyday one in Hellenistic times; to a man of Dionysius's culture it would certainly suggest the Athenian institution, and we may be sure he chose it intentionally, to convey to an educated Greek reader that the Roman system of classes and tribes resembled that of the *summoriai*. Should we infer from this that, just as each class (or century?) had to provide about the same number of soldiers as the rest (so that the lowest centuries, with the largest membership, were the least heavily burdened), it was also liable collectively for an equal share of the *tributum?* We can also imagine another kind of equilibrium, viz. among the tribes. As we shall see, there is a tendency to reconstruct the entire history of the tribes on the basis of what is known about them in the last century of the Republic, when they were extremely unequal in size and population—a state of affairs which was deliberately maintained, especially after 89 BC. But it is quite possible that originally care was taken to keep these subdivisions of the city more or less equal to one another. In that case each Roman tribe, like each Attic *summoria,* would have been responsible for providing the same number of troops and the same war-tax in case of need; while within the tribe, which comprised different classes and centuries, the burden would have been shared in accordance with the census.

The classes and centuries played a part in the process of collecting the tax, but may not have been necessary as far as assessment was concerned. The procedure must have been as follows. To begin with, an estimate was made of the whole amount of the *tributum* required, and this figure was then compared with the total of the citizens' census ratings, arrived at by a simple though laborious process of addition. The ratio between the two figures was expressed as a percentage, and each individual could then be taxed accordingly without the need to work through centuries or tribes.

In the actual process of collection, however, these groups may well have played an important part in the same manner as the *summoriai.* We have curiously little information about the way in which *tributum* was collected at the end of the Republic, after it had been suspended for a whole century. It is usually thought to have been carried out by the quaestors, who specialized to some extent in financial questions: in 196, for instance:

> Money was needed because it had been decided to pay to the private lenders the last instalment of the money contributed for the war [in 210]. The quaestors demanded it of the augurs and pontiffs because they had not paid the taxes during the war. (Livy 33.42.3)

However, while this makes it clear that the quaestors were responsible from the accounting point of view, it does not say who actually collected the tax. We know for certain that at the end of the Republic it was the special duty of the *quaestores urbani* to receive sums due to the *aerarium* and make payments from it on their own responsibility; but it is doubtful whether this was originally the case as regards the *tributum,* which was levied for the sole purpose of paying the army. The troops were paid in early times not by the *quaestores militares* (who, as senior magistrates, would not in any case have done more than verify the total amount) nor by the military tribunes of the legions (as was to be the case at the end of the Republic and under the Empire), but by special 'tribunes of the treasury' (*tribuni aerarii*).[13] The lexicographers and jurists preserve the memory of this ancient office. Festus says 'They were called so because they distributed the bronze [*aes*]' (i.e. the money paid out), and Varro: 'Those to whom the money was assigned that they might pay it to the soldiery were called *tribuni aerarii* ("treasury tribunes")' (*De lingua latina* 5.181). The soldiers had a legal claim on these tribunes in respect of their pay, and if they did not receive it they could invoke the procedure of *pignoris captio*, one of the oldest in Roman law, consisting of distraint without the need for a judicial sentence. This right ceased to be available to private persons at an early date, while remaining fully valid as far as the state was concerned:

> *Legis actio* by *pignoris captio* rested in some cases on custom, in others on statute. By custom it was established in the military sphere. For a soldier was allowed to distrain for his pay on the person responsible for paying it, if he defaulted; money given to a soldier by way of pay was called *aes militare*. He might also distrain for money assigned for the buying of his horse, this being called *aes equestre*; likewise for money assigned for buying barley for the horses, this being called *aes hordiarium.* (Gaius 4.26-7)

These details are helpful to an understanding of what the *tribuni aerarii* really were, for the money which paid for the cavalry's mounts and fodder did not originally pass through the *aerarium*: it was contributed directly by widows and orphans, who were not liable to pay the *tributum*. (The system by which certain kinds of expenditure fell directly on a particular class of taxpayers is exactly similar to the Greek 'liturgy'). Now from a legal point of view the *tribuni aerarii*, who were responsible for paying the troops, were in the same position as widows and orphans, and this indicates, in my opinion, that they not only had to issue the soldiers' pay but, first of all, to collect the *tributum* for the purpose. In that case it is highly probable that they first had to advance the sum in question, just as the Attic *summoriai* did when they paid the *eisphora*. In each *summoria* there were two or three rich men, the *proeispherontes*, whose function, as the word indicates, was to advance the money to the state.[14] They were supposed to recover it from the members of their *summoria*, but there is evidence that they often failed to do so or voluntarily waived the debt in order to acquire a reputation for generosity. They thus paid more than their share of the *eisphora*, a fact which was in the logic of the system. In Hellenistic times the system of *proeisphora* became compulsory in certain cities, e.g. Priene, and was evidently an additional fiscal burden, imposed with the dual object of tapping the wealth of rich landowners and giving them an opportunity to appear as public benefactors.

What we know of the *tribuni aerarii* corresponds perfectly to this pattern. To begin with, they were unquestionably rich, as is shown by the possibility of *pignoris captio*. But in addition, for a long time after the *tributum* fell into abeyance, from the very end of the second century to the end of the first, they still constituted an *ordo*, i.e. an official group the register of which was kept up to date by the censors. When a *senatus consultum ultimum* imposing martial law was decreed, e.g. in 100 BC, this *ordo* was one of the corporate bodies which were called to arms to put down subversion along with the consuls and magistrates:

What shall we say of the Roman knights, most honourable men and best citizens, who on that occasion combined with the Senate in defence of the Republic; or of the *tribuni aerarii* and the men of all other classes who on that occasion took up arms to defend the common liberty? (Cicero, *Pro Rabirio* 27)

In 70 a judiciary law on the selection of jurymen to try promagisters accused of embezzlement laid down that they should be recruited as to one-third each among senators, *equites* and *tribuni aerarii*, and this system lasted until 46. The *ordo* was subdivided according to tribes: in 54 Cicero, defending Cn. Plancius against a charge of electoral bribery, called as witnesses in his favour the knights and *tribuni aerarii* of Atina belonging to the Teretina tribe (*Pro Plancio* 21). There seems to have been an official register, kept up to date in case of need, of rich and respectable citizens who, if a *tributum* was decreed, could be called on to advance the money, to pay it out to the troops (which is why they bore the military title of 'tribune') and, no doubt, to recover it from the taxpayers. The fact that they advanced it is attested by Fabricius's words, reported by Dionysius:

[Instead of enriching myself] I enriched my entire army, [and] gave back to the private citizens the special taxes which they had paid in advance for the prosecution of the war. (Dionys. 19.16.3)

It also appears from the lively speech in Plautus's *Aulularia* in which the miser Megadorus reckons up the likely costs of an ill-considered marriage:

The cleanser, the ladies' tailor, the jeweller, the woollen worker—they're all hanging round. And there are the dealers in flounces and underclothes and bridal veils, in violet dyes and yellow dyes, or muffs, or balsam-scented foot-gear...When you've got all these fellows satisfied, along comes a military man, bringing up the rear, and wants to collect his pay. You go and have a reckoning with your banker, your military gentleman standing by and missing his lunch in the expectation of getting some cash. After you and the banker have done figuring, you find you owe *him* money too, and the military man has his hopes postponed till another day. (*Aulul.* 508-31)

It is clearly implied that Megadorus has to pay the soldier out of his own pocket, so that he is discomfited when he finds that, rich though he is, his wife has denuded his bank account: one of the embarrassments attendant on the honourable station of a tribune of the treasury! Some day he may get the money back from the taxpayers, but in the meantime it is he who will receive a summons from the soldier and is in danger of being distrained upon.

The Roman citizen as a taxpayer

But Rome was not Greece: the system of recognized public benefactors was late in taking hold, and never became so widespread as in the Hellenistic world. As Polybius remarked (31.27), a Roman was not in the habit of paying so much as a penny before it was due. We may safely assume that very few *tribuni aerarii* failed to collect the tax or recover any advances they had made. Hence, as long as the tax was levied it fell on those who owed it in the normal way; and these, as we have seen, were those persons whom the censor classed as *assidui*. In other words, the tax was levied not exactly on all capital, but on that belonging to adult male citizens. If the head of the family was no longer present to declare his property, and if there was no adult heir, the tax might fail to be collected, as happened in 215 after the ruinous casualties of the Second Punic War:

> Necessary expenses were met only by the *tributum*; the number of those who paid that tax had been diminished by the great losses of troops at Lake Trasumennus and also at Cannae; if the few who survived should now be burdened by a much greater levy, they would perish by another malady. (Livy 23.48.7-8)

Hence in the following year, when the financial strain was still acute, the custodians of widows' and orphans' property were persuaded to 'deposit' their wards' money, coined or otherwise, with the treasury, with permission to draw on it for daily needs (Livy 24.18.11-15): this was no doubt the only way in which it could be made available to the state.[15]

Just as the citizen had no legal power to oppose or sanction a *dilectus,* in the same way he was not consulted about taxation. Once the *tributum* was introduced as a direct consequence of the decision on soldiers' pay, it became an unquestioned feature of everyday life. It was not for the people to judge the need for it, which was bound up with the City's very existence. In this respect Rome differed from most Greek cities, especially Athens. There, every *eisphora* had to be sanctioned by a popular vote (*psephisma*) preceded, in the fourth century at least, by an *adeia* or act of indemnity protecting the author of the proposal, which was certain to be unpopular, against changes of illegality which might do him serious damage. Without this, it is probable that few would ever have had the courage to propose new expenses. At all events, taxation could only be imposed with popular consent.[16]

In Rome, on the other hand, the people was not supposed to take any part in the discussion on the *tributum*, which, like the *dilectus*, was a matter for the magistrates and the Senate. At the beginning of the fiscal year, i.e. in principle when the provinces were allotted to new magistrates, the Senate voted the necessary financial arrangements; in the case of the *tributum*, as we have seen, it formulated a global estimate, e.g. in the terms: 'The Senate decided that this year a double *tributum* would be levied.' This measure, belonging to the Senate's ordinary sphere of administration, was called a *decretum*. The matter then passed into the jurisdiction of the magistrate who ordered the collection of the tax, usually in a form similar to that of an edict; the technical term was *indicere tributum*. Then came the actual collection, known as *exactio*; the act of payment was called *conlatio*.

In all this the people were not consulted, nor had they any right of appeal except that which lay open to all citizens against ordinary acts by the magistrates, viz. the *auxilium* of the *tribuni plebis*. This, however, could only operate in favour of individuals, and only if they invoked it themselves. Livy, it is true, says that in 401 the tribunes 'forbade the gathering of the war-tax' in general (5.12.3 and 5.13), which may signify a veto of the Senate's decree, and he mentions a similar occurrence in 378 (6.31.5), but these dates are so ancient that no certainty is possible. In 196, when (as we saw) the quaestors demanded arrears of tax from the augurs and pontiffs, the latter appealed to the tribunes, who, however, refused to intervene. It would seem that there was no political recourse against direct taxation, i.e. no collective, institutional means of resisting it.

But reality was sometimes stronger than constitutional rules. Just as there is some evidence of resistance to the blood-tax, so there are records of protest and objection to the *tributum*. Some of these are anachronistic projections into the past, like the complaint of the old centurion imprisoned for debt in 495:

> During his service in the Sabine war not only had the enemy's depredations deprived him of his crops, but his cottage had been burnt, all his belongings plundered, and his flocks driven off. Then the taxes had been levied, at an untoward moment for him, and he had contracted debts. When these had been swelled by usury, he had first been stripped of the farm which had been his father's and his grandfather's, then of the remnants of his property. (Livy 2.23.5)

This is clearly anachronistic, since the *tributum* was not introduced until 406; moreover, another imprisoned centurion appears in 385 BC (6.14.3), when Manlius Capitolinus makes himself the *vindex* of the plebs. The picture of a peasantry ruined by debt (if not taxes) and by the military levy corresponds notably to what Sallust (*Jugurtha* 41), Appian (*B. Civ.* 1.102) and Plutarch tell us of the 'agrarian crisis' in the second century BC, but it also bears a striking resemblance to the collective protests which Livy ascribes to the tribunes and plebeians some years after the introduction of the *tributum*:

> The more they increased the number of the soldiers, the more money they required for pay. This they tried to collect by taxation; but those who remained at home contributed with reluctance. The tribunes of the plebs declared that the senators had instituted pay for the troops in order that they might ruin one half of the plebs with fighting and the other half with taxation. The commoners were being taxed to their last penny, so that when they at last dragged home their bodies spent with toil, with wounds, and with old age, and found that everything had gone to waste during their long absence, they might pay tribute out of their diminished property, and return to the state many times, as it were with usury, the wages they had received as soldiers. (Livy 5.10.5-9, abridged)

As has been suggested recently, this account may contain anachronistic traces of a much later situation; for the idea of a *tributum* weighing thus heavily on the plebeians is contrary to the original logic of the system.

There is clearer and more reliable evidence of complaints and opposition during the Second Punic War, when there is convergent and incontestable evidence of a general financial crisis due essentially to the war. This is not the place for a detailed study of the measures adopted between 215 and 210, but they throw much light on the fundamental nature of financial relations between the state and its citizens. Strict measures of a traditional kind alternated with innovations of very different scope. For the first time Rome resorted to borrowing: it negotiated loans from Hiero of Syracuse and improved its monetary system in about 214 by instituting the denarius, a new silver currency, and aligning the bronze currency with it, reducing the *as* to a sixth of a pound in weight. It also contracted internal loans of a special type with its suppliers (the *publicani* in 215 and 214) or creditors, such as the owners of Sempronian slaves. The deposit of widows' and orphans' assets with the treasury also dates from this period. Loans from one city to another, or from a city to a rich foreigner or one of its own citizens, were common in Hellenistic times; most of the cases we know of are part of the benefactor system ('euergetism'), but a few are reminiscent of what happened at Rome in the dark years of the war. The most important, the loan which Miletus contracted with its own citizens in 205-4 (*Delphinion*, No. 147) in exchange for an annuity, belongs to a later date. But Rome naturally also resorted to taxation. By the force of events the *tributum* came to be levied annually during the war; it was even doubled, as we have seen, in respect of 216 (and perhaps other years, though we do not know this). When extraordinary expenditure became necessary in the course of a financial year, other measures had to be devised. To equip the fleet in 214, citizens were required to provide slaves (who became the state's property and were no doubt freed after completing their service) and money to pay them with:

> Owing to the lack of sailors the consuls, in accordance with a decree of the senate, issued an edict that a man who in the censorship of Lucius Aemilius and Gaius Flaminius had been rated — either he or his father — at from 50,000 to 100,000 *asses*, or whose property had since increased to that amount, should furnish one sailor provided with six months' pay; that one who had more than 100,000 and up to 300,000 should furnish three sailors and a year's pay; he who had over 300,000 and up to a million *asses*, five sailors; he who had over a million, seven; and that senators should furnish eight sailors and a year's pay. The sailors furnished in accordance with this edict went on board armed and equipped by their masters, and with cooked rations for 30 days. It was the first time that a Roman fleet was manned with crews secured at private expense. (Livy 24.11.7-9)

As Livy makes clear, this was a service directly rendered to the state in the manner of a liturgy. But it was not only proportional, since it affected citizens in accordance with a census classification which passed over the last three Servian categories, taking account only of those rated at more than 50,000 *asses* in 220 and also those worth more than the first class, i.e. upwards of 100,000 *asses*; it was also progressive in that senators as such, whatever their wealth, were taxed at a higher rate than others. So, probably, were the *equites*, since Livy later describes this liturgy as being organized 'according to citizens' census and classes' (26.35.3).

However, when in 210, the treasury being still empty, the consuls issued an edict ordering private citizens 'according to their census and classes, as before' to furnish oarsmen with pay and rations for 30 days (26.35.1-3), this demand aroused resistance which almost turned into an uprising. Livy describes the indignation of the plebs:

> Next after the Sicilians and Campanians the consuls, they said, had taken upon themselves the task of ruining and mangling the Roman populace. Exhausted by tribute for so many years, they themselves had nothing left but the land, bare and desolate. Their houses had been burned by the enemy, the slaves who tilled the soil had been taken away by the state, either by purchase at a low price for military service, or by impressing them as oarsmen. If a man had any money in silver or bronze, it had been taken away for the pay of oarsmen and the yearly taxes. As for themselves, they could not be compelled by any force, by any authority, to give what they did not have. Let their property be sold, let their bodies — all that remained — be harshly treated; not even for the purposes of a ransom was anything left to them. Such were the complaints of a great multitude, not in secret, but openly in the Forum and even before the eyes of the consuls, as they flocked about

them. And the consuls, now upbraiding, now consoling, were unable to
quiet them. Thereupon they said that they would give the people three days
for reflection, while they themselves looked into the matter and sought a
solution. (26.35.4-9)

Next day the consuls convoked the Senate, and several senators expressed
the opinion that 'refusal on the part of the populace was fair'. Fair or not,
however, the money had to be found. Then Laevinus made a novel proposal:

> As magistrates were superior to the senate in dignity, and as the senate
> was superior to the people, so ought they themselves to be leaders in
> shouldering all that was hard and drastic. 'If there is a duty which you wish
> to lay upon an inferior, and you first accept the same obligation as regards
> yourself and your family, you more readily find everyone submitting. And
> the outlay is not burdensome when they see every prominent man taking
> upon himself more than his share in it. Accordingly, if we wish the Roman
> people to have fleets and equip them, and private citizens to furnish oarsmen
> without protest, let us first impose that obligation upon ourselves.'
> (26.36.2-5)

A series of specific proposals followed. The senators were to hand over all
their gold and silver except for certain rings, *bullae* (amulets) for their sons
etc., the horse-trappings of former curule magistrates and one or two vessels to
be retained for sacrificial purposes; only one silver pound was to be allowed to
each senator, and 5,000 *asses* to each paterfamilias. Everything else was to be
deposited with the *triumviri mensarii* (bank commissioners), without any prior
decree by the senate, so as to excite a spirit of emulation first among the *equites*
and then among the plebs (26.36.7-9). Such were the measures adopted in this
exemplary upsurge of national unity.

It would be interesting to know who were the protesters in 210. They must
have belonged at least to the third Servian class, with a capital of at least 50,000
asses, as laid down four years earlier; so they were, if not rich, at any rate well-
to-do. They possessed saleable property (no doubt lands, the *nuda terra* of
which they speak); they had owned slaves, but had had to provide at least one
for the fleet in 214, while the rest — 8,000 in all, though we do not know how
many each individual possessed — were bought and then set free at the state's
expense in 216 (Livy 22.57.11; 24.14.5, 16 and 19; Appian, *Hann.* 27). In
short, the protesters at the bottom end of the scale consisted of smallholders or
landed proprietors of middle rank. As for the voluntary contribution proposed
by Laevinus, it fell on the *principes,* referred to later as *equites* (Livy 26.36.12;
consensum senatus equester ordo est secutus, equestris ordinis plebs). We do not
know whether the protesters were themselves liable for military service, but
the fact that they were in Rome suggests that they were mostly elderly.

It is clear that those affected by the contribution of 210, as by that of 214, were people who had been hit financially but were not actually poor: military and economic catastrophe had not yet shaken the timocratic basis of the state. The 'progressive' character of the tax was accentuated by the fact that Laevinus turned it into a 'voluntary loan'. It was repaid in instalments: the first in and after 204 (29.16.3), the second (not mentioned by Livy) in 202, and a third in 200: this took the form of *trientabula* (31.13.3-9), i.e. lands from the *ager publicus*, on which the state levied a token *vectigal* to preserve its eminent domain. The last remainder was paid back in 196 with the aid of the arrears of tax paid by the priests (33.42.3). We thus know that at least some of the *privati* preferred to be repaid in 200 by a chance to speculate on the value of the *ager publicus* rather than to be reimbursed in cash. At that stage, ten years after the loan, it is interesting to note the procedure: the *privati* in question appealed to the Senate (*frequentes*, according to Livy, but they cannot in fact have been very numerous) and 'accepted' its decree. Instead of the angry crowd of 210 we have the impression of a small group of some political and financial importance. We do not know whether the loan bore interest.

The episode is highly instructive, showing as it does how a fiscal system of the classical civic type, bearing more heavily on the rich than on the poor, was replaced by a voluntary contribution that was in fact a loan; then, as victories succeeded defeats and state confiscations led to the large-scale accumulation of capital in the form of land, the operation turned into a profitable speculation for a small privileged group. The mass of the civic population were not affected. The contributions would in any case have borne on the upper classes only; transformed into a loan, they were of interest only to the very rich. But the people had not much to complain about: they had escaped any aggravation of the ordinary fiscal burden, and in 186 they were reimbursed, in part at least, for the contributions during the war years. The reversal of the military and political situation enabled Rome to begin the process which eventually led to her entire fiscal burden being transferred on to the shoulders of the conquered. Around the beginning of the second century BC a war in which Rome's very survival was at stake turned into a series of overseas conquests which, besides other benefits, enriched the treasury (indemnities from Carthage and Macedon), the soldiers and their generals, and ensured that Rome's fiscal burden was henceforth borne by the provinces. When the state had to appeal to its own citizens as well, it did so in the form of loans which were profitable for all concerned.

Indirect and provincial taxation

The privilege of relief from direct taxation, granted to Roman citizens for the first time in 167 BC, was to continue for 124 years. Accordingly the provinces, outside Italy, are the proper place in which to study the effects of Roman conquest from the fiscal point of view — the precise level of taxation, its social and geographical distribution, in short the financial cost of subjugation to Rome.[17] It is not our purpose to go into this subject here, as we are concerned with the citizens of the master nation. It is not entirely true, however, to say that Roman citizens paid no taxes whatever after 167. In the first place, it was not until the Social War that all Italians acquired what Diodorus calls the 'much desired' privilege of citizenship. The allies were subject to military and fiscal obligations of which we do not know a great deal, but which we have no reason to think were discontinued in 167. Even Roman and Latin colonies had obligations of the same kind. Those which were punished in 204 were subjected to an annual *tributum* at the rate of one per mille. The others, no doubt, had to contribute a sum fixed each year on the basis of the expected cost of the campaign and divided among them in proportion to their census rating; here again there is no reason to think that the system changed after 167. The grievances which the Italians formulated from 125 onwards and which came to a head in 90 did not, ostensibly at least, relate to fiscal matters but rather to the arbitrary behaviour of Roman magistrates, the exclusion of allies from the suffrage and from the benefits of land reform. There are some signs, however, that their claims developed against a background of financial oppression which was rendered more and more burdensome by the increasing arbritrariness of the Roman government.

But there were other taxes besides the *tributum*. We know of customs and harbour dues (*portoria*) and a whole range of what may be called quasi-fiscal charges, such as rights of pasturage on public land (*scriptura*). We may also perhaps class as indirect taxes the rents and revenues (hard to distinguish, as they are grouped under the very general term *vectigalia*) that the state derived from the *ager publicus,* either by directly exploiting the forests, mines etc. or by imposing a recognitive tax on those who occupied and cultivated portions of it. Finally there was a special indirect tax (the *vicesima libertatis*) of 5 per cent on the price of manumitted slaves; this was presumably paid by the master when the act was his initiative and by the slave when he bought his freedom. The revenue from this tax was kept in the form of gold, to be used only in extreme emergency. The tax was formally introduced by a law voted in 357 BC at the instance of the consul Cn. Manlius Capitolinus, not in Rome itself but in the camp at Sutrium, the men voting by tribes. (Livy 7.16.7)

It is impossible to evaluate the total yield of these fiscal charges, and difficult to say upon whom they fell; but, like most indirect taxes, they correspond to some extent to a tax on consumption. It has been suggested that the various dues and tolls may at times have had purposes other than fiscal, for instance economic or sumptuary. Policies of this kind have sometimes been detected in certain Hellenistic states, but it is more than doubtful whether they were pursued in Rome during our period. It is not clear which authority was competent to impose such taxes. Livy says obscurely that the censors in 199 'let out the contract' for the collection of the sales tax and a *portorium* at Puteoli (Pozzuoli), Capua and Castrum (?) (32.7.3), while in 179 they 'established many port-dues and taxes' (*vectigalia*) (40.51.8); the censors on these occasions seem to have acted on their own authority, without any intervention by the people. In 123, on the other hand, a tribune, C. Gracchus, 'established new customs duties' (*portoria*) (Velleius Paterculus, 2.6.3). He could hardly have done so except by means of a law, or in his capacity as an agrarian triumvir appointed by law. The abolition of customs dues and tolls in Italy in 60 BC was effected by a law originating with a praetor and voted by the people with the Senate's consent.

Although we cannot estimate the total value of the tax—we do not even know the rate of customs duty in Italy, but have to infer it from the provincial rates, which are known for the republican or imperial period—we do at least know how it was collected.[18] All the duties in question were farmed out by the censors at public auction to contractors known as *publicani*. In certain cases, and in early times, there might be a large number of small contracts assigned to isolated bidders, but soon, at all events by about the year 200, they were on a much larger scale, often covering a whole province. As individual resources were no longer sufficient the lessees formed associations which were similar to commercial companies, but subject to a special legal regime as public contracts were involved.[19] This is not the place to study the origin and development of the companies of *publicani*, which played an increasingly important part in the political, economic and social life of Rome in the second and first centuries BC. Especially after C. Gracchus's *Lex de Asia* in 123 they became elaborate administrative organizations with a superintending board in Rome, directors elected annually, vice-directors (*promagistri*) in the provinces and a host of employees, both free men and slaves, to staff the local collection offices (*stationes*). These employees might be armed (they were called 'guards', *custodes*) and enjoyed a measure of public authority. Any system of taxes and dues is disagreeable to its victims, but one which allows private persons to batten both on the state and on the taxpayer is doubly odious.[20] Moreover, it was in the logic of the Roman timocratic system that the benefit of the operation was limited to a clearly determined social group. The state naturally looked for guarantees when concluding contracts with individuals; the *publicani*, whether singly or in companies, had to provide substantial personal guarantees and sureties to the magistrate in charge of the adjudication. One way of simplifying this requirement was to lay down that contracts might only be farmed out to citizens with a certain property rating. Hence it is very likely that at a certain time, perhaps in 123, it was specified by law that in future only an *eques* was entitled to bid for some important contracts, or to be a member or representative of one of the great provincial companies.[21] That is to say, a prospective contractor must be worth at least 400,000 sesterces and be on the register of the *ordo*, which was kept up to date by the public authorities.

Thus, by degrees, a central position in public finance came to be occupied by a small group of men, an *ordo* which already enjoyed an honourable place in state affairs. This was the more important as, contrariwise, it was forbidden to senators (and no doubt their descendants) to take any direct part in public contracts. It has sometimes been said that by virtue of these provisions the whole Roman fiscal system became a kind of closed shop, a field abandoned by the Senate and the people to the all-powerful equestrian order. I do not propose to go into the arguments here, but this view is much too one-sided. Although the fiscal administration was leased to *publicani* it remained under the triple control of the adjudicating magistrates (*promagistri* in the provinces), the Senate and the people, who, through the tribunes, intervened in these matters more and more often from 200 onwards. No doubt the tax-farming companies made huge profits from time to time, but they might also be restrained by the antagonism or fair-mindedness of magistrates; they might suffer losses through miscalculation or ill-luck, or through the Senate's hostility and its deliberately mistrustful methods. In 167, for instance, the Senate decided to shut down the Macedonian mines rather than let them be exploited by *publicani*. In 61-59 the tax-farmers of Asia, who had signed over-optimistic contracts, put forward illegal and scandalous demands for their revision, which Cato and the Senate resisted for three years. The provincials were not entirely without recourse against exactions on the tax-farmers' part. If the provincial governor had connived at them, the inhabitants could always sue him for extortion and ensure that their complaint was adduced in evidence, as happened in Gaul over the wine duties introduced by Fonteius. They could also appeal directly to the Senate by sending a delegation to Rome. Greek epigraphy records a fair number of such complaints which were settled to the taxpayers' satisfaction. As regards revenues from the *ager publicus,* the agrarian law of 111 provided that disputes between the *publicani* and those liable for tax should be settled by *recuperatores* chosen by the praetor from the first class of property-owners.

None the less, and while making allowance for the citizen's natural dislike of taxation in general, it is certain that the tax-farming system was universally unpopular. It continued right through the imperial period, when measures were adopted (in the first, and especially the second and third centuries) regulating very precisely the rights and duties of tax-farmers and taxpayers alike; from these we may gather that it was not so much the laws and regulations that caused trouble as the risks of abuse, high-handedness and corruption. *Publicani* and their agents, who had to recoup their investment and had no fixed salaries, lost no opportunity of adding illicit gain to their legal profit. Even in Italy, with the Roman judicial machine close at hand, these abuses were almost beyond endurance. Cicero, a clear-headed man who could hardly be suspected of prejudice against the equestrian order, wrote to his brother about the hatred of *publicani* in the province of Asia:

What bitterness of feeling this question of the *publicani* causes the allies we have gathered from those citizens who recently, on the abolition of port-dues in Italy, complained not so much of that duty itself as of certain malpractices on the part of the customs officers. I know pretty well what happens to allies in distant lands from the complaints I have heard from citizens in Italy. (*Ad Quintum fratrem* 1.1.33)

And, when he wishes to stigmatize the behaviour of his own former quaestor Vatinius, sent to Puteoli in 63 to investigate and prevent the export of precious metals from Italy, Cicero can find no more opprobrious term than 'customs officer':

While thus employed, thinking that you had been sent, not as a guard to keep, but as a customs-house officer to share out the merchandise, you searched every house, warehouse, and ship like a thief indeed, entangled businessmen in iniquitous legal proceedings, frightened merchants when they disembarked and hindered them when they went on board. (*In Vatinium* 12)

Legal documents and anecdotes, some unfortunately of post-republican date, give us an idea of the day-to-day relations between tax-farmers' agents and the public. True, in republican times the rights and duties of the *publicani,* and hence of the taxpayers, were a matter of public knowledge, unlike the position under the Empire up to and including Nero's reign. It was a firm principle of Roman fiscal law that the adjudication (*locatio*) must take place openly, that is to say by word of mouth, in the Roman forum, under the eyes of the Roman people, as Cicero says.[22] The register indicating among other things the exact amount of the tax to be collected had to be proclaimed after giving sufficient notice and in a sufficiently public manner, so that every taxpayer should know precisely what the law required. In the early Empire things were different. In 58 Nero was led by repeated complaints against the excesses of *publicani,* not to abolish indirect taxes altogether as he had thought of doing, but to issue several edicts the first of which once again made public the terms of the contract for each tax (Tacitus, *Annals* 13.51.1). From then on, a taxpayer could no longer plead ignorance of the law (as a constitution of Hadrian recalls: *Digesta* 39.4.16.5). As to customs, a list of dutiable articles had to be exhibited at *stationes* or at any rate the principal ones: imperial inscriptions of this kind have been discovered, e.g. at Zraia (Zarai) in Algeria. Marcianus, in the *Digesta,* gives a list of goods that were taxed at the Italian *portorium;* these were no doubt of Eastern origin, as when Caesar re-established the tolls and duties abolished by the *Lex Caecilia* in 60 he did so, according to Suetonius, only as regards foreign goods (*peregrinae merces*), i.e. presumably luxuries. The traveller or merchant had to make a declaration (*professio*) of the goods, and under the

Empire this had to include non-taxable articles as well. No doubt this was also the case in republican times, but we have little more than a chance reference in Lucilius to 'those who carry out secretly from a harbour unregistered wares (*non inscriptum*) so that they may not have to pay the customs due' (Luc. 753-4 W).

The traveller was taken into the customs office to make the declaration. A pleasant anecdote in the *Life of Apollonius of Tyana*, late or fictitious though it may be, shows the clairvoyant sage having a joke at the expense of a slow-witted official:

> As they fared on into Mesopotamia, the tax-gatherer who presided over the Bridge (*Zeugma*) led them into the registry and asked them what they were taking out of the country with them. Apollonius replied: 'I am taking with me temperance, justice, virtue, continence, valour, discipline.' And in this way he strung together a number of feminine nouns or names. The other, already scenting his own perquisites, said: 'You must then write down in the register these female slaves.' Apollonius answered: 'Impossible, for they are not female slaves, that I am taking out with me, but ladies and mistresses.' (Philostratus, *Life of Apollonius* 1.20)

Slaves were always dutiable, as it was suspected that they were being taken out of the country for sale. One of the few documents on fiscal matters dating from republican times, a fragment of the *Lex censoria* of the Sicilian customs,[23] indicates that an exception was made only for slaves accompanying their master to his home 'for his own use' (*suo usu*). But this proved to be an ambiguous formula, and distinctions were drawn by jurists to whom, no doubt, both *publicani* and taxpayers had appealed:

> Alfenus Varus (consul in 39 BC) in Book 7 of the *Digesta:* The censorial contract for the Sicilian customs states that 'slaves whom a man is taking home for his own use are not liable to duty.' ...Question: what is meant by 'for his own use'?

Alfenus ruled that the phrase referred to slaves attached to their master's person and attending to his everyday needs; all others, even if not intended to be sold, were liable to duty. Such rigid interpretations naturally encouraged smuggling, which, as far as slaves were concerned, most often took the form of disguising them as freemen. In the first century BC this practice became a common topic for exercises in schools of declamation, no doubt because of the many picturesque variations that could be made upon it. The *publicani* and their agents had a wide range of remedies. In the first place they could search travellers and their luggage; women, however, were usually exempt from search (Quintilian, *Declamationes* 349). Customs officers may have been allowed to open private correspondence, to judge from a passage in Plautus:

'Don't you suppose the lad knows his father's signet ring?'—'Oh, stop fussing! Hundreds of explanations can be invented—he lost the one he had and then got himself a new one. In fact, even if the letters aren't brought sealed, he can say they were unsealed and examined at the custom-house.' (*Trinummus* 789 ff.)

If the customs officers detected a case of smuggling they could seize the goods, which became their property (*commissum*), and sell them at auction. We have many details of these operations as far as imperial times are concerned, but lack of precise information for the republican period except for what the Verrine Orations tell us about conditions in Sicily. We shall revert to this in the chapter on relations between the citizen and the administration, as it is perhaps the most alarming revelation of corruption on a huge scale.

Each customs office kept a day-to-day register of goods in transit, and perhaps a list of smuggled goods that had been confiscated (*capturae*). Monthly summaries of this information were stored at provincial headquarters, in the promagister's office, and a copy sent to Rome and filed by the company's directors for that year (*magistri*). Verres' case throws a lurid light on relations between the civil governor of the province and the company in charge of the customs. A provincial governor, apparently, was not legally exempt from paying duty on goods he imported or exported on his own account. Verres, from the first months of his propraetorship, exported to Rome whole shiploads of loot in the form of money, purple dye, ivory and grain (he had, incidentally, got the city of Messina to present him with a ship of his own). Through the Syracuse office alone, in the first few months of his governorship he exported goods to the value of 1,200,000 sesterces, without paying the 5 per cent *ad valorem* tax that applied to all exports (the *vicesima portorii*: 2 *Verr.* 2.185); thus at Syracuse alone he had defrauded the company of 60,000 sesterces. The head of that office, one Canuleius, started to take careful note of these 'oversights' and sent a list of them to Rome. But Verres, while still refusing to pay duty, managed to get on excellent terms with L. Carpinatius, promagister of the company which leased the Sicilian pasture-land and, at this time, the customs as well. He did this by the simple means of sharing with Carpinatius, and no doubt with the company as a whole, the profits of which he defrauded the government in all sorts of ways. In particular he deposited with the company, which no doubt profited substantially from it, the money provided by the state for the purpose of buying wheat (which he obtained by force without paying for it). In return the *magistri* of the company, one of whom was a close friend of Verres', took care to expunge Canuleius's evidence from the official archives.

In Italy itself the most important indirect tax besides the customs was that on pastures (*scriptura*): this must have been of huge value in view of the size of the *ager publicus* and the practice of transhumance.

> Flocks of sheep are driven all the way from Apulia into Samnium for summering, and are reported to the tax-collectors, for fear of offending against the censorial regulation forbidding the pasturing of unregistered flocks. (Varro, *Res Rusticae* 2.1.16)

Documents of the imperial period mention *stationes* at which this tax was collected. By then transhumance had probably developed on a scale unknown during the Republic owing to the multiplication in southern Italy of large estates devoted to extensive stock-farming, like those of Domitia Lepida in Calabria (Tacitus, *Annals* 12.65.1) or the freedman C. Caecilius Isidorus, who owned 7,200 head of cattle and 257,000 of other livestock. But it is only in medieval and modern times that the fiscal supervision of this activity has led to the setting up of a regular administration, and there is no evidence of this having been so under the Republic. In any case the tax on public pastures, fully attested by Varro, was never farmed out to a single company in Italy as it was in Sicily or Asia. But in Italy as elsewhere the *publicani* were legally interposed between the state and the taxpayer, and their existence was recognized by the agrarian law of 111, lines 19-21 of which deal with the status of portions of the *ager publicus* which were made over to their occupants in full ownership (though it is not clear whether the law maintained or abolished the rights by which the holdings were encumbered).

The *publicani* employed numerous agents, most of whom were slaves, and citizens thus had to deal directly with persons who were juridically irresponsible, not being servants of the state or of any specific master. There were probably too many of these petty officials; they were inadequately supervised, enjoyed making trouble for taxpayers and were particularly disliked. Provincial complaints against the *publicani* often speak with aversion not only of the *equites* who were chiefly responsible for abuses, but of the slaves who carried out their orders. In Italy itself a famous criminal case in 138 BC showed how dangerous these hordes of slaves could be:

> I still remember an anecdote which I heard from Publius Rutilius at Smyrna: how in his early youth the consuls Publius Scipio and Decimus Brutus, I believe, were instructed by a resolution of the senate to investigate a great and shocking crime. It seems that in the forest of Sila murder had been committed, resulting in the death of well-known men; and that slaves of the company's household were under accusation, as well as some free members of the corporation which had leased the pine-pitch product from the censors Publius Cornelius and Lucius Mummius. The senate therefore decreed that the consuls should investigate the charges and pass judgement. The case for the corporation was presented by Laelius with great thorough-

ness, as was his wont, and with finish and precision. When at the end of the hearing the consuls announced that on the advice of their counsel the question should be postponed to a further hearing, after a few days' recess Laelius spoke again with greater pains and more effectively, and the case was adjourned as before. The members of the corporation escorted Laelius to his house and thanked him, begging him not to relax his efforts on their behalf. To this he replied that what he had done he had done with studious care, out of regard and honour for them, but that he believed their case could be defended with greater force and effect by Servius Galba, because of his more ardent and more pungent style of speaking.

Therefore on the advice of Laelius the corporation carried its case to Galba. ... To make a long story short: with expectation raised to the highest pitch, before a great audience, and in the presence of Laelius himself, Galba pleaded this famous case so forcibly and so impressively that almost no part of his oration was received in silence. Thus, with many moving appeals to the mercy of the court, the associates in the corporation were that day acquitted of the charge, with the approbation of everyone present. (Cicero, *Brutus* 85-88)

The civil wars: beginning of a new system

Caesar began his personal regime with a financial act which shocked contemporaries by its impiety: he forced open the treasury, the keys to which had been removed by the consuls when they fled the city, and even threatened to kill Caecilius Metellus, tribune of the plebs, when he offered resistance. Caesar's action was not only high-handed since, as a mere pro-magistrate and a rebel to boot, he had no right to touch funds that only the consuls and quaestors were entitled to handle on behalf of the Senate; it was also *impietas,* as he raided in particular the *aerarium sanctius,* the special gold reserve representing the accumulated yield of the five per cent tax on manumissions, which, by order of the Senate, was only to be drawn on in special emergencies. His action was not only impious but a political blunder, as it dispelled once and for all the myth of Caesar's wealth. Until then, his announcements of victory and his largesse had given the impression that he had seized all the gold in Gaul, but when he robbed the treasury people were undeceived. His use of threats and force against Metellus destroyed his reputation for mildness and clemency, and gave Cicero a chance to maintain that this was merely a ploy to gain popularity. Altogether Caesar's action seems to have swung public opinion against him in a few days, even though most of Rome had till then been on his side, if only because most of his declared adversaries had already left the city. It is noteworthy that this incident played such an important part in the polemics of those troubled days. Caesar states that

The consul Lentulus came to open the treasury for the purpose of providing a sum of money for Pompeius in accordance with a decree of the senate, but as soon as ever he had opened the inner treasury he fled from the city. (*De bello civili* 1.14.1)

On the other hand, Cicero (*Ad Att.* 10.4.8) says that Caesar's act aroused popular indignation, while Dio Cassius remarks (41.17.2) that: 'Far from receiving at that time the money he had promised them, the people had to give him all that remained in the treasury for the support of his soldiers, whom they feared.' The episode was a kind of presage of the financial troubles that successive civil wars were to bring upon the City. The finances of the period from 48 to 44 have been insufficiently studied. True, we are ill-informed as to the exact chronology of some of Caesar's measures, e.g. the sumptuary law or the reimposition of customs duties on foreign goods (Suetonius, *Caesar* 43.1), or even certain very specific laws such as that on the working of quarries in Crete. But it is certain that at the beginning of the period, during the fighting against Pompey's partisans in Macedon, Spain, Africa and Asia, Italy underwent not only a budgetary but a financial crisis which extended by degrees to most sectors of economic life, especially rent on buildings, interest rates and the settlement of debts. This crisis became acute in 48-47, when it gave rise to serious political and social unrest which it is not my purpose to study here.[24] On the other hand, Caesar's victories enabled him rapidly not only to replenish the treasury but to inaugurate a policy of largesse to the Roman people, both in money and in kind, on an unprecedented scale. Unlike Augustus, Caesar did not live long enough to compile a list of his benefactions for the admiration of posterity. However, ancient authors record payments of 600 million sesterces to the treasury in 45 (Velleius 2.56.3) and another of 20,414 pounds of gold and 60,500 silver talents (i.e. 1,620 million sesterces) at the time of the triumph of 46 (Appian, *B. Civ.* 2.102); from this latter amount should, however, be deducted gifts to the citizens at the rate of 400 sesterces per head, to the veterans at 20,000 and to the centurions and military tribunes at 80,000. The treasury was thus in a prosperous state without any need for direct taxation, and Caesar left at his death the sum of 700 million sesterces, all of it, to be sure, confiscated from his opponents (Cicero, *Phil.* 1.17).

After the Ides of March the public coffers emptied dramatically in the space of a few months. Cicero naturally blamed this on Antonius, but he was not alone in doing so: Atticus told him the same thing in April 44 (*Ad Att.* 14.14.5). When, in December 44 – January 43, the Senate resolved to send the consuls Hirtius and Pansa to Cisalpine Gaul to relieve the proconsul Decimus Brutus, whom Antonius was besieging at Modena, the *tributum* had to be revived for the first time in more than a century. Cicero foresaw this in November 44:

Where are the 700 millions entered in the account-books at the Temple of Ops? Moneys, ill-omened, it is true, but which, if not returned to their owners, might yet set us free from property taxes. (*Phil.* 2.93)

In May 43 Cicero wrote to Cornificius, proconsul in Africa, that he could not help him over military expenses because

> the money in the public treasury is incredibly scarce — money that is being called in from every quarter to fulfil the promise made to the troops who have served the state so well; and I do not think that can be done without imposing a property tax. (*Ad fam.* 12.30.4)

The *tributum* of 43 seems to have amounted to 4 per cent of each citizen's census rating, but there were also additional demands: senators had to pay another 'four obols' (i.e. perhaps ten *asses*) for each roof-tile on houses owned or rented by them in the City (Dio 46.3.3). Dio adds that

> The very wealthy contributed not a little in addition to this, while many cities and individuals manufactured weapons and other accoutrements for the campaign free of charge... These contributions were given readily by those who favoured Caesar and hated Antony; but the majority were vexed, being burdened alike by the campaigns and the taxes. (31.4)

In a letter to Brutus of July 43(?) Cicero mentions a tax of 1 per cent on the rich which may be different from the *tributum* of 4 per cent and which, he says, has brought in far less than expected because of the shameless way in which those concerned undervalued their property (*Ad Brutum* 18.5).

Rome, in short, was overtaken by a financial blizzard which was to last until Octavian's victory over Sextus Pompeius in 36 BC and even until the battle of Actium. The chief reason was, of course, the civil wars, with the large-scale mobilization and depredations that they implied. Another factor was the need to finance the more or less demagogic measures that each party felt obliged to introduce so as to gain the goodwill of the soldiery (as we have already seen) or the populace. Once the triumvirate was established, a good deal of this money came from confiscating and selling the goods of those outlawed. And, as Dio remarks (47.6.5),

> Since the triumvirs stood in need of vast sums of money and had no other source from which to satisfy the desires of their soldiers, they affected a kind of common enmity against the rich.

Lepidus and Antonius, as Dio tells us (47.8.5), also took money from those whom they spared. But, apart from these acts of violence, the triumvirs resorted to financial devices of a more traditional kind. Without going into detailed chronology, which is often difficult to establish, we may list as follows the old or new taxes imposed on Italy between 43 and 40 BC:

1. The *tributum* of the end of 43, already mentioned, consisting perhaps of 4 per cent of everyone's estimated wealth, plus 1 per cent surtax for the rich, plus the roof-tile tax for senators.

2. Tax on house property: one year's rent if the house was let, six months' if owner-occupied; assessed on the value of the building in each case (Dio 47.14.3).

3. Tax on country estates: half the year's 'revenue' (Dio 47.14.2).

4. Tax on 'sales and rents' (Appian 4.5): this was a *telos,* i.e. an indirect tax.

5. Special liturgies imposed on senators, who had to provide seamen for the navy (slaves and their pay, no doubt, as in 214 BC) and to maintain highways at their own expense.

6. Taxes on slave-owners: first levied in 43, as Dio briefly mentions (47.16.3); repeated by Octavian in 40 to finance his war against Sextus Pompeius:

> An edict was published that the owners of slaves should pay a tax for each one, equal to one-half of the 25 drachmas that had been ordained for the war against Brutus and Cassius [in 43], and that those who acquired property by legacies should contribute a share thereof. (Appian, *B. Civ.* 5.67)

This last edict provoked one of the riots which punctuated Roman political life during this period, as individuals found themselves increasingly hard hit by taxation. Dio paints a sombre picture of the financial situation of Rome and Italy during the triumvirate:

> When Marcus Lepidus and Lucius Plancus became consuls [in 42 BC], tablets were again set up, not involving the death of any one this time, but defrauding the living of their property. For the triumvirs found themselves in need of more money, since they already owed large sums to large numbers of soldiers, were spending heavily on undertakings then being carried out by them, and expected to spend far more still on the wars in prospect; they therefore proceeded to collect funds. Now the reintroduction of the taxes which had been formerly abrogated, or the establishment of new ones, and the institution of the joint contributions, which they levied in large numbers both on the land and on the slaves, caused the people some little distress; but that those who were in the slightest degree still prosperous, not only senators or knights, but even freedmen, men and women alike, should be listed on the tablets and mulcted of another 'tithe' of their wealth aroused great indignation. It was in name only that a tenth of each one's property was exacted; in reality not so much as a tenth was left. For since they were not ordered to contribute a stated amount according to the value of their possessions, but had the duty of assessing the value of their own goods, they were liable to be accused of not having made a fair assessment and to lose in

addition what they had left. And even if some persons did somehow escape this fate, they were nevertheless brought into straits by the assessments, found themselves terribly short of ready money, and so, like the others, were deprived of practically everything.

Moreover, the following device, distressing even to hear about, but most distressing in practice, was put into operation. Any one of the proscribed who wished to do so was permitted, if he would abandon all his property, to put in a claim afterwards for one-third of it, which meant getting nothing and having trouble besides. For when they were being openly and violently despoiled of two-thirds, how were they to recover the other third, especially since their goods were being sold for an extremely low price? In the first place, a great deal of property was being offered at auction all at once and most people were without gold or silver, while the rest did not dare to show by buying that they had money, lest they should lose that too, and consequently the prices were lowered; and, in the second place, anything would be sold to the soldiers far below its value. Hence none of the private citizens saved anything worth mentioning; for, over and above all the other exactions, they had to furnish slaves for the navy, buying them if they had none, and the senators had to repair the roads at their individual expense. Only those, indeed, who bore arms gained great wealth. (Dio, 47.16.1 to 17.4)

Fiscal pressure on this scale was bound to produce violent reactions, despite the tyranny exercised by the group in power. We know of two such riots during the triumvirate, no doubt because they took place in Rome itself and involved persons of note, while in one case at least there were tragic consequences. Similar disturbances must have occurred in the Italian *municipia* which were singly or collectively attacked by the triumvirs. We get an idea of them from Appian's account of the impulse of gratitude which led many Italians who had been, or feared to be, dispossessed to throw in their lot with the consul Lucius Antonius, brother of the triumvir, at the time of the Perusian war in 41 BC:

For the soldiers demanded the cities which had been selected for them before the war as prizes for their valour, and the cities demanded that the whole of Italy should share the burden, or that the cities should cast lots and that those who gave the land should be paid the value of it; and there was no money. They came to Rome in crowds, young and old, women and children, to the forum and the temples, uttering lamentations, saying that they had done no wrong for which they, Italians, should be driven from their fields and their hearthstones, like people conquered in war. The Romans mourned and wept with them, especially when they reflected that the war had been waged, and the rewards of victory given, not on behalf of the commonwealth, but against themselves and for a change of the form of government; that the colonies were being established in order that democracy should never again lift its head — colonies composed of hirelings settled there by the rulers to be in readiness for whatever purpose they might be wanted.

Octavian explained to the cities the necessity of the case, but he knew that it would not satisfy them; and it did not. (*B. Civ.* 5.12)

Lucius Antonius, on the other hand, saw an opportunity to make himself popular:

He alone received kindly, and promised aid to the agriculturists who had been deprived of their lands and who were now the suppliants of every man of importance. (5.19)

The first of the riots referred to earlier occurred in 43. Notwithstanding the money received from the proscriptions, the triumvirs still needed 20 million 'drachmas' (about the same number of denarii). They summoned an assembly and proposed to the people that 1,400 rich and high-born women should be ordered to declare their wealth and pay a proportion of it to be fixed by the triumvirs. Deception and concealment were to be severely punished, and informers would be rewarded. Although Appian does not say so, the reason for this measure probably was that owing to the civil wars many estates had fallen to female heirs and thus escaped taxation, which, as we have seen, was still on a personal basis. The women in question tried without success to get Antony's wife Fulvia to intervene. They then made their way to the Forum — an extraordinary if not unprecedented occurrence — and assembled near the rostra, while Hortensia, Brutus's mother by adoption and daughter of the consul of 69, made a long speech on their behalf. Appian's version of it is no doubt reliable, as the terms of the speech were preserved (Valerius Maximus 8.3.3 etc.):

'You have already deprived us of our fathers, our sons, our husbands, and our brothers, whom you accused of having wronged you. If we have done you wrong, as you say our husbands have, proscribe us as you do them. But why should we pay taxes when we have no part in the honours, the commands, the statecraft, for which you contend against each other with such harmful results? Our mothers did once rise superior to their sex and made contributions when you were in danger of losing the whole empire and the city itself through the conflict with the Carthaginians. But then they contributed voluntarily — not from their landed property, their fields, their dowries, or their houses, without which life is not possible to free women, but only from their own jewellery, and even then they gave not according to fixed valuation, not under fear of informers or accusers, not by force and violence, but only what they themselves were willing to give.'

The triumvirs were angry that women should dare to hold a public meeting when the men were silent; that they should demand from magistrates the reasons for their acts, and themselves not so much as furnish money while the men were serving in the army. They ordered the lictors to drive them away from the tribunal, which they proceeded to do until cries were raised by the multitude outside; then the lictors desisted and the triumvirs said they would postpone consideration of the matter. On the following day they reduced the number of women who were to present a valuation of their property from 1400 to 400, and decreed that all men who possessed more than 100,000 drachmas, both citizens and strangers, freedmen and priests, and men of all nationalities without a single exception, should (under the same dread of penalty and also of informers) lend at interest a fiftieth part of their property and contribute one year's income to the war expenses. (Appian, *B. Civ.* 4.32-34, abridged)

Thus the matrons' energetic protest aroused sympathy among the urban plebs, and the triumvirs had to give in, not without imposing a forced loan (we do not know if it was ever repaid) and an annual tax at an uncertain rate.

The second episode, which we have already mentioned in connection with the army, ended in a very different way. In 40 BC Octavian, preparing for war against Sextus Pompeius, published an edict imposing a tax on slave-owners and an estate duty (perhaps the first of its kind in Rome). However, the indignant people

banded together, with loud cries, and stoned those who did not join them, and threatened to plunder and burn their houses, until the whole populace was aroused. Octavian with his friends and a few attendants came into the forum intending to intercede with the people and to show the unreasonableness of their complaints. As soon as he made his appearance they stoned him unmercifully, and they were not ashamed when they saw him enduring this treatment patiently, and offering himself to it, and even bleeding from wounds. When Antony learned what was going on he came with haste to his assistance. When the people saw him coming down the Via Sacra they did not throw stones at him, since he was in favour of a treaty with Pompeius, but they told him to go away. When he refused to do so they stoned him also. He called in a larger force of troops, who were outside the walls. As the people would not allow him even so to pass through, the soldiers divided right and left on either side of the Via Sacra and the forum, and made their attack from the narrow lanes, striking down those whom they met. The people could no longer find ready escape on account of the crowd, nor was there any way out of the forum. There was a scene of slaughter and wounds, while shrieks and groans sounded from the housetops. Antony made his way into the forum with difficulty, snatched Octavian from the most manifest danger and brought him safe to his house. After the mob had been dispersed, the corpses were thrown into the river in order to avoid their gruesome appearance. It was a fresh cause of lamentation to see them floating down the stream, and the soldiers stripping them, while certain miscreants, as well as the soldiers, carried off the clothing of the better class as their own property. This insurrection was suppressed, but with terror and hatred from the triumvirs; the famine grew worse; the people groaned, but did not stir. (*B. Civ.* 5.67-8)

We may wonder if the ferocity with which the troops put down the rioters was not all the greater because they knew that they themselves were the indirect beneficiaries of the taxation complained of. In any case the incident, including the proposal for an estate duty, emphasizes the insoluble financial problems that arose from the establishment of a military regime.

As soon as he was able to — viz. in 36 BC, after the defeat of Sextus Pompeius — Octavian lifted all the taxes, both regular and extraordinary, that had been decreed since 43; he cancelled outstanding debts from private citizens and from the tax-collectors and may even have repaid the loan of 40 BC (Appian, *B. Civ.* 5.130). No doubt this was one reason for his increasing popularity. From then onwards the citizens expected every new regime to lift once and for all the threat of a direct tax on capital (or on certain forms of income), which they regarded more than ever as a badge of servitude. The strength of their opposition led to the gradual and cautious introduction of a new fiscal device, that of death duties, which were seen as a rough-and-ready compromise between the citizens' traditional privileges and the inflated needs of a state based on a standing army. From this point of view the history of the *vicesima hereditatum* is significant:[25] it was the only direct tax levied under the Empire, and the only one that affected citizens and no one else (Pliny, *Panegyricus* 37). There had never been such a tax under the Republic; it existed in Egypt, and the idea may have been adopted from there. As we saw, it was first introduced for a brief time in 40 BC, and may have been in part the object of the *Lex Falcidia de legatis*; but these estate duties were repealed, most probably in 36.

In AD 6, however, following the creation of the *aerarium militare*, fresh resources had to be found. Augustus, having himself contributed a large sum to the *aerarium militare*, asked the senators for written suggestions as to how it should be maintained; according to Dio, however, he had already made up his own mind, and instead of adopting any other proposal he 'established the tax of 5 per cent on inheritances and bequests' (55.25.5), declaring that he had found this plan in Caesar's papers. While we know that the tax was permanently introduced in AD 6, we do not know in what juridical form, e.g. whether by an edict, law etc. In any case the Senate as such does not appear to have been involved in the enactment. In AD 13, still according to Dio (56.28.4-6), as trouble threatened over the application of the tax Augustus again asked the Senate to suggest alternative sources of revenue. As the senators seemed prepared to agree to anything except the 5 per cent tax, Augustus 'changed it to a levy upon fields and houses; and immediately, without stating how great it would be or in what way imposed, he sent men out everywhere to make a list of the property' (Dio 56.28.6). Although this account is elliptical and ambiguous, apparently the threatened levy brought the Senate to heel, and the *vicesima* was maintained. It does not appear what purpose was served by consulting the Senate a second time, but it is not very surprising that Augustus should have acted as though he were applying to the letter a precept enunciated by Cicero 50 years earlier, in Book 2 of *De Officiis*, outlining a kind of 'fiscal morality' for governments:

> If any state (I say 'any', for I would rather speak in general terms than forebode evils to our own; however, I am not discussing our own state but states in general)—if any state ever has to face a crisis requiring the imposition of such a burden, every effort must be made to let all the people realize that they must bow to the inevitable, if they wish to be saved. (*De Off.* 2.74)

'To let all the people realize': the need for a public debate and a reasoned explanation was asserted throughout Republican history, up to the dawning of the imperial monarchy. Doubtless Augustus had firmly decided to revive the *vicesima* in AD 6 and again in 13, but, whether from legalistic scruple or for fear of a repetition of the riots of 43 and 40 BC, he called for suggestions, counter-proposals and even a Senate debate, so that constitutionally the procedure was very like that of the debates recorded during the Second Punic War. In AD 6 and 13 the position was just what it had been in 214 and 210 BC, in that the state's financial demands were presented as necessary if the citizens 'wished to be saved' (*si salvi esse velint*), so that they could not reasonably be refused. Hence, up to and including Augustus's tax on legacies, and apart from the civil wars of abhorrent memory, the Roman fiscal system was of an essentially 'civic' type in conformity with the traditional canons of the pseudo-Aristotle, according to which taxation is at times a painful necessity, but is always to be regarded as a counterpart to the citizen's privileges. Even the *vicesima* was a proportional tax and therefore more readily imposed on the rich than on the poor. There was, however, an essential difference in that the *vicesima*, established by law, was a permanent tax and not an exceptional measure like the *tributum*. When first instituted it may appear to have been accepted voluntarily; but it was instituted for all time, with no opportunity of alleviation, as the future would show, other than the prince's sense of fairness. This was very different from the traditional *tributum*, an exceptional, non-permanent tax which had to be agreed to on each occasion and the annual yield of which was fixed by the Senate. In this way Roman finances evolved from a 'civic' to a 'monarchic' system.

Distributions of grain and money

But the Roman citizen's financial—or, more broadly, economic—relations with the state were a two-way affair: he was not only a taxpayer, but a beneficiary as well. As we have seen, the oldest and for a long time the only tax was a kind of returnable advance, an investment in the next season's campaign. As a result of sharing in the spoils of war, or of the refunding of his stake after the fight was over, a citizen, even though non-combatant, might in the end receive more than he had originally paid. Ancient Rome knew nothing of the modern idea that it is a citizen's duty to contribute to the functioning of the state as such, let alone the juridical doctrine that every citizen is a debtor to the exchequer.

In most Greek cities current opinion was still more favourable to the citizen. Not only was it accepted that for ordinary purposes the state should rely as little as possible on citizens' contributions, voluntary or otherwise, but it came to be thought natural for the state to provide them with the means of subsistence, at all events in part. This tendency appeared at its strongest and from the earliest date in Athens, where it was also the subject of most argument for and against, in speeches and other texts that have come down to us.[26] There was a simple and exemplary reason for this: the grants of all kinds from which the Athenian citizen had come to benefit by the fourth century, and which were distributed from the fund known as the *theorikon*, were so large as to compete directly with the rest of the city's budget, in particular that of the army and navy. There was much criticism of this state of affairs, but for that very reason the welfare fund was constitutionally protected; it was treated as a 'sacred cow' by the democratic system, and it was illegal to propose any modification of it.[27] Demosthenes had to observe infinite caution in his many attempts to have the *theorika* devoted to purposes of defence. In a famous passage he sought to reverse the accepted values by declaring that:

> Just as each one of us has a parent, so ought we to regard the collective citizens as the common parents of the whole State, and so far from depriving them of anything that the State bestows, we ought, if there were no such grant, to look elsewhere for means to save any of their wants from being overlooked. (*Phil.* 4.10.41)

It was the city's duty to provide for the subsistence of needy citizens, but at the same time the latter resisted military service. In the fourth century, it is true, there was not much money to be made out of soldiering. Athens' last attempt to organise an empire in which the cost of mutual defence was borne by her allies failed in 357, when the danger from Macedon put an end to any hope of expansion or even of a successful war. But, while there was nothing to encourage the citizen to take up arms, he had no intention of relinquishing the advantages that he had enjoyed for over a century thanks to direct democracy and the pressure of the *ekklesia*. His refusal, and the defeat to which it led, put an end to the existence of Athens as a great power.

It is very hard to estimate the exact scale of the burden which the *misthophoria* imposed on the Athenian state, and even its effect on the city's budget. It should be noted that civic activities in the ordinary sense were remunerated directly in so far as they took up the time of gainfully employed citizens and involved them in a loss of income. By degrees civic activity became a profession in that it provided a livelihood, though no doubt a modest one, to the poor and destitute (Aristophanes, *Wasps* 306). In return for attendance at the *ekklesia*, the performance of public duties assigned by lot, jury service and participation in religious ceremonies, the citizen received a *misthophoria*, theoretically an allowance or compensation. This accounts for a distinctive feature of poor relief in Athens, viz. that it was very largely carried out by the city itself, depending less than elsewhere on private benevolence or euergetism. The doctrine of the city's responsibility towards its poorest citizens is reflected in its fullest form in a law mentioned by Aristotle (*Ath. Pol.* 49.4):

> The Council also inspects the Incapables; for there is a law enacting that persons possessing less than three minae and incapacitated by bodily infirmity from doing any work are to be inspected by the Council, which is to give them a grant for food at the public expense at the rate of two obols a day each.

Although this measure may originally have applied only to disabled ex-soldiers, it was also perhaps inspired by the ideology of a 'truly constitutional' policy, dear to Aristotle, in which the middle classes were statistically and politically dominant.

But apart from the *misthophoria*, which as far as we know was peculiar to Athens, both there and in other Greek cities an indirect form of public assistance was in force. This is of interest to us because it was the only one practised in republican Rome, apart from the agrarian laws and the distribution of land to veterans. It consisted of selling corn and sometimes oil at a reduced price (or subsidizing it in order to revert to a normal market price), and even distributing these basic commodities free of charge at certain times. Food supplies were naturally among the Greek city's primary concerns,[28] and special magistrates were appointed to supervise a market which, in principle, was supposed to be kept plentifully stocked and accessible to all. In its relations with foreign powers the city was keenly interested in obtaining extra quantities of these goods, which were always a welcome present. One of the earliest known examples is that of Psammeticus, king of Egypt, who, hoping to ally himself with the Athenians, sent 30,000 medimni of corn to the Piraeus during the famine of 445. The people, after devoting a share to the goddesses at Eleusis, distributed the remainder to all citizens equally. After several thousand names had been removed from the civic register under a recent law which severely restricted the grant of citizenship to resident aliens, altogether 14,240 persons received a share of the distribution.[29] There is no indication that the poor received any preferential treatment; on the contrary, it was emphasized that to be included in the distribution was a mark of privilege and citizenship. There may on that occasion have been diplomatic and economic grounds for this policy. But a century later, in 329-324,[30] when the circumstances were similar — a food shortage, distribution at a controlled price, aid from private benefactors and subscriptions — we find once again that the poor were apparently not especially favoured. At most we may suppose that the rich citizens, *metoikoi* or even foreign merchants who considered it a duty, and no doubt an honour, to contribute to these special funds were not expected to come forward as recipients, even if they were entitled to do so. In any case it is perhaps an anachronism to raise the question of the social differentiation of those who benefited from such distributions, which were still emergency measures in times of actual or threatened shortage. On such occasions, as in wartime rationing, rich and poor are in principle treated alike. It is certainly over-complicating the issue to suppose that prices were controlled for the benefit of the poor and allowed to find their own level as far as the rich were concerned. As A. R. Hands observes, it must not be forgotten that in Athens and other cities the grain market was as a rule controlled by foreign merchants or *metoikoi* (often Rhodians in the third and second centuries BC), and that to allow a black market to develop would have been to the detriment of the whole city, rich and poor alike. The documents we have on the control of the grain market in other cities, particularly an inscription from Samos,[31] similarly show that the purpose of the institution was to assure supplies to all citizens free of charge or at reasonable prices.

The situation at Rome was very different. The first fundamental contrast with Athens is that the Romans never had any idea of rewarding citizens for performing their civic duties. It is true, as we have already seen and shall be showing in detail later on, that the Roman timocratic system, unlike the Athenian democracy, was carefully devised to exclude the poorest citizens from civic and especially political functions, with the important exception that in and after the first century BC they were virtually the only citizens who served voluntarily in the army. Broadly speaking, therefore, Rome and Athens developed in opposite directions. But although the poorest Roman citizens did not take part in political life and *a fortiori* were not paid for doing so, they benefited economically in a different way. Neither in Greece nor in Rome did the citizen believe in doing something for nothing, except perhaps in the very earliest times or in an idealized and somewhat suspect historical past. The state might be compared to an association for purposes of security and profit-making; the Roman citizen, as a partner in the enterprise, received his reward in two complementary ways which were diametrically opposite to what took place in Athens and elsewhere in Greece. In the first place, from 100 BC onwards the poorest citizens, who provided practically the whole of the armed services, found in military service a modest but regular source of income, supplemented after every victory by capital grants in the form of land or money. Secondly Rome, like the Greek cities, took steps at a very early date to keep the urban population supplied with cereals and sometimes oil, as plentifully and regularly as possible. Rome, however, did not rely for this purpose on an extensive network of diplomatic relations (like fourth-century Athens, which cultivated the friendship of the Bosporan kingdoms), or, as the Greek cities also did, on the bounty of foreigners and its own rich citizens. Instead, taking advantage of its dominant position, Rome after 123 BC set about directly organizing the supply of food to its citizens at treasury expense. Thus indirect assistance from the state in the form of soldiers' pay and booty, far from distracting citizens from their civic and especially their military duties, provided an incentive to perform them, and played no small part in fostering the spirit of conquest. As for direct assistance from the treasury, it similarly involved a shifting of the load on to the only taxpayers who still remained after 167, i.e. Rome's provincial subjects, whose role it became to 'feed' the master people in the most literal sense. For these two reasons the effect of state aid to the Roman citizenry was totally different to what it had been in Greece.

Originally, however, until the *Lex Sempronia* of 123 BC, the problem of grain supplies in Rome was not handled very differently from the Greek or Hellenistic method. The chronicles of early times, down to the third century, often speak of shortages and famines, as of other 'natural' catastrophes.[32] There is no reason to doubt what they tell us: we know that in the *Annales,*[33] the oldest Roman historical documents, the market price of corn was carefully noted from year to year, as the difficulty of transport in the ancient world caused it to vary greatly throughout the Mediterranean basin. At a very early stage the state took on itself to remedy shortages in various concurrent ways. In the first place certain ordinary magistrates (no doubt the *aediles plebeii* when first instituted, and afterwards the *aediles curules*) were given the task of ensuring that the market was regularly supplied with grain at a reasonable price. Secondly, in time of emergency extraordinary magistrates or commissions were appointed. (However, the accounts of a first 'praefecture of the *annona*' in 440 BC are almost certainly anachronistic; this office is first reliably attested in 104 BC, when it was held by Aemilius Scaurus: Cicero, *Pro Sestio* 39, and *De Haruspicum Responsis* 43). These magistrates, who might sometimes be the consuls, resorted to the whole range of remedies used by the Greek states: purchasing commissions were sent to neighbouring and far-off countries in search of grain at a low price, merchants and wholesalers were forced to bring stocks on to the market, envoys were sent to ask friendly states or monarchs for cheap or free deliveries. In most of the cases we know about, these measures were taken on the Senate's initiative and financed from public funds: unlike the Greek cities, Rome seems always to have taken an adverse view of private charity in a field so sensitive politically as that of feeding the urban proletariat.

This mistrust is well illustrated by the famous though perhaps half-legendary affair of Spurius Maelius in 439 BC. He is described by Livy and Dionysius as a wealthy man, perhaps a grain merchant, who at a time of shortage took the initiative of buying up corn in Etruria on his own account and distributing it to the plebs at a low price or gratis.[34] In a Greek city such an act would have been rewarded with an honorific decree, a wreath or even a statue. The Roman historical tradition, however (certainly inspired and contaminated by events of the Gracchian era), presents him as a blackguard, seeking cheap popularity in furtherance of his tyrannical ambitions. The Senate, we are told, thought the matter so serious that they ordered the consuls to appoint a dictator, who caused Maelius to be arrested and executed by his Master of the Horse. It does not greatly matter what really happened: the story shows that Roman suspicion of private generosity, at all events on the part of a non-magistrate, was chiefly an aristocratic reaction and was due to acute mistrust of the urban plebs.[35]

A survey of our information on free or cheap distributions before the *Lex Sempronia* of 123 BC shows that the grain was mostly obtained from the provinces officially and at public expense. Thus in 203:

> The year was marked by a great conflagration and by floods, but also by the low price of grain, because not only was all Italy open by reason of peace, but also a great quantity of grain had been sent from Spain; and Marcus Valerius Falto and Marcus Fabius Buteo, the curule aediles, distributed this to the populace by districts at four *asses* a peck (*modius*). (Livy 30.26.5-6)

Sometimes the grain seems to have been provided by the aediles themselves. In 196:

> The curule aediles, Marcus Fulvius Nobilior and Gaius Flaminius, distributed to the people one million measures (*modii*) of grain at two *asses* per measure. The Sicilians had brought this to Rome as a mark of respect to Gaius Flaminius himself and to his father. (Livy 33.42.8)

Most often, however, the authorities kept Rome supplied at moderate prices by using money obtained from taxation, especially tithes, or purchasing grain abroad out of public funds (Polybius 38.2: purchases at Rhodes in 169). Details of this can be studied from the operation of 196. The aediles distributed a million *modii* (about nine million litres or 250,000 bushels) of grain at a price 50 per cent higher than in 203. The minimum ration per person, as we shall see, was estimated at five *modii* per month at the end of the second century and the beginning of the first. If the city population had to make do with one million *modii* for the year 196, at the rate of 60 per person it could only have sufficed for a population of 16,666: this is certainly much too low, whatever our estimate of the population of Rome at that date. We must conclude therefore that the cheap distribution of one million *modii* was a supplement to what was available in the ordinary market, but that it sufficed to keep prices fairly low throughout that year; cf. the effect on prices of a sudden arrival of supplies from overseas, in Livy 30.38.5.

Thus the magistrates and the people were accustomed from early times to use treasury funds or the yield of provincial taxes, as occasion arose, to ensure a more or less steady supply of grain at an acceptable price. But until 123 there was no general and permanent arrangement for state control, apart from the supervision of markets by the aediles; steps were only taken in case of need, if there was a shortage or if prices rose too rapidly. And, if foreign or military policy so required, the interests of the urban populace might be sacrificed to those of the army in the field, as for instance in 191, when grain consignments were diverted from Rome to provinces in which troops were being mustered.[36]

All this was changed by C. Gracchus,[37] who for the first time introduced a law to regulate permanently the distribution of cheap grain to the plebs at regular intervals:

[Gracchus] made the unprecedented suggestion that a monthly distribution of corn should be made to each citizen at the public expense. (Appian, *B. Civ.* 1.21)

[Among Gracchus's measures was] a law that grain should be sold to the plebs for six and one-third *asses*. (Livy, *Per.* 60)

We do not know how much each person received under this law, but probably the ration was five *modii* per month (for each paterfamilias?), as this figure is attested by the corn laws of 78 and 73 which evidently go back to the precedent of 123 BC. As to the number of beneficiaries, according to Appian it must have been equal to that of the citizens. In any case C. Gracchus gave no special treatment to the poor: the rich received their share, as is shown by the celebrated anecdote concerning an opponent of the law, L. Calpurnius Piso Frugi (tribune in 149 BC):

The famous Piso, named Frugi, had spoken consistently against the corn-law. When the law was passed, however, in spite of his consular rank, he was there to receive the corn. Gracchus noticed Piso standing in the throng; he asked him in the hearing of the Roman people what consistency there was in coming for the corn under the terms of the law which he had opposed. He replied: 'I shouldn't like it to come into your head, Gracchus, to divide up my property among all the citizens; but if you were to do so I should come for my share.' (Cicero, *Tusc.* 3.48)

However, although grain was distributed to all and sundry, it was naturally the poor who benefited most, as Plutarch clearly says.[38] This accounts for the aristocracy's opposition to the law; according to Cicero they complained, firstly that it was a drain on the treasury and secondly that it encouraged idleness among the plebs (*Pro Sestio* 103). The corn law (*Lex frumentaria*), along with the agrarian and judiciary laws, became an issue of party politics,[39] as the various leaders from time to time produced skilfully calculated proposals that were either more or less generous (or demagogic) according to the needs of the moment. These changes, as far as can be made out, related either to the price charged to individuals, the number of beneficiaries or the amount of grain allowed to each.

The *Lex Sempronia* no doubt remained in force at least until 100 BC, when the tribune L. Appuleius Saturninus proposed a law of which we know only that it related to the price at which grain was sold. If we accept as it stands the only text that refers to his proposal, it appears that the price was to be five-sixths of an *as* per *modius*, or barely a tenth of what it was under the *Lex Sempronia*. The radical nature of this proposal accounts for its stormy reception:

> When Lucius Saturninus was about to introduce the grain law concerning the five-sixths of an *as*, Quintus Caepio, who was city quaestor at that time, explained to the Senate that the treasury could not endure so great a largess. The Senate then decreed that if Saturninus should propose that law before the people he would appear to be doing so against the common weal. Saturninus proceeded with his motion. His colleagues interposed a veto; nevertheless he brought the lot-urn down for the vote. Caepio, when he saw Saturninus presenting his motion against the public welfare despite his colleagues' veto, attacked him with the assistance of some conservatives (*viris bonis*), destroyed the 'bridges', threw down the ballot boxes, and blocked further action on the motion. Caepio was brought to trial for treason. (*Rhetorica ad Herennium* 1.21)[40]

We have some idea of the trial that ensued: the advocates of the law accused Caepio of acting contrary to the people's vote and the will of its magistrates, while Caepio retorted that he had defended the treasury and resisted the unbridled ambition (*libido*) of wicked men. Caepio was presumably acquitted (if his trial took place immediately, which is not certain), since as quaestor he was responsible with his colleague Piso for an issue of currency that was no doubt intended to pay for grain purchases: the coins were inscribed AD FRUM [ENTUM] EMUN [DUM] EX SC and showed the two magistrates seated on a bench between two ears of corn. Some infer from this that the *Lex Appuleia* was adopted and that the Senate ordered the quaestors to finance it after its author's death.[41] Given the account of Caepio's attitude and that of the Senate, this seems to me very unlikely. It is far more probable that a substitute measure was passed (like those of Livius Drusus in 123 or Cato's proposal in 62) to compensate the people for the rejection of Saturninus's proposal. The food situation was difficult owing, no doubt, to the Servile Wars in Sicily, and the Senate ordered one or two exceptional distributions without committing itself for the future. This seems to me to be confirmed by the fact that the *Lex Sempronia* was still in force some years later, when it was repealed at the instance of a tribune, M. Octavius, whose term of office must be placed in 95-90 rather than before Saturninus's *rogatio:*

Marcus Octavius, son of Gnaeus, whose authority and words availed to abrogate the grain law of C. Gracchus by the votes of a full assembly. (Cicero, *Brutus* 222)

Gaius Gracchus inaugurated largesses of grain on an extensive scale; this had a tendency to exhaust the exchequer. Marcus Octavius inaugurated a moderate dole; this was both practicable for the state and necessary for the commons. (*De Officiis* 2.72)

We do not know in what way the *Lex Octavia* modified the *Lex Sempronia*: whether as regards the price or quantity of grain or the number of recipients, or perhaps all three.

It is generally held that Sulla rescinded the corn laws, but this is based only on an ambiguous remark attributed by Sallust to Lepidus in 78 BC: 'the Roman people...an object of contempt, without the means to live, does not even still enjoy the rations of slaves' (*Oratio Lepidi cos.* 11). In any case, Lepidus in that year brought in the *Lex Aemilia* which established or re-established a monthly ration of five *modii* (Licinianus, 33 F). This may have been less than the amount provided by C. Gracchus. In 73 the consuls introduced a new law, the *Lex Terentia Cassia,* which certainly provided for a distribution of five *modii* per month (Sallust, *Hist.* 3.19) at a price of six and one-third *asses* (Asconius, 8 C). By piecing together various bits of information about this law we can form an idea of the scale of operations involved.[42] We know that the yield of the Sicilian tithes in 73-70 was used in the main to supply the Roman *annona*; and at that time most of the available grain undoubtedly came from Sicily, though there may have been other sources in Africa, Sardinia or Spain. Cicero gives some figures in his denunciation of Verres: Apronius, the latter's accomplice, received as his own share 33,000 *medimni* (i.e. 198,000 *modii*), or 'enough to supply the populace of Rome for nearly a month' (2 *Verr.* 3.72). Dividing this figure by the five *modii,* the number of recipients appears to be 39,600. Allowance must be made for rhetoric, however: this figure is certainly too low for the *plebs frumentaria* in the first century BC. But Cicero provides further evidence on the financial side. Taking as a basis the sums allocated to Verres as praetor of

Sicily for three years to enable him to purchase, at a price fixed by the Senate, what was called the 'second tithe' (over and above the tax proper, which naturally cost nothing), and also to pay for requisitioned corn at the official prices indicated by Cicero, we can calculate that the two tithes plus the requisitioned grain from Sicily amounted to 6.5 million *modii* per annum, i.e. enough to feed 108,000 people per month at five *modii* each. This number of recipients is much more likely than the 40,000 derived from the first calculation. By a supplementary reckoning, less certain because it depends on an exact knowledge of the 'market price' of grain, we can estimate roughly how much the operation cost the state: perhaps two million denarii or eight million sesterces. This, as we shall see, is reinforced by a remark of Cicero's about Clodius's law of 58 BC, to the effect that the free distribution of corn deprived the treasury of one-fifth of its revenue (which was much augmented at that time by Pompey's conquests). Two passages of Plutarch mention a figure: he records that at the end of 63 or the beginning of 62 Cato the Younger, in order to disarm a movement of unrest among the urban plebs in favour of Caesar, obtained a decree from the Senate which increased the allowance in one way or another:

> Cato, fearing above all things a revolutionary movement set on foot by the poorer classes, who were setting the whole multitude on fire with the hopes which they fixed upon Caesar, persuaded the senate to assign them a monthly allowance of grain, in consequence of which an annual outlay of 7,500,000 drachmas was added to the other expenditures of the state. (Plutarch, *Caesar* 8.4; cf. *Cato Minor* 26.1)

Some have deduced from this that Cato's proposal was to increase the number of recipients from 108,000 to something like 270,000; but Plutarch does not say so. We do not know whether the *Lex Terentia* had limited the number in any way; it may be that Cato merely proposed to increase the ration.

The next step was taken by Clodius in 58. The principal effect of the *Lex Claudia* was to make distributions absolutely free, 'remitting', as Cicero says, the six and one-third *asses* per *modius* that had been paid till then; this measure, as Cicero later pointed out (*Pro Sestio*, 55), cost the state nearly a fifth of all its revenues (*vectigalia*). Other sources (Dio 38.13; Asconius 9 Or.) confirm that the distributions were made free, a principle that was never again departed from. From this point of view Clodius's law was an essentially new departure; but it presented other features that modern scholars have generally overlooked. It certainly instituted a kind of general administration of the *annona*, which Clodius caused to be entrusted to a client of his (possibly a former scribe), Sextus Cloelius or Clodius, who was also his adviser and was supposed to have helped in the drafting of the law. For this purpose Cloelius was put in possession of 'all supplies both public and private, all the corn-supplying provinces [?], all the contractors and all the keys of the granaries' (Cicero, *De Domo* 25). These were some of the responsibilities that were to be entrusted to Pompey in 57 in his capacity as *curator annonae*. We do not know in what way the distributions were carried out, but the organization may well have been connected with another of Clodius's laws, that on *collegia* and sodalities, which lifted the ban on associations, particularly local ones, imposed by a *senatus consultum* of 64, and set up new bodies of this kind. We know that in 57—when, despite the corn law of 58, the food situation became acute—the citizens or freedmen enrolled in the new associations demonstrated violently during a theatrical performance, under the leadership of men whom Clodius had put in charge of organizing the new *collegia*: L. Sergius, M. Lollius, Lentidius and Plaguleius (*De Domo* 13 and 89). It may be, therefore, that these associations were intended to provide the framework for corn distributions under the *Lex Claudia*. Another consequence of this law, providing for free distribution to all citizens, was a sudden sharp increase in the number of manumissions. This is attested by Dio Cassius for the year 57:

> Pompey encountered some delay in the distribution of the grain. For, since many slaves had been freed in anticipation of the event, he wished to take a census of them in order that the grain might be supplied with some order and system. (Dio 39.24.1)

Dio adds that this was a wise measure, but that Pompey was blamed for it at the consular election of 56 for 55. Dionysius, for his part, speaks of these manumissions as a regular feature of his own time, in Augustus's reign:

> Some are freed in order that, when they have received the monthly allowance of corn given by the public or some other largess distributed by the men in power to the poor among the citizens, they may bring it to those who granted them their freedom. (Dionys. 4.24.5)

We shall revert to the question of the lists used as a basis for the distributions. According to Dio, Pompey only maintained a register of those newly enfranchised, but there must also have been a general one; indeed we have evidence of it in the first century BC, as it was modified by Caesar in 46:

> He made the enumeration of the people [*recensum*: not a regular census] neither in the usual manner nor place, but from street to street aided by the owners of blocks of houses, and reduced the number of those who received grain at public expense from 320,000 to 150,000. And to prevent the calling of additional meetings at any future time for purposes of enrolment, he provided that the places of such as died should be filled each year by the praetors from those who were not on the list. (Suetonius, *Caesar* 41)

Caesar's restriction was not arbitrary: Dio attests (43.21.4) that it was aimed at those who had got themselves on to the list on false pretences. As the only qualifications, since the time of C. Gracchus at least, were to be a Roman citizen and domiciled in Rome, presumably it was mainly these two points which were checked. There is no evidence that Caesar, any more than his predecessors, wished to restrict the benefit of the law to the poor.[43] A more interesting point is that a ceiling was placed on the number of recipients, only those who died being replaced. At the same time Caesar appointed two new aediles, the *Cereales,* with particular responsibility for the public granaries.

The restrictions imposed by Caesar were overridden after his death, thanks to the civil wars and by the fault of his heirs. Thus, in carrying out Caesar's bequest of 75 denarii to every citizen (the first instance of a *congiarium*), Octavian doled out the money to all comers without scrutinizing their credentials; for, as he himself states, his various bounties never affected fewer than 250,000 persons (*Res Gestae* 15). Once firmly in power, however, Augustus reverted to Caesar's system. In 5 BC he issued a *congiarium* of 240 sesterces to the 320,000 members of the 'urban plebs' (his own expression), but in 2 BC, like Caesar, he revised the list so as to reduce the number of recipients (*plebs qui frumentum publicum accipiebat*) to 200,000 (*Res Gestae* 15; the figure is confirmed by Dio, 55.10.1). By way of compensation, however, he decreed a *congiarium* of 60 denarii or 240 sesterces per head.

Despite the calculated generosity of which he smugly boasts in the *Res Gestae,* Augustus was in fact profoundly hostile to the *frumentationes*: in this he was faithful to the aristocratic Roman tradition voiced by Cicero. Suetonius quotes several anecdotes illustrating his reluctance:

> In times of scarcity he often distributed grain to each man at a very low figure, sometimes for nothing, and he doubled the money tickets. But to show that he was a prince who desired the public welfare rather than popularity, when the people complained of the scarcity and high price of wine, he sharply rebuked them by saying: 'My son-in-law Agrippa has taken good care, by building several aqueducts, that men shall not go thirsty.' Again, when the people demanded largess which he had in fact promised, he replied: 'I am a man of my word'; but when they called for a grant which had not been promised, he rebuked them in a proclamation for their shameless impudence, and declared that he would not give it even though he had intended to do so. With equal dignity and firmness, when he had announced a distribution of money and found that many had manumitted and added to the list of citizens, he declared that those to whom no promise had been made should receive nothing, and gave the rest less than he had promised, so as to make the appointed sum suffice. Once, in a time of great scarcity when it was difficult to find a remedy, he expelled from the city the slaves that were for sale, as well as the schools of gladiators, all foreigners except

physicians and teachers, and some of the household slaves; and when grain at last became more plentiful, he writes: 'I was strongly inclined to do away forever with distributions of grain, because through dependence on them agriculture was neglected; but I did not carry out my purpose, feeling sure that they would one day be renewed through desire for popular favour.' But from that time on he regulated the practice with no less regard for the interests of the farmers and grain-dealers than for those of the populace. (Suetonius, *Augustus* 41-2)

The corn distribution certainly required the establishment of an elaborate administration. Unfortunately we do not know much about its workings in the republican period; only from the reign of the emperor Claudius onwards do inscriptions provide some detailed information. At that time its headquarters were sited at the Porticus Minucia in the Campus Martius. The portico was divided into arcades with 45 'gates' (*ostia*) specially constructed for the purpose of distributing tokens, if not the actual corn. Each arcade was allocated to a group of recipients whose names were carved on bronze tablets displayed beneath the portico. The officials manning the gates were for the most part imperial freedmen. The distribution was on a monthly basis, but did not take place on the same day for everyone; each citizen was assigned to a particular gate and day of the month,[44] which he could quote if necessary, as the following inscription shows:

> Ti. Claudius, freedman of Augustus / Januarius, curator [of the *collegium funerarium*] / registered at the Porticus Minucia, the 13th day of the month / Gate 42, and / Avonia Tyche his wife [etc.] (*CIL* 6, 10223)

To have received a state issue of grain was a proof of enfranchisement, and in funerary inscriptions concerning children of freedmen we often read, for instance, 'He received his grain ration on the 10th day, Gate 39' (*CIL* 6, 10224) or 'on the 7th day, Gate 15' (ibid. 10225).

This flexible and efficient organization, in force from Claudius's time onwards, coincided with the transfer of financial responsibility for the dole from the *aerarium*, administered by the Senate, to the imperial exchequer, and with the direct nomination by the emperor of *praefecti frumenti dandi*: these officials, first appointed by Augustus, subsequently came under the supervision of the *praefectus annonae*, who was of equestrian rank and was in charge of the City's food supply in general.

It is very likely that at least an embryonic organization of this kind existed from the time when distributions were made regular by the *Lex Sempronia*. For that remote period the only evidence we have is that a system of public granaries was set up by C. Gracchus. Some of these were in Rome, as Festus tells us (p. 290); others were situated in what Cicero calls the *provinciae frumentariae*, e.g. Sicily, Macedon, Asia, Syria and no doubt Sardinia, which produced corn and shipped it to Rome by way of tax (*De Domo* 25); others again were at the important entrepot of Delos (*Lex Gabinia Calpurnia*). However, it is doubtful whether distribution was centralized in Gracchus's time as it was under Claudius. As we have seen, when exceptional distributions took place at the beginning of the second century they were carried out *vicatim,* street by street. Probably C. Gracchus used the existing framework of public life for his new institution. Only one text has survived concerning the formalities with which citizens had to comply at the distributions. Unfortunately it is incomplete and its date has been disputed; for a long time it was thought to belong to Caesar's time, and the regulations it describes were thought to relate to his restrictive *recensus* of 46. It now seems, however, that it goes back to the years between 80 and 75 — about the time of the Social War, Sulla, the *Lex Aemilia* of 78 and the *Lex Terentia Cassia* of 73. The document in question is the *Tabula Heracleensis* (lines 1 to 19), which also contains regulations about the activity of aediles and census operations in *municipia* and colonies. It indicates that certain persons had to make 'declarations' concerning the corn distribution and that the magistrates were forbidden to issue grain to those who, on the basis of these declarations, were excluded from the list:

If a person, required by this law to make the aforesaid declaration before a consul, shall be absent from Rome at the time when the declaration ought to be made, then his agent or representative shall on his behalf make the same declaration before a consul, in the same manner and on the same days as the said person would be required by this law to make the declaration if he were in Rome.

[Here follow provisions concerning persons in the care of guardians, and others to the effect that if the consul is absent from Rome the declaration shall be made to the *praetor urbanus* or *peregrinus,* or in their absence to a tribune of the plebs.]

In the case of every declaration required of any person by this law, it shall be the duty of the magistrate before whom the declaration is made to see that the name of the person, his declaration, and its date are entered in the public records; he shall further see that the entries made by him in the said public records shall be copied in black letters on a white board and exposed in the forum, during the greater part of every day, at the time and place in which corn is distributed to the people, so that it may be plainly read from the level of the ground.

Whosoever shall distribute corn or cause others to distribute corn to the people shall neither give corn, nor order nor permit corn to be given, to any of those persons whose names shall have been given in to a consul or praetor or tribune, and in accordance with this law placed in the list upon the notice board. Whosoever, contrary to this law, shall give corn to any such person, shall be condemned to pay a fine to the people of 50,000 sesterces for every measure of wheat so given, and may be sued at will by any person for the said sum.

All that can be said with certainty is that under this law, whatever its date, certain individuals were required to make a declaration (*professio*) the effect of which was to exclude them from the distribution. Those who, like von Premerstein, assign the law to Caesar's time suppose that before he died Caesar intended to restrict the *frumentationes* to the indigent population, and that the *professio* must have been a declaration of personal wealth, those above a certain threshold being excluded. But there is no evidence that Caesar or his predecessors intended this. It must not be forgotten that the *Tabula Heracleensis* was found in a *municipium*, a long way from Rome. Its last sections belong to the climate of the years following the Social War, and clearly concern Italian communities recently integrated into the Roman *civitas*. We may thus suppose that the object was rather to exclude the new *cives* domiciled in Italy from the benefit of the distributions that had till then been confined to *cives Romani* living in Rome. The declaration would then be simply that executed by those who wished to benefit from the laws on citizenship.[45] In any case it shows that a check was operated, no doubt by comparing general lists of authorized persons and special lists, to which publicity was given, of those who were not entitled to cheap or free corn. Now the only text which mentions 'black lists' of this kind is that quoted above from Dio Cassius concerning Pompey's efforts in 57 to make a register (*anagraphè*) of those who had been specially freed for the occasion. The two procedures seem very similar.

There is an interesting sidelight on this point. When Pompey as *curator annonae* drew up a list of those enfranchised recently, no doubt since the *Lex Claudia*, he must also have ordered a revision of the general list of beneficiaries. Now we know from two or three allusions by Cicero that Clodius, among other misdeeds, had caused his henchmen to set fire to the Temple of the Nymphs in order 'to erase the national records of the censor's registration that were printed in the national rolls' (*Pro Milone* 73).[46] The word *recensio*, which Cicero here uses for the only time, is used by Suetonius especially to designate the revisions of the distribution lists carried out by Caesar and Augustus. It is very tempting to suppose that Clodius's express purpose was to destroy the new lists, drawn up by Pompey in 57, which excluded persons who had benefited under the *Lex Claudia*.

The Temple of the Nymphs has recently been identified with a temple which, in the Severian marble plan, is situated in the centre of the Porticus Minucia; its ruins bear traces of a fire which can be dated to the middle of the first century BC. Thus it appears that from the last days of the Republic the documents relating to the corn distribution were preserved in a temple around which the *Porticus Minucia frumentaria* was subsequently built, perhaps in Claudius's reign. As to the original Porticus Minucia, it is now identified with the one immediately to the west which surrounded the four republican temples of the Largo Argentina. We may note, however, that there was an ancient tradition, attested by coins dating from the very end of the second century BC, according to which the family of Marcus Minucius, consul in 109 and builder of the Porticus Minucia, was associated with the distribution of corn rations. It is possible therefore that even the *Minucia vetus* in republican times had some connection with the distribution.

We cannot reconstruct the process of distribution in the republican period, but we know that from Augustus's time onwards it was carried out by means of tokens (*tesserae frumentariae* or *nummariae*). This was a very ancient method, practised also in Greece where the tokens were known as *symbola*.[47] The token was of wood, bone or metal, with a distinguishing mark or inscription; the holder presented it on the due date and obtained his ration in exchange. Under the Empire, every member of the *plebs frumentaria* probably had two documents: a *tessera* which, in principle, he kept all his life (though, as we shall see, it might sometimes be sold or alienated) and another for each separate distribution of grain or money, issued no doubt on presentation of the permanent *tessera* and exchanged, at the gate of the Porticus or elsewhere, against the citizen's ration. The permanent kind of *tessera* might be sold or bequeathed, as Juvenal and some legal texts inform us.[48] Representations of it are rather few and difficult to make out: they seem to show a kind of small oblong tablet, perhaps with a ring to hold it by. In any case, this system of identity documents and tokens is only attested in imperial times, chiefly at the end of the first and during the second century AD. Under Augustus there may have been only a single species of token, valid for one occasion only. At one time Augustus had in mind altering the frequency of distributions:

> He revised the lists of the people district by district, and to prevent the commons from being called away from their occupations too often because of the distributions of grain, he determined to give out tickets for four months' supply three times a year; but at their urgent request he allowed a return to the old custom of receiving a share every month. (Suetonius, *Augustus* 40)

Thus each token was exchangeable for a quantity fixed by law: normally five *modii*, and 20 for the special tokens devised by Augustus. In exceptional circumstances, however, their value could be arbitrarily altered, as in AD 6:

> In times of scarcity too he often distributed grain to each man at a very low figure, sometimes for nothing, and he doubled the money tickets.[49] (Ibid. 41; cf. Dio 55.26.3)

This rudimentary system is evidence of the essentially public and civic character of the corn distributions. It is noteworthy that it exactly resembles the system of vote-casting at the *comitia;* as we shall see, after a certain date (the first century BC at the latest) the voter presented a special *tessera* and received in return a *tabella* which, like the five *modii,* was a mark of citizenship, a right and a privilege. From Augustus's time onwards the *plebs frumentaria* was only a part, and not the largest part, of the population of Rome: its official name was 'the urban plebs of the 35 tribes', i.e. Roman citizens (whichever their original tribe) legally domiciled in Rome. A citizen resident in the provinces and temporarily in Rome was excluded, however ancient his lineage. Freedmen only qualified if they had been formally placed on the register by their patron or by the authorities. The lists were carefully kept up to date, as documents of the republican period already show, and we have imperial inscriptions listing by name the members of each tribe who belonged to the *plebs frumentaria.*[50] It is clear that while the ration itself was always worth having, what was really valued was that it constituted a proof of freedom and citizenship, with the rights and privileges that these entailed. This was not very different from C. Gracchus's original purpose, in so far as his law benefited citizens only. As we have seen, his adversaries accused him of bankrupting the treasury and encouraging sloth; his own motives are perhaps expressed in Florus's dictum, 'What could be juster than that a people in want should be maintained from its own treasury?' (Florus, 2.1.3).

Gracchus, however, may have had other motives as well: in particular, that of preventing the supply of corn (as distinct from its distribution) from becoming a pretext for unscrupulous political manoeuvre. More than half a century before, 'bounties' in money or kind had been used to further electoral ambitions, e.g. by the former consul Manius Acilius Glabrio when he stood for the censorship (Livy 37.57.8). Gracchus, who wished to change the electoral system, may have hoped to reform the standards of public life by making the distribution of corn a state monopoly and placing it on a regular footing. His law in fact only provided for distribution on a modest scale and at a reasonable price, designed to regulate the market rather than to maintain the plebs in idleness. The five *modii* a month were scarcely more than the ration of an infantryman in the field: this, according to Polybius (6.39), was two-thirds of an Attic *medimnus,* i.e. 36 litres or about a bushel, while five *modii* are equal to 44 litres. One could hardly feed a family on this, and it is clear that the cheap or free corn distributed by the state was only a small part of what was consumed in Rome by all those not on the register, and even by the beneficiaries themselves. It is equally clear, as G. E. Rickman has recently shown,[51] that in addition to the corn delivered by way of tax from Sicily, and in Augustus's time from Egypt and Africa, which was chiefly used for official distributions, there were private commercial exports which kept Italian centres regularly supplied. The Roman plebs were not regularly 'fed' by 'free' corn provided from taxation or private bounty. In normal times the distribution merely helped to sustain the free market; in lean years it ensured the bare subsistence of the most privileged and turbulent part of the Roman population, the only part which counted politically.

What is true of the Empire was already true at the end of the Republic, as is shown clearly by the situation in 58-57. Clodius radically altered the nature of the *frumentationes* by proposing to make them entirely free of charge, undoubtedly as a means of ensuring his own popularity; but he underestimated the economic consequences. Despite the general delegation of authority to Sextus Clodius as regards corn obtained by taxation and requisition and also that in private hands, the supervision of granaries, tax-collectors etc. (*De Domo* 25), the supply situation in 58-57 grew steadily worse. Cicero, in an ambiguous passage, hints that this had something to do with speculation by producers and dealers:

> What more justifying occasion could there have been than a famine, than faction, than the projects of you [Clodius] and your adherents, who thought that now that an opportunity was offered to you of inflaming the minds of the ignorant mob, you might make the price of grain a pretext for renewing the robbery which spelt ruin for them? The reason for the famine was partly that the corn-growing provinces had no corn; partly that it had been exported to other countries, the demands of the dealers being, as we are asked to believe, extortionate; partly that it was being kept stored in custody, in order that its alleviating effect in the actual throes of famine might be more gratifying. (*De Domo* 10-11)

Clodius and his friends, in any case, sought to turn the situation to political advantage:

> The oppressive prices of grain and the great scarcity of provisions, which made men apprehensive not merely of a long period of dearness, but of absolute famine, are denied by none. That this was the pretext for pursuing his incendiarism, murder, and rapine which that enemy of peace and tranquillity was ready to grasp at, I would not have you, gentlemen, even suspect, unless you shall see it with your own eyes. ... Seeing that it was with such men as L. Sergius and M. Lollius that, at a time of high prices, you were plotting a sudden onset upon the consuls, the senate, and the property and fortunes of the rich, alleging as a pretext the cause of the destitute and ignorant; seeing that tranquillity offered you no loophole of safety, and that you, with your desperate subordinates, had at your back armies of rascals whom you had already told off to their several functions, was it not the duty of the senate to take measures to prevent your laying the torch of ruin to all that fuel that stood ready to burst into the flames of civil strife?

The occasion, then, was such as to justify a new policy: consider now whether mine was not the rôle almost of a protagonist. In connexion with the incident of the stone-throwing, whose name was mentioned by your minion Sergius, or by Lollius, or by those other scourges? Who did they say should make himself responsible for the price of grain? Was it not myself? Again, was it not from me that your nocturnal troupe of partisans (personally coached by yourself) demanded corn? As if I forsooth, had been placed in charge of supplies, or had made a corner in wheat, or had any authority at all in that direction by any powers either of control or of jurisdiction. And yet, with his whole mind bent on slaughter, [Clodius] had proclaimed my name to his partisans, and openly hinted it to the ignorant mob. When a crowded senate, with his voice alone opposing, had passed in the temple of Jupiter Best and Greatest a decree for the restoration of my position, suddenly upon that very day the extreme dearness of corn gave way to an unexpected cheapness. Some asserted (and I agree with them) that the immortal gods had given a clear intimation of their approval of my restoration, while there were many who reasoned as follows: since all hope of peace and tranquillity lay in my return, whereas my departure had meant a daily apprehension of turmoil, it was the almost total vanishing of the fear of war which was responsible for the change in prices; and since on my return they had again become more oppressive, it was to me, whose arrival loyal citizens had constantly asserted would produce cheapness, that they appealed to influence them.

The upshot of the matter is that it was not merely your partisans who, acting on your suggestion, named me, but, after the defeat and scattering of your forces, it was the whole Roman people, who had gathered to the Capitol, who, since on that day I was in poor health, expressly demanded my presence in the senate. My arrival was eagerly anticipated; and after several speeches had been made I was called upon to speak. The policy which I proposed was one that was highly salutary to the state and most necessary for myself. I was asked to procure plentiful supplies of corn, and a decrease in its price; but whether I had any powers in the matter or not was never taken into account. I was besieged by the urgent complaints of patriots; but it was the sarcasms of the disloyal that I found hard to bear. I entrusted the settlement of the demand to a friend who was wealthier than myself, not from a desire to shelve the responsibility on to one who had deserved so well of me — rather would I have sunk beneath the burden myself — but because I saw that Gnaeus Pompeius, by his loyalty, wisdom, courage, influence, and, last but not least, his proverbial felicity, would realize with the greatest ease the hopes which we and all had reposed in him. (*De Domo* 12-16)

In the last resort it would seem that the interests of Clodius, Cicero and Pompey in this matter coincided, at least for the time being. Clodius wished to cast on to others the blame for the food scarcity which his law had helped to bring about; Cicero, to appear as the arbiter of Roman politics and even of the price of corn; and Pompey, as usual, to assert his own importance. None the less, it was he who probably lost most in the end. Although the powers conferred on him in 57 at Cicero's instance were far-reaching, they were less so than his friend the tribune C. Messius had advocated (*Ad Att.* 4.1.7), and, as we have seen, his task proved particularly arduous on account of the large numbers enfranchised as a result of Clodius's law. More than a year later, in April 56, Pompey had to be voted supplementary credits of 40 million sesterces (Cicero, *Ad Quintum fratrem* 2.5.1); these had to be found by making budgetary cuts and postponing the share-out of Campanian lands under the *Lex Julia* of 59, an expedient which did not suit either Caesar or Pompey. This is only one example of the fact that a policy of increasing grants came up against the shortage of public resources and involved sacrificing other measures, in this case an agrarian law that was mainly for the benefit of veteran soldiers.

Thus we find the same conflict of interest as was noted at the end of the chapter on military matters. During the civil disturbances that marked the last years of the Republic, the essential division was not between rich and poor but, within the large mass of *proletarii* or the proletarianized, between those who had chosen the profession of arms and meant to do as well out of it as possible, and the civilians, whether they were rich or not. The ordinary budget of the Roman state, which was not organized as such, was insufficient to provide simultaneously a decent rate of soldiers' pay, grants of land and money to veterans, and a free minimum ration of food to the 200,000 or 300,000 members of the *plebs frumentaria*. For a long time the circle could only be squared by foreign conquests that were no longer justified by the law of nations but only by the cupidity of the master race. It has recently been suggested that each of the principal corn laws—the *Lex Sempronia* of 123, the *Lex Terentia Cassia* of 73 and the *Lex Claudia* of 58—was financed by fresh revenues from provinces which it was decided to exploit, organize or conquer for that express purpose: Asia in 123, Cyrenaica in 75 and Cyprus in 58.[52] In other words, the Roman plebs could only feed themselves by plundering the world. We have seen that the civil wars may be considered from one point of view as a war of rapine directed inwards instead of outwards: what could no longer be extorted from foreigners was to be obtained by proscribing one's fellow-citizens and confiscating their property for the benefit of conquerors and ex-soldiers. As far as the corn distributions are concerned, we do not hear of confiscations for the purpose of maintaining them, but matters developed similarly in the end. The distributions depended on the benevolence of a supreme ruler who, apart from the regular funds in the *aerarium*, periodically dipped into his private purse (filled essentially by the proceeds of civil war) to support an urban plebs whose obedience and contentment had to be secured at all costs. The novel dependence of the Republic on a single man who had made himself the richest in the world by conquering and despoiling his fellow-citizens is admirably shown by Augustus's complacent enumeration, incomplete though it is, of his personal donations to the Roman people:[53]

To each member of the Roman plebs I paid under my father's will 300 sesterces, and in my own name I gave them 400 each from the booty of war in my fifth consulship, and once again in my tenth consulship I paid out 400 sesterces as a largess to each man from my own patrimony, and in my eleventh consulship I bought grain with my own money and distributed 12 rations apiece, and in the twelfth year of my tribunician power I gave every man 400 sesterces for the third time. Those largesses of mine never reached fewer than 250,000 persons. In the eighteenth year of my tribunician power and my twelfth consulship I gave 240 sesterces apiece to 320,000 members of the urban plebs. In my fifth consulship I gave 1,000 sesterces out of booty to every one of the colonists drawn from my soldiers; about 120,000 men in the colonies received this largess at the time of my triumph. In my thirteenth consulship I gave 60 denarii apiece to the plebs who were then in receipt of public grain; they comprised a few more than 200,000 persons.

Lands and grants to veterans

I paid cash to the towns for the lands that I assigned to soldiers in my fourth consulship, and later in the consulship of Marcus Crassus and Gnaeus Lentulus. The sum amounted to about 600,000,000 sesterces paid for lands in Italy, and about 260,000,000 disbursed for provincial lands. Of all those who founded military colonies in Italy or the provinces I was the first and only one to have done this in the recollection of my contemporaries. Later, in the consulships of Tiberius Nero and Gnaeus Piso, of Gaius Antistius and Decimus Laelius, of Gaius Calbisius and Lucius Pasienus, of Lucius Lentulus and Marcus Messalla and of Lucius Caninius and Quintus Fabricius I paid monetary rewards to soldiers whom I settled in their home towns after completion of their service, and on this account I expended about 400,000,000 sesterces.

Aid to the public treasury; the military treasury

Four times I assisted the treasury with my own money, so that I transferred to the administrators of the treasury 150,000,000 sesterces. In the consulship of Marcus Lepidus and Lucius Arruntius, when the military treasury was founded by my advice for the purpose of paying rewards to soldiers who had served for 20 years or more, I transferred to it from my own patrimony 170,000,000 sesterces.

Personal gifts in the absence of treasury funds

From the consulship of Gnaeus and Publius Lentulus onwards, whenever the taxes did not suffice, I made distributions of grain and money from my own granary and patrimony, sometimes to 100,000 persons, sometimes to many more. (Augustus, *Res Gestae*, 15-18; tr. P. A. Brunt)

CHAPTER VII

COMITIA
The citizen and politics

As ALREADY POINTED OUT, it is not the object of this book to give a description
or history of Roman public law. As in the case of military and fiscal obligations,
we are concerned in this chapter to investigate how far citizens were able in
practice to exercise their political responsibilities in the strict sense in accordance
with their social status, and how far they actually did so.[1] There are two errors
to be guarded against here. The first is that of taking a purely legal view; this is
particularly dangerous where public law is concerned, especially in Rome.
Both ancient and modern jurists, in their anxiety to present the juridical 'system'
of the Roman 'constitution' in all its rigorous coherence, are sometimes led to
depart quite consciously from the known facts of history. To give only one
example: taking a logical view of the law of magistracies, which was the mainstay
of Roman public law, the various magistracies endowed with the *imperium*
come to be considered as autonomous, self-sufficient realities, deriving their
powers and legitimacy from a long line of investitures which went back to the
original monarchy, and conducting their relations with the people as one power
vis à vis another.[2] This interpretation is sometimes offered by jurists to account
for certain vestiges of legal custom that survived into the fully historical period.
No doubt it is necessary to point out this underlying juridical aspect of the
Roman magistracy, which perhaps goes back to its origins, in order to understand
its early history. But clearly such principles no longer correspond to reality at
the period we are concerned with, when the relationship between the magistrates
and the people was quite different. Thus one cannot be guided merely by
principles and the letter of the law. But there is also an opposite risk to be
avoided. Although the Roman people did not have much power from the
strictly juridical viewpoint, some contemporary documents might lead one to
suppose that it was all-powerful.[3] These, as would be expected, are speeches
addressed to the people itself for interested motives, and are often the only
surviving evidence on a particular issue. For obvious reasons such speeches
often magnify the citizens' role and their actual influence; they openly flatter
one social category or another, or paint an ideal, wish-fulfilling picture of
Roman political life. No speaker who wishes to get agreement or force a decision

will admit to his audience that their decisions are not really free or that their powers are limited. Consequently there is a twofold obstacle to our understanding the inner history of decision-taking by the official organs of the Roman state. On the one hand, institutions with their usual rigidity perpetuate legal fictions that may at times act as a brake or a smoke-screen; on the other, speeches, slogans and propaganda, illusions and pious hopes, tend to give an equally misleading impression of voluntarism and popular sovereignty.

At the same time, one clearly cannot outline the history of the Roman citizen's participation in political life without first recalling its institutional framework. In the first place, while institutions are the product of a certain type of political society, they also in turn give a character to that society: opinions take a different shape, for instance, according to whether voting is individual or by 'estates'. Secondly, it is generally when institutions are challenged and transformed, whether gradually or by violence, that we are able to judge how far citizens were really masters of their own destiny, and how the system of power-sharing appeared to them and to their leaders.

The people's role in a 'mixed constitution'

The earliest systematic account of the Roman 'constitution' that has come down to us, and doubtless the first ever attempted, is that by the Greek historian Polybius, which dates from about 150-140 BC but purports to describe the position at the time of the Second Punic War and at the beginning of the second century BC. This text, most of which is preserved in what remains of Book Six of Polybius's *Histories*, is of prime importance to us and was of the greatest interest to the Romans themselves: it was their first introduction to the methods of Greek political thought, of which Polybius was in a sense the heir. A historian and philosopher with a sound knowledge of the art of rhetoric, he analysed Roman institutions in terms of schemes which were equally foreign to the Romans' historical fictions and to their juridical formalism. For this reason his account was a great success with the Roman public, although written in Greek and probably intended for Greeks. It was drawn upon to a great extent, a century later, by Cicero, the first and most considerable of Roman political philosophers, who set out to provide Latin literature with works that would stand comparison with Plato, Aristotle or Isocrates: the *De Republica* in 54 BC and the *De Legibus* and *De Oratore* in 51. Thus Polybius's priority is not only chronological but theoretical and practical as well.[4]

From the point of view we are concerned with, Polybius's analysis is clear: he considered the Roman constitution to be an example, perhaps the best, of what he calls 'composite constitutions', corresponding more or less to what Plato, Aristotle and later Greek philosophers called 'mixed constitutions'.[5] The term is an ambiguous one, partly because different authors define the various kinds of constitution, including mixed ones, in different ways, and partly because two different types of concept are involved. On the one hand are properly juridical considerations concerning the relative competence and interrelation of the city's various 'organs'; on the other, especially in Aristotle, such economic and social factors as the relative importance of the rich, poor and middle classes, the composition of the citizen body—more or less open, according to the part played by wealth and heredity—and the ease or difficulty of access to public office according to the same criteria. The Greek philosophers, moreover, took other aspects into account as well, for instance the manner in which rulers were selected. The only really democratic method, according to them, was by drawing lots, with the least possible restriction on grounds of wealth; election was universally considered to be an 'oligarchic' or 'aristocratic' device, according to whether it was based on wealth or on real or supposed merit.

In Polybius's time political science had a history of two hundred years behind it and had greatly elaborated on these classifications and distinctions. His own description of the Roman constitution as 'mixed' is based on yet another viewpoint, however, being deliberately pragmatic and not juridical. He distinguishes in the Roman city three 'parties' or organs—the magistrates with the two consuls at their head, the Senate and the people—each of which has it own 'share' of responsibility, or powers as we should say. To outward appearances, he says, and according to one's point of view, the Roman constitution might seem to be either monarchical (in view of the consuls' powers), aristocratic (in view of the Senate's role and influence) or democratic (on account of the authority enjoyed by the people). Naturally all these aspects must be considered at once, and that is why the constitution is 'composite'. But that is not all: these three organs, independently of their respective spheres of authority, need one another and come into conflict for reasons that are sometimes not institutional but social or psychological. Thus there is, in law or in fact, a whole system of checks and balances, compromises and concessions, which, in practice at least, make for a reasonably stable and coherent system.

The great merit of this analysis, as can be seen, is that it invokes constitutional law, history and what we may call political science to outline a system, perhaps even a 'structure', in which the relative position and value of the various elements can be discerned. It is not a question of what the Senate, magistrates and people are legally entitled to do, but of what they can do and what they do in practice. Sometimes the observable facts are quite different from what is supposed to happen. Some may regard this as nonsense from the juridical point of view, and certainly Polybius seems at times to have failed to understand the origin or true nature of this or that procedure; but in general he gives an illuminating interpretation of the essential realities of Roman politics.

Beginning with the consuls' powers, Polybius remarks that if they were considered in isolation 'one may reasonably pronounce the constitution to be a pure monarchy or kingship' (6.12); he then proceeds to the Senate, and says that 'to one residing in Rome during the absence of the consuls, the constitution appears to be entirely aristocratic.' Then he speaks of the people's role:

> After this we are naturally inclined to ask what part in the constitution is left for the people, considering that the Senate controls all the particular matters I mentioned, and, what is most important, manages all matters of revenue and expenditure, and considering that the consuls again have uncontrolled authority as regards armaments and operations in the field. But nevertheless there is a part, and a very important part, left for the people. For it is the people which alone has the right to confer honours and inflict punishment, the only bonds by which kingdoms and states and human society in general are held together. For where the distinction between these is overlooked, or is observed but ill applied, no affairs can be properly administered. How indeed is this possible when good and evil men are held in equal estimation? It is by the people, then, in many cases that offences punishable by a fine are tried when the accused have held the highest office; and they are the only court which may try on capital charges. As regards these the Romans have a practice which is praiseworthy and should be mentioned. Their usage allows those on trial for their lives, when found guilty, liberty to depart openly, thus inflicting voluntary exile on themselves, if even only one of the tribes that pronounce the verdict has not yet voted. Such exiles enjoy safety in the territories of Naples, Praeneste, Tibur, and other *civitates foederatae*.
>
> Again it is the people who bestow office on the deserving, the noblest reward of virtue in a state; the people have the power of approving or rejecting laws, and, what is most important of all, they deliberate on the question of war and peace. Further in the case of alliances, terms of peace, and treaties, it is the people who ratify all these or the reverse. Thus here again one might plausibly say that the people's share in the government is the greatest, and that the constitution is a democratic one. (6.14)

But, as we have seen, it is not enough to study the positive attributions of the various organs, whether in public law, criminal law or ordinary practice, without also considering their relations of mutual opposition or dependence. Thus it appears, first of all, that the consuls depend on the Senate and on the people:

> The consul...in fact requires the support of the people and the senate, and is not able to bring his operations to a conclusion without them. For it is obvious that the legions require constant supplies, and without the consent of the Senate, neither corn, clothing, nor pay can be provided; so that the commander's plans come to nothing, if the Senate chooses to be deliberately negligent and obstructive. It also depends on the Senate whether or not a

general can carry out completely his conceptions and designs, since it has the right of either superseding him when his year's term of office has expired or of retaining him in command. Again, it is in its power to celebrate with pomp and to magnify the successes of a general or on the other hand to obscure and belittle them. ...As for the people, it is indispensable for the consuls to conciliate them, however far away from home they may be; for, as I said, it is the people which ratifies or annuls terms of peace and treaties, and what is most important, on laying down office the consuls are obliged to account for their actions to the people. So that in no way is it safe for the consuls to neglect keeping in favour with both the Senate and the people. (6.15)

Next we see how the Senate, wide though its powers are, depends on the mass of the people:

The Senate again, which possesses such great power, is obliged in the first place to pay attention to the commons in public affairs and respect the wishes of the people, and it cannot carry out inquiries into the most grave and important offences against the state, punishable with death, and their correction, unless the *senatus consultum* is confirmed by the people. The same is the case in matters which directly affect the Senate itself. For if anyone introduces a law meant to deprive the Senate of some of its traditional authority, or to abolish the precedence and other distinctions of the senators or even to curtail their private fortunes, it is the people alone who has the power of passing or rejecting any such measure. And what is most important is that if a single one of the tribunes interposes, the Senate is unable to decide finally about any matter, and cannot even meet and hold sittings; and here it is to be observed that the tribunes are always obliged to act as the people decree and to pay every attention to their wishes. Therefore for all these reasons the Senate is afraid of the masses and must pay due attention to the popular will. (6.16)

Finally, the people in its turn depends on the Senate and the consuls:

Similarly, again, the people must be submissive to the Senate and respect its members both in public and in private. Through the whole of Italy a vast number of contracts, which it would not be easy to enumerate, are given out by the censors for the construction and repair of public buildings, and besides this there are many things which are farmed, such as navigable rivers, harbours, gardens, mines, lands, in fact everything that forms part of the Roman dominion. Now all these matters are undertaken by the people, and one may almost say that everyone is interested in these contracts and the work they involve. For certain people are the actual purchasers of the contracts from the censors, others are the partners of these first mentioned, others stand surety for them, others pledge their own fortunes to the state for this purpose. Now in all these matters the Senate is supreme. It can grant extension of time; it can relieve the contractor if any accident occurs; and if the work proves to be absolutely impossible to carry out it can liberate him from his contract. There are in fact many ways in which the Senate can either benefit or injure those who manage public property, as all these matters are referred to it. What is even more important is that the judges in most civil trials, whether public or private, are appointed from its members, where the action involves large interests. So that all citizens, being at the mercy of the Senate, and looking forward with alarm to the uncertainty of litigation, are very chary of obstructing or resisting its decisions. Similarly everyone is reluctant to oppose the projects of the consuls, as all are generally and individually under their authority when in the field. (6.17)[6]

As will be seen, this scrupulous analysis combines elements of what are in principle quite different orders of ideas. The people's financial 'dependence' on the Senate, for instance is not only due to the fact that the Senate controls the ordinary and extraordinary budget, votes the credits allotted to magistrates and decides upon taxes; it is also due to the fact that citizens who enter into public contracts with the state — although these contracts have come within the authority of the censors, who are responsible for them on the state's behalf — still depend in practice on the Senate, which exercises a kind of supervision over the way the contracts are executed and could, at least after 184 BC, have them cancelled or amended. Moreover, legal disputes arising out of such matters are judged by senators appointed for the purpose (*recuperatores*). This *a posteriori* control exercised by the Senate over public contracts and the acceptance of tenders is a relatively recent constitutional practice with no juridical foundation other than the Senate's 'authority'. As to the recruitment of judges (for disputes not involving public law), this is not a constitutional problem but, let us say, a sociological reality. But it does not matter that the arguments are hybrid: from an empirical point of view Polybius's diagnosis is admirable. One thing, however, is missing, for understandable reasons: he does not say a word about the sociological composition of the citizen body, or trouble to explain to his Greek readers the classification of the *populus* on a property basis. He mentions the election of magistrates (placing it, from his point of view, on the same footing as 'punitive' judgements) without specifying who votes and in what way. His readers would not in fact have been misled by this. The great majority of Greek constitutions in Polybius's day were timocratic: as a rule only the rich and noble could belong to the civic body or at any rate hold high office. When Polybius speaks of the Roman 'people' or 'citizens', he is thinking naturally of the rich: those who serve in the army, who can tender for public contracts etc., and from his point of view there is no need to spell this out.

It is not my purpose to study the historical evolution which led to the Roman people exercising the powers described in Polybius's account. Since the early history of Rome has been, with no small difficulty, purged of anachronisms, we know that the people did not always elect the magistrates and that its decisions were not always sovereign, as for a long time they had to be ratified by a subsequent resolution of the Senate. We shall see, on the other hand, that by the end of the second and during the first century BC the people's sphere of direct action was considerably enlarged, while the actual forms of its participation also underwent changes.

Rome, like any other city, had its assemblies, which in principle represented the only way in which the people, i.e. the community as a whole, could be involved in politics, deliberating and taking decisions. The Romans' reconstruction of their own origins seems, it is true, to present on an equal footing two independent realities, the king and the people, whose mutual consent was the only way in which the city's sovereign will could find expression. This is doubtless a fictitious picture, but one which represents the initial independence of the Roman magistracy and perhaps its sacral origins.[7] This conception is reflected in the legend according to which the city's founder, Romulus, derived his title of *rex* from his divine descent. The *rex* did not embody the city in his own person, since he could not act alone on its behalf; and consequently the legend attributes to Romulus — but only after the city had come into being — the creation of the Senate and the acknowledging of certain popular rights. The curious passage in which Dionysius describes the 'constitution of Romulus' may therefore not be wholly false or anachronistic, despite the Caesarian or Augustan overtones that some have detected in it:[8]

To the populace he granted these three privileges: to choose magistrates, to ratify laws, and to decide concerning war whenever the king left the decision to them; yet even in these matters their authority was not unrestricted, since the concurrence of the Senate was necessary to give effect to their decisions. The people did not give their votes all at the same time, but were summoned to meet by *curiae*...(Dionys. 2.14.3)

Such were the difficulties that the Romans encountered when they tried to explain the historical development of their institutions. Unlike Polybius, they saw it as a convergence of elements which, at the outset, had been radically different. However, when in the last century of the Republic Cicero set about analysing the foundations of the City from a consciously philosophical point of view, it is interesting that he took the basic element of communal life to be the *consilium*, i.e. rational debate and decision-taking. From this point of view he described the different types of constitution as follows:

A people is not any collection of human beings brought together in any sort of way, but an assemblage of people in large numbers associated in an agreement with respect to justice and a partnership for the common good. The first cause of such an association is not so much the weakness of the individual as a certain social spirit which nature has implanted in man. (*De Republica* 1.39)

Every people, which is such a gathering of large numbers as I have described, every city, which is an orderly settlement of a people, every commonwealth, which, as I said, is 'the property of a people', must be governed by some deliberative body if it is to be permanent. And this deliberative body must, in the first place, always owe its beginning to the same cause as that which produced the State itself. In the second place, this function must either be granted to one man, or to certain selected citizens, or must be assumed by the whole body of citizens. (Ibid., 1.41-2)

It is true that in the last century of the Republic the *consilium*, i.e. the community's will and power of action, was more within the people's control than at any other time in Roman history: in modern terms, we may say that the sovereignty of the people was that much more clearly affirmed. But this is a piece of political language which does not take account of the juridical substratum. The people as such does not represent the whole state, which may equally be represented by a magistrate exercising his ordinary powers. For example, a magistrate can, as far as the law permits, alienate part of the public domain. But there are very many cases in which an act by a magistrate cannot commit the state unless he associates with it, as if by a real contract, the totality of citizens who make up the *populus*. The election of magistrates depended increasingly on the people, and the idea of exclusive popular sovereignty began to be dimly perceived. But Roman thought never overcame certain restrictions inherent in the fundamental conception of which matters were 'public', i.e. fell within the people's real capacity for action. The first of these was that the people could not act alone. Even if its will, once expressed, was paramount, it was still necessary for an outside agent to bring about the expression of that will, first by calling an assembly and then by inviting the people, as by a kind of contract, to join in what, as Mommsen says, must in the last resort be a bilateral act, whether a law, a judgement or an election; we shall see in due course how this was done. Next, as the people could only act by being party to a contract, the contractors must themselves be present: the modern idea of political representation[9] was unthinkable in the Roman context. Finally, the 'contract' which expressed the people's will concurrently with that of the magistrate who proposed a course of action had to be effected in accordance with necessary forms and procedures. In other words there was a code of 'comitial' law, of rules for the holding of assemblies; the most ancient of these no doubt belonged to the realm of custom, or at least were not laid down in formal acts that are still extant, but the more recent were actual statutes. Clearly these procedures will be of particular interest to us, as they largely determined the way in which political rights were exercised in practice.

Thus the Roman people, the citizenry as a whole, had an existence of its own independent of that of its constituent parts; but that existence was, so to speak, virtual, or similar to the position of a minor represented by a turstee or guardian. A magistrate or even a private individual (as was seen during the years of revolution in the first century BC) could always claim to be deliberating or acting in the interest of the *res publica* of the Roman people; but in that case the people itself is not acting, formulating a policy or giving orders. If, on the other hand, it is brought into action by an official body, then its potential and virtual character turns into active reality. Instead of an abstraction it becomes a concrete reality with a name, form and temporal location of its own: the assemblies of the Roman people. These regular assemblies, the juridical capacity of which has just been described, are invariably designated by the neuter plural *comitia*; it is noteworthy that the formularies contain an old verb *comitiare*, used almost exclusively of the king and signifying 'to convoke the assembly'. If it was deemed necessary or desirable for the people to participate in an act in the full juridical sense, this could only be done by summoning *comitia*. Other popular assemblies indeed existed, under the names of *contiones* and *concilia*; but the first were preliminary assemblies at which no decisions were taken, and in the fifth century the term *concilium* denoted an assembly of the plebs and not the patricians, i.e. only part of the *populus,* so that it could not speak for the whole people or compete with the *comitia* in any way. The *comitia*, as we have seen, only existed in so far as they were summoned by a magistrate. But not all magistrates had the same rights *vis à vis* the people. The nature of their powers varied, and some were not entitled to summon an assembly or, as the phrase went, 'treat with the people' (*agere cum populo*), i.e. propose courses of joint action to it.

This is not all. As we saw earlier, while the citizen possessed full juridical capacity, he did not necessarily enjoy a plenitude of political rights. In other words, the *civitas* was not merely the sum of a number of individuals with equal rights but consisted, properly speaking, of intermediate groups which had to express themselves severally to constitute an expression of the people's will. The *populus* consisted of an indefinite number of *cives* (citizens) but a very precise number of subdivisions, viz. the curiae, centuries and tribes. By the end of the Republic a citizen had to belong to at least two of these formations; in the earliest days all citizens belonged to curiae as well, but that was no longer true in our period. This elaborate classification, as we have seen, was a reflection of different viewpoints. The tribe was originally a territorial grouping: it retained its topographical associations until the end, even though it became hereditary to some extent and, in the case of freedmen, was determined by birth. It was unusual for a man to change his tribe, which was a permanent feature of his civil status and even his name: he was X, son of Y, of the Z tribe.

Membership of a century, on the other hand, was broadly determined by age and census rating, i.e. in part by wealth, and might vary in the course of a man's life. What concerns us at present, however, is that the expression of the people's will was not a mere matter of counting heads but depended, according to circumstances, on a majority in the curiae, the centuries or the tribes. This was the fundamental rule, and it is significant that Livy, for instance, uses expressions like 'the centuries appointed So-and-So', or 'the tribes adopted or rejected the proposed law', as synonymous with 'the people appointed' etc.

At first sight this is very different to what seems to have been the practice in most Greek cities of the classical or Hellenistic period. So, at least, Cicero maintained, for rhetorical purposes it is true, when defending Flaccus in 59 BC; disparaging the way in which Greek cities in Asia took decisions, he declared that:

> Those fine resolutions...are not based upon considered votes or affidavits nor safeguarded by an oath, but produced by a show of hands and the undisciplined shouting of an inflamed mob.
>
> Oh, if only we could maintain the fine tradition and discipline that we have inherited from our ancestors!...Those wisest and most upright of men did not want power to reside in the public meetings. As for what the commons might approve or the people might order, when the meeting had been dismissed and the people distributed in their divisions by centuries and tribes into ranks, classes and age groups, when the proposers of the measure had been heard, when its text had been published well in advance and understood, then and only then did they wish the people to give their orders or their prohibitions. In Greece, on the other hand, all public business is conducted by the irresponsibility of a public meeting sitting down. And so ...that Greece of ancient times...fell through this single evil, the excessive liberty and licence of its meetings. When untried men, totally inexperienced and ignorant, had taken their seats in the theatre, then they would decide on harmful wars, put troublemakers in charge of public affairs and expel from the city the citizens who had served it best. (*Pro Flacco* 15-16)[10]

The contrast, in fact, is over-simplified. In the first place, when opposing 'Greece' to Rome one is too apt to think only of Athens, ignoring the great variety of different constitutions in Greek cities. In oligarchies, of which there were many, the whole *politeia*, and in particular membership of the civic body and elegibility for high office, was regulated on a property basis (*timema*). Citizens were divided into classes by census ratings, if not within the electorate then at least as far as qualification for magistracies was concerned. Probably in some cities there were in fact electoral classes as in Rome. No example is known for certain, but when Plato in the *Laws* devises a detailed constitution for an imaginary city—a possible one, not a Utopia—he envisages a different voting system within the four classes, based on property, which are each to elect 90 councillors (*bouleutai*).[11] He may possibly have had in mind some actual Greek example here, for even at Athens the assembly did not always function on the 'one man, one vote' principle described by Cicero. Classes based on wealth were still in being in the fifth and fourth centuries, and still provided the qualification for elective magistracies, i.e. military commands and financial duties. Only the archons, the *bouleutai* and, of course, the jurymen (*heliastai*) were not subject to this qualification, and as regards the archons, according to Aristotle their exemption was rather a matter of turning a blind eye at the time of the *dokimasia*. But while the ordinary assemblies at the Pnyx, at which elections were held and decrees voted, were convoked irrespective of property qualifications or voters' origins, this was not the case when decisions were taken affecting the status of individuals: ostracism, indemnity (*adeia*), the adoption or expulsion of a citizen. In such matters the Athenians invariably voted in the more precise and limiting framework of the ten (later 12) tribes. The votes no doubt were reckoned as a whole, but they could only be cast within each tribe and in writing.

At the eighth prytany the people first decided, in the assembly, whether an ostracism should take place. If so, a round wooden enclosure was constructed on the Agora with ten passages through which the citizens, ordered in tribes, proceeded to deposit their *ostraka,* without showing the names they had written upon them. (Philochorus, 79 b Müller)

One object of this system was certainly to facilitate checking the identity of the voters, who were more numerous at these special assemblies (the quorum for which was 6,000) than at ordinary ones (2-3,000 on the average in fourth-century Athens). It must also not be forgotten that the election or casting of lots for appointment to Athenian magistracies took place on the basis of preliminary lists of candidates submitted by the tribes or demes (Attic municipalities); so that even in Athens, a democratic city *par excellence*, the people was less haphazardly organized than Cicero makes out. None the less, when it finally expressed its will, particularly in the form of decrees, it did so as a single body, the decision depending on a majority of the votes of individuals and not of constituent groups.

The Roman assemblies and their powers[12]

Despite the predominant part played by the Senate, at least until the second century BC, and the prestige of the higher magistracies, we have seen that the Roman people often intervened decisively in the city's destiny. One question which we shall try to answer in the following chapters is whether these interventions were a matter of real politics and not merely of juridical formalism, the people's presence being required for a public act to be fully valid. It is not enough to say that only the people was competent to say what the law should be: we must know what area was covered by the law, what part was played by popular initiative in introducing and discussing bills, and what means the other public powers—the Senate and magistrates—had at their disposal for opposing or circumventing a law. From the purely formal point of view, however, the people's activity in the Republican period was on a considerable scale. It was exercised in three main fields: the electoral, the legislative and the judicial. Since there were three types of assembly, each with powers of its own in one or more of these spheres, and each assembly differed in its procedures and purpose according to whether it was summoned by one magistrate or another, the electoral system was extremely complicated. The difficulty of understanding it is increased by the fact that it did not remain unchanged but was modified in law or in practice during, especially, the last two centuries of the Republic; moreover our sources are vague or deficient on some points, such as the role of the patricians in the *comitia tributa*. The only texts of electoral laws that we have are late ones of the imperial period: a municipal law from Malaca in Spain, dating from Flavian times, and a law of AD 5 on the creation of a special preliminary assembly for the election of praetors and consuls.

The oldest Roman assembly was certainly that of the curiae. According to tradition these 30 *co-viriae* (groups of fighting men) were subdivisions of the original three gentilitial or ethnic tribes. It is more than likely that the curiae were in some way linked with the *gentes*. Originally each citizen no doubt belonged to a curia, though this may not have been so at all subsequent times. In any case, by the end of the Republic most Romans were unable to name the curia they belonged to; this did not matter much, as from the third century onwards, if not before, each curia was represented by a lictor. In our period the *comitia curiata* met only for formal reasons, for religious purposes or legal matters affecting the *gentes:* e.g. the inauguration of certain priests, transfers of patricians to the plebs, or wills involving adoption. Caesar, for example, convoked this assembly in 59 BC, in his capacity as *pontifex maximus*, to transfer Clodius to the plebs by having him adopted by the plebeian P. Fonteius, a proceeding which Cicero challenged as illegal. Politically, the essential role of the *comitia curiata* was to vote the *Lex de imperio* of the *magistratus minores* and *majores* (except the censors). The origin and nature of this formality, which was required as late as 49 BC, are still a matter of debate. It may have been a political investiture which complemented the sacral investiture, but perhaps preceded it in the early days of the Republic. It has been pointed out that the powers of the magistracies were never expressly defined by a basic law,[13] but were defined in a *Lex curiata* each time a magistrate was elected or confirmed. At the end of the Republic this law still had to be passed: otherwise, Cicero says, the consuls could not 'have anything to do with military matters' (*attingere rem militarem*)

(*De Lege Agraria* 2.30). The ancients themselves were puzzled by these subtleties: they understood the legal effect of the formality, but not its origin. Cicero tried to invent one by imagining that the twofold investiture was a way of giving the people a chance to express second thoughts:

> Our ancestors willed that you should give your votes twice for the election of each magistrate. For when a law of the centuries was proposed for the censors, and a law of the curiae for the other patrician magistrates, a second decision was arrived at in regard to the same men, so that, if the people repented of the favour they had bestowed, they might have the power of taking it back. Now, Romans, while you have kept those as the chief *comitia,* the *centuriata* and *tributa,* the *comitia curiata* have been retained only for the sake of examining the auspices...So then let there be decemvirs appointed neither by the genuine *comitia,* that is by the votes of the people, nor by that *comitia* which, in form and to keep up the ancient practice, is imperfectly represented by the thirty lictors, for the purpose of taking the auspices. (*De Lege Agraria* 2.27 and 31)

Thus the *Lex curiata* no longer really concerned the people. The only two assemblies which were of importance throughout the later republican period were the *comitia centuriata* and the assemblies by tribes, viz. the *concilium plebis* and the *comitia tributa.* The *comitia centuriata* were assemblies of the whole people, patricians and plebeians, divided, as we have seen, into property-classes and voting units within the classes known as centuries. Traditionally they were attributed to the initiative of King Servius Tullius, about the middle of the fifth century BC. It is not impossible, though we cannot know for certain, that the division of citizens into groups on a property basis, which the Etruscans are known to have practised, was introduced in Rome in the form of the class-system during the period of the Etruscan kings. In any case, this classification had an obvious military purpose: the census classes were also classes of warriors whose equipment, and hence their role in battle, depended on their census rating. The military aspect is confirmed by the fact that each class was also divided into age-groups, the *juniores* from 17 to 45 and the *seniores* from 45 to 60(?). For army purposes we have here a division between regular forces and the reserve; the *seniores,* when called up, were used for garrison duties. It may be, as some ancient lexicographers and antiquarians suggest,[14] that men over 60 were at a certain point excluded from the roll of classes and centuries. The essentially military character of the centuries is also attested by the description of each class's equipment – which broadly corresponds, from the archaeological point of view, to the hoplitic type of infantry equipment used in Italy from the seventh century to the fifth and fourth – and by the fact that the five 'unarmed' centuries added to the 170 centuries of infantry included carpenters, blacksmiths and buglers who, in early times, had an obvious military role.

According to Roman tradition this classification of citizen-soldiers on a property basis provided, from the very outset, the framework of a political assembly. Livy, Dionysius and Cicero state that when Servius Tullius established the classes and centuries he decided to have them vote in hierarchical order on questions on which he might seek their advice. There is good reason to doubt this, for it is not at all certain that there was any popular assembly during the royal period. However, when the Republic was established — i.e. when the king was replaced by one or more collegia of magistrates who held office for one year, no doubt by election — such an assembly must have played an increasingly important part. It was probably at this time that the comitial aspect of the Servian system was superimposed on its military aspect by virtue of the principle observed in all cities whereby, as we have seen, benefits and disadvantages were shared among the members of a given civic body on the basis of 'geometrical equality'.

Once the classes and centuries had become the framework within which citizens expressed the will of the 'people', there had to be room in them for non-combatants also. From then on, no doubt, the centuriate system gradually ceased to be an exact representation of the army in the field and became merely a framework for the call-up (*dilectus*) or the assessment of the *tributum*, as we have already seen. Henceforth each century had to supply a certain number of men in the event of mobilization. The number of its actual members was no longer of importance: it might be much more or much less than a hundred according to circumstances. The size of the centuries naturally varied according to the census class — there were fewer citizens in a century of the first class than in one of the fifth — and it might also vary from one census to another. Hence it is pointless, in my opinion, to try to discover any mathematical ratio between the numbers of centuries provided by the Servian system and those of the Roman army, which are very imperfectly known to us, at any particular stage of its history. It is clear, on the other hand, that the system as described by our two principal sources, Livy and Dionysius (see below) is itself the result of a long evolution. For instance, there certainly was a time when all the citizens wealthy enough to be called up comprised only one class and not five; the *proletarii* were then designated by the expression *infra classem*. On the other hand, the figures of property qualifications on which Livy and Dionysius are agreed (as well as Cicero, save for a minor variation), are expressed in *asses* (or drachmai in the case of Dionysius), which can only be *asses sextantarii*, worth one-tenth of a denarius, the new monetary unit which we now know to have been introduced no earlier than about 214 BC. This proves, at least, that the canonical version of the Servian system as our authors present it is subsequent to that monetary reform.

The system as described by Livy and Dionysius may be summed up in the following table.

Order of vote	*Juniores*	*Seniores*	*Total*
Equites (6 ancient centuries plus 12 new ones)			18
First class (rating of over 100,000 *asses*)	40	40	80
Second class (rating of over 75,000)	10	10	20
Third class (rating of over 50,000)	10	10	20
Fourth class (rating of over 25,000)	10	10	20
Fifth class (rating of over 11,000 (?12,500))	15	15	30
Plus 4 centuries of artisans and musicians voting with the first or second and the fourth class; plus 1 'unarmed' century of *capite censi* and *proletarii*			5
Total			193

Livy, Dionysius and Cicero present minor and unimportant variations as to the rating of the fifth class (which, as we have seen, was certainly lowered during the second century) and the question of where the artisans and musicians voted. But all three are quite definite as to the total of 193 centuries, so that the figure needed for a majority was 97, i.e. just over half. We shall revert to this when discussing the voting procedure. The whole matter would be relatively clear if it were not for certain texts which suggest that this 'original' system, in force in the fifth and fourth centuries, was considerably modified at a date which is hard to determine exactly but is generally thought to have been towards the end of the third century or, more probably, the beginning of the second. The changes, it appears, did not affect the total number of votes cast at the *comitia* but did affect the number assigned to each class, the relationship between the centuries and tribes, and especially the order of voting.[15] Livy and Dionysius, after describing the system set out above, go on to say, unfortunately in obscure language:

Nor ought it to cause any surprise that the present organization, which exists since the increase of the tribes to 35 [in 245 BC], and the doubling of their number in the matter of the junior and senior centuries, does not correspond with the total established by Servius Tullius. For, having divided the City according to its inhabited regions and hills into four parts, he named them 'tribes'...; but these tribes had nothing whatever to do with the distribution or the number of the centuries. (Livy 1.43.12-13)

This form of government was maintained by the Romans for many generations, but has been altered in our times and changed to a more democratic form. The change, forced by some urgent needs, was effected, not by abolishing the centuries, but by no longer observing the strict ancient manner of calling them to vote—a fact which I myself have noted, having often been present at the elections of their magistrates. (Dionys. 4.21.3)

Cicero's *De Republica*, in a lacunary passage which is not well established by the MSS (and which, from the dating of the imaginary dialogue, purports only to describe the position at the time of Scipio Aemilianus), gives a breakdown of the votes which seems, after the corrections of a learned medieval scribe, to imply that the first class no longer included 80 centuries but only 70. It is usually deduced from this that there were two centuries for each tribe, one of *juniores* and one of *seniores*. Hence an absolute majority would have to include not merely the first class (80 centuries under the old system) plus the 18 of *equites,* but also eight centuries of the second class:

> If this system were not well known to you, I should describe it, but you are already aware that the arrangement is such that the centuries of knights with their six votes, and the first class, with the addition of the century composed of the carpenters... make up a total of 89 centuries. Now if, out of a total of 104 centuries—for that is the number left—only eight centuries should vote with the 89, the whole power of the people would be exerted. And the remaining 96 centuries, which contain a large majority of the citizens, would neither be deprived of the suffrage, for that would be tyrannical, nor be given too much power, for that would be dangerous. (*De Republica* 2.39-40)

It is a pity that this text, which is clear enough in what it implies as regards the change in the number of centuries of the first class, and the noteworthy fact that the total was kept at 193, rests only on a medieval correction of the otherwise illegible text of the only MS of *De Republica.* None the less, we can accept this account of a minor 'reform' of the system, partly because the record of centuriate elections during the Second Punic War shows that there were in the first class a century of *juniores* and one of *seniores* of each tribe (i.e. 70 centuries?), and partly because we know that at the consular elections in 44 BC not only the first but also the second class was made to vote (there being apparently no votes against),[16] which implies that some second-class votes were necessary for a legal majority. This being so, and with the total number of centuries remaining at 193, one can only guess at the distribution of the centuries of the third, fourth and fifth classes. Taking as a basis the mathematical ratio of tribes to centuries in the first class (one century each of *juniores* and *seniores* per tribe = 70), scholars from the sixteenth century onwards have applied this summarily to all the classes and arrived at a figure of 350 centuries for the whole infantry.[17] This is not attested by any text, however; and so large a number of voting units would have made the electoral operation impossibly cumbersome. In the last century Mommsen conjectured that even if each class in each tribe continued to comprise two centuries from the census point of view, these units must have been grouped in some way or another at elections so as to make only 100 'voting' centuries. This astute hypothesis has been confirmed by the discovery in 1947 of an inscription (the *Tabula Hebana*) showing that certain centuries were thus grouped in accordance with an electoral law of Augustus's time; but we can only guess at the way in which operations were conducted in detail.

As to the exact date of the reform, opinions vary between the latter years of the third century (Q. Fabius Maximus's censorship in 220) and the early part of the second. Livy speaks of a change in the voting system in 179 which may well be identical with the reform: 'The censors changed the method of voting and constituted the tribes according to districts and to the classes and situations and occupations of the members' (or their age and wealth?) (40.51.9).

In any case, the centuriate assembly continued until the end of the Republic to be the most important in law by virtue of its composition and powers. In the first place it comprised the whole *populus,* patricians and plebeians alike: it was thus, as A. Magdelain has recently shown, the *comitiatus maximus* or 'sovereign assembly'.[18] This term appears in the Law of the Twelve Tables, but must be a third-century addition rather than part of the decemviral text dating from the fifth century BC. Cicero speaks of:

> Two excellent laws taken over from the Twelve Tables, one prohibiting laws of personal exception, and the other providing that cases in which the penalty is death or loss of citizenship must be tried before the greatest assembly. (*maximo comitiatu*) (*De Legibus* 3.44, quoting Table 9.1.2).

Cicero comments:

> Our ancestors... also desired that decisions affecting the fate of individuals should be made only in the *comitia centuriata;* for when the people are divided according to wealth, rank, and age, their decisions are wiser than when they meet without classification in the assembly of the tribes. (ibid.)

Thus, according to Cicero the *comitia centuriata* were really the most 'authoritative' (*justa: Post Reditum in Senatu* 27), not because they were the oldest or largest assembly but because they were, strictly speaking, sovereign. It was they who elected the higher magistrates: consuls, praetors and censors. (Jurists based this distinction of rank on the difference between the *auspicia majora* and *minora:* Aulus Gellius 13.15.4). For the purpose of such elections they were presided over by the consuls. They also had pre-eminent powers with regard to legislation: originally only they were competent to pass laws that were binding on the whole people, except for the sphere of private law. Only a higher magistrate, with the right to *agere cum populo,* could propose legislation to them. True, the number of centuriate laws steadily diminished after 286, when the *Lex Hortensia* gave legal status to plebiscites voted on the initiative of a tribune. But the legislative powers of the *comitia centuriata* remained intact, and until the end of the Republic bills were submitted to them from time to time when it was desired to give the resulting law a solemn and irrevocable character. The clearest case is that of Cicero's recall from exile, the proposal for which was put forward by the two consuls on the Senate's initiative, endorsed by all but three of the magistrates (including the tribunes) and submitted to the *comitia centuriata* so that 'the same centuries which had made me consul now expressed their approval of my consulship' (*Post Reditum in Senatu* 27). Finally, the *comitia centuriata* also had jurisdiction over capital crimes. This was seldom invoked after the end of the second century BC because the standing courts, representing an entirely different system of justice, dealt with most criminal cases. But the centuriate assembly continued, archaically and by way of exception, to try accusations of high treason (*perduellio*). Thus it was they who pronounced final judgement in 63 on C. Rabirius, who at a previous stage had been convicted by the *duumviri perduellionis,* Caesar and his cousin L. Julius; we know this because Caesar's accomplice Q. Metellus Celer at the last minute had the red flags hauled down from the Janiculum, which was customary when the centuriate assembly was in session (Dio 37.28). But this judicial procedure was very rare, and the role of the *comitia centuriata* was essentially an electoral one.

The comitia tributa *and the* concilium plebis

By the end of the Republic, as we shall see, the assembly which met most frequently and, while not the most prestigious, was of the greatest practical importance, was the *comitia tributa,* the tribal assembly. It elected the junior magistrates—quaestors, aediles and military tribunes—as well as the 'magistrates' of the plebs, especially the ten *tribuni plebis* who, especially from the Gracchi onwards, were of prime importance practically and constitutionally. It also elected most of the extraordinary magistrates such as agrarian triumvirs or decemvirs, who often had considerable influence on the City's affairs. Being the only assembly with which the tribunes could legally act, it was the proper forum for the discussion of laws of tribunicial origin, i.e. practically the whole of Roman legislation. The majority of popular trials were held before this assembly at the instance of tribunes or aediles, at least until permanent courts began to be established towards the end of the second century. Thanks to these various powers, which were even more important politically than constitutionally, the *comitia tributa* became the essential organ of popular sovereignty in Rome. It is all the more curious that we know so little of its origin and development. Whereas tradition, rightly or wrongly, assigns an exact date to the *comitia centuriata* and ascribes their foundation to one man's 'design', the *comitia tributa* make their appearance surreptitiously, as it were, in 471(?)[19] for the election of tribunes of the plebs, who are supposed till then to have been elected either by the curiae (which is highly improbable), by an informal assembly, or even, according to some, by the classes based on census ratings. The difficulty of tracing their origin lies in the fact that at the time of the struggle between the plebs and the patricians—i.e. until about the end of the fourth century or even the beginning of the third—there was also a purely plebeian assembly which was called unambiguously a *concilium* – i.e. an assembly that was not part of the state machine, as opposed to the *comitia*. The *concilium* met, on what basis we do not know, to elect the representatives of the plebs (tribunes and aediles) who were not yet properly integrated into the system of state officers, and to take decisions (*scita*) which concerned and were binding on the plebs only.

We do not clearly know what part was played at this time by the tribes, whose number periodically increased with the enlargement of the Roman state; in particular, it is uncertain whether, before Appius Claudius's reform at the end of the fourth century, all citizens belonged to a tribe, or only those who were landowners. At all events the patricians were automatically excluded from the *concilium* of the plebs; but Roman constitutional history down to the end of the fourth century is so obscure and cumbered with anachronisms that it is useless to probe into the question further. In any case the *Lex Hortensia* of 286 made decisions of the plebs binding on the whole people, so that from then on *plebiscita* and laws meant more or less the same thing.[20] The ancients themselves from the time of the Gracchi onwards ceased to have an exact idea of these juridical niceties dating from a shadowy past. We see this from the fact that when the unknown drafter of the agrarian law of 111 wished to refer to the agrarian bill proposed (no doubt to the *comitia tributa*) by C. Sempronius Gracchus in 123, to be on the safe side and avoid any procedural error he described it as 'the law or *plebiscitum* introduced by C. Sempronius, son of Tiberius, tribune of the plebs' (*Lex Agraria* 22).

In practice, by the end of the Republic the terms *concilium* and *comitia tributa* meant almost exactly the same thing. The former was a meeting of the 35 tribes presided over by a magistrate of the plebs, an aedile or tribune. It is not certain – we shall revert to this – that patricians (of whom there were very few left by the end of the Republic) were automatically excluded from it at this time; they were still ineligible for the plebeian magistracies, but that is another matter. The *comitia tributa* was an assembly, presided over by any magistrate, of the whole Roman people classified by tribes. It should be said at once that these distinctions of language were not always observed in practice. Many ancient authors refer to assemblies presided over by magistrates of the plebs as *comitia tributa* when, in strict law, they may have been simply *concilia plebis*. Legal formulae preserved the distinction between *populus* (people) and *plebs* (commons): in 210, for instance, the Senate

> decreed that, before leaving the city, the consul should ask the people whom they preferred to have named dictator...that if the consul should refuse, the praetor should ask the people; in case of his refusal also, the tribunes should bring the matter before the commons. (Livy 27.5.16)

And, in 51, a senatorial decree cited by Caelius to Cicero stated that: 'The present consuls, with praetors and the tribunes of the plebs, shall bring the matter before the people or the plebs.' (*Ad Fam.* 8.8.5)

Virtually the only real distinction between these assemblies was the question of what magistrate summoned and presided over them. Perhaps, too, there was a distinction in the religious rites that guaranteed their formal validity. Assemblies for the election of tribunes and aediles did not depend on the auspices, i.e. signs of Jupiter's approval or disapproval of the decisions to be taken; unlike the legislative assemblies, therefore, they could not be interrupted or prevented by the announcement of adverse omens (*obnuntiatio*) by which tribunes of the plebs might interfere with any assembly.

Such, in outline, were the composition and powers of the various kinds of assembly that played a regular part in Roman public life. As we shall see, they met in different places at different periods, in accordance with their functions and character. In the following pages we shall try to discover, as a matter of fact and not only of law, the degree to which the citizen took part in political life, and to follow step by step the operations which preceded and accompanied the actual voting. The table [see p. 228], borrowed from L. Ross Taylor (*Roman Voting Assemblies*, Ann Arbor, 1966), is a useful summary which will save frequent cross-reference.

Composition of the electorate

Unlike certain Greek oligarchies, where a clear distinction was drawn between the whole body of citizens (*politeia*) and the smaller number of those possessing 'political rights' (*politeuma*), at Rome in our period all citizens were endowed with full rights and particularly the suffrage. At Cyrene, for example, under the constitution probably granted by Ptolemy Soter towards the end of the fourth century, which is known from an inscription, the *politeuma* comprised only 10,000 citizens, those who were worth at least 2,000 drachmai (a fairly low sum).[21] At Rome, on the other hand, even the poorest citizens and, as we shall see, even the freedmen were electors, although their vote carried less weight than that of the rich because of the system of voting in groups, on a territorial or property basis. This equality of civil rights was a distinctive feature of the City's government, but it had not always been so. As we saw in Chapter I, until about the end of the third century or the beginning of the second there was a section of the population, namely resident aliens, who were citizens for military and fiscal purposes but did not possess a vote and were not eligible to public office. These were known as *cives sine suffragio* or *minuto jure*. No one was perturbed by their somewhat ambiguous legal status, but it disappeared early in the second century as the result of a gradual movement of integration. Thus in 188 BC a law was passed granting the inhabitants of Arpinum full citizenship and enrolling them in the *tribus Cornelia* (Livy 38.36.7-9). It is doubtless not accidental that around this time we hear of debates or polemics between Roman politicians about the connection between civil rights and voting rights. It seems to have become accepted that the vote could no longer be taken away from a citizen, even one of recent date such as a freedman.

About this time, then, we may consider that the legal electorate, i.e. those on the voting registers, coincided most closely with the whole body of citizens. This is probably why the Romans at this period ceased to grant citizenship freely to the Italian allies, as they could no longer do so in the form of *civitas sine suffragio*. The only question that arises henceforth is therefore that of the assignment of electors to different tribes or property groups, or the checking of the registers at election time. The question of how far citizens duly enrolled as electors actually took part or abstained, and in the latter case whether the cause lay in unsurmountable physical difficulties, is one we shall consider later when surveying the Roman system of assemblies as a whole. But the first question is that of how the electoral rolls were made up.

As we have seen, this problem essentially concerns two classes of citizens: on the one hand freedmen, on the other the Italian 'allies' who had become, or wished to become, fully-fledged citizens. When we study the workings of the *comitia tributa* we shall consider the somewhat different question of the assignment to rural tribes (*tribus rusticae*) of a large part of the urban plebs or the population in the second and first centuries BC.

The place of freedmen in the system of tribes and centuries was always a subject of argument and dissension in Rome.[22] As we saw on p. 85, it was regulated by the censors until the time when the people intervened directly in these matters by legislation. We know nothing of the real status of freedmen until about the end of the fourth century. According to tradition, in 312 the patrician censor Appius Claudius 'gave each citizen the right to be enrolled in whatever tribe he wished' (Diodorus 20.36.4); Plutarch alone states expressly that this included freedmen. Livy says only that Appius distributed the lowly (*humiles*) throughout the tribes, and that Q. Fabius, who succeeded him as censor in 304 together with P. Decius, 'in order that the elections might not be in the hands of the basest of the people, culled out all the market-place mob and cast them into four tribes, to which he gave the name of "urban".' (9.46.14). As L. Ross Taylor observes,[23] there would not be much point in this if all the freedmen in question were townsfolk; the political significance of the measure must have been that it related also to rural freedmen, i.e. clients of nobles or rich families who might have lived on the latter's estates or even acquired land themselves. In any case the number of manumissions increased again in the third century and apparently freedmen were once again found in rural tribes, as the censors of 234, 230, 225 or 220 relegated them once more to the four urban tribes (Livy, *Per.* 20). In the years after the Second Punic War the censors took alternating measures, particularly in 189 (under pressure of a law: Plutarch, *Flamininus* 18.1) and 179. It is hard to discern the exact scope of their action in 179, but it may have concerned the place of freedmen not only in the tribes but also in the centuries. In 169, at any rate, the censors found that

	Comitia Curiata	*Comitia Centuriata*, military organization	*Comitia Tributa*	*Concilium plebis*, often called *Comitia Tributa*
			Assemblies of the tribes, local divisions of Roman territory	
Voting units	30 *curiae*, 10 each from 3 ancient clan tribes, Tities, Ramnes, and Luceres	193 centuries: 18 of *equites*; 170 of *pedites*, classified after 241 within the 35 local tribes into centuries of 2 age groups and 5 classes based on property; 5 unarmed centuries	35 tribes, classified into 4 urban and 31 rural tribes	
Citizens in attendance	People not present; in late Republic each *curia* represented by a lictor	Open to all citizens	Open to all citizens	Open to plebeians; patricians excluded
Presiding officer	Consul or praetor or, for religious purposes, *pontifex maximus* (with auspices)	Consul or praetor or, before 201, dictator; if no consul was in office at the beginning of the year, an *interrex* for consular elections (with auspices)	Consul or praetor; sometimes for jurisdiction curule aedile (with auspices)	Tribune of the plebs; aedile of the plebs (without auspices)
Elections		Of consuls, praetors, censors	Of curule aediles, quaestors, lower officers, special commissioners	Of tribunes and aediles of the plebs and certain special commissioners
Rogationes (bills) a) Legislative	Passed *lex curiata*, confirming *imperium* of magistrates and power of lower officers; under *pontifex maximus* confirmed adoptions and certain wills	Once the chief law-making body of the state; rarely used after 218 except for declarations of war and confirmation of power of the censors. Passed law recalling Cicero from exile	Legislation of any type except that restricted to the *Comitia Centuriata*	The majority of the laws were proposed by the tribunes of the plebs; their measures, properly called *plebiscita*, had the validity of *leges* after 287 BC
b) Judicial (most functions transferred to public courts by late 2nd century)		On capital charges; limited after late second century (period of the Gracchi) mainly to charges of *perduellio*, ancient form of treason	For crimes against the state punishable by a fine	Frequent judgements under tribunes, especially before institution of the public courts
Meeting place	Comitium (Capitol)	Outside *pomerium*, nearly always Campus Martius	For elections, at least in the late Republic, Campus Martius For legislation and judgements, the Forum (originally the Comitium?) or the Area Capitolina; in one case the Circus Flaminius	

'freedmen had been distributed among the four city tribes except for those who had a son over five years old...and those who had an estate or estates in the country valued at over 30,000 sesterces' (i.e. the first and second property classes) (Livy 45.15.1). Livy's text is unfortunately mutilated, but apparently one of the censors wished to deprive freedmen of the vote in one way or another, perhaps by making them *aerarii;* but Claudius

said that it was impossible for a censor without a decree of the people to deprive any individual of his ballot, let alone a whole class. For if, said Claudius, the censor could remove a man from his tribe, which was exactly what ordering him to change his tribe meant, he could remove him from all 35 tribes, that is, deprive him of citizenship and status as a free man...This was argued between the two censors; finally they resorted to the following solution; they drew lots publicly in the Hall of Liberty for one of the four city tribes, to which they would consign all those who had been slaves. The lot of the Esquiline tribe was cast. (Ibid. 4-5)

This solution, it will be seen, was exactly similar to that adopted until 89 BC for the Latins, who, although not enrolled in any tribe, voted in one selected by lot at the time when the vote was taken. Cicero praises the censors' action in 169, saying that without it 'we should long ago have lost the constitution' (*rempublicam jamdiu nullam haberemus*) (*De Oratore* 1.38). But the tendency for freedmen to move into the rural tribes, whether of their own accord or thanks to certain politicians who looked to them for support, recurred again and again. It would seem that in 115 Aemilius Scaurus, the influential leader of a kind of 'third party', tried to secure a following in this way, and apparently he and his friends were the target of an ironic apostrophe quoted by Cicero:

'Hush! Silence! What is all this noise? Have you,
Who neither have a father nor a mother,
Such confidence? Away with all that pride!'

(*De Oratore* 2.257)

Debate on this question did not again arise until the period from 88 to 52 BC. P. Sulpicius Rufus in 88[24] and perhaps Cinna in 87 wished once more to permit freedmen to register in all the tribes, as the newly enfranchised Italians were being allowed to do. There is little doubt, however, that Sulla, while not daring to revoke the enfranchisement of the Italians or confine them to particular tribes, managed in 82 to curtail the rights of freedmen; this alone can explain that in 67 and 66 the tribunes C. Cornelius and C. Manilius attempted to revive P. Sulpicius's measure of 88. Cornelius proposed several interesting laws against the oligarchic clique which dominated the Senate: these dealt with such matters as electoral corruption, praetors' edicts, foreign loans and legal dispensations. His proposal concerning freedmen failed to gain acceptance but was reintroduced by Manilius on 29 December 66, a few days after he took office. It was passed, but quashed by the Senate on 1 January for non-observance of the *trinundinum,* and Manilius did not pursue it as he was more concerned with his law appointing Pompey to lead the army against Mithridates.[25] The plan, according to Dio, was to allow freedmen to vote in the tribe of whoever enfranchised them. It was probably once again revived in 63 by the eminent jurist Ser. Sulpicius Rufus, a candidate for the consulship of 62 and a friend but adversary of Cicero's, as part of a much broader electoral reform to which we shall return. Finally an attempt was made by the celebrated Clodius in his campaign for the praetorship in 52. According to Cicero the project was well advanced: 'Laws were being engraved at his house which were to make us over to our own slaves' (*Pro Milone* 87); Asconius comments: 'I.e. so that freedmen, who could only vote in the four urban tribes, should also be able to do so in the rural tribes which are reserved to the free-born.' Clodius already had a considerable following of freedmen in at least two of the urban tribes, the Palatina (*Pro Sestio* 114) and the Collina (*Pro Milone* 25). The matter was all the more urgent because of the many slaves who had been freed in consequence of the laws on grain distribution, especially that of Clodius in 58 which provided a free ration for every citizen in Rome:

> Some are freed in order that, when they have received the monthly allowance of corn given by the public or some other largesse distributed by the men in power to the poor among the citizens, they may bring it to those who granted them their freedom. (Dionys. 4.24.5)

Pompey, who was put in charge of the corn-supply in 57, attempted to regulate the distribution:

> Pompey encountered some delay in the distribution of the grain. For, since many slaves had been freed in anticipation of the event, he wished to take a census of them in order that the grain might be supplied with some order and system. (Dio 39.24.1)

Under Caesar and Augustus the question of freedmen in the *comitia* became less important in so far as the latter had less influence. However, two of the urban tribes, the Esquiline and the Suburran, retained a stigma of marked inferiority as late as Augustus's reign; the Colline and Palatine, on the other hand, were more highly regarded during this period, as they included some patrician demagogues like Clodius himself. Some communities outside Rome were attached to these two tribes, e.g. Ostia and Puteoli to the Palatine, while many new citizens from the provinces were assigned to the Colline as individuals.

Apart from freedmen, citizens for whom enrolment in the tribes presented numerous problems were the Italians, whether Latins or allies. As we have already seen, the Latins were not full citizens and were not individually registered in tribes, but they were not entirely deprived of the suffrage either. At voting time a tribe was chosen by lot, in which Latins present in Rome voted as well as its own members: this is shown by the episode of the trial of the publicans Postumius Pyrgensis and Pomponius Veientanus before the *comitia tributa* in 212:

The tribunes provided witnesses [at a preliminary *contio*] and cleared the people out of the enclosure, and the urn was brought so that they might determine by lot in which tribe the Latins should vote. (Livy 25.3.17)

This procedure is confirmed by the much later electoral law of the *municipium* of Malaca:

Every person holding the *comitia* in the said *municipium* for the election of duumvirs or aediles or quaestors shall out of the curiae [local equivalent of the Roman tribes] appoint one by lot, in which resident aliens, being Roman or Latin citizens, shall register their votes, and for such persons the registration of votes shall be in that curia. (c. 53)

This limited voting right, which might help to turn the scale if the vote was very close, was the reason why on various occasions steps were taken to remove resident or visiting Latins from Rome on voting day. According to Appian (1.23), C. Gracchus thought of enlisting their vote in favour of his proposals, which included full citizenship for Latins and voting rights for Italians; hence his adversaries violently opposed the Italians in the crisis of 122. The consul C. Fannius made a demagogic speech reminding the Romans that their privileges were threatened:

'If you give the city to the Latins, do you think you will have as much room as you have now at public meetings like this one, or at the games, or for your festivities? Don't you see that they will crowd you out?' (O.R.F.² p. 144)

Just before the vote was taken, the Senate ordered the consuls to give the following public notice, 'Nobody who does not possess the right of suffrage shall stay in the city or approach within forty stades of it [about five miles, the limit of the original *ager Romanus*] while voting is in progress concerning these laws.' (Appian, *B. Civ.* 1.23)

C. Gracchus was powerless to prevent the allies from being expelled by force under his very eyes (Plutarch, *C. Gracchus* 12).

We have already seen that the denial of the Italians' plea for full civil rights was the root cause of the fearful outbreak of revolt in the Social War of 91. In 95 the consuls L. Licinius Crassus and Q. Mucius Scaevola passed a law setting up a special court to try Italians who passed themselves off as citizens by getting their names on the roll illicitly at census time.[26] The tribune Livius Drusus defended the Italians' cause in 91 and once more put forward proposals for their enfranchisement, but when it became clear that he had failed in his purpose the Italians rebelled with the avowed object of setting up a non-Roman state, apparently of federal character, and a coalition to combat Roman hegemony. What their aims really were is a complicated question. Why were they so anxious to acquire Roman citizenship? No doubt many motives were at work, and they must have varied from one nation and social class to another. But the demand for voting rights occurs so often in accounts of their claims and of political conflicts after the war that it must have been very real, at least to the local aristocrats and oligarchs who hoped by this means to get into Roman politics and in time make their way into the senatorial and equestrian orders. Contrariwise, their last-ditch Roman opponents did not contest the grant of citizenship, which was never called in question after 89 BC, but only the Italians' voting rights and particularly their distribution among the tribes. When Sulla landed at Brundisium six years after the law was passed conferring citizenship on the Italians, it was on this point that the legal government negotiated with him:

> Sulla and Scipio...met between Cales and Teanum and came to an agreement upon the laws and conditions concerning the authority of the Senate, the suffrages of the people, and the right of citizenship. (Cicero, *Phil* 12.17)

The grant of citizenship had been confirmed by several successive and complementary laws between 90 and 88. The first and most important, the *Lex Julia,* which must date from the winter of 90-89, enfranchised the Latins and allies who had remained loyal to Rome or agreed to lay down their arms forthwith, provided their cities formally agreed (Velleius 2.16). There followed, probably in 89, the *Lex Plautia Papiria,* granting citizenship to all allies in Italy who were not resident in their original municipalities, on condition merely that they applied to the praetors within 60 days. Finally the *Lex Calpurnia* in 90 empowered generals to grant citizenship to auxiliary troops as a reward for good behaviour.

There remains the question of the application of these laws in practice and particularly the distribution of communities and individuals among the tribes. We cannot know exactly how they worked, but Appian and Velleius agree, if not on the details, at least on the fact that the Romans tried at the outset to restrict the Italians to a limited number of tribes, as they had done in the case of freedmen:

> The citizenship had been given to Italy with the proviso that the new citizens should be enrolled in only eight tribes, so that their power and numbers might not weaken the prestige of the older citizens, and that the beneficiaries might not have greater power than the benefactors. (Velleius 2.20.2)

How was this result to be achieved? The new voters might be registered in a limited number of existing tribes, or tribes might be created specially for them as used to be done before 245 BC. This seems to be indicated by a fragment of Sisenna's *Historiae* which says simply: 'Lucius Calpurnius Piso, following a degree of the Senate, created [?] two new tribes...' Appian appears to be more explicit, but unfortunately his text is not quite certain and is somewhat difficult to follow:

> The Romans did not enrol the new citizens in the 35 existing tribes, lest they should outvote the old ones in the elections, but selected by lot one tribe out of ten [rather than 'divided the Italians into ten groups'?] and created new ones in which they voted last. So it often happened that their vote was ineffective, since a majority was obtained from the 35 tribes that voted first. This fact was either not noticed by the Italians at the time or they were satisfied with what they had gained, but it was observed later and became the source of a new conflict. (Appian, *B. Civ.* 1.49)

It is generally supposed, in any case, that the upshot was to distribute the Italians among ten tribes only, which may have been created for the purpose. Curiously, however, we are nowhere told the names which must have been given to these new tribes even though the census operations were delayed by the Social War and civil wars and were never properly completed. Since, moreover, we know that there were never more than 35 tribes throughout the republican period, the idea that eight or ten new ones were created seems more than doubtful. As W. Seston first pointed out, Appian's phrase (*dekateuontes apephenan heteras*) must signify grammatically that the tribes, not the new citizens, were 'decimated', i.e. one out of every ten was chosen by lot. Was not this exactly the procedure, multiplied by ten as it were, that applied to the Latins' votes before the Social War; and may we not therefore suppose that the Romans selected one tribe in ten (e.g. the tenth, twentieth and thirtieth on the list), continuing for as long as the number of new voters made necessary, and thus created duplicate tribes in the same way as Clodius in 58 formed a 'new Collina'[27] composed of freedmen? In these tribes, whose voting power was perhaps doubled, the new citizens would vote last in order; or rather, the original 35 tribes would all vote first and then a vote would be taken of the new tribes, with old names, in which the new citizens were registered. Some such procedure must surely be imagined rather than a creation of new tribes *ex nihilo*, which could not have completely escaped our sources.

In any case, whatever the exact provisions of the law, in later years the new citizens were in fact distributed throughout the tribes. For example, when the Latin colonies were integrated they were enrolled in 16 tribes, apparently on a basis of geographical proximity or on demographic grounds: none were incorporated in very large tribes such as the Falerna or the Quirina. As to the allies, their final enrolment under the regime of Marius and Cinna in 87-85 was for the most part governed by politics: some whole peoples were assigned to a single tribe, which diminished their influence, while others, like the Etrurians, were distributed through several. These artful arrangements were related, as we shall see, to voting procedures in the *comitia tributa*. An influx of new citizens could profoundly alter the political complexion of a tribe, and by manipulating several tribes in this way a leader or party might be assured of a majority. Most of the Italians were finally registered by the census of 70/69 BC, nearly 20 years after the passage of the relevant laws. From then on the political map of Italy was more or less finally drawn, with the important exception of Cisalpine Gaul; which explains why the Transpadane region took on fresh importance in the political contest and in election campaigns between 70 and 51.[28] Pompey's father, as early as 89, granted Latin rights to native cities north of the Po, which meant that their magistrates were Roman citizens and thus belonged to a tribe. Caesar in 60 'sent to the Latin colonies which were in a state of unrest and meditating a demand for citizenship; and he might have spurred them on to some rash act' (Suetonius, *Caesar* 8). Crassus attempted to register them when he was censor in 65. We shall see that Cicero in 64 showed his sense of the importance of Gual in the electoral geography of Italy by spending two months of his candidacy there (*Att.* 1.1.2); 13 years later the same was done by M. Antonius when candidate for the priesthood (Caesar, *B. Gall.* 8.50), and also by Caesar himself. From what we know of the distribution of the Gaulish cities among the tribes, their importance was certainly due to their being assigned to so many small tribes that any modification of the electoral roll was a sensitive and important matter.

Elections and candidates

As we have seen, the two essential functions of Roman assemblies at the end of the Republic were the electoral and the legislative, the judicial function having almost entirely disappeared. There was enough to be done in these fields to take up a great deal of the citizens' time; we shall see presently how much activity they represented in a normal year. Some brief calculations may be given at this stage. Most of the magistracies were filled by annual elections, so that the whole corps of high officers was renewed every 12 months. The *comitia centuriata* elected the two consuls and a variable but increasing number of praetors (one in 367, two from 242 onwards, four in about 230, six in 198, eight under Sulla, ten in 46, 14 in 45 and 16 in 44; reduced to eight in 27, raised to ten in 23); also two censors every five years. The *comitia tributa* or *concilia plebis* elected the aediles (two from 496, two more—the curule aediles—from 367, six from 47, plus two *cereales* added by Caesar to look after grain distribution): also the quaestors (four from 421, eight from 267, 20 under Sulla and up to 40 under Caesar (Dio 43.47)), and ten tribunes of the plebs. In addition the *comitia tributa* elected other magistrates or quasi-magistrates such as the 24 military tribunes of the first four legions, the *triumviri monetales* and *capitales* (supervisors of the mint and prisons), and members of the agrarian commissions. As we shall see, the voting for each set of offices took at least a day, often two or even three: as simultaneous procedures were not used, the length of the vote was proportionate to the number of posts to be filled. The people were summoned to Rome at least seven times a year, at varying seasons, for elections that might last 15 days or so altogether, not counting the time spent in local elections.

Legislative activity cannot be quantified in the same way, but there was no limit to the number of laws any magistrate might propose during his term of office. According to our sources C. Gracchus introduced at least 15 bills during his two years as a tribune, and we know that many of his colleagues such as C. Rubrius and M. Livius Drusus brought in a great many during the same period. This activity was only limited indirectly for various procedural reasons. In the first place, there were many days on which it was not lawful to *agere cum populo*, i.e. summon an assembly and put a proposal to it: by the end of the Republic the *dies fasti*, on which this was permitted, were no more than 194 or 195 in number, distributed unequally round the year. From these had to be deducted the days fixed for electoral assemblies and for sessions of the Senate; in theory these might coincide, but the magistrates had to be present at both and could not sit in two places at once. Finally rules of procedure enacted in the second and first centuries BC restricted the activity of magistrates and especially tribunes. For instance, under the *Lex Aelia* and *Lex Fufia* (c. 150 BC) they could not introduce bills immediately before the elections. The complication of these religious and civil rules (which were modified in 304 and 287 BC) is well shown in the following extracts from Macrobius:[29]

Court days, or 'days of utterance' (*fasti*), are the days on which the praetor may pronounce the three prescribed formulas: 'I grant, I pronounce, I adjudge'; and opposed to these days are the days on which these words may not be uttered (*nefasti*). Assembly days are the days on which a motion may be brought before the people in assembly. And, although on court days it is possible to plead in court but not possible to bring a motion before the people, on assembly days each process is permissible. Adjournment days (*comperendini*) are those on which it is permitted to order recognizances to be given for reappearance in court. Appointed days (*stati*) are those which are fixed for the hearing of an action with a foreigner...

On the other hand, Julius Caesar, in the sixteenth Book of his treatise on *Auspices,* says that a public meeting cannot be convened — that is, a matter cannot be referred to the people — on a market-day, and so an assembly of the Roman people cannot be held on these days. Cornelius Labeo too, in the first Book of his *Calendar,* declares that market-days are rest days. A careful reader will find the explanation of this difference of opinion in the works of Granius Licinianus, in his second Book, where he says that market days are rest days sacred to Jupiter, since it is the custom for the wife of the flamen to sacrifice a ram to that god in the Royal Palace on every market day, but that the Hortensian Law made market days court days in order that the country people, who used to come to Rome to market, might have an opportunity to settle their legal disputes; for the praetor might not pronounce the prescribed words (*fari*) on a day which was *nefastus.* Those, then, who say that market days are rest days have the ancient usage to protect them from a charge of inexactitude, but the opinion expressed by those who hold the opposite view is also true, if they are taking into account only the time that has elapsed since the passing of the law to which I have referred.

The first establishment of the market day is attributed to Romulus, who, it is said, after sharing his royal power with Titus Tatius and instituting certain sacrifices and associations, also prescribed the observance of those days. And this is what Tuditanus maintains; but Cassius [Hemina] says that they were a device of Servius Tullius, designed to enable country folk to meet in Rome and arrange matters that concerned both town and country. Geminus says that is was after the expulsion of the kings that a market-day was first held, because most of the common people used to offer sacrifice in memory of the late Servius Tullius on those days; and Varro too agrees with this account. However, according to Rutilius, the Romans instituted market days in order that the country people, after working for eight [*recte* seven] days in the fields, should leave their work there on the ninth [*recte* eighth] day and come to Rome to sell their wares and to get information about the laws; and also that there might be a larger concourse of the people to hear the popular and senatorial decrees which might be brought before them, for matters published for a period of three market-days would readily come to the knowledge of one and all. That too was the origin of the custom of promulgating a law for a period of three market-days, and also of the practice by which candidates for office used to come to the assembly of the people on a market-day and take their stand on raised ground, that they might be seen clearly by everyone present. But all these usages fell more and more into neglect and eventually disappeared, when with the growth in numbers of the people the assemblies were well attended even in the period between two market-days. (*Saturnalia* 1.14-16)

Despite these multiple prohibitions, there were years in which legislative activity was extremely heavy. As the law required several preparatory assemblies to be held during a period of at least 27 days before the actual vote, the civic calendar was generally overloaded. A Roman citizen who wanted to play a full and effective part in political life would be summoned at least 20 times a year for operations which might last altogether 40 or 60 days. Much of his time was thus spent attending to public duties in the Campus Martius and the Forum. It is hardly an exaggeration to say that being a citizen was a full-time profession.

We do not know the exact origins and early development of Roman electoral procedures. As we have seen, it is probable that for a long time the people assembled by the magistrate in office had no right other than that of accepting or rejecting his proposed successor or successors. From the third century onwards, however, the election appears more and more as a real choice enabling the people to put forward candidates and indicate their preference. None the less their freedom was narrowly limited by procedural rules which gave the presiding magistrate a leading role in the election.[30]

In the first place it was he who announced to the people that an electoral meeting was necessary, and appointed its date by an *edictum* in customary form. As a rule the date of the edict was governed by the fact that the assembly had to take place during the term of office of the outgoing magistrate and in good time before the new one took office, so that the various elections were held at more or less regular dates; they are not well known to us, however, as we do not know the exact dates on which the various magistrates assumed their duties before the first century BC. For a long time the consuls and no doubt the praetors took office at widely different times of the civil year.[31] In 225, shortly before the Second Punic War, the date was fixed at 15 March, when military operations began (Livy 31.15); but from 154-153 it was decided that the civil and consular years should start on the same date:

> In the five hundred and ninety-eighth year after the founding of the city, the consuls began to enter upon their office on January first. The reason for changing the elections was the uprising of the Spaniards [?] (Livy, *Per.* 47, confirmed by the *Praenestine Fasti*)

From then on the curule aediles and military tribunes also took office on the same date; the quaestors, however, did so on the Nones (5th) of December, 25 or 27 days earlier. Finally the tribunes of the plebs took up their duties on 10 December from at least the second century BC (as we know for certain), and probably earlier still, either from their first creation or at any rate from the Decemvirate. The reason for this tradition is unknown. The various dates, with their modifications, naturally affected the times of the respective elections.

These however, depended in part on practical reasons and were less obligatory than the dates of assuming office, since they did not affect the length of the official's term or the continuity of power. Throughout the republican period the elections were supposed to be held within a particular time-span, but for accidental reasons they sometimes had to be advanced or postponed. In 170, for example, the Senate decided to replace ahead of time the consuls Aulus Atilius and Marcius Philippus, being dissatisfied with their conduct of affairs in Macedonia:

> The Fathers decided that Aulus Atilius the consul should proclaim the assembly for the election of consuls so that it might be completed during the month of January, and that he should return to the city at the first possible moment. (Livy 43.11.3)

On the other hand, during the civil disturbances towards the end of the Republic the elections were often postponed almost indefinitely. In 110, for instance, the tribunicial elections could not be held because of disputes among the tribunes (Sallust, *Jugurtha* 37). In 55-50 this happened more or less constantly. With these exceptions, however, consular and praetorian elections took place around January until 153 BC (when the consuls took up their duties on 15 March), in November from 153 until Sulla's reforms, and afterwards in July. This last date was made possible by the fact that the consuls no longer had to leave Rome during their term of office to command troops in the field; it was no doubt chosen to bring the consular election close to that of the tribunes, traditionally held in July, which was becoming the more important of the two. The specific evidence that we have for this period (about a dozen instances)[32] shows that the rule was to elect the higher magistrates such as the tribunes and aediles in July, but that various circumstances might bring about a postponement until October, November, or even the following January. In 60 BC, for example, the Senate wished to allow a tribune time to bring in a law against bribery; as it was illegal to introduce a bill within 25 days of an election, the date of the *comitia* was postponed:

> The tribune Lurco, who entered on his office under another law, has been freed from the obligations of the Aelian and Fufian laws, so that he may propose his law about bribery. He had luck in publishing it in spite of his deformity. Accordingly the elections have been postponed till the 27th [?31st] of July.) Cicero, *Att.* 1.16.13)

However, a decision to postpone the *comitia* was not always taken by the Senate in due form; it might be due to physical force or violence or to the personal interests of the presiding official. In 57 Milo, supported by the *optimates*, used every means to secure the postponement of the elections at which Clodius intended to stand for the aedileship:

Marcellinus posted up his resolution which he had in writing when he delivered it — it provided that my entire case should be included in the trial, the attack on my building-ground, the arson and the assault on my person, and that all these should precede the election — and Milo gave notice that he intended to watch the sky for omens on all the election days.

Disorderly meetings were held by Metellus, wild meetings by Appius and raving mad meetings by Publius. But the end of it all was that the elections would have taken place, if Milo had not reported evil omens in the Campus Martius. On the 19th of November Milo took up his position in the Campus before midnight with a large force; while Clodius, in spite of his picked gangs of runaway slaves, did not venture to show himself. Milo, to the huge delight of everybody and to his own great credit, stayed there till midday: and the three brethren's struggle ended in disgrace, their strength broken and their pride humbled. Metellus, however, demanded that the prohibition should be repeated in the forum on the next day. There was no necessity, he said, for Milo to come to the Campus at night; he would be in the Comitium at six in the morning. So on the 20th Milo went to the Comitium in the early hours of the morning. At daybreak Metellus came sneaking into the Campus by something like bypaths. Milo caught the fellow up 'between the groves' and served his notice: and he retired amid loud jeers and insults from Q. Flaccus. The 21st was a market-day, and for two days there were no meetings.

It is now three o'clock on the morning of the 23rd as I am writing. Milo has already taken possession of the Campus. Marcellus, the candidate, is snoring loud enough for me to hear him next door. I have just had news that Clodius' hall is utterly deserted, save for a few rag-and-bobtails with a canvas lantern. His side are complaining that I am at the bottom of it all. (Cicero, *Att.* 4.3.3-5)

But these are the last convulsions of a Republic in its death-throes. Although, since the Gracchi at least, the elections often gave rise to keen rivalry, it would be wrong to suppose that they were always marred by such illegal manoeuvres. During the second century and a good deal of the first, the precise rules devised to ensure their regularity worked fairly well.

Once the precise date had been fixed in accordance with the permitted calendar (as we saw in the extract from Macrobius), the next task of the magistrate appointed to organize and preside over the election was to announce the list of candidates. The position as to this varied a great deal until it was finally regulated by law towards the end of the Republic (perhaps not before 62 BC). Originally the power of the presiding magistrate to designate his own successor was practically absolute: his task, according to the formula, was to 'ask (*rogare*) the people' to appoint the next holder of the office, by presenting them with one or several names to accept or choose from. Naturally his discretion was limited by the general rules which came by degrees to govern magisterial appointments: property qualification (at least an equestrian rating was required for most magistracies, except perhaps that of a *tribunus plebis*), age, ability (shown by previous holding of an official post), etc. But it is certain that originally a candidate did not have to appear in person or even declare his willingness to stand. We know of cases in which the people elected (and the magistrate must therefore have proposed) persons who did not wish to be chosen. Thus in 211 one of the two men proposed for the consular election was T. Manlius Torquatus, who had already been consul in 235 and 224. When the election had begun and the *centuria praerogativa* had already voted for him, he interrupted the proceedings as soon as his name was called out, making it clear that he did not wish to be elected:

> When a crowd gathered before Manlius, who was present, in order to congratulate him, ... surrounded by a great crowd he came to the tribunal of the consul, begged him to hear a few words from him, and bade him recall the century which had cast its vote. While all were in suspense, waiting to know what he was going to demand, he gave the condition of his eyes as an excuse. (Livy 26.22.5-6)

On the whole, however, such refusals were rare, and no doubt it soon became customary for candidates to announce themselves openly by what was called a *professio*. For a long time no time-limit was set for this, and it might take place at the election itself. In 211, at the (extraordinary) election of a proconsul for the Spanish command, at first no candidate came forward:

> People had waited for those who thought themselves deserving of so important a command to give in their names. When that hope was disappointed, there was renewed grief for the disaster they had suffered and regret for the lost generals. And so the citizens mourned, being almost devoid of any plan; nevertheless on the election day they went down into the Campus. And turning towards the magistrates they scanned the faces of the leading men, who were looking at one and another of their number, and there were complaints that the situation was so desperate that no man ventured to accept the command; when suddenly Publius Cornelius, son of that Publius Cornelius who had fallen in Spain, being about 24 years of age, declared that he was a candidate, and took his place on higher ground from which he could be seen. All faces were turned towards him. (Livy 26.18)

A candidate might thus declare himself at the last moment, and equally he might withdraw when the election was about to be held. A celebrated case is that of C. Cicereius, who stood for the praetorship in 175/174 at the same time as L. Cornelius Scipio (son of Africanus), whose scribe he had once been:

> To the people's great displeasure, chance brought together on the Campus Martius two candidates for the praetorship: Scipio, son of the first Africanus, and his former scribe Cicereius... Cicereius, however, turned this freak of fortune to his own credit. Once he saw that all the centuries preferred Scipio to him, he came down from the platform, threw off his whitened toga and began to canvass for his opponent. (Valerius Maximus 4.5.3; see, however, p. 277 and note 77 below).

As a rule, however, the candidate's declaration was made in time for the presiding magistrate and the people to take account of it and, in the first place, determine whether he was eligible. From the middle of the second century onwards there were no doubt arrangements to prevent last-minute candidates from forcing the issue after the fashion of 211. At the consular election of 169, for instance, there was a strong current of opinion in favour of L. Aemilius Paullus (who, despite his resistance, was in fact elected for the second time), but the voters were not content until he formally agreed to stand:

> [All his friends and kinsmen] urged him to give ear to the people when it summoned him to the consulship. At first he was for declining the appeals of the multitude, and tried to avert their eager importunities,... but when they came daily to his house and called him into the forum and pressed him with their clamours, he yielded; and when he presented himself among the candidates for the consulship, he did not seem to come into the Campus in order to get office, but as one who brought victory. (Plutarch, *Aemilius Paullus* 10.3)

The word *professio* always means a declaration made before a competent authority.[33] Candidates for election made their declaration before the magistrates, for the good reason that only they were empowered to judge whether it was admissible and whether the candidate was eligible or not. Until a time-limit was fixed for nominations, the magistrate in charge of the *comitia* might reject a candidate at any stage. In the last century of the Republic a schedule was adopted similar to that for the tabling of proposed legislation, and no doubt inspired by it: the list of candidates had to be drawn up at least a *trinundinum* (25 or 27 days) before polling day. From then on the list could not be altered and all candidates were eligible, as it was the presiding magistrate's duty to make known his decision regarding the admissibility of each: the technical terms for considering and accepting a nomination were *rationem habere* and *nomen accipere* respectively. From 62 onwards a candidate had to make his *professio* in person, thus putting an end to what had been the widespread and accepted practice of candidature *in absentia* whereby a promagistrate serving abroad could be elected to office: Marius, for instance, was re-elected consul for each year from 106 to 101 while fighting the Cimbri and Teutones in Gaul. Apparently the rule had not yet been changed in 63, as Cicero says in his speech of that year on the agrarian law proposed by P. Servilius Rullus:

> He must be there in person as a candidate [for the office of agrarian decemvir]—so the law bids him—a thing which no other law has ever required, not even for the regular magistrates. (*De Lege Agraria* 2.24)

But the requirement existed in 61, as Caesar sought exemption from it when standing for the consulate:

> He was making preparations outside the walls for a most splendid procession, during the days when candidates for the consulship were required to present themselves. It was not lawful for one who was going to have a triumph to enter the city and then go back again for the triumph. As Caesar was very anxious to secure the office,... he sent to the Senate and asked permission to go through the forms of standing for the consulship while absent, through the agency of friends, for although he knew it was against the law it had been done by others. Cato opposed his proposition and used up the last day for the presentation of candidates in speech-making. Thereupon Caesar abandoned his triumph, entered the city, offered himself as a candidate, and waited for the *comitia*. (Appian, *B. Civ.* 2.8)

Candidature *in absentia* was a vexed question in 51-50, when Caesar's proconsular powers in Gaul expired and he wished to stand again for the consulship without relinquishing his command and possible right to a triumph. He could not afford to come to Rome as a simple *privatus,* as he was vulnerable from the judicial point of view and his enemies would certainly have brought charges against him. Consequently in 52 he induced the ten tribunes to move that he should be allowed to stand for office in 50 without leaving Gaul. Pompey agreed, and undertook to modify in that sense a law he had himself introduced when sole consul, and which seems to have dealt with electioneering or the powers of magistrates:

> When Pompey proposed a bill touching the privileges of officials, in the clause where he debarred absentees from standing for office he forgot to make a special exception in Caesar's case, and did not correct the oversight until the law had been inscribed on a tablet of bronze and deposited in the treasury. (Suetonius, *Caesar* 28)[34]

The procedure was illegal, as a bill might not be amended directly before the vote, and was naturally treated as void by Caesar's enemies, including the consul Claudius Marcellus, who moved in 50 that Caesar's candidature should be ignored (Suetonius, ibid.)

Apart from the question of a time-limit, the admissibility of nominations was considered from other points of view. The personality and qualifications of would-be candidates were scrutinized with care. To have been indicted on a capital charge was probably a disqualification:

A little later Catiline was charged with extortion and prevented from standing for the consulship, because he had been unable to announce his candidacy within the prescribed number of days. (Sallust, *Cat.* 18)

In any case everything in this field depended on the magistrates who were to preside over the assembly. This does not mean that there was no debate (the magistrates might seek the advice of their *consilium* and of course the Senate), and there might even be open conflict, e.g. with the tribunes of the plebs, who could threaten to block the election if their advice for or against a particular candidate was not heeded. Such incidents occurred, for instance, in 185 at what might be called a by-election to the praetorship:

When this strife had calmed down, another straightway arose as a consequence of the death of Gaius Decimius the praetor. The candidates were Gnaeus Sicinius and Lucius Pupius, who had been aediles the preceding year, and Gaius Valerius the *flamen Dialis* and Quintus Fulvius Flaccus—he, because he was curule aedile elect, did not wear the *toga candida*, but was canvassing more energetically than the rest. The contest was between Fulvius and the *flamen*. Fulvius seemed at first to be on equal terms with Valerius and then even to be passing him, but some of the tribunes of the people declared that his candidacy ought not to be accepted because one man could not seek or hold two offices simultaneously, especially curule offices; others thought that he should be exempted from the operation of the laws, so that the people might have the opportunity of electing whoever they wished to the praetorship. Lucius Porcius the consul was at first of the opinion that he should not accept his name; then... calling together the Fathers, he said that he was referring the matter to them because there was neither any law nor any precedent, acceptable in a free state, that a curule aedile elect might seek the praetorship; if they agreed, it was his intention to hold the election in accordance with the law. The Fathers accordingly voted that Lucius Porcius should appeal to Quintus Fulvius not to prevent the election of a praetor being held in accordance with the law.

When the consul made this appeal in accordance with the decree of the Senate, Flaccus replied that he would do nothing which was unworthy of himself. By this ambiguous answer he created, in the minds of men who interpreted it to suit their own desires, the hope that he would yield to the authority of the Fathers. At the election he continued to canvass even more actively than before, charging that the consul and the Senate were wresting from him the gift of the Roman people and were arousing hostility to him by their talk of duplicated offices, as if it were not evident that when elected praetor he would immediately resign the aedileship. When the consul saw that Flaccus's stubbornness increased and that the favour of the people was turning more and more to him, he adjourned the assembly and summoned the Senate again. A full meeting declared that, since the authority of the Fathers had had no influence with Flaccus, an appeal to him should be made before the assembly. When the consul had called an informal meeting and presented his plea, Flaccus, not even then moved from his position, expressed his gratitude to the Roman people because as often as the opportunity to declare their desires had been granted to them, they had shown such enthusiasm to make him praetor: it was not his intention to disappoint these desires of his fellow-citizens. This speech, obstinate though it was, aroused so much support for him that he would have been praetor beyond a doubt if the consul had accepted his candidacy. Then the tribunes had a great argument, both among themselves and with the consul, until the Senate was convoked by the consul and passed a resolution to the effect that since the stubbornness of Quintus Flaccus and the base desires of men prevented the election to fill a vacancy among the praetors from being held according to law, the Senate decreed that there were enough praetors; Publius Cornelius should hold both jurisdictions in the City and should preside at the games in honour of Apollo. (Livy 39.39.1-10)

In 67 there was a conflict over Lollius Palicanus's candidature for the consulship. A tribune in 71 and a praetor in 69, he had attracted attention by favouring the restoration of tribunicial powers; his candidature, though treated with contempt by Cicero, was apparently quite in order. The consul C. Calpurnius Piso could not refuse to accept it, but said that he would not declare Palicanus elected even it the people voted for him:

C. Piso, in very critical circumstances, upheld his consular dignity with admirable firmness, as the following incident will show. M. Palicanus, a most seditious citizen, had ingratiated himself with the people by pernicious flattery, and every effort was being made in the *comitia* to raise him to the consulship. It was a high disgrace to seek to confer the supreme magistracy on this man, whose odious conduct deserved exemplary punishment rather than the least honour. The people's enthusiasm was abetted by the unbridled agitation of the tribunes, who can be relied on to stir up popular fury when it is slumbering and to stoke the fires once they have broken out. At this juncture, so deplorable and shameful to the Republic, the tribunes surrounded Piso, hustled him on to the platform and held him there like a prisoner, urging him to say that he would declare Palicanus consul if the people voted for him. At first he replied that he could not believe his fellow-citizens so blind as to commit such an outrage. But the tribunes pressed him, saying: 'Yes, but what if they did so vote?', and in the end Piso replied: 'No, in that case I would not declare him elected.' This firm reply made it certain that Palicanus would not obtain the consulship; and thus Piso braved many dangers rather than relax his noble austerity of mind. (Valerius Maximus 3.8.3)

A year later, in 66, the consul L. Volcatius Tullus rejected Catiline's candidature:

Catiline having announced his candidature, L. Volcatius Tullus publicly summoned his *consilium* to advise whether it should be accepted, as he had been charged with embezzlement. Accordingly Catiline withdrew from the election, [postponing his candidature by one year]. (Asconius p. 89 Or.)

Naturally these formal rules on time-limits and legal qualifications did not prevent most candidates, whether above suspicion or not, from starting to canvass well before the date on which the lists were closed. *Petitio*, the general term for canvassing, included a 'walkabout' (*ambitus*) with plenty of 'handshaking' (*prensatio*). We shall study a typical campaign in more detail later on, from the voter's rather than the candidate's point of view. For the present, an essential difference should be noted between electioneering and a campaign to get up support for a law or *plebiscitum*. Whereas in the latter case it was normal and legal for the author of the proposed law, or the magistrates who opposed it, to hold regular preliminary meetings (*contiones*) at which it was presented and discussed, in an election campaign there was no preliminary meeting except on voting day, immediately before the vote was taken; moreover it probably consisted simply of the presiding officer announcing the list of candidates which had already been publicly displayed. Election meetings in our sense, while not unknown, were very rare. They could not be called by the candidates themselves, who by definition were *privati* and not entitled to summon public assemblies. Only a magistrate such as a consul, praetor or tribune could do this, and as far as we know it only happened in exceptional times, when the atmosphere was particularly tense. We saw an example in 67, when the tribunes summoned the consul Piso to a *contio* to dissuade him from his intention of not declaring Palicanus elected.

Meetings of this sort were probably held when Pompey and Crassus stood for the consulship in 71, for at the time the tribunes, and Lollius Palicanus in particular, were fighting to recover their powers and must certainly have summoned the candidates to *contiones* in order to extract promises (which were given and kept) of their assistance in this respect. However, the only specific evidence we have (Appian, *B. Civ.* 1.121 and Cicero, I *Verr.* 45) is of *contiones* held by Pompey and Crassus after they were elected and before they took office.

Summoning of the assembly: voting procedure

The fundamental Roman principle of voting by groups and not individually made the conduct of elections an extremely precise and formal operation. Preliminary obstacles and difficulties having been cleared away, it was for the people to express its will subject to the overriding responsibility of the presiding officer. It would be ideal to have a full and detailed description or theoretical analysis of the way in which the *comitia* worked. Failing either of these we have to make do with scraps of information, hints and elliptical references, in order to form an idea of the atmosphere of a voting assembly and the rules by which it was governed. This is all the more difficult as the rules varied a good deal during our period and also according to the type of assembly: whether *comitia centuriata* or *tributa,* or whether its purpose was electoral, legislative or judicial. In this chapter we are concerned only with electoral assemblies. These were held at varying dates, as we have seen, and originally in varying places: the *comitia centuriata* and *tributa* met in different locations at different periods and according to the purpose for which they were summoned.

The centuries, in any case, could only assembly outside the *pomerium,* the sacred enclosure of the City, because they represented the people in arms (*exercitus urbanus*):

> It is impious for the assembly of the centuries to be held within the *pomerium,* because the army must be summoned outside the city, and it is not lawful for it to be summoned within the city. (Aulus Gellius 15.27)

The centuries might on occasion assemble in various places: the Porta Flumentana, the Petelian grove (*lucus Petelinus*), perhaps the Aventine[35] (under Tiberius; but what exactly were the *improbae comitiae* [sic!] denounced in a certain inscription?). In fact, however, with one or two exceptions they nearly always met in the Campus Martius, on the flat ground encircled by a loop of the Tiber. Thus the official formula cited by Cicero in connection with Rabirius's trial: *in Campo Martio comitiis centuriatis, auspicato in loco (Pro Rab.* 11).[36] The Campus, as its name indicates, was originally an open space for military activities of all kinds: young men's training, the muster following the *dilectus,* army exercises, and certain parts of the census operation, including the *lustrum.* It was adapted for these various purposes from early times: in particular, the 'public farmhouse' (Villa Publica), a complex of buildings and shaded gardens, was created as a setting for the census operations when these were instituted in 435

(Livy 4.22). The *comitia centuriata* met for electoral purposes on consecrated ground immediately adjacent to the Villa. Here the necessary arrangements were made, including a *templum*—i.e. an area in which the magistrate could take the auspices and, in later times, address the people—and an enclosure carefully marked out by ropes and wooden barriers, and in late republican times by permanent constructions, in which the voting units could assemble. Around this was a free space for the various movements involved, as we shall see presently when studying the election process in more detail.[37]

There was no fixed place for the electoral assembly of the plebs, which met according to tribes from at least the fifth century onwards, either as a *concilium* to elect the plebeian magistrates or as *comitia* to elect the lower magistrates, military tribunes and quaestors. There is even one instance of the tribes voting a law outside the City, in the army camp at Sutrium in 357; but this was never repeated. A *concilium plebis*, i.e. an assembly of the plebs presided over by tribunes, could naturally only be held in the City, which was the latter's sphere of competence and activity. We shall see that for legislative and judicial purposes the *comitia tributa* generally assembled in the Forum as late as imperial times.

From a very early date a consecrated place of assembly existed in the heart of the City: the Comitium, which the lexicographers tell us was originally used for the *comitia curiata* (Varro, *De Lingua Latina* 5.155). This was close to the old Curia Hostilia, the Senate's meeting-place in the north-east corner of the Forum. Archaeology is of great assistance here: excavations in this part of the Forum have shown that in the second century BC there was a circular stepped area with an open space in the middle, in front of the Curia but at a lower level. This is exactly the same layout as that shown for the fourth to second centuries BC, but much more completely, by excavations at the Roman colony of Cosa. There the Comitium is situated just in front of the Curia, and the steps on which the people could stand (rather than sit) in large numbers encircled a raised platform in front of the building from which speakers could conveniently address them. At Rome the first speaking platform was built above the steps, perhaps between the Comitium and the Forum: it was called the Rostra because its base was decorated with the bronze beaks of ships captured at the victory of Antium, in 338 BC (Livy 8.14.12). Until 145 BC the *comitia tributa* may have been held in the Comitium. But in that year the tribune Licinius Crassus for the first time had a law passed not in the Comitium but in the Forum, where there was much more room (Cicero, *De Amicitia* 96; Varro, *Res Rusticae* 1.2.9). At that time the only Rostra that could have been used were still those of Antium, which must therefore have been between the Forum and the Comitium. (Cf. plan, p. 375)

Later, but doubtless not before 117, speakers and magistrates used as a platform (still called Rostra) the steps of the newly rebuilt temple of Castor.[38] Meetings were held in other places also: the Circus Flaminius on the Tiber bank north of the Forum Holitorium, and especially on the Capitol, in the precincts of the temple of Jupiter Capitolinus, where for a long time the electoral *comitia tributa* took place (Livy 34.53). It was long supposed on the strength of Appian's account that the last assembly held by Tiberius Gracchus on the Capitol in 133 to secure his re-election to the tribunate was an electoral assembly. But L. Ross Taylor has shown that it was in fact a legislative one, at which, as we shall see, the tribes voted successively, thus requiring much less space than an electoral assembly in which they all voted at once (Appian, *B. Civ.* 1.15 and Plutarch, *Ti. Gracchus* 16-18); Plutarch twice indicates that at that fatal assembly, which lasted two days, the result could be followed as the voting went on, which implies a successive vote.[39]

Whatever the facts about the assembly of 133, it is certain that in 124, and probably much earlier, the electoral meetings of the *comitia tributa* were held in the Campus Martius. At the election of 124, at which C. Gracchus was elected tribune, Plutarch tells us that:

> So great a throng poured into the city from the country and took part in the elections that many could not be housed and since the Campus Martius could not accommodate the multitude, they gave in their voices from the house-tops and tilings. (*C. Gracchus* 3)

This passage is rather puzzling, since by that time votes were cast in writing and people could not have 'voted' from the house-tops. Possibly, however, it refers to a crowd for whom there was no room in the voting enclosure, and who expressed their views by shouting; or they may have been Italians who did not yet possess the franchise. At any rate, the vote took place on the Campus Martius. Probably the choice of a new venue for the *comitia tributa* elections was connected with the fundamental innovation of casting votes in writing by means of tablets (*tabellae*): this was adopted in 139 for elections, in 137 for trials and in 129 for voting on laws. As we shall see, this required semi-permanent arrangements for the voting process, including supervision. It also made it possible for all the tribes to vote at once in *comitia tributa* elections,[40] which was hardly possible when votes were cast orally. The site therefore had to be such as to permit all the tribes to assemble and to file past the voting-urns. At the end of the second century the number of voters increased and the *comitia tributa* revived in importance, tending to become the central body for legislation as well as the election of tribunes. In any case, during the whole of the last century of the Republic the electoral *comitia tributa* were held in the enclosure assigned to the *comitia centuriata*. This meant that it was always possible, after summoning the people to an assembly of the *comitia tributa*, to convert it at the last moment into the *comitia centuriata*. This happened under Caesar's presidency in 44 BC:

At all events you were not in the Campus Martius when, after the opening of the Comitia for the election of quaestors, at the second hour, the chair of Q. Maximus, whom Caesar's party declared to be consul, was duly set in place; and then, on the announcement of his death, that same chair was taken away. But the great man, having taken the auspices for the *comitia tributa,* also held the *comitia centuriata;* and at the seventh hour he announced the election of a consul to hold office till January 1st, which would be the next morning. (Cicero, *Ad fam.* 7.30.2)

The dialogue in Book Three of Varro's *Res Rusticae* (we shall revert at length to this valuable text) takes place on a day of elections to the aedileship in a year between 55 and 50 BC, and shows the protagonists at various stages of their activity as voters.[41] When the voting is over they wait to hear the result, and, as the sun is too strong on the Campus Martius, one of the company suggests that they move to the shade of the Villa Publica close to the electoral enclosure. It is clear from this that the Campus Martius is by now the place where the elections are held, whether *centuriata* or *tributa.* The temporary structures erected there were equally well adapted to either, since from the end of the third or the beginning of the second century there was an arithmetical ratio between the number of centuries and that of the 35 tribes. An enclosed space, also known as the *ovile* or 'sheepfold',[42] was divided by barriers (*saepta*) into a number of lanes or corridors along which the voters advanced. It should be noted that there were also *saepta* in the Forum and other places where legislative assemblies were held (Cicero, *Pro Sestio* 79). An important change was made in the last days of the Republic, when Caesar, with the help of Oppius and Cicero, decided to erect a handsome building on the Campus Martius as a venue for the people's civic activities, especially elections. Very probably, as L. Ross Taylor suggests, this was a by-product of Caesar's rivalry with Pompey, who in 55 presented to the people a fine theatre surrounded by gardens, with a Curia alongside it for meetings of the Senate. In 54 Cicero describes the Campus Martius project as a 'most magnificent affair':

In the Campus Martius we are going to make polling-barriers (*saepta*) of marble for the tribal assemblies, roof them over, and surround them with a lofty colonnade a mile in circumference.[43] And at the same time we shall join this to the Villa Publica. (*Att.* 4.16.8 (4.17 in Loeb edition))

The bill for this work, including expropriations, amounted to a cool 60 million sesterces — Gallic gold, no doubt. The building, to which the triumvir Lepidus also contributed, was only completed in 26 BC, by M. Vipsanius Agrippa. It is mentioned by various authors, including Frontinus, and appears, with sufficient detail to enable its design and exact position to be known, on the marble plan, dating from the reign of Septimius Severus, of which many fragments have been found, and which was originally displayed in the Forum

Pacis near the later Basilica of Maxentius.[44] Thanks to the full publication of this plan in 1960, Italian archaeologists and subsequently L. Ross Taylor have been able to reconstitute the appearance of Caesar's *saepta* with great certainty. Moreover, the outer wall of the west portico has been traced alongside Agrippa's Pantheon, where it can be seen today. The representation seen on the plan, and the vestiges that have been excavated, date, it is true, from the second or third century AD, when the *comitia* had almost completely disappeared; the building was destroyed by fire in AD 80, but in all probability it was piously rebuilt on the foundations laid by Caesar and Agrippa. It was a large rectangular enclosure, measuring 94 by 286 metres and facing more or less north and south. It was a consecrated place, a *templum*, and consequently the entrance was in the centre of its northern end. The surrounding wall had a certain number of openings on the northern side, and the plan shows another in the south-west corner. There cannot have been many more, as the object of the enclosure was partly to facilitate supervision of the vote. At the narrow south end is a construction added by Agrippa, the *diribitorium* in which the votes were counted. Within the enclosure and in front of the *diribitorium* the plan shows lines which no doubt represent the base of a platform, the *tribunal* which was necessary for all *comitia* meetings: this was where the magistrates and candidates waited while the voters came up to place their *tabellae* in the urns. The immense space in front of the tribunal was divided into 35 lanes or columns, one for each voting unit, up which the voters advanced one by one towards the urns and the superintending officials.

Even in Agrippa's construction the partitions, whether wooden or consisting of ropes, were temporary and were placed in position whenever a vote was taken; for the enclosure, as an inscription of 14 BC indicates, was also used for meetings of the Senate. We shall study the arrangement of the *tribunal* in more detail when we come to describe the actual casting of votes. It is possible that in L. Ross Taylor's reconstruction the divisions are too long, as they would hardly leave room for the informal *contio* which had to precede every election. The same scholar calculated the number of people whom the building could accommodate: each division, being 260 metres long and 2.5 metres wide, might hold about 2,000 citizens, giving a total of 70,000. As we shall see, the average attendance at *comitia* was certainly much less than this; but in any case the arrangements were clearly planned on a lavish scale.

How elections were conducted

The holding of assemblies, like all other official acts by Roman magistrates, could only take place after an assurance had been obtained that they were pleasing to the gods. For this purpose auspices were taken on the morning of the appointed day, by the augurs unless the magistrate was an augur himself.

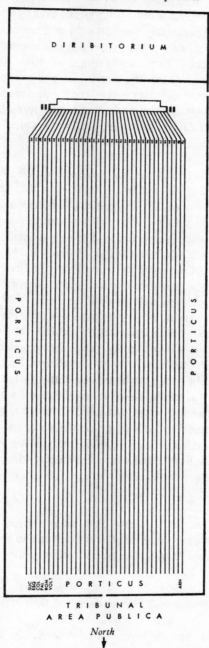

II *Saepta:* reconstruction of interior as arranged for voting, Drawing by Lucos Cozza. (Cf. L. Ross Taylor, *Roman Voting Assemblies*, p. 53).

The only exception was for assemblies presided over by a tribune of the plebs. By the end of the Republic this 'auspication' was no more than a precaution to ensure the religious validity of the proceedings. It also made possible various forms of sharp practice. The presiding magistrate could break up the meeting at any time if he did not like the way it was going, and other magistrates, especially if they were augurs themselves, could claim at any moment that they had seen an adverse omen and, using the consecrated formula, have the assembly adjourned to another day. The example of Marcus Antonius in 44 will suffice; according to Cicero:

> First of all, although Caesar had made it clear that, before he set out, he would order Dolabella's election as consul—and they say that the man who was always both doing and saying something of that kind was not a king!—well, when Caesar had said this, then this eminent augur [Antonius] asserted that he was invested with a priesthood of such a character that he could by the auspices either hinder or nullify the election, and he assured us he would do so. Here, first of all, mark the incredible stupidity of the man. For look you! This act, which he asserted he was able to do by right of his priesthood, would he have been less able to do if he were not an augur but consul? Surely, even more easily. For we augurs have only the right of report, the consuls and the rest of the magistrates the right also of observing the heavens. Well, let it be: this was his inexperience; for we can't require knowledge from a man never sober. But mark his impudence! Many months before, he said in the Senate he would by the auspices either forbid Dolabella's election, or would do what in fact he did. Can anyone divine what flaw there will be in the auspices except the man that has determined to observe the heavens? But it is illegal to do this during an election; and he who has observed is supposed to make his report not when the election has taken place, but before it is begun. But his ignorance and his impudence are mixed up, and he does not know what an augur should know, or act as a modest man should. (Cicero, *Phil.* 2.80-82)

The auspices were taken from a platform set up on consecrated ground (*templum*) on which a tent (*tabernaculum*) was erected in accordance with ritual. In the second century BC religious scruple might still be genuinely felt:

> The consuls Scipio and Figulus resigned their office when the augurs rendered a decision based on a letter written by L. Gracchus to the effect that those consuls had not been elected according to augural law. (Cicero, *De Divinatione* 2.74)

After the augural ceremony, or more probably while it was still going on, the citizens were solemnly convoked. This, as described by Varro, was a dual procedure. A herald made a proclamation from the *templum* on the magistrate's order, while another went round the walls blowing a trumpet and summoning the people to attend and obey the magistrate's commands. We do not know the formulae in which meetings for the election of consuls, praetors or quaestors were summoned, but they were no doubt very similar to two forms recorded by Varro, the first of which was used by the censors on the day of the *lustrum;*

From the Censors' Records: When by night the censor has gone into the sacred precinct to take the auspices, and a message has come from the sky, he shall thus command the herald to call the men: 'May this be good, fortunate, happy, and salutary to the Roman people – the Quirites – and to the government of the Roman people – the Quirites – and to me and my colleague, to our honesty and our office: All the citizen soldiers under arms and private citizens as spokesmen of all the tribes, call hither to me with an *inlicium* ("invitation"), in case any one for himself or for another wishes a reckoning to be given.'

The herald calls them first in the sacred precinct, afterwards he calls them likewise from the walls. (Varro, *De Lingua Latina* 6.86-7)

The second formula relates to a centuriate assembly held to try a case brought by a quaestor. The only variation is that the herald also has to sound the trumpet in front of the accused person's house:

That someone was regularly sent around the walls, *inlicere* ('to invite') the people to that place from which he might call them to the gathering, not only before the consuls and the censors, but also before the quaestors, is shown by an old *Commentary on the Indictment* which the quaestor Manius Sergius son of Manius brought against Trogus, accusing him of a capital offence; in which there is the following:

'You shall give your attention to the auspices, and take the auspices in the sacred precinct; then you shall send to the praetor or to the consul the favourable presage which has been sought. The praetor shall call the accused to appear in the assembly before you, and the herald shall call him from the walls:...You shall send a horn-blower to the doorway of the private individual and to the Citadel, where the signal is to sound. You shall request your colleague that from the speaker's stand he proclaim an assembly, and that the bankers shut up their shops, You shall seek that the senators express their opinion, and bid them be present; you shall seek that the magistrates express their opinion, the consuls, the praetors, the tribunes of the people, and your colleagues, and you shall bid them all be present in the temple; and when you send the request, you shall summon the gathering.'

In the same *Commentary on the Indictment*, this is the summing up of the edict written at the end:

'Likewise those who have received from the censors the contract for the trumpeter who gives the summons to the centuriate assembly shall see to it that, on that day on which the assembly shall take place, the trumpeter shall sound the trumpet on the Citadel and around the walls, and shall sound it before the house-entrance of the accused Titus Quintius Trogus, and that he be present in the Campus Martius at daybreak.' (ibid. 6.90-92)

The trumpet was of the army type known as *classicum,* and the herald who sounded it was called *classicus.* This was an honourable office and was farmed out for a fee, as the above-quoted text (*qui de censoribus classicum... redemptum habent*) indicates. Other rites too were connected with the military origin of the *comitia centuriata,* such as the hoisting of a red flag (*signum*) on the citadel of the Capitol. In 186 Postumius, in a speech denouncing the illegal meeting of Bacchic *thiasoi,* declared:

Your ancestors did not wish that even you should assemble casually and without reason, except when the standard was displayed on the citadel and the army was assembled for an election, or the tribunes had announced a meeting of the plebeians, or some of the magistrates had called you to an informal gathering. (Livy 39.15.11)

As the army was supposed to be occupied in voting, to guard against surprise a guard was posted on the Janiculum, on the Etruscan bank of the Tiber, and another red flag hoisted to show that no enemy was in sight. If this flag was lowered by a magistrate's order the assembly was automatically dissolved: we shall see a celebrated instance of this at the judicial *comitia* of 63 BC.[45]

The citizens, forewarned by the edict of convocation, did not in practice await the herald's summons but proceeded to the Campus Martius at the first or second hour, i.e. at dawn. As we saw earlier, when Milo wished to prevent the election of aediles from taking place he occupied the Campus Martius from midnight for several days in succession. When the presiding magistrate judged that enough people had arrived he would no doubt announce the opening of the election assembly itself. As in the case of legislative assemblies, this began with a preliminary gathering known as the *contio.*

Prior to the actual vote the people assembled in the enclosure[46] without distinction of centuries or tribes, and were there officially apprised of the matter to be laid before them (which they already knew from the edict). This was essential and not a mere formality: an assembly of the Roman people could only take a decision in reply to a question formally put to it by a responsible magistrate. In the case of legislative and judicial assemblies the reply consisted of answering Yes or No to a question of which we know the exact formulation and of which traces are seen in the drafting of laws. But the same was true of elections, where the presiding officer asked the people to give its opinion on the candidates who presented themselves.

Before putting the question the magistrate recited a propitiatory prayer (*carmen*), which may have been repeated when results were announced at nightfall. In general all addresses to the people began with a prayer:

> I prayed to the immortal gods according to the traditional usage of our ancestors that [Murena's] election should bring all good fortune to myself, my trust, my office and to the people and commons of Rome. Today I pray again to those same immortal gods that Murena's acquittal may preserve him for his consulship, that your opinion given in your verdict may tally with the wishes of the Roman people expressed in their votes, and that this agreement may bring peace, calm, tranquillity and harmony to yourselves and to the people of Rome. Believing that that customary election prayer, hallowed by the auspices taken by a consul, has the force and religious weight that the majesty of the Republic demands, I prayed too that the election over which I presided should bring to the successful candidates all good fortune and prosperity. (Cicero, *Pro Murena* 1.1; cf. Livy 39.15.1 and Dionys. 7.59)

As to the terms in which the question was put at election time, some laws which tradition ascribes to the fifth century, but which may be later, are couched as follows: 'He who called upon the Roman plebs to elect tribes should continue to call upon them until he shall effect the election of ten' (Livy 3.65.4). Mommsen reconstructed the formula for consular elections as: 'Do you desire and order, O Quirites, if I ask you to appoint consuls, that these men shall be consuls for the coming year?' This formula might at a pinch be adequate if there were only two candidates, but as soon as there were more than two and the object of the election was to choose between them, the question must have been differently put. It may have varied according to the procedure used, e.g. whether the vote was by word of mouth or, as later, in writing. We shall see that it was probably put in simple, non-committal terms such as: 'Among the candidates whose names I have announced, which is he (who are they) whom you desire to appoint consul, praetor etc.?'[47]

The list of candidates was not merely announced orally but posted up on voting day. We know this, albeit for a late period (AD 5), from the procedure laid down by the *Lex Valeria Cornelia* inscribed on the *Tabula Hebana:*

> [The presiding magistrate] shall cause to be displayed, in places where they can be conveniently read, whitened tablets of wood on which the candidates' names are written. (11.20-21)

There can be no doubt that this practice dated from much earlier. Plutarch, as already noted, says that in 170 BC the people were not content until they 'saw' the name of Aemilius Paullus among those of candidates for the consulship. The same custom is attested by the municipal electoral law of Malaca in Spain, which dates from the Flavian period, but certainly had a long tradition behind it and no doubt conformed closely to Roman procedures; we shall make use of it more than once to explain the complex mechanism of Roman *comitia*.[48] Section 51 governs the details of the *professio,* and provides for the event of there not being enough candidates:

> If, up to the day when the names of candidates should properly be announced, either the name of no candidate shall be announced, or those of fewer candidates than the number to be elected, or if, out of those whose names are announced, those whose candidature may properly by this law be allowed at the elections shall be fewer than the number to be elected, then the person responsible for conducting the elections shall post up, so that they may be read from level ground, the names of as many persons, qualified by this law to stand for the said magistracy, as shall be necessary to make up the number proper to be elected by this law. Each of the persons whose names are so posted up shall, if he so desire, go before the magistrate who is to conduct the said elections and nominate one person of his own choice.

Voting will now shortly begin, but first the president has several more formalities to perform. Firstly he must dissolve the preparatory assembly (*contio*) and announce that the vote will be taken by classes, centuries or tribes. The technical expression for this is *summovere populum,* 'to disperse the people'. In the case of *comitia centuriata* or *tributa* no one was excluded at this point: the citizens were merely told to take position in the 'lanes' appropriate to their units. At a *concilium plebis,* on the other hand, this announcement was probably the signal for the patricians to withdraw. Livy expressly says so on several occasions (2.56; 2.60; 3.11), perhaps reflecting a procedure of his own day.[49] But the expression *summovere populum* was also used for all other assemblies and meant simply that the *contio* was moved to a distance from the tribune so as to permit the citizens to regroup, the temporary partitions to be installed, the urns to be set up etc. The fact that a space was cleared in this way is well attested for a tribal assembly held on the Palatine in 212 to try the accused *publicani* (Livy 25.3.16). No doubt the same was done on the Campus Martius, and for that reason L. Ross Taylor's plan, reproduced above, perhaps represents the lanes leading to the platform as longer than they actually were. To dissolve the *contio* the presiding officer used the formula '*Discedite, Quirites,*' attested by Asconius in the case of a legislative vote:

When the time came for vote-casting the officer who proposed the law to the people ordered them to 'disperse', i.e. to dispose themselves in tribes for the vote. (p. 70 Or.)

The next operation was the casting of lots, again of course related to the basic system of voting by units. We shall study in a moment the order of voting, which raises many problems and varied a great deal according to the period and type of assembly. In some kinds of assembly all the units voted at the same time; in others the order was apparently prescribed by the constitution, while in others again it was determined entirely by lot. Even in the former case, however, lots were cast to decide the order in which the results were announced, as we shall see below, or, above all, to determine which unit or even which person should vote first. All regular Roman assemblies were subject to the religious rule, which soon became a political one also, according to which the first vote cast had the effect of a presage or omen and consequently influenced all the rest. Sometimes, too, lots were cast to decide in which unit non-citizens should vote. As we saw, at the trial of the *publicani* in 212, just as the tribe for the Latins' vote was being determined in this way, the accused men rushed into the empty space in front of the tribunal and stopped the proceedings; while the *Lex Malacitana* provides for the choice by lot of a curia for resident aliens. Lots were generally cast by throwing differently coloured or numbered balls (*pilae*) into a jar called a *sitella;* the same method was used for judicial proceedings. Certain laws lay down that the balls must be 'carefully polished and made as equal as possible' (*quam maxime aequatae*).[50] The *Tabula Hebana* of AD 19 states that the vessel used for determining by lot which tribes are to form new centuries shall be a 'revolving urn' (*urna versatilis*). What this meant is shown by an illustration on a mosaic at Carthage and another in a Roman painting: it was a sphere revolving on a horizontal axis fixed to two uprights, like the contrivance used for drawing numbers in a lottery.[51]

While these preparations were going on, the president called upon the voters to approach the urns. Here again the formula is recorded by Varro:

> In the *Consular Commentaries* I have found the following account:
> He who is about to summon the citizen-army shall say to his assistant (*accensus*): 'Gaius Calpurnius, call all the citizens hither to me, with an *inlicium* (invitation).' The assistant speaks thus: 'All citizens, come ye hither to the judges, to an invitation meeting (*inlicium visite*).' 'Gaius Calpurnius,' says the consul, 'call all the citizens hither to me, to a gathering.' The assistant speaks thus: 'All citizens, come hither to the judges, to a gathering (*conventio*).' Then the consul makes declaration to the army: 'I order you to go by the proper way to the centuriate assembly.' (*De Lingua Latina* 6.88)

The technical term for calling on the units to cast their vote as required by law was *introvocare* (summon within) or *introducere* (lead in). Livy, for instance, describing the election of Q. Fabius Maximus to the consulate in 297, says that the people, encouraged by the tribunes despite Fabius's refusal, 'proceeded to the election, and every century, as it was summoned within, in no uncertain terms named Fabius consul.' (Livy 10.13.11). The tribes, as we shall see, were summoned in the same manner as the centuries. Finally the direct order to vote was given (*in suffragium vocare* or *mittere*).[52]

The praerogativa

We must now go back a little to explain the system of elections. The question of exactly how the different operations were conducted, in what order the votes were cast and how they were counted, is a very complex one; the procedure was complicated in itself and underwent many changes in course of time, so that we are in danger of falling into anachronisms. However, the work of modern scholars, especially P. Fraccaro, and the recent discovery of the *Tabula Hebana* have made it possible to reach definite or very probable conclusions. It is certain, for instance, that an essential distinction is to be drawn between legislative or judicial assemblies on the one hand and electoral ones on the other. In the former case the electors (i.e. each voting unit, tribe or century) had to give a simple reply to a Yes or No question, or a verdict of guilty or not guilty. Counting the votes, whether oral or written, would be a relatively simple and rapid procedure, with an absolute majority determining the result. In the case of a law, for instance, it was sufficient for it to be approved or rejected by 18 tribes, i.e. one more than half. It was possible, therefore, to have the tribes vote successively and proclaim the result at once. If the first 18 tribes voted in the same sense there was no need to go on, as the majority had been reached. We have direct evidence that this is how a legislative or judicial vote was held in the *comitia tributa*, during the period of oral voting and also that of the secret ballot.[53] This had an effect on the question of venue: since only one tribe voted at once, i.e. on the average a thirty-fifth part of the electorate, there was nothing to prevent the operation being held in a limited space: the Comitium in early times, the Forum, the Capitol etc. A single supervised enclosure was sufficient, the tribes entering and leaving it one after the other. This has been firmly established by Fraccaro, but many problems remain: how did voting take place within the tribes, in what order were they summoned, etc.? We shall consider these in due course.

Another point which emerges with certainty is that in the case of electoral tribal assemblies (i.e. the election of minor magistrates by the *comitia tributa* and of tribunes by the *concilium plebis*) all the tribes were called upon to vote simultaneously, *uno vocatu*, at least after the adoption of the secret ballot. There is abundant evidence of this for the late republican period,[54] and again it is confirmed by the *Lex Malacitana:*

> The person holding the *comitia* in accordance with this law shall summon the citizens to register their votes according to their curiae, calling all the curiae to the vote by a single summons, in such manner that the said curiae, each in a separate voting booth, may register their votes by means of tablets. (c. 55)

Thus the order of voting in electoral meetings of this type is fairly well understood. Problems still exist, however, as to how exactly the vote was expressed when several magistrates (e.g. up to 20 quaestors) had to be elected, how the ballots were counted and the results announced; we shall discuss these matters in their turn.

As compared with tribal assemblies, we are much less certain about the exact voting procedure in centuriate assemblies for the election of consuls, praetors and censors. At first sight it would seem that in the centuriate assembly the classes at least must have voted successively, beginning with the first class which included the centuries of *equites,* proceeding to the second and so on:

> For the knights were called upon to vote first; then the 80 centuries of the first class; if there was any disagreement there, which rarely happened, it was provided that the centuries of the second class should be called; and they almost never descended so far as to reach the lowest citizens. (Livy 1.43.11)

> The first centuries that [Servius] called to express their opinion were those with the highest rating, consisting of the 18 centuries of cavalry and the 80 centuries of infantry...If these were not all of the same mind, then he called the 22 centuries of the second class; [etc.] (Dionys. 4.20.3)

And Cicero, it will be recalled, explains that:

> the centuries of knights with their six votes, and the first class, with the addition of the century of the carpenters,...make up a total of 89 centuries. Now if, out of a total of 104 centuries—for that is the number left—only eight centuries should adhere to the 89, the whole power of the people would be exerted. (*De Republica* 2.39)

It would thus definitely seem that the classes voted one after the other. In another passage, describing a judicial assembly it is true, Dionysius gives a more detailed version of Cicero's account.

> The populace was wont to assemble in the field of Mars before the city,

drawn up under their centurions and their standards as in war. They did not give their votes [Dionysius here refers mistakenly to voting tablets] all at the same time, but each by their respective centuries, when these were called upon by the consuls. And, there being in all 193 centuries, and these distributed into six classes, the class that was first called and gave its vote...comprised 18 centuries of horse and 80 of foot...

If, in the case of the first centuries,...97 centuries were of the same opinion, the voting was at an end and the remaining 96 were not called upon to give their votes. (7.59)

But this was a judicial vote pro or contra, and in principle still an oral vote. In elections the procedure must perforce have been somewhat different, as the voters had to choose among several candidates.

As long as voting was by word of mouth, it is very probable that the centuries voted separately within each class. We know this to have been so in the case of the *praerogativa*, which was selected by lot for the purpose of voting first. As we shall see, this practice was one of the most specific institutions of the Roman *comitia*, and was maintained even when simultaneous voting was introduced for the other centuries. It corresponded fairly closely to the custom of choosing by lot a tribe (the *principium*) which voted first, or whose vote was announced first, in legislative or judicial *comitia tributa* (see next Chapter). The term *praerogativa* is sometimes also used of tribes, but no doubt loosely: in technical language it always refers to a century in the *comitia centuriata*. It is not certain, however, that a single century was always chosen by lot: originally, and no doubt until the centuriate system was 'reformed' around 200 BC, the oral vote took place successively and the 18 centuries of *equites* were called upon to vote first. Possibly the term *primo vocatae* ('first-called') was applied to them collectively. Thus in 296:

No one doubted that Fabius would by the common voice of all be for the fifth time elected; and in fact the prerogative centuries and all those which were summoned first were naming him consul, together with Lucius Volumnius. Fabius then made a speech. (Livy 10.22.1)

But within the next hundred years there was certainly a change. In three separate passages where Livy describes in detail incidents that took place when the *praerogativa* was voting in the *comitia*, it is clear that lots were cast and that they fell on what were almost certainly centuries of infantry of the first class.[55] In 215 the consul *suffectus*, Q. Fabius Maximus, returned from Campania to Rome to hold the consular elections. He took the precaution of not entering the City itself but going directly to the Campus Martius:

On the appointed day the right to vote first fell to the century of the younger men of the Aniensis tribe, and it named Titus Otacilius and Marcus Aemilius Regillus as consuls. Thereupon Quintus Fabius, after calling for silence, made a speech against these two candidates...'Lake Trasumennus and Cannae are sad examples to recall...Herald, summon the Aniensis century of the younger men to vote again!' [Otacilius protested, and Fabius had him restrained by his lictors.] Meanwhile the leading century proceeded to vote, and named as consuls Q. Fabius and M. Marcellus. The rest of the centuries without exception voted for them also. (Livy 24.7.12-9.1)

A somewhat different incident took place in 211:

While Fulvius was conducting the election for the choice of consuls, the century of the younger men of the Veturia tribe, having the right to vote first, declared in favour of Titus Manlius Torquatus and Titus Otacilius. When a crowd gathered before Manlius in order to congratulate him, he came to the tribunal of the consul and begged him to recall the century which had cast its vote, giving the condition of his eyes as an excuse. If Fulvius approved, he said, let him order the Veturia century of the younger men to vote again...But the century *en masse* cried out that they would not alter their opinion and would vote for the same men as consuls. On this Torquatus said: 'Neither could I as consul put up with your manners, nor you with my authority.' Then the century, moved by the prestige of the man, begged the consul to summon the Veturia century of the older men. They wished, they said, to confer with their elders and to name consuls on their authority. When the older men of the Veturia had been summoned, they were allowed to confer secretly with them. The elders pronounced in favour of Quintus Fabius, Marcus Marcellus and Marcus Valerius Laevinus. So, after deliberation had been allowed, the elders were sent away, and the younger men cast their vote. They voted for Marcus Claudius and Marcus Valerius as consuls, both being absent. The authority of the leading century was followed by all the rest. (Livy 26.22.2 ff, abridged).

Finally, in 210, when *comitia* were being held by the dictator Q. Fulvius, the prerogative fell by lot on the young men of the Galeria tribe, who voted for Q. Fulvius himself and Q. Fabius as consuls; the 'centuries called in the legal order' (*eodem jure vocatae;* perhaps 'selected in the same manner', i.e. by lot?) were inclined to follow their choice, when the tribunes intervened. The conflict between them and the dictator was resolved by the Senate (Livy 27.6.2-12).

These three incidents all seem to show that the prerogative was no longer given to the *equites* as a matter of course, for there is no trace anywhere of the equestrian centuries being divided into tribes or even into age-groups; *seniores* and *juniores* among the *equites* are only heard of under the Empire. From Livy's text it appears that each tribe was represented in the centuriate vote by two centuries, one of *juniores* and one of *seniores*. As we know that in a centuriate assembly the first class voted first, and as it appears from *De Republica* 2.40, quoted on page 000 above, that after a certain date the first class comprised only 70 centuries instead of 80, it is very tempting to see in the practice described above the first application of the 'reform' of the *comitia*. The first class, at any rate, would include a century of *juniores* and one of *seniores* of each tribe, and the *praerogativa* would be chosen by lot among the *juniores*, which would mean in practice choosing a tribe by lot. Expressions of the type 'Galeria century of the younger men' should thus be understood as meaning 'a century consisting of younger men of the first class, members of the Galeria tribe'. Under this reform, the honour of voting first would belong to infantrymen of military age who had the most direct interest in the choice of consuls and praetors. This is not to say that the vote of the *praerogativa*, important and even decisive though it was thought to be, could never be called in question. Three times during the Second Punic War we have seen this vote contested and even reversed by the presiding magistrate, the tribunes or even one of the candidates. Yet its propitiatory value was fully recognized: the ancients accounted for it by various convergent explanations:

> According to Varro, centuries are called upon as *praerogativae* [*sic*, plural] so that Romans from country districts who do not know the candidates may be able to consider them more easily. But Verrius Flaccus judges with more probability that after candidates were designated by the *praerogativae* the people began to discuss their greater or less merit, and the other centuries voted with more attention. (Festus, p. 290 L)

A late scholiast of Cicero (Pseudo-Asconius, p. 139 Or.) says: 'The prerogative tribes are those that vote before the ones regularly called. For it was the custom, so as to consolidate the people's agreement at the *comitia*, to have them vote twice on the same candidates'.

The custom of choosing a prerogative century by lot is well attested in the first century BC. Cicero speaks of it as a matter of course, especially for consular *comitia*. In his speech defending Cn. Plancius, who was elected aedile in 55 after the *comitia* were several times annulled or postponed under Pompey's chairmanship, he makes the following comparison:

> But, after all, in the previous election Plancius had already been marked down for the aedileship.... The century which votes first carries of itself such weight that no candidate for the consulship has ever secured its vote without being ultimately declared first consul either at that very election or at any rate for the following year; and is it possible that you should be surprised at Plancius' election to the aedileship, when not merely a small fraction [a century], but the whole of the electorate, has given a clear intimation

of its will regarding him? In conferring this distinction upon him, it was not a section of a single tribe that gave the lead to the rest, but it was a whole electorate giving the lead to the ensuing election. (*Pro Plancio* 49)

In the same year 55 the importance of the prerogative in praetorian elections is shown by Pompey's trick to prevent Cato of Utica from being elected:

[Cato stood for the praetorship, but the consuls] Pompey and Crassus feared that he would make the praetorship a match for the consulship. In the first place, therefore, they suddenly, and without the knowledge of the majority, got the Senate together, and had a vote passed that the praetors-elect should enter upon their office at once, without waiting for the time prescribed by law to elapse, during which time those who had bribed the people were liable to prosecution. Secondly, now that by this vote they had freed bribery from responsibility, they brought forward henchmen and friends of their own as candidates for the praetorship, themselves offering money for votes, and themselves standing by when the votes were cast. But the virtue and fame of Cato were superior even to these measures, since shame made most of the people think it a terrible thing to sell Cato by their votes, when the city might well buy him into the praetorship; and therefore the first tribe called upon voted for him. Then on a sudden Pompey lyingly declared that he heard thunder, and most shamefully dissolved the assembly, since it was customary to regard such things as inauspicious, and not to ratify anything after a sign from heaven had been given. Then they resorted again to extensive bribery, ejected the best citizens from the Campus Martius, and so by force got Vatinius elected praetor instead of Cato. (Plutarch, *Cato* 42)

As we shall see, there was a strong temptation for candidates who did not shrink from bribery to concentrate their financial efforts on the prerogative century, even though they did not know in advance which one it would be. In 54 two candidates promised to give this century 10 million sesterces if it would vote for them and against one of their competitors (Cicero, *Ad Quintum fratrem* 2.14.4). In 44, when Dolabella was elected consul *suffectus,* the comitial procedure still included lot-casting for the prerogative vote:

Now comes the day of Dolabella's election. The right of the first vote is determined by lot: he remains quiet. The result is announced. (Cicero, *Phil.* 2.82)

The prestige of the *praerogativa* derived from the ancient religious roots of the *comitia* system: the first vote to be cast was regarded as an omen and a good augury. Thus Cicero in 63:

If the religious feeling of elections has always been so strong that the votes of the first century have been regarded as an omen, there is no cause for surprise that Murena's reputation for luck and talk about it had a powerful effect. (*Pro Murena* 38). [Elsewhere he says:] In the case of the prerogative tribe or century, our forefathers determined that it should be the 'omen' of a proper election. (*De Divination* 1.103)

The religious associations of the *comitia* were invoked, as we shall see, under Augustus and later under Tiberius, when it was desired to place the vote of a restricted assembly of senators and knights, whose function was to 'destine' candidates for the office of consul or praetor, under the patronage of princes of the imperial family who had died an untimely death and were accorded quasi-divine honours, including that of lending their name and protection to the ten (later 15) centuries of the new assembly. The religious aspect is also confirmed by the fact that, after the reform of the *comitia* in the third or second century BC, the prerogative was assigned to a century of *juniores* (men of military age) of the first class.

Order of voting in centuriate assemblies

As we have seen, the *comitia centuriata* were, so to speak, hierarchical by definition. Not only were the classes not called on to vote simultaneously, but the system was such that if the first class was unanimous on any question it only needed another eight centuries of the second class to produce the necessary majority of 97. It remains to be seen, however, in what way the centuries, starting with the first and most important, voted within each class.

The procedure changed when oral voting gave place to the secret ballot. Until then the centuries probably voted one after the other, starting, as Livy and Dionysius tell us, with the 18 equestrian centuries. We have seen an example of this in 296 BC. The system is clearly described by Livy for the previous year: '[Despite Fabius's reluctance] the people proceeded to the election, and every century, as it was summoned within, in no uncertain terms named Fabius consul' (10.13.11). We do not know how the 80 centuries of the first class were distributed and designated before the reform of the third or second century. After it, as we have seen, matters were much simpler: in each tribe all the *juniores* formed one century and all the *seniores* another. Probably, however, the citizens were regrouped in this manner in advance of the *comitia*. The division into centuries was effected by the censors (cf. p. 85 above concerning the *aerarii*), who must also have designated the two principal members of each: the head of the century, called 'centurion' as in the army, and the *rogator* or teller. Every citizen was a *centurialis* or member of a century to which he was assigned before the vote,[56] in the same way as he was a *tribulis* or member of a tribe, and each man knew who his fellow-voters would be.

After the reform it is very probable that the first class voted in order of tribes,[57] unless all the tribes were chosen by lot. The results of the oral vote were officially proclaimed as each century voted, as the above-quoted text has shown. After the first class the second was naturally summoned: cf. Dolabella's election in 44, also quoted above. The only problem is that of the place and voting order of the centuries of *equites*. It is generally thought that these 18 centuries did not all vote together, but that 12 of them — those with the highest property rating, traditionally created by Servius Tullius — voted first, with the first class and no doubt before the infantry; then six more centuries, dating from the time of the elder Tarquin (with ancient and honorific names: *Ramnenses priores* and *posteriores, Titienses* and *Luceres* ditto), voted, it is thought, between the first and the second class, these being known as 'the six votes'.[58] But this complicated and rather surprising pattern is only a reconstruction, and the evidence for it consists only in obscure or ambiguous texts of Festus, Cicero or Livy. What is certain is that if these six centuries existed they were certainly not 'patrician centuries'; while Cicero in his *De Republica,* which purports to describe the situation in 129 BC, refers to their vote as being grouped with that of the other centuries of *equites*. In any case, until the time of the Gracchi the senators voted in the equestrian centuries for the good reason that they were mostly ex-magistrates and in order to become a magistrate one had to have an equestrian rating.[59] The senators kept their 'public horse' beyond the equestrian time-limit, for those not seeking public honours, of ten years' service and 27 years of age, and could thus considerably affect the vote of the *equites* as a whole. Thus Cicero says elsewhere:

> How conveniently the orders are arranged, the ages, the classes, the knights, among whom the votes of the senators also are included! Too many foolishly desire to abolish this useful system in their search for a new distribution of money through some resolution of the plebs providing for the return of the horses. (*De Republica* 4.2)[60]

It is certain, on the other hand, that the senators had ceased to belong to the equestrian centuries by the first century BC. Perhaps these centuries were by then reserved for *juniores:* this seems to be implied by Quintus Cicero in his 'candidate's *vade mecum'* addressed to his brother Marcus in 64:

> The centuries of knights can, I think, be secured much more easily, with care. First you should get to know the knights (there are not many); then, try hard to win them (young men of that age are much more easily gained as friends). Further, you have with you those of the best breeding and highest culture among the young generation; and then, as the order of knights is on your side, they will follow its authority, if you take the trouble to secure its

centuries not only by the general goodwill of the order, but by individual friendships. Young men's enthusiasm in winning support, visiting electors, carrying news and attending on you is amazingly important, and confers credit on you. (*Commentariolum petitionis* 33)

This is a very ambiguous text, and perhaps Q. Cicero is only referring to the help that can be expected from young *equites* (including, no doubt, senators' sons who are not old enough for office) during an election campaign as well as on the actual polling day. It must be admitted, however, that the importance attached to the *equites'* vote in 64 as in 129 BC is hard to reconcile with the idea that six equestrian centuries voted after the first class.

But, while the precedence of classes and the fact that the centuries voted successively are certain for the period of oral voting, this is not the case for the period of the secret ballot. This new technique, the working of which we shall study presently, made it possible to speed up the voting (if not the counting of votes) and to have all the units vote at once if space permitted, as it certainly did on the Campus Martius. We shall see that for the electoral *comitia tributa* the tribes were summoned to vote together in writing, *uno vocatu* as the legal texts say; and there is no reason why the centuries should not have voted in the same way. If the first class consisted of 35 plus 35 centuries it would have been very easy to use for this purpose the enclosure with its 35 divisions as it was arranged for the tribes. Each century—first the *juniores*, then the *seniores*—would assemble in its division, each citizen would deposit his voting tablet, and when everyone had done so the votes could be counted and the result announced for the whole class. This is what Cicero says about Dolabella's election:

> The first class is called: its vote announced; then, as usual, the 'six votes' [?]; then the second class is called; all this is done quicker than my description. When the business is finished the good augur...says 'On another day.' [i.e. the omens are unfavourable] (*Phil.* 2.82)[61]

As this passage shows, the result of a consular election was decided as soon as the second class had voted, or, more probably, its first eight centuries only, as would be expected.

We also know, broadly speaking, the voting order of electoral units in the *comitia tributa*.[62] Before written voting was introduced the tribes certainly voted successively at elections, as they did for laws and judgements (and in these two cases successive voting was the rule at all times):

> Gnaeus Flavius, being in attendance upon the aediles, and perceiving that the tribes were supporting him for aedile, but that his name was thrown out because he was acting as a recorder, put away his tablet and took an oath that he would keep no record. (Livy 9.46.2)

After the introduction of the secret ballot, however, the tribes voted simultaneously. Once again the chief evidence is the *Lex Malacitana,* which says, as already quoted:

> The person holding the *comitia* in accordance with this law shall summon the citizens to register their votes according to their curiae, calling all the curiae to the vote by a single summons, in such manner that the said curiae, each in a separate voting booth, may register their votes by means of tablets. (c. 55)

Thus lots are only cast for the purpose of deciding the order in which the count for each tribe is announced. This order was of importance, as we shall see, because, paradoxical as this may seem at first sight, it could affect the final result.

Introduction of voting tablets

As we have seen, the electoral procedure was profoundly modified by the introduction of voting tablets (*tabellae*). The adoption of the secret ballot was certainly due to political rather than technical reasons. It took place in stages at the end of the second century BC, in accordance with laws proposed by tribunes of the plebs; these were mostly *populares*, and the new system did not fail to arouse opposition. Its purpose was not to make voting technically easier but to protect civil liberties by the secrecy and anonymity of the vote (cf. Figs. 13 and 14).

Under the oral system there was certainly no guarantee of this kind. Each member of a group, tribe or century was called on, perhaps by name, to walk up to the *rogator*, who repeated the question put by the president of the assembly and asked him for his vote. We shall see later how the answer was recorded for counting purposes. Like the *centurio*,[63] the *rogator* was probably appointed for each century by the censor; he was usually a man of note, such as a senator. We know from an anecdote reported by Cicero that in 180 an ex-magistrate, M. Cornelius Scipio Malagunensis, was *rogator* in his century (*De Oratore* 2.200). But the most typical example of the pressures to which the citizen was exposed when voting aloud was the occasion of Aemilius Paullus's triumph in 168. Prompted by the military tribune Servius Galba, the first tribe refused to vote for the triumph on account of the general's strict discipline and the niggardly distribution of booty. Then the ex-consul M. Servilius asked the tribunes to allow him to speak and to start the vote over again. He ended, according to Plutarch, with a scarcely veiled threat:

'Take these people off to their voting; and I will come down and follow along with them all, and will learn who are base and thankless and prefer to be wheedled and flattered in war rather than commanded.' (Plutarch, *Aemilius* 31.7)

Plutarch adds that this speech effectively changed the soldiers' minds, so that all the tribes voted for Aemilius's triumph.

Cicero speaks of the voting-tablet as 'guaranteeing freedom by its secrecy' (*vindex tacitae libertatis; De Lege Agraria* 2.4), and says elsewhere: 'A law to provide for voting by ballot was proposed by L. Cassius. The people thought that their liberty was at stake' (*Pro Sestio* 103). He also says: 'The people cherishes its privilege of voting by ballot, which allows a man to wear a smooth brow while it cloaks the secrets of his heart, and leaves him free to act as he chooses while giving any promise he may be asked to give'; (*Pro Plancio* 16). The best account of the various provisions of the *leges tabellariae* and the reasons adduced for them, as well as the resistance they encountered among the upper classes, is in Cicero's *De Legibus*, which dates from about 54-51 BC. In his 'draft for a revision of the constitution' Cicero suggests a modification of the secret ballot in somewhat cryptic terms: 'When elective, judicial and legislative acts of the people are performed by vote, the voting shall not be concealed from citizens of high rank, and shall be free to the common people' (3.10). He explains his reasons at length, first by an indictment of the secret ballot:

Everyone knows that laws which provide a secret ballot have deprived the aristocracy of all its influence. And such a law was never desired by the people when they were free, but was demanded only when they were tyrannized over by the powerful men in the State. (For this very reason we have records of severer condemnations of powerful men under the oral method of voting than when the ballot was used.) Therefore means should have been found to deprive powerful leaders of the people's undue eagerness to support them with their votes even in the case of bad measures; but the people should not have been provided with a hiding-place where they could conceal a mischievous vote by means of the ballot, and keep the aristocracy in ignorance of their real opinions.

For these reasons no man of high character has ever proposed or supported a measure like yours. There are indeed four such balloting laws in existence. The first is concerned with the election of magistrates; this is the Gabinian Law, proposed by a man who was unknown and of low degree. That was followed two years later by the Cassian Law, which referred to trials before the people; it was proposed by Lucius Cassius, who was a nobleman, but—I say it without prejudice to his family—stood apart from the aristocracy, and, by favouring popular measures, was always seeking the fickle applause of the mob. The third law is that of Carbo, which applies to the adoption or rejection of proposed laws; this Carbo was a factious and mischievous citizen, who could not gain his personal safety from the aristocracy even by returning to his allegiance to their party. The method of oral voting, then, appeared to have gone out of existence except in trials for treason, which even Cassius omitted from his balloting law. But Gaius Coelius provided the ballot even for such trials; however, he regretted to the end of his days that he had done such an injury to the republic in order to destroy Gaius Popilius. And indeed our grandfather, during his whole life, opposed with the greatest energy the passage of a balloting law in this town, although his wife was the sister of Marcus Gratidius, the man who was proposing such a law. For Gratidius raised a storm in a wine-ladle, as the popular saying goes, just as his son Marius did later in the Aegean Sea. Indeed...to our [grandfather]...when the matter was reported to him, Marcus Scaurus the consul said: 'Marcus Cicero, I wish you had chosen to dedicate your efforts to the welfare of the state with the same spirit and energy which you have shown in the affairs of a small town.'

Wherefore, since we are not now simply reviewing the actual laws of Rome, but restoring old laws which have been lost, or else originating new ones, I think you ought to propose, not what can be secured from the Roman people such as it is at present, but what is actually the best. Your beloved Scipio received the blame for the Cassian Law, since his support is said to have made its enactment possible, and if you propose a balloting law, you must take the responsibility for it alone. For it will not receive my approval, nor that of Atticus, so far as I can judge from his expression. (3.34–37)

Then Cicero defends his own proposal:

Well, I see that you have rejected my law without the use of the ballot! But let me explain — though Scipio has given a sufficient defence of these ideas in my former work — that I am granting this freedom to the people in such a way as to ensure that the aristocracy shall have great influence and the opportunity to use it. For the text of my law in regard to votes is as follows: they shall not be concealed from citizens of high rank, and shall be free to the people. This law implies the repeal of all the recent laws which ensure the secrecy of the ballot in every possible way, providing as they do that no one shall look at a ballot, and that no one shall question or accost the voters. The Marian Law even made the passages [*pontes*, see p. 271 below] narrow. If such provisions as these are made to interfere with the buying of votes, as they usually are, I do not criticize them; but if laws have never actually prevented bribery, then let the people have their ballots as a safeguard of their liberty, but with the provision that these ballots are to be shown and voluntarily exhibited to any of our best and most eminent citizens, so that the people may enjoy liberty also in this privilege of honourably winning the favour of the aristocracy.

By this means the result which you just mentioned, Quintus, is already accomplished — that the ballot condemns a smaller number than were condemned by the oral vote, because the people are satisfied with possessing the power; let them but keep that, and in everything else they are governed by influence and favour. And so, to leave out of account the corrupting effect of general donations upon the people's votes, do you not see that if bribery can ever be got rid of, the people, before they vote, will ask the opinion of the aristocracy? Hence our law grants the appearance of liberty, preserves the influence of the aristocracy, and removes the causes of dispute between the classes. (3.38-39)

Cicero's proposal is clearly rather confused.[64] He and his contemporaries evidently regarded the secret ballot as a demagogic measure that was partly to blame for the growing and pernicious influence of the common people on certain decisions. Cicero's family tradition was opposed to the laws in question, as his grandfather had fought successfully all his life to prevent or delay their extension to the local assemblies at Arpinum. Other relatives of his, however, including the great Marius and his nephew by adoption, M. Marius Gratidianus, who was Cicero's own cousin, were fervent advocates of the secret ballot. Cicero himself thought that once a thing has been conceded to the people it is practically impossible to get it back again; he therefore wished to make the innovation as harmless as possible. His plan was, while allowing the masses to vote in secret if they chose, to make it legal for better-class citizens to give their vote openly in the hope that they would influence the rest, and to allow them to check the vote of the *humiles* if the latter did not object. In short, under Cicero's plan the secret ballot would be optional instead of compulsory — a compromise solution typical of his subtle policy. As I have suggested, it may have been inspired by certain passages in Plato's *Laws*,[65] which he obviously had in mind when writing *De Legibus*. Plato devised a method of voting publicly in writing, with the same object as Cicero's: so that the better class might affect the voting by their example, without depriving voters of the protection of secrecy. Even if Cicero did not consciously follow Plato, the similarity of their ideas is significant and need not cause any surprise.

The voting process

Having noted the main lines of the voting procedure and the reasons for the introduction of the secret ballot, we may consider how individuals actually voted within their units.

The secret ballot led to modifications in the physical design of the electoral enclosure. The citizens no longer had to file past a *rogator* who would record their votes on a *tabula*, afterwards counting them and reporting the result to the presiding officer. The voters were now furnished with tablets which they would drop into an urn. For once we have some visual idea of how things worked, as voting scenes are represented on three coins of the late republican period, struck by officials of the mint who wished to recall to memory some aspects of the elections.[66] The clearest of these dates from about the end of the second century and was probably intended to commemorate the ballot laws, perhaps especially that introduced by Marius in 119. It shows three figures, two of whom are citizens in the process of voting. They are advancing from left to right across a gangway of which only one of the two parapets is visible: this is one of the *pontes* ('bridges'), the temporary passageways that were already used in the days of oral voting and over which the citizens advanced one or two at a time. The *Lex Maria* of 119 reduced their width so as to prevent voters from being pestered by candidates' friends at the last minute, but they must still have been wide enough to allow room for the scrutineers as well. The *pontes* gave the voters access to the president's tribunal where the urns were; they were thus level with the tribunal and at a certain height above the floor of the enclosure. We do not know what that height was in the *saepta*, but to judge from the *tribunalia* used in the Forum, which were simply the *podia* of certain temples (e.g. that of Castor), it might have been between two and three metres. There would be steps leading up to the *pontes*, which extended over empty space for a length of several metres; this accounts for the way they are referred to in ancient sources. The Romans had a proverbial saying: 'Men of 60, off the bridge!', which some explained as follows:

At the time when it first became the custom to walk across a bridge in order to vote, the *juniores* cried that men of 60 and over should be 'pushed off the bridge', as they no longer had any public duties, and it was for them, the *juniores*, to elect generals. (Festus, p. 452 L)

In 44 the senators who conspired against Caesar hesitated whether to assassinate him on the Campus Martius during the elections,

so that while some hurled him from the bridge as he summoned the tribes to vote, the rest might wait below and slay him. (Suetonius, *Caesar* 80)

If this text is taken literally, perhaps we must suppose that the 35 lanes for the different tribes all terminated at a single platform from which the *templum* was reached, and which might itself be divided into 35 passages. In any case the voters certainly had to ascend some steps to reach the level of the *templum*; their existence can be surmised from the attitude of the figure on the left of the denarius of Licinius Nerva.

In what order did the individual citizens vote, in their centuries or tribes? As we shall see, in legislative *comitia* the name of the first man to vote was noted and recorded. We do not know for certain if he was selected by lot or designated by the president. Very likely there was a sort of roll-call. This is what occurred in the procedure of *destinatio* as laid down by the *Lex Valeria Cornelia* of AD 5; after selecting a tribe by lot, the president 'shall call on the members of that tribe who are senators or have the right to address the the Senate, to approach the first urn and cast their vote' (1.28).[67] We may suppose that each century possessed an *album* or register in which its members were listed by name. A passage in Pseudo-Asconius (p. 103, Or.; cf. above, p. 85) says that one who was declared *aerarius* ceased to be registered in the *album* of his century. Roman inscriptions of the first century AD with lists of recipients of grain distributions give their names alphabetically under tribes and centuries. Very possibly men were summoned to vote in the same way. In any case there must have been some identity check to prevent fraud, or how, for instance, could a law have been applied such as that of 95 which denied the vote to non-citizens? There is evidence of such a check, in any case, in 115, when Marius was elected praetor.

> Suspicion was chiefly aroused by the sight of a servant of Cassius Sabaco inside the palings (*saepta*) among the voters; for Sabaco was a special friend of Marius. Sabaco was therefore summoned before the court, and testified that the heat had made him so thirsty that he had called for cold water, and that his servant had come in to him with a cup, and had then at once gone away after his master had drunk. Sabaco, however, was expelled from the Senate by the censors of the next year, and it was thought that he deserved this punishment, either because he had given false testimony, or because of his intemperance. (Plutarch, *Marius* 5)

The method of supervision no doubt varied. Originally it would have been the duty of the heads of civilian centuries and the *curatores* of tribes to know all their members. Later, we can be sure that the *divisores* — a well-established and almost honourable profession — whose task it was to distribute public or electoral largesse within the tribes, had a good memory for faces and knew all their electors by sight. Rome, after all, was largely a word-of-mouth civilization, and visual or aural memory must still have played a very large part. Senators had slaves called *nomenclatores* whose duty was to remind them of people's names at the right moment.[68] But it is also very possible that, at least by the first century BC, less subjective means of control were used at elections as they were for grain distribution. As we have seen, the names of those entitled to receive grain were inscribed on a bronze tablet at the appropriate 'gate' of the Porticus Minucia or elsewhere, and the *tessera frumentaria* became a permanent document, a sort of identity card. On a coin of the reign of Antoninus in the second century AD[69] it can be seen as an oblong tablet with a ring on top. An exactly similar object appears on a unique coin of the Caesarian period, a sestertius of Lollius Palicanus.[70] As this type of *tessera frumentaria* did not yet exist in republican times, may we not suppose that the sestertius depicts an earlier form of 'identity card' used in the *comitia?* This is supported by a passage in Book Three of Varro's *Res Rusticae*, the action of which takes place during the counting of votes for an election to the aedileship:

> Pantuleius Parra comes and tells us that a man was caught, while they were sorting the ballots in the office, in the act of casting ballots into the ballot-box; and that he was dragged off to the consul by the supporters of the other candidates. (3.4.18)[71]

These 'ballots' (*tesserulae*) are certainly not voting tablets (*tabellae*), and the 'ballot-box' (*loculus*) has nothing to do with the urn, always called *cista*, into which the *tabellae* were cast. May it not have been a receptable into which the *custodes* or scrutineers dropped each *tessera* as it was handed in by the voter, to make sure that there were the same number of *tesserae* as of ballots (*tabellae*)? In that case the man caught interfering with the ballot-box would have been hastily filling it up because, no doubt, his accomplices had cast more votes than the tribe in question was entitled to.

We now come to the exact procedure of the individual vote. During the period of oral voting it appears to have been quite simple. The *rogator* at the far end of the *pons* had a list (*tabula*) of approved candidates, no doubt a smaller copy of the one posted up on the tribunal. He would ask each voter to indicate his choice for consul, praetor etc., and would make a mark (*punctum*) on the line opposite each name. When the whole century or tribe had passed through, the marks obtained by each candidate were added up, and the one with the highest number was declared to be the first choice of that century or tribe. The process was then continued for as many names as there were posts to be filled. Each unit was certainly supposed to vote for several candidates (two for the consulship, etc.), as is shown by the texts quoted above concerning the prerogative century. That the votes were originally counted by adding up the marks (*puncta*) obtained by each candidate is confirmed by the anecdote mentioned earlier concerning Cornelius Scipio Malagunensis in 180. When the *praeco* put the formal question to him on the president's behalf: 'What of Lucius Manlius?' (i.e. how many votes for him?), he replied, absent-mindedly or otherwise, 'I take him for an honest man and a capital fellow-citizen' (Cicero, *De Oratore* 2.260).

The counting procedure was not essentially modified by the introduction of written voting. In each voting unit, the results still gave a certain number of *puncta* for each candidate. We have some details, for instance, for 55 BC, when Cn. Plancius was elected aedile. At his trial for malpractice the prosecuting counsel, as quoted by Cicero, exclaimed:

> 'Can you doubt that collusion was employed, seeing that Plancius and
> Plotius together carried the votes of so many tribes?' But could they have
> been elected together, if they had not carried the votes of the tribes together?
> 'Yes,' he objects, 'but in some of the tribes they scored an almost exactly
> equal number of points.' Naturally, since they had both come to the poll
> with their election and declaration virtually accomplished at the previous
> election [which, it will be recalled, had been annulled]. Yet even this
> circumstance should not involve them in any suspicion of collusion; and
> indeed our ancestors would never have provided for the election of aediles
> by lot, had they not foreseen the possibility of two candidates receiving the
> same number of votes. (*Pro Plancio* 53)

The *Lex Malacitana* expressly provides for the eventuality of several
candidates obtaining the same number of votes in each curia; in that case a
married man takes precedence over a bachelor, a paterfamilias over a childless
man etc.; failing all else, a lot is to be cast (ç. 56).

A puzzling question arises, however, in connection with the written vote
and perhaps even with the oral one: viz. for how many candidates did each
elector cast his vote? Logically it would seem that he should have given as
many names as there were posts to be filled. This would have been practicable
enough in a consular election (two posts only) or even the election of aediles
(four posts). But what happened in the case of collegia comprising ten posts
(like the tribunate), 20 (like the quaestorship after Sulla) or even the praetorship?
For these, each voter would have had to utter ten or 20 names, or later to write
the same number, albeit in abbreviated form, on his voting tablet. Is this really
conceivable, or should we suppose, as Mrs Ursula Hall first suggested,[72] that
each man only voted for a single candidate, and that the right number of
candidates were declared elected, in order, on the basis of the votes thus obtained?
The texts and documents do not enable us to solve the question; at most, there
are one or two pieces of evidence which do not rule out the supposition. If it
were correct, the result could sometimes have been that some posts were unfilled
even after all the centuries or tribes had voted. This situation, which could not
happen on any other hypothesis, does seem to have occurred fairly regularly in
tribunicial elections and at least once in consular ones. One example is the
election of 217, at which C. Terentius Varro, who as consul suffered defeat at
Cannae, stood for office as an opponent of the nobility:

> When the plebs had been inflamed by these harangues, though there were
> three patrician candidates...and two plebeians of families which had already
> been ennobled,...Gaius Terentius was the only consul elected, and the
> assembly called to choose a colleague for him was therefore under his control.

The nobles, finding that Varro's competitors had not been able to command the necessary strength, thereupon obliged Lucius Aemilius Paullus to stand, though he held out long and earnestly against their importunity. ...On the next election day all those who had been Varro's rivals withdrew their names, and the consul was given Paullus, rather as a competent opponent than as a colleague. (Livy 22.35.1-4)

If each citizen had had to vote for two candidates it is hard to imagine that a second nomination would not have emerged, even if Varro was well ahead of the rest. Livy in fact expressly says that the nomination of Varro alone was a manoeuvre by his partisans to ensure that he would preside over the *comitia* for the election of his successor, either next day or subsequently. Their stratagem failed because, as all the rival candidates withdrew on the following day, the voters were bound to elect the sole remaining candidate, who represented the nobility. We also know that sometimes the vote did not produce enough names to fill up the number of the college of tribunes. In that case the presiding officer was bound to repeat the procedure for several days, or as long as might be necessary.[73]

The citizen, then, was provided with one or more *tabellae* on which to record his vote. We know little more about these tablets, except that in AD 5 they were coated with wax and were therefore written on with a stylus, like private letters and memoranda. In 123 C. Gracchus's followers, who had assembled for a legislative vote, used their styli as defensive weapons when attacked.[74] The *Tabula Hebana* states that before voting began the tablets were placed in front of the president on the tribunal, beside the urns, but unfortunately it does not say exactly when they were given to the voters. We may suppose from Licinius Nerva's coin that the citizen was given a tablet, perhaps in exchange for his *tessera* of identity, when he mounted the steps leading to the *pons*; the person seen at a lower level, half-hidden by the barrier, would then be the *rogator* or one of his assistants, handing the voter his ballot. We can form an idea of the tablets' size from those used in the courts; these were four inches long, coated with wax and inscribed with a letter A (*absolvo*) on one side and D (*damno*) on the other. The juryman was supposed to erase one letter or the other and drop the tablet into an urn without showing which way he had voted.[75] Similar tablets were probably used, as we shall see below, for legislative and judicial *comitia;* but what about elections? All we know for certain is that the voter was supposed to write on unmarked tablets in his own hand: for if two ballots were found marked in the same handwriting it was regarded as evidence of fraud. A friend of Cato's, M. Favonius, was defeated at the election of aediles in 54, but Cato, who was his 'teller', noticed that 'the voting tablets were all inscribed in one hand' (Plutarch, *Cato* 46.2); he protested to the tribunes and the election was quashed. Probably, according to Roman custom, the voters could, if they wished, write only the initials of the candidate or candidates of their choice; Cicero tells of a schemer who 'realized that if he renounced the aedileship there was a chance of his being returned praetor by Lucius Piso the consul [in 58], if only it turned out that there was a rival candidate with the same initial as himself' (*De Domo* 112).

Finally, the voters could write whatever they liked on the unmarked tablets: in 44 Caesar's opponents at the consular elections wrote in the names of two tribunes, Caesetius and Marullus, whom he had removed from office the year before, although they were not candidates (Suet., *Caesar* 80).[76] In elections where several posts had to be filled it seems doubtful that the voter would have had time to write ten or 20 sets of initials. But this is not absolutely conclusive, and it must remain uncertain whether he voted for several candidates or for one only.

The urn belonging to each voting unit was supervised by guards, *custodes*. There were several of these: one at least appointed by the presiding officer, and others by the candidates. Again the *Lex Malacitana* lays down precise regulations:

> [The president] shall likewise see that three of the citizens of the said *municipium* are placed at the voting box of each curia, not themselves belonging to that curia, in order to guard and count the votes, and that before performing such duty each of the said three citizens shall take oath that he will deal with the counting of the votes and make report thereon with all good faith. Furthermore, he shall not hinder candidates for an office from each placing one guard at every several voting box. And the said guards, both those placed by the person holding the *comitia* and those placed by candidates for office, shall each register his vote in that curia at whose voting box he shall be placed on guard, and the votes of the said guards shall be as lawful and valid as if each had registered his vote in his own curia. (*c.* 55)

The same procedure is attested at Rome for our period, except that no doubt each candidate could appoint several *custodes* for each century or tribe. It was a great honour to be asked to act as *custos*, and even more so to be entrusted with the *prima tabula*, i.e. the register of votes (*puncta*) of the *centuria praerogativa*. People of note were selected for these responsibilities, e.g. Cicero was given the *prima tabula* by his future adversary L. Piso (*In Pisonem* 11). When recalled from exile in 57 Cicero declared that the *rogatores* and *custodes* were the most distinguished ever seen on the Campus Martius; they had no doubt been appointed by the sponsors of the law for his recall, i.e. all the magistrates. The tellers' names were recorded in the archives: thus Cicero says 'I see indubitably for myself — what indeed the public records prove — that you were the collectors, the tellers and the custodians of the voting-tablets' (*In Pisonem* 36).

Later, at the beginning of the Empire, a body was set up consisting of 900 men eligible to serve as *custodes* at election time (Pliny, *N.H.* 33.31); they were selected from all the 'decuriae of the judges', i.e. senators, some *equites* and wealthy members of the first class. This was enough to provide nine tellers for each urn at the *comitia centuriata*, assuming 100 centuries actually voted, and 15 each at the *comitia tributa*. Most probably, as we have seen, only 35 urns were provided at the *saepta*, even for the *comitia centuriata* (each class voting in two sections), so that no doubt the 900 did not all have to serve at once.

Counting of votes and announcement of results

The system of voting by units each of which was counted as a whole introduced complications and sometimes paradoxical results from a modern point of view. It is certain that in some cases the results for each unit were announced before other units had even voted, as it depended on those results whether they would be called on to vote or not. This was clearly the case in the centuriate assembly, electoral or legislative, where, as we have seen, it was customary to stop at the second class (Cicero, *Phil.* 2.82). In legislative or judicial assemblies where the tribes voted successively the results were certainly announced as each one voted; as we shall see, when a majority was almost reached there was always a dramatic pause, as new elements might suddenly change the situation radically. This was true of elections only when the units voted successively, as they perhaps did before balloting was introduced. This may have been what happened at Scipio's election, in 174 no doubt, when his former scribe Cicereius stood down 'once he saw that all the centuries preferred Scipio to him' (i.e. those which had already voted).[77] But what happened in the days of the written vote? It would seem that all the centuries of the first class were then called on to vote at once (in two batches, since there were only 35 divisions of the *saepta*). For the *comitia tributa* the 35 tribes were called on *uno vocatu*. With votes cast in writing, time was required to scrutinize and count the ballots and record the result of *tabulae*. In these circumstances (and perhaps the same procedure applied to the vote of a single class in the *comitia centuriata*) the *Lex Malacitana* shows how the count was effected and the result proclaimed, and *c.* 56, already quoted, indicates how the results were calculated in each curia:

> The person holding the said *comitia* shall return that candidate who has more votes than the rest as elected and created by that curia, and then the next in order, until the number of people to be elected is made up.

(Unfortunately, as we saw, while this text shows that the curia as a whole must vote for as many persons as there are posts to be filled, it does not say whether each individual voted for one candidate or several). These partial results were naturally essential in determining the final results. The text does not say when they were ascertained, but it is natural to suppose that the count for each unit began as soon as it had finished voting; since the units differed greatly in size, this would have meant a different time for each. It was certainly the business of the *rogatores* to record their unit's vote on a *tabula* and submit it to the presiding magistrate. When all the separate returns were in, the final result would be calculated:

> The person holding the *comitia*...shall, when the voting lists of all the curiae have been brought in, subject the names of the curiae to the lot, and draw out one by one the names of the several curiae by lot, and as the name of each curia is drawn, he shall order those candidates elected by the said curia to be declared in the order in which the several candidates shall have secured a majority of the curiae; he shall, after they have...taken oath and given security for public money, return the same as appointed and created, until the number of magistrates proper to be created by this law is made up. If two or more persons shall have the same number of curiae, he shall take the same course concerning such persons as has already been set forth concerning those who obtained an equal number of votes... (*c.* 57)

Thus, even when the units voted simultaneously, the casting of lots to determine the order in which the partial results were declared affected the priority of candidates in the formal announcement of results. Usually the result would most probably be in accordance with the relative number of votes polled. A candidate, for instance, was more likely to be declared first in the *comitia tributa*, i.e. chosen by 18 tribes, if he was preferred by the great majority of voters altogether, for instance if he was the first choice of each separate tribe. But it could happen, as Pernice first observed in the last century,[78] that this method of announcing the tribal votes in an order determined by lot (and in the reformed *comitia centuriata* the results for the first class, which were decisive, must have been announced in the same manner) meant that a candidate declared to be elected in first place had fewer votes than one who was returned subsequently, or even than a defeated candidate. The practice of deciding the order of the *renuntiato* by lot thus introduced an element of arbitrariness, perhaps not more serious than a modern electoral law such as, for example, the British one under which a party can obtain a majority of seats in the Commons although it has not an absolute or even a relative majority of the votes cast.

When voting was by word of mouth, the announcement of partial results which were known at least informally after each unit had voted may have affected the choice of those who had not yet cast their vote. Even with votes in writing, this must certainly have happened in legislative or judicial matters. But in the case of electoral assemblies with the secret ballot, all the votes having been cast, it is not clear, despite the opinion of U. Hall and E. Staveley, how the announcement could have had this effect. If could not do so in the electoral *comitia tributa*, and we have seen that under the *Lex Malacitana* the results for all the tribes were brought to the president simultaneously. True, as we saw in the previous chapter, partial results may have been announced informally as they became available. In that case the units which voted last, and which had the most members, might have altered their choice in the light of the votes already cast, but on the whole this does not seem likely. Cicero would hardly have been referring to such an event when he said to C. Antonius, his rival for the consulate in 64: 'Don't you know that I was the first to be elected praetor when you only managed a third place thanks to your competitors withdrawing, to the rallying of certain centuries and, above all, thanks to me?' (Asconius, p. 85 C).

These were centuriate elections, and very possibly after the first class had voted there might be withdrawals and switching of votes in aid of a candidate in difficulties. In any case, when any college of magistrates was elected, although in theory each of them was equal to the others in rank and powers, the order in which the names were announced (and which must usually have been that of the number of votes cast) was of great importance to their dignity and authority. Cicero, who was elected time and again with flying colours, constantly refers to this: e.g. 'The Roman people by their general suffrages returned me high on the poll as quaestor, and successively as first aedile and first praetor' (*In Pisonem* 1.2). We have quoted his proud words to Antonius about the praetorship, and his election to the consulate was more triumphant still. When Servilius Rullus proposed that the triumvirs appointed under his agrarian law should be elected by only 18 tribes, chosen by lot, he retorted that 'It was not the last sorting of the voting-tablets, but those first hastening to the polling-booths — not the individual voices of the criers, but the unanimous voice of the Roman people that proclaimed me consul' (*De Lege Agraria* 2.4). In other words, Cicero probably had all the centuries on his side. Of his two chief competitors, Antonius was favoured by only a few centuries more than Catiline (Asconius, p. 94 C): As each century, if not each voter, had to nominate two consuls, this means that out of the 87 centuries that were required, Antonius did not achieve second place until a large number had voted: for instance all those of the second class (perhaps 35) and even some of the third. We may say, in any case, that whereas the first centuries were unanimous in favouring Cicero, they were divided as to whether Antonius or Catiline should have the second place.

The counting operations took time; they too were placed under divine protection, and sometimes they gave rise to incidents. To our great advantage, Book Three of Varro's *Res Rusticae* consists of a dialogue which is supposed to take place on a day of elections to the aedileship:

> During the election Quintus Axius, the senator, a member of my tribe, and I, after casting our ballots, wished, though the sun was hot, to be on hand to escort the candidate whom we were supporting when he returned

home. Axius remarked to me: 'While the votes are being sorted, shall we enjoy the shade of the Villa Publica, instead of building us one out of the half-plank (*tabella dimidiata*) of our own candidate?' 'Well,' I replied, 'I think that the proverb is correct, "bad advice is worst for the adviser," and also that good advice should be considered good both for the adviser and the advised.' So we go our way and come to the Villa. There we find Appius Claudius, the augur, sitting on a bench so as to be on hand for consultation if need should arise. (2.1-2)

The conversation thus skilfully introduced turns on the subject of *villae*. A minute or two later,

A shouting arose in the Campus. We old hands at politics were not surprised at this occurrence, as we knew how excited an election crowd could become, but still we wanted to know what it meant; thereupon Pantuleius Parra comes and tells us that a man was caught, while they were sorting the ballots in the office, in the act of casting ballots into the ballot-box; and that he was dragged off to the consul by the supporters of the other candidates. Pavo arose, as it was the watcher for his candidate who was reported to have been arrested. (5.18)

Shortly after, Appius's bailiff comes with a message from the consul that the augurs are summoned (7.1). When Appius returns, the others ask him what happened. Finally Pavo comes back and says:

'If you wish to weigh anchor, the ballots have been cast and the casting lots for the tribes is going on; and the herald has begun to announce who has been elected aedile by each tribe.' Appius arose hurriedly, so as to congratulate his candidate at once. [Varro remains behind with Axius, knowing that his own candidate will come and find them. The discussion on rustic matters continues.] Then a noise was heard on the right, and our candidate, as aedile-elect, came into the villa wearing the broad stripe. We approached and congratulated him and escorted him to the Capitoline. (17.1; 17.10)

All these operations required time, even if no special incidents arose. Varro's dialogue takes nearly two hours to read at a conversational rate. We have another indication from 44, when Caesar held improvised *comitia* for the consulship instead of the *comitia tributa*; although there was only one post to be filled, the operation lasted from the second to the seventh hour. The duration of course depended on the number of candidates and actual voters in this or that assembly, both of which were extremely variable. We have seen several examples in Livy of assemblies which had to be extended for some days because not all the posts had been filled by the first evening. In general, while precise information is lacking, we may take it that an election lasted a whole day at least.

Legislative and judicial assemblies

Many of the details we have given for electoral assemblies are equally valid for judicial and legislative ones. Generally speaking, however, it is clear that their procedures were simpler in so far as the vote was a matter of Yes or No, acquittal or conviction. This, as we have seen, made it possible to continue the practice of consecutive voting in these assemblies even after the secret ballot was introduced. When voting was by word of mouth this meant that each vote was known as soon as it was cast; but the same must have been the case with the secret ballot also, for only this can explain the fact that a decision was often announced as soon as the eighteenth tribe had voted. The best-known of these occasions was the vote on the law by which Tiberius Gracchus sought to depose his fellow-tribune M. Octavius, who opposed his agrarian law (but in 133 legislative votes still took place orally):

> When Octavius was not to be persuaded, Tiberius introduced a law depriving him of his tribuneship, and summoned the citizens to cast their votes upon it at once. Now there were 35 tribes, and when 17 of them had cast their votes, and the addition of one more would make it necessary for Octavius to become a private citizen, Tiberius called a halt in the voting, and again entreated Octavius...Octavius was not altogether unmoved...But when he turned his gaze towards the men of wealth and substance who were standing in a body together, his awe of them, as it would seem, and his fear of ill repute among them, led him to take every risk with boldness....And so the law was passed. (Plutarch, *Ti. Gracchus* 12)

This episode, however, does not mean that the vote was stopped as soon as a majority was obtained, for Plutarch later quotes Gracchus as saying:

> If it is right for him to be made tribune by a majority of the votes of the tribes, it must be even more right for him to be deprived of his tribuneship by a unanimous vote. (Ibid. 15)

What actually happened was that the presiding officer dramatically interrupted the proceedings so that Gracchus's adversary could accept the decision with a good grace. The introduction of written voting made no difference to this procedure, as we may see from the vote in 67 on the *Lex Gabinia*, by which Pompey was put in charge of operations against the pirates. The tribune Gabinius was opposed by L. Trebellius, and similarly proposed a measure removing him from the tribuneship:

As L. Trebellius persisted in intervening—he had promised the Senate that he would die rather than allow the law to be passed—Gabinius began to call a vote of the tribes on the question of dismissing him from the magistracy, in the same way as Ti. Gracchus had once done in regard to his colleague M. Octavius. For some time Trebellius was undaunted and continued to oppose the law, as he thought Gabinius was bluffing and would not push his proposal to the uttermost. But when 17 tribes had voted for the law and only one more was needed to make it valid, he desisted from his intervention. This was how Gabinius succeeded in carrying his law against the pirates. (Asconius, p. 72 C)

We have other evidence of consecutive voting in judicial *comitia centuriata* and *tributa*. The most typical is that of 169, when the censors C. Claudius and Ti. Sempronius Gracchus were indicted on two charges of high treason (*perduellio*) by a tribune of the people, P. Rutilius. Such cases could only be tried by the *centuriata*, so the tribune requested the *praetor urbanus* to appoint a day for the judicial assembly. The praetor named the eighth and seventh days before the calends of October, showing that the trial was expected to be a long one.

Claudius pleaded his cause first; and when out of 12 centuries of knights eight had condemned the censor, along with many other centuries of the first class, at once the leading men of the state, in the sight of the people, laid aside their gold rings and put on mourning, in order to go about entreating the commons. Chiefly, however, Tiberius Gracchus is said to have changed men's minds, because, although there was everywhere shouting from the commons that Gracchus was in no danger, he solemnly swore that if his colleague were condemned he would not await the outcome of his own trial, but would accompany Claudius into exile. None the less, so near did the defendant come to the last ray of hope that only eight centuries were lacking for condemnation. When Claudius had been acquitted, the tribune of the people said that he did not care about the case of Gracchus. (Livy 43.16.14-16)

Thus 89 centuries (97 less eight) voted for Claudius's conviction and at least 97 for his acquittal. On this occasion, for once, we can deduce how far the vote extended: at least 186 centuries voted, which means that it went as far as the fifth class. Each class was divided in its views (the censors had gravely offended the *equites*), and, as Livy says, in the first class alone eight out of 12 equestrian centuries and several infantry ones had voted against him. This passage is often cited as evidence that the knights voted in two separate groups, first the

12 newer centuries and then the others; but the Latin does not show whether '12' or 'the 12' is meant. In any case we know that in judicial *comitia tributa* the vote continued even after a majority was secured:

As for Gaius Lucretius, on the day set for his trial [in 170 BC] the tribunes accused him before the people and proposed a fine of one million *asses*. When the vote was taken, all the 35 tribes approved his condemnation. (Livy 43.8.9)

The assemblies most used for judicial and legislative purposes, at least towards the end of the Republic, were the *comitia tributa*. Very few laws were passed by the *centuriata*; in the first century BC we only know of the law recalling Cicero from exile, which was no doubt passed in this way to give it more authority and perhaps to give scope to Cicero's partisans, who were certainly more numerous in the first classes than in the last. As for judicial matters, the *comitia centuriata* only met as a high court to try cases of *perduellio*: here again we know of only one example, that of Rabirius in 63. All other business, including the great bulk of legislation, was transacted by the *comitia tributa*. As we have seen, the tribes must have voted consecutively, but it is hard to say how the order was determined. There was, it is true, an official 'order' of the tribes,[79] attested by Cicero (but without details) when protesting at the proposal in Rullus's agrarian bill to have decemvirs elected by only 18 tribes selected by lot:

In the first place, what is the meaning of the arrogant and insulting idea of cutting off part of the Roman people and upsetting the order of the tribes; of assigning land to the country people who have it already before the city people...(*De Lege Agraria* 2.79)

Varro gives the first few names on the list: Suburana, Palatina, Esquilina, Collina, Romilia (the first of the rural tribes);[80] the last rural tribe was the Arnensis (*De Lege Agraria* 2.79). This traditional order was certainly not a hierarchical order, for we know that the Arnensis was highly respected and the urban tribes rather looked down upon, as they included freedmen. We also know that, contrary to what Mommsen thought, when laws were voted on a tribe (known as the *principium*) was selected by lot to cast its vote first. Careful note was taken of its name (like that of the curia which voted first in the legislative *comitia curiata*) and the name of that member of it who voted first. There were no doubt several reasons for this: in the first place it gave the act a kind of accreditation, and for this reason the information was included in the short title (*praescriptio*). There are several examples, e.g. the *Lex Agraria* of 111: 'the...tribe voted first; the first to vote in the name of his tribe was Q. Fabius', and particularly a document cited by Frontinus, the *Lex Quinctia* of 9

BC on the subject of aqueducts:

> The consul Titus Quinctius Crispinus duly put the question to the people, and the people duly passed a vote in the Forum, before the Rostra of the temple of the Deified Julius on the thirtieth day of June. The Sergian tribe was to vote first. On their behalf, Sextus Virro, the son of Lucius, cast the first vote. (*De Aquaeductu* 129)

We may wonder, however, whether the *principium*, which in effect played the same part as the *praerogativa*, was really chosen at random, or whether the hand of chance was not guided by the presiding magistrate. Cicero makes some curious remarks about the famous *Lex Julia* in favour of tax-farmers, introduced by Caesar in 59 BC. The *publicani*, and especially their leader Cn. Plancius, had put forward an impudent demand for the revision of a contract concluded with them in 61. The Senate resisted for a long time, until Caesar satisfied the claim by this law. When Plancius's son, who had become an aedile, was charged in 55 with electoral corruption, his accusers did not fail to bring up the suspicious circumstance that Cn. Plancius had been the first to vote for the *Lex Julia*. Cicero replied:

> As regards the fact that he was the first to vote for the law that dealt with the tax-farmers, on an occasion when a consul of supreme distinction accorded to that body through the medium of the popular assembly a privilege which he would have accorded them through the medium of the Senate had he been permitted to do so, if you say that his giving his vote is a chargeable offence, who was there among the tax-farmers who did not give his vote? If the offence lies in the fact that he was the first to vote, do you impute this fact to chance, or to the proposer of the law? If you impute it to chance, then you have nothing to charge *him* with; if to the consul, then you admit that our highest magistrate accounted Plancius to be the leading man of his order. (Cicero, *Pro Plancio* 35)[81]

We also know, from an inscription, of a law proposed in 58 by the consuls A. Gabinius and L. Calpurnius, the first vote for which was cast by another A. Gabinius who has been shown to be the consul's cousin.[82] Again Cicero states that when Clodius passed the law condemning him to exile he arranged for the first vote to be cast by C. Fidulius, the head of one of his (Clodius's) organized bands of slaves — who later asserted that he was not even in Rome on the day in question.

> Was not Publius Clodius able, after subverting the Republic, to rob of his citizenship a man of consular rank, by the mere summoning of a meeting, and the hiring of gangs, not merely of ne'er-do-wells but even of slaves, with

Fidulius as their ring-leader, who now states that on that day he was not at Rome? But if he was not at Rome, what greater audacity than yours [Clodius's] to have had his name engraved? What more desperate plight than to have been unable, even by lying, to find a more reputable promoter of your measure? But if he was the first to give his vote, as indeed is easily conceivable, seeing that, being without a roof to cover him, he had spent the night in the forum,[83] why indeed should he not swear that he was at Gades, when you yourself on one occasion endeavoured to prove that you were at Interamna? (*De Domo Sua* 79-80)

All this seems to show that, while it might be difficult to rig the selection of the first tribe to cast its vote, it was easy for the president on voting day to get an accomplice, who might simply be a voter desirous of supporting him, to vote first among members of that tribe. But what happened next? Were all the tribes selected by lot one after the other? If so, it is hard to see why there was such agitation in 89 over the enrolment of new citizens in certain tribes and not others. Probably, on the contrary, the official sequence of tribes was followed, either from the beginning (excluding, of course, the one which had voted first) or starting with that one, continuing until the thirty-fifth and then going back to the first.

When written ballots were introduced the procedure was the same as for elections, except that when voting on laws, at least in the first century BC, the tablets were inscribed with the letters V and A, standing respectively for *uti rogas* ('as you propose') and *antiquo* ('I maintain things as they are'). We do not know whether these letters were on two separate tablets or, for instance, on both sides of a single one, as in the case of trials. A reference by Cicero suggests that there were two: when a vote was taken in 61 on the *Lex Pupia Valeria de incestu P. Clodii*, setting up a special court to try Clodius, the latter had the *pontes* occupied by his myrmidons and 'the voting was so managed that no *placet* forms were given out' (*Att.* 1.14.5).

Preparatory assemblies and election meetings

We have seen that one of the main differences between electoral assemblies and judicial or legislative ones was that in general there were no election meetings at which issues were debated. Votes at elections were canvassed in a different manner, which we shall describe below. For judicial decisions or voting on bills, however, preliminary assemblies were not only permitted but compulsory. In the case of trials the accused and accusers had to be allowed time to speak, and the actual *comitia* were only the last of a succession of proceedings which were really judicial instances. Cicero's speech on behalf of C. Rabirius in 63, which was essentially a legal plea, was addressed to a preparatory meeting of this kind. In the case of bills, the law required that they should be given due publicity so that the public knew what it was voting about.[84] A proposed law had to be posted up at least a *trinundinum* (25 days) before voting day. In the last century of the Republic precautions were introduced against possible manoeuvres and forgery. During the 25 days it was forbidden, for example, to amend the text of a bill.[85] This rule may not have applied in the previous century: it seems possible that Ti. Gracchus, faced with opposition to his first agrarian bill, at once substituted another which diverged considerably from it. But apart from extreme cases provided for by law, it was in the sponsor's own interest to make known what he proposed and to get as much support for it as possible. It was customary, if no longer compulsory, to inform the Senate first of all; the tribunes themselves, out of deference, submitted most of their proposals to this body in the first instance. But above all the sponsors of a bill were entitled to hold 'deliberative', i.e. non-voting assemblies (*contiones*) at which all were free to defend or even oppose the measure. Any magistrates who disapproved of it could call similar meetings of their own. These assemblies were the setting for the great speeches for or against a law which were a particularly important form of eloquence and action in Roman politics. Many of the speeches of the great orators that have come down to us in whole or in part are *suasiones* or *dissuasiones* of this kind. All forms of pressure, oratorical and other, were naturally exerted in order to obtain the desired decision. The types of argument that were used successfully naturally varied from one period and from one assembly to another. It is probable too that, just as in modern times, the audience at political meetings varied a good deal according to the matter in hand or the personality by whom the assembly was summoned.

Until the middle of the second century BC there seems to have been considerable freedom of speech and fairness of debate, approval or hostility being expressed in a fairly restrained manner. As far as we can judge, the climate began to change a few years before the time of the Gracchi; from then on the *contiones* were often disorderly and sometimes marked by violence and murder. Naturally they were as a rule summoned by tribunes of the plebs. Sometimes they were used to expound a whole programme: thus C. Gracchus delivered a speech 'On the Promulgation of Laws' which certainly dealt with the law on citizenship, among other matters.[86] Speeches could also be made in defence of others' proposals, e.g. Cicero's *Pro Lege Manilia* was delivered at a *contio* summoned by Manilius: the purpose of the law was to entrust Pompey with the command against Mithridates, and its sponsor was glad of the support of a praetor in office who was already recognized as one of the great living orators. At the same meeting the bill was opposed by Q. Catulus and Q. Hortensius. Cicero's speech, as he himself tells us, was his first non-forensic one, a fact which throws an interesting light on the political level of those (other than the tribunes themselves) who were allowed to speak at *contiones*: apparently they were seldom below the rank of praetor. The speech is also valuable for the indications it gives of arguments previously used, at the same *contio* or an earlier one:

> What then says Hortensius? That if one man is to be put in supreme command, the right man is Pompeius; but that supreme command ought not to be given to one man....It was you yourself, Quintus Hortensius, who...denounced Aulus Gabinius before the Senate, when he had introduced a measure for the appointment of a single commander against the pirates; and also from this platform you spoke at length against the same measure. ...It remains, I think, that I should speak of the opinion expressed by Quintus Catulus. When he asked you on whom you would set your hopes if anything should happen to Gnaeus Pompeius, in the event of your staking everything upon him, he received a great tribute to his own high character and position when almost with one accord you all asserted that in that case you would set your hopes upon himself. (*Pro Lege Man.* 52, 59)

Not all proposed laws were so courteously debated. Sometimes tribunes by-passed the Senate and took little trouble to secure the magistrates' agreement. A curious example is that of Servius Rullus's land bill in 63, at the very beginning of Cicero's consulship. Rullus was a friend of Caesar's and his proposal was calculated to put Cicero in a difficulty, yet the latter was not consulted or even warned:

> Being told at the outset, when I was consul-elect, that the tribunes-elect were drawing up an agrarian law, I felt a desire to learn their intentions;... But when I attempted to get on such terms with them that we could converse without reserve, I was kept in the dark, I was shut out; and when I gave them to understand that, if the law seemed to me likely to be useful to the Roman plebeians, I would support and help to pass it, they scorned my generous offer, and declared that I could never be brought to approve of any kind of largesse....At last the tribunes entered upon office, and I waited for the man's expected law and speech. At first no law is proposed. He orders an assembly to be summoned for the 12th of December. A crowd gathers round on tiptoe of expectation. He unrolls a very long speech in very fine language. The only fault I had to find was that, among all the throng, not one could be found who was able to understand what he said....The more intelligence persons in the assembly suspected that he meant to say something or other about an agrarian law.
>
> At last, however, as soon as I was elected, the law was publicly proposed. By my instructions a number of copyists came running up all together, and brought me an exact transcript of it. I took this law into my hands with the feeling that I wanted to find it advantageous to you and such that a consul who was a friend of the people in reality, not in words, might honourably

and gladly support it. But from the first article to the last, Romans, I find
that the only idea of the tribunes, their only aim in what they do is to
appoint ten kings of the treasury. (*De Lege Agr.*, 11-15)

Sometimes the *contiones* provided an opportunity to pillory the highest officers
of state. Clodius was a past master in the art of whipping up popular support
in this way. He showed this abundantly as a tribune (Plutarch, *Pompey* 48.5-6),
and in 56 took advantage of Milo's trial to have Pompey shouted down by
hecklers in his pay:

> On the 6th of April [56 BC] Milo again appeared for trial. Pompey spoke,
> or rather such was his intention; for when he got up, Clodius's hired gangs
> raised a yell, and that is what he had to endure the whole time he was
> speaking, being interrupted not only with shouts, but with insults and abuse.
> When he had finished his speech (he showed great fortitude in the circumstances;
> he never quailed, he said all he had to say, and now and then silence was
> compelled by his impressive personality), but, as I say, when he had finished
> his speech, up got Clodius. He was met with such a deafening shout from
> our side (for we had determined to give him as good as he gave), that he lost
> all control over his faculties, his voice, and his countenance....Maddened
> and white with rage, he asked his partisans (and he was heard above the
> shouting) who the man was that starved the people to death; his rowdies
> answered 'Pompey'. Who was bent upon going to Alexandria? They answered
> 'Pompey'. Whom did they want to go? They answered 'Crassus'. (*Ad Quintum
> fratrem* 2.3.2)

We shall see that similar incidents sometimes arose during the examination
of witnesses in court proceedings, though the public was less directly concerned
in these. the actual voting of laws could also give rise to violent scenes and
riots, as on the occasion when Ti. Gracchus was killed. We have a still more
detailed account of such an event when a *rogatio* by the tribune. C. Cornelius
was rejected in 67 BC. Cornelius had intended to introduce a measure forbidding
loans to foreign ambassadors, but the Senate, whom he had notified, rejected it
on the ground that a senatorial decree of 27 years earlier made it unnecessary.
Cornelius, incensed at this, held a *contio* to denounce usury in the provinces
and submitted his bill to it, with a clause to the effect that no one could be
dispensed from the operation of a law except by the people (so that it could not
be evaded by a mere *senatus consultum*). Influential senators took a hostile view
of this proposal and induced another tribune, P. Servilius Globulus, to oppose
it:

> When, on voting day, the herald accompanied by the scribe was about to
> proclaim the terms of the law to the people, Globulus forbade the scribe to

hand him the text (*codex*) and would not let the herald read it; so Cornelius began to read it himself. When the consul Piso protested vehemently that this was illegal and that a tribune had interposed his veto, the people raised a violent outcry. Piso ordered the lictor to arrest those who were threatening him, but the crowd broke the *fasces* and some at the back even threw stones at the consul. Alarmed at this disorder, Cornelius immediately broke off the meeting. (Asconius 58 C)

The law of course punished this kind of interference, as it was an affront to the people to prevent it manifesting its sovereign will. Nevertheless, during the Second Punic War some tax-farmers who were about to be condemned upset the voting-urns at the last moment, and Ti. Gracchus's adversaries did the same when his first land bill was being voted on. There is as yet no systematic study of these preparatory legislative or judicial assemblies,[87] although plenty of unmistakable references to them exist in addition to the not always reliable accounts of Livy or Dionysius. They were an extremely interesting way of consulting public opinion, in advance of and on different lines from the regular *comitia*. Anyone could attend a *contio,* including groups which were normally excluded from the *comitia*: Cicero indicates this *à propos* of Jews and Syrians in 59 (*Pro Flacco* 66-7). Often a question already debated in the Senate was made the subject of a *contio,* whether the senators so desired or not. There is room for an extremely detailed analysis of all the occasions of which we have information, studying closely differences of vocabulary and reasoning, types of argument and the various political techniques used by the leaders at different periods and in different circumstances: in this way an idea could be formed of the type of public which attended the meetings and of its reactions. The discussion of a particular measure in the Senate and before the people respectively, the names of the speakers on either side and the results of the voting, would provide exemplary material for the analysis of the Roman political system. For the present we merely point this out as a line of research, to be followed up elsewhere.

The elector's role

It has been seen throughout this book that one of the fundamental activities of the Roman people was the exercise of its political rights. From the third century onwards, whether for the purpose of voting laws, passing legal judgements or electing magistrates once a year, the people, duly assembled in its tribes and centuries, was practically sovereign. Legally its decisions were binding on one and all. But what exactly was meant by the 'people'? We have seen in previous chapters that the degree of participation in civic duties varied a great deal according to social class, geography and occupation. Are the same variations to be noted when it comes to decision-taking by means of the suffrage? We have seen that in principle, at least from the second century onwards, no one could be legally prevented from exercising this right: every citizen was *ipso facto* an elector. Even those penalized by the censors (we are not, of course, speaking here of those convicted by process of law) were not wholly deprived of rights: they were not expelled from the tribes or centuries altogether, but were moved from one tribe to another or relegated to a century created for the purpose. But we have also seen that the electoral system itself imposed certain limits on this participation. In the centuriate assembly it was very unusual for the last classes to be actually called on to vote. While there was no distinction of classes in tribal voting, the tribes differed substantially as regards size and geographical location. The essential question we have to examine is thus: Who voted in Rome, how often and with what real influence?

It should first be noted that there was no obligation to vote. Unlike the situation as regards the census, the *dilectus* or the *tributum*, no legal penalties were visited on an elector who abstained from voting. An electoral assembly might be more or less well attended (*frequens*), but we never hear of a quorum being necessary in Rome as it was in Athens (6,000 for an ostracism).[88] All we know, from a statement of doubtful import by Cicero, is that in certain legislative votes by the *comitia tributa* some tribes might be represented by only five electors, and even these were not all really members of it.[89] If he is not speaking of deliberate fraud, we must infer that the presiding officer was empowered to assign certain electors arbitrarily to certain units so that these should not be entirely unrepresented. On the other hand, towards the end of our period it could happen that some tribes were deliberately excluded from voting: the *Lex Valeria Cornelia* of AD 5 provided for ten centuries named after the *principes juventutis*, composed of senators and knights, to be formed by casting lots among only 33 tribes, excluding the Suburrana and Esquilina. This presumably means that there were very few members of these tribes in the assembly. If there were any, however, the law laid down a procedure which is not stated precisely but no doubt consisted of choosing another voting unit by lot (lines 32-33).

In any case there was no compulsion to vote, and it was for candidates or the sponsors of laws, or their opponents, to do their best to secure a large enough turn-out. Consequently we cannot estimate either the average number of voters, or the highest and lowest figures. As we have seen, some archaeologists calculate that the *saepta* of Caesar and Agrippa might have had room for 70,000 people. This is not many if one recalls that the number of Roman citizens in Italy who had the vote and were able to use it was perhaps of the order of 1,700,000 adult males in 28 BC, while in 225 BC they may already have numbered close on 300,000.[90] The figure of 70,000, moreover, is only a theoretical maximum. It may be that in exceptional circumstances a large number of electors turned out: as we have seen, when C. Gracchus was first elected tribune in 124, according to Plutarch the crowds overflowed the Campus Martius and occupied the roofs of neighbouring houses.

Another way of estimating the number of voters is to calculate it on a time basis. In 45 an election to a single consular post, which no doubt only one candidate, took five hours in all for the casting and counting of votes, probably by 97 centuries. Assuming that the voters in their 35 columns advanced at the rate of two a minute, and that the voting as opposed to the counting lasted four hours, we get a figure of about 16,800 voters, which is quite plausible. These, however, would have been only the voters of the first two classes.

All the foregoing, it need hardly be said, is entirely conjectural. What is symptomatic is that our sources never give a number of votes or individual voters on any occasion, but at most a number of tribes or centuries to indicate how a given result was obtained. In Roman eyes the result of an election did not depend on a total of individual votes but on the agreement or disagreement of the centuries or tribes. It was not of concern to the state as such whether electors turned out or not, and accordingly they were not obliged to. But their numbers were naturally of great concern to politicians interested in their own careers and projects. It was part of the political game to win elections, and for this purpose to make sure that a maximum number of one's supporters voted. This was not so easy, as it was not just a matter of routing out lazy or apathetic voters, but also of their actually getting to the polls. Votes could only be cast in Rome, so that citizens who did not live there had to travel what might be a long distance and often remain in the City for a considerable time. This state of affairs throws into relief a series of contrasts which were to be decisive for the fate of the *comitia*. Firstly between the Urbs and its outlying territory, between citizens who lived hundreds of miles from the Forum and Campus and those who could go there every day, or even spend the night encamped in a strategic spot.[91] Secondly between elections and votes of other kinds: the former took place more or less regularly and the elector could make plans accordingly, but judicial and legislative votes were a different matter. Despite the requirement of advance notice which was in force from the second century onwards, they might take place at any season of the year, so that a special information and propaganda campaign was necessary, if the issue was controversial, to induce people to leave their business and come to Rome for the vote. Thirdly, the system affected different kinds of voters to a different extent: country dwellers were much more tied to their lands, to the rhythm of the seasons and the calendar of rural labour and holidays, while city folk were more available at all times, even if some of them had jobs and were not perpetually at leisure.[92]

Within these large masses, too, there were subtle but definite contrasts of status and social order. In the first place, the weight and influence of the different groups varied according to the type of assembly. In the centuries the senators, *equites* and members of the first class with a capital of 10,000 denarii

(25,000 sesterces) were predominant, whereas in the tribes every vote counted, and those of the poorest classes might determine the result. In the last century of the Republic, moreover, all questions were decided by the tribes except the election of consuls, praetors and censors, charges of *perduellio* (extremely rare), and deprivation of civil rights. Thus it is not quite correct to say that the strength of moral and political pressure to frequent the *comitia* was proportionate to a man's social standing; this only applied to the centuriate elections, but it was certainly true of these, as many examples show. At that level, indeed, there was no marked contrast between ordinary citizens and what might be called the 'political class' of senators and magistrates. Bonds of friendship and personal patronage, and the subtle ties of electoral give-and-take, were strong enough to prevent those involved from deserting the Forum even if they were tempted to do so. True, in the first century BC there are traces of a kind of rift between the senatorial and the equestrian order, as for the first time we find knights refusing to embark on the *cursus honorum*. But these were a minority of the order, and although they no longer wished to be magistrates or senators they still acted as jurymen (as the law required), while many became tax-farmers. They also took an active part in political life, either when matters affecting them came up for debate (as they often did), or when their friends and relations aspired to high offices of state. This being so, it would have been pointless and dangerous for them to shirk their civic duties, e.g. by not voting; and all the evidence is that candidates in fact relied most firmly on the influence, wealth and connections of people of this sort.[93]

The task of professional politicians, as we shall see, was not only to rally supporters in sufficient number but to see that they were all distributed in different voting units, i.e. basically in the tribes.

In studying any episode of Roman politics, whether one of routine or a dramatic and exceptional event, what we should like to know as precisely as possible is how many and what kind of people took part in the relevant assemblies, and what was their social origin. As a rule we know none of these things, but there are some hints from time to time. The most informative case is perhaps the key event of 133, the adoption of Ti. Gracchus's agrarian law. We know that Gracchus's bill was not an improvisation but had been discussed at length, perhaps already during his electoral campaign which lasted through the previous year. It was carefully drafted with the aid of some of the chief authorities in the Senate, although Gracchus did not submit it beforehand to that body. The discussions naturally became more intensive during the *trinundinum* before the vote, which must have been set for as early a date as possible, in the winter of 134 or the spring of 133. Appian and Plutarch record that Gracchus made a major speech in support of his proposal, of which we have a summary and also a verbatim extract, and in which he advanced all kinds of arguments. Probably, as Brendan Nagle has suggested,[94] the speech was repeated several times and communicated to country voters, if not in writing then orally by the efforts of his numerous clients. We know that Gracchus's object was to benefit the rural population rather than the townsfolk; according to Appian (1.14) it was only towards the summer of 133, when campaigning for re-election, that he was obliged to seek urban support. Until then his chief supporters and adversaries had naturally been those directly interested, one way or the other, in land reform:

> This was extremely disturbing to the rich because, on account of the triumvirs, they could no longer disregard the law as they had done before... They collected together in groups and accused the poor of appropriating the results of their tillage, their vineyards, and their dwellings. Some said that they had paid the price of their land to their neighbours. Were they to lose the money with the land?...On the other side were heard the lamentations of the poor—that they were being reduced from easy circumstances to extreme penury, and also to childlessness because they were unable to rear their off-spring. They recounted the military services they had rendered, by which this very land had been acquired, and were angry that they should be robbed of their share of the common property....While these classes were thus lamenting and indulging in mutual accusations, a great number of others, composed of colonists, or inhabitants of the free towns, or persons otherwise interested in the lands and who were under like apprehensions, flocked in and took sides with their respective factions. (*B. Civ.* 1.10)

It is certain that large numbers of Tiberius's followers flocked in from the countryside to vote for his bill:

> The crowds poured into Rome from the country like rivers into the sea. They were buoyed up with the hope of effecting their own salvation, since their champion was a man subject neither to favour nor to fear—a man, moreover, who for the sake of restoring the land to the people was determined to endure any toil or danger, to his last breath....
> On the other hand, [Octavius's] was not a group just recently assembled and drawn from many tribes, but comprised the most politically alert and well-to-do segments of the populace. Since, then, the strength on both sides was evenly balanced, and the scales tipped now this way, now that, the two parties, being assembled many thousands strong, clashed violently...like waves of the sea. (Diodorus 34/35.6)

These countryfolk, rich and poor—but chiefly the latter—had to stay in Rome longer than they expected, on account of the obstacles of all kinds raised by Gracchus's adversaries: riots and breaking of the urns, opposition by Octavius, debate in the Senate and the introduction of an amended bill. These delays were no doubt to the advantage of the rich, who could afford to remain longer in Rome. Finally the law was passed. Attempts have been made to discover the place of origin of its partisans from the pattern of land allotments as far as it can be reconstructed, on the perhaps doubtful assumption that they would have been given a better deal under the law. But Ti. Gracchus died in the summer of 133, and there is no certainty that his successors followed this principle even if he himself did.

In any case, the departure of his rural supporters was the direct cause of his failure and death. That summer he decided to stand for the tribunate a second time, which no doubt made it necessary first to pass a law for the purpose; as Appian says:

> As the day for voting approached it was very evident that the rich had earnestly promoted the election of those most inimical to Gracchus. The latter, fearing that evil would befall if he should not be re-elected for the following year, summoned his friends from the fields to attend the election, but as they were occupied with harvesting he was obliged, when the day fixed for the voting drew near, to have recourse to the plebeians of the city. (*B. Civ.* 1.14)

'Plebeians of the city' here signifies not the four urban tribes but the members of all tribes who lived in Rome. On the day of the riot in which he was killed, Gracchus had only 3,000 supporters with him (Plutarch, *Ti. Gracchus* 20.3), a figure which agrees with that of the few thousand electors to be expected in a tribal assembly.

Other episodes of political history illustrate the fact that countryfolk came to Rome for important votes: Marius was elected thanks to them, and Saturninus and Glaucia were helped by them to pass certain laws. The problem of accommodating and feeding these fairly large crowds must have arisen frequently. No doubt these migrations must be thought of in terms of a society which still preserved traces of nomadism, as do some countries in modern times. In the Greco-Roman world it was not uncommon for whole populations to go on the move, especially for religious festivals, games, gladiatorial fights and so on. Political assemblies were one reason for travelling among many others; we know that in the second and first centuries BC well-to-do members of the Roman upper class did not shrink from quite long journeys, even for purely social purposes. Moreover, the various reasons for large numbers of people coming to Rome often coincided: e.g. after Sulla's time the elections took place in July or August, at the same season as the Megalensian games, and in 70 BC they also coincided with the beginning of the census. Thus Cicero declared at the beginning of August: 'I will not permit the settlement of this case to be delayed until after the departure from Rome of these multitudes that have simultaneously assembled from all parts of Italy to attend the elections, the games and the census' (*I Verr.* 18.54). Such a triple event was rare but not unique. Again, the voting of the law on Cicero's recall attracted many to Rome, though the interested party no doubt exaggerated the size of the crowd, so flattering to himself. On that occasion, however, it is true that what may be called the machinery of government, or at least that of the most influential politicians in Rome, was put into action, slowly but powerfully. Pompey, at last emerging from the wings, had decided to lend his support to those who, with advice from Atticus and Quintus, were endeavouring to secure the introduction of a proposal for Cicero's return. In January 57 the new consul P. Lentulus induced the Senate to pass a decree to the effect, as Cicero put it,

> that all men throughout Italy who had the safety of the state at heart should concentrate their resources upon the restitution and defence of a broken and all but shattered man like myself; so that the same command which had been but thrice uttered by a consul in the cause of the state since the foundation of Rome, and then had merely been addressed to those within earshot of his voice, might now be uttered by the Senate in order to rally from their fields and townships all the citizens of all Italy for the protection of a single life? (*Post reditum in senatu* 24)

Cicero's Italian supporters were in fact already on the road to Rome. They were stirred up by Pompey, who caused a decree in favour of Cicero's return to be voted by the newly-founded colony of Capua, of which he was a duumvir (*Pro Milone* 39; *Post reditum in senatu* 29); then, according to Cicero, he toured the municipalities to persuade influential electors to come to the City:

> During his own tenure of office, in a recently established colony, where none had been bribed to interpose his veto, Pompey attested by the authority of honourable men and by official documents the arbitrary and cruel nature of a law directed against an individual, and was the chief supporter of the view that the resources of all Italy should be solicited on behalf of my safety. (*Post reditum in senatu* 30)

> He was approaching the municipal towns on my behalf, and interceding for the loyal support of Italy. (*In Pisonem* 80)

In June 57 the Senate, meeting in the temple of Honour and Virtue (chosen symbolically in memory of Marius, another great 'native son' of Arpinum), urged Roman citizens throughout Italy to come and vote for the law, thus fortifying the Senate's own authority. Those who were already in Rome showed their approval of this invitation by a spontaneous demonstration at a public spectacle, to which we shall return (*Pro Sestio* 117-26). But what chiefly interests us here is the campaign in the *municipia* and colonies. Consular letters were issued in Cicero's favour and decrees were voted by local assemblies — in every single town, according to Cicero—as well as by *pagi,* collegia and tax-farming companies:

What public deliberative body is there, important or unimportant, in the whole world, whose verdict upon my achievements has not been such as to meet my highest desires and my proudest ambitions? The supreme deliberative body of the Roman people, and indeed of all peoples, nations, and kings, is the Senate; and the Senate decreed that all who had the safety of the Republic at heart should rally to my sole defence, and intimated that the state could not have survived had I not existed, and would be annihilated should I not be restored. Immediately below this exalted body is the equestrian order; and all the companies for the collection of all the public revenues passed resolutions concerning my consulship and my achievements which were most laudatory and enthusiastic. The secretaries, who assist us in the charge of public accounts and records, expressed in unmistakable terms their judgement and conclusion upon my services to the state. There is no guild in this city, no community, whether of the villages or the highlands (for it was the will of our ancestors that the city proletariat too should have its committees and councils of a kind), which did not register most complimentary decrees dealing not only with my restoration but also with my merits. Why should I enlarge upon the heaven-inspired and never-to-be-forgotten decrees of the municipalities and colonies, and indeed of the whole of Italy—a ladder, for so I account them, whereby not merely did I return to my country, but climbed to heaven? But what a day was that, Publius Lentulus, when the Roman people itself saw you proposing a measure dealing with me, and when it realized my greatness and my eminent merits? For it is generally recognized that at no previous meeting of the assembly had the Field of Mars ever shone with so brilliant a concourse of all ranks, all ages, and all orders of men. I forbear to mention the unanimity of judgement and opinion with regard to my services displayed by communities, tribes, provinces, kings, and, in a word, by all the world...(*De Domo* 73-5)

On two occasions Cicero claimed that as a result of the Senate's exhortation there was 'not a single citizen who would have thought himself dispensed, on grounds of age or health, from registering his vote for my recall' (*Post reditum in senatu* 28; *Pro Sestio* 112). (He actually uses here the technical term *excusatio,* signifying a discharge from public duty). There was certainly a huge attendance at the *comitia centuriata* which voted for Cicero's recall, and perhaps an even greater crowd when he actually returned in August, 'borne shoulder-high by the whole of Italy'. On this occasion we have a sidelight as to the effect on a still fragile economy of such a mass movement of population, as Clodius, to avenge his recent defeat, stirred up fresh trouble by claiming that the current scarcity of food was due to the influx of Cicero's supporters:

The occasion, then, was such as to justify a new policy: consider now whether mine was not the rôle almost of protagonist. In connexion with the incident of the stone-throwing, whose name was mentioned by your minion Sergius, or by Lollius, or by those other scourges? Who did they say should make himself responsible for the price of grain? Was it not myself? Again, was it not from me that your nocturnal troop of partisans (personally coached by yourself) demanded corn? As if I, forsooth, had been placed in charge of supplies! (*De Domo*, 14-15)

But the circumstances of 57 were exceptional. In a normal year, so to speak, the *comitia* were certainly much less well attended. It could not be expected that a majority of citizens from the *municipia* and colonies would come to Rome, and so the localization of national political activity gave a substantial initial advantage to the City's inhabitants. Contemporaries were fully conscious of this imbalance; as we shall see, Augustus sought an original remedy for it, but by then it was far too late. Nor was the difficulty confined to political matters. There was a fundamental ambiguity in that Rome, while the capital of a huge territory, was itself administered as a town of modest dimensions; the nature of its institutions required citizens to be present for innumerable day-to-day activities and formalities. As we shall see, even in imperial times important trials could only be held in Rome, and only there could the solemn ceremonies be held whereby citizens were enrolled in the higher orders of the state, whether senatorial or equestrian after the latter *ordo* was restored by Augustus. To modern minds this would seem an intolerable restriction; the Romans perhaps did not consider it as burdensome as we should do.

Clients and electioneering

If the Roman electoral system had been a direct democracy based on universal suffrage, these geographical inequalities would soon have become unendurable and a means would have been found of enabling the great majority of citizens to vote in their own localities. But we have seen that the system of voting by groups made it unnecessary in normal times for the whole electorate to cast its vote. It was sufficient to command a certain number of voting units; to gain the firm support of certain tribes in the *comitia tributa*, or of the first class and the knights for the *comitia centuriata*. It was a matter of rallying tribes and centuries rather than individual voters. This accounts for the fact that the rules of an electoral or political campaign in ancient Rome were so different from what we are accustomed to in modern representative democracies.

The gradual evolution of these rules may be dated from about the end of the third century BC. It is noteworthy that, according to tradition, the earliest legislation forbade practices that were afterwards regarded as perfectly legal.[95]

It was resolved, in order to do away with canvassing, that the tribunes should propose a law forbidding anyone to whiten his toga for the purpose of announcing himself as a candidate. This may now appear a trivial thing and scarcely to be considered seriously, but at that time it kindled a furious struggle between the patricians and the plebs. (Livy 4.25.13)

In 358 the first law was passed against bribery at elections (*de ambitu*); 'by this measure', Livy tells us (7.15.12), 'they thought to suppress corrupt practices, particularly on the part of men risen from the people, who used to haunt country fairs and gathering-places.' Yet the two practices in question— whitening one's toga as a sign that one was standing for office, and canvassing in villages and market-places round about the City—were so customary that in spite of laws against them they finally became the approved practice. The whitening of the toga gave rise to the term *candidatus*, which has passed into most modern languages, while *ambitio* was used to signify 'going about' to solicit votes; it had no pejorative sense in itself, whereas *ambitus* denoted corrupt practices. The two *plebiscita* just mentioned probably did not entail any penal sanctions against offenders. Legislation in this field was reinforced at the beginning of the second century, and again in 181 and 169, by a series of measures of which we know little. Towards the end of that century we find that there was already a standing court (*quaestio*) to try such cases; a succession of trials for electoral malpractice in 116, particularly that of Marius, presuppose the existence of such a court.[96]

Further laws, with increasingly severe penalties, were passed during the last century of the Republic: the *Leges Cornelia* (81), *Calpurnia* (67), *Tullia* (63), *Licinia* (55) and *Pompeia* (52). But their very multiplication shows that illegal practices were more and more frequent and difficult to prevent. During this period—on the eve of the civil wars and *coups d'état* which practically put an end to the republican regime based on free electoral competition, narrowly restricted though this was to a small governing circle—the nature of electoral corruption underwent a change. It was no longer a matter of limited abuses affecting only a part of the electorate, but of generalized practices which implied an entirely new conception of the voter's role, one might even say of his profession.

Admittedly it is extremely hard to draw a line in this field between the normal and the exceptional, what is lawful and what is forbidden. Practically all our information comes from the accusations and arguments in trials for corruption of which record exists. It would be interesting to know how frequent such prosecutions really were, so as to form an idea as to the 'normality' of practices virtuously denounced or repudiated by the lawyers on either side. The only text which might enable us to see how far it was possible to go while remaining within the law is the *Commentariolum petitionis* or Electioneering

Handbook, a long letter purportedly addressed to Marcus Cicero by his brother Quintus towards the end of 65 or the beginning of 64 BC, just before the elections for the year 63. It is a fascinating text in which precise details are mingled with robust attacks on Cicero's chief competitors, Catiline and C. Antonius (the latter of whom became his fellow-consul in 63). Unfortunately its authenticity has been questioned, perhaps mistakenly, but in any case it can be shown that, forgery or not, the letter was composed with the aid of unimpeachable documents, including Cicero's lost speech to the Senate in support of a bill *de ambitu* which was being opposed by a tribune.[97]

Cicero, who was no novice in politics, was at this time embarking on a decisive and particularly delicate stage of his career. He had been elected aedile and praetor with apparent ease, securing the first nomination in both cases despite strong intrigue against him for the aedileship. He was now trying for the consulship although a *novus homo*, i.e. member of a family which had never held high office: his father, apparently for health reasons, had remained an *eques*, and the family was a provincial one from Arpinum. Cicero's social standing was in fact not as low as it might seem: his family had matrimonial connections or links of friendship and patronage such as would normally pave the way for him to enter the senatorial class, and had already brought him as far as the praetorship.[98] His grandmother was connected by marriage with the *gens Maria* (the famous Marius and his brother), and he was also related to the Aelii Tuberones. His grandfather had been one of Aemilius Scaurus's many friends at Arpinum. No one grudged Cicero his rise so far, and if he had stopped at the praetorship his son might in the ordinary way have become consul without any opposition on grounds of birth from the *nobiles*, i.e. the narrow circle of men of consular family. But Cicero wanted to reach the top himself, and entered the contest for the consulship in 65. He bagan his campaign on 17 July, the earliest date permitted by law, which was also that of the tribunicial elections. Shortly before, he explained his intentions at length to Atticus:

With regard to my candidature, in which I know you take the greatest interest, things stand as follows...P. Galba is the only canvasser who is already hard at work; and he meets with a plain, simple, old-fashioned No. People think this unseemly haste of his in canvassing is by no means a bad thing for my interests: for most refusals imply a pledge of support to me. So I have hope that I may derive some advantage from it, when the news gets abroad that my supporters are in the majority. I had thought of beginning to canvass in the Campus Martius at the election of tribunes on the 17th of July, the very time when, Cincius tells me, your man will be starting out with this letter. It seems certain that Galba, Antonius, and Q. Cornificius will be standing against me. I can imagine your smile or sigh at the news. To make you tear your hair, there are some who think Caesonius will be a candidate too. I don't suppose Aquilius will. He has said not, pleading his illness and pressure of business in the law courts in excuse. Catiline will be sure to be standing, if the verdict is No sun at midday. Of course you will know all about Aufidius and Palicanus, without waiting for letters from me.

He then refers to some of his supporters:

> I shall take the greatest care to fulfil all a candidate's duties: and, as Gaul's vote counts high, I shall probably get a free pass and take a run up to visit Piso, as soon as things have quietened down in the law courts here, returning in January. When I have discovered the views of the 'upper ten', I will let you know. The rest I hope will be plain sailing, with my civilian rivals at any rate. For our friend Pompey's followers you must be responsible, as you are quite close to them. Tell him I shall not take it amiss if he does not come to my election. (*Att.* 1.1.1-2)

Cicero then enters into details of an interesting behind-the-scenes matter, apologizing for his inability to act for Atticus's uncle Caecilius, a well-known banker, in a lawsuit against one Satyrus:

> Now there is hardly a day but Satyrus pays me a visit. He is most attentive to L. Domitius and after him to me, and he was of great assistance to me and to my brother Quintus when we were canvassing. I am really embarrassed on account of the friendliness of Satyrus himself and of Domitius, who is the mainstay of my hopes.

Having begun his campaign Cicero finds that he is in danger of not being supported by the nobility, and he appeals to Atticus in a much more pressing tone:

> I badly want you back soon: for there is a widespread opinion that some friends of yours among the upper ten are opposed to my election, and I can see that you will be of the greatest assistance to me in winning their good will. So be sure you come back to town in January, as you proposed. (1.2.2)

Quintus's 'Electioneering Handbook' deals with electoral tactics in full detail. The first thing is to reckon up all the ties of friendship and obligation on which the candidate can rely. Accordingly Cicero should contact all those to whom he had done a good turn in the past, especially by defending them successfully in the courts or furthering their political designs: e.g. Pompey, for whose benefit he supported the *Lex Manilia* in 66. Quintus speaks of four men in particular:

> In these last two years you have laid under obligation four sodalities run

by men of great influence in electioneering, C. Fundanius, Q. Gallius, C. Cornelius, and C. Orchivius. I know (for I was present) what the members of the sodalities undertook and assured for you when they entrusted you with the briefs for these four. So what you have to do is to exact from them on this occasion what they owe you. (*Comm. Pet.* 19)[99]

[Then] there are men of influence in their own neighbourhoods and towns, persistent and prosperous persons who, even if they have not felt inclined to exercise their influence before, still can easily make efforts at a moment's notice for someone to whom they are indebted or well disposed...[New friends must also be cultivated.] Take care to secure all the centuries through many friends of different sorts. First—and this is obvious—attach to yourself senators, Roman knights, active and influential men of all other ranks. Many energetic city folk, many influential and active freedmen are about the Forum; as many as possible should be most diligently brought by yourself or by mutual friends to desire your success; pursue them, send agents to them, show them how you esteem the benefaction. Then, reckon up the whole city—all the Colleges, the suburbs, the environs; if you strike up a friendship with the leading men among their number, you will easily, through them, secure the masses that remain. After that, visualize the whole of Italy divided into its tribal divisions, and let there be no town, colony, rural district, or indeed any place where you have not a sufficiency of support, inquire and seek out men everywhere, get to know them, pursue them, secure them, see that they canvass their localities for you and act like candidates on your behalf...Small-town and country folk think themselves our friends if we know them by name. To the rest, especially to your competitors, they are total strangers, whereas *you* know them or will easily get to know them—without which there can be no friendship. Yet merely to know them, though important, is not enough unless it is followed by the hope of advantage, so that you are seen to be a good friend and not only a recollector of names. (Ibid. 24, 29-32)

Naturally the candidate must first pay attention to his own tribe. He should be able to count on it as a matter of course, and it is a disgrace if, on election day, he does not secure a majority of it; 'for in these days electioneering experts have worked out, with all their eager will and resources, how to get what they want from their fellow-tribesmen' (Ibid. 18).

The services to be rendered to one's own people are of the most varied kinds. Quintus drops a discreet hint:

Take special pains to recruit and retain those who have from you, or hope to have, control of a tribe or a century [or perhaps: a military tribunate or the rank of centurion], or some other advantage. (Ibid. 18)[100]

Quintus goes on to say that Cicero's origins and past activities ought to ensure the support of certain kinds of people who are particularly influential in the assemblies. He belongs to the equestrian order, and will thus enjoy the goodwill of the tax-farming companies and jurymen (this, we know, is perfectly true). Young men of the equestrian centuries, some of whom are of noble birth, will be attached to him because of their taste for eloquence and culture (Cicero was already a literary 'classic' at this time, his speeches being published and commented on):

> Young men's enthusiasm in winning support, visiting electors, carrying news and attending on you is amazingly important, and confers credit on you. (Ibid. 33)

Quintus next speaks of 'attendance' (*adsectatio*): troops of supporters were supposed to follow candidates wherever they went, their numbers being an index of expected success at the *comitia*. This was one of the most striking features of Roman society, based on calculated display and competitive showmanship:

> As to attendance, you must take care to have it daily, from all sorts and ranks and ages, for the very numbers will give an idea of the resources of strength you will have at the poll itself. This subject falls into three parts: the first, callers at your house; the second, escorts from your house; the third, attendants in general. (Ibid. 34)

Finally efforts must be made to reach all those with whom the candidate has no specific ties. We thus move out of the domain of personal association and friendship into something more like politics as we know it in modern times. It has often been claimed that the *Commentariolum* shows conclusively that Roman elections were not about political programmes or attitudes but were purely on a personal level; but this is too hasty an assertion, as the document itself makes clear:

> Having said enough of friendships, I must now speak of the other part of the canvass, which is about how to deal with the people. This requires a memory for names, an ingratiating manner, constant attendance, generosity, publicity, a good political image. (Ibid. 41)

> Next, generosity...is to be shown in banquets, to which you and your friends should often convoke the people at large or tribe by tribe. (Ibid. 44)

> You must achieve the result...that the people itself, instead of hearing at second hand from these acquaintances of yours, shares their devotion to you. You have already won over the city masses and the favour of their

political managers by advancing Pompey, by undertaking the case of Manilius and defending Cornelius;...See that your whole canvass is a fine show, brilliant, resplendent, and popular...Above all, it must be shown that high hopes and good opinions are entertained for your political future. Yet, during your canvass, you must not deal with politics either in the Senate or in political meetings of the people. Instead, you must keep in mind that the Senate should deem you, on your life's record, to be in future an upholder of its authority; the Roman knights and men of worth and substance should believe you, from your past life, to be devoted to peace and quiet times; the masses, to be favourably inclined to their interests, since you have been 'popular' at least in your speeches in political meetings and lawcourts. (Ibid. 50-53)

Quintus sums up with the observation:

I see that no election is so polluted with bribery that some centuries do not return, without bribes, the candidates with whom they have a very special bond. (Ibid. 56)

From all this it can be seen what should be the main themes of an electoral campaign for the consulship, at least for a 'new man' who has no hereditary patronage and cannot claim a God-given right to supreme honours, such as certain others seem to invoke with a clear conscience and with the ready approval of the mass of electors. A *novus homo* must build up his own contacts and connections with unremitting energy, but he must also place himself on the political map, as Cicero did not fail to do. In the course of his candidature he had the good fortune to be involved in political troubles (the so-called first Catilinarian conspiracy) which gave an opportunity to former Sullanians and challenged Pompey's newly-established leadership; this made it possible for Cicero to play a political game, i.e. to attack the established links of patronage or loyalty *vis à vis* his adversaries and create new ones for his own benefit. This objective became evident at the end of his consulate, in November-December 63, when he was faced with a conspiracy far more serious than expected, which threatened to degenerate into civil war.[101] On this occasion the 'new man' from Arpinum disclosed his real aim and deep-seated design, which was nothing less than to force on Pompey a kind of division of influence and, basing himself on the equestrian order and the chief men of the *municipia*, to create a new 'party' capable of breaking down the barriers that hedged the nobility. These had been his ambitions as far back as 66 BC, but in view of his modest forces he was careful not to reveal them too soon, while seeking to assure himself of the support from all quarters that he would need in future. Contrary to what is generally maintained, this was a typically political manoeuvre aimed at transforming the pattern of patronage and support in terms not merely of personal loyalty, but also of specific opinions and interests.

All that we read in the *Commentariolum* about the practical conduct of an election campaign is abundantly confirmed by other, more direct sources. We have seen that Marius was elected consul in 108 thanks in part to the *suffragatio*, the active propaganda, of *equites* who were in Africa either with the army, as officers or in the ranks, or as *negotiatores*. In 63 the equestrian centuries were still important enough in the elections for the charge of bribing them to figure prominently in the indictment of L. Murena, consul in 62. The son of Murena's accuser, himself still a member of those centuries, charged L. Natta, another *eques* who was Murena's stepson, of having acted as his stepfather's agent (*Pro Murena* 73). Again, in 44 we find Cicero seeking the support of the same centuries on behalf of L. Aelius Lamia, who was standing for the praetorship. He writers to Brutus in Gaul: 'Since you hold in your hand certain centuries of the *equites*, among whom you are king, send a message to our friend Lupus to secure those centuries for us' (*Ad Fam.* 11.16.3).

Cicero's speeches on behalf of clients sued for fraud throw light on practices that are delicately hinted at in the *Commentariolum* (which does not by any means imply that Cicero was himself given to corruption). A candidature for the consulate began to all intents and purposes several years earlier, when the candidate was still an aedile. In that office, far-sighted people might cultivate a reputation for 'generosity' and enlisting popular gratitude. As Cicero says to Ser. Sulpicius, Murena's accuser:

> Do not treat with such complete contempt the fine arrangements for his games and the splendour of his show which helped him so much. Need I mention that games have a great attraction for the people and the ignorant herd? There is nothing less surprising. Yet that is enough for my case; elections are decided by the people and the masses. (*Pro Murena* 38)

Cicero goes on to tell Sulpicius that he did himself the worst possible service, during his campaign for the consulship, by preparing charges against his rivals and pressing, in his senatorial capacity, for laws against corruption and electoral reforms (which we shall discuss later). 'Your voice demanded a heavier penalty for the commons; the anger of the poorer people was aroused' (Ibid. 47). This, as will be seen, related to bribery and the selling of votes in general. As to the electoral reforms, their effect would have been to reduce the influence of members of the first centuries:

> Men of standing, influential in their neighbourhoods and towns, objected to a man such as you fighting to remove all distinctions of prestige and influence. (Ibid.)

Cicero then proceeds to refute the charges against Murena one by one, and in so doing follows the sequence of practices forbidden by the law:

'But he was followed by a large crowd.' Show that they were paid, and then I shall admit that a crime was committed. What accusation do you make, if that charge is dismissed? 'What need is there,' my opponent says, 'of this retinue?' Am I the man to ask what is the need of something that we have always had? Men of small means are only able to earn favours from our order or pay us back in one way, and that is by helping us and following us about when we are candidates for office. It is not possible and it cannot be asked of us senators or of Roman knights that they should attend for whole days their friends who are candidates. If they come in large numbers to our houses and on occasion accompany us down to the Forum, if they condescend to walk with us the length of a public hall, we think that we are receiving great attention and respect. It is the poorer men, those who have sufficient time, who provide the constant attention that is habitually given to men of standing and to those who confer benefits.

Do not, then, Cato, take from the lower class this fruit of their attention. Allow the men who hope for everything from us to have something to give us in return. If poor men have nothing but their vote, then, even if they use it, their support is valueless. Finally, as they are always saying, they cannot plead for us, stand surety for us, or invite us to their homes. They ask us for all these favours but think that they can only repay us for what they receive from us by personal service....'But shows were given to the tribes and invitations to dinner were given indiscriminately.' Even though Murena took no part in this, and his friends followed traditional practices with moderation, the occasion prompts me to recall, Servius, the number of votes that these complaints in the Senate lost us. Can we or our fathers ever remember a time when there has not been this wish — whether self-interested or out of a disinterested generosity — to provide a seat in the circus and the Forum for our friends and fellow-tribesmen? Those are the rewards and bounties that poorer men receive from their fellow-tribesmen by ancient custom.

[Part of the speech is lost here]

[If they attack Murena] for providing seats for his fellow-tribesmen on a single occasion when he was only a personal adjutant, what will they do to our leading citizens who have provided whole blocks of seats in the Circus for theirs? These charges relating to retinues, shows, public banquets, have all alike been put down by the people to your officiousness, Servius; but Murena has the authority of the Senate to back him against them. How so? The Senate does not think that it is illegal to go out to meet a candidate, does it? 'No; only if payment was made.' Prove that it was. To be escorted by a large crowd? 'No; only if they were hired.' Show that they were. To provide a seat at a show or give an invitation to dinner? 'Not at all; unless it was given indiscriminately throughout the city.' What does 'indiscriminately' mean? 'Given to everybody.' If, then, Lucius Natta, a young man of good birth —and we see his character and the sort of man that he is going to become —wanted to win favour with the centuries of knights in order to fulfil the obligation of his close relationship with Murena and with an eye to the future, no injury or charge will be suffered by his stepfather as a result. If a Vestal Virgin, a relative and friend, has given Murena her seat at the gladiatorial games, her gift is a mark of affection and his acceptance of it above reproach. All these acts are the obligation of friends and relatives, the services of poorer men and the duties of candidates. (*Pro Murena* 70-73)

It will be seen that every social class had its part to play in helping or hindering a candidature. People of low degree could be of little or no service by their votes, but they could show enthusiasm by swelling the retinue by whom their candidate was attended, and in their case the laws and senatorial decrees placed no restriction on numbers (*Pro Murena* 17).

However, canvassing methods were not always so innocent as Cicero represents them to be when defending his heir apparent. Citizens' votes were not prompted exclusively by deference or gratitude, but were openly bought and sold. As early as 102 Marius was accused of having secured his sixth election to the consulate *in absentia* by distributing money lavishly to all the tribes.[102] Such bribery became almost a recognized institution in the first century BC. Its agents, known as *divisores*, had a quasi-official status, as it was their function to supervise legal distributions when there were any, including perhaps the grain ration until its administration was regulated by Augustus. The tribes, as legal corporations, were entitled to receive gifts and legacies (Appian, *B. Civ.* 2.143; 3.23), and there had to be machinery for handling these sums. The *divisores* were appointed officially according to regulations that are known to us but which certainly took account of their census rating.[103] They might be respected members of the equestrian order: we hear of one who was a friend and relative of Verres' father, himself a senator, while another was of the same tribe as Atticus, perhaps an acquaintance of his, and had a son who was a tribune of the plebs (*Att.* 1.18.4). The *divisores* lived in Rome, but they were naturally expected to know all the members of their tribe individually, including those who lived in remote districts and only appeared at election time. L. Ross Taylor plausibly suggested that the country tribes had headquarters in Rome, at which residents in the city could foregather with those who came up from the country. Funerary inscriptions indicate that there was a burial-place belonging to members of the Pollia tribe, showing that the tribes could own real estate. As for the *loca tribuum*, they may have been located near the Circus Flaminius and later the Porticus Minucia, where the grain administration was later set up. In any case it was the *divisores* who handled the electoral 'slush-fund'. In 70 Verres, who was in trouble with the law, did his best to prevent Cicero from being elected aedile:

> I learnt from certain persons who were my regular detectives that a number
> of baskets of Sicilian coins [illegally brought back by Verres from his govern-
> ship] had been transferred from a particular senator to a particular knight,
> that some ten or more of these baskets were left at this senator's house for a
> purpose connected with my own candidature, and that a meeting of the
> bribery-agents for all the tribes was held one night at Verres' house. One of
> these agents, a man who felt bound to give me all the help he could, called
> on me that same night, and told me what Verres had been saying to them: he
> had reminded them how liberally he had dealt with them, both when he was
> himself a candidate for the praetorship some time ago, and at the recent
> elections of consuls and praetors; and then had at once proceeded to promise
> them whatever they chose to ask for turning me out of my aedileship. At
> this, some of them had said they would not dare to try it, others had replied
> that they did not believe it could be managed; however, a stout ally turned
> up from among his own kinsmen, Quintus Verres of the Romilian tribe, a
> fine old specimen of the bribery-agent, who had been the pupil and friend
> of Verres' father; this man undertook to manage the business for 500,000
> sesterces down, and some of the others said after all that they would join
> him. In view of all this my friend very kindly warned me to take every
> possible precaution.
>
> Within the same short space of time I had now to face more than one
> pressing anxiety. My election was upon me; and here, as in the trial, a great
> sum of money was fighting against me. The trial was approaching; and here
> also those baskets of Sicilian gold were threatening me. I was deterred by
> concern for my election from giving my mind freely to the business of the
> trial; the trial prevented my devoting my whole attention to my candidature;
> and to crown all, there was no sense in my trying to intimidate the bribery-
> agents, since I could see they were aware that the conduct of this present
> trial would tie my hands completely. It was just at this moment that I heard
> for the first time how Hortensius had sent the Sicilians word to call on him
> at his house — and how they had behaved like free and independent men,
> refusing to go when they understood why they were being sent for. And
> now began my election, which Verres supposed to be under his own control
> like all the other elections of this year. He dashed about, this great potentate,
> with his amiable and popular son, canvassing the tribes and interviewing the
> family friends — to wit, the bribery-agents — and summoning them to the
> fray. As soon as this was noticed and understood, the people of Rome, with
> prompt enthusiasm, saw to it that I was not thrust out of office by the money
> of a man whose wealth had failed to lure me out of my honour.
>
> Once relieved of the heavy anxieties of my candidature, I began, with a
> mind much less occupied and distracted, to devote my thoughts and energies

to the trial alone. (*I Verr.* 22-5)

The *divisores* must have been fairly numerous, certainly more than one per tribe. In 67 they were powerful enough to cause a kind of a riot in the Forum when the *Lex Cornelia de ambitu* was being voted on (Asconius 75 C), so that its author took flight: the consul Calpurnius had to come to his rescue and ensure the passage of the law by calling to the *comitia* 'all who desired the well-being of the state.'

We have some undoubted evidence of large-scale money handouts at election time. In the first place, the law sometimes condemned the guilty party to pay out the sums he had promised, even if defeated at the election, e.g. to the amount of 3,000 sesterces per tribe, each year until his death (*Att.* 1.16.13). In 54, as we have seen, Memmius and Domitius, candidates for the consulship, together promised 10 million sesterces to the prerogative century alone (*Ad Quintum fratrem* 2.14.4) — a small fortune for each man, if we reckon their number at a few hundred. In the same year, we know from Cicero and Plutarch that candidates for the tribunate — at least ten in number, and probably more — each deposited 500,000 sesterces with Cato the Younger in an attempt to eliminate malpractice,

> on the understanding that they would canvass according to his instructions, and any of them failing to do so would be condemned by him. And if that election proves free from all corruption, as it is supposed it will, Cato will have proved himself more powerful than all the laws and jurors put together. (Cicero, ibid.)

These sureties thus totalled between 5 and 10 million sesterces. The raising of sums of the order of 15-20 million sesterces for the elections alone naturally had repercussions on the money market, pushing up the rate of interest from 4 to 8 per cent. Bribery continued under the Principate: in 18 BC Augustus enacted a *Lex Julia*, and the *Lex Valeria Cornelia* of AD 5 was also in part an anti-corruption measure. But bribery had to be fought by its own methods. To prevent the Fabia and Scaptia tribes, of which he was a member, from being corrupted, Augustus distributed 1,000 sesterces per head from his private purse on election day, 'so that they should not expect anything from any of the candidates' (Suetonius, *Augustus* 40).[104]

The laws against corruption forbade virtually all the practices we have mentioned, such as giving banquets for fellow-tribesmen or the populace in general, or assembling crowds to welcome a returning pro-magistrate or attend on a candidate during his campaign; a special law, the *Lex Fabia,* limited the size of these and the numbers of senators and *equites* who might take part (*Pro Murena* 71). There was even a senatorial decree forbidding propaganda in favour of third parties (Plutarch, *Cato Minor* 49). What the law was intended to prohibit, of course, was not these advantages as such, but the practice of paying for them; it was thus a valid defence to show that one had obtained them for nothing.

Other practices were more emphatically condemned and were made the subject of a special law in 55: viz. the formation of unlawful soceieties (*sodalicia*) for political or electoral purposes, and collusion (*coitio*) between candidates who traded votes instead of fighting fairly.[105] Private associations and clubs were always carefully watched in Rome; in principle they were absolutely forbidden, except for religious and funerary purposes. Almost all the societies that existed, such as professional guilds, purported to be religious colleges. Towards the decade 80-70, and perhaps earlier, associations began to appear which, though the language did not differentiate them clearly from the others, were more or less exclusively devoted to electoral purposes. They were forbidden by a *senatus consultum* of 65 (*Ad Quintum fratrem* 2.3.5), but Clodius in 58 passed a law which permitted them once again: 'Not only were those guilds (*collegia*) restored which the Senate had abolished, but countless new ones were called into being from the slave-dregs of the city' (Cicero, *In Pisonem* 9). The new associations certainly included slaves, or at any rate freedmen, among their members. Cicero says in several places that the latter were enlisted in separate sections of the town and enrolled into squads of ten:

> And with the same consuls looking on, a levy of slaves was held in front of the Tribunal of Aurelius on the pretext of forming clubs; men were enlisted street by street, formed into squads and incited to deeds of violence, murder and robbery. (*Pro Sestio* 34)

It is hard to see how Clodius could have recruited other men's slaves in this fashion. Perhaps, however, the law of 58 was connected with the law on grain distribution which he introduced at the same time. Clodius had decided that grain would henceforth be distributed free to those entitled to receive it, but he had his friend Sex. Cloelius put in charge of preparing the lists and carrying out the distribution (*De Domo* 25). The 'slaves' were perhaps about to be freed by their masters so that they could be maintained by the state: this, as we know, was one of the causes of the food scarcity which Pompey had to remedy in 57. Clodius may have seen in this situation a useful opportunity to recruit gangsters cheaply, organizing the mass of slaves or men newly freed into groups for the purpose of the grain dole so as to provide him with gangs of unscrupulous followers in the city itself. In order to get rid of Sex. Cloelius a new measure, the *Lex Cornelia Caecilia*, was introduced in 57 and carried with Cicero's support (*De Domo* 26), transferring the superintendence of the *annona* to Pompey.

However, Clodius was not alone in making use of the associations that were once again permitted. He no doubt managed to have a large number of the new citizens enrolled in urban tribes, including the Palatina which was his preferred instrument in 58 and 57 (*Pro Sestio* 114): he may have got some into the Collina in 57 despite Pompey's control (*Pro Milone* 25, but this is inconclusive). The new sodalities and *decuriae* were dissolved by a *senatus consultum* of 56 (*Ad Quintum fratrem* 2.3.5), and violators were liable to a charge of disorderly behaviour; but apparently the decree was not enforced, as Crassus enacted a further measure against sodalities in 55, under which Cn. Plancius was prosecuted in that year (having just been elected aedile). This was supposed to be a recapitulation of all the previous laws against corruption: it forbade in particular 'the systematic organization of the tribes and the electorate into sections and the restriction of the freedom of the poll by bribery' (*Pro Plancio* 45). Plancius was accused of having bribed his own tribe in particular, the Teretina (he was a native of Atina in Campania), and also the Voltinia. To this Cicero naturally replied that Plancius owed his support in both tribes not to corruption but to services rendered in the ordinary way, to his family's patronage at Atina and round about, and also — which was no doubt true — to the pride which members of hitherto obscure *municipia* felt at seeing a fellow-townsman launched on the Roman *cursus honorum*.

Another charge was one of electoral collusion between Plancius and Plotius, an opponent of his who had also been elected and who, like him, was a *novus homo*. The charge was based on the fact that the two candidates had obtained almost the same number of votes in the same tribes (*Pro Plancio* 54-5; we have already referred to this). Plancius was supposed to have promised the Teretina to Plotius, and Plotius the Aniensis to Plancius; some cash discovered in the Circus Flaminius was said to be evidence of illegal distribution (ibid. 55).

Illicit practices were not confined to the campaigning period but might also occur on polling day, as we have already seen. The most blatant was the use of violence, including injury to life and limb, overturning the urns and so on; but there was also the fraudulent distribution of ready-marked voting tablets, the casting of votes by unauthorized persons, and sharp practice in connection with the scrutiny and counting. Offences of this kind were generally alleged by unsuccessful candidates, in ancient Rome as in our own day. In Orson Welles' film *Citizen Kane* the central character is defeated in the election for governorship of New York State; expecting the result, he has a special edition of his newspaper printed with the headline 'Fraud at Polls!' This was exactly the course followed by Cato and Ser. Sulpicius Rufus on the day after the consular elections of 64 for 63.

The fate of the comitia

Elections in the last years of the Republic were certainly not very edifying. The relative probity in public affairs which had excited Polybius's admiration as late as 150 BC had gravely declined. Nevertheless, hasty generalizations should be avoided. The history of this period as it has reached us is largely a chronicle of gossip and scandal, with a somewhat suspicious predominance of sensational incidents. We are also hampered by insufficient information concerning trials for electoral corruption, and the impossibility of obtaining statistics which would show how frequent it was. Some limits were imposed on malpractice by the electoral system, with all its archaic features. The *comitia centuriata* were heavily weighted in favour of the rich, the equestrian centuries and the first property class, and it is unlikely that these privileged persons were much tempted to let themselves be bribed. In any case, if the results of prosopography are used to study the outcome of elections, it appears that the system did not necessarily operate in favour of what might be called plutocracy. There is no known example of a *nouveau riche* freedman or plebeian attaining high office by dint of wealth alone. On the contrary, the supreme offices of state, and particularly the consulship, remained in the hands of a hereditary 'status group', the nobility, which maintained its position less by wealth than by the prestige of illustrious names, a network of friendships, influence and patronage, and finally the conservatism and snobbery of an electorate which respected traditional values. If a 'new man' succeeded in making his way into the circle it was either thanks to an upsurge of revolutionary feeling (Terentius Varro in 216) or pressure on his part for fuller rights (Marius in 108) or, as in Cicero's case, a mobilization of public opinion in times of trouble and dramatic change. The centuriate assembly, which was certainly oligarchic and conservative, was for that very reason less vulnerable to overt corruption. The tribal assembly is another matter, but here again it is too often placed in a wrong perspective: the assembly is supposed to have been dominated by the urban plebs, who are thought of as the dregs of the population. But, to begin with, the urban tribes as such — comprising freedmen and, no doubt, the lesser fry of artisans and shopkeepers — were a minority in the *comitia tributa*, with only four votes out of 35. It was still the rural tribes which carried the elections. As far as they were concerned, those of their members who lived in Rome certainly had the electoral advantage: these were country folk who had migrated to the city since the beginning of the second century BC in search of jobs or a livelihood from private or public charity.[106] These were certainly the most influential voters, and those whom it was easiest or most tempting to court. But we have also seen that the effect, if not the object, of the complicated system was to achieve a kind of *de facto* if not *de jure* representation of the citizens of *municipia* or colonies who lived too far away to come to Rome *en masse* and exercise their vote regularly. They were reinforced by delegations — there is no other word — composed of local notabilities who came to assure their chosen candidates of their votes within the tribal system. It is too often assumed that these were always knights, prominent persons or members of the first class. Cicero expressly indicates the opposite:

Must not so many Roman knights, so many tribunes of the treasury — not to mention the plebs, who were present to a man at the election, and who have now been dismissed from this court — must not all these have lent vast material and moral support to my client's candidature? (*Pro Plancio* 21)

We should not underestimate the Italians' ambition, especially after the Social War, to introduce members of their local families into the Roman corridors of power: support of this kind must often have been more effective than overt corruption, which, as we have seen, was employed without success against Cicero in 70 BC.

Naturally this is not to say that the system was perfect. Its archaism leapt to the eye: in 44 it was still functioning in the form adopted during or shortly after the Second Punic War, in spite of the huge expansion of the electorate during the decades which followed the Social War. Several attempts were made to modify it, one apparently by C. Gracchus in 123: this is known to us only from a passing reference by Sallust, or an author using his name, in a kind of open letter of advice to Caesar, a curious document which may be dated to the beginning of the Civil War (49 BC):[107]

First of all, deprive money of its importance. Let no one be given greater or less opportunity, according to his wealth, to serve as a juror in cases involving life or honour; just as no consul or praetor should be chosen because of his riches, but because of his worth. In the case of a magistrate, the people can easily decide; but for jurors to be selected by a faction is tyranny, and for them to be chosen on the basis of money is shameful. It therefore seems to me fitting that all citizens of the first class should be eligible as jurors, but that they should serve in somewhat greater numbers than at present. Neither the Rhodians nor the citizens of any other state have ever had occasion to be ashamed of their courts, where rich and poor alike, according to the accident of the lot, decide indiscriminately matters of greatest or of slight importance.

As regards the election of magistrates, I for my part very naturally approve the law which Gaius Gracchus proposed in his tribunate, that the centuries should be called up by lot from the five classes without distinction. In this way money and worth are put on an equality and each man will strive to outdo his fellow in merit. (*Ep. ad Caesarem* 11, 7.10-8.2)

It is unlikely that this *rogatio* by C. Gracchus was ever carried. In any case the hierarchical system of voting by classes continued throughout the first century BC. P. Sulpicius Rufus, in 88, may have changed the voting order in some way, but when Sulla marched on Rome in that year he certainly re-established the old system 'of King Servius Tullius'. In 63, at the height of the contest for the consulship between Catiline, Murena and Servius Sulpicius

Rufus, the latter may have put forward a proposal in the Senate which to some extent revived C. Gracchus's plan. This eminent lawyer, a friend of Cicero and a declared adversary of Catiline, had more original and profound ideas of constitutional law and Roman politics than most of his contemporaries. A former praetor and certainly not a *popularis*, while campaigning for the consulate he made a series of proposals to the Senate which, as we have seen, surprised and embarrassed his friends. The first was a tightening-up of the *Lex de ambitu* of 67. Cicero had to adopt this suggestion and, at the Senate's behest, put forward a proposal of his own on corruption, with increased penalties for *divisores* and candidates guilty of malpractice. Other proposals by Servius Sulpicius were rejected, but are worth attention. He attempted to reintroduce the law on voting by freedmen, carried by the tribune C. Manilius in 67 but annulled by the Senate on procedural grounds on 1 January 66. But Sulpicius certainly went further, for Cicero describes his proposals in terms which would hardly apply to a law which related to the *comitia tributa* and nothing else:

> You demanded a random order of voting for the centuries,...equal distribution of influence, prestige and voting. But men of standing, influential in their neighbourhoods and towns, objected to men such as you fighting to remove all distinctions of prestige and influence. (*Pro Murena* 47)

These terms are exactly the same as those which traditionally defined the 'degrees of dignity' reflected in the system of classes and centuries. It is probable, therefore, that Servius Sulpicius wished to reform the class organization in some way, and his unsuccessful proposal may have been a revival of that put forward by C. Gracchus in 123 and cited by Sallust in 49.

Caesar, in any case, had no intention of taking Sallust's advice. His concern with the electoral system was not to reform it but to use it to his own advantage, while retaining power to appoint most of the magistrates. The Triumvirate likewise designated the magistrates in advance as it saw fit, and the regular elections, sometimes carried out under the threat of armed force, were no more than a farce. However, when Augustus in 27 took on himself to 'restore' the Republic, he also revived the *comitia*, and immediately electoral corruption flourished more than ever. Perhaps wishing to induce citizens to take an interest in public affairs once again, Augustus tried to devise original solutions of the evident contradiction caused by extending the franchise to all Italy and even some of the provinces, while maintaining an electoral system confined to the city of Rome. One solution might have been a representative regime, such as was already familiar in the federal states and leagues of antiquity. But Augustus also wished to maintain the fiction of *mos majorum* and to restore the past greatness of the Republic. He resorted to an innovation, known to us only from an allusion by Suetonius, which had interesting possibilities and might have applied to other fields besides elections:

After having thus set the city and its affairs in order, he personally established 28 new Italian colonies; furnished many parts of Italy with public buildings and revenues; and even gave it, at least to some degree, equal rights and dignity with the city of Rome, by devising a kind of vote which the members of the local senate were to cast in each colony for candidates for the city offices and send under seal to Rome against the day of the elections. (*Augustus* 46)

According to Suetonius, Augustus also planned to regulate admission to the equestrian order in this way:

To keep up the supply of men of rank and induce the commons to increase and multiply, he admitted to the equestrian military career those who were recommended by any town. (Ibid.)[108]

I have suggested elsewhere that these knights promoted *ex commendatione publica* are to be identified with the 'military tribunes designated by the people' who are mentioned in Italian inscriptions dating from Augustus' reign. Unfortunately Suetonius does not tell us in what way the colonies' votes, sent under seal to Rome, were counted on voting day. But it happens that the chief electoral reform of Augustus's time, smuggled in, so to speak, in AD 5 on the occasion of the funeral honours paid to the *principes juventutis*, provides for a preliminary vote by certain categories of citizens, whose ballots were to be deposited and kept under seal until the day of the *comitia* and then integrated, in some way or another, in the total count. Nothing was known of this basic reform until it was spectacularly revealed by an inscription discovered in 1947, the *Tabula Hebana*.[109] Although some key passages are unfortunately missing, this document (the *Lex Valeria Cornelia*) provided for a restricted assembly of senators and all the *equites* enrolled in the judicial *decuriae* (but no others), for the purpose of 'destining' candidates for the offices of praetor and consul; only these would then be voted on by the people. The system, as can be seen, was based on several precedents. It was in some degree an extension of the *praerogativa* to ten centuries (raised to 15 in AD 19) of the city's *élite*. It was also a means of preventing corruption, for these centuries were not permanent and pre-existing but were chosen by lot on a tribal basis at voting time; they thus answered to Sulpicius's desideratum of a 'random order of voting'. Finally it was a deferred vote, like that of the *decuriones* of the colonies, which had to be registered in advance; and a means enabling some of the provincial *élite* to take part in the election, since the *equites* in the judicial *decuriae* often came from very distant provinces.

This effort to rationalize or moralize the *comitia*, however, came too late. Despite the appearance of freedom that the Princeps left to the assemblies, and the fierce competition that there might still be for the magistracies, the prize was devoid of substance, since the Republic was dead and the Princeps was its master. It is significant that Augustus's attempt to place the assemblies on a sound moral basis came in the midst of a series of semi-divine honours which the Senate conferred on princes of the imperial family, showing its devotion to the dynasty with a zealous servility that was imitated by most cities of the Empire. It was poetic justice that Augustus and his immediate successor, having in vain sought to reanimate the ghosts of ancient liberties and the old Republic, met with nothing but servility from their contemporaries. But the Republic had been dead since rule by the sword was introduced through the military *coups d'état* of Sulla, Caesar and Octavian himself. It had died at the same time as Cicero's rhetoric, and could not be revived by the feeble devices of the *Lex Valeria Cornelia*.

CHAPTER VIII

LIBERTAS
The citizen and the authorities

The ruling class and the rule of law

THE FOREGOING CHAPTERS will, I hope, have given an idea of the multiple and reciprocal links by which the Roman citizen was attached to the City. In the most literal sense, the citizen did not even exist until the community, represented for this purpose by the censors, had taken cognizance of his physical and biological reality, expressed in a declaration which included particulars regarding age, sex, parentage, *gens* and family, civil status (wardship etc.), domicile, tribal membership and property. On the strength of this declaration, made in public and duly verified, the City solemnly conferred on him a place in a complex organization which determined his rank and dignity and thereby gave him a precise part to play in the manifold relationships of civic life—a part which, in principle, involved an approximate balance of rights and duties, advantages and disadvantages. We have seen to some extent how this balance worked out in the three essential aspects of the citizen's life: military, fiscal and political. As a soldier, a taxpayer or recipient of public bounty, and an elector, the Roman was made to realize at every stage of his life that he was a *civis*, a member of a community that existed because of him and for his benefit. During the last two centuries of the Republic, as we have tried to show, these mutual relationships formed a fairly coherent system. Each of the three depended on the other two and was justified and limited by them, thus producing a remarkably balanced whole.

So far, however, we have said little about an essential aspect of this communal life: the distance and the more or less frequent relations that exist in almost any political society between the governors and the governed, between those who embody or monopolize the state, on the one hand, and the rank and file on the other:[1] that is to say, relations between the citizen and the authorities. At first sight this may not seem very important: in an ancient city state, governed by assemblies, councils and magistrates who are elected or chosen by lot, the distinction reduces to a minimum. Such indeed was the ideal which the Roman constitution professed to embody:

We must have magistrates, for without their prudence and watchful care a

State cannot exist. In fact the whole character of a republic is determined by its arrangements in regard to magistrates. Not only must we inform them of the limits of their administrative authority; we must also instruct the citizens as to the extent of their obligation to obey them. For the man who rules efficiently must have obeyed others in the past, and the man who obeys dutifully appears fit at some later time to be a ruler. Thus he who obeys ought to expect to be a ruler in the future, and he who rules should remember that in a short time he will have to obey. (Cicero, *De Legibus* 3.5)

But in practice things were not so, for the simple reason that the Roman polity was based on wealth, so that not everyone had the same right or opportunity to achieve high office. Contrary to what is often stated, there was a property qualification for the first step in the *cursus honorum*, viz. the quaestorship, as well as all the rest which depended on it. Originally one had to be at least a member of the first property class in order to attain this office, and even to be one of those whom the censors certified as entitled to serve in the cavalry.[2] In fact, one could not stand for any public office whatever without first serving in the cavalry for ten years. Towards the mid-second century the property qualification for the rank of *eques* was fixed, probably at 400,000 sesterces, and this was also the requirement for those who aspired to be quaestors, magistrates or senators.

These restrictions clearly eliminated a large number of citizens at the outset — the only possible exception being the tribunate of the plebs, to which they are not known to have applied. But that was not all. In practice the recruitment of magistrates and senators was even more narrowly based, since from the earliest days of the Republic there was a *de facto* trend towards heredity at various levels. In this way there grew up a ruling class based largely on birth and only enlarged at long intervals, generally after a sharp political contest. It is not my intention to discuss this situation here, but it meant that within the apparent unanimity of the Roman city there was an increasingly clear distinction between a minority of families and citizens who really took part in every aspect of civic life, especially the magistracies, and, on the other hand, the masses who played a much more restricted role. They were practically excluded from public counsels (the Senate) and from the magistracies, and their part in civic affairs was confined to military service, taxpaying and the receipt of rations, and membership of the assemblies, which itself was on a strictly graded and hierarchical basis.

Thus, in the nature of things, a ruling class was confronted by the mass of citizens. We have seen something of their mutual relations in connection with the army and the financial system; while our study of the workings of the assemblies has touched on the complex and often ambiguous relations between candidates and voters. But relations between the citizen and the authorities also found expression in two spheres that we have not yet considered: that of day-to-day administration (to use a modern term whose application will have to be examined and justified) and that of justice and the courts.

I shall not go into the question of political relations between the Roman magistrates and the people as a whole, i.e. the citizen body. This is a field which has been studied with some thoroughness, partly because the Romans themselves, rightly or wrongly, had a very precise idea of their internal history as a slow but steady conquest, by the people, of freedom and equal rights. In this largely idealized schema the authority of the supreme magistrates was thought of as having been from the outset particularly imposing and coercive, after the fashion of a military command. The whole Roman tradition emphasized the solemn, mandatory and in a sense religious character of the exercise of power and its symbolic manifestations, so that in some cases the mere presence of the consuls or dictator with all the accoutrements of *imperium* was sufficient to imbue the people with superstitious terror. This was seen in 439 at the time of the 'conspiracy' of Spurius Maelius, when L. Quinctius, the newly-appointed dictator, and his Master of the Horse, Servilius Ahala, made a dramatic appearance in the Forum:

> The next day, after disposing guards at several points he went down into the Forum, where the novel and surprising sight drew upon him the attention of the plebs. (Livy 4.14.1)

To the Greeks, this external panoply of Roman power was a source of surprise and terror even in much later times. Thus the Macedonians in 167:

> Although they were used to a royal court, yet the ceremonial of a new master with frightening as it met their eyes — the consul's bench, his entrance after the way had been cleared, the herald, and the orderly, all things novel to their eyes and ears, which might have inspired terror in allies, to say nothing of conquered enemies. (Livy 45.29.2)

The essentially repressive and coercive nature of Roman authority was shown first of all by the display which surrounded it in both republican and imperial times: the magistrate invariably appeared in public preceded by his lictors, bearing on their shoulders the axe surrounded by a bundle of rods. Those who were not entitled to lictors and fasces were escorted by *viatores* armed with clubs, as well as heralds and other attendants. In case of need they were allowed to use military force despite the rule that the citizen army might not assemble within the *pomerium*: we have seen examples of this under Sulla, and even in 52 during Milo's trial. The same principle applied in public law. Magistrates possessing the *imperium* were not only entitled to institute a public trial which might result in corporal penalties being inflicted on the offender; they also had the right of *coercitio*, i.e. exacting obedience to their lawful orders by any means including physical force and, in early times, even putting recalcitrants to death. The only difference between these sanctions and those which might follow a criminal trial was that they were not inflicted by judicial sentence but were simply enforcement measures.

It thus appears at first sight that public authority had every advantage over the citizens, either as a body or as individuals. In reality this was not altogether so, as there operated (in circumstances which are still a matter of dispute) a safeguard of the people's individual and collective rights which the Romans regarded as the linchpin of their political and social system. This was the office of tribune of the plebs and its immediate corollary, the right of *provocatio* or 'appeal to the people'.[3] These institutions were the essential guarantee of *libertas*, the supreme attribute and privilege of the citizen. I am not concerned here to analyse this concept, which was a particularly vivid and concrete one in Roman eyes; but we may note that it is perhaps the best translation of the Greek word *demokratia*, denoting a regime in which the whole people exercises power as directly as possible. At Rome, as Polybius saw, power was actually shared between the people in its assemblies, the Senate and the higher magistrates, each being in a sense autonomous, but dependent on the others in order to exercise its competence to the full; and the question was not so much whether the people 'governed' but whether it was 'free', i.e. able to make full use of its rights. *Libertas* is perhaps the key concept of the Roman civic and political vocabulary, invoked by everyone at all levels: by the people as a whole *vis à vis* the dominant oligarchies (patricians and senators), and by the plebs against members of the old *gentes*. It was also appealed to by particular groups within the city: by the Senate against pressure from magistrates or the threat of personal power, and by magistrates against the claims of tribunes.

From the individual's point of view *libertas* was primarily a guarantee of equality under the law—established, in principle, by the Twelve Tables in the mid-fifth century—and later, from the end of the fourth century, an assurance that the rules of judicial procedure would be known, published and impartially applied. But—and here we come much closer to an effective guarantee against public authority—it also stood for the certainty that the magistrates' coercive power was not unlimited. In particular, whenever this power threatened the citizen's physical or civil personality, his life or liberty, the whole people would have a say in the matter if the individual concerned chose to appeal to it. This *jus provocationis*, the right of appeal to one's fellow-citizens against the arbitrary decision of a magistrate, is unanimously extolled in Roman literature as the essential achievement and most precious privilege of Roman freedom. Traditionally, and no doubt anachronistically, it was dated from the very beginning of the Republic in 509. It naturally took time to be consolidated and entrenched in public and criminal law, but this was achieved by the beginning of the second century with the series of *Leges Porciae* and was further supplemented by a law of C. Gracchus in 123 BC. After this the citizen could no longer be coerced, let alone condemned, without the right of appeal coming into play automatically: i.e. the case had to be publicly debated before a court, and in criminal matters the only competent court was the people itself in its assemblies. Liberty, associated with the right of *provocatio* and the tribunate of the plebs through which it was exercised, was not only a sentiment or a moral climate but a specific right interposed, in a concrete and highly efficacious manner, between the citizen and the shadow of power: an imprescriptible human right on the lines of habeas corpus, which it antedates by 18 centuries.

This protection conferred by the people on each and every citizen eventually became the common patrimony of all Romans. In the first century every 'party' and political grouping claimed it as their heritage, even though it might lapse in the course of political struggles (the alternation of revolutions and repressions from 133 onwards). The content and overtones of the term might vary greatly according to political allegiance and circumstances, but the honour paid to it was all the greater. The most eloquent hymn to the liberty of the citizen, which had been flouted by a Roman pro-praetor, is in the famous passage of the Verrine orations on the torture and execution of Gavius of Compsa at Messana (Messina) in 70 BC:

[Verres] suddenly ordered the man to be flung down, stripped naked and tied up in the open market-place, and rods to be got ready. The unhappy man cried out that he was a Roman citizen, a burgess of Compsa; that he had served in the army under the distinguished Roman knight Lucius Raecius, who was in business at Panhormus and could assure Verres of the truth of his story. To this Verres replied that he had discovered that Gavius had been sent to Sicily as a spy by the leaders of the fugitive army—a charge which was brought by no informer, for which there was no evidence, and which nobody saw any reason to believe. He then ordered the man to be flogged severely all over his body.

There in the open market-place of Messana a Roman citizen, gentlemen, was beaten with rods; and all the while, amid the crack of the falling blows, no groan was heard from the unhappy man, no words came from his lips in his agony except 'I am a Roman citizen.' By thus proclaiming his citizenship he had been hoping to avert all those blows and shield his body from torture; yet not only did he fail to secure escape from those cruel rods, but when he persisted in his entreaties and his appeals to his citizen rights, a cross was made ready—yes, a cross, for that hapless and broken sufferer who had never seen such an accursed thing till then.

Does freedom, that precious thing, mean nothing? nor the proud privileges of a citizen of Rome? nor the law of Porcius, the laws of Sempronius? nor the tribunes' power, whose loss our people felt so deeply till now at last it has been restored to them? Have all these things come in the end to mean so little that in a Roman province, in a town whose people have special privileges, a Roman citizen could be bound and flogged in the market-place by a man who owed his rods and axes to the favour of the Roman people? When the fire and hot metal plates and the like were brought to torture him, even if his agonized entreaties, his pitiful cries could not stay your hand, was your soul untouched even by the tears and the loud groans of the Roman citizens who then stood by? You dared to crucify any living man who claimed to be a Roman citizen?...If you, Verres, had been made prisoner in Persia or the remotest part of India, and were being dragged off to execution, what cry would you be uttering, save that you were a Roman citizen? You, a stranger among strangers, among savages, among a people inhabiting the farthest and remotest regions of the earth, would have been well served by your claim to that citizenship whose glory is known throughout the world. What, then, of this man whom you were hurrying to execution? whoever he was, he was unknown to you, and he declared himself a Roman citizen: could not that statement, that claim of citizenship, secure from you on your judgement-seat, if not remission, yet at least postponement of the sentence of death?

Poor men of humble birth sail across the seas to shores they have never seen before, where they find themselves among strangers, and cannot always have with them acquaintances to vouch for them. Yet such trust have they in the mere fact of their citizenship that they count on being safe, not only where they find our magistrates, who are restrained by the fear of law and public opinion, and not only among their own countrymen, to whom they are bound by the ties of a common language and civic rights and much else beside: no, wherever they find themselves, they feel confident that this one fact will be their defence. Take away this confidence, take away this defence from Roman citizens; lay it down that to cry 'I am a Roman citizen' shall help no man at all; make it possible for governors and other persons to inflict upon a man who declares himself a Roman citizen any cruel penalty they choose, on the plea that they do not know who the man is; do this, accept that plea, and forthwith you exclude Roman citizens from all our provinces, from all foreign kingdoms and republics, from every region of that great world to which Romans, above all other men, have always had free access until now. (*2 Verr.* 5.161-3, 167-9)

Whatever the advocate's motives in a particular case, the praise of liberty as well as of the laws is an unmistakable leitmotiv throughout Roman literature, both historical and juridical. The demand may be partisan or one-sided: Catiline invoked liberty no less eloquently than Cicero and died for the idea of it that he had implanted in his own followers, as Cicero in turn died for a more austere kind of freedom, aristocratic and parliamentarian, and as Brutus and Cato died for liberty after taking up arms in its defence. Admittedly there is a shift, in this series of examples, from civic to political liberty, which latter perhaps means no more than freedom to oppress others. This, in Rome, concerned at most the few thousand members of the political class; but the original, juridical liberty of the citizen is quite another matter.

However, while the 'rule of law' represents an immense conquest, it is not everything. The essential question in a given society is perhaps that of how the law is set in motion and applied. The Romans well knew this, with their saying that 'the magistracy is a speaking law, governing the people' (Cicero, *De Legibus* 3.2). In principle the law protected the Roman citizen against arbitrary administrative action by magistrates, and assured him first of equal treatment in judicial matters and then of the fullest possible guarantees. But what guarantee was there that the law would be applied and respected? Were not arbitrary treatment and oppression reintroduced hypocritically by the back door, as the law remained a dead letter? And, if so, distinctions must again be drawn: if there was arbitrary action despite the law, it must have differed in its effect on different individuals and groups. In short, what is needed is a social and differential history of Roman liberty and its relations with the state.

A general point must be made here. We have many accounts of what may be called oppression or repression suffered at one time or another by some or all Roman citizens. These consist for the most part of 'speeches' attributed by historians to orators or political leaders seeking to persuade an audience. It follows that they raise difficult problems of interpretation, in the first place as to whether they tell the truth or were ever really delivered. All those in Dionysius or Livy which relate to the obscure period down to and including the fourth century BC are highly suspect of anachronism. But this does not mean that they are negligible as evidence, since, following the rules of annalistic elaboration, they sometimes reflect with great accuracy uses of language, attitudes and events which are perfectly real and interesting for their own time although much later than the period they purport to describe. A speech by Manlius Capitolinus in 390 BC, as reported by Livy, is almost a carbon copy of one delivered by the tribune Mamilius Limetanus in 109 according to Sallust's version (*c.* 40-30 BC), itself perhaps derived from one by Licinius Macer, a historian and political speaker in the years 75-65.[4] One may suppose from this that the vocabulary and ideas of the speeches attributed to 390 and 109 respectively in fact belong only to the period after Sulla. But this is not all. The complaints of oppression are 'speeches', which means that even if the ancient historian endorses them they represent only a point of view, a partial (in both senses) account of the matter at issue, in fact a contribution to a debate. This is the essential point: oppression (by a man or a group, a constitutional organ like the Senate, a class, the 'nobility' or those in power) is presented not so much as an objective fact but rather as an argument in a public debate. However harsh or unjust it may seem to us, at least it is displayed in full daylight and not in the obscurity of a prison cell, and, in Republican times at least, such discussion was never forbidden. By the laws of the game a revolutionary speech or one expressing demands presupposes a speech containing counter-arguments. This, moreover, was not simply an accident or a cultural fashion: it was an organic part of the city's life, in which, even if real power was confined to an oligarchy, the process of government, justice and administration was supposed to be carried on and debated in public. It is not until the last years, when military dictatorship was in the offing—the years of Sulla, the triumvirate and Augustus —that we find arbitrary decisions being prepared in the secret counsels of the dictator or *princeps* and suddenly imposed on the public without discussion or appeal, like Sulla's proscription or Octavian's confiscations. But by then the Republic was already doomed.

A final remark: in most cases, protests against injustice or oppression or the infringement of civil liberties were aimed against individuals (such as Sulla) or specific groups (such as a party in the Senate), not against the state or justice in general; in Roman eyes oppression was not a natural feature of the state, but a negation and depravation of it. To restore liberty would also signify restoring the *respublica*. This is what Caesar, by his own account, says to his troops when about to march on Rome:

> A new precedent had been introduced into the state whereby the right of tribunicial intervention, which in earlier years had been restored by arms, was now being branded with ignominy and crushed by arms. ...He had not quitted his province with any evil intent, but...to restore to their position the tribunes of the people who had been expelled from the state, and to assert the freedom of himself and the Roman people who had been oppressed by a small faction. (Caesar, *De bello civili* 1.7, 22)

The same language was used 28 years earlier by another rebellious consul, Aemilius Lepidus, denouncing Sulla's regime:

> I looked upon freedom united with danger as preferable to peace with slavery. If you are of the same mind, citizens of Rome, rouse yourselves and with the kindly aid of the gods follow Marcus Aemilius, your consul, who will be your leader and champion in recovering your freedom! (Sallust, *Historiae* 1.55.27)

Administration and the civil service

This confidence in the old Republic goes some way to reply to the questions we raised earlier about relations between the citizen and the administration. In Roman eyes, oppression was not an inescapable feature of civil life but an accident of history. And indeed the attributes which, since Engels perhaps, we are inclined to take for granted as part of the idea of a state were almost entirely lacking in Rome. To begin with, despite the imposing spectacle of the magistrates' retinue, the apparatus of government and what may be called the civil service of republican Rome were of a most rudimentary kind. This was a city, the only one in the ancient world, which grew to the size of a modern state, with several million inhabitants in Italy alone after 89 BC, and several million citizens. But it had only the sketchiest of means with which to maintain order, which may be regarded as the essential function of a state, and carry on the administration. There was no police force in the proper sense; in emergency recourse was had to the army, which, as we have seen, regarded itself as a citizen militia for much longer than is commonly supposed. The magistrates had their right of *coercitio* and officials to help them maintain it, but the 24 lictors to whom the two consuls were entitled can hardly be called a repressive force. Even if we add to these the 'public slaves' and contingents of certain allies (the Bruttii) who were recruited in the second century to serve outside Rome as a bodyguard or even as executioners, it remains true that the majesty of public authority consisted in the respect it inspired and in consensus rather than force. The baneful institution of the praetorian guard did not make its appearance until the Empire. In republican times, what we should call police duties and the maintenance of public order were the general responsibility of all the magistrates: consuls, praetors, aediles, in some cases tribunes (since they had jurisdiction of their own) and lesser magistrates, among whom the *tresviri capitales* were particularly concerned with enforcing penalties. These magistrates had staff to assist them, as we shall see, but certainly not on the scale of an armed force, so that when necessary they made use of their own freedmen or slaves. The prison system was so little organized that in Cicero's time prisoners were sometimes detained in magistrates' homes in a kind of 'house arrest':[5] this happened in the case of Catiline's chief accomplices, who were quite prominent individuals. Roman prisons, in fact, were seldom used for citizens, who were generally protected by the tribunes' intercession or the right to put up bail; they were reserved for slaves, captives or non-citizens, as is shown by the 'prison conspiracy' of 198 BC which Livy describes:

> The Carthaginian hostages were confined at Setia. With them, since they were sons of prominent men, were a large number of slaves. Their number was increased, as was natural after the recent African war, by numerous prisoners of war of that nation, bought up out of the booty by the people of Setia themselves. These formed a conspiracy and sent messengers from their company to stir up other slaves, first in the Setine territory, then around Norba and Cerceii. Complete preparations having been made, they agreed to attack the crowd at the games which were soon to be held at Setia; they captured Setia in the confusion, but failed to take Norba and Cerceii.... Shortly after this, word was received that some of the remnants of the same conspiracy were about to occupy Praeneste. Lucius Cornelius the praetor went there and executed about 500 who were implicated in the crime. The

state feared that the Carthaginian hostages and prisoners had contrived the plot. So at Rome watchmen patrolled the streets, the minor magistrates were ordered to make inspections, and the three officials in charge of the quarry-prison to increase their vigilance, and the praetor sent letters around to the Latin confederacy that both the hostages and the prisoners should be guarded, the former in private custody, with no opportunity to come out into public places, the latter loaded with chains of not less than ten pounds' weight, just as if they were confined in a public prison. (Livy 32.26.5-1f.)

We shall revert to the question of guarantees for the citizen when speaking of the legal system and especially criminal law. But the state's authority is not encountered solely in the form of repression, whether political or judicial. In modern states, the ordinary citizen's day-to-day relations with the administration present increasingly serious problems of a psychological or political order. These relations with the community and its representatives were just as close and frequent in antiquity as they are at the present day, and were certainly more restrictive than, for instance, in nineteenth-century France, Britain or the USA. We may therefore suppose that they presented the same kind of problems: the citizen confused by complex procedural requirements, the difficulty of communication between an individual uncertain of his rights and officials, often underlings, who are tempted to abuse their authority or their position; corruption in all its forms, denial of justice and privileged treatment for the rich, the cultivated and the powerful, those with influence and official connections. We must consider all these aspects and try to see how far modern difficulties were paralleled in ancient Rome.

One preliminary point is to ascertain the importance and actual competence of what may be called the Roman civil service, interposed between the citizen-elector and the magistracy elected by him. In other words, was there in Rome at this time an established hierarchy of long-service professionals with security of tenure, responsible for the practical execution of official decisions under the magistrates' supervision? As a rule this question is answered in the negative. Most historians consider that a Roman 'bureaucracy' did not take shape to any great extent until the reign of Claudius, when the Empire had been in existence for some decades; they regard the lack of administrative cadres as a distinctive feature of the Republic, and perhaps one of the causes of its downfall.

This view, however, requires some qualification. At least by the last century of the Republic the gradual but steady increase in the number of magistrates (who, for their part, bore no resemblance to a bureaucracy) naturally involved a similar increase in the number of officials under their orders. We are not concerned here to describe this apparatus in detail, but merely to give some indication of the various ranks. These included lictors, apparitors, scribes, *viatores*, heralds of all kinds (*praecones, calatores* etc.) and *nomenclatores*. For all official business within their competence the magistrates were surrounded by subordinates of this kind who acted as a buffer between them and the citizens, and who occupied different levels of the administrative, political and social hierarchy. At the top were the *apparitores* and especially the scribes (clerks or secretaries), who had to be citizens and were generally of free birth, but sometimes freedmen. These officials multiplied in number towards the end of the Republic. For instance, when the quaestors were increased to 20 they had 36 specialized scribes at their disposal; two of these accompanied each of the 11 provincial quaestors to their provinces each year, while 14 remained in Rome in the service of the urban quaestors.

The aediles had secretaries too, as did the tribunes of the plebs and no doubt the censors, though they may have gone under another name. Thus there were certainly more than a hundred of these high officials, who played an essential part in current administration. But there were also the extraordinary magistracies, which often entailed a whole administrative apparatus. The best example is the independent commission of ten magistrates set up under Servilius Rullus's land bill of 63 BC, of which Cicero says:

> Then he provides them with apparitors, clerks, secretaries, criers, and architects and in addition with mules, tents, provisions, furniture; he draws money for their expenses from the treasury and supplies them with more from the allies; 200 surveyors from the equestrian order, and 20 attendants for each are appointed as the servants and henchmen of their power. (*De Lege Agraria* 2.32)

The surveyors (*finitores*) played an essential part, being sworn officials who, in the last resort, decided upon the ownership and boundaries of disputed lands; their rank of *equites* placed them well up in the hierarchy; they enjoyed delegated authority and their arbitral awards were final.[6] The scribes were no less responsible; in general they supervised all public accounts, i.e. they were not merely in physical charge of them (with the aid of copyists known as *librarii*) but saw to it that they were kept in accordance with the rules of the official audit.[7] Their position and power *vis à vis* the magistrates were considerable: as Cicero put it, the 'legal responsibility' (*periculum*) of the high officers of state was in their hands. There is much evidence that many magistrates, out of laziness or ignorance of their jobs, left matters entirely to them. But the quaestors' scribes also played an important part, inasmuch as the treasury was also the public records office. The reports and yearly accounts of magistrates and promagistrates were filed there, as were the texts of laws, treaties and *senatus consulta*. Moreover, the scribes were in touch with individual citizens as public auditors and revenue officers: in the provinces, for the purpose of collecting certain taxes and levies in kind, and in Rome, where they had dealings with debtors and creditors of the treasury. The system by which sureties were required in most financial relations between the state and individuals (contracts for public works, supplies and tax-farming) called for elaborate records, and here again the scribes played an essential part.

We have not much evidence as to how they discharged their duties. Livy mentions an isolated case of malversation by scribes in the service of the aediles in 203:

> Having secretly abstracted money from the Treasury, clerks and messengers of the aediles were condemned on evidence of an informer, not without disgrace for Lucullus as aedile. (30.39.7)

In the first century BC, on the other hand, corruption seems to have almost reached the level of an institution. We need hardly mention peculation in the provinces, where scribes who were well out of reach of the courts or public opinion depended wholly on the governor and took their cue from him. Verres' entourage, especially his scribes Maevius and Volcatius, followed his example and turned everything into a source of private revenue: judicial favours, documents of all kinds, and the assessment and collection of tithes and other taxes for which the pro-praetor was directly responsible. Apart from sums which passed from hand to hand and thus were not recorded in any way, Verres' scribes instituted or revived abusive practices which enabled them to levy, with the appearance of legality, a whole range of alleged 'duties' at the expense of taxpayer and treasury alike:

> From the full sum that you should have paid to those farmers deductions were regularly made under one pretext or another. The first was for 'inspection and exchange', the second for something called 'wax-duty'. All these terms, gentlemen, are not names for real things: they are names for impudent pieces of theft. How can there be any exchange, when a single coinage is in universal use? As for 'wax-duty' — why, how can such a term have any connexion with magistrates' accounts and public money? The third kind of deduction, on the other hand, wore the air of being permissible — of being desirable — of being entirely necessary. Two-fiftieths of the whole of the payments made were subtracted under the heading 'clerk'. But who gave you leave for that? what law, what authority from the Senate, and moreover what principle of justice, gave leave for your clerk to carry off all that money, whether from the farmers' resources or from the revenues of the Roman nation? If that amount can be deducted without injustice to the farmers, let the nation have it, especially with the treasury depleted as it now is; if the nation has willed that it should be paid to the farmers, and if it is just that it should be so paid, shall a fellow whom the nation pays a few shillings a week to work in your office go preying upon the farmers' property?

And is it in defence of such a system that Hortensius seeks to rouse the whole clerical class against me, declaring that I am endangering its interests and attacking its rights? As if clerks had any precedent for doing what that man did, or any recognized right to do it? I need not go back to the old days, nor speak of those clerks whom we all know to have been men of blameless honour. I am not unaware, gentlemen, that ancient precedents are now listened to, and regarded, as romantic inventions, and I will confine myself to our own unhappily degenerate days. You, Hortensius, were a quaestor not many years ago, and how your clerks behaved you can best tell us: how mine behaved I will now tell you. In this same province of Sicily I had with me as clerks two thoroughly honest men, Lucius Mamilius and Lucius Sergius; and when I was paying the cities money for their corn, not only was the Verrine deduction of two-fiftieths not made, but not one penny was deducted from the payment made to anyone.

For this, gentlemen, I should take the whole credit to myself, if those men had ever asked my permission to do otherwise, or ever thought for one moment of doing so. Why, indeed, should there be deductions for the clerk? why not, instead, for the mule-driver who has brought the money, the postman whose arrival with the advices enabled them to apply for it, the attendant who bade them come in and get it, the porter or temple slave who took away the empty basket? The clerk's share in the business is not so laborious or so valuable as to entitle him to receive, in addition to his salary, so large a share of the money itself. (*2 Verr.* 3.181-3)

Verres was no doubt an extreme case, and was brought to book for his misdeeds; but he was certainly not the only one. In Rome itself, at the centre of the treasury administration, the situation around 60 BC was little better. Tradition has preserved the memory of the younger Cato's tenure of the quaestorship in 64, when, either out of moral conviction or as a shrewd political move, he made an attempt to cleanse the Augean stables:

Although the office of quaestor was open to him, he would not become a candidate for it until he had read the laws relating to the quaestorship, learned all the details of the office from those who had had experience in it, and formed a general idea of its power and scope. As soon as he had been instated in the office, he made a great change in the assistants and clerks connected with the treasury. These were fully conversant with the public accounts and the laws relating thereto, and so, when they received as their superior officers young men whose inexperience and ignorance made it needful that others should teach and tutor them, they would not surrender any power to such superiors, but acted as superiors themselves. Now, however, Cato applied himself with energy to the business, not having merely the name and honour of a superior official, but also intelligence and judgement. He thought it best to treat the clerks as assistants, which they really were, sometimes convicting them of their evil practices, and sometimes teaching them if they erred from inexperience. But they were bold fellows, and tried to ingratiate themselves with the other quaestors, while they waged war upon Cato. Therefore the chief among them, whom Cato found guilty of a breach of trust in the matter of an inheritance, was expelled from the treasury by him, and a second was brought to trial for fraud. This person was defended in court by Catulus Lutatius the censor, a man who had great authority from his office but most of all from his virtue, being thought to surpass all Romans in justice and discretion; he also commended Cato's way of living and was intimate with him. Accordingly, when Catulus had lost his case on its merits and began to beg openly for the acquittal of his client, Cato tried to stop him from doing this. And when Catulus was all the more importunate, Cato said: 'It would be a shameful thing, Catulus, if you who are the censor and should scrutinize our lives, were ejected from the court by our bailiffs.' When Cato had uttered these words, Catulus fixed his eyes upon him as if he would make reply; he said nothing, however, but either from anger or from shame went off in silence, much perplexed.

However, the clerk was not convicted, since, when the votes for condemnation exceeded those for acquittal by a single ballot, and one Marcus Lollius, a colleague of Cato, was kept by sickness from attending the trial, Catulus sent to him and begged him to help the man. So Lollius was brought in a litter after the trial and cast the vote that acquitted. Notwithstanding this, Cato would not afterwards employ the clerk, or give him his pay, or in any way take the vote of Lollius into the reckoning.

By thus humbling the clerks and making them submissive, and by managing the business as he himself desired, in a little while he brought the quaestorship into greater respect than the Senate, so that all men said and thought that Cato had invested his office with the dignity of the consulship. For, in the first place, when he found that many persons owed debts of long standing to the public treasury and the treasury to many persons, he saw to it that the state was no longer defrauded and ceased to defraud others. From its debtors he rigorously and inexorably demanded payment, and to its creditors he promptly and readily made payment, so that people were filled with respect as they saw men making payments who had tried to defraud the state, and others receiving payments which they had ceased to expect. In the next place, though many used improper methods to get writings filed with the quaestors, and though previous quaestors had been accustomed to receive false decrees at the request of those whom they wished to please, nothing of this sort could be done now without Cato finding it out. Indeed, on one occasion when he was doubtful whether a certain decree had actually passed the Senate, though many testified to the fact, he would not believe them, nor would he file the decree away until the consuls had come and taken oath as to its validity.

Again, there were many persons whom the famous Sulla had rewarded for killing men who were under proscription, at the rate of 12,000 drachmas. All men hated them as accursed and polluted wretches, but no one had the courage to punish them. Cato, however, called each of these to account for having acquired public money by unjust means, and made him give it up, at the same time rebuking him with passionate eloquence for his illegal and unholy act. After this the men were at once charged with murder, were brought before their judges condemned beforehand, one might say, and were punished. At this all were delighted, thinking that with their deaths the tyranny of that former time was extinguished, and that Sulla himself was punished before men's eyes.

Moreover, the multitude were captivated by Cato's continuous and unwearied attention to his duties. For no one of his colleagues came up to the treasury earlier than he, and none left it later. Besides, he never failed to attend sessions of the assemblies or senate, since he feared and kept close watch on those who were ready to gratify people by voting remissions of debts and taxes, or promiscuous gifts. And so by exhibiting a treasury which was inaccessible to public informers and free from their taint, but full of money, he taught men that a state can be rich without wronging its citizens. At first some of his colleagues thought him obnoxious and troublesome, but afterwards they were well pleased with him, since he took upon his own shoulders exclusively the burden of the hatred arising from refusal to give away public moneys or to make unjust decisions, and furnished them with a defence against people who tried to force requests upon them: they had merely to say 'It is impossible; Cato will not consent.'

On the last day of his term of office, after he had been escorted to his home by almost the whole body of citizens, he heard that many friends and men of influence had beset Marcellus in the treasury and were trying to make him register some remission of moneys due. Now Marcellus had been a friend of Cato from boyhood, and when associated with him had been a most excellent magistrate. When acting alone, however, he was led by a feeling of deference to be complaisant towards suppliants, and was inclined to grant every favour. So Cato at once turned back, and when he found that Marcellus had been forced into registering the remission, he called for the tablets and erased the entry, while Marcellus himself stood by and said nothing. After this had been done, Cato conducted Marcellus away from the treasury and brought him to his house, and Marcellus had no word of blame for him either then or afterwards, but continued his intimate friendship up to the end.

Not even after he had laid down the quaestorship did Cato leave the treasury bereft of his watchful care, but slaves of his were there every day copying the transactions, and he himself paid five talents for books containing accounts of public business from the times of Sulla down to his own quaestorship, and always had them at hand. (Plutarch, *Cato Minor* 16-18)

The way in which these scribes were recruited and organized perhaps explains the prevalence of corrupt practices, which Cicero reluctantly admits in another passage (2 *Verr.* 3.181-4).[8] They were not engaged at random: from the second century onwards, and probably before, they were organized in an *ordo* or professional corporation under state supervision, in which each man was listed by name. To be a scribe one not only had to possess qualifications — reading, writing, arithmetic, knowledge of the rules of auditing, public records and doubtless also some law — but to have those qualifications recognized by the state. The censors no doubt kept a separate register of scribes, as they did of tax-farmers. From time to time the scribes are referred to as a corporate body: when martial law was proclaimed and the consuls called on the 'estates of the realm' to come to its assistance, the scribes were mentioned directly after the senators, knights and tribunes of the treasury (whose status we have discussed earlier).[9] In addition to other qualifications they would have had to be in a position to give surety for the handling of public moneys. But their organization is particularly well illustrated by a chapter of Sulla's law on the 20 quaestors, showing that the *ordo* potentially comprised more members than there were posts in any given year. The chapters of this law that have survived concern *viatores* and *praecones*, but no doubt the scribes were recruited and organized in the same way. The *ordines* were divided into *decuriae* or sections, doubtless three in number, each containing 12 *viatores* and *praecones*. Each *decuria* functioned for a year, during which the other two were in reserve. After Sulla's reform, no doubt to prevent collusion between magistrates and scribes, lots were drawn three years in advance to determine which clerks would be appointed to which magistracy; thus they were not engaged by the magistrate himself. Apart from saying that they must be Roman citizens the law does not prescribe qualifications, but it says significantly that: '[The consuls] shall choose all the said messengers and heralds according as they believe them worthy of the said rank' (C.I.L. I², 587, 1.31).

The whole body of scribes and apparitors assembled at the treasury for the lot-casting ceremony. On 5 December 63 BC, the day on which Cicero delivered his fourth speech against Catiline, he took advantage of their presence to affirm that the whole city stood behind his policy:

> I see that the same zeal to defend the Republic has gathered here the gallant tribunes of the treasury. I see too that the entire body of clerks, who happen to be here at the treasury today, have been diverted from waiting for the drawing of their lots, out of concern for our common safety. (*In Cat.* 4.15)

But in our period, if not earlier, a new practice was introduced. It was the rule that professional apparitors and scribes could, if they chose, retire from 'active service' and present a substitute or successor, known as *vicarius*, to the magistrate in charge of the lot-casting. The *vicarius* naturally had to have the same qualifications as the man he was replacing. At the close of the Republic it became a recognized practice to effect this substitution in return for money, i.e. the scribe's office was put up for sale: the phrase was *emere decuriam*, 'to buy a place in a *decuria*'. A well-known case is that of the poet Horace, a freedman's son, who, after serving as a military tribune in Brutus's army in 42, bought himself a position as *scriba quaestorius*. (For an auction sale see *Scholia ad Juvenalem* 5.3). Thus scribes' and apparitors' posts in Rome were by now purchasable. This had come about for two reasons. In the first place, the job was salaried and thus represented a source of income. We do not know what the pay was, but we do know the figure for magistrates' clerks in the Julia Genativa colony founded by Caesar at Urso (Osuna) in Spain: the four chief officers of state had 38 officials all told, their annual salaries totalling 8,000 sesterces. The best paid were the duumvirs' scribes at 1,200 sesterces each. In Rome salaries were certainly much higher, and the purchase price of the post must have been at least sufficient to yield interest on this scale. But there was another reason why the position of a scribe or *viator* was coveted: it could be bought by a plebeian or freedman and in practice offered an almost certain guarantee of eventual admission to the equestrian order. As a rule it sufficed merely to apply for this: if the scribe had the necessary capital (and, if he did not have it at the time of purchasing the post, there was every chance that he would after a year or two in office!), all he then had to do, if a former slave, was to erase the stigma of his birth. This meant receiving the 'golden ring' which senior magistrates were entitled to bestow at the end of their term of office, as a British prime minister draws up an honours list. The scribe could then call himself an *eques*, a member of the second highest order in the Roman state, unless debarred from it by some exceptional measure of scrutiny.

The position of a scribe was thus honourable and lucrative, it was not beneath the dignity of an *eques* by birth, and its holder could often become an *eques* if he were not one already. But in the closing years of the Republic this enhancement of civic status did not have the same moral implications as earlier. Men of doubtful probity saw the purchase of a *decuria* as a cloak of respectability, and we may be sure that they intended to make it pay for itself. Hence there was a tendency to corruption, just as the ever-increasing cost of electoral campaigns made it almost inevitable that magistrates in office would be guilty of malpractice:

'The clerk's profession' you tell us 'has a high standing'. Who denies that? and what has it to do with the matter in hand? It has, in fact, a high standing because its members are entrusted with the public accounts and the reputations of our magistrates. Go then to those clerks who are worthy members of their profession, honest and reputable family men, and ask them what those deductions of two-fiftieths mean. You will soon find that all of them regard the whole thing as a scandalous innovation. But please let me refer the question to such clerks as these. Do not consider the men who have scraped together enough cash, from the presents of wasters or the gratuities of actors, to buy themselves membership of the profession, and then boast of having risen from the front rank among the playhouse rowdies to the second rank in the public service. On the charge before us, you and I must take the opinion of clerks who resent the membership of such men as that: though the fact is that, when we find a number of unfit persons in an order intended for men of industry and character, we can hardly wonder that some people should disgrace themselves in a position that is open to anyone who will pay for it. (Cicero, *2 Verr.* 3.183-4)

Justice and the courts

The administration of justice was an essential part of Roman public life, and, rightly or wrongly, the Romans are thought of as inveterate litigators. The majestic and unified construction known as 'Roman law', which stands as the essential basis of most modern legal systems, might lead us to suppose, with its elaborate logical provisions and definitions concerning persons, communities and property, that every Roman citizen could be regarded as an abstract entity, a subject and object of legal rights, to whom the law afforded total and permanent protection. This would be a mistake, however. In the first place, 'classic' Roman law is a late creation, historically speaking: paradoxically, it dates in the main from the third and fourth centuries AD, by which time the Empire had developed into a bureaucratic monarchy of a fairly despotic kind. Moreover, it only became what it is through the patient, long-term activity of generations of officials and jurists supported by imperial authority, and at the period we are concerned with this slow process had not even begun. Indeed it must be admitted that our period presents a repellent image of Roman justice, in which corruption seems to have flourished to an unparalleled extent.

A distinction must be drawn, however. In Roman law there were two kinds of trial, public and private, corresponding broadly to our criminal and civil cases. Public trials (*causae publicae*) concerned all matters in which the City was involved in one way or another. As we have seen, while the right of *provocatio* originally fell within the direct jurisdiction of magistrates, it soon came to involve an appeal to the people. This was a substantial guarantee, despite the cumbrous procedure, the uncertainty of public opinion and the inconstancy of the mob. But the defendants in public trials (except perhaps those on trial for murder) seem generally to have been members of the political class or citizens who had fallen foul of the state on account of desertion, non-payment of taxes etc. It is doubtful whether the man in the street was often involved in a public trial: in the last century of the Republic, at least, this form of justice represented a first-class spectacle rather than a scene in which he himself was likely to play a part. However, at the end of the second or the beginning of the first century BC an important change took place in this border-line area between politics and criminal justice. Responsibility was gradually transferred from the supreme popular assembly to what were called 'commissions of enquiry' (*quaestiones*), originally *ad hoc* and afterwards permanent, consisting of large juries (numbering from 50 to 75) under the chairmanship of a magistrate who might be a praetor or an aedile.[10] The sentences of these courts were not subject to appeal by *provocatio*. The first of them were set up to deal with specific crimes, e.g. the Bacchanalia in 186 BC. By degrees, up to and including Sulla's time, many others were created by specific laws in which their scope was clearly defined. Meanwhile in 149 the idea of standing courts (*quaestiones perpetuae*) was introduced. Thus within a century or so most crimes and misdemeanours were fairly closely defined by law and assigned to appropriate standing courts or 'divisions' with their own procedures.

This, it might be thought, was an advance on the old system, even if the right of appeal had gone. It would have been so but for the fact that the composition and therefore the integrity of juries was open to grave question from the outset. Until 123 BC the jurymen were chosen from the Senate, and hence reflected the average moral level of that socio-political group. Consequently —and this was the main subject of complaint against them—they were inclined to be too lenient with members of their own order, and in addition they openly took bribes. In 123 Caius Gracchus replaced some or all of them by *equites*, against whom the same accusations were soon made; they were in fact a constant theme throughout republican times and under the Empire. Making all allowance for rhetoric and polemics, we are left with the strong impression that neither plaintiffs nor defendants entirely trusted the Roman courts. This was the more serious because, as I have observed, the 'crimes' in question were on the border-line between law and politics. Politics were almost constantly involved in cases of this sort, even e.g. the murder of Oppianicus in 66 or that of Roscius in 81. The ability of lawyers, their political links with those in power, and the personality of the accused (who were often magistrates or senators, and still more often *equites*) all played a part in determining the sentence, but money played a larger one. Between 74 and 66 a whole series of celebrated and scandalous trials brought the whole body of jurymen (drawn at this time from the Senate, which Sulla had much enlarged) into the gravest disrepute: Hortensius, a well-known lawyer, actually had voting-tablets of different colours distributed to those whom he had bribed, so as to ensure that he received value for money. The multiplication of legal safeguards against these abuses is not an encouraging sign. Still more serious was collusion between criminals and those in power. Verres, for instance, hoped (although mistakenly) to escape the punishment he knew he deserved by spinning out the trial until his friends were elected to the consulate, and setting aside a third of his ill-gotten gains to buy those who would be his judges (*1 Verr.* 19; 40).

But, as many contemporary historians realized, criminal justice was largely a political matter and affected a small circle of men in public life, not the man in the street in his ordinary affairs. Civil lawsuits (*causae privatae*), on the other hand, concerned day-to-day matters of every kind: estates, debts, obligations. A civil action consisted of two stages: in the first (*in jure*) a magistrate, the praetor, laid down the procedure (*dare actionem*), i.e. defined the object and scope of the dispute; in the second (*in judicio*) a single judge, appointed by the praetor, acted as an arbiter, i.e. gave judgement on the question of fact but not that of law.[11] In principle this *judex unus* had to possess certain social and moral qualifications, many of the archaic kind proper to a rural civilization in which neighbourhood and reputation counted for a great deal; he must be a *vir bonus*—a man of property with a degree of personal authority, and a good citizen whose word was his bond. He should be the embodiment of *fides*, good faith: it did not matter much whether he knew law; it was not for him but for the praetor to expound the workings of justice; his task was rather to pronounce an equitable sentence. These were excellent principles; doubt has been expressed as to whether the civil courts in republican times really conformed to this somewhat idealized picture, and whether the lowliest citizens were really equal before the law.[12] It has been noted that the oldest *actiones* or legal forms said nothing about how a party to a dispute could be compelled to answer a charge, or how a man without wealth or connections could obtain redress against a man of influence. It has also been pointed out that until the end of the second century BC the *judex unus* was recruited exclusively from the senatorial order, and in the first century from the senators and knights, i.e. the privileged classes as far as wealth and honours were concerned; while this did not mean they were necessarily biased, it did not make for 'democratic' justice either. The senatorial judges were not beloved by popular orators: here is a portrait by C. Titius, about the middle or end of the second century:

Describing how men of prodigal habits would go to the Forum full of drink, to act as judges, and the customary tone of their conversation on the way, Titius says: 'They are devoted to gambling and spend their time at it drenched in scent and surrounded by a crowd of harlots. At the tenth hour they summon a slave to go to the comitium and inquire what business has been transacted in the Forum: who have spoken for and who against a bill, and how many tribes have supported and how many have opposed it. After that they make their way to the Place of Assembly, in time to escape a charge of absence from duty, and being gorged with wine they fill all the urinals in the alleys as they go. On arrival at the comitium they gloomily bid proceedings begin. The parties state their case, the judge calls the witnesses and retires himself to make water. When he comes back, he says that he has heard everything, calls for the documentary evidence, and glances at what is written, although he can hardly keep his eyes open for the wine he has drunk. They retire to consider a verdict, and then they say to one another: "Why should I be bothered with these silly people? Why are we not better employed in drinking mead mixed with Greek wine and eating a fat thrush and a fine fish —a genuine pike caught between the two bridges?"' (Macrobius, *Saturnalia* 3.16.13)

It is true, on the other hand, that in some civil suits we can discern in the pleadings that have come down to us a suspicious tendency by one side or the other to emphasize the inequality between the two parties and the responsibility of the judge called on to dispense justice to the weaker man attacked by the stronger:

Two things which have most power in the state, namely influence and eloquence, are both working against us to-day; the one, Gaius Aquilius, fills me with apprehension, the other with dread. That the eloquence of Quintus Hortensius may embarrass me in my pleading is a thought that causes me some disquietude; that the influence of Sextus Naevius may injure the cause of Publius Quinctius—of that I am gravely afraid. Yet I should not consider the possession of these great advantages by my opponents to be so greatly deplored, if our side possessed at least a moderate share of either; but the position is such that I, who have little natural ability and insufficient experience, am pitted against a most accomplished advocate, while my client Quinctius, whose resources are small, who has no opportunities and only a few friends, has to contend with a most influential adversary....

The more numerous these disadvantages are, Aquilius, the greater should be the indulgence with which you and your assessors listen to our words, so that truth, weakened by so many unfavourable conditions, may at last be vindicated by the impartiality of men so eminent. But if you, in your capacity as judge, show that you can afford no protection to loneliness and distress against violence and interest; if, before such a tribunal, the cause is weighed in the balance of influence and not in that of truth, then assuredly neither sanctity nor purity any longer exists in the state, nor can the authority and integrity of the judge afford any consolation to a humble citizen. Either truth will prevail before you and your assessors, or, driven by violence and interest from this tribunal, it will be unable to find a place wherein to rest. (Cicero, *Pro Quinctio* 1.1-2, 4-5)

The preliminary stage before the praetor (*in jure*) was crucial to the case as a whole, and was wide open to abuse. The praetor-elect, at least until 66 BC, had considerable latitude in drawing up his *edictum*, i.e. declaration of the principles and procedural rules he intended to follow when in office. The rules for doing so were not yet codified, and while the *praetor urbanus* naturally paid attention to his predecessors' rulings, he still had plenty of opportunity to indulge his own inclinations at the expense of justice. The praetorship of Verres in 74 BC is an exceptionally flagrant example. Later, from 73 to 71, this 'new man' and former supporter of Sulla was the plague of Sicily, extorting 40 million sesterces from its inhabitants without distinction of class or race (*2 Verr.* 1.27). In his case there was no question of party favour or preference: his sole interest was that of Gaius Verres. He made his début as a quaestor, changing sides politically so as to hold on to the money-bags; then, as legate and pro-quaestor in Asia and Cilicia, he left behind him a trail of ruinous exactions. As praetor-designate his sole thought was how to turn his future office into a source of profit. During this period, when according to law he was supposed to be preparing his *edictum*, he contacted some persons whose cases he was to try (chiefly questions of inheritance involving large sums) and offered, for a reward, to bend procedures in their favour; hence his 'procedural fantasies', as they have been called. The go-between in these proceedings was his mistress, a freedwoman named Chelidon:

> Just as, between his election and his entry upon office, he composed the whole of his edict to suit those who were trafficking in justice with him to serve their own ends, so during the tenure of his office he had no scruple about giving decisions that contradicted the edict itself. The result was that Lucius Piso filled a pile of note-books with records of the cases in which he vetoed decisions by Verres as inconsistent with Verres' own edict. I imagine you have not forgotten this—what a streaming crowd of people would regularly gather round Piso's judgement-seat during Verres' year of office. But for his having Piso for a colleague, Verres would have been buried in the Forum under a shower of stones. As it was, the wrongs he did appeared more tolerable because people found, in the equitable character and legal knowledge of Piso, an always available refuge, of which they could make use without trouble or unpleasantness or expense or even an advocate's help.
>
> Pray recall to your memories, gentlemen, the wanton character of Verres' administration of the law, the lack of uniformity in his decisions, the trafficking that went on; how unfrequented were the houses of all the experts in civil law whom it is the practice to consult, how densely crowded was the house of Chelidon. As often as that woman came up to him and whispered in his ear, he would call back the parties to a case that he had already judged, and alter his judgement; at other times he would, without the least scruple, deliver in one case a judgement directly opposed to that which he had delivered in the previous case a few minutes before. Hence those people whose indignation went so far as to make them humorists: some of these made the remark you have often heard repeated, that *jus verrinum* ['Verre' justice', or

'pork gravy'] was pretty poor stuff: others were still sillier, only that their irritation passed them off as good jesters, when they cursed Sacerdos [the name means 'priest'] for not sacrificing such a miserable hog. I should not recall these jokes, which are not particulaly witty, no, moreover, in keeping with the dignity of this Court, were it not that I would have you remember how Verres' offences against morality and justice became at the time the subject of common talk and popular catchwords. (*2 Verr.* 1.119-20)

The praetor had other responsibilities as well: from Sulla's time onwards, when the censors were not in office it was his task to farm out certain public works. In connection with the maintenance of the temple of Castor, Verres planned with an accomplice to extort a large sum of money from the contractor — a minor whose guardians were persons of high rank. In order to put their case before the praetor these men of respectable age and position had to solicit Chelidon's favour. Cicero describes their sense of humiliation:

Yes, they went to see Chelidon: Gaius Mustius, knight and collector of revenue, as honourable a man as lives; the boy's uncle, the honest and upright Marcus Junius; and his guardian Publius Titius, respectable and conscientious, than whom no man of his rank is esteemed more highly. Ah, Verres, how many there are to whom your praetorship has brought pain and misery and shame! To speak of nothing else, I bid you think simply of the feelings of shame and disgust with which such men must have entered the dwelling of a harlot. For no consideration would they have brought themselves to stoop so low, had not regard for duty and friendship compelled them. They went, as I have said, to see Chelidon. Her house was full: decisions, judgements, methods of procedure — none ever heard of before — were being applied for: 'make him give me possession', 'don't let him take it from me', 'don't let him pronounce against me', 'get him to award me the property'. Some were paying her cash, others were signing promissory notes: the house was filled, not with a courtesan's usual visitors, but with the crowd that attends a praetor's court.

As soon as they were allowed, the gentlemen I have named approached the woman. Gaius Mustius explained the facts, asked for help, and promised her money. Her reply, for a woman of that type, was not ill-natured: she would gladly do her best, and would certainly talk to Verres about it — let them return later. They left her, and returned the next day; she then told them that the man was inexorable, and that he said there was a really big sum of money to be made out of this business. (Ibid. 1.137-8)

Episodes of this kind throw a lurid light on Roman judicial procedures, but their significance must be assessed with caution. To discover whether Verres was typical or exceptional one would have to make a study, which has never been attempted, of the frequency of such behaviour by Roman magistrates and judges. One should not take at face-value the stereotyped laments of each successive generation on the theme of 'growing corruption' and moral decadence. It is also a matter for enquiry how far measures were in force which limited corruption in practice or ensured that offenders paid the penalty. Verres, after all, was in the end bankrupted, exiled and punished for his exactions, though not until he had enjoyed the pro-praetorship of Sicily to the full; his downfall was due to a political change in Rome itself, which enabled Catulus and Cicero to rouse public opinion and led to a reform of the judicial system. Verres' depredations in Sicily duly formed part of the charges against him. The muliplication of punitive laws against magistrates and even (in 61, 59 and later) against their staff and entourage does not merely show that offences were on the increase; there were spectacular trials, some eminent persons were disgraced, exiled or driven to suicide. Justice might be slow and unreliable, but sometimes it struck effectively.

But the politico-judiciary system also contained two built-in safeguards of appreciable importance. In the first place, the collegiate system enabled a magistrate discreetly to supervise his colleague and sometimes to rectify his acts: thus the *praetor peregrinus* in 74, Calpurnius Piso, did what he could to put a spoke in Verres' wheel. Secondly, the tribunes of the plebs exercised their right of intervention freely, in criminal if not in civil affairs. Important trials took place under the eyes of the Roman people; they were closely followed by public opinion, and this could sometimes be mobilized. Abbius Oppianicus, a petty landowner from Larinum who distinguished himself at the time of Sulla's victory, was convicted on a charge of violence in 74. Rightly or wrongly, he claimed that the judges were corrupted. A tribune of the plebs took the matter up, made a political issue of it and aroused public opinion in Abbius's favour. Another safeguard of judicial probity was the censor's *nota*, a mark of ignominy which could lead to a citizen being expelled from the Senate or reduced in status.

To sum up, while Roman justice left a great deal of scope to the praetor's initiative, the judge's discretion and the freedom of juries, it was none the less subject to various controls — legislative, judicial, social or political — which made the situation tolerable from the citizen's point of view. It may be shocking to our ideas that the courts explicitly took account of influence (*gratia*) or social standing; but this could not be otherwise in a society imbued with hierarchical values and with a sense of the multiple and diverse ways in which citizens were linked together so that each had his proper place and part to play in society. The network of influence and patronage did not work only one way, and the system provided some advantage for almost everyone. Members of the lower orders, *tenues*, could not exist unaided and had no thought of trying to do so: they depended on patrons, whether natural, hereditary or acquired by fortune, from whom they expected help in judicial and other matters, and for the patrons to refuse this would have been contrary to the law of gods and men. In this way a humble litigant was able, by proxy as it were, to stand before a judge or magistrate with confidence:[13] but it was naturally unusual for only one party to a suit to be thus supported. Any important dispute would involve by degrees a whole series of interventions on either side which were considered perfectly legitimate, being part of the recognized operation of the patron-client system, and doubtless to a large extent cancelled each other out, except in times of civil upheaval. Another effect of *gratia* was to multiply references, applications, appeals and testimonies, so that judicial debates and administrative acts were brought fully into the light of day. In this way the Roman citizen was more or less protected against the most insidious of evils, namely official secrecy and *raison d'Etat*.

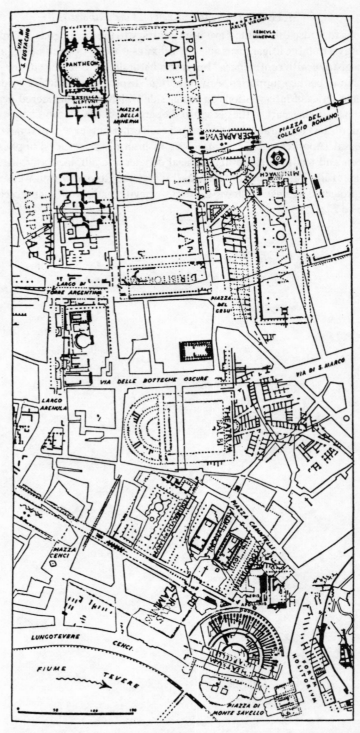

III Centre of the Campus Martius; area of the *Circus Flaminius, Porticus Minucia* and *Saepta Julia* (planimetry by G. Gatti)

CHAPTER IX

POPULARITAS
The rise of 'alternative' institutions

S O FAR we have examined the ways in which the citizen was integrated into the City by means of its regular institutions. We have seen the majestic regularity, governed by the years and seasons, of his ceremonial participation in political and social life. Entered on the censorial roll, as a child, by his father or guardian, registered as a *junior* at the age of 17 and subjected from then on to intensive training as a soldier and citizen, we have seen him answer the consuls' call to arms; then, as a recruit, he experienced the harsh constraint of a war machine which, none the less, appealed to his *virtus* and civic conscience rather than to passive obedience, and offered solid opportunities, if he chose to take them, of social and political advancement. As a taxpayer the country appealed to him to meet its extraordinary expenses, which recurred only too often as long as Rome was on the defensive. In this field, however, the City's demands were moderate, as citizens contributed only according to their means, and the state did not assert any regalian rights in fiscal matters: Roman taxation was neither recognitive nor permanent. On the contrary, the close and fundamental solidarity between the citizen and the City appears clearly from the fact that taxes were refunded when possible and ceased to be levied for more than a century after Rome's wars became victorious. Further, the exploitation of the provinces, regarded as a reward from Destiny, enabled the citizen, as the privileged member of a dominant community, to share individually in the prosperity of the Roman treasury: he was entitled to part of the spoils and, from the end of the second century BC, to the relative security of a basic food ration supplied by the state, first at low cost and shortly free of charge.

Finally there remained the all-important field of participation in government decisions, or at least in the choice of governors. Here we must recall that the whole structure of Roman civic life was pervaded and organized by the differential system. Citizens were classified in terms of a civic hierarchy which did not precisely coincide with the spontaneous social hierarchies, nor was it wholly distinct from them. While Romans were assured, in theory, of equal liberty and equality before the law, the system acknowledged their different degrees of *dignitas,* i.e. of real participation in the life of the community. The place rigorously assigned to them in the hierarchy of sub-groups and orders was governed by several criteria, but most of all by wealth and repute (*nomen*), which chiefly meant heredity. An individual's census rating was the basis for various rights and duties which, in principle at least, were carefully counter-balanced. Thus, in each of the fields we have mentioned (military service, finance and politics, elections and the voting of laws) the citizen body varied in size and composition: it expanded or contracted according to circumstances, and different parts of it were involved or consulted to a different extent. Society was honeycombed with divisions and contrasts, sometimes overlapping and sometimes not: between the poor, the less poor and the rich; between members of the higher and privileged orders—senators, knights and officials—and the rest; between City-dwellers and country-dwellers, 'new' and 'old' citizens, former slaves and the free-born. Consequently, as I have emphasized, any account of the ordinary Roman citizen's participation in the life of the City, as opposed to that of the narrowly political class, must be a differential one. But, however sharp these differences and contradictions, the dominant fact remains that for at least 200 years, from the middle of the fourth to the middle of the second century BC, they were resolved within the normal institutional framework, without recourse to violence and without exceeding the traditional bounds of debate and discussion among magistrates, decisions by the Senate or by the people in its assemblies. A tradition which, whether true or false, was unanimously accepted by the Romans was that the fiercest political struggles of their distant past had never degenerated into armed revolt, let alone into civil war, until the fatal tribuneship of Tiberius Gracchus in 133 BC:

> The plebeians and Senate of Rome were often at strife with each other concerning the enactment of laws, the cancelling of debts, the division of lands, or the election of magistrates. Internal discord did not, however, bring them to blows; there were merely dissensions and contests within the limits of the law, which they settled by making mutual concessions, and with much respect for each other.... The sword was never carried into the assembly, and there was no civil butchery until Tiberius Gracchus, while serving as tribune and bringing forward new laws, was the first to fall a victim to internal commotion; and with him many others, who were crowded together at the Capitol round the temple, were also slain. Sedition did not end with this abominable deed. Repeatedly the parties came into open conflict, often carrying daggers; and from time to time in the temples, the assemblies, or the forum, some tribune, or praetor, or consul, or candidate for those offices, or some person otherwise distinguished would be slain. (Appian, *B. Civ.* 1.1-2)

But recourse to violence, in various forms that we shall summarize rapidly (since they are not our immediate subject in this book), was not the only sign of a change in the language of politics. Clearly the three areas of participation we have referred to—military, fiscal and politico-judicial—were far from covering all the manifold, proliferating relationships of Roman civic society. Families and tribes, relations of kinship, neighbourhood and patronage, cultic and religious affinities, economic and cultural groupings and philosophical beliefs all divided the Roman population in some respects and united it in others, so that individuals were involved in a multiplicity of interacting hierarchies. But it is a long time before we find these various groups playing a recognizable and distinctive part in civic life. The official institutions of the army, the census and the *comitia* imposed limits and discipline on them and curbed their exuberance, at any rate after the fourth century BC, when traces can no longer be discerned of such archaic and (to us) little known institutions as the *gentes* and *curiae*.

After the second century BC, however, we find emerging what may be called parallel or alternative forms of civil life, outside the traditional domain of public law, and offering fresh opportunities of integration and participation to one group of citizens or another: the variation of these groups according to circumstances is again of interest to a differential study. In some cases there was a positive change in the scene and object of the conflict. There came into being a new language involving new methods, new techniques of communication, a different way of approaching men, securing their support and manipulating them. Public life of course continued largely to run in traditional channels, but other settings came into view, new ceremonies and a different ritual which gradually tended to rival and even obliterate the old ones. At the end point of this evolution, the circus and the amphitheatre take the place of the Forum and the Curia; instead of a dialogue between the people and its elected magistrates, punctuated by the proclamation of election results, the interchange is between the *princeps* and the urban plebs, and it takes place to the accompaniment of largess and public games.

It would require a further book to trace this evolution in detail. Here we may point out the chief manifestations of the 'alternative City' which was concealed by the façade of regular institutions but which, from the first century BC, tended on occasion to predominate over the official one. While leaving out of account what was exceptional and transitory, we shall try to exhibit facts that recur often enough to become quasi-institutional in their turn.

First of all we may class together a number of ceremonies which have one evident feature in common, that of being spectacles presented by some citizens to others. Private, semi-private or public, such spectacles—as in most civilizations, but still more so in the extrovert world of the ancient city-state—naturaly involve a subtle dialectic between actors and their public. The latter, being physically present, reacts in a manner that may or may not be foreseen and affect the course of the spectacle itself, distorting its development and purpose. This is one way in which public opinion, whether spontaneous or organized, can find expression outside institutional forms. The chief spectacles of this kind are funerals, triumphs, theatrical and gladiatorial shows, and the seeing-off or welcoming-back of magistrates. Such ceremonies, of whatever origin (generally religious), existed in Rome at all times and were, in principle, perfectly normal aspects of social life. What interests us here is the stage at which they became detached from their original purpose and turned into manifestations or occasions of political conflict.

Funerals

A good example of this kind of distortion is provided by funeral ceremonies.[1] A funeral, in principle, was a private rite *par excellence,* a performance of the simple duty of *pietas* which relatives owed to the dead. From the outset, however, this pious homage took on a manifold significance. It was the role of the dead man's relatives to show that his life had been well spent and, in the case of exalted servants of the state, to exalt his civic virtues in an almost didactic manner. The pride of families and the glory of the City were inseparable, the first consisting in the exaltation of the second and in the accolade of public recognition: this is a civilization based on display, on overt praise and blame. A great man's funeral was, as it were, the last service he could render to the City, and the last recompense from his fellow-citizens. Polybius, depicting Roman institutions (in the wider, not merely the political sense) as they were in about 200 BC, carefully points out all the features which seem to him to explain the City's marvellous cohesion, the source of its power and cause of its victories. He is at pains to show that Roman public life is full of powerful inducements to *virtus* and self-sacrifice, based on a highly coherent system of rewards and punishments. Among these he gives prominence to funeral ceremonies:

> A single instance will suffice to indicate the pains taken by the state to turn out men who will be ready to endure everything in order to gain a reputation for valour.
>
> Whenever any illustrious man dies, he is carried at his funeral into the forum to the so-called rostra, sometimes conspicuous in an upright posture and more rarely reclined. Here with all the people standing round, a grown-up son, if he has left one who happens to be present, or if not some other relative mounts the rostra and discourses on the virtues and successful achievements of the dead. As a consequence the multitude and not only those who had a part in these achievements, but also those who had none, when the facts are recalled to their minds and brought before their eyes, are moved to such sympathy that the loss seems to be not confined to the mourners, but a public one affecting the whole people. Then, after the interment and the performance of the usual ceremonies, they place the image of the departed in the most conspicuous position in the house, enclosed in a

wooden shrine. This image is a mask reproducing with remarkable fidelity both the features and complexion of the deceased. On the occasion of public sacrifices they display these images, and decorate them with much care, and when any distinguished member of the family dies they take them to the funeral, putting them on men who seem to them to bear the closest resemblance to the original in stature and carriage. These representatives wear togas, with a purple border if the deceased was a consul or praetor, whole purple if he was a censor, and embroidered with gold if he had celebrated a triumph or achieved anything similar. They all ride in chariots preceded by the fasces, axes, and other insignia by which the different magistrates are accompanied according to the respective dignity of the offices of state held by each during his life; and when they arrive at the rostra they all seat themselves in a row on ivory chairs.

There could not easily be a more ennobling spectacle for a young man who aspires to fame and virtue. For who would not be inspired by the sight of the images of men renowned for their excellence, all together and as if alive and breathing? What spectacle could be more glorious than this? Besides, he who makes the oration over the man about to be buried, when he has finished speaking of him recounts the successes and exploits of the others whose images are present, beginning with the most ancient. By this means, by this constant renewal of the good report of brave men, the celebrity of those who performed noble deeds is rendered immortal, while at the same time the fame of those who did good service to their country becomes known to the people and a heritage for future generations. (Polybius 6.52-4)

This complex scene involving the family and the state, with the funeral oration and ceremonial display of the masks of ancestors (the only outward sign of the only nobility recognized in Rome, that of public service), was a pledge of a certain social order and also an opportunity for the public, represented by throngs of clients mustered for the occasion, to associate itself with the ostentatious rivalries of great families. For a long time exhibitions of this kind actually meant what Polybius says they did, an exaltation of the nation's unity in the persons of its great men. The most notable example, and perhaps the one Polybius had in mind, is the funeral of Aemilius Paullus, the victor of Pydna, which is thus described by Plutarch:

Three days afterwards he died. He was fully blessed with everything that men think conducive to happiness. For his funeral procession called forth men's admiration, and showed a desire to adorn his virtue with the best and most enviable obsequies. This was manifest, not in gold or ivory or the other ambitious and expensive preparations for such rites, but in good will and honour and gratitude on the part, not only of his fellow citizens, but also of his enemies. At all events, out of all the Iberians and Ligurians and

Macedonians who chanced to be present, those that were young and strong of body assisted by turns in carrying the bier, while the more elderly followed with the procession, calling aloud upon Aemilius as benefactor and preserver of their countries. For at the times of his conquests he had treated them all with mildness and humanity, and during all the rest of his life he was ever doing them some good and caring for them as though they had been kindred and relations. (*Aemilius* 39)

In this particular case the influence of certain Greek customs can be seen: in Hellenistic cities the dead were frequently honoured by the *kataphora eis agoran*, by being carried shoulder-high into the market-place by grateful citizens.[2] More specifically Roman is the funeral oration, the right to deliver which was perhaps originally confined to former magistrates, and at the end of the Republic to men who had deserved well of the state. It was not for a long time that the women of great families were granted such funeral honours; and, when they were, it was the sign of a certain distortion and politicization of the ceremony, as we shall see in the case of Julia, Caesar's aunt. The unanimity of civic funerals culminated, however, in the exceptional honour of official or state funerals, which were the occasion for a particularly grandiose ceremony. The most striking instance, symbolic of the whole political future of Rome, was the funeral of the dictator Sulla, who divested himself of power and retired to die at Cumae; although his political achievement was already threatened, he was still all-powerful in the eyes of the Roman people. Sulla's case shows how the death of a leader itself became a 'subject of dissension', as Appian puts it, and acquired a political significance of its own:

A dissension sprang up in the city over his remains, some proposing to bring them in a procession through Italy and exhibit them in the forum and give him a public funeral. Lepidus and his faction opposed this, but Catulus and the Sullan party prevailed. Sulla's body was borne through Italy on a golden litter with royal splendour. Trumpeters and horsemen in great numbers went in advance, and a great multitude of armed men followed on foot. His soldiers flocked from all directions under arms to join the procession, and each one was assigned his place in due order as he came, while the crowd of common people that came together was unprecedented, and in front of all were borne the standards and the fasces that Sulla had used while living and ruling.

When the remains reached the city they were borne through the streets with an enormous procession. More than 2,000 golden crowns which had been made in haste were carried in it, the gifts of cities and of the legions that Sulla had commanded and of individual friends. It would be impossible to describe all the costly things that were contributed to this funeral. From fear of the assembled soldiery all the priests and priestesses escorted the remains, each in proper costume. The entire Senate and the whole body of magistrates attended with their insignia of office. A multitude of knights followed with their own decorations, and, in their turn, all the legions that had fought under him. They came together with eagerness, all hastening to join in the task, carrying gilded standards and silver-plated shields, such as are still used on such occasions. There was a countless number of trumpeters who in turns played the most melting and dirge-like strains. Loud cries of farewell were raised, first by the Senate, then by the knights, then by the soldiers, and finally by the plebeians. Some really longed for Sulla, while others were afraid of his army and his dead body, as they had been of himself when living. Looking at the present spectacle and remembering what this man had accomplished they were amazed, and agreed with their opponents that he had been most fortunate for his own party and most formidable to themselves even in death. The body was shown in the forum on the rostra, where public speeches are usually made, and the most eloquent of the Romans then living delivered the funeral oration, as Sulla's son, Faustus, was still very young. Then strong men among the senators took up the bier and carried it to the Campus Martius, where only kings were buried, and the knights and the army marched past the funeral pyre. Such was Sulla's end. (Appian, *B. Civ.* 1.105-7)[3]

The unanimity at Sulla's funeral was apparent only: the impressive military apparatus was designed to recall the origin of his power, and was not more than was needed to restrain his numerous enemies and partisans. Before long, funerals became a normal occasion of party strife. Caesar, in particular, was skilled at exploiting the susceptibility of the urban mob to this new language, as he showed during his quaestorship by delivering the funeral oration of his aged aunt Julia (in accordance with the *mos majorum*) and subsequently that of his young wife. The former enabled him to recall that Julia was the wife of Marius, and thus, as Plutarch says, to bring back the dead general's honours 'as it were from Hades': Caesar exhibited Marius's images for the first time and extolled his services to the state, while not forgetting the divine and royal pretensions of the *gens Julia* (Suetonius, *Caesar* 6). The speech at his wife's funeral, which was quite contrary to custom, aroused popular sympathy: the crowd took to him as to a man 'gentle and full of feeling' (Plutarch, *Caesar* 5). Here we see a master of political psychology, a man who 'knew his political ABC' (cf. Suet., *Caesar* 77), playing on the nostalgic sentiments of a section of the crowd while making a show of private *pietas*.

A further step was taken when the crowd itself began, more or less spontaneously, to take part in a leader's obsequies. This, it is true, was in exceptional circumstances, the leader in question having been assassinated; but on two occasions, in the closing years of the Republic, the state was in imminent danger of being overthrown as the result of an outburst of mourning at a funeral ceremony, a kind of collective hallucination. The first was in 52, after the murder of Clodius by Milo:

> Clodius's body reached Rome before the first hour of the night, and a large crowd of common people and slaves surrounded it with a great display of sorrow in the hall of his house where it was laid. Horror at the murder was increased by Clodius's wife Fulvia...showing his wounds. At dawn on the next day a still greater crowd of the same kind appeared, and several men of note lost their lives [reading *elisi* for *visi*]. [Urged by T. Munatius Plancus, Sulla's grandson on his mother's side] the ignorant crowd took the body, naked and mud-stained, as it had lain on the funeral couch and, so that its wounds might be seen, took it to the Forum and deposited it on the Rostra. There, in front of the assembly, Plancus and Pompeius, who were supporting Milo's opponents, aroused people's anger against Milo. Led by the scribe Sex. Cloelius, the crowd carried the corpse to the Curia, where they made a funeral pyre by burning the benches, daises, tables and registers. The Curia itself caught fire, and the Porcian basilica next to it was destroyed. The crowd also attacked the house of the interrex M. Lepidus...and that of Milo, who was absent; but they were driven off by arrows. (Asconius, p. 32 C)

Cicero afterwards mocked Clodius's followers for having deprived their hero of a decent burial. None the less, the crowd's action unquestionably altered the course of public events. By setting fire to the Curia they initiated a political process which, by way of the appeal to Pompey and the extraordinary *dilectus* carried out by him with Caesar's agreement in Cisalpine Gaul and Italy, led straight to the confrontation of civil war.

Caesar's own funeral is a striking example of the part that skilful stage-managing could play in the manipulation of crowds. In the feverish days which followed the Ides of March all groups and factions were in a state of confusion. Cautious negotiations went on in the dark between the various parties—the magistrates in office, Caesar's murderers (most of whom were themselves magistrates), the Senate, the army, the veterans and the urban plebs—each trying to bargain with all the others and fearful of losing its footing in the general turmoil. Each of them tried to appeal to the people, i.e. the crowds which usually attended *contiones,* pleading its own cause and offering benefits of one sort or another. Zvi Yavetz has made a pioneering study of these strange debates, which should be followed up by a detailed examination of the various arguments and motives. Some, like Brutus and Cassius, clearly mistook the age they were living in and the kind of public they were addressing: it was pointless to invoke the 'ancient constitution' and proclaim the restoration of liberty to a crowd that had not felt Caesar's tyranny and was grateful for his 'generosity'. The funeral took place on 20 March, five days after his death, and significantly it was at that stage that disturbances broke out. We need not believe Cicero when he makes Antony responsible for everything that happened: the cruel splendour of the ceremony itself was quite sufficient to inflame the mob. The cult of Caesar appears as a spontaneous, natural consequence of his death, independent of any action by those in power or even by the most highly-placed of his followers. There seems to have been only one person, among all those who had reason to lament Caesar's death, who tried to turn these spontaneous movements to his own advantage: this was an agitator such as Rome had seen before in troubled times, the 'Pseudo-Marius', who claimed to be a grandson of the great general and, from 45 onwards, had recruited a large number of clients and followers in Rome and the rest of Italy, in the evident hope of insinuating himself among the beneficiaries of the regime.[4]

> Suddenly two men with swords by their sides and brandishing a pair of javelins set the pyre alight with blazing torches, and at once the throng of bystanders heaped upon it dry branches, the judgment seats with the benches, and whatever else could serve as an offering. Then the musicians and actors tore off their robes, which they had taken from the equipment of Caesar's triumphs and put on for the occasion, rent them to bits and threw them into the flames, and the veterans of the legions sacrificed the arms with which they had adorned themselves for the funeral; many of the women too, offered up the jewels which they wore and the amulets and robes of their children. At the height of the public grief a throng of foreigners went about lamenting after the fashion of their various countries, above all the Jews, who flocked to the place for several successive nights.
>
> Immediately after the funeral the commons ran to the houses of Brutus and Cassius with firebrands, and after being repelled with difficulty, they slew Helvius Cinna by mistake for Cornelius Cinna, who had the day before made a bitter indictment of Caesar and for whom they were looking; and they set his head upon a spear and paraded it about the streets. Afterwards they set up in the Forum a solid column of Numidian marble almost 20 feet high, and inscribed upon it. 'To the Father of his Country.' At the foot of this they continued for a long time to sacrifice, make vows, and settle some of their disputes by an oath in the name of Caesar. (Suetonius, *Caesar* 84-6)

> There was a certain pseudo-Marius in Rome named Amatius. He pretended to be a grandson of Marius, and for this reason was very popular with the masses. Being, according to this pretence, a relative of Caesar, he was grieved beyond measure by the latter's death, and erected an altar on the site of his funeral pyre. He collected a band of reckless men and made himself a perpetual terror to the murderers....
>
> It was said that Amatius was only waiting an opportunity to entrap Brutus and Cassius. On this rumour, Antony, making capital out of the plot, and

using his consular authority, arrested Amatius and boldly put him to death without a trial. The senators were astonished at this deed as an act of violence and contrary to law... The followers of Amatius, and the plebeians generally, feeling indignation especially because the deed had been done by Antony, whom the people had honoured, determined that they would not be scorned in that way. With shouts they took possession of the forum, exclaiming violently against Antony, and called on the magistrates to dedicate the altar in place of Amatius and to offer the first sacrifices on it to Caesar. Having been driven out of the forum by soldiers sent by Antony, they became still more indignant, and shouted more loudly, and some of them showed places where Caesar's statues had been torn from their pedestals. One man told them that he could show the shop where the statues were being broken up. The others followed, and having witnessed the fact, they set fire to the place. Finally, Antony sent more soldiers and some of those who resisted were killed; others were taken prisoner, and of these the slaves were crucified and the freemen thrown over the Tarpeian rock. (Appian. *B. Civ.* 3.2-3)

Episodes of this kind are a long way from the dignified and moral atmosphere of the traditional funerals extolled by Polybius, or the official manifestation of unity that Sulla's obsequies were supposed to be. The *populus,* decimated or terror-stricken, had disappeared in the whirlwind of civil war. All that was left were power-obsessed leaders on the one hand and a brutish multitude on the other, the centurion's sword and the irrational hero-worship of the urban plebs. Rome had already become the Empire.

Triumphs[5]

A similar evolution can be seen in the case of another great civic ceremony, the military triumph. A symbol of Roman power and its remorseless expansion, its very frequency (there were over 360 triumphs in eight centuries of history) presented citizens with a tangible and recurrent image of their own glory. We are not concerned here with the origin of the institution, which may have been Etruscan. Its religious character is evident: the victorious *imperator* to whom the City granted a triumph by law or senatorial decree was, with his special costume and attributes, the embodiment of a divine blessing conferred by the City's supreme protector, Jupiter Capitolinus, to whose temple he repaired to offer thanks. Making his solemn entry into a city from which warriors under arms were excluded at all other times, the victorious general embodied religious and magic forces which were, so to speak, canalized and controlled through him. Much could be said about the fundamental nature of the triumphal rites, which may well have been composite and diverse in origin; but it is fortunately easier to define its collective and social meaning in historical times and as it was conceived by the spectators. It too, like the funeral cortège, was a public display of the first order: the City admiring itself in its victorious army, and the conqueror offering himself to be admired.

While the ritual and religious aspect was never lost sight of, it seems clear that in the last centuries of the Republic the spectacular element became a fundamental aspect of the triumph. The route and character of the solemn procession are well known. Starting from the Campus Martius near the Villa Publica it entered the *pomerium* by the Porta Triumphalis, passed through the Circus Flaminius, crowded with spectators, and the Circus Maximus, continued along the Via Sacra and across the Forum, and finally made its way up to the Capitol. Temples and streets along the route were decorated. The magistrates and senators, at the head of the procession, were followed by the essential part of the spectacle, viz. the display of booty, considered as the personalized spoils of the enemy: costly weapons, standards, vessels and precious metals, coined and uncoined. In the second century, when the element of display came to the fore, it became customary to represent vanquished peoples, battles, captured towns etc. by means of paintings, small-scale models or a kind of caricature in the form of *tableaux vivants*. Next were exhibited the honours—generally golden crowns—conferred on the general, after the Greek manner, by the peoples he had conquered. Then the white bulls, sacrificial victims, sometimes to the number of hundreds. Then, to stimulate the nervous excitement of the crowd, came the human captives, spared for the express purpose of enhancing the triumph, exalting the majesty of the Roman people and humiliating its enemies. Some of these might themselves be kings, like Perseus, Jugurtha and Vercingetorix. Pompey in this way paraded 324 captives of high degree, whom he afterwards freed and treated with much honour. Then appeared the lictors, followed by the triumphal chariot in which the *imperator* stood clothed in almost divine array, resplendent in purple and gold; his sons, if any, stood with him in the chariot or rode alongside, and his chief officers, the *cohors praetoria*, followed behind. Next came the soldiers in marching order, in full uniform with decorations. Far from keeping a religious silence, they bawled out a triumphal song interspersed with jokes at their chief's expense, which were perhaps of ritual origin but sometimes had a political bearing as well.

A triumph took hours to pass by, and at the close of the Republic, party rivalries having played their part in extending its length, it might last several days. That of Aemilius Paullus in 167 took three days; Pompey's in 61 two days, the first for spoils and booty and the second for the troops and captives. Caesar celebrated five triumphs, four of them in 46 and the fifth in 45 BC, which surpassed in richness, splendour and baroque effects all military and civic festivals previously known to the Romans. Everything assumed fantastic proportions, from the forty elephants bearing torches which accompanied the *imperator* back from the Capitol after the sacrifice, to the colossal feast with 66,000 guests which followed the ceremony.

We know too little of the character and exact significance of the first Roman triumphs, in royal times or at the outset of the Republic, to be able to judge whether they possessed a certain gravity and simplicity despite the importance of the desacralizing rites. From Livy's description they sound fairly similar to those of later times, but can we be sure? In any case there is something very Hellenistic about the way in which a purely military and religious ceremony was gradually turned into an enormous show with elements of clowning, a pretext for festivities of all kinds and a means of whipping up excitement among crowds who, by that time, had no idea what a real battlefield was like. Nothing is more symptomatic than the ruinous emulation (similar to a North American 'potlatch') which arose in 166 between Aemilius Paullus, the conqueror of Macedonia, who had already celebrated his victory in advance at Amphipolis with games and a full-scale parade, and the young Antiochus IV, king of Syria, who sought to restore his prestige in the Greek world by an even more imposing ceremony:

When this king heard of the games celebrated in Macedonia by Aemilius Paullus the Roman general, ambitious of surpassing Paullus in magnificence he sent out embassies and sacred missions to the towns to announce the games he was about to give at Daphne, which made people in Greece very eager to visit Antioch. The festival opened with a procession headed by 5,000 men in the prime of life, armed after the Roman fashion and wearing breastplates of chain-armour. Next came 5,000 Mysians, and immediately behind them 3,000 Cilicians armed in the manner of light infantry, wearing gold crowns. Next came 3,000 Thracians and 5,000 Gauls. They were followed by 20,000 Macedonians of whom 10,000 bore golden shields, 5,000 brazen shields and the rest silver shields. Next marched 250 pairs of gladiators, and behind them 1,000 horsemen from Nisa and 3,000 from Antioch itself, most of whom had crowns and trappings of gold and the rest trappings of silver. Next to these came the 'companion cavalry', numbering about a thousand, all with gold trappings, and the regiment of 'royal friends' (*epilektoi*) of equal number and similarly accoutred; next 1,000 picked horse followed by the so-called 'agema', the crack cavalry corps, numbering about a thousand. After them marched the 'cataphract' or mailed horse, the horses and men being armed in complete mail, as the name indicates. Of these too there were about 1,500. All the above wore purple surcoats, in many cases embroidered with gold and heraldic designs. Next came 100 chariots drawn by six horses and 40 drawn by four horses, then a chariot drawn by four elephants and another drawn by a pair, and finally 36 elephants in single file with their housings.

...The quantity of gold and silver plate may be estimated from what follows. The slaves of one of the royal 'friends', Dionysius, the private secretary, marched along carrying articles of silver plate none of which weighed less than 1,000 drachmae, and 600 of the king's own slaves went by bearing articles of gold plate. Next there were about 200 women sprinkling the crow with perfumes from golden urns; these were followed by 80 women seated in litters with golden feet and 500 in litters with silver feet, all richly dressed. (Polybius 30.25)

A more noteworthy feature, however, in the transformation of the Roman triumph is the citizens' attitude towards the victor.[6] It is virtually certain that at the outset all credit for the victory was given to the gods. But before long the citizens felt, and some of them expressed, the need to establish a direct link of gratitude between themselves and the conqueror, isolated and exalted above his fellows. The link between the citizens and the city tended to give place to direct allegiance between a man and the masses who regarded him as a personal saviour. Victory was seen, so to speak, as an act which had saved the greatest number from slavery, and the masses felt towards the conqueror the same kind of gratitude and personal loyalty as a freedman towards the patron to whom he owed his liberty. This kind of collective devotion is already seen in the curious episode, clearly touched-up by the annalist, which in 216 BC put an end to the unhappy rivalry between the dictator Fabius Maximus and his (elected) master of the horse, Minucius Rufus. Fabius and his army had had to rescue Minucius, who committed his troops contrary to orders. After victory, Minucius made solemn amends:

> The master of the horse advanced in front of the rest and called upon Fabius by the name of Father, and his entire army saluted the dictator's soldiers who had gathered round them as their patrons. (Livy 22.30.2)

Prisoners liberated by victory were clearly in a situation of this kind, particularly as the Romans did not usually hold them in high esteem. The attitude of such prisoners was significantly expressed by Q. Terentius Culleo, who had been in captivity at Carthage and whom Scipio, who was already his patron, had had released in 204 BC; in 201 he followed Scipio's triumphal procession wearing a freedman's cap, thus showing clearly to whom he owed his liberty (Livy 30.45.4). In 196 all the Roman prisoners liberated by Flamininus's victory (they had been previously captured by Hannibal and sold into Greece) followed in his triumph, their heads shaven (Livy 34.52.10). The ideology of victory as manifested in the triumph came more and more to resemble that of the individual saviour, which had been widespread in the Greek world since the dawn of Hellenistic time. Sulla was the first Roman general to benefit from this transference:

> His triumph, which was imposing from the costliness and rarity of the royal spoils, had a greater ornament in the noble spectacle of the exiles. For

the most distinguished and influential of the citizens [those who had been banished by Marius's supporters], crowned with garlands, followed in the procession, calling Sulla their saviour and father, since it was through him that they were returning to their native city and bringing with them their wives and children. (Plutarch, *Sulla* 34)

It will be seen what a change has taken place here: for the first time, the victory of one party over another is regarded as the token of salvation, the personal link between the masses and their deliverer. Some in after years tried, of course, to give a republican flavour to such honours: Cicero, for instance, when he received the same title as Sulla — *parens patriae* — for saving the City from Catiline's conspiracy. But in fact what we have here is a new form of affiliation in civic life, the same which was eventually to produce the Empire.

Escorts and demonstrations

Funerals and triumphs were official, public manifestations in which the City was in principle always a spectator of its own display, were it only the physical progress of an ordered, hierarchical procession. It was only gradually that they degenerated into a paroxysmic encounter between a mass of people heedless of hierarchical distinction and an individual, living or dead, whom they regarded as their saviour and for whom their feelings were not those of citizens for a magistrate but of a client for his patron, or a devotee for his god. The ancestral framework of the City was designed in part to prevent this very polarization, and its progressive weakening certainly owed much to Greek influence.

Although political funerals and triumphs were frequent enough to be schematically described, as we have tried to do in very brief outline, in the last resort they were exceptional occasions. They afforded a brief opportunity for political and civic structures of a non-traditional kind to manifest themselves; but the traditional forms were not yet effaced or superseded. This does not mean, however, that the Roman people had no ordinary means of self-expression other than the traditional ones of the census and electoral or legislative assemblies. On the contrary, in the last century of the Republic various forms of public action took on fresh importance, if they did not appear for the first time, and became remarkably frequent. Developing outside the constitutional sphere in the narrow sense, such activities became an integral part of civic and social life. They form a sort of counterpoint to the official scene, no less important though involving different forms and different actors; or, to change the metaphor, they constitute a new language or grammar of politics.

As a first category we may notice what might be called symbolic manifestatons or demonstrations, i.e. private and unofficial gatherings. We have already seen that the regular assemblies at which public matters were decided according to law — whether electoral, legislative or judicial — were preceded by one or more *contiones* at which the issues were debated. These were fully official meetings, which could only be summoned by a magistrate entitled to 'treat with the people' or the plebs. When public life became corrupt they might degenerate into riots, but that did not affect their regular status. But, apart from *contiones* and *comitia*, the Roman people or sections of it also took part in public gatherings outside the constitutional structure. Some became recognized institutions and were for the most part peaceful, such as the custom of turning out in large numbers to welcome magistrates or pro-magistrates on their entry into the City or to see them off on their departure. This was in no way official, but was an almost automatic mark of respect. What is interesting is that while the escort, whether spontaneous or not, consisted essentially of friends and clients, it also usually included representatives of corporations, especially the tax-farming companies. This happened, for example, in Verres' case, showing that he was not on such bad terms with the Sicilian Company:

> Carpinatius [the *promagister* at Syracuse] was writing even more frequently to the company, hoping that if possible, the effect of his earlier letters [accusing Verres] would be completely wiped out. Finally, when Verres was about to leave Sicily, he wrote urging them to assemble in force and meet him on his arrival, to express their thanks, and to promise to execute zealously any commands he might have for them. The company accordingly observed the traditional practice of revenue-contractors... (Cicero, 2 *Verr.* 2.172)

Turn-outs of this kind were a barometer of political popularity; thus Cicero derided Piso for the quietness of his entry into the City, as a sign that he had no friends or was of bad character:

> Why not admit that scarcely a single person came, even among prospective candidates for office — a class who are even most punctilious in courtesy — although they had received general warnings and requests to do so on the actual day and on many previous days? (*In Pisonem* 55)

In the same way it was frequent enough for an office-seeker to be accompanied, while canvassing, by a large and faithful retinue of friends including magistrates, *equites* and *publicani*, corresponding as far as possible to the electorate whom he hoped to win over, i.e., as a rule, the City organized after the pattern of the *comitia centuriata*. In such cases a distinction might be observed between the habitual escorts of different candidates, reflecting differences between their *clientelae*, supporters or voters. Thus Licinius Murena, Cicero's candidate for the consulship in 63 and a friend of the *optimates*, was accompanied by a very different sort of people than Catiline:

Again, if all the companies to which many of the jurors belong, if a host of our own distinguished order, if the whole of that tribe of candidates, always so ready to please and allowing nobody to enter the city without due honour, if even our own prosecutor Postumus came in person to meet him with a good large crowd of his own, what is surprising in the size of the throng? I leave out the clients, neighbours, fellow-tribesmen, the whole army of Lucullus which was present at the time for his triumph...(*Pro Murena* 69)

At the same time Catiline appeared, brisk and cheerful, accompanied by his troop of youths, entrenched behind informers and assassins, buoyant with the hopes of his soldiers and the promises which he said my colleague had made to him, surrounded by an army of colonists from Arretium and Faesulae, a throng with here and there men of a very different type, victims of disaster at the time of Sulla. (Ibid. 49).

But in more exceptional and dramatic circumstances a very different kind of demonstration might take place, such as that which preceded Cicero's departure into exile after Clodius introduced his first bill threatening the ex-consul. Clodius was supported by his armed bands and by the urban plebs in general, having gained its favour by abolishing payment for grain distributions, organized through the restored *collegia*. As against this, Cicero and his friends tried to present the public image of another City composed chiefly of the 'respectable orders', the *equites* and most of the senators, with the purpose of inducing the consuls and the Senate as a body to stand up to Clodius's demagogy. In a great demonstration on the tenth day before the calends of March, 58 BC, over 20,000 people, according to Cicero's account,[7] put on mourning together with him, proceeded to the Capitol while the Senate was in session, and sent in a delegation of knights and senators to ask the consuls to intervene. The consuls retorted by issuing an edict of banishment against one of the leading knights, L. Aelius Lamia, and forbidding the Senate to act on a motion it had just passed at the instance of L. Ninnius Quadratus, that all senators should put on mourning:

At this point the Senate became anxious; you, Knights of Rome, were aroused; the whole of Italy was deeply moved; in fact, men of every rank and class were of opinion that help must be sought for the supreme interests of the State from the consuls and from their supreme authority—although they were the only persons except that raving tribune, those two whirlwinds that swept over the State, who not only failed to come to the support of their country when it was falling headlong, but lamented because it was collapsing too slowly. They were daily importuned by the complaints of all patriotic men, even by the entreaties of the Senate, to take up my cause, to do something, in fact, to bring the matter before the House; but not only with denials but also with mockery did they continue to assail every man of mark in that body. And then, straightway, when an amazing throng had assembled on the Capitol from the whole city and from the whole of Italy, all men deemed it their duty to put on mourning and to defend me in every possible way by measures of their own, since the State had lost its public leaders. At the same time the Senate had assembled in the Temple of Concord, the very temple that recalled the memory of my consulship, and the whole order with tears entreated the consul with curly hair—for the other one, shock-headed and grave, carefully kept at home. (*Pro Sestio* 25)

We have already seen that Cicero's party combined these street demonstrations, involving essentially the senatorial and equestrian orders, with a campaign aimed at other sections of society, which they continued until their leader was finally recalled from exile:

There was no borough, no colony, no prefecture in Italy, no company of tax-farmers in Rome, no club nor association, nor, in short, any deliberative body, which had not at that time passed a decree in the most complimentary terms concerning my welfare, when suddenly the two consuls published an edict that senators should resume their usual dress. (Ibid. 32)

Meanwhile Clodius for his part had created an organization of quite a different kind. Making all allowance for polemic exaggeration, it could be said that two communities of different origin and structure were confronting each other in the same City. Clodius had passed a bill making legal the clubs and sodalities that the Senate had forbidden in 64 as contrary to public order. In addition— though he was not alone in this—he enrolled a large number of supporters in gangs of military type (according to Cicero); their organization in *decuriae* may have been identical with that of the *collegia* and, I suggest, the *plebs frumentaria,* which was under the thumb of Clodius's scribe Sex. Cloelius. We do not know how far Clodius's *collegia* and *decuriae* differed from electoral organizations of the kind which all candidates, e.g. Plancius, maintained during the decade 60- 50 BC; but it is certain that in one or other of these organizations Clodius did not shrink from enrolling slaves, not to speak of wage-earners and even shopkeepers. It was one of Cicero's key arguments against the law exiling him that it had only been got through the *comitia tributa* by emptying every corner shop in Rome—exactly what Catiline's accomplice Lentulus had tried in vain to do in 63 (*Cat.* 4.16-17).

It is not my purpose here to study these new forms of association, which were first made use of by some *tribuni plebis* in 67-66, like Manilius, and afterwards by such as Catiline and especially Clodius, who was practically master of the Roman populace between 61 and 52. Such a study would, however, show that new channels of participation in politics were being opened up, which were more accessible to the urban plebs than the traditional framework of the City. It would also show how the parties were regrouping and splitting along different lines. It was no longer a question of groups of electoral supporters on a gentilitial or geographical basis, as in the second century, nor even, as with the Gracchi and as late as Saturninus, of fairly large social groups with specific common interests like the agrarian law, but of 'parties' of a completely new type. The dividing line was not a social one: Catiline and Clodius drew their supporters from every sphere of society, although the former's conspiracy was on a much higher level as far as his chief assistants were concerned. What is novel is the militarization of these new parties. Catiline's plans were strictly military: the abortive insurrection in Rome was to have been the signal for a full-scale uprising, carefully prepared in various parts of Italy. Clodius, who had fewer lines out to the countryside, managed with scarcely and interruption to control the assemblies and the rabble in Rome itself, thanks to the revived *collegia* and the organization he had created in outline in 61 and perfected in 58 under cover of the grain distribution law.

Clodius's supremacy continued until others, using similar means, challenged him on his own ground, with armed and paid troops of professional soldiers. None of them, however, could afford to neglect public opinion, as they also needed the support of the masses. The corn law was a powerful weapon in Clodius's hands: it affected the immediate interests not only of the urban proletariat but of the whole population of Rome, though many of Clodius's chief lieutenants were, as might be expected, of Italian origin.[8] Against this organization, the counter-offensive prepared by Cicero's friends during his exile and prolonged until about 56 BC was more original than is commonly recognized. He too launched a direct appeal to public opinion with the means appropriate to his personality and background. He sought support from what he regarded as the 'true' Roman people, tightly organized around an élite composed of the respectable and well-to-do and of local notabilities. In a series of famous passages which are also manifestos or professions of faith, he refers to the philosophy of these groups as the *consensus omnium bonorum*. This consensus was triumphantly expressed in the law of 57 recalling him from exile and in his astonishing journey home from Brundisium. We have seen in the previous chapter the part played in this scenario by the appeal to municipalities and the official votes of the corporations and orders, headed by the *equites*. The point to be noted here as regards the realignment of grass-roots Italy is that Cicero tried in the following year (56) to prolong it on a wider basis. This he sought to do, in a way that was quite novel in Roman politics, on the basis of a doctrine and not merely of personal loyalty or the defence of certain interests. The doctrine, expressed at length in *Pro Sestio* and afterwards in more ambitious works such as *De Republica* and *De Legibus,* consisted of establishing a political regime which should be exactly that of the *boni*: within the framework, practically unchanged, of the traditional *respublica* and the mixed constitution, it would offer better chances of participation to the Italian bourgeoisiè and to rich and enterprising citizens (and even freedmen) who wished in their turn to embark on the *cursus honorum*.

This desire to mould public opinion by speeches and writings, offering a whole political and constitutional programme under the guise of a Platonic fiction, was a completely new departure on Cicero's part and was not followed by anyone else except perhaps Caesar's supporters, if their ideas in 51 and 46 are rightly interpreted in the *Epistulae* attributed to Sallust.[9] None the less — and this must be our final point — in the last century of the Republic, convulsed as it was by civil wars, riots and revolutions, public opinion had become a redoubtable force. It is true, as we have already seen, that Rome was from the very beginning a self-contained community in which everyone was supervised by everyone else and no one existed except in so far as all the others recognized his proper place and value. It can be said that a city of this kind is already a city fundamentally ruled by public opinion. But as long as the rigid framework of the census system endured together with the quasi-military command structure of the magistracies, and while the Senate, a small group of former magistrates, possessed the monopoly of a quasi-religious *auctoritas*, public opinion could only find expression within narrow limits, on rare occasions which were carefully stage-managed, and in accordance with regular forms. The citizen of old Rome only gave his opinion when asked for it ritually under the vigilant eye of his natural mentors. He voted, but he did not debate. Thus he might, at a given moment, reject one leader or improve the chances of another, but he had little or no control over his own career, which was entirely in the hands of his peers and meticulously governed by official rules.

Games, festivals and theatres

This restraint did not mean, however, that public opinion had no other way of expressing itself. In the first place, although there was virtually no means of general information and discussion corresponding to the press in modern times, there was a good deal of *ad hoc* literature in which ideas were ventilated. I shall not describe this in detail here, as it was chiefly of concern to those directly involved in politics.[10] But our study will have shown that in the last century of the Republic the standard of literacy must have been quite high in order for citizens to perform their duties at assemblies and even in the army (voting tablets, a written password etc.) We may thus safely assume that literary propaganda reached a fairly wide circle of readers and helped to form public opinion at a higher level. The existence of *libelli* or pamphlets, which were sometimes posted up clandestinely, indicates that there must have been a fairly large and appreciative urban public for this kind of material. A century later, in a different sphere, the electoral inscriptions on the walls of Pompeii, with their stereotyped slogans and a few surviving graffiti of a more original or satirical character, point to the existence of a body of opinion which sometimes verged on high politics, for instance in its criticism of Nero.[11] There are few traces of such activity in Rome itself except for a short flurry of pamphlets and posters during the months preceding the Ides of March, but there can be no doubt that it existed there also. We have, on the other hand, fairly abundant evidence of literary propaganda in the form of letters, treatises, published books and speeches, which flourished in more strictly political circles.

There was, however, one type of occasion on which the masses could express their feelings effectively, viz. during religious festivals and the various shows — chariot-races, gladiatorial fights, tragedies, comedies and mimes — which were their main popular attraction.[12] These gatherings played no less important a part in public life under the Republic than under the Empire: occurring regularly and frequently, they were still marked by a high degree of religious solemnity, and by bringing together the masses indiscriminately on a vast scale they were conducive to the expression of popular feelings and attitudes. The liturgical calendar, as we may call it, was full of such occasions. By the end of the Republic at least seven great series of games were regularly held: the Roman and Plebeian, those in honour of Ceres and Apollo, the Megalensia, the Floralia; games commemorating Sulla's victory for a number of years, and, after 46, those commemorating Caesar's. Some of these were lengthy: the Ludi Romani lasted 15 days, the Plebei 14 and the Cerealia eight. Under the Empire, by the fourth century AD no fewer than 175 days in the year were holidays. The number was certainly much less in the last century of the Republic, but to those already mentioned must be added 'private' games held by magistrates on particular occasions, such as Pompey's dedication of his magnificent theatre in 56 BC.

The Roman year was thus punctuated by celebrations held at a fixed date, or one announced well in advance, which brought together the urban plebs and the élite and also drew to Rome a large part of the population of the Italian *municipia* and colonies. In 70, for instance, at the time of Verres' trial, Rome was full of citizens from Italy because of the coincidence of three solemn or festive occasions: the *comitia*, the games and the census (1 *Verr.* 54). We can form an idea of the size of audiences by the capacity of the various buildings involved. The Circus Flaminius and the Circus Maximus (the latter rebuilt and enlarged by Caesar) had room for tens if not hundreds of thousands:

Tarquinius also built the Circus Maximus... dividing the places among the 30 curiae, he assigned to each curia a particular section... This work also was destined to become in time one of the most beautiful and most admirable structures in Rome. For the Circus is three stades and a half [700 metres] in length and four plethra [120 metres] in breadth. Round about it on the two longer sides and one of the shorter sides a canal has been dug... Behind the canal are porticos three stories high, [forming a] single portico like an ampitheatre, eight stades [1600 metres] in circuit and capable of holding 150,000 persons. ... There are several entrances and ascents for the spectators, so that countless thousands of people may enter and depart without inconvenience. (Dionys. 3.68)

We do not know how large the Circus Flaminius was, but it can hardly have been smaller. The Romans, unlike the Greeks, did not build any theatres in stone until quite late: throughout the second century BC the Senate firmly opposed the idea of permanent buildings on the Greek model, perhaps because it was thought dangerous to provide a place where the masses could assemble of their own accord. As we have seen, it was customary for those attending Roman assemblies to stand (Cicero, *Pro Flacco* 17), and a senatorial decree introduced by Scipio Nasica in 151 forbade citizens to be seated at the public games. The ban was evaded, but only temporary wooden seats were used.[13] Audiences were no smaller on that account. Pompey's stone theatre, completed in 52 BC, seated 17,580; that of Cornelius Balbus in 13 BC had 11,500 seats, while Marcellus's (a later building) had 20,000. The temporary structures of earlier times must have held about the same numbers. Thus the crowds at public shows were comparable in numbers to those who attended the *comitia*. Several spectacles might be in progress at the same time: Caesar, at his triumphs in 46 BC, had performances given in all parts of Rome and in all languages.

Gatherings of this size were clearly calculated to encourage mass movements. Cicero bears witness to the fact that nothing delighted the Roman people so much as public shows, and they also gave the spectators an opportunity to express their views on quite other matters. As Cicero says in the course of a sustained argument in one of his most important speeches, 'The opinion and feeling of the Roman people in public affairs can be most clearly expressed on three occasions: at a meeting (*contio*), an assembly, or a gathering for plays and gladiatorial shows' (*Pro Sestio* 106). This can be better understood from an outline of the way in which performances were organized.[14] They were thoroughly official: being associated with public religious festivals they were entrusted to magistrates, generally the aediles. The state bore only a small part of the expense, and the rest fell on the magistrates themselves. This fact alone is politically significant and accounts for the fact, which appears from all the evidence we have, that towards the end of the Republic the aedileship had a decisive effect on a man's further career, owing to the popularity he could gain by presenting the public with lavish and original performances on a large scale. This had its bearing on the behaviour of the political class — Caesar in 65 BC is a noteworthy example, but we are not concerned with this aspect for the moment. The organizing magistrates naturally decided what shows to put on, but sometimes, for political reasons, their colleagues or superiors might step in and alter the arrangements (Cicero, *Ad Att.* 16.2, 5; cf. p. 371 below). In some circumstances the choice of play might be a very delicate matter: the theatre, even more than chariot-racing or gladiatorial shows, lent itself to demonstrations which could be embarrassing to the organizers. There is much evidence of the number and frequency of such demonstrations. The spectacle had a twofold aspect: the crowd might be excited by reading a topical meaning into the play, and in addition it could manifest its feelings to magistrates or leaders who were present in the audience: for it was a civic obligation to attend performances, even for those who did not enjoy them or shrank from confronting the multitude. The theatre was a kind of testing-ground, alongside the *comitia*, where citizens could say what they thought without too much risk and public men could assess their own popularity rating. Hence theatrical events played a prominent part in the correspondence of politicans skilled at interpreting the signs:

> If you have any news of practical importance, let me hear it; if not, give me full details as to who was cheered by the people at the mimes, and the actors' epigrams. (Cicero, *Ad Att.* 14.3.2: April 44).

When Cicero was proconsul in Cilicia he enjoined Caelius not only to keep him *au courant* of events in Rome (as to which he had other sources), but to give him an intelligent picture of what was going on; in doing so, Caelius gave prominence to theatrical events:

> The day after the acquittal [of M. Valerius Messala, accused of corruption] Hortensius [his lawyer, suspected of having suborned the jury] entered Curio's theatre, to give us the chance, I suppose, of showing that his joy was ours. Instantly you heard
> Din and uproar, crash of thunder, and the hissing of the shrouds,
> which last was all the more remarked upon because Hortensius had reached a venerable age unscathed by a single hiss. But now he was hissed heartily enough to satisfy anyone for the whole of his life, and to make him sorry that he had ever won this case. (*Ad Fam.* 8.2.1)

Thus the regular attendance of all politicians and party leaders at theatrical shows was a constant source of significant incidents. Sometimes public reaction was unanimous, while at other times it varied considerably between different classes and orders; for the audience at these official performances was socially stratified and reflected the organization of the City even in the order of seating. From at least 194 BC senators had separate seats in the orchestra and the front rows:

> At the Roman Games given by these aediles, the senate for the first time looked on segregated from the common people. This caused gossip, as every novelty usually does, some thinking that this distinction, which should have

been granted long before, was at last bestowed upon a most honourable body; others taking the view that whatever was added to the majesty of the senate was subtracted from the dignity of the commons, and that all such discriminations, which tended to draw the orders apart, were dangerous to impartial harmony and freedom. For 558 years, they said, people had looked on from seats chosen at random; what had suddenly happened to make the Fathers unwilling to have the plebeians mingle with them in the crowd, or the rich man scorn the poor man as his neighbour at the show? This was a novel and arrogant caprice, never desired nor practised by the senate of any other people. It is reported that in the end even Scipio Africanus repented that in his consulship he had suggested this innovation. (Livy 34.54.4-8)

In 123, in all probability, C. Gracchus went a step further by reserving the first 14 rows for *equites*. This unpopular measure was probably reversed by Sulla but was revived by L. Roscius Otho, tribune of the plebs in 67.[15] The equestrian order was pleased, as it had been when the privilege of supplying criminal juries was partially restored to it in 70, but the plebs were discontented for a long time. In 63 Roscius, who was probably then praetor, was hissed at the theatre, which provoked Cicero's eloquent intervention:

A proof of the charm of Cicero's discourse may be found in an incident of his consulship connected with the public spectacles. In earlier times, it seems, the men of the equestrian order were mingled with the multitudes in the theatres and watched the spectacles along with the people, seated as chance would have it. Marcus Otho was the first to separate the knights from the rest of the citizens, which he did when he was praetor, and gave them a particular place of their own at the spectacles, which they still retain. The people took this as a mark of dishonour to themselves, and when Otho appeared in the theatre they hissed him insultingly, while the knights received him with loud applause. The people renewed and increased their hisses, and the knights their applause; then they turned upon one another with reviling words, and disorder reigned in the theatre. When Cicero heard of this he came and summoned the people to the temple of Bellona, where he rebuked and exhorted them; whereupon they went back again to the theatre and applauded Otho loudly, and vied with the knights in showing him honour and esteem. (Plutarch, *Cicero* 13)

This arrangement of the audience in classes, which continued and became stricter under the Empire, naturally made it easy to identify the source of demonstrations. In 59, during Caesar's consulship, it could be seen that it was chiefly the knights who applauded Curio boisterously, gave Caesar a cool reception and Pompey a hostile one, all of which the common people took much amiss (Cicero, *Ad Att.* 2.19). But at other times it was possible to note, and draw the moral from, a unanimous public reaction. Cicero refers to this in the following passage, which perhaps contains a play on the expressions 'high', 'middle' and 'low' — since at the theatre people of rank occupied the lowest seats, while commoners sat in the 'gallery':

> I indeed am one that always despised such applause when awarded to popularity-hunting citizens: at the same time, when it comes from the highest, from the middle, from the lowest grade, when in a word it comes universally, and when those that used to follow the popular verdict stand aside, I do not regard it as applause, but as a judgement. (*Phil.* 1.37)

Sometimes hostile demonstrations turned into riots. It was easy for gangs to burst in from outside the theatre and break up a performance, as the seats prevented the audience from moving freely and the exits were few and narrow. On two occasions Clodius, who was expert in urban guerrilla warfare, disrupted performances in this way. During the Apollonian Games in July 57 he 'collected a crown of commoners and, having excited their anger at the price of corn, made them drive all the spectators out of the theatre' (Asconius, p. 48 C). Next year, when he was an aedile, he did the same thing at the Megalensian Games:

> Innumerable bands of slaves that had been mustered by this scrupulous aedile from every quarter of the city, and had been incited for the occasion, were suddenly let loose upon us from every archway and entry, and at a given signal burst on to the stage. Then it was that you, Lentulus, showed the same courage as your great-grandfather showed of old...In your support the senate and the knights of Rome and all true patriots rose to their feet, after Clodius had exposed that senate and that Roman people to the mercies of a mob of jeering slaves, imprisoned and rendered powerless as they were in the tightly packed seats of the auditorium, and hampered by the confusion of the narrow exits. (Cicero, *De Haruspicum responsis* 22)

But much the most interesting feature of theatrical demonstrations of this kind was that they were not only directed at persons present in the audience. They were generally touched off by something in the play itself: either its political content as intended by the author, or something read into it by the organizers or the actors. A remarkable taste for allusion came into play here. The extreme politicization of the Roman theatre is a notable fact, no doubt derived largely from the first beginnings of dramatic art.[16] In Rome, as in Athens three centuries before, tragedies were staged in order to draw public attention to great national questions,[17] the subject being either taken from a traditional repertoire or intentionally depicting a current military or diplomatic issue. The first *fabula praetexta* of this kind, Naevius's *Clastidium*, represented the new-won victory of M. Claudius Marcellus over the Insubrian Gauls (222

BC), while Ennius's *Ambracia* celebrated the capture of that town by M. Fulvius Nobilior in 189. Subsequent generations followed suit: Pacuvius wrote at least one patriotic tragedy (*Paullus*), and Accius two (*Decius* and *Brutus*). The subject did not greatly matter in itself, for political ingredients could be added to the actual content. It is pretty certain, for instance, that Accius, who lived at the time of the Gracchi, filled his tragedies, even those on Greek subjects, with plain allusions to the events of 133 and after, when Rome was overshadowed by growing fears of dictatorship and revolution.

Sometimes the author's text was more topical than he himself intended; but it is remarkable enough that a wide public was sufficiently educated and alert to react to political allusions that were deliberately put into the mouths of tragic characters. Moreover there is abundant evidence that, nearly a century after these tragedies were written, audiences were still on the lookout for any accidental resemblance or allusion that could be read into what were already classic texts, and made their 'recognition' of current events abundantly clear. There are of course many similar examples in modern times; during the French Revolution and Empire, theatre audiences reacted in the same way to the repertoire of the Comédie Française. Cicero gives a clear account of the process when describing at length an episode which redounded to his own glory:

Expressions of public opinion at assemblies and at meetings are sometimes the voice of truth, but sometimes they are falsified and corrupt. At theatrical and gladiatorial shows it is said to be common for some feeble and scanty applause to be started by a hired and unprincipled claque, and yet, when that happens, it is easy to see how and by whom it is started and what the honest part of the audience does. Why should I tell you to-day what men or what class of citizens is chiefly applauded? Not one of you fails to understand. Suppose applause to be a trivial matter, which it is not, since it is accorded to all the best citizens; but if it is trivial, it is so only to a man of character, whereas to those who depend upon the merest trifles, who are controlled and governed by rumour and, as they themselves put it, by the favour of the people, applause must seem immortality, and hissing death. I therefore ask you particularly, Scaurus, you who gave most magnificently appointed shows, did any one of those 'friends of the people' visit your shows, or venture to appear in the theatre before the Roman people? That arch-comedian himself [Clodius], not merely a spectator, but an actor and virtuoso, who knows all the pantomimic interludes of his sister, who is admitted into a party of women in the guise of a harp-girl, neither visited your shows during that fiery tribunate of his, nor any others except once when he scarcely escaped alive. Once only, I say, did that man who was a 'friend of the people' venture to show himself at the games, when in the Temple of Virtue honour was paid to merit, and the monument of Gaius Marius, saviour of our Empire, afforded his fellow-townsman and defender of the State a place for securing his own recall.

What feelings the Roman people entertained at that time was made plain in both ways. First, when the decree of the Senate had been heard, unanimous applause was given to the measure itself, and to the Senate, before they came in; next, to the senators, when they returned one by one from the Senate to see the shows. But when the consul himself, who gave the entertainment, took his seat, people stood up with outstretched hands, giving thanks, and weeping for joy openly showed their goodwill and sympathy for myself. But when Clodius arrived, that raging fiend, at the height of his frenzy, the Roman people could scarcely restrain themselves, men could scarcely help wreaking their hatred upon his foul and abominable person; cries, menacing gestures, loud curses came in a flood from all.

But why do I speak of the spirit and courage of the Roman people, when at last after long servitude they had a glimpse of freedom, in their attitude towards a man whom even the actors did not spare to his face as he sat in the audience, though he was then a candidate for an aedileship! For when a comedy, *The Pretender*, I fancy, was being performed, the whole company, speaking all together in loud tones, bent forward threateningly and looking straight at the foul wretch, loudly chanted the words,

This, Titus, is the sequel, the end of your vicious life!

He sat utterly disconcerted, and the man who used to make his meetings resound with the hoots of a ribald claque was hooted away by the speech of genuine actors. And since I have mentioned theatrical performances, I will not omit to say that, among many and varied reflections in the comedy, there was never a passage seeming, from the poet's words, to have some bearing on our times, where either the whole people failed to grasp the special point or where the actor himself failed to make it clear. And here, gentlemen, I beg you not to think that any spirit of levity has led me to fall into an unusual kind of pleading if I talk about poets, actors, and plays in the course of a trial.

I am not so ignorant of legal proceedings, gentlemen, nor so unaccustomed to speaking, as to hunt for what I intend to say from every kind of subject, and to pluck and cull all kinds of flowers of speech from every source. I know what is due to your dignity, to this body of counsel, that gathering of citizens, what the high character of Publius Sestius, the greatness of his danger, my age, and my position demand. But on this occasion I have undertaken, if I may say so, to instruct our youth as to who are the 'aristocrats.' In making that clear, I must show that not all those are 'friends of the people' who are thought to be so. I shall most easily be able to do that, if I describe the true and uncorrupted judgment of the whole people, and the inmost feelings of the country. What, then, do you think of this? When news had just been brought to the shows and to the stage of that decree of the Senate which was passed in the Temple of Virtue, before a vast audience a great artist who has always played a most noble part in public life as well as on the stage, weeping with joy still fresh, with mingled grief and longing for me, pleaded my cause before the Roman people in much weightier words than I could have pleaded myself! He expressed the genius of a great poet not only by the exercise of his art, but also by his own grief. For when he uttered the words:

> Who with firm spirit helped the public cause,
> Upheld it, ever stood with the Achivi —

with what force he made it clear that I had stood on your side, as he pointed to your assembled Orders! He was encored by all when he went on to say:

> In wavering affairs did never waver
> His life to offer, nor did spare his head.

What shouts of applause greeted this passage, when they took no notice of the acting, but applauded the words of the poet, the earnestness of the actor and the hope of my recall! After the line:

> Our greatest friend, in this our greatest war,

the actor himself added the words

> Endowed with greatest genius

out of friendship for me, and perhaps the spectators approved owing to some regret for my absence.

A little later in the same play, how the Roman people groaned when they heard the same actor utter the words:

> O my father!

He thought that it was I, I in my absence, who ought to be lamented as a father, whom Quintus Catulus and many others in the Senate had often called 'Father of his Country.' How he wept as he spoke of the burning and destruction of my house, when lamenting an exiled father, his afflicted fatherland, his house burnt and ruined! His acting was so pathetic that after having described the man's former prosperity he turned to the audience with the words

> All these things I have seen in flames,

and drew tears even from my enemies and my detractors! And then again, by heaven, how he declaimed these other words! — words which seemed to me to have been so delivered and written that they might well have been uttered even by Quintus Catulus, had he come to life again; for he was in the habit of freely censuring and blaming rashness by the people or error by the Senate:

> O thankless Argives, disobliging Greeks,
> Forgetful of past kindness!

No, that was not true, for they were not ungrateful, but unfortunate, because they were not permitted to save him who had saved them, nor has anyone ever found one person more grateful to anyone than they have all been to me. But, be that as it may, a most eloquent poet must have written the following words in my interest, and the actor, as remarkable for his courage as for his acting, applied them to me, when he pointed to all the Orders and accused the Senate, the Roman knights, and the entire Roman people:

A banished man you leave him; you consent,

As you consented to his banishment!

How on that occasion the whole audience indicated their feelings, how the whole Roman people declared their goodwill for a man who was not a 'friend of the people,' I heard by report; those who were present can more readily estimate.

And—since my speech has led me thus far—the actor bewailed my lot so often, as he pleaded my cause with such emotion, that that splendid voice of his was choked with tears; nor did the poets, whose talents have always been my delight, fail me in my trouble; and the Roman people showed, not only by applause but also by lamentation, how much they approved of these allusions. Ought then Aesopus or Accius to have pleaded thus for me, had the Roman people been free, or ought the chief men of the State? In the *Brutus* I was mentioned by name:

Tullius, who 'stablished safe the people's freedom.

The line was encored a thousand times. Did the Roman people fail to show how firmly they believed that what scoundrels charged us with overthrowing had in fact been established by myself and the Senate? (*Pro Sestio* 115-26)

It seems clear that on this occasion, during the Floralia of 57 BC, the curule aediles whose task it was to organize the games had concerted with Pompey and a majority of the Senate to select from the repertoire plays which would give Cicero's supporters a chance to make a noisy demonstration of their feelings. At the Apollonian Games of 59, on the other hand, it would seem that the organizers had no special intentions and that the actor Diphilus himself chose to point the allusion against Pompey:

Popular feeling can be seen best in the theatre and at public exhibitions. For at the gladiatorial show both the leader and his associates were overwhelmed with hisses: at the games in honour of Apollo the actor Diphilus made an impertinent attack on Pompey, 'By our misfortunes thou art Great,' which was encored again and again. 'A time will come when thou wilt rue that might,' he declaimed amid the cheers of the whole audience, and so on with the rest. For indeed the verses do look as though they had been written for the occasion by an enemy of Pompey: 'If neither law nor custom can constrain,' etc. was received with a tremendous uproar and outcry. At Caesar's entry the applause dwindled away; but young Curio, who followed, was applauded as Pompey used to be when the constitution was still sound. Caesar was much annoyed: and it is said a letter flew post-haste to Pompey at Capua. (Cicero, *Ad Att.* 2.19)

The intention of those who organised the games on the occasion of Caesar's funeral is clearer still:

> At the funeral games, to rouse pity and indignation at his death, these words from Pacuvius's *Contest for the Arms* were sung: —
> 'Saved I these men that they might murder me?'
> and words of a like purport from Atilius's *Electra,* (Suetonius, *Caesar* 84)

Sometimes, it appears, the authorities foresaw that a particular play might cause an outburst and took precautions against it — the only instance we know of theatrical censorship in Rome. In 44 Brutus as *praetor urbanus* was responsible for organizing the Apollonian Games in July, but when he fled from Rome in April the task was taken over by his fellow-praetor C. Antonius, Mark Antony's brother. Apparently Brutus had intended to organize games on a magnificent scale to win over the populace, and had chosen Accius's play *Brutus* (on the founding of the Republic) as an appropriate theme after the Ides of March. He expected this to benefit him both personally and politically:

> He prefers the games to take place in his absence. He says he will go to Asia at once, as soon as he has handed over the management of the games to those who will attend to it [i.e., no doubt, private contractors]. (Cicero, *Ad Att.* 15.12.1)

At the last moment Antonius cancelled this explosive programme and substituted *Tereus,* another play by Accius. However, this too accrued to the advantage of Brutus and Cassius: the play was a success ('The news I brought him [Brutus] about *Tereus* was no news': *Ad Att.* 16.5), Brutus was largely given credit for it, and the occasion became a demonstration in favour of Caesar's murderers:

> Did the applause bestowed on the Apollinarian Games, or rather the testimony and judgment of the Roman people, appear to you an insignificant thing? Oh, how happy were they who, unable through force of arms to be present in person, yet were present, seated in the hearts and inmost affections of the Roman people! (Cicero, *Phil.* 1.36)

Plutarch gives interesting information as to the care Brutus took to make sure the games would be organized on a grand scale, while Appian indirectly confirms that the whole affair was contrived to sway public opinion in favour of the two chief conspirators. He describes how a paid group shouted for their recall and the rest of the audience was beginning to join in, when Octavian intervened: he had just arrived in Rome and was laying himself out to conciliate the urban plebs and the veterans, especially by grants of money. Then, Appian tells us, 'crowds ran in and stopped the games until the demand for the two men's recall was checked' (*B. Civ.* 3.24).

It is worth reflecting on these various instances, spontaneous or otherwise, of the use of public spectacles to express political feelings. Those who doubt that there was such a thing as public opinion in the ancient world, and Rome in particular, should consider whether its existence is not proved by the fact that a political message (disguised as a literary fiction) could be addressed simultaneously to tens of thousands of citizens with the avowed intention of persuading them to call for Brutus's return and arousing them, if need be, to violent action. If Roman public opinion expressed itself in oblique and allegorical ways, that is a cultural peculiarity which could be paralleled elsewhere, for instance Biblical or Shakespearian allusions in Anglo-Saxon political language. Generally speaking, the system of education in ancient times was such as to make men particularly sensitive to word-play and obscure references of all kinds, which is why we find it so difficult at times to understand Lucilius or the Roman comic writers, or even Cicero's letters. What is interesting is to note the kind of public to whom the allusions are addressed. Clearly, for instance, there is a difference of level between the surviving fragments of the two most celebrated authors of 'mimes' in Caesar's time, Publilius Syrus and his rival Laberius, and classical tragic or even comic writers. The authors of mimes dealt with day-to-day events, somewhat after the fashion of French *chansonniers* (but for a very wide public).[18] They expressly took sides in current political issues, in trenchant verses whose application was not always clear ('*Felix improbitas optimorum est calamitas*: the prosperity of evil is a disaster for the good.') Sometimes they spoke in their own name and joined issue with those in power, like Laberius, an *eques* and a successful dramatist who had the misfortune to fall foul of Caesar. The latter humiliated him by making him appear on the stage himself in 46, thus forfeiting his equestrian rank, but made amends with a present of 500,000 sesterces which enabled him to regain it.[19] This strange duel between Caesar and the satirist, played out at one remove, so to speak, aroused various reactions in different quarters (including Cicero, then a senator); on the whole it redounded to the dictator's credit, as showing him to be a man of humour and clemency.

In the case of Laberius, where the people were witnesses, spectators and actors at one and the same time, the allusions and attacks were transparent enough. The use of classics, including tragedies in the Greek style, seems at first sight more esoteric, and we may wonder what public was literate enough to appreciate it. But, as we have seen, theatre audiences were far from being an undifferentiated mass: senators, magistrates, knights and rich bourgeois were present in their seats of honour, and these cultivated folk would be the first to pick up and relish an allusion. Perhaps, too, we should not underrate the general cultural level of the population: it was often from works of this kind that they first learnt to read. Nor should one exaggerate the difficulty of interpreting classical texts to fit modern events. The texts, after all, generally convey relatively straightforward ideas and sentiments, and one can find in them what one is looking for; while the language had not changed so much in a century or two as to be beyond comprehension. None the less, it must be recognized that Roman theatre audiences in the last century of the Republic were politicized to a remarkable extent.

Trials and lawsuits

Another type of occasion on which public opinion often made itself felt was at important trials. One is inclined to say 'political trials', but this does not really apply to Rome: on the one hand there was no mechanism of the parliamentary type implying the political responsibility of governments, and on the other we know of very few trials that were exclusively political in the modern sense, which is usually pejorative. Happily, the forensic history of republican Rome presents very few parallels to the French Revolutionary tribunal or the Moscow trials. Contrariwise, the idea of political responsibility had not emerged—it is only in modern representative regimes that it has, very slowly, become disentangled from civil and criminal responsibility—and there was thus no legal distinction in Rome between political, criminal and even civil justice. Originally and in principle, offences falling within these categories were judged by the people, i.e., in the last resort at least, by the *comitia centuriata* or *tributa*. The decisive session of the assembly at which the vote was taken was preceded, as we have seen, by a series of official preparatory meetings (*contiones*) at which the charge was brought, the witnesses heard, the defence put forward and the case debated. It is clear that as long as this solemn form of judicial proceeding continued, the whole people, and therefore public opinion, was directly involved in every trial. It expressed itself in accordance with rules and procedures which, on the whole, differed little from those of the legislative and electoral assemblies; thus Polybius (6.14.4) considered that the Roman people 'alone [had] the right to confer honours and inflict punishment' because it elected its rulers and office-holders and was their ultimate judge. We may perhaps imagine or guess, from accounts that may be embellished by tradition, that the setting and atmosphere of a judicial assembly were more dramatic and spectacular than those of an electoral or legislative one. The accused, even if of high rank, must have done all they could to influence the people who were to judge them, and the issue was even more important to them than an election. The people, for their part, did not hesitate to show their feelings; but in any case the final decision rested with them.

Things changed around the beginning of the second century BC, and especially after 149. Criminal justice was gradually withdrawn from the people's competence by the creation, one after the other, of a number of standing courts or 'divisions' each specializing in a particular range of offences; these were defined in special laws, which generally laid down the procedure and duration of the trial, the number of witnesses, the composition and functioning of the jury, the penalty and the manner of passing sentence. Ths multiplication of special courts certainly improved the law by specifying counts of indictment and distinguishing penalties for particular acts. In one important respect it added to the safeguards enjoyed by the accused, as the death penalty was expressly excluded. But the essential though indirect consequence of the new system was to deprive the people in practice of its judicial rights, as there was no appeal against decisions of the standing courts. (For this reason, incidentally, the accused was nearly always given an opportunity, at a particular stage of the trial, to avoid sentence by going into voluntary exile.) Juries, as we have seen, were always recruited on a very narrow basis: until 123 BC, those of the permanent courts were drawn exclusively from the Senate. From 123 to 70 they were senators or *equites*, chosen according to circumstances and to the nature of the crime. From 70 to 46 there was a third panel (*decuria*) of *tribuni aerarii* (cf. Chapter VI above), who were also a privileged order. The only court which could be considered fairly representative of the whole population was that of the *centumviri*, which makes its appearance in the second century BC. This, however, was not concerned with criminal matters but chiefly with important cases of inheritance; the *centumviri* were elected, three from each tribe (thus actually 105 in number), without any special qualifications as far as we know. In fiscal matters, to try disputes between taxpayers and *publicani*, in the provinces at least courts were set up with *recuperatores* (small juries) chosen from among citizens of the first class. Apart from these two exceptions, criminal justice was henceforth in the hands of the privileged orders, to the exclusion of the people.

This was the more important since a large part of 'criminal' justice concerned what might be called political matters, viz. charges which, by their nature, could scarcely be brought against any but magistrates or those who in one way or another exercised a measure of public authority. This applied to perhaps the most celebrated of the standing courts, the *quaestio de repetundis* for the recovery of sums illegally exacted by office-holders. Other offences like that of treason (*majestas*), i.e. any infringement of the state's internal or external sovereignty, might in theory be committed by any citizen, but in practice these charges too were unlikely to be brought against any but members of the ruling class. The same might be said of the embezzlement of public money (*peculatus*) and electoral corruption, which latter could only be practised by candidates or perhaps their agents.

As regards offences by the governing class, therefore, it can be said that most criminal trials were a regular aspect of political life, compensating to some extent for what was otherwise a major hiatus in public law, viz. the absence of political responsibility: for Roman magistrates, unlike those of Greece, were not obliged, in the regular course of things, to render any account of their stewardship other than in a purely financial sense. Our sources hardly enable us to provide any formal statistics, but they make it clear that in the second and especially the first century BC it was far from unusual for a man in public life to be called to account before a jury. Statesmen who, like Cicero, escaped having to face charges in this way can be counted on the fingers of one hand. There are many possible reasons why such trials should have become a kind of institution. The law itself offered temptations to plaintiffs in the form of financial gain and especially perhaps the hope of advancing their own careers by supplanting the magistrates whom they accused; a fair number of such cases are known to us.[20] Ambitious young men of the senatorial or equestrian *ordo* might wish to prove or try their skill in the courts, to make their name by securing a conviction, to win political or monetary rewards, to avenge some family discomfiture or establish themselves as clients of a particular leader. But again, all this was chiefly of concern to the political class. Such trials were also of close interest to the legal profession, since, apart from plaintiffs or defendants who were members of the Senate (and who might themselves be jurists or advocates), there came into being at the close of the Republic a class of lawyers of more modest origin, knights or citizens of *municipia,* who do not appear to have had political ambitions but were content with the fees they received for their services despite the restrictions of the *Lex Cincia.*

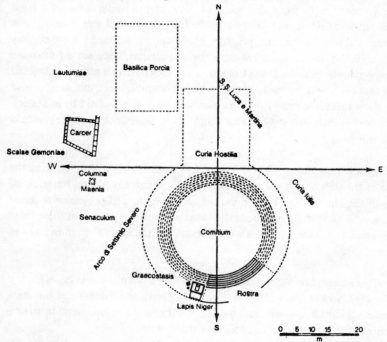

IV Reconstruction of the Comitium in the republican period: the Rostra and the *tribunal Aurelium* (after F. Coarelli). Scale in metres.

Even so, only a narrow circle of a few hundred individuals were thus interested in trials in the same way as in other public events. What of the people itself, and how did citizens react to being almost completely excluded from the administration of criminal justice? Did they remain aloof from the stormy world of the courts which, in some ways, was simply a further dimension of politics, or were court sentences subject to ultimate endorsement or reversal by public opinion? There is no straightforward answer, but at any rate one fact is clear: even when Roman justice was removed into the hands of the privileged orders it continued, until the very end, to be administered publicly, in the full blaze of daylight. A Roman criminal trial never lost the ritual and spectacular character that marked all litigation from the earliest times: it was a set piece, a grandiose performance which lent itself admirably to histrionics and, by its very nature, presupposed an audience. The audience was, of course, in the first place the court itself—a large jury of 50 or 75 members presided over by a senior magistrate, usually a praetor, sometimes in special cases an ex-consul. But besides the court and lawyers there was a multitude of witnesses, friends and clients of the accused and his accusers (who might themselves be numerous), as well as a throng of bystanders and sight-seers, Forum habitués to whom a trial was an absorbing entertainment. In addition—and this is the most important point here—there were crowds of partisans in the modern sense of the term, who did not hesitate to interfere at the behest of politicians and agitators.

Trials in republican times took place in the Comitium or the Forum,[21] the most convenient sites from the point of view of publicity. The only legal requirement was that the venue must not be further out of Rome than the first milestone. Subject to this, the praetors could set up a court wherever they liked; in 210, for instance, to reassure the population, they sat *ad piscinam publicam*, no doubt near the Porta Capena (Livy 23.32.4). The magistrate would take his seat on a wooden dais, attended by his council, assessors, scribes and ushers. Each magistrate had his own court, and all of them could be in session at once. Sometimes two magistrates might even announce that they would hear the same case:

> About the same time [47 BC] the praetor M. Caelius Rufus, espousing the cause of the debtors, at the beginning of his magistracy placed his tribunal close to the chair of G. Trebonius, the city praetor, and promised to assist anyone who should appeal about the valuation and the payments to be fixed by an arbitrator, in accordance with Caesar's arrangements when present in Rome. (Caesar, *B. Civ.* 3.20)

Thus there were days when the Forum was literally 'full of courts', as Cicero put it (2 *Verr.* 5.143). Even the standing courts with their dozens of jurymen sometimes sat simultaneously, and sometimes the jurymen had to go from one to another, which could give rise to shady manoeuvres:

The insane scoundrel [Verres in 70 BC] thought that he could manage a supplementary ballot of the same kind for the judges who were to try himself, by the help of Quintus Curtius, president of his own criminal court. (Cicero, 2 *Verr.* 1.158)

When there was a jury it sat at the foot of the tribunal, but on seats raised above ground level. On either side were benches for the prosecuting and defending lawyers, witnesses and perhaps the public. The term *subsellia* denoted either the 'bar' or the jurymen's bench, so that if a man had been both a juryman and a barrister in the course of his career he was said to have 'sat on both benches' (*in utrisque subselliis*).[22] Whenever possible, courts sat in the open. In bad weather, or for lack of space, use may have been made of the basilicas adjoining the Forum, the Aemilia to the north and the Sempronia to the south; in imperial times there were many more basilicas and the various courts were housed in them. What was perhaps the first permanent structure for judicial purposes, the *Aurelium tribunal* or *gradus Aurelii,* was apparently built around 80 BC; in any case it was new in about 74. It seems to have consisted of a wall in front of which the dais could be placed, and curved tiers of steps as in a theatre. It is unlikely that this building could have sufficed for all the trials that took place, but we do not know according to what rules it was used for one case or another. B. Lugli suggests that it may have been situated behind Caesar's rostrum, and that the semicircular wall that is still seen there may have been part of it.[23] In any case the structure was designed to accommodate a large audience. Cicero even claims that Flaccus's accuser chose it for this reason:

Then there is that unpopularity over the Jewish gold. This is presumably the reason why this case is being heard not far from the Aurelian steps. It was for this particular charge, Laelius, that you sought this site and that crowd. You know how vast a throng it is, how close-knit, and what influence it can have in public meetings. I will speak in a whisper like—this—, just loud enough for the jury to hear; for there is no shortage of men to incite this crowd against me and all men of goodwill. (*Pro Flacco* 66)

In such a setting, and given its basic character, a Roman trial was a spectacle of the first order. The 'stars' were of course the accused in mourning garb, accompanied by their families similarly attired, sometimes their clients and friends. But the magistrates, jurymen and counsel for either side, who were often eminent persons, also attracted a faithful audience. The tempo was determined by the solemn ritual of the oral proceedings. Nothing can have been more impressive than the oath-taking by the jurymen, who for this purpose turned towards the Forum at the foot of the Rostra. All the circumstances were such as to justify and call forth the fieriest eloquence. Roman oratory involved a command of various 'registers'—legal language, of course, but also the kind of rhetoric that appealed to crowds—as well as what the treatises call *actio*, the art of delivery, including appropriate bearing and gestures.[24] The reading of the indictment, the examination of witnesses, the presentation of exhibits, speeches for the prosecution and defence—all this lent itself admirably to theatrical performances by great advocates who were also great artists. There is no more typical example than Cicero's perorations: the eloquence of his appeal turns everyone into actors as well as himself—character witnesses and friends of the accused, the defendant himself and, not least, his family. For instance:

> To this poor boy, a suppliant to you and to your children, gentlemen, you will by your decision give guidance in his way of life. If you acquit his father, you will show him by practical illustration what kind of citizen he ought to be; but if you take his father from him, you will show that you have no reward to offer for a plan of life that has been virtuous, unwavering and responsible. He is now of an age to be affected by his father's grief, but not yet old enough to bring his father help, and so he begs you not to increase his grief by his father's tears nor his father's sorrow by his own weeping. He turns his eyes to me, his expression appeals to me for aid and somehow his tears call upon me to keep faith and remember that position of distinction which I once promised to his father for saving our country. Have pity on his family, gentlemen, on a valiant father, have pity on the son. Whether it be for his family's sake or for his ancient lineage or for the man himself, preserve for the Republic an illustrious and gallant name. (*Pro Flacco* 106)

Public sympathy was constantly appealed to in this way, and the people, although deprived by law of its judicial sovereignty, recovered it in part thanks to an indirect and unofficial, but constant influence over the courts. That influence might at times overstep the bounds of legality, when public reactions impeded the course of justice. An advocate might take advantage of them for his own ends: Cicero, for instance, took advantage of the public's attitude to prevent Verres and his friend Curtius from 'packing' the court to their advantage:

> Had I not had the strong help of the people, who supported my resistance to his move with loud shouts of anger and abuse, Curtius would have proceeded, by means of this supplementary ballot, to draw upon your own panel, to which it was important for me to have the freest possible access, and would without the least justification have secured for his own court the men whom Verres selected for removal. (2 *Verr.* 1.158)

Sometimes public interest in a trial developed into a riot. In 58 Vatinius called in Clodius's bands to halt the proceedings that were being conducted against him by the praetor C. Memmius:

I ask you, Vatinius, whether anyone in this State, since the foundation of Rome, has ever appealed to the tribunes of the commons to be saved from pleading. Has any accused person mounted the tribunal of his judge and violently thrust him down from it, scattered the benches, thrown down the urns, and, in short, in order to upset a trial, committed all those excesses which were the very reason why trials were established? Do you not know that Memmius then took to flight? That your accusers had to be rescued from your hands and from those of your accomplices? That the presidents of the neighbouring courts were turned out of their seats? (Cicero, *In Vatinium* 34)

This type of behaviour was in fact not so uncommon as Cicero makes out. In 212, when justice was still administered by the *comitia*, contractors for supplies to the army in Spain who were being tried on a charge of barratry, having tried in vain to persuade a friendly tribune to intervene, burst into the electoral enclosure with their friends and clients and overthrew the urns just as voting was about to begin. In 89 the praetor A. Sempronius Asellio, who had offered legal protection to some debtors being sued by creditors, was done to death by the latter at his own tribunal—not while hearing the case, it is true, but when sacrificing in front of the temple of Concord (Appian, *B. Civ.* 1.54).

The fact is that trials, which might last several days and even weeks, acquired an importance over and above their judicial character. Taking place regularly in the public eye, they became a pretext and occasion for political agitation when the people either seized on political or ideological issues or sought to discover powerful interests at work behind the ostensible proceedings. There are many well-known examples. It was, for instance, the scandalous acquittal of certain obviously guilty pro-magistrates which moved C. Gracchus in 123 BC to propose his law on the judicial system, the apple of discord of the Republic. *Causes célèbres* like that of the Vestals in 114 and 113, or the trial of Rutilius Rufus in 92, were first-class political events. The mechanism by which they became so was in general very simple: a magistrate, usually a tribune, would take the matter into his hands and summon official meetings (*contiones*) to debate it. Between 74 and 66 a murky story of murder and legacy-hunting involving rich bourgeois of the municipality of Larinum became a political issue on account of their party affiliations. One of them, Aulus Cluentius, accused his stepfather Abbius Oppianicus of having tried to poison him, and secured his condemnation by a senatorial court which he was suspected of having bribed. L. Quinctius, a tribune of the plebs who had defended Oppianicus, unleashed a violent campaign against the court and senatorial justice in general:

Immediately upon the conviction of Oppianicus, L. Quinctius, an ardent demagogue, whose ears were set to catch every breath of private gossip or public harangue, felt that here was a chance of using the unpopularity of the Senate for his own advancement, considering how poor a reputation with the people the Senatorial courts enjoyed at the time. He delivered several violent and impressive harangues, loudly protesting as tribune of the people that the jurors had been bribed to condemn an innocent man: 'This touches every one of us,' he said. 'Fair trial is a thing of the past: not a man is safe who has a rich enemy.' ... The judge Fidiculanius was tried twice: for Lucius Quinctius, with the lawless and unruly mass meetings which he held daily, had excited a violent prejudice against him. (Cicero, *Pro Cluentio* 77, 103)

The pretext was still clearer in another famous case, the trial of Milo for killing Clodius in 52. The murder had first dumbfounded and then roused to fury Clodius's friends and supporters, as well as the urban plebs whom he had won over by means of his grain distribution law and organized in quasi-military bands. Cicero's scholiast Asconius has left us a long and detailed account of the trial. As armed bands were preventing the elections from being held, public opinion called for Pompey to be made dictator. The Senate, after commanding him to take care for the safety of the Republic, appointed him sole consul (Asconius, 14). The tribunes held several meetings to debate the circumstances of the murder.

> Q. Pompeius, C. Sallustius and T. Munatius Plancus, tribunes of the plebs, made especially hostile speeches against Milo and Cicero himself, who had defended Milo so vigorously. Most of the people, too, were hostile not only to Milo but also to Cicero for undertaking the defence. (Asconius, p. 37 C)

Pompey having rushed through a special judiciary law, the trial at last began:

> As M. Marcellus began to interrogate... he was so frightened by the disorderly behaviour of the crowds of Clodius's partisans that Domitius allowed him to take refuge on the tribunal to escape the worst violence, both Marcellus and Milo having pleaded for this. Cn. Pompeius, who was near the *aerarium* at that time, was also alarmed by the shouting and promised Domitius to come down next day to the Forum with a guard, which he did. This overawed Clodius's followers, who kept silent for two days while the witnesses were being heard...
>
> When the court rose at about the tenth hour T. Munatius urged the people to come in large numbers to the next day's session and not allow Milo to escape punishment, but to make their opinion and feelings clear to the

jurymen as they voted. Next day, the most important one of the trial (the sixth before the Ides of April), the shops were shut throughout the City and Pompey placed guards in the Forum and at all the entrances to it. He himself took up a position near the *aerarium*, as he had on the previous day, surrounded by picked troops.

The proceedings began by casting lots for the jurymen, after which the Forum was as quiet as it is possible for a public place to be... When Cicero began to speak he was interrupted by the shouts of Clodius's men, whom even the presence of soldiers could not frighten into silence. Consequently he spoke with less than his usual firmness. (Asconius, pp. 40-2 C)

The intervention of Pompey's soldiers was indeed prophetic: it sounded the knell of the free Republic and, by the same token, of Roman political and forensic eloquence. The Roman mob thought it had gained a victory by intimidating Cicero and driving Milo into exile; but all it had done was to prepare the way for civil war and thereby the Empire.[25]

CONCLUSION
Structure and communication

————·•·————

I HAVE SET OUT in this book to analyse Roman political life at the level of what may be called the civic grass-roots, ignoring the more exalted but much narrower sphere in which the drama of politics was played out. This was the sphere of the 'political class', consisting essentially of the magistrates and pro-magistrates (about 50 persons at most in any given year), the Senate (300 members, afterwards 500 or 600, mostly ex-magistrates who expected to hold high office again), and, from 123 BC, a few hundred *equites* who were on the panel of jurymen. This very small collection of people — an oligarchy in the strict etymological sense — constituted the Roman political class in combination with what may be called their entourage: friends or relatives from the senatorial or equestrian class who had chosen to stay out of the limelight and not go into politics on their own account — Atticus is a typical example — or else members of the dependent classes: clients, freedmen and even slaves. These associates might actually be the moving force behind a given policy, either as the drafters of texts or as managers of the financial interests of their friends and patrons (e.g. the celebrated Philotimus). A study of this class and of its role in the decision-making process would be very interesting as part of an in-depth analysis of Roman political as opposed to civic life. For various reasons I have chosen not to embark on this. In the first place, politics at the level of great men and great decisions is the field about which our sources tell us most, and which has therefore been most fully studied. Earlier and more recent works like those by F. Münzer, M. Gelzer, R. Syme, L. Ross Taylor, E. Badian, myself, C. Meier and E. Gruen have thrown light on its social composition, groupings and divisions and have gone far towards working out what C. Meier calls a 'grammar' of Roman politics, based on such major dichotomies as that between rules and exceptions, the public and the private sphere and so on. The point of view adopted in this book, on the other hand, has hardly been explored up to now, because the relevant facts are largely hidden from us: the ordinary citizen, the 'little man' who is important only in the mass, figures scarcely at all in sources that are generally annalistic and nothing more.

The foregoing chapters, though only a brief outline of the subject, suggest some tentative conclusions which, I believe, are such as to modify the somewhat rigid conception of the Roman city that emerges from a study of public law alone. A few points may be emphasized.

Firstly, civic life in the middle and later period of the Republic presents itself as a genuine structure, a coherent whole with a powerful logic of its own. Naturally each element of this structure stands in a relatively fixed relationship to the others, and any modification of one of them sooner or later brings about a modification of the others. Civic life, as we have seen, went on in three main spheres: military, financial and political (including judicial). In each of these spheres, Roman citizenship signified a complex of rights and duties, advantages and disadvantages. The spheres were intimately linked, as it was unthinkable and perverse for a citizen to be excluded or to exclude himself from decisions that concerned his life and property. Rome, like other ancient cities, saw a very close and direct connection between the greatness and prosperity of the community and that of its individual citizens. Nothing could be more foreign to this mental universe than the kind of alienation whereby a state is thought of as incarnate in a single man or a transcendent cause, a church or a God. To give one's life for the City, as the individual might easily be called on to do, was merely an extreme instance of self-sacrifice for the sake of a well-understood interest, such as the survival of one's own children. Cicero, in a very Stoical passage, enumerates in hierarchical order the social links and the duties they entail: first come duties towards the human race, but the City is uncontestably in second place because it comprises the greatest number of things common to all mankind: 'the Forum [political decisions], temples [religion], colonnades, streets, statutes, laws, courts, rights of suffrage' (*De Off.* 1.17.53). Thus all aspects of civil life form a single system which is both restrictive, as it is concerned essentially with inter-personal relations, and native to the individual, since without it there can be no real life at all. Thus in the last resort all the City's demands (military, fiscal and civic duties) are demands that the citizen makes upon himself. They are not imposed from outside, by some transcendent reality, but proceed from the simple logic of the implicit contract that exists among free individuals. Necessary constraints are only a form of liberty; they are not arbitrary, but form a logical and firmly-based structure.

But, while each citizen is bound to the City by identical legal ties, in practice the degree of participation or, if the term is preferred, compulsion is not the same for everyone. Having first admitted and guaranteed juridical equality, the Roman city at once recognized the *de facto* inequality of different individuals and groups. For a long time this physical, economic and social inequality was treated by the City with indifference, as an accident of nature and fortune. But, having recognized it at the outset, the state was bound eventually to reduce its consequences to an endurable level. Hence, in due course, the City organized itself in accordance with a central principle, the keystone of its structure, designed to allocate rights and duties, burdens and benefits, to each citizen as strictly and precisely as possible in conformity with the common interest. This was the system or structure (*ordo, ratio*) of the census, which, with the various classifications based on it, was the centre and foundation of the Roman state. Everything depended on it: army recruitment, the assessment and collection of taxes, the organization of political assemblies, eligibility for office, and membership of the political class in general. The distinctions on which it was based were no longer merely natural or social; they were recognized as an inherent part of the citizen's identity, conferring on him a definite role and status in the official hierarchy.

It would be wrong, however, to think that the hierarchy was merely one of wealth. By taking responsibility for defining and classifying citizens and, in a sense, assigning to them their specific being, the city to a large extent corrected the accidents of birth and wealth and effected a compromise, varying from one period to another, between individual merit and the collective interest. This voluntary hierarchy among citizens was established through the censors, as far as possible in accordance with the great principle of 'proportional' or 'geometrical' equality. Broadly speaking, military and fiscal duties and political responsibilities were related to the individual's place in the census register. The rich, noble and powerful were expected to supply the main military and fiscal effort and to play the chief part in forming and executing political decisions; those to whom fortune had been unkind were relieved of these various duties and responsibilities.

Such a system deserves to be called a structure, since the test of history shows to what a striking degree its component parts were interdependent. The census system as I have described it worked as it was intended to until about the close of the war with Hannibal, before gradually disintegrating from the mid-second century onwards. First to disappear was the fiscal part of the system: after 167 BC successful overseas conquest made it possible to exempt citizens from direct taxation. This was to the immediate advantage of the most wealthy, who alone paid taxes, and it also created an imbalance by putting an end to the close link between military and fiscal contributions. The poor were not slow to claim a corresponding financial advantage: in 133 parts of the *ager publicus* were directly assigned to them, and in 123 they were assured of a subsistence ration of grain at a price subsidized by the state. Before long a second portion of the structure collapsed: the rich could not long continue to bear the burden of the blood-tax unaided. In the first place there were not enough of them, and secondly their warlike spirit and sense of military vocation declined somewhat towards the mid-second century. At the same time increasingly victorious campaigns were making war a profitable business, so that when, in 107, Marius waived the property qualification he had no trouble finding volunteers among the proletariat. As we have seen, this limited measure did not at once transform the citizens' militia into an army of professionals; the process was much slower, lasting for nearly half a century, and indeed not reaching its final stage until the Empire. None the less, it was of great importance. From Marius's time onward, the section of the civic population which was, so to speak, jostling the political class from below no longer had experience of active service, which was still compulsory for those of higher rank. Meanwhile the proletarianized armies, which after 90 BC were recruited from parts of Italy that had only recently been naturalized, felt less and less affinity with Roman civic traditions; instead they were actuated by personal loyalty to their leaders, professional pride and dislike of civilians, whom they regarded as their natural prey. The army thus became a dangerous instrument of civil war, a party or a state within the state, as was seen after Caesar's death.

Two main elements of the civic structure having suffered profound modification, the third — namely citizens' participation in political decisions — could not long remain intact. In this field the process was lengthier and more complex than in the other two — politics is not an exact science — but within a century the logical conclusion worked itself out: the mass of citizens, relieved of military and fiscal duties, were finally deprived of their role in the assemblies also. Although, as a matter of strict law, the *comitia* survived into the first century AD, they were an empty formality after Augustus's basic reform in AD 5 whereby the election of consuls and praetors really depended on *destinatio* by a preliminary assembly of senators and certain *equites*. Despite these survivals the *comitia* had ceased to be the real locus of political life: Caesar's dictatorship and the Triumvirate, by establishing a system of personal power with a strong military flavour, had shifted the centre of gravity and taken all the meaning out of political elections and the adoption of laws.

This evolution, however, was neither uniform nor straightforward. At the end of the second and beginning of the first century BC the people, including its poorest sections, came to enjoy a larger measure of influence on political decisions. The juridical guarantees of individual freedom against coercion by magistrates were enlarged and improved down to the year 123 BC. Electoral procedures were made more democratic and freed from improper influence by the secret ballot, introduced between 139 and 107. The increasing importance of the *comitia tributa*, in which distinctions of wealth were less important than in the *centuriata*, certainly enabled many citizens of humble degree to make their voice heard during the period before the Social War of 90-89. Despite the two grave crises of 133 and 121, political conflicts were generally settled within the legal framwork and violence was not yet resorted to as a matter of course.

It was not until 101 that a law was passed by men voting under duress from bravoes armed with clubs; only in 88 did a Roman army first march against the City to reverse the *comitia*'s decision as between two rival commanders. Nevertheless the disappearance or transformation of the military and fiscal systems was accompanied by electoral changes which in time profoundly affected the exercise of political sovereignty. The massive influx of Italian citizens during the century which followed the Social War enlarged the civic population from

400,000 to a million or more, though in Rome itself there is no sign of any appreciable increase in the number of actual voters save in exceptional cases such as 70 BC and perhaps 57, on the occasion of Cicero's recall. In this way the gap widened between the citizen's legal status and his exercise of political rights, and this brought about a sharper geographical and sociological cleavage between inhabitants of the City (by birth or residence) and those of the rest of Italy. At the same time there was a reversal of the relative influence of the urban and rural population in the two principal assemblies. Although theoretically confined to four of the 35 tribes, the urban plebs came to predominate. But a distinction must be drawn: the new dominant class really consisted of privileged citizens, still enrolled in their original rural tribes, who lived in Rome or could get there easily to exercise their voting rights. In the absence of any representative principle within the civic body, the inordinate expansion of the City's territory and electorate brought about an inversion of political values. The predominance of the rural masses which can be detected as late as the end of the third century BC gave place to a predominance of rural notables at the very time when the franchise was theoretically enlarged. This suffices to explain the fact that the political 'dialogue' of the *comitia* gives the impression of having become increasingly insignificant.

For this reason I have tried to describe, by way of counterpoint, the birth or development of a kind of political language which increasingly supplanted the official one. The real urban masses—under-represented in the *comitia,* if not wholly absent from them—consisted in the main of freedmen, juridically confined to the four tribes, or new citizens who were rootless and proletarianized. Although without influence in the centuriate and even tribal assemblies, they made their views felt in a fairly effective though unofficial way, on occasions that were less fortuitous than might be supposed. In Rome, as in the Hellenistic cities, crowds assembled periodically for great ceremonies of religious or civic origin, such as triumphs and public games, the regular succession of which came to constitute a kind of liturgical year. The original purpose of these events was certainly to promote social cohesion. They were designed to enable the whole City to contemplate its own glory or rejoicing, and to unite in apparent unanimity the masses and the élite, the citizens and their chosen leaders. By degrees, however, this psychological framework was superseded. These imposing scenes, which were meant to overawe as well as to delight by their splendour, became an opportunity for the expression of something like public opinion. The citizens, assembled in a less orderly and hierarchical manner than in the official *comitia*, took advantage of their leaders' presence at civic displays to express forthright opinions on individuals and matters of public concern, with an astonishing freedom of language and attitude. Although such manifestations had of course no legal status, they were so regular and frequent that they must in the long run have affected the machinery of decision-taking. At least for the political class, they provided what might be significant indices of public opinion.

The more skilful or fortunate leaders were able to manipulate this opinion and sometimes, through it, to influence events more effectively than by the traditional channels.

This alternative political language, which could give or restore a voice to those who lacked one, also had its disorderly and disruptive aspects. A crowd might easily turn into a hired mob or an armed gang, which was more and more likely to be organized on the military pattern that alarmed citizens by its deadly efficacy in Sulla's time. From Lepidus to Catiline, from Clodius to Milo, political leaders (of the second rank, it is true) all cherished the idea of imposing their will at the head of a band of legions: if they had no regular troops they would organize private armies in imitation of the real thing, and the Forum and Campus Martius from time to time became arenas of civil war.

Having spoken of structures, we may now consider mechanisms. A political system may be considered as a living organism or a machine, after Easton's model,[1] designed to respond to stimuli. We shall see presently what kind of questions and responses are involved; but first a remark or two on the way the system worked. We are struck by the very high level and density of relations and communications that united the Roman civic body in every direction. The number of citizens first of all: the demographic dimension of civic life is remarkable in itself and quite extraordinary by the standards of the ancient world. There is no parallel in antiquity to the way in which the Roman state succeeded, without bursting its bounds, in enabling hundreds of thousands of citizens to live and work together for centuries, regularly absorbing individuals and populous communities, bringing the mosaic of Italian peoples into a single Romanized pattern, and conquering the loyalty of all its subjects by the relative freedom of entry into the upper orders of society and the political class. Long before the example of monarchical and republican France at the conclusion of the eighteenth century, or England in 1688, Rome transformed Italy into a nation, unquestionably the first in history, anticipating by two thousand years the famous definitions of French nationalism and Renan's *'vouloir vivre ensemble'*. It is highly characteristic of the Roman system that the Social War, Rome's last conflict with the Italians and the only major one, was fought against 'enemies' who were clamouring for Roman citizenship and, though defeated, obtained it by force of arms.

The citizens of this large body were, moreover, in close and more or less permanent touch with one another. The civic calendar, as we have seen, was an extremely full one. The census took place only once in five years (though senators, *equites* and others might attend it more than once in their lives), but there was a military levy almost every year, combined with the collection of taxes until 167 BC. Elections occupied at least a couple of weeks every year. The voting of laws must have taken up a good deal more time in some years when, as we know, at least a dozen measures were passed. In addition each of these procedures involved several preliminary meetings, attendance at which was not compulsory but which sometimes attractéd crowds. Games and shows occurred regularly and, at the close of the Republic, occupied many weeks of each year. To this were added triumphs, funerals and, as we have seen, escorts for magistrates leaving or returning to the City. Finally the courts sat for most of the year, and the last century of the Republic witnessed an increasing number of trials of great political importance. The citizen's physical presence at all these events was required or vigorously urged with a frequency quite unmatched in our modern democracies. Each of them, moreover, involved thousands and sometimes tens of thousands of people travelling to the City, not only from the surrounding countryside but from the whole of citizen Italy: anyone was allowed to come, and everyone came who could. One has the impression that civic life, even more than economic life, set up continual migratory movements throughout Italy. Groups and individuals travelled regularly to Rome and back, and political life flowed through society like a bloodstream.

Furthermore, these were not inorganic movements affecting individuals only. The social and political structure based firmly on property and also on the tribes, which were partly territorial communities, placed each individual in a group, within which alone his opinion and his vote were effective. In a sense, therefore, Rome was a segmentary society; but solidarity among its members took many forms. There was a geographical dimension; the territorial or urban community, the *municipium* or colony, tribe or region. Here influences and associations were based on local interests and particularism, which were still lively in the first century BC; but these were often transferred to the Roman arena, where conflicts were fought out and alliances came into play within the framework of Roman politics and ostensibly in Roman terms. Groups would come to the City in attendance on one or several notables; there would be meetings and reunions; assurances and watchwords would be exchanged, and the parties would return home discomfited or triumphant. The accidents of political history sometimes made a particular region, tribe or city exceptionally important to the Roman, i.e. national, political game: thus between 65 and 45 there was general competition for the votes of the rich province of Cispadane Gaul, which became a Tom Tiddler's ground for fortune-seekers of all kinds.

In this way horizontal and geographical ties were complicated by vertical and social ones: the patron-client relationship, marriages, friendship, services rendered and returned. Personal links such as these pervaded Roman social life and naturally played a part in politics in the stricter sense; they were reinforced by the segmentary character of civic organization, though the two did not fully coincide. The principal leaders were surrounded by a profusion of groups, parties and influences, some based on family and geographical ties but many on voluntary associations and loyalties sealed on the battlefield or in the Forum, not to speak of financial and commercial links or simply political and ideological affinities. Almost every male citizen was thus involved in a network of relationships of all kinds, their density, ramifications and complications being all the greater because of the intertwining and overlapping of political and social connections, those freely chosen and those imposed by circumstances. This is a very different picture from the isolation of a medieval peasant stuck in his parish, sunk in ignorance and cut off from the world by the nearest forest and the local seigneur's hunting-ground.

The extreme density of Roman relationships implies — and this is what seems to me important — a very high level of communication and an intense mental and social life. Among these men involved in the same civic life there must have been a constant circulation of messages, constituting as a whole a refined political dialect. We have seen that in the Roman city, whatever the case might be in other political systems, everything was on a reciprocal basis. There was a permanent dialogue between the City and the citizen, between the state and its subjects, between those who gave and those who received orders. Even such a mandatory process as enlistment in the army depended in the first place on the individual's voluntary declaration to the censor; when the consul called up the new recruits individual cases could be examined, and there was an ultimate remedy in the shape of an appeal to the *tribuni plebis* against unfair treatment. At the moment of entry into service an oath was taken — hence a further dialogue — and, in the army itself, the commander gave orders in the form of an *adlocutio*, an address to his troops, which presupposed a civic consciousness on the soldier's part: this was the case from the first days of the Republic to its close. In more strictly political matters the need for dialogue was even clearer. Roman politics, as Mommsen said, were a matter of contract: the people had to be consulted, questions for decision had to be formally articulated and answered unambiguously. This involved the exchange and transmission of messages, both short and long, of which we have fairly numerous examples. Eloquence was a prerequisite for decision-taking, as before a question was put to the people it was often necessary to explain the issue, inform the voters and if possible convince them. It will be a new and fascinating task for coming historians to analyse the speeches that have come down to us, making allowance for distortions in the original recording and subsequent transmission, in order to identify as closely as possible the type of public to whom they were addressed. In certain cases, such as Cicero's two speeches on the agrarian law to the Senate and people respectively, it should be possible to make an analysis in depth of the cultural level and collective mentality of the audience concerned.

This line of enquiry leads to a surprising observation. What we already know of the Roman political dialogue, together with the analysis of assembly techniques and procedures, indicates that the cultural level of the Roman voter was remarkably high. Despite the overwhelming importance of eloquence and oral techniques, we should not forget that nearly all the operations and circumstances of civic life involved the frequent use of writing. Declarations to the censor were copied on to registers; texts of proposed laws were posted up, as were the names of candidates for office. Voting-tablets were used, on which the elector himself had to inscribe a few letters at least. Not least remarkable is the army use of tablets, already attested by Polybius, for the system of guard duty and passwords. We never hear of a Roman citizen being at a loss when called on to vote in an election (contrast Plutarch's story of the Athenian peasant asking Aristides to write his own name on an *ostrakon*) or, as in some new democracies at the present day, of ballots on which the candidates are distinguished for the benefit of the illiterate by different colours, pictures of animals etc. Such indications give the impression of what may almost be called a clerical civilization. This, of course, may be accounted for in two alternative ways. We may deduce from it that only a privileged minority generally took part in civic life, since it could not be fully lived without a fairly high degree of literacy, and that this minority, which is assumed to have been a small one, was thus effectively marked off from the poorer classes. Or, on the contrary, we may note the various signs that most of the citizen body took a remarkably large part in the different forms of communal life and, since this involved the use of writing, we may infer that the proportion of literates in the population, including that of Romanized Italy, was unusually high.

In my opinion the second of these interpretations is certainly the right one, unexpected as some of its consequences are. It confirms what is already suggested by other studies as regards the importance and prevalence of the written word in Graeco-Roman civilization.[2] Electoral and other graffiti and private receipts found at Pompeii point to a high standard of literacy among the male population, at least, of that small town. A similar conclusion is suggested by the opinion of certain world historians on the general level of urban Graeco-Roman civilization at its apogee, that in its demographic density and cultural level it achieved a degree of development that was not seen again in Europe until the century of the Enlightenment.[3] Nor is this really so unexpected. The ancient city-state, which was a political and cultural centre rather than a commercial or industrial one, extended a serried network of relationships above the rural community on which it was based. For various reasons a sufficient part of the population enjoyed enough leisure to 'invest' in education and culture, and the advanced development and rationalization of political life was an incentive to take full advantage of this possibility. In an earlier work I have tried to show that social advancement, which always to some extent presupposed political success, required a high level of culture even in the days before Rome possessed a bureaucracy in the proper sense. The first stage in the process was to belong to the wide circle of citizens, and this can hardly be imagined without a minimum degree of education.

It would be of the greatest interest to look beyond the basic requirement of the three Rs and try to discover what impact the need for education had on the political and civic attitudes of the mass of citizens. Certainly there is no lack of complaint, by actors or witnesses of civic life, as to the irrational or passive behaviour, the ignorance and coarseness of the multitude. Cicero remarks humorously that those to whom Rullus first expounded his land bill, despite its popular intention, could not make head or tail of his speech, which apparently was both rambling and bombastic. But there is evidence in a contrary sense: a man like Cicero, a veteran of the Forum and capable of a rabble-rousing speech when he chose, seems on the whole to have thought that men could always be persuaded by an appeal to reason and that if things were properly explained they would understand them. By and large a Roman political speech was a rational one which made the least possible use of surprise, emotional effects and appeals to authority.

Modern political science has introduced the concept of 'system' into the study of political institutions in a wide sense: i.e., according to organic or, less convincingly, cybernetic models, the idea of a set of elements combining to produce a certain effect. In other words, a system is designed to provide responses to stimuli or demands from the environment. In this book I have tried to analyse the political system of republican Rome from a global point of view. The viewpoint that I have deliberately adopted is perhaps not, after all, the best from which to judge its effects and the way it worked, since it is clear that the essential political decisions, those which commit the entire social organism in a profound and lasting way, were as a rule not taken in the popular domain that I have set out to describe. I have several times emphasized the sharp distinction within the citizen body between the mass of *cives* who are the subject of this book and what I have called the political class: broadly speaking, the higher orders of society, senators, knights, *publicani*, scribes and associates of various kinds. The main emphasis in the decision-taking process naturally falls on the Senate as the principal organ of deliberation and the formulation of policy. The study of this fairly small ruling circle is by now almost complete thanks to the convergent efforts of German and British historians in particular, whose researches cover questions of membership, issues, conflicts, divisions and realignments within the group. Of course much detailed study remains to be done, but at least the spade-work has been accomplished.

Less attention, it must be admitted, has been paid to discovering what kind of issues concerned the citizen body as a whole during the two or three centuries with which this book is concerned. Yet it is on the basis of this global appreciation that we can best reply to the fundamental question: how did Roman institutions work, what was their value and significance? As I have shown, a preliminary answer to this question was given by a contemporary historian and statesman, Polybius, who was familiar with the methods and conclusions of Greek political philosophy. His judgement is doubly interesting: in the first place he was writing of a dramatic stage of history, when it was beginning to be clear that sooner or later Rome would bring the whole inhabited world under its sway, and secondly his organicistic conception of human societies and the evolution of institutions is, in a way, very close to certain twentieth-century models. Polybius discussed these matters in a long excursus in Book Six of his *Histories*.

In his view, any global society and any set of institutions are finally to be judged by the degree of cohesion they impart to the nation that uses them. The stronger is the 'will to live together', the more social and political pressure will be exerted on the various parts that compose the whole and the more interdependence there will be between the different organs of the city and of government; in short, the more centripetal forces prevail over centrifugal ones, the more a state will be likely to prosper. From this point of view, according to Polybius, Rome was a privileged and exemplary society for two main reasons. Firstly at the constitutional level, in the narrow sense of governmental institutions: these were so well balanced that it was virtually impossible for any major conflict to arise between them. The people, Senate and magistrates each had a reasonable share of autonomy, of authority to make decisions, of duties and advantages. As a rule they had every incentive to come to terms and collaborate with one another rather than quarrel as in some other cities. Then, on the more general level of institutions, i.e. the totality of 'customs and usages', Rome was imbued with a collective sense of discipline which greatly reinforced social cohesion. This discipline, freely accepted, was not repressive only, but happily combined rewards and punishments, encouragement and repression, so that all Romans were patriotic and devoted to their city.

This clear and vigorous picture can, of course, be criticized in detail. Its chronological limits must also be borne in mind; it seems clear that Polybius himself, towards the end of his life (after 118 BC), realized that the machinery he so greatly admired was beginning to get out of gear. His interpretation is in itself coherent and attractive, but it dates from about 150 BC and describes the position about half a century earlier. The Republic was to last another 120 years, in the course of which the system manifestly went to rack and ruin. First there was a murderous conflict over the agrarian law; violence in the Forum became more and more commonplace; then came the period of wars between citizen armies, with brief monarchical interludes (Cinna, Sulla, Caesar), and finally a new regime, the Empire, which differed radically from its predecessor. All this is well known—perhaps too well: for the tramp of boots and clatter of weapons distract us from studying the real nature of the conflicts that divided citizens and the objectives they strove for. It is clear that a number of issues that our histories place in the forefront—those specifically concerned with power. i.e. attempts at monarchy, successful or otherwise, or with the make-up of the political class—were, in a sense, outside the immediate sphere of interest of the *populus*. The latter's intervention in this domain was always very limited: it could only express a preference between rival candidates belonging to the governing class, in accordance with the legal or traditional rules proper to that class. The Roman people never actually governed: this was ruled out by the property qualification which placed the magistracy out of the direct reach of the great majority of *cives*. In this respect the people was seldom an actor on the political stage, and almost exclusively a spectator.

It remains a problem, however, how in this typically oligarchic situation the people, while apparently deprived of control over its own affairs, nevertheless continued until the very end of the Republic to participate in electoral or judicial rites which seemed to concern only the political class, and how it managed to intervene so often, and with such passion and violence, to bring its views directly to bear. If Roman politics were really reduced to personal or gentilitial rivalries, the operation of the patron-client relationship would not suffice to account for the 'popularity' of one leader or another; nor could it be explained how the settling of accounts between politicians — to take the most typical example, the murder of Clodius by Milo — could have touched off popular movements that were clearly spontaneous to a large extent. In other words, the fact that the great majority of citizens had no chance of becoming magistrates did not in the least prevent them from being interested and concerned by the way in which the magistracy was exercised.

This was because the masses felt that the political game, though apparently confined to a very small group, was being played for stakes that concerned them directly. No doubt we should avoid speaking of 'political parties' and especially a 'popular party' in Rome, as has been too often done since the last century. On the other hand there was a type of political behaviour to which the phrase *populariter agere* applied perfectly well, and which was amply defined and exemplified in theoretical works, by Cicero in particular, and in the actions of those who practised it. To be a *popularis* was to curry favour with the populace, and, as Zvi Yavetz has brilliantly shown, this was not only a matter of political acts or proposals but also of ordinary speech and day-to-day behaviour: simplicity of language, good humour, lack of haughtiness, and a show of interest in the people's pleasures and hardships. From this point of view, for instance, when politicans competing for power and popular favour during the years 58-52 hired and maintained troops of gladiators it was not merely for strong-arm purposes but also to show that they understood and shared popular tastes.

However, popular favour and disfavour were not expressed solely at this elementary level. There was, of course, no such thing as a popular 'programme', but certain measures or proposals recur so often from the end of the second century onwards, in speeches and in political practice, that one is bound to regard them as reflecting some of the real issues that kept alive citizen interest in the contests of the Forum and the Campus Martius. The most obvious were of course those which brought immediate and tangible advantages to all or most of the citizen body: first the agrarian laws under Ti. Gracchus, then the corn distribution under C. Gracchus and his successors, as well as laws, senatorial decrees and praetorian actions against usury and for the relief of debtors. As a rule any politician who wanted to get public opinion firmly on his side had only to raise one or other of these questions. The conservatives were well aware of this and had no scruples about outbidding their 'popular' rivals in this field: examples are Livius Drusus in 123, his son in 91 and even Cato of Utica in 62. Nevertheless we know that proposals of this kind were sometimes defeated even without their opponents resorting to force, and this too must be explained. The most typical case is Rullus's agrarian bill in 63, which was reasonable and well conceived but was rejected as a result of Cicero's eloquence; the range and type of arguments that he used are worthy of close study.

At all events the people were able to discern their own interest, and usually bestowed their favour in return for immediate advantages. Thus, as Cicero often pointed out, the most clear-cut disputes arose between the advocates of 'popular' measures and those who objected on the grounds of the treasury's overriding interests or those of the privileged classes:

> Formerly those who followed this path and principle in affairs of state had far more to fear, for in many ways the desire of the masses and the advantage of the people did not agree with the public interest. A law to provide for voting by ballot was proposed by Lucius Cassius. The people thought that their liberty was at stake. The leaders of the State held a different opinion; in a matter that concerned the interests of the *optimates,* they dreaded the impetuosity of the masses and the licence afforded by the ballot. Tiberius Gracchus proposed an agrarian law. The law was acceptable to the people: the fortunes of the poorer classes seemed likely to be established. The *optimates* opposed it because they saw in it an incentive to dissension, and also thought that the State would be stripped of its champions by the eviction of the rich from their long-established tenancies. Gaius Gracchus brought forward a corn law. It was agreeable to the masses, for it provided food in abundance without work. Loyal citizens were against it because they thought that it was a call to the masses to desert industry for idleness, and saw that it was a drain upon the Treasury. (*Pro Sestio* 103)

> But they who pose as friends of the people, and who for that reason either attempt to have agrarian laws passed in order that occupants may be driven out of their homes, or propose that money loaned should be remitted to the borrowers, are undermining the foundations of the commonwealth. First of all they are destroying harmony, which cannot exist when money is taken away from one party and bestowed upon another: and second, they do away with equity, which is utterly subverted if the rights of property are not respected. (*De Officiis* 2.78)

> What is the meaning of an abolition of debts, except that you buy a farm with my money; that you have the farm, and I have not my money? We must, therefore, see to it that there is no indebtedness of a nature to endanger the public safety. It is a menace that can be averted in many ways; but, should a serious debt be incurred, we must not allow the rich to lose their

property while the debtors profit by what is their neighbour's. For there is nothing that upholds a government more powerfully than its credit; and it can have no credit unless the payment of debts is enforced by law. Never were measures for the repudiation of debts more strenuously canvassed than in my consulship. Men of every sort and rank attempted with arms and armies to force the project through. But I opposed them with such energy that this plague was wholly eradicated from the body politic. Indebtedness was never greater, but debts were never liquidated more easily or more fully; for the hope of defrauding the creditor was cut off and payment was enforced by law. (Ibid. 84)

But the masses were not only sensitive to their material interests. The popular 'programme' also included political and judicial measures aimed simply at making the system work better by eliminating some of the most glaring inequalities: for example the *leges tabellariae*, which increased the freedom of the ballot, or the tribune Cornelius's proposals in 67 on *privilegia,* senatorial decrees and praetorial ẽdicts. The great struggle between 75 and 70 for the restoration of the rights of tribunes of the plebs, as far as we can follow it from Sallust's account, likewise shows that in spite of some hesitation the masses finally understood where their true interest lay.

During the last 30 years of the Republic, however, the nature of the conflict changed once again. A new theme comes into prominence, rivalling and sometimes outweighing the simple appeal to immediate material interests: the defence of peace and public order in the face of mounting dangers and the spectre of civil war. Nothing is more typical of this than the younger Curio's action as tribune on the eve of the collision between Caesar and the Senate. Whatever were the real motives of this ambitious man, who assumed the mantle of Clodius, he aroused general enthusiasm with his repeated proposals in the autumn of 50 BC that armed conflict should be avoided by dismissing both Caesar and Pompey:

Curio, aided by Antony and Piso, prevailed so far as to have the opinion of the senate taken. He moved that those should withdraw to one side who wished that Caesar only should lay down his arms and that Pompey should remain in command; and the majority withdrew. But when he moved again that all those should withdraw who wished both generals to lay down their arms and neither to remain in command, only 22 favoured Pompey, while all the rest sided with Curio. Curio, therefore, felt that he had won the day, and with a joyful countenance rushed before the people, who clapped their hands in welcome and pelted him with garlands and flowers. (Plutarch, *Pompey* 58.3-5)[4]

In the last resort it is this profound repugnance to disorder and civil war, after the experience of 82 BC, which explains Cicero's success in opposing Rullus's agrarian bill at the beginning of 63 and again in November, when he managed to convert the urban plebs from supporting Catiline by convincing it that the latter, after his many repulses, was preparing to take up arms and set fire to the City. In 50 BC the people certainly hoped until the last moment that a return to the horrors of Sulla's time could be avoided.

It is thus clear that, oligarchical as one may suppose it to be, the Roman system implied a certain degree of communication, not all of it one-way, between the masses and the political class. Formally the initiative seems to rest primarily with the latter, as magistrates or candidates for election; we can only estimate the extent to which they had regularly to seek support for their plans, and we have seen the part played in this by the spoken and the written word. But within certain limits the system could also work in the opposite direction: the masses could successfully assert some of their essential claims and manifest their elementary needs and preferences in such a way that the political system had to take account of them. It did so in its own fashion, by the interplay of groups and individuals: for a cause to be successful there had to be a champion who was more inclined to defend it than others were, because at the time he had more need of *popularitas* than they. On the whole, the Roman political system was diversified enough to ensure that this function was always assumed, in case of need, by one party or another. The real and supreme objective of each member of the political class was perhaps his own *gloria* and *dignitas*; it is, however, characteristic of the system that these essential notions, defining the mentality and psychology of a whole social group, should by nature be collective ideas which imply exchange and reciprocity. The typical Roman oligarch, whether Catiline, Clodius or Caesar, was eager for glory, honour and dignity, but in the last resort these had to be bestowed on him by others and at a price. The people was certainly not all-powerful in Rome, but it did count for something.

The issues that directly concerned the mass of citizens, however, belong to a kind of subterranean history that is generally not much emphasized, although light is thrown on it by some texts that are too seldom studied. The first of these, and it would be wrong to forget it, was simply the survival of Rome as a city and of its individual citizens. Ancient cities lived dangerously, in a world without international safeguards; and Rome, at the periphery of the Greek world, was more exposed than most. The war against Hannibal was the last of the great wars in which every Roman knew that he was fighting not only for his country but for his own life and liberty. We should not underrate the effect that awareness of this very real danger had on the public mind and willingness to accept discipline. Naturally, as what may be called foreign policy was involved, there were other interests at stake, including both economics and personal ambition. These divided the political class and might find an echo among the masses, but they were secondary compared with the overall solidarity compelled by the rules of war in the ancient world.

This fundamental sense of common interest gradually faded when it became clear that the war was definitely won and that Rome was no longer directly threatened; it revived, however, with the Third Macedonian War in 171, the Teutonic invasion in 106 and even what was regarded as a threat from the Gauls in 63-58. It is none the less true that the nature of the issue changed around the middle of the second century BC, when war became a profitable enterprise and there was increasingly keen competition for the spoils. This affected the masses through the agrarian law, the question of war booty and the distribution of revenue from the provinces. As we know, these unforeseen conflicts were resolved, after many uncertainties, in terms of benefit to the citizens as a whole. Rome was by now a 'going concern', and its prosperity aroused envy. The distribution of profits induced avid crowds to press against the City's gates; centripetal forces caused a rush towards the paradise that was Rome. A million Italians forced the gates in a paradoxical war, a kind of conquest in reverse. Rome, having conquered Italy, was conquered by it, because she had also conquered the world. The progress of 'democracy' and the outcome of 'social' and political conflicts were determined by the constant growth of the organism and its repeated external successes.

The other great collective interest was freedom. The term *libertas*, it should be recalled, was seldom used alone but was usually completed by the expressions *aequa libertas* and *aequum jus*, signifying equality before the law. Provided this was assured, social and political inequalities were held of no account. *De facto* aristocracies were easily endured, personal power tolerated or even accepted, provided they upheld the autonomy of law; and the status of a citizen continued to be the indispensable and sufficient guarantee of this form of liberty. From time to time it might be endangered by the slaughter and confusion of civil war, but it is noteworthy that each successive restoration—Sulla's, or the Empire—was marked by an advance in the rule of law. When all is said and done, it was not the least paradoxical feature of the imperial monarchy that, despite the disappearance of political liberty, it nevertheless maintained an endurable juridical regime. This was symbolized and guaranteed by the appeal to Caesar, which descended directly from the appeal to the people, and above all by the codification of laws. Until about the middle of the second century AD Roman citizens, who were steadily increasing in numbers, felt equal before the law even if they shared a condition of political servitude, which on the whole they did not mind much. This essential acquisition of the Roman system was eclipsed during the long centuries of the Germanic Middle Ages; but it was never lost, and has re-emerged triumphantly in the modern world. We are all Roman citizens.

NOTES

NOTES TO INTRODUCTION

1. This book is not, properly speaking, a sequel to my *L'Ordre équestre à l'époque républicaine* (Vol. I, Paris, 1966; Vol. II, 1974), since that work dealt with problems of the definition and recruitment of an *ordo* rather than its civic or political activities. But I have touched on questions concerning the Roman 'political class' in several detailed studies, e.g.: *Rev. ét. lat.*, 1960, pp. 236-63; *Latomus*, 1963, pp. 721-32; *Rev. ét. lat.*, 1964, pp. 212-30; *Mél. Carcopino*, 1966, 1966, pp. 691-709; *Rev. ét. lat.*, 1967, pp. 267-304; *Mél. Arch. hist.*, 1967, pp. 26-76; *Rev. ét. lat.*, 1969, pp. 55-64; J.-P. Brisson (ed.), *Problèmes de la guerre à Rome*, 1969, pp. 117-56; *Latomus*, 1970, pp. 72-103; *Annuaire Ecole pratique Hautes Etudes, IVe section*, 1971-2, pp. 251-8.

2. R. Syme, *The Roman Revolution*, 1939, p. 7: 'In all ages, whatever the form and name of government, be it monarchy, republic or democracy, an oligarchy lurks behind the façade.'

3. For the first appearance of this official formula see W. Porzig, 'Senatus Populusque Romanus', *Gymnasium*, LXIII, 1956, pp. 318-26.

4. The famous 'law of Delphi' setting up a command against pirates (*Fouilles de Delphes*, III, No. 37 = *F.I.R.A.*, No. 9). A new version of this text was recently discovered at Cnidos: M. Hassall, M. Crawford and J. Reynolds in *Journal of Roman Studies*, 1974, pp. 195-220.

5. The most recent study of this movement is A. J. Wilson, *Emigration from Italy in the Republican Age of Rome*, Manchester, 1966. Cf., however, F. Cassola, 'Romani e Italici in Oriente', *Dial. Arch.* 1970-1, pp. 305-29.

6. For its juridical content cf. Chapter I below, notes 1 and 2.

7. Christian Meier, *Respublica amissa*, Wiesbaden, 1966, pp. 116-50 and 162-206.

8. P. A. Brunt, *Italian Manpower 225 B.C. – A.D. 14*, Oxford, 1971, pp. 121-30.

9. Cf. C. Nicolet, 'Le cens sénatorial sous la République et sous Auguste', *JRS* 1976, pp. 20-38.

10. Besides the article quoted in the previous note, written in 1973, cf. A. Chastagnol, 'La naissance de l'*ordo senatorius*', *Mél. Ecole franç. de Rome*, 1973, pp. 583-607.

11. Cf. my remarks in *Recherches sur les structures sociales dans l'Antiquité classique*, Paris, C.N.R.S., 1970, 'Introduction', pp. 1-18.

12. The expression is of course inappropriate, as there was no judicial 'power': cf. my remarks in *Aufstieg und Niedergang der römischen Welt*, I, 2, Berlin, 1972, pp. 197-214, and the essential work by E. Gruen, *Roman Politics and the Criminal Courts, 149-78 BC*, Cambridge, Mass., 1968.

13. See, by way of comparison, G. Ardant, *Histoire de l'Impôt*, Paris, 1971, vol. I, pp. 107-21; and, e.g., for France under the *ancien régime*, Y. Durand, *Les Fermiers généraux au XVIIIe siècle*, Paris, 1971, pp. 45-59 and 398-443.

14. But see the criticism of this doctrine by A. J. Jones, 'The Roman civil service', *JRS* 1949, pp. 38-55.

15. Cf. B. Cohen, *The Roman Ordines*, thesis, Tel Aviv University, 1972.

16. Prosopography, the 'poor man's demography', consists of analysing and collating all the known information about individual members of a particular historical society. The word was used in the eighteenth century in connection with the juridical history of the Lower Empire, but it is only since the end of the nineteenth that it has come to denote a scientific method, or rather practice. On its history and value for other periods cf. Laurence Stone, 'Prosopography', in F. Gilbert and S. Graubard (ed.), *Historical Studies Today*, New York, 1972, pp. 107-40; for Roman history C. Nicolet, 'Prosopographie et histoire sociale: Rome et l'Italie à l'époque républicaine', *Ann. E.S.C.*, 1970, pp. 1209-28, and A. Chastagnol, ibid., pp. 1229-35. I have tried to show the two principal directions in which prosopography has developed: social history (composition and recruitment of the *ordines* and magistracies) and political history. For the first of these see e.g. P. Willems, *Le Sénat de la République romaine*, vol. I, Louvain, 1878; W. Drumann (2nd edn. P. Groebe), *Geschichte Roms...*, Berlin, 1889-1908 (6 vols.); articles on individuals in the *Real-Encyclopädie* (those for the republican period are mostly by F. Münzer); to some extent T. R. S. Broughton's monumental and extremely useful work *The Magistrates of the Roman Republic*, 2 vols. and Supplement, N.Y., 1951-60; J. Suolahti, *The Junior Officers of the Roman Army in the Republican Period*, Helsinki, 1952; id., *The Roman Censors*, Helsinki, 1963; C. Nicolet, *L'ordre équestre*, I, 1966 and II, 1974; S. Treggiari, *Roman Freedom during the Late Republic*, Oxford, 1969; and T. P. Wiseman, *New Men in the Roman Senate*, 139 B.C.-A.D. 14, Oxford, 1971.

17 By a justified reaction against the 'constitutionalism' of Mommsen's school, prosopography has transformed our ideas of structures and conflicts in the field of political history: cf. my article quoted above, *Ann. E.S.C.*, 1970, pp. 1214-16. The turning-point came with F. Münzer's *Römische Adelsparteien und Adelsfamilien*, Stuttgart, 1920. Since then the method has been systematically used and refined by what may be called the Anglo-American school: R. Syme, *The Roman Revolution*, 1939: H. H. Scullard, *Roman Politics, 220-150 B.C.* (first edn. 1951); E. Badian, *Foreign Clientelae 264-70* [BC], Oxford, 1958; it seems to have reached its highest point in E. S. Gruen, *The Last Generation of the Roman Republic*, Univ. of California Press, 1974.

18. J. Rubino, *Untersuchungen über römische Verfassung und Geschichte*, 1839; R. von Jhering, *Geist des römischen Rechts*, 3 vols. (4th edn.), 1878-83; T. Mommsen, *Römisches Staatsrecht*, 3 vols. (3rd edn., 1887; French translation *Le Droit public romain*, 8 vols., Paris, 1887-91); F. De Martino, *Storia della costituzione romana*, 6 vols., Naples, 1951-72 (2nd edn. of vols. I-V, 1972-5).

19. On the caution required in assessing types of society radically different from our own cf. L. Dumont, *Homo Hierarchicus*, Paris, 1966, pp. 13-55. Roman civil law for a time reflected egalitarian principles (*aequum jus*: Cicero, *De Republica* 1.49). But neither criminal nor public law, nor even private law in practice, were egalitarian: cf. P. Garnsey, *Social Status and Legal Privilege in the Roman Empire*, Oxford, 1970; J. Kelly, *Roman Litigation*, Oxford, 1966.

20. Cf. below, Chapter III, note 6.

21. Cf. below, Chapter VII, note 12.

22. Z. Yavetz, 'The living conditions of the urban plebs in republican Rome', *Latomus*, 1958, pp. 500-17; L. Ross Taylor, *Roman Voting Assemblies*, Ann Arbor, Mich., 1967.

23. G. Carettoni, A. M. Colini, L. Cozza and G. Gatti, *La Pianta marmorea di Roma Antica*, Rome, 1960; but the real progress as regards the Campus Martius is due to the exact locating of the Circus Flaminius (G. Gatti in *Capitolium*, XXXV, 1960, p. 3) and the Porticus Minucia Frumentaria (L. Cozza in *Quaderni dell'Istituto di Topografia Antica dell'Università di Roma*, V, 1968, pp. 9-22). See now F. Coarelli, *Guida archeologica di Roma Antica*, Verona, 1974.

24. But rather the 'history of politics' as rehabilitated by J. Le Goff, 'Is politics still the backbone of history?' in F. Gilbert and S. Graubard (ed.), *Historical Studies Today*, N.Y., 1972, pp. 337-55.

25. The value of political anthropology and political science for the study of classical antiquity was discussed by G. Balandier, A. Michel and the present writer during a symposium at Madrid in September 1974 (proceedings in *Bulletin de l'Association Guillaume Budé*, 1975, pp. 213-95).

26. Students of the ancient world may be suspected of bias, but certainly not G. Balandier: cf. his *Anthropologie politique*, Paris, 1967, p. 5.

27. C. Nicolet, 'L'idéologie du système censitaire et la philosophie politique grecque' in *Actes du colloque 'Droit romain et philosophie grecque'*, Accad. Nazionale dei Lincei, Rome, 1973 (1976), pp. 111-37, and 'Polybe et les institutions romaines' in *Polybe*, Fondation Hardt, Entretiens, XX, 1973, Geneva, 1974, pp. 209-58.

NOTES TO CHAPTER I

1. On Aelius Aristides see J. H. Oliver, 'The Ruling Power', *Trans. Amer. Philos. Soc.*, Philadelphia, 1953, pp. 900 and 919; also Dio Chrysostom, *Peri Homonoias* 41.9; on the 'Antonine constitution' most recently W. Seston, 'La citoyenneté romaine au temps de Marc-Aurèle et de Commode', *C.R.A.I.*, 1961, pp. 317-23, and 'Un dossier de chancellerie', *C.R.A.I.*, 1971, pp. 468-90; C. Sasse in *Journ. Jur. Papyr.*, 1962, p. 109, and 1965, p. 329.

2. On *provocatio* and its significance under the Empire see A. H. Jones, 'I appeal unto Caesar' in *Studies...David M. Robinson*, II, 1951, pp. 918-30 = *Studies in Roman Government and Law*, Oxford, 1960, pp. 51-65; A. W. Lintott, 'Provocatio' in *Aufstieg und Niedergang...*, Berlin, I, 2, pp. 263-7. The transfer to Rome of three Romans from Cyrene in 7-6 BC, mentioned in the second 'Edict of Cyrene', doubtless has no connection with *provocatio* (F. de Visscher, *Les édits d'Auguste découverts à Cyrène*, 1940, pp. 78-86). On difficulties of

interpretation in St Paul's case cf., however, P. Garnsey in *JRS,* 1968, p. 51.

3. On this question see basically W. Seston, *La citoyenneté romaine, Rapport au Congrès Int. Sc. Hist.,* Moscow, 1970; A. N. Sherwin-White, *The Roman Citizenship,* 1st edn., 1939; 2nd edn., 1973; id., same title, in *Festschriften J. Vogt,* I, 2, 1972, pp. 23-58.

4. R. E. Palmer, *The Archaic Community of the Romans,* Cambridge, 1970; E. Kornemann, 'Polis und Urbs', *Klio,* 1905, p. 72.

5. E. Benveniste, *Vocabulaire des institutions indo-européennes,* Paris, 1969, I, pp. 335-7 and 367 (translation, *Indo-European Language and Society,* London, 1973, pp. 273-4 and 298-9); L. Labruna, 'Quirites', *Labeo,* VIII, 1962, pp. 340-8.

6. Inscription in Conway, *Italic Dialects,* No. 292; cf. R. E. Palmer, *The Archaic Community,* p. 63.

7. For wills attested by curial assemblies (*comitia calata*) see Aulus Gellius 15.27.3 and Gaius 2.101; for adoptions, Aulus Gellius 5.19.4-6 and Cicero, *De Domo* 13, 34; G. W. Botsford, *The Roman Assemblies,* N.Y., 1909, pp. 152-67.

8. A. Alföldi, *Early Rome and the Latins,* Ann Arbor, 1966; J. Gagé, *Recherches sur les Jeux séculaires,* Paris, 1934, p. 51.

9. Cf. J. Carcopino, 'La Table claudienne de Lyon' in *Les étapes de l'impérialisme romain* (1934), 1969, p. 1974.

10. Besides A. N. Sherwin-White cf. A. Rosenberg, *Der Staat der alten Italiker,* Berlin, 1913; H. Rudolph, *Stadt und Staat im römischen Italien,* Leipzig, 1935.

11. Pseudo-Acro, *Schol. ad Hor. Ep. 1.6.62*; Pseudo-Asconius, p. 189, Stangl; M. Sordi, *I rapporti romano-ceriti e l'origine della civitas sine suffragio,* Rome, 1960.

12. E. Manni, *Per la storia dei municipi fino alla guerra sociale,* Rome, 1947; M. Humbert, *Municipium et civitas sine suffragio,* Ecole Française de Rome, 1978.

13. J. Heurgon, *Recherches...sur Capoue préromaine,* 1938, pp. 157-207. The progressive disappearance of *civitas sine suffragio* around 180-160 BC is no doubt connected with debates on the voting rights of freedmen (Livy 45.15.4-5); cf. page 227 below.

14. E. T. Salmon, *Roman Colonization under the Republic,* London, 1969.

15. *C.I.L.* I² 594 = *F.I.R.A.,* No. 21.

16. A. N. Sherwin-White, op. cit., pp. 31, 107; G. Tibiletti, 'Ricerche di storia agraria', *Athenaeum,* 1950, p. 231; E. T. Salmon, *Colonization...,* p. 173; C. Saumagne, *Le droit latin et les cités romaines sous l'Empire,* Paris, 1965, pp. 1-36; A. Bernardi, *Nomen Latinum,* Pavia, 1973.

17. P. Brunt, *Italian Manpower,* op. cit., pp. 28, 538.

18. *C.I.L.* I² 1529 = *I.L.L.R.P.* 528

19. *C.I.L.* II 1964 = *F.I.R.A.,* No. 24, chap. 53.

20. Appian, *Hisp.* 84, 89; A. E. Astin, *Scipio Aemilianus,* 1967, pp. 136, 169.

21. Aulus Gellius 10.3.14 = H. Malcovati, *Orat. Rom. Frag.,*², p. 26, No. 58.

22. H. Malcovati, *O.R.F.*², p. 144.

23. P. 67 Clark.

24. Cf. also Cicero, *Phil.* 12.2.2 for the interview between Pompey and the Marsic leader Vettius Scato.

25. For the 'Italian question' from 126 to 88 cf. E. Badian's recent summing-up

'Roman Politics and the Italians, 133-91 BC' in *Dialoghi di Archeologia*, 1970-1 (1972), pp. 373-409. See also, however, E. T. Salmon, 'The cause of the social war', *JRS*, 1965, pp. 90-109.

26. W. Seston, *Municipium fundanum* (comm. Instit. Droit Rom., Paris, 1975).

NOTES TO CHAPTER II

1. T. Mommsen, *Droit public*, op. cit., IV, pp. 1-108 and VI, pp. 180-223; J. Suolahti, *The Roman Censors*, Helsinki, 1963, pp. 20-79; G. Piéri, *L'histoire du cens jusqu'à la fin de la République romaine*, Paris, 1968; T. P. Wiseman, 'The census in the 1st century BC', *JRS*, 1969, pp. 59-75.

2. C. Nicolet, 'Les justifications idéologiques du système censitaire', Colloque des Lincei, Rome, 1973.

3. E. Benveniste, *Vocabulaire...*, op. cit., II, 143 (English translation, p. 418); G. Dumézil, *Servius et la fortune*, 1942, pp. 78 f. and 166 f.

4. G. Piéri, *L'histoire du cens...*, pp. 54-68.

5. The hereditary character of political office, at least in practice, is well illustrated by the formation, from the third century onwards, of a *nobilitas* composed of members of consular families, and by the low proportion of *novi homines* at all levels of the Senate; cf. E. Gruen, *The Last Generation...*, op. cit., pp. 508-23. For the equestrian order also, the idea of *locus* (family origin) became dominant in the first century BC: cf. Nicolet, 'Les *finitores ex equestri* loco de la loi Servilia', *Latomus*, 1970, pp. 72-103.

6. This interpretation of the centuriate system was already put forward by H. Le Tellier in *L'organisation centuriate et les comices par centuries*, Paris, 1896.

7. The census ended in a religious ceremony on the Campus Martius, the *lustrum* performed by the censors; the curious expression for this was *condere lustrum*, to 'found' the lustrum. It involved a circular procession and the sacrifice of an ox, a sheep and a pig (*suovetaurilia*). I shall not go into its significance here; cf. R. M. Ogilvie, 'Lustrum condere', *JRS*, 1961, pp. 31-9, and G. Piéri, *L'histoire du cens*, pp. 77-98.

8. Cf. most recently *La pianta marmorea*, op. cit., pp. 100 f.; F. Coarelli, 'Il tempio de Bellona', *Bull. Comm. Archeol. Com. Roma*, LXXX, 1965-7 (1968), p. 61 f.

9. F. Coarelli, 'Il tempio di Bellona', op. cit., p. 64; id., 'L'identificazione dell'Area sacra dell'Argentina', *Palatino*, 1968, p. 367.

10. Plutarch, *Sulla* 30; *Strabo* 5.249; Livy *Per.* 88; Valerius Maximus 9.2.1; Seneca, *De Clem.* 1.12.2; etc.

11. Platner-Ashby, *Topographical Dictionary of Ancient Rome*, p. 56; G. Lugli, *Roma Antica*, p. 101.

12. F. Coarelli, 'L'identificazione...', op. cit., pp. 365-73. Cf. below, p. 199.

13. F. Schulz, 'Roman registers of birth and birth certificates', *JRS*, 1942, pp. 78-91, and 1943, pp. 55-64; J. P. Lévy, 'Les actes d'état civil romains', *Rev. Hist. Droit*, 1952, pp. 449-86; 'Nouvelles observations sur les *professiones liberorum*', *Etudes J. Macqueron*, Aix-en-Provence, 1970.

14. *C.I.L.*, I², 583, lines 13, 17, 23.

15. 'The ceremony of purification was completed later than usual because the censors had sent men to the various provinces to report the number of Roman citizens in each of the armies.'
16. L. Capogrossi-Colognesi, *La struttura della proprietà nell'età repubblicana,* Milan, 1969.
17. F. Cancelli, *Studi sui censores,* Milan, 1957.
18. C. Nicolet, 'Eques Romanus ex inquisitione', *BCH,* 1967, pp. 411-22.
19. Livy, 21.63.2; Cicero, 2 *Verr.* 5.45.
20. Cicero, *De Off.* 1.42; cf. C. Nicolet, *L'ordre équestre,* I, 1966, pp. 360-1.
21. C. Nicolet, *L'ordre équestre,* op. cit., vols. I and II; B. Cohen, *The Roman ordines,* Tel Aviv, 1972.
22. L. Ross Taylor, *The Voting Districts of the Roman Republic,* American Academy, Rome, 1960.
23. On this question see. P. Fraccaro, 'Tribules et aerarii...', 1931 = *Opuscula,* II, pp. 149-70; and C. Nicolet in *Annuaire Ecole Pratique Hautes Etudes,* IVe Section, 1974, pp. 378-81.
24. For a detailed study of this monument, its origin and date, see F. Coarelli, 'L'"ara di Domizio Enobarbo" e la cultura artistica in Roma nel II sec. a.C.', *Dial. Arch.* 1968 (1969), pp. 302-68. Cf. also J. Harmand, *L'armée et le soldat...*(see Chapter III, note 6), pp. 55-98, and P. Mingazzini, 'Sui quattro scultori di nome Scopas', *Rivista Ist. Arch. Stor. Arte,* 1971.
25. M. Torelli, *Il rilievo storico romano. Problemi di struttura e di linguaggio,* Rome, 1976.

NOTES TO CHAPTER III

1. The whole of G. Dumézil's work is relevant here.
2. Cf. J. P. Vernant (ed.), *Problèmes de la guerre en Grèce,* Paris, 1968.
3. J. P. Brisson (ed.), *Problèmes de la guerre à Rome,* Paris, 1969.
4. C. Nicolet, 'Armée et société à Rome sous la République: à propos de l'ordre équestre' in *Problèmes de la guerre à Rome,* op. cit., pp. 117-56; id., 'Tribuni militum a populo', *Mél. Arch. Hist.,* 1967, pp. 29-76.
5. There is an excellent recent study of juridical aspects of the *militia* by V. Giuffre: *La letteratura 'de re militari',* Naples, 1974, especially pp. 26-42 on the Republic.
6. All these questions have been revived in a number of recent studies, including several by E. Gabba, now collected in *Esercito e società nella tarda repubblica romana,* Florence, 1973; those of G. R. Watson, collected in *The Roman Soldier,* London, 1969; those of P. A. Brunt in *Italian Manpower,* Oxford, 1971; and J. Harmand, *L'armée et le soldat à Rome de 107 à 50 av. notre ère,* Paris, 1967.
7. Polybius 6.19.1; Cicero, *De Republica* 2.40.
8. Cassius Hemina, fr. 21 Peter.
9. H. I. Marrou, *Histoire de l'éducation dans l'Antiquité,* Paris, 1965, pp. 345-55.
10. As regards the origin, use and topography of the Campus Martius the best synopsis, although subsequently challenged in detail, is still F. Castagnoli,

'Il Campo Marzio nell'antichità', *Mem. Accad. Lincei*, Ser. 8, 1948, pp. 93-193; on Mars (as a warrior, not an agricultural god), G. Dumézil, *La religion romaine archaïque*, Paris, 1966, pp. 208-45. On the military use of the Campus see Livy 3.27.3; Suetonius, *Claudius* 21; Horace, *Odes* 4.1.37 and 1.8; on the fact that the Campus Martius was 'covered with grass throughout the year', Strabo 5. 3, 8 (Castagnoli, p. 172).

11. J. Marquardt, *L'organisation militaire*, Paris, 1891, pp. 10, 81, 87, 147; T. Mommsen, *Droit Public*, op. cit., vol. VII, pp. 282-8; id., *Die Conscriptionsordnung der röm. Republik, Ges. Schriften* VI, pp. 20-117; F. Liebenam, *Dilectus*, in *Real-Encyclopädie* (1903); R. Cagnat, *Dilectus*, in *Dictionnaire des Antiquités*.

12. It is probable, however, that towards the end of the second century laws were passed to regulate what might otherwise have been an arbitrary procedure. C. Gracchus's *Lex Sempronia* of 123 BC 'ordained that clothing should be furnished to the soldiers at the public cost, that nothing should be deducted from their pay to meet this charge, and that no one under seventeen should be enrolled as a soldier' (Plutarch, *C. Gracchus* 5); youths below this age had been enlisted, for instance, in 212 (Livy 25.5.8). The *Lex Sempronia,* which also provided for less severe discipline, was repealed in 109, together with other laws, by a *Lex Junia* introduced by the consul M. Junius Silanus, who stated that previous laws had 'diminished the number of campaigns' (Asconius, p. 68, Or.).

13. P. A. Brunt, *Italian Manpower*, p. 377; A. Astin, *Scipio Aemilianus*, Oxford, 1967, p. 42.

14. *C.I.L.* I², 583, lines 77-8.

15. Livy 23.48.8 and 25.1.4; C. Nicolet in *Ann. ESC* 1963, p. 463; id., *L'ordre équestre* I, 289; 'Armée et société...', 1969, p. 133; *L'ordre équestre* II, 991 and 996.

16. S. Tondo, 'Il "Sacramentum militiae" nell'ambiente culturale romano-italico', *Stud. Doc. Hist. Iur.* 1963, pp. 1-123; A. Momigliano in *JRS* 1967, pp. 253-4; id., 'Sacramentum militiae', *S.D.H.I.* 1968, pp. 376-96.

17. This is a famous episode, but its picturesque and horrible details do not fit well in to the general context of Livy's account of the Samnite wars. It is accepted by Tondo, art. cit., p. 72 (following Festus 102 L, and F. Altheim), but is vigorously challenged by E. T. Salmon in *Samnium and the Samnites*, Cambridge, 1967, pp. 103-5 and 146.

18. Cicero, *De Off.* 1.36-7.

19. F. Lammert, 'Kriegsrecht', *R.E.* Supp. VI, pp. 1351-62 (1935); E. Sanders, 'Militärrecht', *R.E.* Supp. X, 395-410 (1965); C. E. Brand, *Roman Military Law*, Austin, Texas, 1968; Neumann, 'Disciplina militaris', *R.E.* Supp. X, p. 142; especially for the imperial period G.R. Watson, *The Roman Soldier*, 1969, p. 117 f.; and recently V. Giuffre, *La letteratura 'de re militari'*, Naples, 1974.

20. Livy 4.29.6 and 8.7 (on the *imperia Postumiana,* Aulus Gellius 1.13.7); also Valerius Maximus 2.7.1-15; 2.9.1 and 7; 6.3.3 and 4. Cf. H. W. Litchfield in *Harvard Studies in Classical Philology*, 1914, pp. 1-71.

21. The existence of a military code (*jus militare*) is not attested until imperial times. The first jurist to concern himself with specifically military law was L. Cincius, a contemporary of Cicero and Augustus (cf. Aulus Gellius 16.4.2-5; 6; V. Giuffre, *La letteratura 'de re militari'*, pp. 35-41). I leave aside the vexed

question of whether soldiers enjoyed the *jus provocationis ad populum*. In principle this could only be exercised through the tribunes, who were not allowed to leave Rome. Under the *Leges Prociae* at the beginning of the second century a citizen could 'appeal to the people' against flogging or execution, i.e. it was forbidden to subject him to these punishments; but according to Polybius they were used in the army, apparently without arousing any protest. However, there are coins of Porcius Laeca which certainly allude to a *provocatio* (they bear the inscription PROVOCO) and show a magistrate, dressed as an *imperator*, threatening a citizen. Does this mean that after a certain date executions could not be carried out in the field but that the culprits had to be sent to Rome? This is suggested by the case of Q. Pleminius in 205 (Livy 29, 21 and 22) and the contrary instance of the Latin T. Turpilius in Africa in 109 (Sallust, *Jugurtha* 69.4), and by the fact that a mutineer, C. Titius, was sent to Rome for trial in 88 BC (Dio Cassius, frag. 100). But, on the other hand, Cicero declares in *De Leg*. 3.3.6 that *provocatio* was not in force in army camps, and we know that Crassus still 'decimated' troops during the war against Spartacus. Perhaps therefore we should revert to the interpretation offered by A. H. J. Greenidge in 'The Porcian coins and the Porcian laws', *Classical Review*, 1897, pp. 437-40, viz. that the coin represents a *dilectus* in Rome itself. On these problems cf. the opinions and recent summaries of evidence by C. E. Brand, *Roman Military Law*, 1968, p. 67; E. Sander, 'Römisches Militärstrafrecht', *Rhein. Mus.*, 1960, pp. 289-319; J. Martin, 'Die Provokation in der klassischen und späten Republik', *Hermes*, 1970, 72; A. W. Lintott, 'Provocatio' in *Aufstieg und Niedergang der römischen Welt*, I, 2 (1972), p. 249 f.

22. On this text cf. C. Nicolet, 'Polybe et les institutions romaines' in *Polybe*, Entretiens de la Fondation Hardt, XX, Geneva, 1974, pp. 209-65.

23. Livy 8.30-36; Valerius Maximus 2.7.8 and 3.2.9. I am not concerned here with the army as a means of social advancement: cf. 'Armée et société', 1969, p. 134, n. 47, and p. 147 f. When M. Fabius Buteo was appointed dictator in 216 to fill up the number of the Senate he included in it some men who had been decorated for outstanding services; their rank and origins are not stated (Livy 23.23.6).

NOTES TO CHAPTER IV

1. On these points, besides earlier work such as that of A. Klotz (*Philologus*, 1933, pp. 42-89) or A. Afzelius (1944), see A. Toynbee, *Hannibal's Legacy*, London, 1965, II, pp. 45-100 and 647-54; P. A. Brunt, *Italian Manpower*, pp. 391-434 and 625-99.

2. In the old army based on property assessment, the soldiers had to provide their own food and equipment. The introduction of pay made it possible to share the burden between those on active service and the others. According to Polybius's account (6.39.15) the basic equipment was provided by the state and only the cost of additional items was deducted from pay. But Polybius says earlier (6.23.15) that defensive weapons varied from one class to another: only soldiers assessed at over 10,000 drachmas (= 100,000 *asses*) wore a coat

of chain-mail. On all these points, which are far from having been clarified, see J. Harmand, *L'armée et le soldat*, pp. 55-97, 179-97 and 262-72. On the provision of togas and tunics for the armies of the Second Punic War see Livy 27.10.11 and Plutarch, *Cato Major* 4; for war supply contracts (supervised in 90 BC by L. Calpurnius Piso, whose son was consul in 58) cf. Cicero, *In Pisonem* 87.

3. G. R. Watson, 'The pay of the Roman army. The Republic', *Historia*, 1958, p. 113; for a recent date, C. Gatti in *Acme*, 1970, pp. 131-5.

4. Pliny, *N.H.* 33.45; H. Mattingly, 'The retariffing of the denarius at 16 *asses*', *Num. Chron.* 1934, pp. 81-91; P. A. Brunt, 'Pay and superannuation in the Roman army', *Papers of the British School in Rome*, 1950, pp. 51-3; T.V. Buttrey, 'On the retariffing of the Roman denarius', *American Numismatic Society, Mus. Notes*, 1957, P. 57; Watson, op. cit., pp. 89-91; J. Harmand, *L'armée et le soldat*, p. 263; and recently P. Marchetti, 'Solde et dévaluations monétaires pendant la deuxiéme guerre punique', in *Actes du Colloque 'Les dévaluations de la monnaie romaine'*, C.N.R.S. — Ecole Française de Rome, 12-15 Nov. 1975.

5. Suetonius, *Caesar* 26.3; Tacitus, *Annals* 1.17.6.

6. Cicero, *Pro Rosc. Com.* 28.

7. J. Harmand, op. cit., p. 166 f.

8. A. Aymard, 'Le partage des profits de la guerre dans les traités d'alliance antiques', *Rev. Hist.* 1957, pp. 233-49; on the Thyrreion inscription R. G. Hopital, 'Le traité romano-étolien de 212 av. J.-C.', *Rev. Hist. Droit*, 1964, pp. 18-246.

9. L. Shatzman, 'The Roman general's authority over booty', *Historia*, 1972, pp. 177-205.

10. Durrbach, *Choix Inscr. Délos*, No. 159.

11. On these points see C. Nicolet, 'Armée et société...', pp. 153-6; cf. the case of C. Fusius Cita, Caesar, *B. Gall.* 7.3.

12. Livy 7.39-41, esp. 41.3-8; Appian, *Samn.* 1.2.

13. The only general study of mutinies in the republican period is still W. S. Messer, 'Mutiny in the Roman Army, the Republic', *Class. Phil.*, 1920, p. 158-75, which is very inadequate. Cf. Toynbee, op. cit., II, pp. 80-6.

14. Livy 45.38-9. Cf. C. Nicolet, *Les idées politiques à Rome sous la République*, 1964, pp. 85-6.

NOTES TO CHAPTER V

1. Cf. also Valerius Maximus 2.3.1. In addition to the studies by E. Gabba (*Esercito e società*, pp. 30-45), J. Harmand (*L'armée et le soldat...*, pp. 9-23) and P. Brunt ('The army and the land in the Roman Revolution', *JRS*, 1962, pp. 60-86), see M. Sordi, 'L'arruolamento dei capite censi nel pensiero e nall'azione politica di Mario', *Athenaeum*, 1972, pp. 379-86.

2. Appian, *B. Civ.* 1.39; for the freedmen ibid. 1.49.212; Livy *Per.* 74; Macrobius 1.11.32; P. A. Brunt, *Italian Manpower...*, pp. 94 and 435-40.

3. R. Cagnat, 'Evocati' in *Dict. Ant.*; Cicero, *Fam.* 3.6; Appian, *B. Civ.* 3.40.

4. P. A. Brunt, in 'The army and the land..', op. cit., pp. 85-6, gives an excellent

picture of the geographical origin of the levies from 87 to 49 BC. See also J. Harmand, *L'armée et le soldat*, pp. 409-31.

5. Suetonius, *Caesar* 33; C. Nicolet, *L'ordre équestre*, I, p. 58.

6. The *Tabula Heracleensis* (*C.I.L.* I², 593 = *F.I.R.A.²*, 13) thus makes an exception to the age classes in favour of ex-soldiers; cf. H. Legras, *La table latine d'Héraclée*, Paris, 1907, p. 117.

7. We lack a study of the civil wars as a form of political conflict. P. Jal, *La guerre civile à Rome* (Paris, 1963) discusses only the literary aspect of the narratives concerning them; for our period cf. E. Gabba, *Appiano e la storia della guerre civili*, Florence, 1956, and his editions of Appian, Books I and V (Florence, 1967 and 1970).

8. C. Nicolet, *L'ordre équestre*, II (1974), p. 847.

9. Appian, *B. Civ.* 1.29-30: 'The tribune Appuleius appointed the day for holding the *comitia* and sent messengers to inform those in country districts, in whom he had most confidence because they had served in the army under Marius. As the law gave the larger share to the Italian allies the city people were not pleased with it. A disturbance broke out in the *comitia*;...the rustics, rallied by Appuleius, counter-attacked the city folk with clubs, overcame them and passed the law.'

10. Caesar, *B. Civ.* 1.7; Suetonius, *Caesar* 31 (Suetonius records a speech at the crossing of the Rubicon, *Caesar* 32).

11. Cf. B. Rödl, *Das Senatus Consultum Ultimum und der Tod der Gracchen*, Erlangen, 1968; J. Ungern-Sternberg v. Pürkel, *Spätrepublik. Notstandrecht*, Munich, 1970; E. Erdmann, *Die Rolle des Heeres in der Zeit von Marius bis Caesar*, Neustadt, 1972, pp. 86-101.

12. C. Nicolet, 'Consul togatus...', *Rev. Et. lat.*, 1960, pp. 236-63.

13. Livy 29. 8.7 to 9.10; Toynbee, *Hannibal's Legacy*, II, pp. 613-21.

14. Cf. a single example, in the provinces (Cicero, *Att.* 5.21.5): 'The richer states used to pay large sums to escape from having soldiers billeted on them for the winter.'

15. Cicero, *In Cat.* 2.20; Sallust, *Cat.* 19.4.

NOTES TO CHAPTER VI

1. I have discussed the subject of this Chapter at greater length in *Tributum. Recherches sur la fiscalité directe...sous la République*, Bonn, 1976.

2. Plutarch, *Aemilius Paullus* 38; Valerius Maximus 4.3.8; Pliny, *N.H.* 33.56.

3. Practically nothing has been written on Roman public finance since J. Marquardt, *L'organisation financière*...(French translation 1888), pp. 211-20; T. Mommsen, *Droit public*..., IV, p. 66; VI, 2, p. 252; VII, p. 338; G. Humbert, *Essai sur les finances et la comptabilité publiques chez les Romains*, 2 Vols., Paris, 1886; L. Clerici, *Economia e Finanza dei Romani*, I, Bologna, 1943.

4. *Pro Flacco* 80; J. Carcopino, *La loi de Hiéron et les Romains*, 1914, p. 278; J. Hatzfeld, *Les trafiquants italiens...*, 1921; A. N. Wilson, *Emigration from Italy...*, 1966; C. Nicolet, *L'ordre équestre*, I, pp. 312-13.

5. E. G. Lactantius, *De Mort. Pers.* 23; Libanius, *On Patronage* 7-10.

6. A. Andreades, *A History of Greek Public Finances* (English translation 1933); H. Francotte, *Les finances des cités grecques,* 1909; G. Tozzi, *Economisti greci e romani...*, Milan, 1961.

7. B. van Groningen, *Aristote, le second libre de l'Econ.*, Leiden, 1933, pp. 31-52 (the Budé edition, 1968, is less useful: cf. P. Thillet in *R.E.L.*, 1969, p. 563); L. C. Ruggini in *Athenaeum*, 1966, pp. 199-236, and 1967, pp. 3-88.

8. G. Luzzato, 'La riscossione tributaria in Roma,,,', *Atti Congr. Int. Diritto Rom.*, 1953, IV, p. 63; F. Grelle, *Stipendium vel tributum, Publ. Fac. Giur.*, Naples, LXVI, 1963, pp. 1-21; N. d'Amati, 'Natura e fondamento del tributum romano', *Ann. Fac. Giur., Univ. Bari*, XVI, 1962, pp. 143-69.

9. M. Duverger, *Les Finances publiques,* Paris, pp. 99-100.

10. A tax similar to the tithe, whatever its rate, can of course be regarded as a coefficient tax, as it consists of a certain fraction of the gross product (the harvest). But such taxes were never civic taxes; they were reserved for subject peoples. Citizens subject to the census were always taxed on capital, not income. For the typology of fiscal systems and burden-sharing taxes cf. G. Ardant, *Théorie sociologique de l'impôt*, I, p. 461 f.

11. W. Dittenberger, *Sylloge*[3], 976, (J. Pouilloux, *Choix d'inscriptions grecques*, Paris, 1960, No. 34).

12. For Athens, besides C. Mossé, *La fin de la démocratie athénienne*, Paris, 1962, p. 307, see R. Thomsen, *Eisphora*, Copenhagen, 1964, pp. 34, 103, 119, 135 etc.; T. Wilson, 'Athenian military finances...', *Athenaeum*, 1970, pp. 302-26. On the word *symmoria* see C. Nicolet, *Tributum*, p. 43, n. 75.

13. C. Nicolet, *Tributum,* p. 47, N. 81.

14 H. Schaeffer, 'Proeisphora', *R.E.* Supp. IX, 1962, pp. 1230-5; B. Helly in *Rev. Arch.*, 1971, pp. 15-28; C. Nicolet, *Tributum*, p. 46, n. 79 (*Inschr. v. Priene,* 174).

15. C. Nicolet in *Ann. E.S.C.*, 1963, pp. 415-31.

16. G. Glotz, *La cité grecque*, Paris, 1928, pp. 185 and 348-54.

17. There is no general study of provincial finances; cf., most recently, E. Badian, *Roman Imperialism,* Cornell, 1968[2].

18. R. Cagnat, *Les impôts indirects chez les Romains*, Paris, 1882; S. J. De Laet, *Portorium*, Bruges, 1949.

19. I shall be studying these in a forthcoming book. Meanwhile cf. F. Kniep, *Societas publicanorum*, Jena, 1896; V. Ivanov, *De societatibus vectigalium...*, St Petersburg, 1910; C. Nicolet, *L'ordre équestre*, I, pp. 317-55; E. Badian, *Publicans and Sinners*, Cornell, 1972.

20. For comparison cf. F. Hincker, *Les Français devant l'impôt sous l'Ancien Régime*, Paris, 1971, pp. 82-5 and 145; Y. Durand, *Les Fermiers généraux au XVIIIe siècle*, Paris, 1971, pp. 424-36. Cf., however, Montesquieu, *Esprit des Lois* 13.19, quoted by F. Kniep, op. cit., p. 92.

21. Cf. Lucilius, v. 650-1 W: 'To become a tax-farmer of Asia, a collector of pasture-taxes, instead of Lucilius — that I don't want!'; 647 W: 'I at any rate won't be persuaded to give my own fields in exchange for farmed state-revenues'; C. Nicolet, *L'ordre équestre*, I, p. 337.

22. Cicero, *De lege agr.* 1.7; 2.55 (C. Nicolet in *Annuaire Ecole Pratique des Hautes Etudes*, Ve section, 1974, pp. 279-81).

23. *Digesta,* L, 16, 203.

24. I have done so in 'les variations des prix et la théorie quantitative de la monnaie...', *Annales E.S.C.*, 1971, pp. 1203-27.

25. R. Cagnat, 'Les impôts indirects...', pp. 179-226; F. Stella Maranca, 'Intorno alla lex Julia de vicesima h.', *Rend. Acc. Lincei*, 1921, p. 263; S. J. De Laet in *Ant. Class.*, 1967, p. 29; G. Wesener in *R.E.*, VIII.A.2 (1958), p. 2471.

26 G. Glotz, *La Cité grecque*, 1928, pp. 224, 325, 346-9; C. Mossé, *La fin de la démocratie athénienne*, pp. 158 and 309 f.; J. J. Buchanan, *Theorika*, N.Y., 1962; A.R. Hands, *Charities and Social Aid in Greece and Rome*, London, 1968.

27. G. Glotz, op. cit., p. 347.

28. P. Francotte, 'Le pain à bon marché et le pain gratuit dans les cités grecques', *Mélanges Nicole*, 1905, pp. 135-57; A. Wilhelm, 'Sitometria', *Mélanges Glotz*, Paris, 1932, II, pp. 899-908; L. Robert, 'Inscription de Messénie', *B.C.H.*, 1928, pp. 426-32 = *Opera minora sel.*, I, pp. 108-14; id., *Villes d'Asie Mineure*, pp. 32 and 257-8.

29. G. Glotz, *La Grèce au Ve siècle*, p. 179; Plutarch, *Per.* 37; Philochoros in *Fragm. Hist. graec.*, fragm. 90; J. Labarbe, 'La distribution...de 445 à 444' in *Sozialökonomische Verhältnisse im alten Orient und im klassischen Altertum*, Berlin, 1961, pp. 191-207.

30. Dem. (34) 37-9; (42) 20, 31; W. Tarn, *Hellenistic Civilization*, [3]1951, p. 107; F. Heichelheim, 'Sitos', *R.E.*, Supp. VI, p. 847.

31. Samos inscription, *Syll.[3]*, 976: J. Pouilloux, loc. cit., n. 11 above; cf. also ibid. Nos. 24, 32, 44, 49, 52 and 57. On the importance of Rhodes as a corn market see M. Rostovtzeff in *Social and Economic History of the Hellenistic World*, pp. 169-72 (Polybius 5.90.3), 676-80, 1462, 1485.

32. Texts collected by Tenney Frank in *Economic Survey of Ancient Rome*, I (1933), pp. 24, 97, 158, 192; on the value of these references in the 'dark centuries' cf. A. Momigliano, 'Due punti di storia romana arcaica, I: le frumentazioni a Roma nel V° sec. A.C.', *S.D.H.I.* 1936 = *Quarto contributo...*, Rome, 1969, p. 331. There is no reason to doubt the reality of the famines and purchases recorded by tradition, even for the fifth century B.C. (Cardinali, pp. 225-8; A. Momigliano, op. cit., p. 344); their relation to the annalistic chronology is highly problematical, however. But the connection of the *gens Minucia* with the *frumentationes* seems to be attested from the end of the second century BC by coins which combine frumentary symbols with a reference to the *Columna Minucia*, and no doubt it existed much earlier.

Embassies to Cumae in 507 (Livy 2.9) and to Cumae and Sicily in 492 (Livy 2.34; Dionys. 7.1); purchasing commissions and obligations to sell stocks in 474 (Dionys. 9.25). L. Minucius first *praefectus annonae*(?) in 440 (Livy 4.12.6); the Spurius Maelius affair in 440-439: L. Minucius (*praefectus* or, in another version, eleventh(!) tribune) distributes Maelius's grain to the people (Livy 4.12.8; Pliny, *N.H.* 18.3); the *Columna Minucia* erected in his honour (Platner-Ashby, p. 133). Embassies to Etruria and Sicily in 433 (Livy 4.25.4) and 412 (4.52.5).

33. Cato in Aulus Gellius 2.28.6; C. Nicolet, 'Les variations des prix...', *Ann. E.S.C.*, 1971, p. 1225.

34. Livy 4.13.1; Dionys. 12.1; T. Mommsen, '...Die drei Demagogen', *Hermes*, 1871, p. 228 = *Röm. Forschungen* II, 153; R. Pais, 'Siciliot elements in the earliest history of Rome' in *Ancient Italy*, London, 1908, pp. 232-301; C. Nicolet, *L'ordre équestre* I, pp. 369-72.

35. The Spurius Maelius affair could be quoted in all sorts of ways. Cicero used it with transparent allusions to Catiline and himself; Quintilian (5.23.24) and Diodorus before him gave it an anti-Gracchian slant. On the prices at which corn and oil were distributed from the fifth to the third century see Pliny, *N.H.*, 18.15-17: 1 *as* per *modius* under M' Marcius, L. Minucius and an aedile, Seius (duplicate of the M. Seius attested by Cicero, *De Off.* 2.58, and Pliny, 15.2, for 74 BC); still 1 *as* per *modius* in 250 BC), representing 10 pounds of oil and 30 pounds of wine and figs.

36. Livy 36.2.12 and 4.5-6 (191 BC). G. Cardinali has usefully distinguished, for the pre-Gracchian period, between distributions at public expense (Livy 30.26.6; 31.4.6; 31.50.1); private distributions by aediles (Livy 10.11; Cicero, *De Off.* 2.58); and distributions by aediles as to which it is not clear whether they were public or private.

37. G. Cardinali, art. 'Frumentatio' in De Ruggiero, *Diz. Epigr.*, IV, pp. 225-315 (1922); O. Hirschfeld, 'Annona' in *Philologus*, 1870, pp. 1-96; D. Van Berchem, *Les distributions de blé et d'argent à la plèbe romaine sous l'Empire*, Geneva, 1939, pp. 8-31; A. R. Hands, *Charities...*, op. cit., pp. 101 f.; R. J. Rowland, *Roman grain legislation 123-50 BC* (thesis, Univ. of Pennsylvania, 1964; *non vidi*).

38. Plutarch, C. Gracchus 5: 'for the poor'; Diodorus 35.25. It might be thought that Livy's *'frumentum plebi daretur'* is a technical expression excluding the senators and *equites*; but the story about Piso proves the contrary.

39. J. Martin, *Die Populären...*, thesis, Freiburg, 1965, pp. 155-6; C. Meier, in art. 'Popularis', *R.E.*, 1965, 550-615, is more concerned with the methods of the *populares* than their actual programme (esp. col. 609). Their ideology is well expressed in Florus's words (2.1), no doubt quoting C. Gracchus himself: 'What could be juster than that a people in want should be maintained from its own treasury?'. Cf. C. Nicolet, 'L'inspiration de Tibérius Gracchus', *R.E.A.*, 1965, pp. 155-6.

40. I follow the convincing demonstration by J. G. Schovánek, 'The date of M. Octavius and his lex frumentaria', *Historia*, 1972, pp. 235-43. (This M. Octavius is the second son of the consul of 128 BC).

41. M. Crawford, *Roman Republican Coinage*, Cambridge, 1975, pp. 73 and 331.

42. R. J. Rowland, 'The number of grain recipients in the late Republic', *Acta Antiqua Hung.*, XIII, 1965, pp. 81-3 (with an arithmetical error: 180,000 for 108,000).

43. This has been suggested, however, in particular by J. Elmore in 'The *professiones* of the Heraclean tablet (*lex Julia municipalis*)', *JRS*, 1915, pp. 125-37 (cf. also id. in *Classical Quarterly*, 1918, pp. 38-45). The idea is based on the opening passage of the *Tabula Heracleensis* (quoted below, p. 198) which lays down that certain individuals are to make a declaration, but excludes them from the distribution. Elmore thought these declarations were about wealth, and inferred that under Caesar's measure the rich were not entitled to any allocation. But

the date of the *Tabula Heracleensis* is uncertain.

44. I propose to revert to the question of the material organization of distributions under the Empire and the Republic. The distribution centre, from Claudius's time at least, was certainly the *Porticus Minucia*. But the question is very complicated, since late descriptions of Rome (*Notitia* and *Curiosum*) refer to two porticoes of this name, the *vetus* and the *frumentaria*. The 45 'gates' are attested by the *Chronogr. of 354*, p. 144 (Mommsen; inscriptions attested 42 of them). The Severian marble plan, as has become known recently, shows one *Porticus Minucia* (the *frumentaria?*) on the Campus Martius east of the Largo Argentina and south of the *Saepta*, i.e. on the site of the *Villa Publica*. It is unlikely that monthly distributions to 150,000 or 200,000 people could have all taken place in a single spot; I believe that the *Porticus Minucia* was only the place where the *tesserae* were handed out. Cf. D. Van Berchem, *Les distributions de blé...*, pp. 32-63 and 84-95. M. Rostovtzeff, in *Catalogue des plombs...*, Paris, 1900, suggested that the *tesserae* were identical with stamped pieces of lead that have survived, but Van Berchem in *Rev. Num.*, 1936, believed these to be arithmetical counters. For the location of the *Porticus Minuciae*(?) cf. now F. Coarelli, 'L'identificazione dell'area sacra di Largo Argentina', *Palatino*, 1968, pp. 365-73.

45. For recent comment on this difficult text see E. Schönbauer, 'Die Inschrift von Heraclea — ein Rätsel?' in *Rev. Int. Dr. Ant.*, 1954, pp. 373-434; M. Frederiksen in *JRS*, 1965, p. 183; P. A. Brunt, *Italian Manpower*, p. 519. But it is still necessary to read A. von Premerstein, 'Die Tafel von Heraclea und die Acta Caesaris', *Zeitschrift der Savigny-Stiftung*, 1923, pp. 45-152, and expecially H. Legras, *La Table d'Héraclée*, Paris, 1907.

46. Cf. Cicero, *Pro Caelio* 78; *Paradoxa* 4.51; *De Har, Resp.* 57.

47. E.g. *Syll.*[3] 944, 947; P. Gautier, *Symbola*, Paris, 1973.

48. Juvenal 7.174; *Digesta* 5.1, 52, 1; 31, 49.1; 31.87. pr.; 32.55.pr.

49. This is my provisional understanding of the expression *tessera nummaria*: just as *tessera frumentaria* means a token entitling the holder to receive corn, so a *tessera nummaria* could be exchanged for money. The *tessera frumentaria* mentioned in legal texts of the second and third centuries AD is in fact the equivalent of a perpetual annuity. It made the freedman a member of the *plebs frumentaria*, and careful account was kept of its annual value in terms of corn and money. In the testamentary disputes to which the legal texts refer, the monetary value of these benefits is calculated (*aestimatio*) and interest is charged on any arrears. One spoke of buying a *tessera frumentaria* in the same way as 'buying a tribe', i.e. membership of a tribe of the *plebs frumentaria*: *Dig.* 32.35 pr. The texts do not say whether the *tesserae* were sold by the state or by private individuals. However, the fact that they could certainly be bequeathed, and not necessarily to freedmen (*Dig.*, loc. cit.: to a senator), seems to show that the name of the bearer could be changed; they must presumably have been inscribed with a name so as to prevent fraud. On these matters cf. F. Fabbrini, 'Tesserae Frumentariae', *Nuovo Digesto Italiano*, pp. 266-73.

50. *I.L.S.*, 6045 f. (6046, number of recipients: 4191 in the Palatina, 4068 in the Succusana, 1777 in the Esquilina, 457 in the Collina, but only 68 or 69 in the Romilia).

51. G. Rickman, *Roman Granaries and Store Buildings*, Cambridge, 1971, pp. 307-11.

52. E. Badian, *Roman Imperialism*, ²1968.

53. Cf. P. A. Brunt, *Res Gestae Divi Augusti*, Oxford, 1967, pp. 56-9; J. Béranger, 'Fortune privée impériale et Etat' = *Principatus*, Geneva, 1973, pp. 353-66.

NOTES TO CHAPTER VII

1. As mentioned earlier, there is no book dealing specifically with the subject of this Chapter. There are manuals of public law (Mommsen, De Martino etc.); works specializing in political history, such as J. Carcopino, *Des Gracques à Sylla*, Paris, 1935, and R. Syme, *The Roman Revolution*, Oxford, 1939; and attempts to analyse political mechanisms, such as those of C. Meier, *Respublica amissa*, 1966, and E. Gruen, *Roman Politics and the Criminal Courts*, Harvard, 1968, and *The Last Generation of the Roman Republic*, Univ. of California Press, 1974. All these works deal almost exclusively with the 'political class'. The present study is based in the main on those by G. W. Botsford and L. Ross Taylor.

2. Cf. my 'Polybe et les institutions romaines' in *Polybe*, Entretiens Fond. Hardt, XX, Geneva, 1974, pp. 231-2; also A. Magdelain, 'Notes sur la loi curiate...', *Rev. Hist. Droit*, 1964, pp. 198-203; id., 'Auspicia ad patres redeunt' in *Hommages à J. Bayet*, Brussels, 1964, pp. 427-73.

3. A classic example is Crassus' speech in favour of Caepio's *Lex Servilia* in 106 BC: Cicero, *De Orat.* 1.225; cf. Nicolet, *L'ordre équestre*, I, 531.

4. Cf. F. Walbank, *A Historical Commentary on Polybius*, Oxford, 1957, pp. 635-746, and C. Nicolet, 'Polybe et les institutions romaines', op. cit., p. 242.

5. C. Nicolet, 'Polybe...', op. cit., pp. 225-31; K. von Fritz, *The Theory of the Mixed Constitution in Antiquity*, N.Y., 1953; G. Aalders, *Die Theorie der gemischten Verfassung...*, Amsterdam, 1968.

6. For the interpretation of the passage on the *publicani* see C. Nicolet, 'Polybius VI,17,4 and the composition of the *societates publicanorum*', *The Irish Jurist*, 1971, pp. 163-76, and 'Polybe', op. cit., p. 253.

7. Relations between the *populus* and the magistracy are among the most vexed questions in Roman public law. See R. Monnier, 'A propos de quelques études récentes...', *Iura*, IV, 1953, p. 90; G. Tibiletti, 'Evol. di magistrato e popolo...', *Studia Ghisleriana*, series II, vol. I, 1950, Pavia, pp. 1-22; P. de Francisci, 'Quelques remarques sur la création des magistrats', *Mélanges Levy-Bruhl*, 1958, p. 119; A. Magdelain, *Recherches sur l'imperium*, Paris, 1968, passim, esp. pp. 34-6.

8. See basically E. Gabba, *Studi su Dionigi di Alicarnasso*, I, 'La costituzione di Romolo', *Athenaeum*, 1960, pp. 175-225.

9. Cf. J. O. Larsen, *Representative Government in Greek and Roman History*, Univ. of California, 1955.

10. Cf. also *Pro Sestio* 109.

11. Plato, *Laws* 744 b-d; 765b-757c (election of council). Cf. C. Nicolet, 'L'idéologie du systême censitaire...' Accad. dei Lincei, Rome (1973), and 'Cicéron, Platon

et le vote secret', *Historia*, 1970, pp. 39-66, esp. 59-65.

12. The following sections owe much to certain fundamental works: T. Mommsen, *Droit public*, VI, 1, pp. 180-223, 271-340 and 341-481; G. W. Botsford, *The Roman Assemblies*, N.Y., 1909; F. De Martino, *Storia della Costituzione Romana*, I-IV, ²1972; and above all L. Ross Taylor, *The Voting Districts of the Roman Republic*, American Academy, Rome, 1960, and *Roman Voting Assemblies*, Ann Arbor, 1967. A briefer account is E. S. Staveley, *Greek and Roman Voting and Elections*, London, 1972, pp. 122-235.

13. A. Magdelain, 'Note sur la loi curiate..', *R.H.D.*, 1964, pp. 198-203; *Recherches sur l'imperium*..., op. cit., pp. 5-35.

14. Festus, p. 452 L; Varro, *De Vita Populi Romani*, frag. 71 R.

15. The 'reform' of the centuriate system is one of the most obscure and complicated questions in all Roman history. I have touched on it in 'La réforme des comices de 179 av. J.-C.', *R.H.D.*, 1961, pp. 341-68; but see the subsequent accounts by L. Ross Taylor, *Voting Assemblies*, pp. 85-106 (and her article in *American Journal of Philology*, 1957, pp. 337-54); E. S. Staveley, op. cit., pp. 123-9; and C. Nicolet, *L'ordre équestre*, I, p. 17.

16. Cf. p. 266 below. It may be, however, if one accepts B. Cohen's interpretation, that the vote by centuries (Cicero, *Phil.* 2.82) applies only to the (5 plus 1) centuries of the *tribus praerogativa*. A majority is none the less reached after the second class has voted.

17. This is the so-called 'Pantagathan system' named after the sixteenth-century scholar Ottavio Pantagato or Baccato, who deserves credit for first devising it; cf. C. Nicolet, *L'ordre équestre*, I, pp. 2 and 21.

18. A. Magdelain, 'Praetor Maximus et comitiatus maximus', *Iura*, 1969, pp. 257-86.

19. Livy 2.55.10; Dionys. 9.43-9.

20. Livy *Per.* 11; Aulus Gellius 15.27.4; Diodorus 21.18.2.

21. *S.E.G.*, IX, 1939, pp. 1-4; M. Cary, 'A constitutional inscription from Cyrene', *Journal of Hellenic Studies*, 1928, pp. 222-38; J. Machu, 'Cyrene..', *R.H.*, 1951, pp. 41-55; A. Pagliano in *Studi Calderini*, I, 1956, p. 101.

22. Taylor, *Voting Districts*, pp. 132-49; S. Treggiari, *Roman Freedmen during the late Republic*,. Oxford, 1969, pp. 37-52; Livy *Per.* 20.

23. Taylor, *Voting Districts*, p. 137.

24. Livy *Per.* 77; Appian, *B. Civ.* 1.55; Plutarch, *Sulla* 8.

25. Asconius, 64 and 65 Or.; Dio 36.25; Cicero, *Pro Murena* 47.

26. E. Badian in *Historia*, 1969, p. 490, and in *Dial. Arch.*, 1970-1, p. 406.

27. Cicero, *Pro Milone* 25. There has been much argument as to the meaning of Appian's phrase. The most recent hypothesis, by R. G. Lewis in *Athenaeum*, 1968, p. 273, will not hold water. Cf. E. Gabba, *Appiani Liber I*, ²1967, p. 441, and his 'Mario e Silla' in *Aufstieg und Niedergang*...(H. Temporini, ed.), I, 1973, p. 792, n. 163.

28. E. Gruen, *The Last Generation*..., pp. 409-11 and 460-1.

29. On these questions see P. Grimal, *Etudes de chronologie cicéronienne*, Paris, 1967, pp. 16-25 and 144-66, and A. K. Michels' very detailed study, *The Calendar of the Roman Republic*, Princeton, 1967.

30. This point is specially studied by J. Linderski, *The Roman Electoral Assembly*

from Sulla to Caesar (in Polish), Warsaw, 1966, pp. 23-24; id., 'Constitutional aspects of the consular elections in 59 B.C.', *Historia,* 1965, pp. 423-42.

31. Mommsen, *Droit public,* II, pp. 265-6.

32. Collected by A. K. Michels, op. cit., pp. 58-9.

33. D. C. Earl, 'Appian *B.C.* 1.14 and *Professio', Historia,* 1965, pp. 325-32.

34. For detailed comment on this episode see E. Gruen, *The Last Generation...,* pp. 455-6 and 475-8.

35. The Aesculetum and the Petelian grove extended along the Tiber south of the Campus Martius near the Circus Flaminius. Cf. F. Castagnoli, 'Il Campo Marzio nell'antichità', pp. 124-5; Pliny, *N.H.* 16.37; Livy 6.20.11 and 7.41.3. For the Aventine, *I.L.S.* 6044; cf. R. Syme, 'Seianus on the Aventine', *Hermes,* 1956, p. 263.

36. Cf. F. Castagnoli, 'Il Campo Marzio', *Memorie Lincei,* series 8, vol. I, 1948, p. 122; Varro, *L.L.* 6.92; Aulus Gellius 15.27; Cicero, *Cat.* 2.1, 4.2 etc. On the need to consecrate the place by taking auspices see Cicero, *Cat.* 4.2; Livy 5.52.16; Cicero, *Pro Rab.* 11; this meant, among other things, that the voting enclosure had to be ritually oriented.

37. The question is fully examined in Taylor, *Roman Voting Assemblies,* pp. 15-58, using the most recent archaeological data. See below, plan on p. 375.

38. Taylor, op. cit., pp. 22-6.

39. L. Ross Taylor, 'Was Tiberius Gracchus' last assembly electoral or legislative?', *Athenaeum,* 1963, pp. 51-69.

40. P. Fraccaro, 'La procedura del voto nei comizi tributi romani', *Atti Accad. Torino,* 1913, p. 600 = *Opuscula* II, pp. 235-54.

41. C. Nicolet, 'Le livre III des *R.R.* ...et les allusions au déroulement des comices tributes', *R.E.A.,* 1970, pp. 113-37.

42. *Ovile*: Livy 26.22.11; Lucan 2.197; Juvenal 6.528-9. The best definition of the *Saepta* is that of Servius *ad Virg. Buc. 1.33*: 'The *Saepta* are a place in the Campus Martius, enclosed by wooden barriers, in which the Roman people used to stand when voting.'

43. As F. Coarelli has pointed out to me, Cicero's 'mile' (a Roman mile was 1480 metres) corresponds exactly to the length of the later imperial *Saepta* as shown on the marble plan.

44. G. Carettoni, A. M. Colini, L. Cozza and G. Gatti, *La pianta marmorea di Roma antica,* Rome, 1960 (cf. plan, p. 342).

45. Dio 37.27.3.

46. Varro, *L.L.* 6.91; Festus, 100 and 101 L; Mommsen, *Droit Public,* VI, 459.

47. C. Nicolet, 'Cicéron, Platon et le vote secret', *Historia,* 1970, p. 45, n. 14.

48. C.I.L., II, 1964 (cf. Mommsen, 'Die Stadtrechte der lateinischen Gemeinden Salpensa und Malaca...' = *Gesammelte Schriften* I, 267-382) = *F.I.R.A.²,* p. 208.

49. This was Mommsen's supposition, followed by L. Ross Taylor. (*Roman Voting Assemblies,* pp. 61-2 and 139; cf. Festus 372 L (on the meaning of *plebiscita*) and Aulus Gellius 15.27.4. E. Staveley, in *Athenaeum,* 1955, pp. 1-31 and *Greek and Roman Voting and Elections,* p. 248, maintains that the patricians were no longer excluded at the end of the republican period; his position is based on the confusion between *lex* and *plebiscitum* which prevailed in the

language of public law (cf. *Lex agraria, C.I.L.* I² 585, lines 29, 39), but L. Ross Taylor replied to this in advance: op. cit., pp. 139-40.

50. Florence fragment, *C.I.L.* I² 596 = Bruns⁷, p. 117; first edict of Cyrene, 1.25 (*F.I.R.A.²* p. 405); *Tabula Hebana* 1.23; Asconius p. 39 C (casting lots for judges appointed under Lex Pompeia of 52 BC); cf. C. Nicolet, *L'ordre équestre.* p. 621.

51. Cf. J. W. Salomonson, *La mosaïque aux chevaux de l'Antiquarium de Carthage*, Arch. Stud. Nederl. Hist. Inst. Rome, I, The Hague, 1965, No. 7; A. Ferrua, *Le Pitture della nuova catacomba di Via Latina*, Rome (Vatican City), 1960, Tav. LXXII and LXXIII, 1, p. 74.

52. Mommsen, *Droit Public*, VI, I, p. 461.

53. P. Fraccaro, 'La procedura del voto...', p. 604 = *Opuscula*, II, p., 239. Vote on Aemilius Paullus's triumph in 167: Livy 45.36; Plutarch, *Aem.* 31 (cf. also Livy 6.38; 40.42.10; 4.5.2. *Rogatio Gabinia* of 67: Asconius p. 58 C; Dio 36.30. Deposition of Octavius in 133: Appian, *B. Civ.* 1.12.52; Plutarch, *Ti. Gracchus* 12, etc. Valerius Maximus 8.1.7 (trial of Q. Flavius in 329).

54. Cicero, *Pro Plancio* 49.

55. The expressions used by Livy in these three cases are ambiguous and hard to interpret correctly. Literally the terms *Aniensis juniorum, Veturia juniorum* (or *seniorum*), *seniores Veturiae* (26.22.11) and *Galeria juniorum* must apparently mean 'the young men of the Aniensis tribe' or 'the part of the Aniensis tribe consisting of young men'; that is to say, on the face of it, the young men of all five classes of that tribe. For this reason B. Cohen puts forward a new hypothesis based also on Cicero's words in *Phil.* 2.82, quoted on p. 266 below: viz. that the *praerogativa* was a whole tribe (or rather a half-tribe comprising the *juniores*) in respect of which the five centuries voted successively, representing the five classes. This, in his opinion, would explain the rapidity of the voting operations described in *Phil.* 2.82. This is an attractive conjecture, but there are strong objections to it. The chief one is that the best texts—Cicero, *Q. Fr.* 2.14.4 and especially Livy 26.22.8 and 13—have *centuria* in the singular; it would have to be argued, therefore, that the same word was used to denote either the five classes of *juniores* in a tribe or a single class only. It would also have to be supposed that, for the benefit of the prerogative tribe or century, a unique exception was made to the principle of priority in voting, so that, for instance, the *juniores* of the second class of the Galeria would vote before those of the first class of the next tribe. This is very unlikely.

56. Festus, 184, 15 L; cf. C. Nicolet in *Annuaire Ecole pratique H.E.*, IVe section, 1975, p. 380.

57. P. 283 below.

58. Mommsen, *Droit Public*, VI, I, 331 (119, n. 2); H. Hill, *The Roman Middle Class...*, Oxford, 1952, pp. 208-11; C. Meier, 'Centuria praerogativa', *R.E.* Supp. VIII (1956), pp. 586-7 (all these based on Livy 43.16.14); *contra*, C. Nicolet, *L'ordre équestre*, I, pp. 125-39.

59. This is the conclusion which I now accept; cf. 'Le cens sénatorial à l'époque républicaine et sous Auguste', *JRS*, 1976, pp. 20-38.

60. C. Nicolet, *L'ordre équestre*, I, pp. 103-13. For a somewhat different solution leading to the same result see B. Cohen, *The Roman Ordines*, Tel Aviv, 1972.

61. Cf. note 55 above. If B. Cohen's supposition were accepted it would be impossible to explain how, in a vote involving five or six centuries of the prerogative 'tribe', the result could be known for certain after only two centuries had voted.

62. For the order of the tribes (*ordo tribuum*) cf. p. 283 below.

63. The *centurio* of a civilian century is attested by Festus, p. 184 L, and several inscriptions of the imperial period: *C.I.L.* VI, 33994; *C.I.L.* VI, 200 = *I.L.S.* 6049.

64. On various aspects of this text cf. C. Nicolet, 'Aemilius Scaurus, Arpinum et les Tulli Cicerones', *R.E.L.*, 1967, pp. 276-304, and 'Cicéron, Platon et le vote secret', *Historia*, 1970, pp. 39-66.

65. Plato, *Laws*, 753 c-d. On the secret ballot in Greece see J. O. Larsen, 'The origin and significance of the counting of votes', *Classical Philology*, 1949, pp. 164-81; A. Boegehold, 'Towards a study of Athenian voting procedures', *Hesperia*, 1963, pp. 366-74; E. S. Staveley, *Greek and Roman Voting*, pp. 88-95.

66. Denarius of P. (Licinius) Nerva (Babelon, II, p. 129, No. 1; Grueber, II, 526; Sydenham, 548); denarius of L. (Cassius) Longinus (Babelon, II, No. 10; Grueber, I, 3929; Sydenham, 935). The first of these two types shows the *pontes* and the voting operation; the second represents in a more symbolic fashion a citizen voting for a law. Other denarii, of C. and Q. Cassius, show judicial *tabellae* bearing the letters L(*ibero*), D(*amno*) and A(*bsolvo*), C(*ondemno*). These coins, long used to illustrate the history of the *comitia*, have been particularly studied by C. Nicolet, 'Le déroulement du vote...', *Mél. Arch. Hist.*, 1959, pp. 192-210; T. F. Carney, 'Coins bearing on the age of Marius', *Num. Chron.*, 1959, p. 87; Taylor, *Roman Voting Assemblies*, p. 34 f. (cf. my review in *R.E.L.*, 1968, p. 104, n. 2).

67. Note the hierarchical order. The lists of members of tribes which we have for the *plebs frumentaria* in imperial times show for instance in each tribe the *juniores* divided into a certain number of centuries (up to eight), which may represent the five census classes plus the *accensi, proletarii* and *capite censi*. In each century, designated by the name of its *centurio*, about a hundred names are listed in alphabetical order of *gentes*. For instance:

'Devoted to the eternal peace of the house of the emperor Vespasian Caesar Augustus and his children, the young men of the Succusana tribe. Dedicated on the fifteenth day before the calends of December under the consulate of L. Annius Bassus and C. Caecina Paetus [AD 70]:

'[Century] of Ti. Claudius Nicias: C. Acilius Abascantus, D. Annius Appolonius [etc.: over 100 names];

'[Century] of D. Roetius Secundus: L. Albius Auctus, M. Antonius Fortunatus [etc.: over 90 names] etc.' (*C.I.L.* VI 200 = *I.L.S.* 6049).

The term *centuria prima* is also used: cf. *I.L.S.* 6053. The names do not reveal any difference of social class as between the first and the last century.

68. In the first century AD the theatre ushers who looked after the seats reserved for senators and knights knew their rightful occupants by sight and were quick to expel interlopers: cf. Martial 5.8.12 and 14.11; 3.95.10; 5.23.4; 6.9.2 and especially 5.35.1. The names of this vigilant pair were Leitus and Oceanus:

L. Scamuzzi, 'Studio sulla lex Roscia', *Riv. Stud. Class.*, 1969, p. 303.

69. Mattingly-Sydenham, *Roman Imperial Coinage*, III, p. 123, No. 757 (Pl. V, No. 112). This *tessera frumentaria* is also shown on a funeral bas-relief from Ostia, now in the National Museum in Rome, in the right hand of a figure representing the *Annona* (Inv. No. 40799; R. Paribeni, *Museo delle Terme*, p. 77, No. 102; J. M. C. Toynbee, *The Hadrianic School*, 1943, Tab. XXIII, 2). I shall revert to these representations elsewhere.

70. Babelon II p. 149 = Grueber I, 4017 = Sydenham, 963. I formerly took this for a voting *tabella*, but now think it probably represents an 'identity card' or a *tessera frumentaria*.

71. C. Nicolet, 'Le livre III des *Res Rusticae* et le déroulement des comices tributes', *R.E.A.*, 1970, p. 132, No. 1.

72. U. Hall, 'Voting procedure in Roman assemblies', *Historia*, 1964, pp. 267-306; G. Forni, 'Considerazioni sui comizi romani', *Rend. Istituto Lombardo*, 1972, pp. 543-66.

73. By the *Lex Trebonia* (Livy 3.64.4; 5.10.11-12); cf. also the law of 123 concerning tribunes (Appian, *B. Civ.* 1.29.90) and the *Lex Papiria* of 131 (E. Gabba, *Appiani Liber Primus*, p. 71).

74. Plutarch, *C. Gracchus* 13 ('large writing styles').

75. *Lex repetundarum* (on extortion and bribery) of 123 BC, C.I.L. I^2 583, lines 51-2.

76. C. Nicolet, *R.E.A.*, 1970, p. 127.

77. This story, related by Valerius Maximus (4.5.3), is doubtful: cf. Broughton, I, 399, n. 1 (to p. 398) and 406, n. 2 (to p. 404).

78. Mommsen, *Droit Public*, VI, I, p. 477. Also Fraccaro, 'La procedura...' = *Opuscula* II, 257, and L. Ross Taylor, *Roman Voting Assemblies*, pp. 81-3.

79. L. Ross Taylor, *Voting Districts...*, Chap. 6, pp. 69-78.

80. Varro, *LL* 5.56 (= Festus, 506 L). However, *C.I.L.* VI, 1021 (= *I.L.S.* 6046) gives Palatina, Succusana, Esquilina, Collina, Romilia and Voltinia only; there are other lists, with variations.

81. E.S. Staveley in *Historia*, 1969, pp. 513-20; J. Linderski in *Zeitsch. Pap. und Epigr.*, 1973, pp. 247-52.

82. *C.I.L.* I^2, 2500; cf. E. Badian in *Philologus*, 1959, pp. 97-9; J. Linderski, loc. cit.; C. Nicolet in *R.E.L.*, 1973 (1974), pp. 150-8.

83. B. Cohen supposes that in each tribe, even for a tribal vote, the electors were called on in the hierarchical order of classes (as in the inscription *I.L.S.* 6049). But the above passage of Cicero may simply mean that Fidulius was the first to come forward. And Cicero speaks of a *sortitio*.

84. It was never laid down, however, that all citizens should be able to debate or amend a proposed law (except in Livy's doubtful account of the Twelve Tables: 3.34.4); cf. C. Nicolet, 'Le Sénat et les amendements aux lois...', *Rev. Hist. Droit*, 1958, pp. 260-75.

85. *Lex Junia Licinia de legumlatione* (62 BC): Cicero, *In Vat.* 33; *Phil.* 5.8; *Pro Sestio* 135; *Ad Att.* 2.9.1 and 4.16.5; Suetonius, *Caesar* 28. There may have been precedents.

86. Aulus Gellius 10.3.2; Schol. Bobb., p. 81; Festus, 218 L (H. Malcovati, *O.R.F.*^{2}, pp. 190-3).

87. Except, as regards their venue, by L. Ross Taylor: *Roman Voting Assemblies*, pp. 15-33.
88. Nor was there anything like the system of fines for non-voting, suggested by Plato (*Laws* 756 c-e).
89. Cicero, *Pro Sestio* 109.
90. Brunt, p. 54.
91. Cf. G. Tibiletti, 'The comitia during the decline of the Roman Republic', *S.D.H.I.*, 1959, pp. 94-127.
92. For a reassessment and 'rehabilitation' of the industrious plebs (*tabernarii*, *opifices* etc.) cf. Z. Yavetz, 'The living conditions of the urban plebs', *Latomus*, 1958, pp. 500-17; 'The failure of Catiline's conspiracy', *Historia*, 1963, pp. 485-99.
93. Cf. the league of publicans in 55 in support of the son of one of them, Cn. Plancius (*Pro Plancio* 24; C. Nicolet, *L'ordre équestre*, II, pp. 981-3).
94. B. Nagle, 'The failure of the Roman political process in 133 B.C.', *Athenaeum*, 1970, pp. 372-94.
95. Mommsen, *Droit Pénal*, III, pp. 194-206; Livy 4.25 and 40.19, also *Per.* 47.
96. E. Gruen, *Roman Politics and the Criminal Courts*, 1968, P. 124.
97. Survey of evidence by C. Nicolet and others in H. Temporini (ed.), *Aufstieg und Niedergang...*, I, 3, 1973, pp. 329-77; L. Ross Taylor accepted the text without question.
98. C. Nicolet, *L'ordre équestre*, I, pp. 264-9, and II, pp. 1052-3.
99. The *Lex Cincia* forbade the payment of fees to advocates, but not practices of this kind.
100. Some MSS read *tribunatum* for *tribum*; it is thus not clear whether the text refers to electoral promises or recommendations for a commission in the army (cf. Caesar, *Bell.Afr.* 54 and Cicero, *Ad Fam.* 7.5.2). I prefer the first hypothesis.
101. I have discussed this period and these questions in 'Consul togatus...', *R.E.L.*, 1960, pp. 236-63, and in *L'ordre équestre*, I, pp. 639-86.
102. It is true that the accuser was Marius's sworn enemy Rutilius Rufus (Plutarch, *Marius* 28).
103. C. Nicolet, *L'ordre équestre*, I, pp. 603-4; II, pp. 911, 997, 1068-9.
104. For the consular elections of 52 Milo distributed 1,000 *asses* (62.5 denarii) to each individual in all the tribes. If we suppose that this *largitio* was confined to the first class, say 15,000 electors, this already makes 1 million denarii or 4 million sesterces. Applying this to the figures for 54 would mean 4 or 5 times as many electors for 15 to 20 million sesterces. It is a pity we cannot be certain of this, as it would throw valuable light on the question of the size of the poll (Asconius 33, 21 C).
105. J. P. Waltzing, *Les corporations professionnelles...*, Louvain, 1896, p. 96; F. de Robertis, *Il diritto associativo*, 1938, pp. 71-162; A. Lintott, *Violence in Republican Rome*, 1968, pp. 78-83; S. Treggiari, *Roman Freedmen...*, 1969, pp. 168-77; E. Gruen, *The Last Generation...*, pp. 228-9; J. M. David in *Aufstieg und Niedergang...*, I, 3, 1973, pp. 275-7.
106. Sallust, *Cat.* 37: '*privatis atque publicis largitionibus*'.
107. The text is controversial: cf. recently E. Pasoli, *Problemi delle epistulae sallustiane*,

Bologna, 1970; as to C. Gracchus see C. Nicolet, 'Confusio suffragiorum...', *Mél. Arch. Hist.*, 1959, p. 145; F. De Martino, *Storia della Costituzione*, II³ (1973), p. 528.

108. Cf. C. Nicolet, 'Tribuni militum a populo', *Mél. Arch. Hist.*, 1967.

109. The literature since 1947 is enormous and somewhat confused. Most recently P. A. Brunt in *JRS*, 1961, p. 71; A. E. Astin in *Latomus*, 1969, pp. 863-74; B. Levick in *Historia*, 1967, pp. 207-30; L. Ross Taylor, *Roman Voting Assemblies*, pp. viii, 11, 108 and 159-63.

NOTES TO CHAPTER VIII

1. This aspect is neglected by constitutional law but is part of the subject-matter of political science. As regards Rome see the outlines by J. Gaudemet in Recueil de la Société Jean Bodin, *Gouvernés et Gouvernants*, 1962 (1968), pp. 22-44 and 189-251.

2. This is my present conclusion, despite Mommsen's authority. Cf. my article 'Le cens sénatorial...', *JRS*, 1976, pp. 20-38.

3. A. H. Greenidge's articles are still useful: 'The *provocatio militiae* and provincial jurisdiction', *Classical Review*, 1896, pp. 225-33, and 'The Porcian coins...', ibid., 1897, pp. 437-40. See now A. W. Lintott, 'Provocatio', in H. Temporini ed.), *Aufstieg und Niedergang...*, I, 2, 1972, pp. 226-67.

4. Livy 6.17-18; Sallust, *Jugurtha* 31 and 40, and *Hist.* 3.48 M; C. Nicolet, *Les idées politiques à Rome*, 1964, pp. 99, 113, 118.

5. J. Le Gall, 'Note sur les prisons à Rome...', *Mél. Arch. Hist.*, 1939, pp. 60-80; cf. Sallust, *Cat.* 47; Mommsen, *Droit pénal*, I, p. 358.

6. C. Nicolet, 'Les finitores ex equestri loco...', *Latomus*, 1970, pp. 72-103.

7. There has been no work on the scribes since Mommsen (first in 1847 and 1848, then in *Droit public*, I, pp. 276-422) and E. Kornemann in *R.E.* II, 3, 848 (1921). Cf. L. Ross Taylor, 'Horace's equestrian career', *American Journal of Philology*, 1925, p. 161; S. Treggiari, *Roman Freedmen...*, pp. 153-9; B. Cohen, *The Roman ordines*, Tel Aviv, 1972.

8. P. Louis-Lucas, *Etudes sur la vénalité des charges et des fonctions publiques dans l'Antiquité romaine,* thesis (law faculty), Paris, 1882, pp. 623-40.

9. Cicero, *Cat.* 4.15; *De Domo* 74.

10. To mention only two recent sources: E. Gruen, *Roman Politics and the Criminal Courts,* 1969; C. Nicolet, 'Les lois judiciaires et les tribunaux de concussion', *Aufstieg und Niedergang* (op. cit.), I, 2, 1972, pp. 197-214.

11. J. Mazeaud, *La nomination du judex unus...*, Paris, 1933.

12. J. Kelly, *Roman Litigation,* Oxford, 1966; cf. Val. Max. 8.5.6.

13. This aspect of Roman life partly explains the fact that 'procurators' were drawn from the equestrian order: cf. my *L'ordre équestre*, I, pp. 423-39. There is a typological study of 'letters of recommendation' by one of my pupils, E. Deniaux. Cf., for instance, Cicero, *Fam.* 12.58 (intercession with a praetor).

NOTES TO CHAPTER IX

1. The aspects of life dealt with in this Chapter have never been studied collectively from this point of view. On funerals see J. Marquardt in *Das Privatleben der Römer* (vol. 7 of *Handbuch der römischen Altertümer*), Leipzig, 1879, pp. 330 ff.; French translation, *Vie privée des Romains*, 1893, vol. I, pp. 409-22.

2. L. Robert, 'Enterrements et épitaphes', *Ant. Class.*, 1968, pp. 414-15.

3. J. Carcopino, *Sylla ou la monarchie manquée*, 1931, pp. 226-8; for a parallel with imperial funerals (*principes juventutis*, Augustus, Drusus, Germanicus) see W. Seston in *Rev. Hist. Droit*, 1952, pp. 159-77.

4. For the curious figure of Amatius see Z. Yavetz, *Plebs and Princeps*, Oxford, 1969, pp. 58-74.

5. The aspects with which I am concerned here are scarcely touched on in the latest studies, e.g. H. S. Vresnel, *Triumphus*, Leiden, 1970, and L. Bonfante-Warren, 'Roman Triumphs and Etruscan Kings', *JRS*, 1970, p. 49.

6. A. Brühl, 'Les influences hellénistiques dans le triomphe romain', *Mél. Arch. Hist.*, 1929, p. 77; J. Gagé, 'Les clientèles triomphales de la République romaine', *Rev. Hist.*, 1957, pp. 1-27.

7. Cicero, *Red. Pop.* 8, 11; *De Domo* 55, 56; *Red. Sen.* 12, 16; *in Pis.* 23, 87; Plutarch, *Cic.* 31; Dio 38.16.2.

8. Cicero, *De Domo* 89.

9. I have expressed my view on this in *L'ordre équestre*, I. pp. 639-55 and 673-98.

10. P. Jal, *La guerre civile à Rome*, 1963, pp. 200-30.

11. *C.I.L.* IV, 8075 = M. della Corte, *Case ed abitanti di Pompei*, No. 638 = *A.E.* 1962, 133 (J. Carcopino): a graffito in a house, dating from the reign of Vespasian and referring satirically to 'poison, the finance minister of Nero Augustus'.

12. Nothing has been written on this subject since F. F. Abbott's essay 'The theater as a factor in Roman politics under the Republic', *Trans. Amer. Phil. Assoc.*, 1907, p. 49.

13 L. Ross Taylor, *Roman Voting Assemblies*, pp. 29-32 and 108.

14. The best account is still that by Friedländer in J. Marquardt, *Le Culte chez les Romains*, II (French translation, 1890), pp. 247-349.

15. U. Scamuzzi, 'Studio sulla lex Roscia theatralis', *Riv. Stud. Class.*, 1969, pp. 133-65, 269-319.

16. See most recently P. Grimal, *Le siècle des Scipions*, Paris, ²1974, pp. 65-89, 154 f., 279 f.; id., 'Le Théâtre à Rome' in *Actes du IXe congrès Budé*, Rome, 1973 (1975), p. 246.

17. See, *inter alia*, recent studies by B. Biliński, in particular *Accio e i Gracchi*, Accad. Polacca Roma, 1959, pp. 3-51.

18. P. Hamblenne, 'L'opinion romaine en 46-43 et les sentences politiques de Publilius Syrus', *Aufstieg und Niedergang* (op. cit.), I, 3, 1973, pp. 631-702.

19. On this celebrated incident (Macrobius, *Sat.* 2.7.2; 2.3.10, etc.) cf. F. Giancotti, *Mimo e gnome...*, Messina, 1967; L. Ross Taylor, 'Republican and Augustan Writers...', *Trans. Amer. Phil. Assoc.*, 1968, p. 476; C. Nicolet, *L'ordre équestre*, II, pp. 919-21.

20. L. Ross Taylor, *Party Politics in the Age of Caesar*, Univ. of California, 1949, pp. 112-15.

21. C. Gioffredi, 'I tribunali del Foro', *Stud. Doc. Hist. et Iuris,* 1943, pp. 208-82. The question has recently been reopened, however, by L. Richardson, 'The tribunals of the praetors of Rome', *Mitt. Deutsch. Arch. Institut,* 1973, pp. 219-33, showing that movable daises (*tribunalia*) could be set up on the praetors' orders in various places, generally making use of available rostra. Richardson distinguishes between the *gradus Aurelii* (Cicero, *Pro Cluentio* 94; *Pro Flacco* 66), which he believes to have been part of the tiered seating of the Comitium, and the *tribunal Aurelium,* a new building erected about the beginning of the first century BC, probably in the eastern part of the Forum.

22. Cicero, *Fam.* 13.10.2; C. Nicolet, *L'ordre équestre,* ii, p. 1035.

23. G. Lugli, *Roma Antica. Il centro monumentale,* 1946, pp. 99-100. It was once thought that the *gradus* were identical with some steps excavated near the temple of Caesar (E. Nash, *Bildlexikon...,* II, p. 482; Erik Welin, *Studien zur Topographie des Forum Romanum,* Actes de l'Institut Suédois, Série in-8°, VI, 1953, pp. 104-10); but cf. L. Richardson's article cited in n. 21 above, distinguishing the *gradus* and the *tribunal.*

24. Cicero, *De Orat.,* 1.18 etc.; Plutarch, *Ti. Gracchus* 2-6.

25. E. Gruen, the principal specialist, devotes long chapters to criminal procedure in *The Last Generation of the Roman Republic,* Berkeley, Calif., 1974, pp. 260-404; on p. 444, however, he distinguishes 'riots over economic deprivation or civil rights' from outbreaks due to 'legislative contests, criminal trials, and electoral rivalries, [which] were, on the whole, atistocratic matters.' But in Milo's trial all these aspects were present.

Notes to Conclusion

1. D. Easton, *A Systems Analysis of Political Life,* N.Y., 1965.

2. R. Marichal, 'L'écriture latine et la civilisation occidentale du Ier au XVIe siècle, in *L'écriture et la psychologie des peuples,* Centre Intern. de Synthèse, 1964, pp. 199-247.

3. P. Chaunu, *Histoire, science sociale,* Paris, 1974, pp. 108-10.

4. E. Gruen, *The Last Generation...,* p. 487.

SELECT BIBLIOGRAPHY

Aalders, G. *Die Theorie der Gemischten Verfassung im Altertum*, Amsterdam, 1968
Abbot, F. F. 'The theatre as a factor in Roman politics under the Republic', Trans. Amer. Phil. Assoc., 1907
Alföldi, A. *Early Rome and The Latins*, London, 1966
d'Amati, N. 'Natura e fondamento del tributum Romano', Ann. Fac. Giur. Univ. Bari. XVI. 1962
Andreadès, A. *A History of Greek Public Finances*, Trs. English 1933
Ardant, G. *Histoire de l'Impôt*, Paris, 1971
 — *Théorie Sociologique de l'Impôt*.
Astin, A. E. *Scipio Aemilianus*, Oxford, 1967
 — *'Nominare* in accounts of elections in the early Principate', Latomus, 1969
Aymard, A. 'Le partage des profits de la guerre dans les traités d'alliance antiques', Rev. Hist., 1957
Badian, E. *Foreign Clientelae*, Oxford, 1958
 — *Publicans and Sinners*, Cornell, 1972
 — *Roman Imperialism*, Cornell, 1968
 — 'The Early Career of Aulus Gabinius' *Philologus*, 1959
 — 'Roman politics and the Italians 133 — 91 B.C.', Dial. Arch. 1970-1971
Balandier, G. *Anthropologie Politique*, Paris, 1967
Balandier, G., Michel, A. and Nicolet, C. 'Anthropologie sociale et politique et sciences de l'antiquité', Bull. Ass. Guillaume Budé. 1975
Benvéniste, E. *Vocabulaire des Institutions Indo-Européennes*, Paris, 1969
Béranger, J. 'Fortune privée impériale et état', *Principatus*, Geneva, 1973
Berchern, D. van *Les distributions de blé et d'argent à la plèbe romaine sous l'Empire*, Geneva, 1939
 — 'Tessères ou calculi?' *Rev. Num.* 1936
Bernardi, A. *Nomen Latinum*, Pavia, Italy. 1973
Bilinski, B. 'Accio ed i Gracchi', *Accad. Polacca, Rome*, 1959
Boegehold, A. 'Toward a study of Athenian voting procedures', *Hesperia*, 1963
Bonfante-Warren, L. 'Roman Triumphs and Etruscan Kings', *Journ. Rom. Stud.*, 1970
Botsford G. W. *The Roman Assemblies*, New York, 1909
Brand, C. E. *Roman Military Law*, Austin, 1968
Brisson, J. P. *Problèmes de la Guerre à Rome*, Paris, 1969
Broughton, T. R. S. *The Magistrates of the Roman Republic*, New York, 1951
Bruhl, A. 'Les influences hellénistiques dans le triomphe romaine', *Mél. Arch. Hist.*, 1929
Brunt, P. A., 'The lex Valeria-Cornelia', *Journ. Rom. Stud.* 1961
 — 'Italian aims at the times of the Social War'. *Journ. Rom. Stud.* 1965
 — *Italian Manpower 225 B.C.-A.D. 14*, Oxford 1971
 — 'Pay and superannuation in the Roman Army', *Pap. Brit. Sch. Rome.* 1950
 — *Res Gestae Div. Augusti*, Oxford, 1967
Buchanan, J. J. *Theorika*, New York, 1962
Buttrey, T. V. 'On the retariffing of the Roman denarius', *Amer. Num. Soc., Mus. Notes* 1957
Cagnat, R. *Les impôts indirects chez les Romains*, Paris, 1882
Cancelli, F. *Studi mi censores*, Milan, 1957
Capogrossi-Colognesi, *La struttura della proprietà nell' età repubblicana*, Milan, 1969
Carcopino, J. *La loi de Hiéron et les Romains.*, Paris, 1914
 — 'La table claudienne de Lyon', in *Les étages de l'imperialisme romain*, (1934) 1959
 — *Sylla ou la monarchie manquée*, Paris, 1931 (3rd. Ed. 1950)
 — *Des Graques à Sylla.* Paris, 1935
Cardinale, G. 'Frumentatio', in de Ruggiero, *Diz. Epigr.* IV 1922
Carettoni, G., Colini, A. M., Cozza, L. and Gatti G. *La pianta marmorea di Roma Antica*, Rome, 1960

Carney, T. F., 'Coins bearing on the age of Marius', *Num. Chron.* 1959
Cary, M. 'A constitutional inscription from Cyrene', J. H. S., 1928
Cassola, F. 'Romani e Italici in Oriente', *Dial. Arch.* 1970-1971
Castagnoli, F. 'Il campo Marzio nell' antichità', *Mem. Accad. Lincei. Ser.* 8 1948
Chastagnol, A. 'La naissance de l'ordo senatorius', *Mél. Ecole Fr. de Rome.* 1973
Chaunu, P. *Histoire, Science Sociale*, Paris, 1974
Clerici, L. *Economia e Finanza dei Romani*, Bologna, 1943
Coarelli, F. 'L'"ara di Domizio Enobarbo" e la cultura artistica in Roma nel II sec. a.c.' *Dial. Arch.* 1968 (1969)
— *Guida archeologica di Roma Antica*, Verona, Italy, 1974
— *L'identificazione dell' Area Sacra dell' Argentina*, Palatino, 1968
— 'Il tempio di Bellona', *Bull. Comm. Archeol. Com. Roma*, LXXX 1965-1967 (1968)
Cohen, B. *The Roman Ordines*, Tel Aviv, 1972
Cozza L. 'Pianta Marmorea Severiana: nuove ricomposizioni di frammenti" *Quaderni dell' Ist. di Topografia Antica dell' Università di Roma V*, 1968
Crawford, M. *Roman Republican Coinage*, Cambridge, 1975
Druman, W.-Groebe, P. *Geschichte Roms....*, Berlin, 1899-1908 (2nd ed., 1929)
Dumézil, G. *Servius et la fortune*, Paris, 1942
— *La religion romaine archaïque*, Paris, 1966
Dumont, L. *Homo Hierarchicus*, Paris, 1966
Durand, Y. *Les fermiers gérréraux au XVIII e siècle*, Paris, 1971
Durrbach, F. *Choix Inscr. Délos*
Duverger, M. *Les Finances publiques*, Paris,
Earl, D. C. 'Appian B.C., I.14 and Professio', *Historia*, 1965
Easton, D. *A system analysis of political life*, New York, 1965
Elmore, J. 'The professions of the Heraclean Tablet', *Journ. Rom. Stud.*, 1915
— 'Ciceronian and Heraclean professiones', *Class. Quart.*, 1918
Erdmann, E. *Die Rolle des Heeres in der Zeit von Mariks bis Caesar*, Neustadt, 1972
Fabbrini, F. 'Tesserae Frumentariae', *Nuovo Digesto Ital.*
Ferrua, A. *Le pitture della nuova catacomba di via Latina*, Rome, 1960
Forni, G. 'Considerazioni sui comizi', *Rend 1st. Lomb.*,, 1972
Fraccaro, P. 'Tributes ed aerarii', *Opuscula* II, 1931
— 'La procedura dell voto trei comizi tributi romani', *Att. Acc. Toritro*, 1913
Francisci, P. de, 'Quelques remarques sur la création des magistrats,' *Mélanges Lévy-Bruhl*, 1958
Francotte, H. *Les finances des cités grecques,* Brussels, 1909
Francotte, P. 'Le pain à bon marché et le pain gratuit dans les cités grecques', *Mélanges Nicole*, 1905
Frederiksen, M. 'The republican municipal laws. Errors and drafts', *Journ. Rom. Stud.*, 1965
Friedländer, W. article in J. Marquardt, *Le Culte chez les Romains*, II, (trad. fr. 1890)
Fritz, K. von, *The theory of the mixed constitution in antiquity*, New York, 1954
Gabba, E. *Appiani Liber I*, Florence, (2nd edition), 1967
— *Appiano e la storia delle guerre civili*, Florence, 1956
— 'Aspetti economici e mone tarii del soldo militare', *Les dévaluations à Rome*, Rome, 1978
— *Esercito e società nella tarda repubblica romana*, Florence, 1973
— 'Mario e Silla', *Aufstieg und Niederg*, I, 1973
— *Studi su Dibrigo di Alicarnasso I*, 'la costituzione di Romolo', *Athenaeum*, 1960
Gagé, J. 'Les clientèles triomphales de la République romaine', *Rev. Hist.*, 1957
— *Recherches sur les jeux séculaires*, Paris, 1934
Gall. J. le, 'Note sur les prisons à Rome...', *Mél. Arch. Hist.*, 1939
Garnsey, P. *Social status and legal privilege in the Roman Empire*, Oxford, 1970
— 'The criminal jurisdiction of governors', *Journ. Rom. Stud.*, 1968
Gatti, A. 'Riflessioni sull' istituzione dello stipendium per i legionarii romani' *Acme*, 1970
Gatti, G. 'Dove erano situati il Teabro di Balbo e il Cizco Flaminio', *Capitolium*, XXXV, 1960
Gaudemet, J. 'Gouvernés et gouvernants', *Recueil de la Société Jean Bodin*, 1962, (1968)
Gautier, Ph. *Symbola*, Paris, 1973
Giancotti, F. *Missio o e gnome*, Messina, 1967
Gioffredi, G. 'I tribunali del Foro', *Stud. Doc. Hist. et Iuris*, 1943
Giovannini, A. 'La solde des troupes romaines á l'époque républicaine', Paris, 1978
Giuffre, V. *La Petteratura 'de re militari'*, Naples, 1974
Glotz, G. *La Grèce au Ve siécle*, Paris, PUF, 1931
— *La cité grecque*, Paris, 1928
Goff, J. le, 'Are politics still the backbone of history?', *Histocial Studies today*, N.Y., 1972
Greenidge, A. H. 'The porcian wine and the porcian laws', *Class. Rev.*, 1897

— 'The provocatio militiae and provincial jurisdiction', *Class. Rev.*, 1896
Grelle, P. *Stipendium vel tributum*, Publ. Fac. Giur. Napoli, LXVI, 1963
Grimal, P. *'Études de chronologie cicéronienne'*, Paris, 1967
— *Le siècle des Scipions*, Paris, 1976
— 'Le Théâtre à Rome', *Actes du IX e congrés Bride'*, Rome, 1973 (1975)
Groningen, B. von. *Aristote, le second livre de l'Economique*, Leyde, 1933
Gruen, E. S. *Roman politics and the criminal courts, 149-78 B.C.*, Harvard, 1968
— *The last generation of the Roman Republic*, California, 1974
Hambienne, P. *'L'opinion romaine en 46-43 et les sentences politiques de Publius Syrus'*, Aufstieg und Niedergang I, 3, 1973
Hands, A. R. *Charities and social aid in Greece and Rome*, London, 1968
Harmand, J. *L'armée et le soldat à Rome de 107 à 50 av. notre ére*, Paris, 1967
Hassal, M., Crawford, M. and Reynolds J. 'Rome and the Eastern Provinces at the end of the second century B.C.', *Journ. Rom. Stud.*, 1974
Hatzfeld, J. *Les trafiquants italiens dans l'orient hellénique*, Paris, 1921
Heichelheim, F. 'Sitos', R. E., Sup. VI, 847
Helly, B. 'Une inscription de Kiéron en Thessalie', *Rev. Arch.*, 1971
Heurgon, J. *Recherches sur l'histore, la religion et la civilization de Capoue préromaine*, Paris, 1942
Hill, H. *The Roman Middle Class in the republican period*, Oxford, 1952
Hincker, F. *Les Français devant l'impôt sous l'Ancien Régime*, Paris, 1971
Hirschfeld, O. 'Annona', *Philologus*, 1870
Hopital, R. G. 'Le traité romano—étolien de 212 av. J. C.', *Rev. Hist. Droit.*, 1964
Humbert, G. *Essai sur les finances et la comptabilité publiques chez les Romains*, Paris, 1886
Humbert, M. *Municipium et civitas sine suffragio*, Rome, 1978
Ilari, V. *Gli Italci nelle strutture militari romaine*, Milanci, 1974
Ivanov, V. *De societatibus vectigalium*, Saint-Petersburg, 1910
Jal, P. *La guerre civile à Rome*, Paris, 1963
Jhering, R. von. *Geist des römischen Rechts*, 1878-1883
Jones, A. H. 'I appeal unto Caesar', — *Studies...David M. Robinson*, II, 1951 and *Studies in Rom. Gov. and Law*, Oxford, 1960
Kelly, J. *Roman litigation*, Oxford, 1966
Kniep, F. *Societas publicanorum*, Kena, 1896
Kornernan, E. 'Polis und Urbs', *Klio* 1905
Labarbe, J. 'La distribution...de 445-444', *Sozialök, Verhältnisse im Alten Orient v. im Klas. Altert.*, Berlin, 1961
Labruna, L. 'Quirites', *Labéo*, VIII, 1962
Laet, S. J. de, *Portorium*, Bruges, 1949
Lammert, F. 'Kriegsrecht' R.E. Sup. VI, 1935
Larsen, J. O. 'The origin and significance of the counting of votes' *Class. Phil.*, 1945,
— *Representative government in Greek and Roman history*, Univ. of Calif., 1955
Legras, H. *La table latine d'Héraclée*, Paris, 1907
Levick, B. 'Imperial control of the elections under the early principate. Commendatio, suffragatio and "nominatio"', *Historia*, 1967
Lévy, J. P. 'Les actes d'état-civil romains', *Rev. Hist. Droit.*, 1952
— 'Nouvelles observations sur les professiones liberorum', *Etudes J. Macqueson*, Aix, 1970
Linderski, J. 'Constitutional aspects of the consular elections in 59 B.C.', *Historia*, 1965
— *The Roman elect assembly from Sulla to Caesar* (en polarais), *Varsore*, 1966
Linderski, J. *et al.* 'A Gabinius, A. F. Capito and the 1st voter on the legislative comitia tributa', *Zeits- für papyr u. Epigraphik*, 1973
Lintott, A. *Violence in Republican Rome*, Oxford, 1968
Lintott, A. W. 'Provocatio', *Aufstieg und Niedergang Röm. Welt*, Berlin I
Litchfield, H. W. 'National exempla virtutis', *Harv. Stud. Class. Phil.*, 1914
Louis-Lucas, P. *Etude sur la venalité des charges et des fonctions publiques dans l'Antiquité romaine*, Thése de Droit, Paris, 1882
Lugli, G. *Roma Antica. Il centro monumentale*, Rome, 1946
Luzzatto, G. 'La riscossione tributaria in Roma e l'ipotesi della proprietà-sovrasità', *Atti Congr int Diritto Rom.*, 1953, IV, 1963
Magdelain, A. 'Auspicia ad patres redeunt', *Hommages à J. Bayet*, Brussels, 1964
— 'Notes sur la loi curiate...', *Rev. Hist. Droit*, 1964
— 'Praetor Maximus et comitiatus maximus', *Iura*, 1969
— *Recherches sur l'imperium*, Paris, 1968
Manni, E. *Per la storia dei municipi fino alla guerra sociale*, Rome, 1947
Marchetti, P. *'Historie économique et movétaine de la deuxième guerre punique'*, Brussels, 1978
— 'Paie des troupes et dévaluations monétaires au cours de la deuxième guerre

punique', *les dévaluations à Rome*, Collogne C.N.R.S. Rome, 1978
 − 'Solde et dévaluations monétaires pendant la deuxième guerre punique', *Actes* du Colloque 'les dévaluations de la monnaie romaine' C.N.R.S.
Marichal, R. 'L'écriture latine et la civilisation occidentale du Ier au XVIe siècle', dans *L'écriture et la psychologie des peuples*, centre Interm. de Synthèse, 1964
Marquardt, J. *L'organisation militaire*, Paris, 1891
Marquart, J. *Vie privée des Romains*, Tran. fr. 1893
Marrov, H. I. *Histoire de l'éducation dans l'Antiquité*, Paris, 1965
Martin, J. *Die Populären*, Diss Freiburg, 1965
 − 'Die Provokation in der klass. und späten Republik' *Hermes*, 1970
Martino, F. de, *Storia della Costituz Romana*, Naples, 1951- (2nd ed. I-V, 1972-1975)
Mattingly, H. 'The retariffing of the denarius at sixteen asses', *Num. Chron.*, 1934
Mazeaud, J. *La nomination de judex unus sous la procédure formulaire à Rome*, Paris, 1933
Meier, Ch. *Respublica amissa, eine studie zu verfassung und Geschichte der späten römischen Republik*, Wierbeden, 1966
 − 'Popularis', R.E., 1965
Messer, W. S. 'Mutiny in the Roman Army, the Republic', *Class. Phil.*, 1920
Michels, A. K. *The calendar of the Roman republic*, Princetown, 1967
Mingazzini, P. 'Sui quattro siultori di nome Scopas', Riv. 1st. Arch. Stur. Arte., 1971
Momigliano, A. 'Due punti di storia romana arcaica, I., le frumentazioni a R. nel V° sec A.C.', S.D.H.I., 1936 and *Quarto Contributo*, Rome, 1969
Mommsen, Th. *Die Conscriptionordnung der röm Rep.*, *Gesam. Schrift*, VI
 − *Röm. Staatsrecht*, (3rd ed. 1887-Tran. French *le Droit public romain*, 1887-1891)
Monnier, R. 'A propos de quelques études récentes... *Iura*, IV, 1953
Mossé, C. *La fin de la démocratie athénienne*, Paris, 1962
Münzer, F. *Römische Adelsparteien und Adelsfamilien*, Stuttgart, 1920
Nagle, B. 'The failure of the Roman political process in 133 B.C.', Athenaeum, 1970
Neumann, 'Disciplina militaris', R. G. Sup. X (1965)
Nicolet, C. *L'ordre équestre à l'époque républicaine (312-43 av. J. C.)*
 − *Définitions juridiques et structures sociales*, Paris, 1966
 − *Prosographie des chevaliers*, Paris, 1974
 − *Les Graques, Crise agraire et révolution à Rome*, Paris, 1967
 − *Tributum. Recherches sur la fiscalité directe sous la République Romaine*, Bonn, 1976
 − *Rome et la conquête du monde méditerranéen*
 − Tome 1, *Les Structures de l'Italie Romaine*, Paris, 1977
 − Tome 2., *Genèse d'un Empire*, Paris, 1978
 − 'Les réformes electorales de Caius Gracchus et la politique des *populares' Rev. Et. Latines*, XXXVI, 1958
 − 'Le Sénat et les amendements aux lois à la fin de la République', *Rev. Hist., Droit*, XXXVI, 1958
 − 'Note sur Appien, B.C., I, 100;467. Sylla et la réforme électorale', *Mél. Arch. et Hist.*, LXXI, 1959
 − '*Confusio suffragiorum*. A propos d'une réforme électorale de Caius Gracchus', *Mél. Arch. et Hist.*, LXXI, 1959
 − '*Consul Togatus*: remarques sur le vocabulaire politique de Cicéron et de Tite-Live', *Rev. Et. Latines*, XXXVIII, 1960
 − 'La réforme des comices de 179 av. J. C.,' *Rev. Hist. Droit*, XXXIX, 1961
 − 'A Rome pendant la seconde guerre punique. Techniques financières et manipulations monétaires', *Annales E. S. C.*, XVIII, 1963
 − 'L'inscription de l'autel de Narbonne et la *commendatio* des chevaliers', Latomus, XXII, 1963
 − 'Le *De Republica* VI, 12 et la dictature de Scipion', *Rev. Et. Latines*, XLII, 1964
 − 'L'inspiration de Tibérius Gracchus. A propos d'un livre récent', *Rev. Et. Anc.*, LXVII, 1965
 − 'Rome et les élections', *Rev. Et. Latines*, XLV, 1967
 − '*Eques Romanus ex inquisitione*. A propos d'une inscription de Prousias de l'Hypios' *B.C.H.*, XCI, 1967
 − *Tribuni militum a populo'*, *Mel Ec. Franç. Rome*, LXXIV, 1967
 − 'Politique et tribunaux criminels', *Rev. Et. Latines*, XLVII, 1969
 − 'Armée et société à Rome à l'époque républicaine', in *Problèmes de la Guerre à Rome* J. P. Brisson (ed.) Paris, 1969
 − 'Cicéron, Platon et le vote secret', *Historia*, XIX, 1970
 − 'Le livre III des *Res Rusticae* de Varron et les allusions au déroulement des comices tributes', *Rev. Et. Anc.*, LXXII, 1970

— 'Introduction' to *Recherches sur les structures sociales dans l'Antiquité Classique*, Paris, 1970
— 'Prosopographie et histoire sociale. Rome et l'Italie à l'époque républicaine', *Annales E.S.C.*, XXV, 1970
— 'Les *finitores ex equestri loco* de la loi Seruilia de 63 av. J. C.,' *Latomus*, XXIV, 1970
— 'Polybius, VI, 17, 4 and the composition of the *societates publicanorum*', *The Irish Jurist*, VI, 1971
— 'Culture et société dans l'histoire romaine' in *Niveaux de Culture et groupes sociaux*, Paris, 1971
— 'Les lois judiciaires et les tribunaux de concussion' *Aufstieg und Niedergang der römische Welt*, Berlin, 1973
— 'Polybe et les Institutions romaines', *Entretiens sur l'Antiquité Classique*, XX, 1974
— 'L'idéologie du système centuriate et l'influence de la philosophie politique grecque', *Actes due Colloque de l'Acc dei Lincei, Droit Romain et philosophie grecque*, Rome, 1973
— 'Histoire de l'Antiquité Classique et science politique', *Bull. Ass. Guillaume Bude*, 1975
— 'Tessères frumentaires et tessères de vote' in *Mel. J. Heurgon*, Rome, 1976
— 'Aperçus sur la fiscalité à Rome sous la République,' Ktéma 1976
— 'Le temple des Nymphes et les distributions frumentaires à Rome à l'époque républicaine d'après les dècouvertes récentes', *Compt. Rend. Acad. Inscr.*, 1976
— 'Le cens sénatorial sous la République et sous Auguste', *Journ. Rom. Stud.*, 1976
— 'Les classes dirigeantes romaines sous la République: ordre sénatorial et ordre équestre', *Annales ESC*, 1977
— 'Armée et fiscalité: pour un bilan de la conquête romaine', in *Armées et fiscalités dans le Monde Antique*, Paris C.N.R.S., 1977
— 'Mutations monétaires et organisation censitaire sous la République', in *Les Dévaluations à Rome*, Rome, 1978
— 'Le *stipendium* des alliés italiens jusqu'à la Guerre Sociale', *Papers Brit. School Rome*, XLVI, 1978
— 'Deux remarques sur l'organisation des sociétés de publicains à la fin de la République romaine', in *Points de vue sur la Fiscalité Antique*, Paris, 1979
Ogilvie, R. M. 'Lustrum condere', *Journ. Rom. Stud.*, 1961
Oliver, J. H. 'The ruling power', *Trans. Amer. Philos. Soc.*, Philadelphia,1953
Pais, R. *Ancient Italy*, London, 1908
Palmer, R. E. *The archaic community of the Romans*, Cambridge, 1970
Pasoli, E. *Problemi delle epistulae sallustiane*, Bologna, 1970
Pieri, G. *L'histoire du cens jusqu'à la fin de la République romaine*, Paris, 1968
Platner, S. B. and Ashley, T. *A Topographical Dictionary of Ancient Rome*, Oxford, 1929
Pouilloux, J. *Choix d'inscriptions grecques*, Paris, 1960
Porzig, W. 'Senatus Populusque Romanus', *Gymnasium*, 1956
Premerstein, A. von. 'Die Tafel von Heraclea und die Acta Caesaris', *Zeitsch. Sar. Jif.*, 1923
Rickman, G. *Roman granaries and store buildings*, Cambridge, 1971
Robert, L. 'Enterrements et épitaphes', *Ant. Class.*, 1968
— 'Inscription de Messénie', B.C.H., 1928
— *Villes d'Asie Mineure*, Paris, 1962
Robertis, F. de, *Il diritto associatiro Romano dai collegi della Republica alle corporazioni del Basso Impero*, Bari, Italy, 1938
Rödi, B. *Das Senatus Consultum Ultimum und der Tod der Gracchen*, Erlargen, 1968
Rosenberg, A. *Der Staat der alten Italiker*, Berlin, 1913
Ross Taylor, L. 'Republic and Augustan writers', *Trans. Amer. Phil. Ass.*, 1968
— *Roman Voting Assemblies*, London, 1967
— *The voting districts of the Roman Republic*, Amer. Acad. Rome., 1960
— 'Was Tiberius Gracchus' last assembly electoral or legislative?', *Athenaeum*, 1963
— 'Horace's equestrian career', *Am. Journ. Phil.*, 1925
Rostortzeff, M. *Social and economic history of the Hellenistic World*, 3 vol. Oxford, 1941
— *Catalogue des plombs...du Cabinet des Médailles*, Paris, 1900
Rowland, R. J. 'The number of grain recipients in the late Republic', *Acta Antiqua Hung.* XIII, 1965
— *Roman grain legislation 123-50 B.C.*, Dissert. Un. Penns., 1964
Rubino, J. *Untersuchungen über römische Verfassung und Geschichte*, 1839
Rudolph, H. *Stadt und Staat in römischen Italien*, Lepzig, 1935
Ruggini, L. C. 'Eforo nello Pseudo- Aristotele, *Oec.* II,' *Athenaeum*, 1966, 1967
Salmon, E. T. 'The cause of the social war', *Phoenix*, 1962
— *Roman colonization under the Republic*, London, 1969
— *Samnium and the Samnites*, Cambridge, 1967

Salomonson, J. W. *La mosaïque aux chevaux de l'Antiquarium de Carthage*, Arch. Stud. Nederl. Hist. Inst. I, La Haye, 1965

Sander, E. 'Röm. Militärstrafrecht, *Rhein. Mus.*, 1960
— 'Militärecht', *R.E.*, Sup. X, (1965)

Saumagne, C. *Le droit latin et les cités romaines sous l'Empire*, Paris, 1965

Scamuzzi, U. 'Studio nulla lex Roscia theatralis' *Riv. Stud. Class.*, 1969

Schaeffer, H. 'Proeisphora' R.E. Sup., IX, 1962

Schönbauer, E. 'Die Inschriften von Heraclea — ein Rätzel?' *Rev. Int. Dr. Ant.*, 1954

Schovánck, J. G. 'The date of M. Octavius and his lex frumentaria', *Historia*, 1972

Schulz, F. 'Roman Registers of birth and birth certificates', *Journ. Rom. Stud.*, 1942

Scullard, H. H. *Roman Politics 220-150 B.C.*, 1st ed. 1951

Seston, W. 'Municipium fundanum', *Comm. Inst. Droit. Rom.*, Paris, 1975
— 'La aloyenneté romaine au temps de Marc Aurèle et de Commode', *C.R.A.I. 1961*
— 'La aloyenneté romaine Rapport', Congrès Int. Sc. Hist. Moscow, 1970
— 'Un dossier de chancellerie?' *C.R.A.I.*, 1971
— La Lex Julia de 90 avant J. C. et l'intégration des Italiens dans la aloyenneté romaine, *Comptes-Rendus de l'Acad. des Livres et Belles Lettres*, 1978

Shatzmann, I. 'The Roman general's authority over booty', *Historia*, 1972

Sherwin-White, A. N. *The Roman citizenship*, 1st ed. 1939; 2nd ed. 1973, *Festschriften J. Vogt* I, 1972

Sordi, M. 'L'anuolamento dei capite cersi nel persiero? e nell'azione politica di Mario', *Athenaeum*, 1972
— *I rapporti romano-centi e l'origine della civitas sive suffragio*, Rome, 1960

Staveley, E. S. *Greek and Roman voting and elections*, London, 1972
— 'The role of the first voter in roman legislative assemblies', *Historia*, 1969

Stella Maranca, F. 'Intorno alla lex Julia de vicesima R.', *Rend. Acc. Lincei*, 1921

Stone, Lawrence, 'Prosopography', *Historical Studies today*, N.Y., 1972
(Ed. F. Gilbert — S. Grambard)

Suolahti, J. *The junior officers of the Roman Army in the Republican period*, Helsinki, 1952
— *The Roman Censors*, Helsinki, 1963

Syme, R. *Roman Revolution*, Oxford, 1939

Tarn, W. *Hellenistic Civilization*, 1951

Tellier, H. le, *L'organisation centuriate et les comices par centuries*, Paris, 1896

Tenney, Frank, *Economic Survey of Ancient Rome*, 5 vol., Baltimore, 1933-1940

Thomsen, R. *Eisphora*, Copenhagen, 1964
— From libral aes grave to uncial aes election', *Les dévaluations à Rome*, colloque C.N.R.S., Rome, 1978

Tibiletti, G. 'The comitia during the decline of the Roman Republic', *S.D.H.I*, 1959
— 'Évol. di magistrato e popolo...', *Studia Ghisteriana*, série II, I, 1950, Paris

Tondo, S. 'Sacramentum militiae', *S.D.H.I.*, 1968
— Il 'Sacramentum militiae' nell' ambiente culturale romano-italiano', *Stud. Doc. Hist.*, 1963

Torelli, M. *Il riliero stories romano. Problemi di stuttura e di linguaggio*, Rome, 1976

Toynbee, A. *Hannibal's Legacy*, London, 1965

Tozzi, G. *Economisti greci e romani*, Milan, 1961

Treggiàri, S. *Roman Freedmen during the late Republic*, Oxford, 1969

Ungern-Sternberg von Pürkell, J. *Spätrepublik Notstandrecht*, Munich, 1970

Vernant, J. P. *Problèmes de la guerre en Grèce*, Paris, 1968, (ed. J. P. Vernant)

Vissher, F. de, *Les édits d'Auguste découverts à Cyrène*, Brussels, 1940

Vresnel, H. S. *Triumphus*, Leyde, 1970

Walbank, F. A historical commentary on Polybius, Oxford, 1957

Waltzing, J. P. *Etude historique sur les corporations professionnelles chez les Romains 4 vol.*, Louvain, 1896-1900

Watson, G. R. 'The pay of the Roman army. The Republic', *Historia*, 1958
— *The Roman Soldier*, London, 1969

Welin, E. *Studien zur Topographie des Forum Romanum*, Actes. Inst. Suédois, VI,1953

Wilhem, A.'Sitometria',*Mélanges Glotz*, 1932, II

Willems, P. *Le Sénat de la République romaine*, Louvain, 1878

Wilson, A. J. *Emigration from Italy in the Republican age of Rome*, Manchester, 1966

Wilson, T. 'Athenian military finances, 378/7 to the peace of 375', *Athenaeum*, 1970,

Wiseman, T. P. 'The census in the 1st Cent. B.C.', *Journ. Rom. Stud.*, 1969
— *New Men in the Roman Senate, 139 B.C. — A.D. 14*, Oxford, 1971

Yavetz, Z. 'The failure of Catiline's conspiracy', *Historia*, 1963
— 'The living conditions of the Urban plebs in the republican Rome', *Latomus*, 1958
— *Plebs and Princeps*, Oxford, 1969

INDEX OF SOURCES

Abbreviations of the titles of authors' works usually follow the Oxford Latin Dictionary and the Liddell-Scott-Jones Greek-English Lexicon. Referenes are to be understood thus: APPIAN *BC* 1(60)142=for Appian, *Bellum Civile* Book 1, Section 60, see page 142.

SUBJECT INDEX